The Cambridge Companion to Jazz

The vibrant world of jazz may be viewed from many perspectives, from social and cultural history to music analysis, from economics to ethnography. It is challenging and exciting territory. This volume of nineteen specially commissioned essays provides informed and accessible guidance to the challenge, offering the reader a range of expert views on the character, history and uses of jazz. The book starts by considering what kind of identity jazz has acquired and how, and goes on to discuss the crucial practices that define jazz and to examine some specific moments of historical change and some important issues for jazz study. Finally, it looks at a set of perspectives that illustrate different 'takes' on jazz – ways in which jazz has been valued and represented.

Mervyn Cooke is Professor of Music at the University of Nottingham. He is the author of *Jazz*, *The Chronicle of Jazz*, and *Britten and the Far East*; co-author of *Benjamin Britten: Billy Budd*; editor of *The Cambridge Companion to Benjamin Britten* (1999) and *The Cambridge Companion to Twentieth-Century Opera* (forthcoming) and is currently writing a history of film music for Cambridge University Press. He is also a composer and pianist.

David Horn was Director of the Institute of Popular Music at the University of Liverpool from 1988 to 2002. He was a founding editor of the journal *Popular Music* (Cambridge University Press) and is author of two bibliographies of American music. He is currently joint managing editor of *The Encyclopedia of Popular Music of the World*.

Cambridge Companions to Music

The Cambridge Companion to

JAZZ

. . . .

EDITED BY

Mervyn Cooke
Professor of Music
University of Nottingham

and

David Horn
Director, Institute of Popular Music
University of Liverpool

 **CAMBRIDGE**
UNIVERSITY PRESS

PUBLISHED BY THE PRESS SYNDICATE OF THE UNIVERSITY OF CAMBRIDGE
The Pitt Building, Trumpington Street, Cambridge, United Kingdom

CAMBRIDGE UNIVERSITY PRESS
The Edinburgh Building, Cambridge CB2 2RU, UK
40 West 20th Street, New York, NY 10011-4211, USA
477 Williamstown Road, Port Melbourne, VIC 3207, Australia
Ruiz de Alarcón 13, 28014 Madrid, Spain
Dock House, The Waterfront, Cape Town 8001, South Africa

http://www.cambridge.org

First published 2002
Reprinted 2004

Printed in the United Kingdom at the University Press, Cambridge

Typeface Minion 10.75/14 pt   *System* LaTeX 2_ε [TB]

A catalogue record for this book is available from the British Library

Library of Congress Cataloguing in Publication data

The Cambridge companion to jazz / edited by Mervyn Cooke and David Horn.
p.   cm. – (Cambridge companions to music)
Includes bibliographical references (p.) and index.
ISBN 0–521–66320–2 – ISBN 0–521–66388–1 (pb.)
1. Jazz – History and criticism.   I. Cooke, Mervyn, 1963–   II. Horn, David   III. Series.
ML3506 .C29   2002
781.65 – dc21   2001052671

ISBN 0 521 66320 2 hardback
ISBN 0 521 66388 1 paperback

Contents

Plates

Notes on contributors

David Ake is Assistant Professor of Music at the University of Nevada, Reno. He holds a PhD in musicology and an MA in ethnomusicology from UCLA, as well as degrees in jazz performance from the University of Miami and the California Institute of the Arts. His articles on jazz have appeared in *American Music*, *Echo* and *Encyclopaedia Britannica*, and his book, *Jazz Cultures*, was published by the University of California Press in 2002. As a pianist, he has played alongside Ravi Coltrane, Charlie Haden, James Newton and Bud Shank, and on recordings by Phil Farris, David Borgo and The Collective. He has also formed his own award-winning bands in New York, Los Angeles and Germany. The David Ake Group's first CD for the Posi-tone label, *Sound and Time*, was released in 1998.

Darius Brubeck is a pianist, composer and Director of the Centre for Jazz and Popular Music and Professor of Jazz Studies at the University of Natal, Durban. Named after Darius Milhaud, his father Dave's postgraduate composition teacher, Darius grew up in an intensely musical environment where he learned more by osmosis than through study. He later majored in ethnomusicology and history of religion at Wesleyan University, and during the 1970s he and his brothers, Chris and Dan, toured internationally with Dave Brubeck as Two Generations of Brubeck or The New Brubeck Quartet. At Natal University in 1983, Darius started the first Jazz Studies course to be offered by an African university. In recent years, he has toured extensively, mainly with his own bands from South Africa, visiting England, Italy, France, Germany, Turkey, Thailand, Peru and the US. He has performed regularly with his family and the London Symphony Orchestra, most recently in 2000 when his composition, 'Four Score in Seven', was premiered, and in 1999–2000 he was a Visiting Fellow in Music at the University of Nottingham.

Mervyn Cooke is Professor of Music at the University of Nottingham. He studied at the Royal Academy of Music and at King's College, Cambridge, and was for six years Research Fellow and Director of Music at Fitzwilliam College, Cambridge. He is the author of *Jazz* (World of Art) and *The Chronicle of Jazz*, both published by Thames & Hudson; he has contributed chapters on jazz to the forthcoming *Cambridge History of Twentieth-Century Music* and *The Cambridge Companion to the Flute*. His other books include studies of Britten's *Billy Budd* and *War Requiem* (Cambridge University Press), a monograph, *Britten and the Far East* (The Boydell Press), and *The Cambridge Companion to Benjamin Britten*. He is currently editing *The Cambridge Companion to Twentieth-Century Opera* and writing a history of film music for Cambridge University Press. He is also active as a pianist and composer, his compositions having been broadcast on BBC Radio 3 and Radio France and performed at London's South Bank and St John's, Smith Square.

Robert P. Crease is a Professor in the Department of Philosophy at the State University of New York at Stony Brook, and historian at Brookhaven National Laboratory. His books include *Making Physics: A Biography of Brookhaven National Laboratory* (University of Chicago Press, 1999), *The Play of Nature: Experimentation as Performance* (Indiana University Press, 1993), and a forth-coming study of vernacular dance. He also writes a column, 'Critical Point', for *Physics World*. He is a co-founder of the New York Swing Dance Society, and a former dancer in the Big Apple Lindy Hoppers.

Krin Gabbard has published extensively on literature, theatre, film studies and psychoanalysis. His first book, *Psychiatry and the Cinema* (University of Chicago Press, 1987), has recently been published in a second edition. He was one of the creators of a new jazz studies when he published 'The Quoter and His Culture' in 1991 (in *Jazz in Mind*, ed. R. Buckner and S. Weiland, Wayne State University Press). He later brought the insights of critical theory to jazz study with two anthologies, *Jazz Among the Discourses* and *Representing Jazz* (both published by Duke University Press, 1995). In 1996 he published *Jammin' at the Margins: Jazz and the American Cinema* (University of Chicago Press), the first extended study of the interactions between jazz and film. He is currently writing a book on the representations of masculinity in recent American cinema.

David Horn was Director of the Institute of Popular Music at the University of Liverpool from 1988 to 2002. He was a founding editor of the journal, *Popular Music* (Cambridge University Press), and a founder member of the International Association for the Study of Popular Music (IASPM). His publications include a two-volume bibliography, *The Literature of American Music* (Scarecrow Press, 1977 and 1988), and articles on various aspects of American music, including two on George Gershwin. He has recently edited a special issue of the *Black Music Research Journal*, for which he has also written an essay on Art Tatum. He is joint managing editor of a long-running international project to compile a multi-volume reference work, *The Encyclopedia of Popular Music of the World*.

Travis A. Jackson is Assistant Professor of Musicology at the University of Michigan in Ann Arbor. His scholarly interests include jazz, rock, ethnography, urban space and recording technology. He is currently completing *Blowin' the Blues Away: Performance and Meaning on the New York Jazz Scene*, a book about jazz in the 1990s. In his spare time, he is a guitarist, songwriter and amateur recordist.

Bruce Johnson is Associate Professor in the School of English, University of New South Wales, Sydney, where he lectures across a wide range of areas from the Renaissance to the present day, with particular emphasis on popular cultures. He has written prolifically on popular music, cultural politics and Australian studies, and is the editor of *The Oxford Companion to Australian Jazz*. His most recent book, *The Inaudible Music*, is a study of the connections between jazz, gender and Australian modernity. He is active in music and record production and has established two record labels devoted to Australian jazz. He has worked extensively in arts administration, research and policy formation, and was the prime mover in the establishment of the government-funded Australian Jazz Archives. He is also a radio broadcaster and producer, and performs regularly as a jazz musician.

Dave Laing is Reader in the School of Communication and Creative Industries at the University of Westminster and an editor of the journal *Popular Music*. During a lengthy career as a journalist, editor, researcher and teacher, he has written extensively on music and the music business. His books include *The Sound of Our Time* (1969), *Buddy Holly* (1970), *The Marxist Theory of Art* (1979), *One Chord Wonders* (1985) and *The Guerilla Guide to the Music Business* (2001, with Sarah Davis). He has edited reports on the music business in Europe and the UK for the European Commission and the National Music Council. He was co-editor with Phil Hardy of the pioneering *Encyclopedia of Rock* in the mid-1970s and of the *Faber Companion to Twentieth-Century Popular Music* in the 1990s.

Peter J. Martin is currently Dean of Undergraduate Studies in the Faculty of Social Sciences and Law at the University of Manchester. He graduated from the University of Edinburgh and completed his PhD at Manchester, where he is a former Head of the Department of Sociology. He has particular research interests in the sociology of culture (particularly music), interactional analysis, sociological theory and social stratification, and his publications include *Sounds and Society: Themes in the Sociology of Music* (Manchester University Press, 1995) and, with W. W. Sharrock and J. A. Hughes, *Understanding Classical Sociology* (Sage, 1995). His current projects include the development of a sociological approach to jazz improvisation, studies of musical institutions in nineteenth-century Manchester, and the car in contemporary culture.

Ingrid Monson is the Quincy Jones Professor of African-American Music at Harvard University. She specialises in jazz, African-American music and the music of the African diaspora. She is the author of *Saying Something: Jazz Improvisation and Interaction* (University of Chicago Press), which won the Sonneck Society's Irving Lowens Award for the best book on American music published in 1996. She is currently completing *Freedom Sounds: Jazz, Civil Rights, and Africa, 1950–1967*, which will be published by Oxford University Press. She has published articles in *Ethnomusicology, Critical Inquiry, Black Music Research Journal, World of Music, Journal of the American Musicological Society* and *Women and Music*. She is also a trumpet player.

Stuart Nicholson is the author of five books on jazz. His biographies of Billie Holiday and Ella Fitzgerald have both received 'Notable Book of the Year' citations from the *New York Times Review of Books*. His first book, *Jazz: The 1980s Resurgence* (1990), was a landmark study of an important renascent decade for jazz, and his *Jazz-Rock: A History* (1998) was praised by *Kirkus Review* for its 'impeccable musical scholarship'. His documentary biography of Duke Ellington, *Reminiscing in Tempo: A Portrait of Duke Ellington* (1999), was nominated 'Book of the Week' by the *Mail on Sunday*. Stuart Nicholson is co-author (with Max Harrison and Eric Thacker) of *The Essential Jazz Recordings Vol. 2: Modernism to Postmodernism*.

Thomas Owens, a native of California, studied at El Camino College (AA) and the University of California at Los Angeles (BA, MA, PhD); in addition, he studied privately with Myron Floren (accordion), Sam Saxe (jazz improvisation) and Eduardo Delgado (piano). Though a part-time jazz musician, Owens is primarily a music educator, and has taught at El Camino College (1966–91,

1992–2000) and UCLA (1991–2). He has written for *The New Grove Dictionary of American Music, The New Grove Dictionary of Jazz, Jazz Times, Encarta 97 Encyclopedia, Encarta Africana Encyclopedia* and other publications, and is the author of *Bebop: The Music and Its Players* (Oxford University Press, 1995).

Jeff Pressing was a cognitive scientist, mathematical modeller and internationally recognised composer and jazz/avant-garde keyboard performer. He published extensively in the fields of theoretical chemistry, microbiology, cognitive psychology, motor behaviour and skill, expertise, musical cognition, improvisation, time series analysis, financial prediction and self-organising systems. Formerly Associate Professor of Music at Berklee College of Music in Boston, composer-in-residence with the Australian Broadcasting Corporation and Head of Music at La Trobe University, Melbourne, he was subsequently a tenured researcher in the Department of Behavioural Science at the University of Melbourne, where he was Director of the Intelligenesis Research Group. His World Rhythm Band was active in Australia and he performed internationally as a keyboardist. He was also a music critic for the *Melbourne Age*.

Jed Rasula is a Professor of English at Queen's University in Canada, and has a PhD from the History of Consciousness Programme at the University of California, Santa Cruz. His books include *The American Poetry Wax Museum: Reality Effects, 1940–1990* (1996) and *Imagining Language: An Anthology*, co-edited with Steve McCaffery (1998). Two books on American poetry are forthcoming: *This Compost* and *Syncopations*. He has published widely on various aspects of modern culture, including an essay on jazz history in *Jazz Among the Discourses* (ed. Krin Gabbard), an essay on comic books and juvenile delinquency in *Representations* (1990) and essays on communications technologies and literature in *Sound States* (ed. Adalaide Morris) and *Close Listening* (ed. Charles Bernstein).

David Sager studied trombone from the age of nine, and in 1983–95 worked as a professional musician in New Orleans, from which base he toured the US and Europe with singer Banu Gibson and the New Orleans Hot Jazz. He has performed with Al Hirt, Pete Fountain and the Preservation Hall Jazz Band, and recorded with Branford Marsalis, Danny Barker and John Gill's New Orleans Novelty Orchestra. He currently works in the Recorded Sound section of the Motion Picture, Broadcast and Recorded Sound Division of the Library of Congress, and is trombonist with Dan Levinson's Roof Garden Orchestra (which specialises in jazz of the late 1910s and early 1920s). Alongside his professional work, he is pursuing a postgraduate programme in jazz research and history under Lewis Porter at Rutgers University.

Robert Walser is Professor and Chair of Musicology at the University of California, Los Angeles. He specialises in American music, especially jazz and other popular musics. He is the author of *Keeping Time: Readings in Jazz History* (Oxford, 1999) and *Running with the Devil: Power, Gender, and Madness in Heavy Metal Music* (Wesleyan, 1993); the latter was named an 'Outstanding Academic Book' by *Choice* and won the Irving Lowens Award for Distinguished Scholarship in American Music. A recipient of NEH, ACLS and Whiting Foundation Fellowships, he is co-editor of the Music/Culture Series at Wesleyan University Press and editor of the scholarly journal, *American Music*.

Acknowledgements

The editors gratefully acknowledge the constant enthusiasm and support of the staff at Cambridge University Press throughout work on this project, which would not have been possible without the vision and almost limitless patience of Penny Souster. Special thanks are also due to Sue Dickinson for her skilful copy-editing, to production controllers Louise Howes and Neil de Cort, and to all the book's contributors on both sides of the Atlantic. For contributions to the book above and beyond the demands of their own chapters we are especially indebted to Darius Brubeck, Krin Gabbard, Bruce Johnson and Rob Walser. We also thank Lewis Porter and Graham Lock for their invaluable advice, and Sheila Husson for her research at the Norsk Jazzarchiv and Norske Argus that provided the starting point for Chapter 9.

For permission to reproduce copyright material we are grateful to William P. Gottlieb, Felix Rosenstiel's Widow & Son Ltd, Erik Strøyer, and the Schomburg Center for Research in Black Culture.

With sadness we record the death of contributor Jeff Pressing on 28 April 2002, while this book was in press.

A brief chronology of jazz

1890s The ragtime craze begins with the publication of ragtime songs by Ben Harney, Ernest Hogan and others, and piano rags by William H. Krell and Tom Turpin (1897). Scott Joplin's *Maple Leaf Rag* (1899) quickly becomes a bestseller. The blues is also fully fledged at this time, though not preserved in print or recorded form.

1900 John Philip Sousa's concert band performs ragtime arrangements in Paris. John Stark moves his successful ragtime publishing business to St Louis.

1901 First acoustic recording of piano rags issued by Victor.

1902 New Orleans's Lincoln Park becomes major venue for ragtime. Jelly Roll Morton claimed to have invented jazz in this year (though he was only 12 years old at the time).

1903 Scott Joplin composes his first ragtime opera. Pianist Eubie Blake publishes his first rags.

1904 Cornettist Buddy Bolden is active in New Orleans, fusing elements drawn from both ragtime and the blues.

1905 Ragtime songs criticised for racism in the black press. Morton composes 'Jelly Roll Blues', later to become the first published jazz piece (1915).

1906 Trumpeters Freddie Keppard and Bunk Johnson active in New Orleans.

1907 Buddy Bolden committed to an asylum for the mentally ill. Musicians begin gradual migration from New Orleans to Chicago and New York.

1908 French composer Claude Debussy emulates ragtime in his piano suite, *Children's Corner*. Freddie Keppard takes his New Orleans jazz on tour.

1909 Ragtime publication peaks in this year.

1910 Cornettist King Oliver is playing in New Orleans. Bandleader James Reese Europe founds the black musicians' Clef Club in New York.

1911 Trombonist Kid Ory and clarinettist Sidney Bechet active in New Orleans.

1912 W. C. Handy publishes 'Memphis Blues', the first blues to appear in print. Singer Bessie Smith active in minstrel shows.

1913 James Reese Europe's Society Orchestra records ragtime arrangements in New York. Freddie Keppard tours with his Original Creole Orchestra. The word 'jazz' appears in print for the first time.

1914 George Gershwin begins work, aged 15, as a song-plugger on Tin Pan Alley. W. C. Handy publishes his 'St Louis Blues'.

1915 Clarinettists Jimmie Noone and Johnny Dodds active in New Orleans.
Scott Joplin stages his second ragtime opera, *Treemonisha*, in Harlem.

1916 Johnny Stein's Dixie Jass Band performs in Chicago.
Stride pianist James P. Johnson begins cutting piano rolls.

1917 The Original Dixieland Jass Band performs in Manhattan and makes the first
jazz recordings. Rejected by Columbia, their music is issued by Victor on 7
March, and 'Livery Stable Blues' becomes an instant hit.
The Storyville naval base in New Orleans closes, intensifying the migration of
musicians to Chicago and New York.

1918 Cornettist Louis Armstrong plays with Fate Marable's band on Mississippi
steamboats, then joins Kid Ory in New Orleans.

1919 The Original Dixieland Jazz Band creates a sensation in London.
Will Marion Cook's Southern Syncopated Orchestra tours Europe, where
Sidney Bechet elects to stay.

1920 In New York, singer Mamie Smith cuts the first blues recordings.
King Oliver forms a band in New Orleans.

1921 Jazz is banned in Zion, Illinois, for being 'sinful'.
Pianist Fletcher Henderson directs the Black Swan Record Company in Harlem.

1922 Kid Ory's Sunshine Orchestra records in Los Angeles.
Louis Armstrong joins King Oliver's band in Chicago.
First recordings by pianists Fats Waller and Count Basie, and by the New
Orleans Rhythm Kings.
The first European jazz club opens, in Paris.

1923 A recording boom results in recordings by Bessie Smith, Ma Rainey, King
Oliver's Creole Jazz Band, Jelly Roll Morton, Sidney Bechet and Bennie Moten.
Columbia launches its 'race records' series.
New bands formed by Fletcher Henderson and Elmer Snowden in New York.

1924 George Gershwin composes *Rhapsody in Blue* for Paul Whiteman's 'Experiment
in Modern Music'.
First recordings by trumpeter Bix Beiderbecke, and by Duke Ellington as leader
of The Washingtonians.
Robert Goffin organises jazz parties in Brussels.

1925 Louis Armstrong records variously with Sidney Bechet, Bessie Smith and
Fletcher Henderson, and with his own Hot Five in Chicago.
Electric recording technology introduced.
Dancer Josephine Baker and Sidney Bechet perform in Paris.

1926 Louis Armstrong pioneers 'scat' singing with 'Heebie Jeebies'.
Tenor saxophonist Coleman Hawkins records with Fletcher Henderson.
Jelly Roll Morton records in Chicago with his Red Hot Peppers.
Sidney Bechet visits Moscow.
First critical book on jazz published, in Paris.

1927 Duke Ellington's band takes up its residency at Harlem's Cotton Club.
Bix Beiderbecke plays with the bands of Jean Goldkette and Paul Whiteman.

1928 First recordings by clarinettist Benny Goodman.
Louis Armstrong (who records 'West End Blues' this year) moves to New York, as does Jelly Roll Morton.
Pianist Earl Hines establishes his big band in Chicago.

1929 Count Basie records with Bennie Moten's Kansas City band.
Trumpeter Cootie Williams joins Duke Ellington's band.
Bessie Smith stars in the movie *St Louis Blues*.

1930 Drummer Lionel Hampton records the first jazz vibraphone solo.
Duke Ellington records 'Mood Indigo'.
Paul Whiteman appears in the movie, *The King of Jazz*.

1931 Chick Webb's band plays at Harlem's Savoy Ballroom.
Hungarian composer Mátyás Seiber establishes the first academic jazz class, in Frankfurt.

1932 Louis Armstrong and Fats Waller tour Europe.
Hot Club de France founded in Paris.
Duke Ellington records 'It Don't Mean a Thing (If It Ain't Got That Swing)'.

1933 First solo recordings by pianist Art Tatum, and first recordings by singer Billie Holiday.
Duke Ellington tours Europe.

1934 Coleman Hawkins plays in London.
Ella Fitzgerald is vocalist with Chick Webb's band.
Formation of Quintette du Hot Club de France, featuring violinist Stephane Grappelli and guitarist Django Reinhardt.
Journal *Down Beat* launched in Chicago.
Hugues Panassié publishes his book, *Le Jazz Hot*, in Paris.

1935 Benny Goodman's band phenomenally successful in Los Angeles, playing Fletcher Henderson's arrangements; Goodman also performs small-combo jazz with players of mixed race this year.
Count Basie takes over leadership of Bennie Moten's band in Kansas City.
UK Musicians' Union announces ban on visits by US musicians (revoked in 1954).
Nazi party announces plans to ban all jazz broadcasts in Germany.

1936 Revival of blues-based 'boogie-woogie' piano style.
Count Basie records for Decca, his band including tenor saxophonist Lester Young.
First jazz discography published, by Charles Delaunay in Paris.

1937 Count Basie's band appears at Harlem's Savoy Ballroom and Apollo Theatre, and records 'One O'Clock Jump'.
In Los Angeles, Nat King Cole forms the first jazz piano trio.

1938 Benny Goodman's band appears at Carnegie Hall, New York.
Prominent new bandleaders include Artie Shaw, Harry James and Gene Krupa.
Jelly Roll Morton makes retrospective recordings for the Library of Congress.
Winthrop Sargeant publishes his book, *Jazz, Hot and Hybrid*, in New York.

1939 Arranger Billy Strayhorn joins Duke Ellington, whose band tours Europe this
year.
Glenn Miller records two big-band popular hits, 'In the Mood' and 'Moonlight
Serenade'.
Billie Holiday records the anti-racist song, 'Strange Fruit'.
Coleman Hawkins records 'Body and Soul'.

1940 In Harlem, Minton's Playhouse becomes the venue for early bebop jam sessions.
Broadcasting ban by American Society of Composers, Authors and Publishers
(until 1941).
Big-band recordings include Duke Ellington's 'Concerto for Cootie' and
'Ko-Ko', and Lionel Hampton's 'Flying Home'.

1941 First recordings featuring alto saxophonist Charlie Parker.
Duke Ellington's new signature tune is Billy Strayhorn's 'Take the "A" Train'.
Stan Kenton founds his Artistry in Rhythm Orchestra.
Sidney Bechet records as a one-man band.

1942 Bunk Johnson participates in a revival of the old New Orleans style.
Recording ban by American Federation of Musicians (until 1944).
Charlie Parker and trumpeter Dizzy Gillespie play with Earl Hines's band.
Singer Sarah Vaughan wins talent contest in Harlem.

1943 Glenn Miller and Artie Shaw lead US military bands, and 'V-discs' are
manufactured exclusively for distribution to those on active service (until
1949).
Duke Ellington's band performs 'Black, Brown and Beige' at Carnegie Hall.
Art Tatum forms his piano trio.

1944 First recordings by pianist Thelonious Monk.
Norman Granz founds Jazz at the Philharmonic in Los Angeles.
Pianists Oscar Peterson and Erroll Garner active.

1945 Dizzy Gillespie records 'Be-Bop' in New York, and trumpeter Miles Davis joins
Gillespie and Charlie Parker at venues on New York's 52nd Street.
Pianist Mary Lou Williams appears at Town Hall, New York.
Sidney Bechet and Louis Armstrong reunited in New Orleans.

1946 Charlie Parker records for Dial Records in Los Angeles.
Dizzy Gillespie forms his bop big band.
Igor Stravinsky composes *Ebony Concerto* for Woody Herman's band.
Australian Jazz Convention founded.

1947 Louis Armstrong and Billie Holiday appear at Carnegie Hall, and Armstrong
launches his All Stars at New York's Town Hall.
Miles Davis's first recordings as leader.
Dizzy Gillespie promotes 'Cubop' (i.e., bop with Latin elements).
Art Blakey forms his Jazz Messengers.
Radio debate between jazz modernists and traditionalists in New York.

1948 First major jazz festival, at Nice, features Dizzy Gillespie.
Duke Ellington tours Europe.

Miles Davis's nonet launches 'cool' jazz in New York.
Tenor saxophonist Stan Getz records with Woody Herman.

1949 First Paris Jazz Festival is attended by Charlie Parker, Dizzy Gillespie, Sidney
Bechet, Miles Davis and Kenny Clarke.
Pianist Lennie Tristano experiments with an early form of free jazz.
Miles Davis and Gil Evans make nonet recordings later issued on LP as
The Birth of the Cool.

1950 Charlie Parker tours Sweden, and Benny Goodman tours Europe.
Big bands led by Count Basie and Dizzy Gillespie are forced to disband for
financial reasons.

1951 Pianists Dave Brubeck and John Lewis both form quartets.
Fender launches its Precision electric bass guitar.

1952 Charlie Parker plays with trumpeter/singer Chet Baker in Los Angeles.
John Lewis establishes, with vibraphonist Milt Jackson and others, the Modern
Jazz Quartet.
Californian jazz featured at Carnegie Hall.

1953 Charlie Parker takes bop to Canada.
The Dave Brubeck Quartet begins performing on US university campuses.
Count Basie and Benny Goodman form new big bands.
Sydney Jazz Club founded in Australia.
Frankfurt Jazz Festival founded.

1954 First US jazz festival held at Newport, Rhode Island.
Billie Holiday and Count Basie tour Europe.
Chet Baker records 'My Funny Valentine'; baritone saxophonist Gerry
Mulligan and drummer Shelly Manne also active on West Coast.
Charles Mingus forms his Jazz Composers' Workshop.

1955 A four-hour memorial concert for Charlie Parker (d. 12 March) is held at
Carnegie Hall.
Chet Baker tours Europe.
First recordings by Miles Davis's Quintet, featuring tenor saxophonist John
Coltrane.

1956 Dizzy Gillespie's big band undertakes world tour; European tourers this year
include Louis Armstrong, Stan Kenton and Jazz at the Philharmonic.
Charles Mingus records *Pithecanthropus Erectus*, saxophonist Sonny Rollins
records *Saxophone Colossus* and Miles Davis records a flurry of albums for
Prestige.
Duke Ellington causes a sensation at Newport with 'Diminuendo and
Crescendo in Blue'.

1957 Third stream movement promoted by Gunther Schuller.
Jazz film scores by Miles Davis and John Lewis.
Thelonious Monk records with Art Blakey.
John Coltrane records 'Blue Train'.

1958 Miles Davis and Bill Evans experiment with modal jazz.
First Monterey Jazz Festival, California.
'Bossa nova' launched by Antonio Carlos Jobim.
Overseas tours include Dave Brubeck (Denmark and Middle East), Oscar
Peterson (Holland), Billie Holiday (Europe), Duke Ellington (UK), Woody
Herman (South America) and Jack Teagarden (Far East).
Stan Getz emigrates to Denmark.

1959 Seminal albums recorded this year include *Time Out* (Brubeck), *Giant Steps*
(Coltrane), *Kind of Blue* (Davis) and *The Shape of Jazz to Come* (Ornette
Coleman).
Film scores by Duke Ellington and John Lewis.
International Jazz Jamboree founded, Warsaw.

1960 Free jazz promoted in US by Ornette Coleman, Don Cherry, John Coltrane and
others.
Eric Dolphy collaborates with Charles Mingus.
Stan Tracey becomes house pianist at Ronnie Scott's London club.
Metropol Jazzhus opened, Oslo.
Antibes Jazz Festival founded.

1961 Increasingly negative press for free jazz in US.
Art Blakey, Oscar Peterson and Ella Fitzgerald perform in Tokyo.
Thelonious Monk and Eric Dolphy visit Europe.
Molde Jazz Festival founded in Norway.

1962 Bossa nova further popularised by Stan Getz.
First recordings (as leader) by pianist Herbie Hancock.
Benny Goodman and Teddy Wilson visit Soviet Union.
Pianist Cecil Taylor brings free jazz to Scandinavia.
Saxophonist Dexter Gordon emigrates to Europe.

1963 Miles Davis launches new quintet featuring George Coleman (sax), Ron Carter
(bass), Herbie Hancock (piano) and Tony Williams (drums). Thelonious Monk
performs in Tokyo.
Trumpeter Lee Morgan records his hit hard-bop album, *The Sidewinder*. Charles
Mingus records experimental album, *The Black Saint and the Sinner Lady*.

1964 Wayne Shorter replaces George Coleman in the Miles Davis Quintet.
John Coltrane records *A Love Supreme* and Eric Dolphy *Out to Lunch*.
Berlin Jazz Festival founded.

1965 New impetus to free jazz with the foundation of the Association for the
Advancement of Creative Musicians in Chicago, and John Coltrane's radical
recording, *Ascension*.
Herbie Hancock records *Maiden Voyage*.
Duke Ellington's *First Sacred Concert* premiered in San Francisco.

1966 Virtuosic big band led by trumpeter Thad Jones and drummer Mel Lewis opens
at the Village Vanguard, New York.
Duke Ellington and John Coltrane visit Japan, and Earl Hines plays in the
Soviet Union.

Pori Jazz Festival founded, Finland.

San Sebastián Jazz Festival founded, Spain.

1967 Art Ensemble of Chicago formed.

Down Beat extends coverage to include rock music.

First Montreux Jazz Festival, Switzerland, and first Berkeley Jazz Festival, California.

1968 Newport Festival performers appear at London's Jazz Expo '68.

Anthony Braxton forms his Creative Construction Company.

Black Artists' Group formed, St Louis.

Jazz and Heritage Festival founded, New Orleans.

Gunther Schuller's pioneering book, *Early Jazz*, first published.

1969 Miles Davis popularises jazz-rock with his electrified albums, *In a Silent Way* and *Bitches Brew*.

Tony Williams founds jazz-rock group Lifetime.

Duke Ellington's 70th birthday celebrated at the White House, Washington DC.

Concord Jazz Festival founded, California.

1970 Edition of Contemporary Music (ECM) launched with recording by Norwegian saxophonist Jan Garbarek.

Keyboard players Chick Corea and Keith Jarrett play with Miles Davis; Corea forms Circle with Anthony Braxton.

Trumpeter Ian Carr's Nucleus makes first recording.

1971 Foundation of fusion bands, Weather Report (by keyboard player Joe Zawinul and saxophonist Wayne Shorter) and Mahavishnu Orchestra (by guitarist John McLaughlin).

Sun Ra performs free jazz in Cairo.

Duke Ellington visits Soviet Union.

1972 Chick Corea forms fusion band, Return to Forever.

Thelonious Monk begins a decade of retirement.

Ornette Coleman performs 'Skies of America' with the London Symphony Orchestra.

Bix Beiderbecke Memorial Festival established, Davenport, Iowa.

1973 Bill Evans, Sarah Vaughan and Cecil Taylor perform in Tokyo.

Herbie Hancock's funk success with *Head Hunters*.

Ragtime revival stimulated by success of movie, *The Sting*.

Big band formed by Toshiko Akiyoshi and Lew Tabackin.

1974 Modern Jazz Quartet disbands.

Keith Jarrett collaborates with Jan Garbarek.

Free jazz in Europe expands, with formation of Antwerp Free Music Festival, a European tour by Anthony Braxton, and the foundation of Willem Breuker's Kollectief orchestra.

Ravenna Jazz Festival founded, Italy.

1975 Live recording of Keith Jarrett's solo concert in Cologne becomes a major seller for ECM; also this year, guitarist Pat Metheny records his debut album for the label.

Miles Davis retires following Newport Festival.

Trumpeter-prodigy Wynton Marsalis (aged 14) performs with the New Orleans Symphony Orchestra.

Brothers Mike Brecker (sax) and Randy Brecker (trumpet) record in New York.

1976 Thelonious Monk makes his last public appearance, at Newport.

Brubeck Quartet reunites to celebrate its 25th anniversary.

Ornette Coleman founds his fusion band, Prime Time.

North Sea Jazz Festival founded, The Hague.

Montmartre Jazz Club opened, Copenhagen.

1977 World Saxophone Quartet formed.

Count Basie, Dave Brubeck and Dizzy Gillespie appear at Montreux Festival.

Pat Metheny makes first recording with keyboard player, Lyle Mays.

1978 Don Cherry fuses world music and jazz with his group, Codona.

Soviet pianist Vyacheslav Ganelin records with his trio in Moscow, where a new jazz festival is founded.

Other jazz festivals launched this year include Atlanta (free jazz), Praxis (Athens, for free jazz), Guinness (Cork, Eire), Jazzratya (Bombay), Zurich and Chichester.

1979 Mingus Dynasty formed in memory of the bassist (d. 5 January).

Special Edition formed by drummer Jack DeJohnette and saxophonist David Murray.

Last major recordings by pianists Bill Evans and Horace Silver.

New jazz festivals in Copenhagen, Edinburgh, Chicago and Hollywood (Playboy Festival).

1980 Wynton Marsalis performs with Art Blakey at Montreux.

Art Ensemble of Chicago tours Germany and Italy.

Mike Maineiri and Mike Brecker form Steps.

Swing revived by Savoy Sultans at Newport.

New jazz festivals launched in Paris and Canada (Edmonton/Montreal).

1981 Miles Davis stages his come-back at Newport, then tours in Japan.

Wynton Marsalis forms his own group for a tour of Japan, where the Modern Jazz Quartet are also reunited this year; Marsalis makes his first recordings as leader.

Jazz festivals founded in Madrid and Israel.

1982 Thelonious Monk's death is commemorated by the foundation of the group Sphere, and by Milt Jackson at Ronnie Scott's London club.

Benny Goodman recreates his 1930s quartet.

Bassist Jaco Pastorius forms his own group.

New jazz festivals founded in Umbria and Salzburg.

1983 Keith Jarrett forms a trio to play standards.

Miles Davis plays with saxophonist Bill Evans, guitarist John Scofield and bassist Marcus Miller.

Herbie Hancock's 'Rockit' is no. 1 in pop charts.

Wynton Marsalis wins Grammy awards for both classical and jazz recordings.
New jazz festivals founded at Brighton and Miami (Floating Jazz Festival).

1984 Sun Ra appears at Athens's Praxis 84 Festival.
Miles Davis plays in Denmark and scores a pop success with his version of 'Human Nature'.
The Ganelin Trio tours the UK.
The Dirty Dozen Brass Band reinterprets venerable New Orleans styles.

1985 Blue Note record label relaunched at New York's Town Hall.
New British band Loose Tubes perform at Ronnie Scott's.
Weather Report records its final album.
Chick Corea forms his Elektric Band.
First recordings by singer Cassandra Wilson.

1986 Debut of Gary Giddins's American Jazz Orchestra.
Wynton Marsalis records standards.
Recording debut of British saxophonist, Courtney Pine.
New festivals founded in London (Soho), St Petersburg, Oslo and New York (JVC).

1987 Jazz declared a 'national treasure' by US Congress.
World tour by Dizzy Gillespie's big band celebrates his 70th birthday.
A retrospective celebrates the 80th birthday of saxophonist Benny Carter in New York.
New jazz festivals in Sweden (Åhus) and Vienna (Blue Danube Jazz Summit).

1988 Jazz at Lincoln Center programme launched, under direction of Wynton Marsalis.
Miles Davis performs with pop star Prince.
New Grove Dictionary of Jazz published, under editorship of Barry Kernfeld.

1989 Jazz Messengers reconstituted in Germany to mark Art Blakey's 70th birthday.
Charles Mingus's large-scale work, *Epitaph*, is reconstructed by Gunther Schuller.
Trumpeter Roy Hargrove and postmodernist John Zorn come to prominence.

1990 Jan Garbarek collaborates with Pakistani musicians.
Saxophonist Pharoah Sanders appears in London.
John McLaughlin records with the London Symphony Orchestra.
Top musicians in *Down Beat* annual polls include Ornette Coleman's Prime Time, the Phil Woods Quintet and Sun Ra's Arkestra.

1991 Smithsonian Institution's Jazz Masterworks Orchestra and Jazz Masterworks Edition founded.
Revival of Cubop, New York.
'Women of the New Jazz' Festival launched in Chicago.
Akbank Jazz Festival founded in Turkey.

1992 Montreux Festival renamed 'Montreux Jazz and World Music Festival'.
Special tribute to the music of Jelly Roll Morton mounted at the San Francisco Jazz Festival.

1993 Saxophonist Joe Henderson wins several awards in *Down Beat* polls.
Jan Garbarek's crossover album with medieval music, *Officium,* becomes a
best-seller.
Oscar Peterson wins the Glenn Gould Prize.
Chick Corea's Elektric Band refused permission to perform in Germany on
account of its leader's membership of the Church of Scientology.

1994 Verve Records celebrates its 50th anniversary, and *Down Beat* its 60th.
High-profile recordings by pianists Geri Allen and Maria Schneider.
First International Jazz Festival in Hawaii launched by British
husband-and-wife duo, saxophonist John Dankworth and singer Cleo Laine.
Jazz-rap summit held in New York.

1995 Arts Council conducts major review of the state of jazz in the UK.
Roy Hargrove finally dislodges Wynton Marsalis from top of the *Down Beat*
readers' poll.

1996 Jazz-Fest USA showcases musical talents of US college students.

1997 Wynton Marsalis awarded Pulitzer Prize.

1998 British trumpeter Humphrey Lyttelton celebrates his 50th anniversary as a
bandleader.

1999 Ken Burns makes his epic television documentary *Jazz,* which reportedly
doubles sales of jazz recordings in the USA when broadcast there in 2000. The
series is subsequently aired in the UK (in a shortened export version) during
2001.

The word jazz

KRIN GABBARD

Jazz is a construct. Nothing can be called jazz simply because of its 'nature'. Musical genres such as the military march, opera and reggae are relatively homogeneous and easy to identify. By contrast, the term jazz is routinely applied to musics that have as little in common as an improvisation by Marilyn Crispell and a 1923 recording by King Oliver and his Creole Jazz Band. Developed well outside the more carefully regulated institutions of American culture, early jazz, proto-jazz or *Ur*-jazz was performed by people from an extremely wide variety of backgrounds. Many styles of playing were mixed together and others were split off and acquired different names. If today we call something jazz, it has much more to do with the utterances of critics, journalists, record companies and club owners than with the music itself.

Those who have been most devoted to defining the music and to discriminating between true jazz and false jazz often rely upon tautologies and *ad hominem* arguments. The esteemed poet and jazz writer Philip Larkin, for example, once wrote:

> I like jazz to be jazz. A. E. Housman said he could recognize poetry
> because it made his throat tighten and his eyes water: I can recognize jazz
> because it makes me tap my foot, grunt affirmative exhortations, or even
> get up and caper around the room. If it doesn't do this, then however
> musically interesting or spiritually adventurous or racially praiseworthy it
> is, it isn't jazz. If that's being a purist, then I'm a purist.   [Larkin 1985, 175]

One could argue that Larkin's definition of jazz works only for him. A more suspicious observer might add that he is driven by unarticulated or unconscious agenda that have more to do with ideology and attitudes about race than with music. Indeed, as a jazz writer's manifesto recedes in time, the non-musical agenda behind it become increasingly evident. To speak generously, we can credit certain writers with discovering and publicising what is most vital in certain musical cultures. Speaking critically, we might accuse writers of colonising the music to fit their own prejudices and obsessions.

If critics and other jazz writers have been primarily responsible for creating and sustaining notions about jazz, the musicians themselves have often refused to state their own positions on what the music may or may not be.

Although there have always been highly articulate artists playing the music, not all have been interested in a conversation that creates borders around what they play. At their most whimsical or polemical, musicians have relished the opportunity to mystify rather than clarify. Louis Armstrong's legendary reply to the request that he define jazz – 'If you've got to ask, you'll never know' – is perhaps the best-known statement by a musician who preferred not to be pigeon-holed. Part of the stance of the hipster jazz artist has almost always been to 'signify' on dominant discourses rather than to contribute to them.

The reluctance among some musicians to establish the boundaries of what is and is not jazz has not stopped writers from decrying a musician for selling out, bleaching the music, betraying a legacy, abandoning the audience or playing 'anti-jazz'. Nevertheless, those who would protect the term are on a slippery slope, to say the least. The word has always carried a great many meanings, many of them outside music. Even as a term limited to a type of music, it has gone through radical changes in meaning. And many who have been granted pride of place among jazz artists have tried to disassociate themselves from the term.

According to several researchers, the earliest appearance of the word jazz in written form was probably in San Francisco newspapers. In 1913, Ernest J. Hopkins offered this definition: 'something like life, vigor, energy, effervescence of spirit, joy, pep, magnetism, verve, virility, ebulliency, courage, happiness – oh, what's the use? – JAZZ'. When the word began showing up on the sports pages of the *San Francisco Bulletin*, also in 1913, the term regularly appeared in the column by 'Scoop' Gleeson. For example, Gleeson wrote, 'Everybody has come back full of the old "jazz". What is the "jazz"? Why, it's a little of the "old life", the "gin-i-ker", the "pep", otherwise known as the enthusiasalum' (quoted in Porter 1997, 5). Needless to say, neither Hopkins nor Gleeson linked the term to music. It is not surprising, however, that a sportswriter, who is especially likely to bring terms from slang and oral culture into his published writings, would be one of the first to put a word such as jazz into a newspaper.

By the 1920s, the term was appearing in literary works as a synonym for sexual intercourse. It had almost certainly carried this meaning in oral culture at least since the turn of the century. In the 1970s Dick Holbrook sought early appearances of the word by making inquiries among older graduates of his college who lived in the western United States. One replied that he had heard jazz used as slang for sexual intercourse in California, New Mexico, Arizona and even New Hampshire as early as 1904. Another wrote, 'Yes. Circa 1910 – in Chicago. When you went out for a little Jazz, you just weren't singing *Dixie*' (quoted in Porter 1997, 4). This kind of evidence has led many to believe that the word originally had a sexual reference, per-haps related to the word 'jism', slang for semen. As is often the case with vern-acular terms, jazz lost its obscene connotations as it made its way into more polite discourse in the second decade of the twentieth century. Much the same can be said for the original, sexual meaning of the phrase 'rock-and-roll' and its widely accepted subsequent meaning as a kind of music.

The word jazz almost surely began in African-American slang, but many counter-theories on the term's origins have been advanced. Clarence Major has found an African word from a Bantu dialect, *jaja*, to dance or play music. Because of the French presence in New Orleans during the early years of the music's development, some have suggested that the word comes from the French *jaser*, meaning to banter or chat. The French term *chasse beau* may have been the inspiration for the American term 'Jasbo', and thus for jazz. There was even a bandleader named Jasbo Brown, whose name has been brought forth as a source (Porter 1997, 1). Then there was the dancing slave named Jasper who may have inspired people to shout 'Jas, Jas' as he performed. One of the entries in Bill Crow's *Jazz Anecdotes* cites the use of jasmine oil in perfumes popular in New Orleans: 'To add it to perfume was called "jazzing it up". The strong scent was popular in the red-light district, where a working girl might approach a prospective customer and say, "Is jass on your mind tonight, young fellow?"' (1990, 19).

All of these explanations for the term's genesis are conjectural and cannot be proven. We also do not know when the term jazz became more firmly attached to music, although newspaper articles were making the connection as early as 1915 (Porter 1997, 10). But if the term did originate as sexual slang, then it follows that its more polite association with energy and enthusiasm could have had a middle passage as reference to a scandalous and/or energetic form of dance music. Thus the arguments for how a sexual term associated with jasmine oil came to mean popular music in New Orleans can also be marshalled to explain the trajectory of a slang word for semen.

The shift from 'jass' to 'jazz' is also impossible to explain with certainty, but an enchanting theory involves posters for the Original Dixieland Jass Band, a group that made what are widely considered to be the first jazz recordings in 1917. When people committed mischief on their posters by obliterating the J, the band's leader, Nick LaRocca, decided to change the name to the Original Dixieland JAZZ Band (Crow 1990, 20).

LaRocca was not, however, successful in making the word jazz stick to his or anyone else's music. We now regularly use the term Jazz Age to refer to fast living and night life in the United States in the 1920s; Henri Matisse used the word to characterise a series of paper cut-outs of circus subjects he constructed in the 1930s; and, in one form or another, the word has been used more recently as the brand name for a cologne, a single-use digital camera, a computer software program, and an American basketball team called the Utah Jazz that was founded in New Orleans but subsequently (and oxymoronically) moved to a state known for its religious and political conservatism.

Keep in mind also that in the 1920s Louis Armstrong and a great many other African-American artists who played what we now call jazz would have told you that they were playing blues or ragtime (Peretti 1992, 42). Meanwhile, for most white Americans in the 1920s, Paul Whiteman was 'The King of Jazz', Al Jolson was 'The Jazz Singer', Irving Berlin was 'Mr Jazz Himself', and Sophie Tucker was 'The Queen of Jazz'. The fact that most jazz writers today look past these white entertainers and apply the term to their African-American and Creole contemporaries has resulted in the striking statement by Michael Rogin that the 1927 film that starred Al Jolson as a blackface entertainer, *The Jazz Singer*, 'contains no jazz' (Rogin 1996, 112). While most white Americans in the 1920s thought of jazz as the music of Whiteman, Jolson and George Gershwin, critics today have read more modern forms of music back into the 1920s in order to designate Armstrong, Oliver, Morton, Bechet, Henderson and Ellington as the real jazz artists. Paraphrasing Thomas Kuhn, Scott DeVeaux has pointed out that jazz history, like all history, is usually written backwards (1997, 443; see Kuhn 1970, 138).

Although a few jazz purists were already beginning to stake their claim on the term in the 1920s, not all of what they wrote is consistent with more contemporary meanings of the music. A revealing example can be found in the articles that Roger Pryor Dodge wrote in the 1920s for the English review, *The Dancing Times* (see Dodge 1995). Although Dodge claimed that Whiteman, Gershwin and Berlin did not play jazz, and although he insisted that artists such as Ellington, Henderson and Armstrong did, he included Ted Lewis and the Mound City Blue Blowers in the list of artists who played the real thing. In fact, he listed Lewis *first* in his list of 'true' jazz artists. The parity of Ted Lewis and Duke Ellington that Dodge sincerely posited in the 1920s is unthinkable at the beginning of the twenty-first century.

Disagreements about who did and did not play the real thing became most intense in the 1940s when 'the battle between the ancients and the moderns' was fought on several fronts. As Bernard Gendron has written, the defenders of the contrapuntal music from old New Orleans traded insults with champions of the more sophisticated dance music from the 1930s and 1940s. Writing in journals such *The Record Changer* and *H.R.S. Rag*, proponents of early jazz claimed that it was authentic, emotionally powerful and the music of the folk. In *Down Beat* and *Metronome*, swing was praised for being complex, progressive and technically demanding. A few years later, the same arguments that had been advanced for swing were appropriated to defend the emerging new music, bebop. As Gendron points out (1995, 32), these arguments formed the basis for subsequent assertions that jazz was a legitimate art form. Although they violently disagreed on the definition of jazz, critics in the 1940s tacitly agreed to fight their battles around a set of dualisms – black versus white, art versus commerce, nature versus culture, technique versus affect, European versus native – on which claims about jazz as art have been built ever since.

By the late 1940s, after the bebop revolution had alienated most of the listeners who had followed the big bands, *Down Beat* launched a contest to find a new name for a music that did *not* include bebop but that might win back readers who had abandoned the magazine and the music to which it was devoted. Terms such as 'ragtonia', 'syncopep', 'crewcut music', 'Amerimusic' and 'Jarb' all failed to replace the word jazz (Crow 1990, 21). Although writers had already been struggling over the term for several decades, it was exhibiting surprising durability.

By the 1950s, jazz had become an elite music policed by devoted groups of fans and critics. As the music continued to evolve, still more terms were introduced to account for the fact that jazz musicians were no longer playing what everyone used to call jazz. A phrase which had brief but considerable success was 'third stream', a term to describe music that was carefully composed and inflected with tonalities and concepts drawn from European classical music. Jazz was becoming even more of an art music for the elite, and once again the critics felt the need for a better word. Critics were also likely to coin terms like 'anti-jazz' and 'non-jazz' to describe the sounds of Ornette Coleman, John Coltrane and Eric Dolphy, even if these avant-garde musicians would later be deified as the great priests of jazz when rock influences entered into the music. For most purists, fusion became the new anti-jazz in the 1970s. In the 1980s, music that mixed jazz improvisation with New Age elements was attacked as the latest force that was destroying jazz. In 1997 Eric Nisenson published *Blue: The Murder of Jazz*, in which he argued that Wynton Marsalis, Albert Murray, Stanley Crouch and the staff of Jazz at Lincoln Center were killing the music by enforcing a canon of older musicians and established styles. For Nisenson, jazz would seem to be defined *not* as recognisable stylistic conventions but as constant experimentation and forward movement.

In spite of continuing and often bellicose attempts throughout most of the twentieth century to attach the term to specific kinds of music, critics had lost control of the word almost entirely by the 1970s when departments of dance and physical education in colleges and universities began to offer courses in 'jazz dance'. Students heard music that was more likely to be rock or pop while mimicking moves that recalled musicals choreographed by Bob Fosse. At the end of the twentieth century, when a student said that she was studying jazz, it usually meant a course in modern dance. In health clubs and in private homes with a videocassette recorder, people could even indulge in something called 'jazzercise'.

The musicians themselves, however, did not always feel vindicated when critics determined them worthy of the honorific term. Just as Louis Armstrong and/or Fats Waller allegedly finessed the opportunity to define jazz, other musicians bristled at the idea that they should be confined by a single word. Miles Davis and Anthony Braxton have both objected to a term they found to be inadequate as their musics developed beyond familiar paradigms. Davis explicitly associated the word jazz with slavery (Davis and Troupe 1989, 325). Quoted in 1944, Duke Ellington expressed a preference for the term 'Negro folk music' (Tucker 1993, 218). Much later, writing in his autobiography, *Music Is My Mistress* (1973), Ellington wrote, '"Jazz" is only a word and really has no meaning. We stopped using it in 1943' (452). Beginning in the 1960s, some of the more militant African-American artists insisted that they were playing 'black music'. In 1970 Max Roach ruefully observed that 'Don't give me all that jazz' is synonymous with 'Don't give me all that shit'. He continued, 'Personally I resent the word unequivocally because of our spirituals and our heritage; the work and sweat that went into our music is above shit. I don't know whether anybody else realizes what this means, but I really do, and I am vehement about it. The proper name for it, if you want to speak about it historically, is music that has been created and developed by musicians of African descent who are in America' (A. Taylor 1983, 110).

Nevertheless, the word jazz has proved remarkably durable in designating a number of musics with enough in common to be understood as part of a coherent tradition. Discussions of the music – including this one – would be much less effective without the word. As John Szwed has pointed out, the word jazz now has more meaning outside the music and has a special appeal to a greater audience beyond the circle of devotees and connoisseurs: '"Jazz" (as we might now call this larger area of discussion) has outgrown its original means, moving beyond the music to become what some would call a discourse, a system of influences, a point at which a number of texts converge and where a number of symbolic codes are created' (Szwed 2000, 7). As jazz moved into the twenty-first century, those codes had more to do with urbanity, artistic discipline and romance than with dissipation and drug abuse. Even as late as the 1980s, few would have predicted this shift. Those who care about the music will surely be just as surprised by what the word will come to mean if it survives for a second century.

PART ONE

Jazz times

1 The identity of jazz

DAVID HORN

Among the many historical accounts of jazz, it is above all the discographies that convey most graphically and emphatically just how extensively performed and how diverse jazz has been since it arrived on the public scene in 1916–17. But it is beyond the brief of a discography to do much more than list, and so the nearest thing we have to a record of the sheer scale of jazz diversity and inventiveness is silent on many other questions. Thus, while many discographies take for granted that the diversity they chronicle represents a collective body of music – even if they appear to have built into them particular views of what is and is not 'jazz' – they do not see it as their task to identify what, if anything, might connect the music together (and how and why), even less to consider the question of how the achievements they enumerate belong in, reflect and respond to a wider world. And there is no particular reason why they should. But if we seek to go beyond diversity and extent and look for what made jazz distinctive, we need to ask questions such as: how did jazz acquire its identity in the twentieth century, how was that identity constructed, and what role was played in the formation of identity by the ways in which the music was connected to processes and histories both close to and beyond its immediate environment?

Diversity and connectedness; distinctiveness and conformity. In the complex cultural history of the twentieth century, jazz emerged to live as one music among many, one moreover that bore the imprint of its connections with other musics – musics as diverse as the blues and Broadway show tunes. At the same time, it was a music that continuously asserted its difference, and had its difference recognised. On the face of it, what seems most apparent about the perception of jazz is the strong contrast between different eras, exemplified in the gulf between the way jazz was associated with risk in the speakeasies of 1920s American cities, and the cosy image of 'dinner jazz' put out by end-of-the-century radio programming – from counterculture to counter-indigestion. This does not seem fertile ground on which to search for the consistency necessary to the formation of identity. Indeed, Scott DeVeaux has cautioned us against the assumption, often made in jazz historiography, of an underlying organic essence uniting all of jazz, however disparate, and of the construction of a 'unitary narrative', concepts which lead inexorably to the emergence of the notion of tradition (1991, 526ff., 540).

Accepting that advice, I nevertheless do not want to abandon the idea that there may be consistent factors within the process by which jazz has achieved identity and within the component parts of that identity. I do not mean for one minute to ignore or reduce in importance either the profound changes that took place within jazz or the ways in which jazz was used to support the desire for change, either in the arts or in society as a whole. Nor do I mean to propose a view of jazz as more conservative than radical. Rather I am interested in what LeRoi Jones, in the context of black culture, first termed 'the changing same'. The concept, as taken up by Paul Gilroy (1993, 101), provides an alternative to ideas of fixity on the one hand and a disconnected pluralism on the other. At the same time, a focus on the relationship between continuities and changes should not be confined to the particular stream of practice under scrutiny; instead, we need to see the many ways in which that stream connects to other streams, how it enters and engages in what George Lipsitz and Keith Negus, drawing on Mikhail Bakhtin to write about popular culture and popular music, have thought of as multiple ongoing historical dialogues, dialogues in which 'no one has the first or last word' (Lipsitz 1990, 99; also quoted in Negus 1997).

What follows is an examination of certain features of the history of jazz as it developed in the twentieth century, areas where change has been steady, sometimes relatively straightforward, sometimes contested, but where also particular ideas appear to have emerged that have become strongly associated with the music and may have made a major contribution to its identity. These were not the unadorned invention of jazz – in each case jazz entered a dialogue already in existence – but neither were they dispensable to it. In them, jazz explored the relationship between consistency and particularity that may have been especially significant in enabling it to acquire the identity that it did.

One place to begin – and to establish that we are in no way dealing with an autonomous totality – is to register the many ways that jazz connected itself to particular aspects of twentieth-century experience. In no previous century had cultural, social, economic and technological activity interacted in such a dynamic way (especially where the culture concerned was not identified as high art), nor had cultural products of societies with economic power ever penetrated the cultures of other societies with such rapid and profound effect. As a music that emerged at a time when the motor of these processes was beginning to move rapidly through its gears, it is clearly possible that jazz's identity lay in its existence as a consequence of, a commentary on, even a symbol of the changes that were taking place.

Many specific connections have been made between jazz and twentieth-century experience. Some lie primarily in the realm of artistic life, such

as the influence of jazz on modernism, others in more overtly political
territory, ranging from the role of jazz in wartime, to jazz as oppositional
politics; others concentrate more on the role of jazz in changing social
leisure behaviour, and still others on its role as the first twentieth-century
music to move from local roots to international familiarity. One particular
connection has been frequently seen as problematic: the connection between
jazz and the music industry. Yet there is a persuasive argument that says this
connection played one of the most significant parts in enabling jazz to
establish its identity. It is here I would like to start.

Media and money

It was live performance by the Original Dixieland Jazz Band (ODJB) from
New Orleans that marked the first enthusiastic public response to jazz,
in Chicago in 1916 and, especially, in New York in 1917, but it was the
band's appearances on record that secured their fame and disseminated
their music.[1] Within two years the band was an equal success in London,
where their records had preceded them. Yet, obvious as it would later become
that recording linked to live performance and touring was a highly effective element in promotional strategy, in the late 1910s records still played
second fiddle to publishing, and the publishing–performing link was considered the most productive one. Forty years after the first appearance of
sound recording, and nearly twenty years after the establishment of the
first of what would become major record companies (Columbia, Victor, the
Gramophone Company), there had been numerous commercial successes,[2]
but in the still-developing music business they had not dented the hegemony
of publishers – publishers who had themselves been a new generation, with
very different ideas about their product and its promotion, in the 1890s.

   With the ODJB's success, jazz became part of this business; but the
market potential of jazz records did not develop with any great speed until the record companies began recording African-American music in the
very early 1920s. In retrospect it seems clear that there was more than one
reason for this slowness, and that these reasons were linked. Although the
implications of the fact that a record dealt in performance were apparent
to the record industry – which was, after all, making money from selling
performance – they were still not fully so. The performers who recorded
were mainly performers of pieces of music that had their own separate existence and were usually published as such. The implications of the record's
ability to be at one and the same time both the music *and* the performance –
in other words, to break the sequentiality that had been dominant hitherto –
had not yet fully sunk in. Related to this was a lack of awareness across the

industry as a whole, including the record sector, of what was going on in vernacular culture in general, and in African-American vernacular culture in particular. As W. C. Handy had shown with songs such as 'St Louis Blues' (1914), if the blues could be notated, it could be published and sold with considerable success, but few yet recognised the market potential of a vernacular culture's music that did not require the intervention of notation (as had been the case with ragtime). Furthermore, while African-Americans had undoubtedly bought sheet music, as a group they had never been seen by the industry as major purchasers, and no doubt this contributed to the fact that the industry doubted the existence of a market for its product in those areas of society where vernacular culture flourished most strongly. But the ability of the record to deal primarily in performance, to capture music and re-deliver it, without the need for the intervention of notation, was a different story – or would be, once the connection was made. It was a different story also, of course, for other vernacular musics and their audiences. In due course, the record industry would respond to them, too, but not before music by and for African-Americans had established the trends and patterns.

If the link between jazz and records that developed in the early 1920s was crucial in the emergence of an identity for the music, the story of the link was not a simple one. The recording of African-American jazz owed a great deal to the development of 'race records',[3] *de facto* segregated catalogues of recordings which came into being in the wake of the first successful blues recording in 1920 and whose contents were produced and marketed entirely for black Americans. The race-records initiative convinced the record companies of the commercial opportunity that opened before them.

But the debt jazz owed to race records was not apparent in numerical terms – a great many more jazz records would appear in general catalogues than in race catalogues in the 1920s. In terms of the relationship between recording and public knowledge, jazz had a much better deal than other African-American musics (blues, gospel). It benefited from the race-records development, but public knowledge – and hence the reputation and identity of jazz – was not confined to race records or dependent on them.

There is little doubt that records led to jazz becoming more widely known than would have been the case if knowledge had depended on live performance alone. It is less often stated, but equally clear, that it was jazz above all that introduced into the world of the making and buying of commercial recordings the idea of the record as itself a primary event, not an event at the end of a sequence – a concept with hugely important ramifications for twentieth-century popular music. But, at the same time, the link between jazz and records also ensured that just what it was that jazz was becoming known as and for was not always entirely clear.

For one thing, if jazz was introducing the notion of the potential primacy of the record – a notion without which the studio-only recordings by Louis Armstrong's Hot Five and Hot Seven ensembles, between 1925 and 1928, would probably not have taken place – not all records that passed for jazz were viewed in this way. And if it was becoming apparent that any publishing of a jazz tune in notated form bore only a limited relevance to the music on the records, notated music still held an important sway. In particular, the jazz-influenced dance-band music of leaders such as Paul Whiteman could have been said to have muddied the waters of jazz's identity as a recorded music. In placing syncopated decorum and careful planning so obviously ahead of spontaneity (real or imagined) and physical excitement, and indeed in their support for the term 'symphonic jazz', Whiteman and others conveyed a view of jazz as different only in some of the idiomatic resources available to it.

Further contributions to the growth of knowledge about jazz and the emergence of a sense of identity came from the music's relationships with other sectors of the industry. In the 1930s, for example, radio was a major source of familiarisation. But these relationships ebbed and flowed. Taken over a longer period, the relationship with records was the key music-industry relationship for jazz, one that continued through the numerous technological developments that took place (the arrival of the LP and magnetic tape in the late 1940s, of digital recording in the 1980s). Each of these developments also involved important changes in how the music and the record-industry sector responded to each other, from the increased track time afforded by the LP and its consequences for recorded jazz performance and the marketing image of the records, to the opportunity offered by CDs to reissue 'back catalogue' in such an extensive way that all past histories of recorded jazz became synchronically present.

Throughout these changes, much of the audience for jazz based the process of acquiring, developing and sustaining a knowledge and love of the music firmly around recordings, supplemented by radio listening and attendance at live performance. But the very centrality of the connection has also been a source of tension, or, more accurately, of two tensions. The first was between the record as a document of an event and as the event itself, and centred on arguments about the primacy or otherwise of the unique, unrepeatable performance. Although it had been a virtually inevitable outcome of the encounter between jazz and recording that the jazz record would become so significant, the fact that a record in effect froze one particular performance and had the power to repeat it *ad infinitum* began to be seen, by many involved in jazz (both musicians and the steadily growing ranks of jazz critics), as inimical to the ideology of a lack of closure that was being constructed on the back of the centrality of improvisation. No other twentieth-century music seems to have felt the dialectical push-and-pull of this dilemma quite so sharply as jazz, even if, to a wider public largely unbothered by the finer points of an improvisation aesthetic (we will return to this later), such ambivalence in the end meant mainly a falling-off in the presence that jazz could command in the dominant musical medium.

The second tension was between the record as promoter of interest in the music and as controller of the direction in which the music should go, and centred on art/commerce arguments. In its crudest form the commercial processes were castigated as exploitative, or championed as part of creative endeavour. In these debates the record industry was not the only industrial sector involved, but was often cast as standing for the industry as a whole. Similar tensions with regard to the relationship between music and commercial interests characterised virtually every genre and sub-genre of western popular music to emerge in the twentieth century, and the results were engraved on the identity of many of them. DeVeaux points out the inconsistency in a view of jazz in which the music 'is kept separate from the marketplace only by demonising the economic system that allows musicians to survive' (1991, 530). In other musical areas it was not the plain fact that capitalism interferes that was at issue, but how much space it leaves, or doesn't leave, and how that space can be used. Such concerns were rare among the jazz writers who, from the late 1930s on, lamented the power of commerce over jazz, and who did so in large part in order to develop the idea that jazz was in some way superior. But despite their efforts this idea seems to have taken root mainly among the fraternity of the like-minded. What tended to emerge as part of jazz's identity for the broader public was the image of a music that could not make its mind up, that wanted the best of both worlds – to be both above the marketplace, and to benefit as and when from its promotional know-how.

On the road

Any such observations did not alter the fact that, from the late 1920s on, when the component parts of what would later be known as 'the music business' were being put in place,[4] jazz had been centrally involved in those processes and that its twentieth-century experience was marked by engagement with all those components, individually and collectively. In most of these encounters – with publishing, radio, film, copyright, the live performance circuit – the story of jazz's experience shared many characteristics with those of other musical genres, but sometimes it was significantly different. The apparently inseparable link between copyright concepts and the primacy of the written score, for example, created problems in many generic areas, but peculiarly so in jazz where an improvised solo to all intents and purposes lay outside the boundaries of normal legislative concerns.[5]

One area where connections between jazz and a component part of the industry took on particular significance for jazz was that of musicians' mobility. For many, mobility began with migration to an urban centre, but it was more the role played by touring, from that or another urban base, that contributed to musicians' identity. The modern concept of touring had begun to be developed as early as the 1830s, connected to improvements in transportation. By the arrival of jazz, some element of mobility was endemic to the lifestyle of a great many musicians. For much of the 1920s, while some musicians concentrated on building an audience for their music in one particular place (typically a city, such as Chicago), moving between places to follow possible new opportunities, others leased their services to operations such as the Theater Owners Booking Agency, which organised tours of the African-American vaudeville circuit. By the late 1920s in some parts (such as the so-called 'territories' of the American southwest) and by the 1930s elsewhere, taking their music from place to place had become an integral part of musicians' promotional activity.

For those black bands and musicians whose journeys took them through the southern American states in the early decades of jazz, touring often brought a particularly unpleasant set of problems, but it was not the encounters with racism so much as the sheer stamina needed to survive the gruelling succession of one-night stands that marked the musicians out, black and white, and began to contribute to their identity. Life 'on the road' also put personal relationships under enormous strain, adding a sense of separateness, disconnectedness, even in some case isolation, to the image. The 'road' was also not complete without its antithesis, the big-city base, and this provided a further element in the characterisation of jazz musicians – not of travellers returning 'home' in a conventional sense, but of city-lovers replenishing themselves through contact with their peers and with their 'natural' terrain. Rootlessness and rootedness did not complement each other in the persona of the jazz musician, however, so much as exist in a fascinating ambiguity.

Once in place, these elements of characterisation retained their power. With the increasing prominence of individual musicians in the jazz performance, a further element was added – the expectation that being on the move so often would not result in repetition. Thus it became a further characteristic that the jazz musician on the road was expected, by the audience and by the musicians themselves, to respond creatively to the challenge of a relentlessly changing performance environment.

Jazz in performance

One thing that emerges from even a brief analysis of jazz's connections into these areas of twentieth-century experience is that jazz did not invent the connections, but entered in its own way, and with its own interpretations, into ongoing processes and dialogues. In the example we have just seen, working out ways to deal with the relationship between stasis and mobility, jazz musicians drew on and learned from others who had had to face similar problems in earlier eras. But in acquiring a special significance for musicians (in terms of their lifestyles and opportunities) and for audiences (in terms of their interpretation of what they heard and saw), the particular jazz 'take' on the relationship raised it to a higher level of significance in the formation of identity than it had previously had in any other musical context.

Fundamental to the kind of relationship that grew up between jazz and the examples of twentieth-century experience that we have identified was the fact that jazz was perceived as laying a special emphasis on performance.

At first, the aspects of jazz performance that attracted most attention were its manner and character, particularly its display of those elements that history has often considered superficial or clichéd: energy, vitality and physicality, often exuberance. Not that these were totally absent before jazz arrived – the music for the dancing fashion of the first half of the 1910s was considered liberating (or threatening) in its encouragement of corporeality; and, if exuberance was not dominant in an approach to entertainment in the late 1910s that still bore the strong imprint of the nineteenth century, it was nevertheless present. But, ultimately, that same dance music was tailored mainly to reflect the image of the chaste vitality in the dancing of the sophisticated Irene Castle, while in popular song a good sentimental ballad such as Richard Whiting's 'Till We Meet Again' (1918) could always sell a million copies.

For many musicians, the energy and vitality in the music's performance were part of the attraction of the modern city. William Kenney notes that white Chicago jazzmen's 'initial desire to play this tension-filled, fast-moving music came from their anticipation of the excitement of urban life, their alienation from middle-class Victorian moralism' (1993, 116). Energy and excitement were not enough, however. From a quite early point a related yet substantially different phenomenon, that of *creative* energy in the guise of spontaneity, also became significant; and whilst the manner and character of jazz performance would shift radically – so that at some points 'studious' would be a much more appropriate epithet than 'energetic' – spontaneity was the sign of a performance concept, maybe even an aesthetic, and as such had the potential to become fundamental.

Here, again, however, the basic idea was by no means new. Embellishing the music in an (apparently) spontaneous way and altering its rhythms, especially by syncopation, was part of the performance equipment of many ragtime artists, for example ('ragging' meaning just that); and, as John Whiteoak has shown in studying music-making in Australia, this was not just an American phenomenon but extended its influence far and wide (1999, 112ff). Spontaneity alone was not a sufficient idea in the longer term. As the jazz soloist emerged in the late 1920s, especially after Armstrong's Hot Five and Hot Seven recordings, the key identifiers in the area of performance for musicians, and, increasingly, for the audience also – at least for the knowledgeable audience – shifted towards what spontaneity might signify, namely improvisation.[6]

Jazz's way with performance, especially around the question of improvisation, was a central factor in the hostility to the music that followed its emergence. The antagonism to improvisation that emanated from worried guardians of culture was more aesthetic than moralistic, though the link between art and social morality, even politics, often proved too tempting. The *Musical Courier*, for example, polled a group of classical musicians in 1922 and reported back that they considered 'the "ad libbing" or "jazzing" of a piece . . . thoroughly objectionable'. Not content with that, they indicated that they deemed the 'smashing of the rules and tenets of decorous music' to be 'bolshevistic' and that in its 'excessive freedom of interpretation' the music had held 'makers of the rules of dignified social intercourse' in disregard (N. Leonard 1962, 42).

A somewhat different attack was to emerge later (1941) from the caustic dialectics of the exiled German critic, Theodor Adorno. For Adorno, the proposal that genuine musical individuality could emerge from the improvised performance of jazz was a contradiction in terms. All attempts to prove otherwise were false – the results of what he bitingly termed 'pseudo-individualisation', the music's need to create a veneer of difference in order to maintain interest in its products. Adorno was responding in particular to the music of the swing era that he heard on American radio in the late 1930s, and his ultimate target was not jazz itself, or indeed any other idiom, but the culture industry that produced it. But no subsequent changes in jazz style ever came near persuading him to change his mind, and though his insistence on the connections between twentieth-century popular musics and the imperatives of capital was and remains immensely important, there is a strong residual sense in reading Adorno that what ultimately bothered him was the failure of the music to be sufficiently like great classical music, which operated on principles according to which it was the composer's task to use harmony (especially), melody and structural development to challenge the listener. Performance, whether improvised or not, could not introduce what was not already there; indeed, all its apparent departure from the original could ever do was remind the listener of the inexorable grip of the original, in all its limitations (for which, in the main, read harmonic limitations). Although listeners thought they were experiencing difference in jazz performance, all they were doing was 'differentiating between the actually undifferentiated' (Adorno 1991, 309).

In their different ways neither the 1920s guardians of aesthetic standards nor Adorno could ever distance themselves from the thought that the original composition was bound, in the last resort, to be the most important thing. Though this view, coupled with the stubborn suspicion that performance itself could never be as creative as pre-composition, found echoes in many unsympathetic responses to jazz across the century, neither the listening public nor jazz musicians seem ever to have been especially concerned by it. Rather, what made jazz in performance not only acceptable but distinctive, across different styles, was the way it combined creativity, energy and content. Whereas in other highly public musical idioms musical content generally dictated performance – performance existed so that musical content could be made known – in jazz it seemed more the other way round, that content was subservient to performance. Even in stylistic contexts apparently dominated by pieces and their arrangement, the issue of performance individuality was to become sacred. Thus, Duke Ellington, in his announcements at his orchestra's 1946 Carnegie Hall concert – at a home of the classical repertoire, therefore – was at pains to make clear that the purpose of the concerts was not to render his music (the standards and the new pieces), but was 'primarily to present our instrumentalists in their solo and ensemble responsibilities to the best of their advantage, in appreciation of the fact that they are the inspiration of all the things that are written'.[7]

As jazz established itself, it also established an approach to the relationship between performance and piece that allowed a wide range of options. This did not mean there were no arguments; quite the reverse. But none of these possibilities necessarily negated the value of an original piece or idea (indeed, numerous jazz musicians were keen to enhance their compositional skills), or, equally important, of its arrangement; rather, what the jazz approach did was create a context no longer controlled by notions of what was scripted and what unscripted, with all their value connotations. It was the very fact that a jazz performance appeared as neither scripted nor unscripted that appealed to many, practitioners and listeners.

For a great many musicians, what mattered was the opportunity that this approach offered for individuality of expression. For some – often deemed the 'greatest' musicians by historians – this meant devising ways of meeting the challenge of creativity in performance, of creating afresh for the moment and, perhaps most important, of being motivated by the idea that the exploration of alternative solutions was a justifiable guiding principle. But many others were less concerned with those particular imperatives, yet still supported – believed in – a conception of performance that accorded them, the musicians, the leading roles. In some particular cases, a performance seemed, and still seems, designed to draw attention to the act of performing in itself (listen, for example, to Louis Armstrong perform a perennial favourite, 'Lazy River', on a 1955 recording, with its growled exhortation to his pianist, 'modulate, Billy Kyle, modulate').

What emerges as a constant identifier of jazz in its approach to performance is not so much the single, primary importance of improvisation and all that it might signify, but the fact that jazz performance constantly challenges ideas of set relationships between piece and performance and between preparation and realisation, continuously puts those relationships under its spotlight, and equally continuously validates the idea that the initiative is always with the performer, whether the performer in question is known as a reproducer, an interpreter or an improviser. For all of these types of musician, in different ways and in differing times, the end was not to have an end; the ultimate value lay in the act of performance itself. And it was this rather than improvisation itself that united them and helped fashion their identity across the century.

The jazz event

One might argue that all this shows, in the last analysis, is that a jazz performance which has the absolute minimum of pre-existing material at its starting point is at one extreme end of a spectrum that, at its other end, has performance in apparently complete subservience to composition, and that these extremes and all points in between are somehow conjoined. But taking such a position may miss a crucial point. It may impoverish jazz performance to see it as part and parcel of an ultimately indivisible spectrum of performance possibilities, and it makes more sense to see in jazz performance the development, to quite a high level, of a different concept, one in which the term 'event' is more useful than 'performance'.

If we could explain jazz's conception of and approach to performance by placing it at a variety of points on such a spectrum, it would presumably be possible to do this for another broadly based music that came to prominence in the twentieth century – popular music. And indeed, popular music performance can be seen, from one common perspective, to lie within the dominant tradition of a piece and its realisation, while having many alternatives available to it as to what that realisation may mean and involve. But, as I have argued elsewhere (Horn 2000, 28–30), rather than think of much popular music as structured around pieces and their performance, it is useful to think in terms of popular music 'events'. The event is the sum of a number of occurrences or processes which may include any or all of: the origination, borrowing, development and arrangement of an 'idea', the participation of persons and technical equipment whose task is to produce sound, the relationships between them, the execution of the task, the transmission of the result, the hearing of the result, the context in which hearing takes place. These may link together and proceed in sequential fashion, but, equally, they may not. A musical 'idea', for example, may come at the start of a sequence of occurrences, and be followed by others – arrangement, reception – of which performance is one. But, equally, it may emerge in such a way as to make it impossible to tell who among the many participants in the event was the originator; and what is more, it may not matter. Similarly, although one process may dominate, attempts to establish hegemony are always subject to challenge, because there is no agreement on how the relationship between the various occurrences should be set. If neither established sequences nor the domination by one type of process or occurrence explains how events work, we might think of them instead as structured around an interactive nexus made up of performer, performance and performed. (By 'performed' I do not mean the end result, but the material on which performer and performance work.) This interactive nexus (not spectrum!) is characterised by movement and negotiation and permits many alternatives.

There is no space here to discuss the complexity – and contentiousness – of the relationship of jazz to popular music. But we may note that, at the time when the effects of activity within this nexus of performer–performance–performed began to have an impact on twentieth-century culture (which in its clearest form dates from the intervention of recording and the radio in the 1920s), jazz was well to the fore in popular culture, and continued to be so for some time; and that it is entirely plausible that it played an important role in establishing and disseminating the effect of this activity.

If, taking our cue from the popular music event described above, we speak of the 'jazz event', the two have much in common. For example, neither origination nor borrowing nor performance have consistent places in an established sequentiality. Here, as in popular music, the concept of negotiation within the nexus of performer–performance–performed offers a persuasive alternative to more traditional concepts. What seems to be distinctive about the way jazz handles the nexus is partly due to the music's preferences, each historically arrived at, for the particular character of the contributing elements (for example, the choice of instruments used in performance). In particular, it is due to preference for types of relationship between the participants that provide the space for them to enter multiple dialogues. For example, we might see the nexus as allowing performers to face several ways: to the performed, to fellow musicians, to other musicians who have 'conversed' with the same material, and to the audience. It seems that particular ideas, especially those relating to the performer, have a persistent power, but equally that others are surrounded by uncertainty – for example, the role of the record producer. But the concept of the nexus allows us to see how, given these tendencies, the possibility always exists for dialogue. The role of ECM owner-producer, Manfred Eicher, offers a good example of this – a passionate believer in freedom for performers, his label is also known for its production standards and its own quality of sound.

Jazz as black music

By the latter part of the twentieth century the semiotic messages communicated by jazz were undoubtedly complex, involving many of the aspects of identity we have touched on so far, plus others such as those introduced, for example, by the use of jazz in film soundtracks. In the visual image of jazz, however, one element became particularly common. Marsha Hammel's painting, *Saxman* (see Plate 1.1), depicts a jazz musician playing, with a gracefully curved torso, an equally gracefully curved yellow sax. He is well dressed in a black suit with blue trim and a V-necked white T-shirt. The musician is black; and he is the epitome of 'cool'.

Over sixty years previously, the African-American painter Aaron Douglas, who was closely associated with the Harlem Renaissance, placed a black saxophonist at the centre of his 1934 painting called *Aspects of Negro Life: Song of the Towers* (Plate 1.2). The musician is dwarfed by skyscrapers and (or but), beneath the outstretched sax, which the musician holds one-handed, is seen the distant figure of the Statue of Liberty. As Donna Cassidy, who has discussed the painting at length, observes, the figure of the black jazz saxophonist had many meanings both for Douglas and for other African-Americans, incorporating a sense of cultural achievement, spirituality (the musician's pose recalls that associated with the Angel Gabriel) and social advancement, as well as, in Douglas's words, 'anxiety and yearning from the soul of the Negro people' (Cassidy 1997, 115–46; quotation from Douglas, 140).

A visual image connecting jazz and black culture can mean very different things, in different hands and in different contexts, and it is not my purpose to analyse the phenomenon any further here. But there is no doubting

Plate 1.1 Marsha Hammel, *Saxman*, by courtesy of Felix Rosenstiel's Widow & Son Ltd, London

Plate 1.2 Aaron Douglas, *Aspects of Negro Life: Song of the Towers*. Art and Artifacts division, Schomburg Center for Research in Black Culture, New York Public Library, Astor, Lenox and Tilden Foundations

that the connection itself, whether made visually or by other means, has proved to have an enduring character. By the century's end it had become so widely accepted that any reference to it would typically be regarded as unexceptional. How the connection was interpreted by those close to jazz – musicians, critics or fans – was a different matter. There were many who held the view that, whoever had been most responsible for the music's character and development, jazz had become a *lingua franca*, and as such, was better described as 'interracial' and not constrained by racial boundaries. Others, while they could concur on the spread of the music, insisted on its remaining the cultural property of African-Americans.

The coexistence, if not concurrence, of these views might be viewed as a sign of some kind of a hard-won consensus after years of strife: jazz as somehow both an African-American music and a multi-ethnic music of the world. But it is an uneasy agreement at best, and one which serves equally as a reminder of the profound paradoxes and struggles that underlay the issue of jazz and race throughout much of the century, albeit with changing emphases and perspectives. It also conceals the infinite subtle and not-so-subtle variations that the broad positions contain.[8]

The incontrovertible fact of a strong connection between jazz and black American culture was part of a larger story, of course, that cannot be told or explained solely in regard to jazz. It is a story that involves both the wider contribution of African-Americans to American life and the complex nature of the cultural context in which that contribution was made. Noting both of these things, Ralph Ellison remarked in 1964 that 'white Americans have been walking Negro walks, talking Negro flavored talk ... dancing Negro dances and singing Negro melodies far too long to talk of a "mainstream" of American culture to which they're alien' (256). In sports, too, the influence and contribution were profound. Ellison himself noted this on another occasion, but he also observed that, to him, all these centrally important contributions were, as he put it, 'jazz-shaped', suggesting a crucial dual role for jazz in this process, both as the enabler of the process and as a symbol – or, perhaps, an epitome – of black cultural achievement to date (Ellison 1970).

The issue of the contribution of African-Americans to American culture (and beyond) was itself one aspect of a larger subject, one that was writ large across twentieth-century American history and that played a significant role in the histories of other industrialised and urbanised countries also. Often summarised under the heading 'race relations', it involved the long struggle, by black and white, to persuade white-dominated societies and economies to open up those societies and economies on a fair and equal basis to the racial minorities whose members had been oppressed and/or marginalised in numerous ways. There is no need to rehearse even the outstanding features of this struggle here. The point is, first, to remind ourselves to place 'cultural relations' involving black contributions – and therefore 'jazz relations' – firmly in the wider context of race relations; and secondly to ask: did those 'jazz relations' merely reflect and re-enact, in the particular microcosm of jazz, the larger history, or, allowing for the umbilical connection between them, was the space in which jazz met race any different from other spaces where the racial encounter took place? And, if so, what does that tell us about the identity of jazz?

It was certainly the case that the connection between jazz and black culture had a complex history. If, by the 1990s, a jazz historian could write that 'in creating jazz, black players exercised a kind of cultural leadership in America', he had at the same time to acknowledge that it was a kind of leadership that 'has rarely been permitted or acknowledged' (Peretti 1992, 76). The nature of the relationship between jazz and black culture was often sharply contested, and the contest could be as sharp among participants and *aficionados* as it was among those who disapproved of, or cared little about, the music. Equally, it was also subjected to the kind of power inequalities that could make contest itself very complicated. Not that power was not invariably all on the side of the socially and economically dominant group. As Kenney has shown (1993, 110–11), in 1920s Chicago far more opportunities for performance were available to black musicians than white; but the history of white treatment of black also meant that, although many black musicians let white musicians sit in with them, they were often ambivalent towards them and doubted their motives.

Whatever problems were encountered historically, jazz is rarely cited as much more than a footnote in books on 'the race question', and one reason for this may be that the degree and severity of the particular struggle around jazz never matched the intensity or the importance of other social, economic and political struggles involving race. It may nevertheless have been the case that only in contests around jazz was there found a range of opinion so wide that it could elevate the achievement of black Americans to the realms of high art or denigrate it as the lowest level of imitation, could accord those responsible the status of high priests of style or demean them as coarse servants of white pleasure, lacking even the permission to enter at the same door. What can we make of that? Perhaps that the issues tied up in cultural struggle, although linked to issues tied up in socio-economic and political struggles, were not necessarily identical with them, and that jazz provided a somewhat different space in which the interaction between them was sharply delineated. That space was constructed around a number of elements, of which we may identify four as particularly important: opportunity, ownership, origination and representation.

In considering the part played by jazz in making cultural activity a space where these factors could interact, it is important to recognise that the process had been going on for some time. After the end of Reconstruction in 1877, America saw a retreat from programmes of equality and opportunity (designed to link the black population into American society) and the concomitant rise of segregationist practices, and the black population was thrown back on to its own cultural resources – but with the flavour, as it were, of participation in a wider project still present. Though disillusion was deep, so was the cultural pool to be drawn on in this increased isolation, and one of the (many) things it contained was the knowledge that there was a strength in interpretative activity that could take elements observed in wider society, examine them and, in an encounter with more endemic practices and the particularities of specific contexts, re-create them as something new and original.

These new things were intended for African-Americans themselves, who would understand the significance of the complex give-and-take that lay behind them. But if the 1890s and early years of the new century were characterised by increasing legal and social hostility to African-Americans, they were also a time in which the nascent American popular-culture industry began to notice some of the new products of cultural activity in African-American society and to consider their commercial possibilities. This involved bringing African-American musicians into the industry arena in certain areas, for example that of publishing (ragtime songs and piano pieces). Some doors began to be edged open by African-Americans themselves, most notably in the musical theatre, where Bob Cole and J. Rosamond Johnson so impressed the Broadway production team of Klaw-Erlanger in 1903 that they were given a three-year contract to write distinctively 'Negro' songs for them, and went on to earn over $25,000 a year from the songs in royalties (Woll 1989, 21–2).

But in both publishing and stage performance black musicians had also to deal with well-established expectations regarding how black people were to be represented. The legacy of the minstrel show was very apparent in the vogue for 'coon songs' and in the requirement of stage performers to behave in a minstrel style. Both Cole and Johnson and another duo, Bert Williams and George Walker, began by conforming to the stereotypes (Williams and Walker appeared as 'Two Real Coons'), but determined to free their shows of this inheritance. Partly successful in this, and justifiably proud of their achievement, they could do nothing about the fact that audiences for their shows were predominantly white and that theatres operated strict segregation policies for those blacks who could afford tickets. This practice was still in operation in the early 1920s.

Much more detail could be added to this account, but it should be clear that in the years before jazz the black experience of participation in the twentieth century's popular-culture industry involved many tensions. The ying and yang of these experiences – separation and participation, welcome and rejection, initiation and appropriation, opportunity and precondition, ownership and surrender – also accompanied the emergence and subsequent history of jazz

The history within jazz of each of the factors I have suggested as important – opportunity, ownership, origination and representation – involved many connections between them, as well as many changes within them and many shifts in their ability to generate debate. A few examples must suffice.

Although black jazz bands made some appearances in early Hollywood movies that used jazz, opportunities were very limited, as 'studio personnel worried about showing black faces on the screen in roles equal to (those of) whites' (Erenberg 1981, 174). That the limiting of opportunity was linked to the issue of racial representation in the film industry's mind is clear from the way that Louis Armstrong was required to behave, in a leopard skin in *Rhapsody in Black and Blue* (1932) and singing to a horse in *Going Places* (1938). But as Berndt Ostendorf has shown in another context, 'the racist slur' is 'outdone by the sheer artistry . . . of the performance' (1982, 84). In Krin Gabbard's interpretation, Armstrong's performance in *Rhapsody* in particular is also a specific counter to demasculinisation, a phenomenon with its own long history (Gabbard 1995d, 104–5).

Some thirty years on, the link between opportunity and image was still operating, albeit in a different context and in a different way. That, at least, was the view of many musicians as reported by Frank Kofsky in his depiction of the attitude of what he called 'nightclub capitalism' to the music of John Coltrane, Archie Shepp and others. The opportunity offered by the night clubs, in Kofsky's account, was contingent upon musicians complying with expectations regarding the length of their sets and their doing nothing to discourage the audience from buying drinks. It was predicated on a view of the contemporary black jazz musician 'as some kind of disembodied entity who has no existence except at the moment of artistic creation. If you are a jazz musician you are expected to go on the stand and create on demand, simply because the audience has paid its money . . . You can cease to exist the moment you lay down your horn' (Kofsky 1970, 145).

Questions of origination were present from a very early point, were frequently contested, and remained so, even if the participants in the debate changed. In the public career of jazz, the first to speak on the subject were the white musicians of the Original Dixieland Jazz Band, the product of a multi-ethnic working-class district of New Orleans, whose frenetic music (as we have already seen) became celebrated in 1916–17. Both at the time and in later recollection the members of the band insisted on the total absence of black input into the music. 'The colored', said Tom Browne, 'only play plantation music' (quoted in Peretti 1992, 80).[9] In 1919 the band visited England with huge success. Here, according to Chris Goddard, their denial of any black influence or contribution meant 'it was ten years before the seminal role of the black musician in jazz was understood' (1979, 28–9).

In the late 1910s, black New Orleans musicians had little or no access to any means of public expression in order to put an alternative point of view, but that was not the case for the growing class of black intellectuals in New York. As Ted Vincent has shown (1995, 152ff), among the founders of the new black-run magazines there were some editors, most notably Cyril Briggs of *The Crusader*, who tirelessly promoted both jazz and the blues as new black urban music. By no means all of those involved in the Harlem Renaissance were as enthusiastic for the music or, consequently, as eager to argue for its point of origin or the pre-eminence of black musicians in its execution – or indeed for what jazz signified in terms of black Americans' ability to create their own beauty. The editors of *Crisis*, the journal of the National Association for the Advancement of Colored People, largely ignored both jazz and blues, an attitude possibly caused, in Vincent's view, by a 'reluctance to confuse friendly Whites by trying to explain the value in music that seemed so "wild" – as in "wild African savage"' (172). In contrast, Joel A. Rogers, writing in Alain Locke's compilation *The New Negro*, described jazz as 'of Negro origin plus the influence of the American environment', adding, 'the Caucasians never could have invented it' (quoted in Cassidy 1997, 131). For Langston Hughes, the issue was, ultimately, one of creative independence. The 'blare of Negro jazz bands' was evidence that 'we younger Negro artists who create now intend to express our dark-skinned selves without fear or shame. If white people are pleased, we are glad. If they are not, it doesn't matter' (quoted in Floyd 1995, 133).

Such ideas of differentiation were to reappear in the 1940s, the time of bebop. Here there was no argument, in racial terms, as to who was responsible for the origination of the new idiom. But whereas in the minds of such as Langston Hughes in the 1920s, white understanding of black creativity was viewed with indifference, bebop musicians appear to have made the conscious attempt to create something that whites (musicians and audiences) would struggle to understand. Not only that: they sought to take charge of the image of the musician at the same time. If, as Eric Lott remarks, it is necessary 'to restore the political edge' to bebop, it is not necessarily easy, or correct, to map the politics of culture neatly on to the politics of the socio-economic reality (1995, 245). If we grant that 'the music attempted to resolve at the level of style what the militancy fought out on the streets' (*ibid.*, 246) we may also want to insist that in the encounter between bebop and the political moment, jazz did not merely reflect what it saw, it brought its own meditation on it, and its own way of managing it.

In its particular way of connecting opportunity, ownership, origination and representation, along with related issues such as appropriation, bebop offers us a good example of how jazz continued to provide an opportunity for aspects of the black cultural experience to be in constant – and constantly changing – dialogue, with each other and with wider society. It is perhaps the depth and richness of these explorations, above all else, that lies behind that part of the identity of jazz that connects it so unequivocally to black culture and the black experience.

The sounds of the time and the timing of the sounds

There is one further, fundamental way in which jazz acquired an identity, and that was through its sound, or, more accurately, its combination of sound, rhythm and timing. The establishment of jazz as a distinctive music can, and should, be ascribed to a complex convergence of musical, social, economic and technological factors, but to the public itself there seems little reason to doubt that what separated jazz most clearly from the norms of the day (whether these were old or relatively new) was the interaction of the music's sonic and temporal characteristics. Whatever music jazz found itself along-side, it retained the ability to sound different. In large measure, this was due to the leading roles that were persistently accorded to certain instruments and instrumental families, enabling us to speak of jazz as providing a distinctive sonic experience. But there was also a crucially important – if hard to describe – role for approaches to rhythm and, particularly, timing that could mark something as jazz, even when its sonic characteristics seemed less distinctive. To the distinctive sonic experience, therefore, was added a distinctive temporal experience, especially the inscribing of new patterns on time.[10]

The secular popular-music world into which jazz came was dominated by four sonorities, with distinct but connected histories: the voice–piano combination that was still the mainstay of domestic music-making; the brass, wind and percussion sounds of the public open spaces, especially those of marching bands; the full orchestral sound of the operetta; and the hybrid sound of the vaudeville theatre and dance orchestras. Although the impact of the sound of jazz was considerable, it did not come as a complete surprise. Those who had heard the 'society orchestras', for example, the dance bands that were highly popular in New York around 1913–14, had heard a combination that included violins, plucked strings, unison clarinet and cornet, trombone, piano and drums.

When jazz first attracted the public ear beyond the boundaries of the places – New Orleans especially – where it had been developing, it did so not as a set of unfamiliar sounds, but as familiar sounds in unfamiliar relationships. Most of the wind and percussion instruments making up the first widely heard jazz ensembles in the late 1910s and early 1920s were familiar from their role in band music (whether of the marching or the concert variety), while the plucked string instruments were known from the popular theatre and, in many cases no doubt, the home. With the gradual inclusion of the piano, the instrument that was perhaps the most familiar of all, and the most readily associated with the home, became present also. But we may note that contrasting connotations were being brought together: trumpet with the street, piano with domestic respectability and familial solidity; the banjo with an almost outmoded style of popular theatre.

Jazz, therefore, belonged to the sound world from which it also distinguished itself, but it was the sense in which it broke with norms that gave it sonic individuality. In this it was aided considerably by rhythm and timing. Here, too, jazz emerged into a musical world already deep in rhythmic exploration, but it was also the case that within a very short time there was a considerable contrast between the syncopations of ragtime and dance music and the off-beat phrasing of jazz.

Very early in the history of processes by which jazz was recognised, the music's departure from the norms of sound, rhythm and timing resulted in another further element of distinctiveness: the opportunity for individual musicians to present their own version of this combination – fashioning an instrumental sound and 'individualising' it with a distinctive approach to phrasing (see Bradley 1992, 48ff). Whereas, before jazz, audiences rated musicians highly mainly because they were skilled practitioners of a particular style, they now began to rate them because they sounded different. Not only different, of course; difference was persuasive only when married to skill, expressed within the music's broadly conceived templates. But whilst for the musicians themselves the question of what made a fellow musician or a band distinctive was often to be answered in technical terms, audiences were more likely to be affected by a mixture of pleasure in the new aural and temporal dimensions being evoked and the prospect of more difference to come.

Having forged a distinct sonic identity, jazz was able to preserve this identity through many changes of style. The exact character of jazz's combination of sound, rhythm and timing changed relentlessly as styles of jazz changed, but it remained the case that, whether the style in question was New Orleans revival, big-band swing, bebop, cool or free jazz, the listening public seems to have retained the ability to recognise the space that existed between jazz and other musics, even when specific features that had long been present in jazz, such as the exploration of nuances of timbre and rhythm, expressed in brief moments, began to appear elsewhere (for example, in rock).

The distinctiveness embodied in jazz's combination of sound, rhythm and timing, coupled with the music's apparently built-in opportunities for variety of expression, took on a range of signification beyond the purely musical. For some in the world of the arts in the United States in the 1920s, for example, the general sound of jazz evoked the American city, increasingly different from its European counterpart, while its individuality of sonic and rhythmic expression drew attention both to the possibility of fragmentation within that environment and to what painter Josef Stella called a 'new polyphony' (Cassidy 1997, 59). For others it was perhaps more a case of what the later twentieth century sometimes termed 'attitude' – a self-confidence which, whether exuberant, aggressive or reflective, seemed unbeholden to any kind of external authority. And this, too, spoke to notions of American identity.

One of the connections most frequently made between human experience and the way jazz handled its sonic and temporal resources was in the confusing area where body met mind. To some degree, there was a historical shift here, one which complicates the notion of identity. Especially in its first two decades, the sound, rhythm and timing of jazz were often treated as having a correspondence to somatic behaviour. For early opponents of jazz, they not only connoted indecency, they encouraged it. 'Those moaning saxophones', wrote Fenton J. Bott in 1921, 'and the rest of the instruments with their broken, jerky rhythm make a purely sensual appeal . . . Jazz is the very foundation of salacious dancing' (quoted in N. Leonard 1962, 34). As subtle changes in rhythm, timing and phrasing appeared to break the link between jazz and bodily expression (i.e., in dance), and the increased use of the metallic sound of cymbals for rhythm seemed to speak to mental states where previously lower sounds had encouraged physical movement, so jazz seemed to many to connect more to mental than to somatic process.

But looking over the course taken by jazz in its use of its resources of sound, rhythm and timing, it is evident that, while there were tendencies and tensions, there never were mind–body splits. It made, and makes, little sense to speak of music as varied in its use of these resources as Bix Beiderbecke's 'Singin' the Blues' (1927), Lester Young's solo on Billie Holiday's version of 'All of Me' (1941), or Charles Mingus's 'Shoes of the Fisherman's Wife' (*Let My Children Hear Music*, 1972) in terms of body, mind, or even soul, alone. The way each goes about creating interplay between the aural and the temporal can speak to each, to all three, or indeed to none.

We have said nothing of how sound is organised in jazz – the enormous range, from small-group polyphony and heterophony to homogeneous instrumental sections, to successive individual 'statements'. But even this short list seems to support the idea that a variety of organisational principles can contribute to sonic plurality (Bakhtin's 'heteroglossia') without undermining the music's identity – that, in effect, the sound of jazz displays competing centrifugal and centripetal tendencies but that these are generative more than they are restrictive. It is quite a short step from this observation to one of a more socio-political nature, namely that, although it is clearly true that the issue of how to reconcile regularising forces and aspirations to identity (collective and individual) has characterised many centuries, the twentieth century experienced it more profoundly than any other; and that in jazz it had a very special example in which the threat of domination by either tendency was real, but whose nature it was to go beyond a mere *modus operandi*, an uneasy truce, into a vibrant, creative continuum.

*

Looking back on his life, Sidney Bechet remarked that he was desperate to find 'the part of me that was there before I was' (1978, 4). In its manifold connections with the twentieth century, jazz drew on complex overlapping memories generated before and during its existence. But Bechet also remarked that 'Life isn't just a question of time; it's a way you have of talking back and forth to the music' (202). The identity of jazz lay, ultimately, neither in temporal shifts nor in anything that withstood such shifts, but in multiple dialogues, especially those around some specific themes, and in the particular way it talked back and forth both to prominent aspects of twentieth-century experience and to things that belonged to the particular character of music.

2 The jazz diaspora

BRUCE JOHNSON

As early as 1922, in an article published in the *New York Times Book Review and Magazine,* journalist Burnet Hershey chronicled his recent journey around the world taking in Europe, Africa, Asia and the Orient, and reported that jazz was everywhere:

> No sooner had I shaken off the dust of some city and slipped almost out of earshot of its jazz bands than zump-zump-zump, toodle-oodle-doo, right into another I went. Never was there a cessation of this universal potpourri of jazz. Each time I would discover it at a different stage of metamorphosis and sometimes hard to recognize, but unmistakably it was an attempt at jazz.   [Cited in Walser 1999, 26]

The dominant readings of jazz history have concentrated on chronology: the historical succession from New Orleans jazz to classic jazz, swing, bop and beyond (see, for example, Kernfeld 1988, I, 580–606). While such accounts are not modelled in terms of the diaspora, they are locked into it, since these stages happen also to correspond to diasporic factors. From New Orleans to the classic jazz of Chicago, from Kansas City to the bop hothouse of New York – each stylistic shift is also marked by a geographical shift. In formalist approaches (that is, those centred on musical characteristics), emphasis is on what is seen as 'progress' to higher levels of musical aesthetics, a teleology that continues to underpin powerful institutionalised discourses. Parallel to, but often in tension with, formalist accounts are cultural narratives interested less in what the music sounds like than in its social meanings. In these readings, various themes have remained durable, as, for example, a music of cutting-edge modernist or bohemian individualism, yet of authentic folk collectivity. Both reflect a suspicion of mass culture.

Aesthetic judgements based on these approaches find little value in the 'quaint' sounds of, say, a 1920s Finnish jazz band, a 1940s 'commercial' Russian swing orchestra or a 1960s Australian straw-hat shopping-mall group. Such approaches remain durable in the disdainful mythologies regarding 'authentic' black developments *vis-à-vis* 'ersatz' white derivatives. The discrepancies between musicological and culturalist accounts can be explicated to a great extent by realising that the meanings of the word 'jazz', and the meanings of the cultural practices it has described, were not always uniformly connected. Records of the word (jazz, jass) and its antecedents (jasm, jism – signs of sexual and athletic vigour) predate the first records of the music in 1917 (see, for example, Holbrook 1974). Even as the word came to designate music, the kinds of music it referred to, from hemisphere to hemisphere, often differed radically. It is difficult to hear the generic commonality between, say, 'Sponono' by South Africa's Jazz Revellers Band (1933), 'Hei Hulinaa, Helsinki' by Finnish Matti Jurva and Rytmi-Pojat (Rhythm Boys) in 1935, and the orchestra led by major Russian jazz figure, Alexander Tsfasman, playing 'Vistrij Tanjec' in 1937. The commonality is more likely to be found in the social meanings of the musics rather than in the musics themselves.

The tools of diasporic theory, even if not visibly deployed, are useful in illuminating the points of junction between culturalist (context-based) and formalist (text-based) narratives. The transition from small-group improvisation to, say, big-band swing, for example, which seems to be aesthetically driven, may well make more sense if it is seen as a function of the diaspora – from smaller to larger urban centres and recreational spaces. To relocate the socially grounded reasons for what appear to be artistically driven changes enables us to construct the past more sympathetically and to redeem musical pleasures made guilty by teleological discourses of excellence and authenticity. Jazz practices are often much more revealing both culturally and musically when they diverge from the comfortably canonised styles. These local accents are more prominent in sites that are peripheral to US or Eurocentric jazz narratives, in which difference also equates to inauthenticity. Such sites provide some of the least observed yet most interesting features of the diaspora, and the source of most of my references.

Diasporic channels

Migrations of musicians and audiences

Shortly after the turn of the century, the balance in the flow of entertainers from Europe to the US was reversed, accelerating the internationalisation of African-American entertainment (Gronow 1996, 22–3). Louis Mitchell's Jazz Kings (1917), the Original Dixieland Jazz Band (1918), Will Marion Cook's Southern Syncopated Orchestra with Sidney Bechet (1919) and Sam Wooding's groups (from 1924) were all seen by British and European audiences. Farther afield, Wooding also visited Tunis and South America, and Josephine Baker and a sixteen-piece orchestra visited Finland in 1933 (Kernfeld 1988, I, 502; Goddard 1979, 9–78). Other non-Americans were being exposed to African-American musicians. In 1917, James Reese Europe's 60-piece black band of the 369th US Infantry ('The Hellfighters') presented jazz and ragtime repertoire to Allied soldiers in France, presumably including service personnel from other countries. Two Australian servicemen who heard the Original Dixieland Jazz Band in London returned home and started a jazz band. Valentin Parnakh heard Mitchell's Jazz Kings in Paris in 1921 and returned to Russia to become a major jazz spokesman and organiser (Bisset 1987, 14; Starr 1983, 44). The importance of direct contact is reflected in the case of Finland, bypassed by early American tours of Scandinavia. Finnish jazz recordings as late as 1939, when compared with those of Swedish bandleader Thor Ehrling of the same year, indicate a much closer stylistic correspondence between Ehrling's work and the source materials of jazz/swing. The US influence on Swedish jazz is also disclosed through repertoire, instrumentation and recordings made with visitors such as Benny Carter in 1936 (see Nicolausson 1983).

In a pre-aviation era, shipping traffic was an important conduit. Sydney's contact with early jazz was dependent on its shipping links with the west coast of the US. Finland's jazz scene began in the port towns Helsinki and Kotka. The arrival of the SS *Andania* in Helsinki in 1926 (see below) was a key moment, and in Kotka in the early twenties Edmund Guttormsen was coached in the blues by the engineer of a Dutch freighter; Finnish jazz pioneer, Eugen Malmstén, recalled that he first heard jazz during a visit by the British Navy in 1924 when the band played 'Yes Sir, That's My Baby' during calisthenics (Haavisto 1996, 10, 11).[1]

Mass media

Increasingly, live contacts were overtaken by mass mediations. Although little more than templates of jazz practices, by the early 1920s sheet music emanating from an expanding global music-publishing industry had transmitted African-American repertoire as far afield as Russia and South Africa (Starr 1983, 26; Ballantine 1991, 130–31).[2] Printed commentary both reported jazz activity and provided the earliest definitions, both in the US and beyond (Kernfeld 1988, I, 593–4; Walser 1999, 3–70). Finland's *Rytmi* magazine (established in 1934) and the Australian journal, *Jazz Notes* (established in 1941), played central roles in shaping local perceptions of jazz (Haavisto 1996, 17; Johnson 1998).

For a music generated in performance, however, printed notation was of limited relevance to its dissemination, and the technological mediation of sound and moving image was decisive in the extraordinarily rapid global spread of the music. Film disseminated images of its performance rhetoric and also channelled the music along such lines as class and gender. In Russia, early movie audiences were primarily of the lower middle class; in Australia in the 1920s, 70 per cent of cinema audiences were women; in South Africa, film provided US lifestyle models to urban blacks (Stites 1992, 24; Johnson 2000, 62; Ballantine 1991, 131). Apart from jazz imagery, the silent movie was mediated acoustically through local cinema musicians, including in Russia the young Dmitri Shostakovich; they incorporated US jazz material in their collages, the performance of which also provided one of the most important public opportunities for developing improvisational material (Starr 1983, 27; Whiteoak 1999, 61). US films became major vehicles of jazz mythology, and of the international dance craze with which jazz diasporically intertwined. The world's first jazz 'festival', a 'Jazz Week' at the Globe Theatre in Sydney in 1919, offered the opportunity to learn the latest dance steps from films (Johnson 2000, 61).

For domestic spaces, radio created a new professional category, the studio musician, who had to be *au fait* with the latest material. Music was also broadcast from restaurants and ballrooms. Public radio began in Australia in 1923, and by the mid-1920s jazz and hot dance bands enjoyed significant broadcasting time. From its opening in 1926, the Finnish Broadcasting Corporation presented jazz from restaurants on Saturday nights, and internationally, radio established strong links with swing clubs from the mid-1930s (Johnson 1987, 73; Haavisto 1996, 63). But the single most significant medium in the international dissemination of jazz was the sound recording.

Until the late nineteenth century, the mass dissemination of culture was dominated by print. The advent of sound recordings bypassed notation and released music from the limits of its symbolic order and specialised knowledge restricted on grounds such as class, gender, ethnicity and physical location, giving direct access to music as sound. Apart from private purchase, recorded sounds were disseminated publicly on radio, often supplied from private collections which also serviced group discussions. In the 1930s, the collections of Bill Miller in Australia and Sergei Kolbasev in Russia were influential in places remote from northern-hemisphere touring circuits. The sound recording also altered jazz and its meanings, embodying an evanescent oral music in a commodity, shifting it into a different political economy. Among urban black South Africans, owning the latest record was valued not only as a music delivery system, but also as a marker of status (Johnson 1987, 212–13; Starr 1983, 119; Ballantine 1991, 130).

The recording industry globalised with impressive speed. Gramophone Company representatives had arrived in St Petersburg by the turn of the century, establishing the first of several pressing plants in 1902, in Riga. By 1907, 500,000 gramophones had been sold in Russia and record sales had reached 20 million by 1915, constituting a major market until post-revolutionary nationalisation. Likewise, until nationalisation Japan enjoyed strong indigenous record production. Its earliest factory was established with Columbia in 1908 and by 1913 there were three smaller local companies (Gronow 1996, 165; Starr 1983, 23; Gronow, 86, 91). In Australia in the early 1920s imported records were dumped at reduced prices, one label alone shipping in 100,000 records per month. By 1925, when local production began, it was estimated that there were already one million phonographs owned in Australia (Johnson 1987, 72; Johnson 2000, 9).[3] In 'The Green Rolls Royce' (1923), the poet Kenneth Slessor included the sound of phonographs in Sydney apartments in his inventory of contemporary urban experiences. The first Finnish records were produced in 1901 by Gramophone, with about 50 released annually from 1905 to 1915. Production was interrupted by political instability, but resumed in time to participate in the international 'gramophone fever' of 1929, with sales of over one million in a population of only 3.4 million. In Japan in that year sales reached ten million, and it is estimated that between one third and one half of all households in North America and Western Europe now owned a record player (Gronow 1996, 61, 46; Gronow 1989, 4). In spite of the massive slump in the early 1930s, however, the sound recording had already had a decisive effect.

The globalisation of recording also meant the internationalisation of American music, since the industry was controlled to a significant extent by the US. By 1910 the leading record companies were the US Victor Talking Machine Company and the Gramophone Company (Hayes, Middlesex), which was half-owned by Victor. By agreement, Victor operated in the Americas and the Far East, Gramophone in the rest of the world (Gronow 1996, 40). Wherever recordings penetrated, so did US jazz. Australians could buy a wide range of predominantly white US jazz performances from the early 1920s and, with the inauguration of such projects as Parlophone's 'rhythm style' series in 1930, they could hear a growing sample of black jazz musicians. Australia's most important pioneer, trombonist and trumpeter Frank Coughlan, was converted to jazz by recordings of Miff Mole. In Finland, increasing demand for recorded music in the late 1920s emphasised jazz. Toivo Kärki, from a religious family tradition, went on to unparallelled power in the Finnish music industry as a composer and record-industry executive. His turning point was hearing a recording of Louis Armstrong in a local café in 1928 (Johnson 1987, 72–3, 133; Gronow 1989, 4; Gronow 1986).

Along with sound film, jazz recordings also circulated US vocal accents, timbres and contemporary narratives, with implications which went beyond musical form. To non-American ears, the accent erased the class markers inscribed in English voices, and the expansion of timbral effects characteristic of jazz paved the way for the distinctive voice of twentieth-century pop. Jazz-related lyrics also gave public voice to the everyday narratives of modernity.

The link between the internationalisation of jazz and the record industry was equally striking when it was severed. The isolation which followed the revolution seems to be one reason for the difficulties Russian musicians had in assimilating the non-notatable aspects of the music. During World War II, Australian musicians found access to the latest US jazz blocked by a lack of recordings brought about by material shortages and the recording embargo imposed by the American Federation of Musicians. When bop records arrived, around 1946, the style was therefore virtually incomprehensible as having any connection with jazz (Starr 1983, 48; Johnson 2000, 17–18).

Sound technology was thus both channel and filter, determining which forms and examples of jazz would be disseminated, depending on access to recording, marketing and distribution. Paul Whiteman's record sales made him a major influence on the perception of what 'jazz' meant, occluding the New Orleans and classic styles during the 1920s (Kernfeld 1988, I, 587). The selectivity of jazz dissemination because of the politics of the mass media thus set up definitions of the music that only became contested by later revelations. Because of what was available on record, one of the most important figures in Russian jazz, Leonid Utesov, took white vaudevillean Ted Lewis as his model. From Russia to black Africa, a major jazz inspiration was Glenn Miller, largely because of the films, *Sun Valley Serenade* (1941) and *Orchestra Wives* (1942). African-American musicians themselves exhibited preferences based on what was available to be heard, which have puzzled or embarrassed later fans. Louis Armstrong and his colleagues listened admiringly to broadcasts by Guy Lombardo's orchestra (Collier 1984, 219). Lester Young's revolutionary style was developed by listening to recordings of white musicians, including Jimmy Dorsey, Frank Trumbauer and classical virtuoso Rudy Wiedoft (Starr 1983, 147–9; Stites 1992, 126; Ballantine 1991, 131–2; Buchmann-Møller 1990a, 21–5).

The conditions of dissemination thus determine which aspects of a tradition migrate, with performers later regarded as derivative and peripheral exercising disproportionate influence. None the less they had already become crucial diasporic influences: their stature is not merely illusory. Uncomfortable though it may well be for guardians of the jazz aesthetic, Glenn Miller's band was more influential in shaping the global jazz sound than, say, Luis Russell's (see Sudhalter 1999). The fact that, for most of the century, access to the mediations has been easier for white Anglo-US males has shaped two versions of jazz history in its diasporic phase. On the one hand, a 'popular' history emerged from early diasporic media representation. Against this, reactive narratives attempted retrospectively to occlude influential jazz activity which was inconvenient to criteria of folk authenticity at one extreme, and artistic integrity at the other. Such accounts produced their own mythologies: poor Bix Beiderbecke having to endure Whiteman's band, Armstrong 'selling out' in the 1930s and, most pervasively, the generalised assertion that whites can't play 'real' jazz. This reductionist narrative has obscured the diversity of musical and ethnic streams in jazz, both in the US (white country, rockabilly, Jewish cantor and commercial Tin Pan Alley) and powerful regional accents in the international diaspora.

The jazz diaspora is thus a case-study of the negotiation between local cultural practices and global cultural processes, between culture and mass mediations. In such negotiations, diaspora is the condition of the music's existence and character. Jazz was not 'invented' and then exported. It was invented in the process of being disseminated. As both idea and practice, jazz came into being through negotiation with the vehicles of its dissemination, and with conditions it encountered in any given location. The complexities of diasporic reinvention are not simply the outcome of which particular versions of jazz were exported. The conditions that these exports encountered reconfigured the music and its meanings even further.

Each diasporic site presented its own distinctive conditioning features. In Finland, such apparently non-musical events as the civil war and the emergence into independence produced lines of force relating to national identity and imperialist pressures from Russia and Sweden. These reverberate within particular musical and cultural influences, in turn implicated in attitudes to New World cultures. In Australia, the distinctive function of Anglo-Celtic traditions in a 'remote' outpost of civilisation, the schematic social stratification institutionalised in a penal settlement, the particular balance between English, Scottish and Irish influences, the bush–city binary, and related gender issues – all these contributed to the formation of a local jazz movement. In South Africa, the relationship between race and urbanisation influenced jazz reception. In post-revolutionary Russia, a society with access to the most extreme measures of cultural engineering was faced with resolutely unauthorised popular tastes, a tension producing an approved proletarian jazz and a decadent bourgeois form.

Language was a mediating factor, especially apparent in different language groups such as Finno-Ugrian. Jalkanen has shown how the prosody of Finnish produced a distinctive local tango. A study of Finnish lyrics superimposed on jazz material may well cast light on the acculturation process. Apart from metrical and rhythmic features, Finland's linguistic profile affected who had access to what, introducing considerations of class and demography. Members of Finland's Original Buddie Orchestra, established in 1926, spoke Swedish, facilitating contacts with Swedish musicians who in turn had more exposure to touring Americans. When jazz musician Tommy Tuomikoski arrived from the US on the *Andania* in 1926, his fluency in Finnish increased his effectiveness as a jazz conduit for Helsinki musicians. In the 1930s, Finnish jazz was promoted vigorously by middle-class students whose knowledge of languages other than Finnish gave them access to internationalist culture (Jalkanen 1993, 5; Haavisto 1996, 12, 13; Jalkanen 1989, 398). Jazz also had to negotiate with the local musical 'language', including traditions of form, accent and instrumentation, all emerging from particular social conditions. Though ardent converts to jazz, musicians retained powerful residues of the musical culture that nurtured their tastes and competencies. All these spontaneous interstitial syncretisms in the otherwise seamless jazz histories are crucial to the jazz diaspora. They are most audible in the early phase, which is one of the main reasons that this overview will concentrate on the period between the two world wars.

Diaspora within the US

Jazz was a music already in motion as a convergence of diverse traditions of the New World when it began circulating across the US through entertainment circuits and the peregrinations of individual musicians, sometimes encountering other regional versions. Its most influential early impact was in Chicago.[4] This was not just a question of jazz moving its operations. The shift from New Orleans (where venues included picnics, parades and funerals, as well as bars, brothels and dances) to Chicago and beyond produced more professional opportunities with higher pay, and an increasing focus on indoor nocturnal entertainment. These shifts accentuated the division between music and everyday social practices, including an increased quarantining of music from the acoustic quotidian; it became a contained commodity to which access was controlled by considerations of race, economics and gender. The shift also foregrounded particular artistic profiles, including the artist-as-separate, the individual genius. At the same time, however, the music became available to ideologues of the new politics growing out of contemporary urban societies. Garveyism linked up with jazz in an attempt to mobilise the urban African-American as the 'new negro', as opposed to the bumbling Stepin Fetchit, country boy. In the process, jazz acquired new cultural meanings that would affect its international migrations. This dimension of the music gave it particular appropriateness, for example, as a model for the growing population of urban working-class blacks in South Africa (Chilton 1987, 27, 28; Eyerman and Jamison 1998, 83–4; Ballantine 1991, 121–9). The northward diaspora of jazz musicians from New Orleans was therefore a movement historically and geographically into the high-density urban milieu of the twentieth century, and brought musicians into different kinds of performance space as well as differing relationships with their audiences.

The global diaspora

Diasporic meanings

Jazz became the music of urban modernity. In the US journal, the *Etude Music Magazine*, in 1924, visiting European violinist Franz Drdla described jazz as 'the characteristic folk music of modernity'. For many it was thus a threat to traditional values: an 'expression of protest against law and order', asserted the *Ladies' Home Journal* in August 1921 (cited in Walser 1999, 44, 35). This semiosis in the US pervaded the international diaspora, traversing all local differences. The jazz migration coincided with an emancipative reaction against nineteenth-century traditions, and the musical marker was provided by the 'New World'.

In every way – origins, musical form, aesthetics, the vehicles of diaspora, generic syncretism, performance practices – jazz in its early diasporic forms was seen by friend and foe as the musical embodiment of the twentieth century. In *The Appeal of Jazz*, published in London in 1927, R. W. S. Mendl maintained that modern America was expressed in the 'swift-moving, bustling, snappy restless rhythms of syncopated dance music . . . in the cunning quips and cranks of the jazz orchestra' (Walser 1999, 67–8). The German Georg Barthelme saluted jazz in 1919 as 'the logical development and completion of an idea that is called to introduce a new and better age' (Starr 1983, 12). To black South Africans, jazz was a rallying call to a new era of emancipation. Australian women found in jazz the articulation of sexual and social freedom. Although entering pre-revolutionary Russia at the upper levels of society, jazz was a racy challenge to the old imperial culture (Ballantine 1989, 308, 309; Johnson 2000, 59–76; Starr 1983, 21). Its friends often included the avant-garde. Apart from oft-mentioned names like Hindemith, Milhaud and Stravinsky, Finnish composers Uuno Klami and (Russian-born) Ernest Pingoud, and the radical artists and writers known as 'The Torchbearers', all found messages of modernity in jazz. In Russia, Valentin Parnakh promoted jazz among the avant-garde in the early 1920s. Kurt Kranz recalled that Bauhaus students formed their own 'Bauhaus Band', a mixture of a sort of Dixieland and something 'partly inspired by' Hindemith. When they walked the streets of Dessau, mothers would warn their daughters that they were from the Bauhaus: 'we were the punks of Dessau' (Helasvuo 1987, 6; Jalkanen 1989, 395; Starr 1983, 45–6).[5]

This moral panic discloses the other side of the coin. Cultural power blocs agreed with this coding of jazz, but read it as threat rather than promise. Jazz embodied the unruliness of twentieth-century mass-disseminated culture, 'popular' in its most obvious sense: in Finland, jazz musicians were making twice the salary of the members of the Helsinki Orchestra by the late 1920s. A professor of musicology at Helsinki University called for the music to be extirpated, and the Finnish Musicians' Association, founded in 1917, remained suspicious of the music until the late 1940s. In Australia, the Union lobbied to ban imported US jazz orchestras, drawing on a pervasive racism that made much of the 'negroid' origins of the music. The first occurrence of the word 'jazz' in a Finnish publication in 1919 also described jazz as 'one of the more savage, senseless, and of course uglier forms of jumping that Negro brains have invented' (Haavisto 1996, 14; Jalkanen 1989, 396; Haavisto, 61; Johnson 1987, 6; Haavisto, 6).

The charge of primitivism foregrounds the perplexed anxiety induced by jazz, since it was also being demonised as the sound of a corrupt modernity. Films made as far afield as Russia and Australia agreed that jazz was the music of the twentieth-century city, a morally suspect site which exposed decent people to transgressive possibilities, often embodied in the sexually ambiguous 'flapper' (Stites 1992, 59; Johnson 2000, 61, 69). The menace presented by jazz was deeply rooted in the fear that the fundamental values of civilisation itself were at risk. *Does the Jazz Lead to Destruction?* asked the title of an Australian film of 1919, and the advertising for the 'Jazz Week' it accompanied cheerfully indicated that, indeed, it did (Johnson 1987, 4). Where the threatened values resided changed from place to place: early opposition to jazz in Finland was particularly strong among the upper and middle classes, while in neighbouring Russia it was regarded as an evil associated with the capitalist bourgeoisie (Jalkanen 1989, 396; Starr 1983, 92). Jazz threatened the aesthetic, moral and political controlling mechanisms of the entrenched cultural gatekeepers, and most fundamentally it reversed the mind/body hierarchy that formed the basis of Enlightenment rationalism. 'I do not approve of "jazz" because it represents, in its convulsive, twitching, hiccoughing rhythms, the abdication of control by the central nervous system – the brain';[6] it was not music, but an 'irritation of the nerves of hearing, a sensual teasing'.[7] It undermined cognitive regulation and embraced randomness: an 'anything happens music', complained Finnish pianist Asser Fagerström, who later, however, became a fan. Unleashing the sensual, the abandoned, the ecstatic in everyman, jazz was too revolutionary – for which read too decadent – for the theorists of the proletarian revolution. Both Gorky and Lunacharsky regarded jazz as a capitalist plot designed to subject man to the control of his sexuality (Haavisto 1996, 12; Starr 1983, 89–93).

Diasporic practices

Jazz as musical form

Jazz articulated musical modernity on a global level, but with local inflections – manifested in instrumentation, repertoire, musical structures, performance protocols and even emotional range – which grew out of local traditions. In Australia, the earliest colonial administrators were *de facto* prison warders, establishing a tradition of nervous watchfulness over the threat presented by demotic recreations. Scored art-music and its satellites provided the ruling classes with a constant bearing by which to navigate mentally back to civilisation through a physical and cultural environment regarded as hostile, savage and criminal. This produced an arts establishment that was literally conservative, resistant to signs of the breakdown of order, as in the onset of an era of mass-disseminated culture. Unlike in many other countries, jazz therefore found no place of any consequence within the art-music landscape. Rather, it aligned itself with 'trivial' demotic forms notable for an apparent lack of aesthetic *gravitas*. First performed in vaudeville or music-hall settings, its range was narrowed emotionally to low comedy, and musically to extroverted novelty routines.

In diasporic sites, jazz instrumentation quickly became standardised. An Australian reviewer wrote in 1918:

> The Jass band consists of a pianist who can jump up and down, or slide
> from one side to the other while he is playing, a 'Saxie' player who can
> stand on his ear, a drummer whose right hand never knows what his left
> hand is doing, a banjo (ka)plunker, an E flat clarinet player, or a fiddler
> who can dance the bearcat.   [Johnson 1987, 4]

The fiddle as optional foreshadows the displacement of softer instruments; many violinists began to double on saxophone through the 1920s. Drums also were a key addition. Finland's first 'jazz' orchestra, led by Hugo Huttunen at the Konsertti Café in 1923, was simply the traditional salon band line-up of violin, cello and piano, with a drummer added for the jazz credentials. Likewise the saxophone was a particularly strong diasporic marker of jazz. In Finland, the use of 'saxophone' in the band name established its status as 'jatsi'. In Russia, Valentin Parnakh singled out the saxophone as the instrument of jazz dissonances and, for the authorities, to ban the instrument was virtually to extirpate the music (Haavisto 1996, 10; Konttinen 1987, 21; Starr 1983, 46–7, 85, 216).

What was played on these instruments in the earliest diasporic performances remains unclear in the absence of sound recordings. Already coded as iconoclasm, it was assumed that performance should incorporate acoustic anarchy. Reviews of Australian jazz performances in 1917 mention gunshots, kitchenware, bells, rattles and even the hurling of instruments about the stage. In Europe, a similar interpretation of jazz established an alliance with Italian futurism through what was called 'noise music', a connection audible in German 'Lärmjazz', which was exported to other German-influenced regions including Finland (Johnson 1987, 4; Starr 1983, 47–8; Haavisto 1996, 7).

With more conventional jazz instrumentation, regional practices evolved distinctive instrumental textures. In Finland, early attempts to fuse jazz with local traditions produced a robust working-class 'accordion jazz', as represented by the important group called Dallapé (Haavisto 1996, 15; Jalkanen 1989, 393). Hybrid structures also emerged in jazz performance. In South Africa, jazz was implicated in attempts to preserve Bantu music and black national identity. This produced township jazz fusions with their own generic designations such as *mbaqanga, majuba* and *msakazo*, in which the local marabi form and repertoire are conspicuous, generating one of the most strikingly distinctive diasporic jazz traditions (Coplan 1985, 161). On aural evidence, such distinctive fusions seem to be especially powerful when jazz encountered robust local, and especially non-Anglophone, narrative and musical traditions. Early Finnish jazz is heavily stamped with the Russian and German influences that pervaded local popular music, as well as 'native' influences as embodied in the *Kalevala* tradition, the latter accentuated by the country's emergent nationalism at the time of independence in 1917. In 1929, Yrjö's Orchestra recorded 'Raatikkoon Blues' and 'Isoo-Antti', both jazz adaptations of Finnish folk songs, sung in Finnish (the second celebrating a romanticised outlaw); the language of what came to be regarded as the first Finnish jazz standard, The Ramblers' 1932 recording of the local composition 'Muistan Sua, Elaine', was also the vernacular (Jalkanen 1993, 1–4; Haavisto 1996, 16).

Jazz as social practice
The social spaces occupied by diasporic jazz also proclaimed its meaning and function, broadly speaking by emphasising its role in the escape from entrenched regimes. In South Africa, it became associated with transgressive behaviour such as illicit drinking and indoor nocturnal recreation which circumvented local street curfews on urban blacks (Ballantine 1991, 122, 135–6). The South African case is also representative of a diasporic connection between jazz and recreational dance. The global spread of dancing as a public and private recreation in the early twentieth century (see Chapter 4) drew largely on US models linked with the ragtime and jazz performed in specialised spaces such as restaurants and dance halls (Starr 1983, 29–36; Haavisto 1996, 10; Johnson 2000, 63–9).

The significance of this connection is profound. Dancing is among the most democratic and least mediated forms of self-expression. The dancer is the dance. In addition, the alienating distance between producer and consumer is all but dissolved in the *act* of dancing. The dancer is a vigorous producer of culture and the global popularity of dance in the early twentieth century is a striking manifestation of a spirit of cultural 'mass production'. Furthermore, in its earliest diasporic manifestations, jazz was not simply music made by musicians. 'The jazz is a dance', reported Australian lifestyle journal *Table Talk* in August 1919. In Russia, Parnakh made the same connection (Starr 1983, 44). 'The jazz', 'jazzing', the modern girl 'jazzes': these now slightly confusing grammatical constructions, common in the 1920s, tell us how thoroughly jazz was imagined and practised as a dance, like 'the foxtrot' or 'the tango'.[8]

Again, however, the connections between jazz and dancing were articulated differently, and to different effects, in various diasporic sites. The connection was sometimes erratic. In 1926, the Andania Yankees were booked into the Ylä-Opris Restaurant, where dancing was not permitted. One consequence was that the 'concert' format provided other local musicians with the opportunity for instructive, focused attention (Haavisto 1996, 13). Starr's incisive account of 'Russia's Roaring Twenties' discloses the linkage between jazz and dancing as the expression of demotic cultural power. In the early 1920s, Russian youth embraced US music and dances. Two black American jazz bands, led by Bennie Peyton and Sam Wooding, arrived in 1926. While the conservatory music community discussed Wooding's 'concert' jazz, with its regimented listeners, it was Peyton's band that fuelled a public jazz craze, with dancing audiences. The different audience protocols reflected the great gap between elite minority cultural custodians and mass urban culture, emphasised in the USSR where the cultural engineers had powerful enforcement mechanisms. Attempts to interest the populace in ideologically sound popular music were of little avail, however, leading to the unsuccessful search for a version which reconciled proletarian emancipation with revolutionary puritanism (Starr 1983, 54–78).

Jazz as social meanings

The case of Russia schematises the collaboration between the jazz diaspora and the socio-political changes of the early twentieth century. In South Africa, too, jazz was far more than simply an imported recreation, but provided musical modellings of such changes. Ballantine identifies a range of these for urban blacks, from the link between individual musical success and the possibility of escape from the ghetto, to the achievement of more radical changes that would abolish the ghetto altogether. Yet this apparently straightforward message of black emancipation was intersected by conflicting lines of force relating to the emergence of a black middle class that disapproved of the jazz milieu (Ballantine 1993, ch. 3). This reproduced a pattern that had been evident in New Orleans and most diasporic sites. But nowhere could this be reduced to a simple formula of increasing resistance as we ascend the social scale, since this in turn was traversed by other factors. Middle-class youth, bohemians and a chic *nostalgie de la boue* cut across the class factor.

So too, to a profound degree, did gender. The phenomenon of the jazz flapper with her androgynous figure and her threatening invasion of male spaces is deeply embedded in the image of 'The Jazz Age'. In Finland, she gave her name to The Flappers Dance Band. In Australia, she appeared in the silent film, *Should a Girl Propose?* (1926), in jazz lyrics ('Flappers in the Sky'), wearing lifestyle accessories (the 'jazz corset'). (See Haavisto 1996, 14; Johnson 1987, 6, 8.) In the deeply patriarchal conservativism of public life in Australia, the alliance between women and jazz was a powerful marker of cultural change. Apart from the fact that dancing (and therefore 'jazzing', as discussed above) was a feminised activity, women were also far more prominent in jazz and improvisational performance and related media technologies than masculinist histories have recognised. This was in turn one of the most audible proclamations of the decisive role played by women in Australia's transition to modernity (Whiteoak 1999, 66; Johnson 2000, ch. 3). A similar pattern prevailed in South Africa, where black women were involved in early jazz groups, thus finding a public space through which they became models of female independence. As in the notable case of Johanna 'Giddy' Phalane, whose musical energies were complemented by explicit racial and gender activism, such women challenged conservative gender politics operating in both black and white communities (Ballantine 1991, 141; Ballantine 1993, 46–50). Yet again, local circumstances could reconfigure the dynamic, as in the case of Russia where, while greater employment opportunities gave women a strong public presence, this also reduced the leisure time available for popular recreations (Stites 1992, 61).

Inevitably the emancipative coding of diasporic jazz attracted the attention of local political interests of oppositional and dissenting inclinations. In both South Africa and Australia, the left courted jazz, providing various forms of patronage and infrastructural support. South Africa's Commercial Workers' Union and Communist Party hired jazz bands, likewise the youth arm of the Australian communist movement, the Eureka Youth League, which also made its premises available for independently organised jazz functions (Ballantine 1993, 50–55; Johnson 1987, 100–101). This is not to imply that the musicians themselves were highly politicised, however, and in both countries the courtship was only erratically reciprocated in the early years. As Starr has documented, the relationship between jazz and political dissent in Russia was a rather more volatile affair, characterised by a perennial paradox of the post-revolutionary regimes: the disparity between what the ideologues defined as proletarian culture and what the proletariat wanted.

The erratic fate of jazz in the Soviet Union draws attention to a further factor which determined the diasporic trajectory. The situation of Soviet jazz was to a large extent a weather vane of current relations with the US, but in less theatrical ways the same was true of other countries. A response to jazz was often an elliptical summary of the historical relations with other aspects of American culture. Finland's first major contact with jazz was just such an incandescent moment. Finland was part of the archipelago of European communities for whom the US was a destination – a place you went *to* – offering material and spiritual fulfilment in exchange for honest enterprise. Through migration and through reports, letters, photographs and visits back home, the US was becoming meshed with Finnish identity. Finnish communities in the US reported home on their American-ness: new possessions, occupations, land, children. But they also retained practices and tokens of their Finnishness, such as kantele, song and narrative traditions. By the 1920s they had established a distinctive Finnish-American musical presence. This reciprocity was reflected in the record industry: most Finnish-American records made by Columbia in the late 1920s were marketed in Finland.[9]

In 1926, the passenger ship SS *Andania* docked in Helsinki carrying around 600 returning emigrés or their descendants, and an orchestra, the Andania Yankees, which included several Finnish speakers. Its arrival was a significant moment in the mythology of renewal and reinvention, and the music which articulated that renewal was jazz. The Yankees played a month's season in a Helsinki restaurant, and for the first time Finnish audiences and musicians heard jazz live directly from the US, and played by *Finnish*-Americans. In terms of instrumentation (there were no violins), solo improvisation and rhythm, it was a revelation. Several of the Finnish-speaking musicians stayed on, working in local bands which were formed in the wake of the *Andania*'s visit, including Wilfred 'Tommy' Tuomikoski, who later founded a saxophone school – the first 'jazz studies' programme in Finland.[10] Curiously, then, there were significant affinities between this non-Anglophone society and African-American music, which were not present in the latter's relationship with Anglophone outposts such as Australia.

Relations with the US were of course starkly engraved with the onset of World War II, which thus reconfigured the jazz diaspora in complex and often contradictory ways that can only be sketched here. Music in Australia, a wartime base for around one million US service personnel, became conspicuously Americanised. Swing regained the momentum that it had lost in the late 1930s, and a new generation of young musicians enjoyed an accelerated development that prepared them to absorb the post-war impact of progressive styles like bop. At the same time, wartime mobility and encounters with visiting service musicians such as Max Kaminsky, who recorded with Roger Bell in Melbourne, nurtured what would become the internationally influential Australian traditional jazz movement (Johnson 1987, 23–31). In Russia, the opening of Germany's 'second front' in 1941 saw US

Plate 2.1 Wartime mobility and encounters with visiting service musicians: Morris Goode (New York) and Roger Bell (Australia). Source: Bruce Johnson

jazz and swing suddenly enjoy official favour, especially among the armed services, with even the NKVD ('People's Commissariat of Internal Affairs') putting together its own jazz bands. This brief sunshine period gave Russians a glimpse on film of Glenn Miller, who accordingly established considerable influence before the resumption of austerity and the 'jazz purges' that accompanied the Zhdanov proclamations following the end of the war (Stites 1992, 104–18; Starr 1983, 181–234). Wartime alliances produced the reverse effect elsewhere. Finland's strategic alliance with Germany, together with an officially engineered patriotic solemnity which included a ban on public dancing, virtually silenced jazz as an authorised entertainment (Haavisto 1996, 22–4; Gronow 1992, 31). Japan suffered the same drought, that was to be suddenly ended with the presence of American troops of occupation in the post-war years (J. Moore 1998, 265–6; Hosokawa *et al.* 1991, 13). Even in a region as remote from the European and Pacific theatres as South Africa, the war affected the reception and impact of jazz. Ballantine includes wartime inflation and increasingly dense urban black ghettoes among the factors that produced a growing 'New Africanism' and associated localised jazz idioms (Ballantine 1993, 54–61).

The post-war period takes us beyond the boundaries defined at the outset of this chapter, but subsequent tendencies can be tentatively identified. Up until the mid-1960s, diasporic jazz seems to have achieved a higher level of homogeneity than the diversely localised sounds that emerged between the wars, in part because of the increasingly systematic international marketing of US culture from the mid-1950s. This disseminated a canon, as well as contemporary developments, neatly encapsulated on LP albums and sleeve notes, in conjunction with an emerging consensus among historians as to central developments. More recently, in conjunction with a growing interest in local identities and hybridities, musical fusions have muddied the migratory paths into something approaching unintelligibility. Yet this is no more than the intensification of a mediating process that began the moment the idea of jazz came into existence. Even so cursory a sketch as this tends to confirm the thrust of the body of this chapter, that the deeper lessons concern the usefulness of some of the terms deployed to talk about cultural forms and the processes of their dissemination.

It is generally observed that there was little international consensus about the meaning of the word 'jazz' throughout the 1920s, and it is easy to jump from that observation to the suggestion that the understanding of the word was vague. Yet in all countries, each individual usage, and indeed that of many groups – whether for or against the music – is anything but vague. There is no equivocation in the declaration that jazz is 'an irritation of the nerves . . . a sensual teasing'. It is in such statements that jazz is being 'invented' in a particular diasporic site. Rather than dismissing such statements as 'vague' or misguided according to some definition evolving in a homogeneous jazz narrative produced by later generations, it is useful to try to respect and understand these definitions on their own terms. We may smile when we read a categorical declaration from a white Australian fashion writer in the 1920s that 'the jazz is a dance'. But the resolute fact is that for a host of readers, dancers and musicians, this *was* jazz. As a cultural form, jazz was invented as much in its diasporic spaces as in the dance halls of New Orleans, the speakeasies of Chicago, the nightclubs of Kansas City, the bars of New York.

It was only through diasporic (mis)conceptions as to what jazz was that it came to be the international anthem of the twentieth century. There is little if any evidence that the musicians coming out of New Orleans thought of themselves as bearing such a message. Indeed, upon arriving in the northern cities they were more likely to feel like country hicks. The construction of jazz throughout the 1920s as the music of modernity was the work of precisely those witnesses who were at a distance from its 'roots', and whose accounts and practices are often now disdained. Louis Armstrong might have *made* music of the twentieth century, but it was not he who *made it* the music of the twentieth century – for that we have to go to culturally and geographically diasporic spaces, Whiteman and white men, American Jews like Gershwin, Anglo-European commentators and the fans, readers and musicians who were in some ways guided by them. Especially in the 1920s, jazz was to a significant degree the invention of diasporic discourses and practices, of non-African-Americans.

It is an axiom of cultural studies that cultural forms and meanings are socially constructed. In those 1920s diasporic pronouncements on the nature and meaning of jazz, we are watching precisely that process. We cannot plausibly argue the social construction of meanings if we then invoke essentialist notions like 'authenticity' as markers of value. Ultimately, the idea of 'authenticity' – so powerful in the critical discourse of jazz in its native and diasporic forms – is of very little relevance in understanding and evaluating those forms. Each established its own 'authentic' identity in the convergence between music and place. With increasingly effective mediations, these diasporic forms and discourses (how people played, what they valued) then rippled across the whole field, including back to what is constituted as the centre. Ultimately, the source and the diaspora fold into each other.

Australia provides an instructive case study. By the mid-1940s, under the influences of US recordings and wartime contacts, a robust local traditional jazz movement had become established. In 1947 the Eureka Youth League proposed to Melbourne pianist Graeme Bell that he take his jazz band to the International Youth Festival in Czechoslovakia to represent Australia. Overcoming considerable logistical and economic obstacles, the band arrived in Prague where their performances created a sensation. For the Czechs emerging from the Nazi era, jazz was deeply encoded as music of resistance, and their only access to the music had been via illicit broadcasts, and through what was regarded as the enfeebled versions peddled by authorised swing and dance orchestras. The mood of liberation converged with the buoyant informality of the Australians and their music, heard in concerts, broadcasts, a season in a Prague restaurant and a regional tour. Performances were reviewed as being the first exposure to 'real' jazz, and Australia came to be regarded as a major source of the music. Recordings made by the group for Supraphon during their visit were canonised by the jazz bands that sprang up in its wake as their 'Bible', according to a description given by a fan to Graeme Bell when he revisited as the guest of the Czech government in the early 1990s. The band's influence touched a range of subsequent popular musics, and even appears to have affected cultural policy under the Communist regime in a way reminiscent of the impact of jazz in the Soviet Union. The traditional jazz movement in Czechoslovakia was launched by an Australian band.

After four months, the Australians then proceeded to the United Kingdom where, as British subjects, they were not subject to the same embargo as US bands. For eight months they played concerts, broadcast, recorded and toured, including Continental Europe on their itinerary. They introduced new repertoire (including their own compositions) and instrumentation (two members doubled on saxophone). Perhaps most significantly, they transformed the audience for, and social functions of, English jazz. They opened their own jazz club in London, and insolently broke with the traditional concert/lecture format of jazz-club functions by advertising their music for dancing. The club opened the jazz scene to a youthful audience who flocked to this den of boisterous recreation in the austere postwar English climate. The breezy, swaggering extroversion of their music was identified as a distinctive Australian jazz style, with multi-instrumentalist Ade Monsbourgh particularly influential. The reputation of the 'Australian style' spread: Bell later reported having met US saxophonists who named Monsbourgh as a model.[11]

The case of the Bell band in Europe exemplifies the complexity of the jazz diaspora. During its migrations jazz has traversed most points on the continuum from mass to high culture, from folk-form to art-form, from popular to elitist. It has journeyed longer and farther across the terrain of musical categorisation and politics than any other twentieth-century music. As such it has been the most versatile and durable register of the complex influences of twentieth-century mass mediations, their role in the negotiations between hegemonic and subaltern musical cultures, and thus the political and aesthetic dynamics of twentieth-century western music. Since jazz circulated

Plate 2.2 The Graeme Bell band in 1952 on its return from its second European tour (1951–2). Back row, left to right: Don 'Pixie' Roberts (reeds), Bud Baker (guitar/banjo), Lou Silbereisen (bass), Graeme Bell (piano/leader). Front row, left to right: Roger Bell (trumpet), John Sangster (drums), Deryck Bentley (trombone), Ade Monsbourgh (reeds/trombone). The breezy, swaggering extroversion of their music was identified as a distinctive Australian jazz style. Source: Bruce Johnson, Mike Sutcliffe.

around the globe it has challenged rudimentary notions of cultural dissemination. Simple migratory patterns based on movements between centres and margins have become densely cross-hatched. Margins jostle and connect with margins, producing new cultural fusions that challenge the idea of spatial and discursive 'centres'. It has been a long time since it could be reasonably declared that there is only one significant source from which jazz is disseminated and its meanings and practices controlled. Notwithstanding the continuing perception of certain geographical locations as jazz wellsprings, they are increasingly ritualistic sites of preservation and commemoration, pilgrims' destinations. Increasing access to mass mediations redefines the sources and sites of power. The original lines of migration have thickened and criss-crossed into a worldwide web, mapping a polyspora.

DISCOGRAPHY

Australian

Roger Bell's Jazz Gang (with Max Kaminsky), 'Oh! That Sign', Ampersand 1, rec.
19 September 1943

Don Roberts Wolf Gang (with Max Kaminsky), 'Ja-Da', Ampersand 1, rec. 19
September 1943

The Supraphon sessions made by the Graeme Bell band in Czechoslovakia,
referred to as a group in the foregoing, are listed in detail in Mitchell 1988.
They were reissued on several discs, including *Graeme Bell & His Dixieland Jazz
Band: Czechoslovak Journey*, Supraphon 0 15 1455, 1973

Finnish

Markus Rautio with Yrjö's Orchestra, 'Raatikkoon Blues', Columbia 17804, rec.
1929. Reissue: *Suomalaista Jazzia, Vol 5: Laulajia jazztunnelmissa* (*Finnish Jazz,
Vol 5: Singers in a Jazz Mood*), F[azer] Records 0630-16713-2, 1996; 'Isoo-Antti',
Columbia W 37456, rec. 1929. Reissue: *Finnish Jazz 1929–1959, Vol 1,
1929–1945*, F[azer] Records 440302, 1994

Leo Adamson with The Ramblers, 'Muistan Sua, Elaine' (I Remember You,
Elaine), H-O 23141, rec. 1931. Reissue: *Finnish Jazz 1929–1959, Vol 1,
1929–1945*, F[azer] Records 440302, 1994

Matti Jurva and Rytmi-Pojat, 'Hei Hulinaa, Helsinki' (Hey, Helsinki Hullabaloo),
6247 GR/MILP 245, rec. 1935. Reissue: *Finnish Jazz 1929–1959, Vol 1,
1929–1945*, F[azer] Records 440302, 1994

Bruno Laakko and Lepakot Orchestra [Dallapé], 'Kissa Vieköön' (Jeepers
Creepers), Columbia CY 278 (as listed in the following reissue), rec. 1 July
1939. Reissue: *Suomalaista Jazzia, Vol 5: Laulajia jazztunnelmissa* (*Finnish Jazz,
Vol 5: Singers in a Jazz Mood*), F[azer] Records 0630-16713-2, 1996;
'Aleksanterin Jazzyhtye' (Alexander's Ragtime Band), label/cat. no.
unavailable, but likely as above, rec. 1 July 1939. Reissue: *Finnish Jazz
1929–1959, Vol 1, 1929–1945*, F[azer] Records 440302, 1994

Arvi Tikkala with Rion Tanssiorkesteri, 'Milloin Luotta Voin Sinuun?' (When Can
I Trust You?), HMV A. L. 1409, rec. 1939. Reissue: *Finnish Jazz 1929–1959,
Vol 1, 1929–1945*, F[azer] Records 440302, 1994

Russian

Orkestr Pod Upr. Alexander Tsfasman, 'Vistrij Tanjec' (The Sound of Dance),
SSSR (SU) G-6376, rec. 1937. Reissue: *Harlequin History of Jazz Series
Vol. 3 – Jazz and Hot Dance in Russia*, Harlequin HQ 2012 [1984?]

South African

Jazz Revellers Band, 'Sponono' (Sweetheart), Columbia AE 45, rec. 1933. Reissue:
Marabi Nights – Early South African Jazz and Vaudeville, cassette published with
Ballantine 1993

Swedish

Benny Carter med Sonora Swing Band, 'Some of These Days' and 'Gloaming',
Sonora 3188, rec. 12 September 1936

Thor Ehrling, 'Lady Be Good', Odeon D3031, rec. 1 January 1939. Reissue: *Thor
Ehrling – Jazz Highlights 1939–55*, Dragon DRCD 236, 1993; 'The Flat Foot
Floogie', Odeon D3031, rec. 10 February 1939. Reissue: *Thor Ehrling – Jazz*

Highlights 1939–55, Dragon DRCD 236, 1993; 'Runt Om Ett Enrissnår' (Stop Beating Around the Mulberry Bush), Odeon D3037, rec. 6 March 1939. Reissue: *Thor Ehrling – Jazz Highlights 1939–55*, Dragon DRCD 236, 1993; 'Royal Strut', Odeon D3037, rec. 14 April 1939. Reissue: *Thor Ehrling – Jazz Highlights 1939–55*, Dragon DRCD 236, 1993

3 The jazz audience

JED RASULA

Once the Dixieland revival found an audience in the 1940s, the mono-lithic façade of swing began to splinter into the interest groups that have populated the subsequent history of jazz: bop, cool, third stream, free jazz, fusion, neo-traditionalist. Jazz as music is inseparable from the African-American experience, and Duke Ellington rightly insisted that 'the Negro is the creative voice of America, is creative America' (Tucker 1993, 147). The question of the jazz audience, on the other hand, encompasses a more inde-terminate populace. One could approach the topic of audience by offering a demographic profile of various constituencies of fans, but this would lend tacit assent to consumerism as validating criterion. There was an audience for jazz before there were consumers, in part because 'the Jazz Age was born . . . almost before there was jazz' (Schiff 1997, 87). 'Jazz' was initially so mercurial a term that it was applied to music intermittently: the audience responded to a social spectrum in which music was only a part. None the less, historians have gravitated to the narrative magnetism of giants shaping the music to their personal visions, and 1923 is often cited as an inaugural moment because it marks the first recordings of Louis Armstrong, Jelly Roll Morton, Sidney Bechet and Bessie Smith. Gunther Schuller even refers to a 'pre-1923 era' (1968, 71). But if we de-prioritise recordings, a significant fact appears: jazz had already had a worldwide impact before 1923. As a case in point, consider a different artifact from 1923, Russian constructivist Alexander Rodchenko's photomontage for Vladimir Mayakovsky's book of poetry, *About This* (see Plate 3.1). The history of jazz has been so obses-sively narrated as an American phenomenon that Rodchenko's image forces a perspectival adjustment. If it was launched with those famous recordings of 1923, how did jazz make it to Moscow so quickly, and what did it mean? To answer this question is to discover that the jazz audience was responsive to a culture complex in which modernism, fashion, dance and Americanism were inseparable from the music.

It is not hard to trace the routes by which jazz reached Moscow. Jazz was initially disseminated by the spread of new dances such as the foxtrot, which arrived in England in the summer of 1914 and crossed the Channel the next year. The chanteuse Gaby Deslys spent part of the war in New York, returning to the Casino de Paris with a jazz band in 1917, and black American soldiers were being conscripted by the Parisian avant-garde for fêtes in 1918. The

Plate 3.1 Alexander Rodchenko, photomontage for Vladimir Mayakovsky's poetry book *About This*. At the base of the montage we read 'Die Jazz-Band', above which, in smaller type, is 'ORIGINAL – JAZZ' (a Russian work cites jazz in German and English). At the top of the collage, somewhat obscured by a bottle of schnapps or brandy, are references to popular dances in decorative lettering: 'Jass-Two-Step', 'Fox-Trot' and 'Shimmy'. Rodchenko's montage incorporates other elements of the milieux in which 'jass' made its European debut, including dancing couples, café tables, high-heeled shoes and the looser style of women's dress suited to the new dances. There are several bottles of liquor as well as a large cigar floating into the centre of the montage like the Hindenberg blimp.

arrival of jazz coincided with the devastation of the Great War, marking it with a singular intensity in the European context. R. W. S. Mendl repeatedly emphasises the connection in his 1927 book, *The Appeal of Jazz*, calling jazz a 'musical alcohol' affording stimulating relaxation to soldiers on leave from the front, while being itself 'a reflection of the elemental instincts of war fever' (95). The hostilities delayed further diffusion, and it was only in 1918 that Germans experienced the foxtrot and the tango. Thereafter, jazz was rapidly infused with a cosmopolitan aura.

Almost as soon as jazz became a fad it was attracting attention as a serious cultural phenomenon. By 1923 it had become common for classical composers to incorporate jazz syncopation into their works (Stravinsky and Milhaud most famously, but also Hindemith, Martinů, Křenek, Erwin Schulhoff, Louis Gruenberg, John Alden Carpenter, John Powell and Henry F. Gilbert). Students at the Bauhaus, the German bulwark of international modernism, organised a jazz band in 1923. The previous year a vanguard yearbook, *Devetsil*, appeared in Prague, in which several of the contributors addressed the phenomenon of the jazz-band (invariably hyphenated) as part of a culture complex including football, cabaret, variety shows, circus, kino, Charlie Chaplin and modern dance. This nexus of associations was perpetuated by those European authors who wrote the first serious studies of jazz: Coeuroy and Schaeffner (1926), Bernhard (1927), Mendl (1927), Burian (1928), Bragaglia (1929) and Goffin (1932).

For Americans and Europeans alike, jazz was a phenomenon inextricably bound up with the issue of modernity. In *Yankee Blues*, Macdonald Moore calls jazz 'a scavenger symbol for the cultural traumas of the 1920s'. 'As they unpacked the metaphor of jazz, critics "discovered" the secret of modernism', he writes, as '"jazz" lent perceptual coherence to phenomena as discrete as European musical avant-gardism, bureaucratic and scientific rationalization, even contemporary faddism' (1985, 82–3, 119). Walter Kingsley evoked the sensation of jazz for *New York Sun* readers in 1917: 'Imagine Walter Pater, Swinburne and Borodin swaying to the same pulses that rule the moonlit music on the banks of African rivers.' 'The laws that govern jazz', he clarified, 'rule in the rhythms of great original prose, verse that sings itself, and opera of ultra modernity' (Walser 1999, 7). 'Modernity' and 'modernism' went into circulation just about the time that jazz became available as one among many instances of what these terms meant. Fred Lewis Pattee gave the title *Tradition and Jazz* (1925) to a collection of literary criticism on such topics as 'The Old Professor of English: An Autopsy'. Jazz in this context had no musical connotation but meant defiance of the *passé*. Musically, jazz could be affirmed as 'the characteristic folk music of modernity because America is the most modern country of the world' (Drdla in Walser 1999, 44). For Clive Bell, jazz was a broad cultural movement that 'took its name from music – the art that is always behind the times'. He was writing just before the Jazz Age was named as such, but Bell clearly thought the term applicable to a range of cultural manifestations. Its most distinctive feature, syncopation, 'has given us a ragtime literature which flouts traditional rhythms and sequences and grammar and logic'. He singled out T. S. Eliot and Stravinsky as the supreme practitioners of jazz in their respective media, and in literature cited Woolf, Cocteau and Cendrars appreciatively, while disparaging Joyce: 'he rags the literary instrument' with 'talents which though genuine are moderate only' (Bell 1928, 215, 223, 224).

Bell's arts of 'jazz' include post-impressionism, symbolism, primitivism and neo-classicism: a formidable medley, but similar to those proposed by other commentators. In 1913 an article in the *San Francisco Bulletin* speculated on the vivacity of this 'futurist word which has just joined the language' (Sudhalter 1999, 8). It is unclear whether the reference is to Italian futurism, but modern art movements provided handy comparisons. 'The ferment which produced the innovations in the other arts which we call "jazzy" was at work in Europe long before its influence was felt here. Germany had her Sandburgs and Steins before we did', Henry O. Osgood informed American readers in 1926 (245). A German commentator greeted jazz as a 'musical revelation, a religion, a philosophy of the world, just like Expressionism and Impressionism' (Georg Barthelme in Starr 1983, 12). Robert Goffin informed French readers that 'What Breton and Aragon did for poetry in 1920, Chirico and Ernst for painting, had been instinctively accomplished as early as 1910 by humble Negro musicians' (Walser 1999, 86). For American painter Stuart Davis, the incentive to modernise himself as an artist arose from 'the numerical precisions of the Negro piano players in the Negro saloons' (1971, 23–4). Eric Hobsbawm later observed that 'Jazz was, and is, for deviant members of the American middle class what surrealism and existentialism were for deviant French members of it' (Newton 1960, 242). Recognition was not a one-way street. 'That Dada Strain' was the title of a jazz tune, and musicians recognised in other artistic events a comparable incentive. Mezz Mezzrow claims that *The American Mercury* was 'the Austin High Gang's Bible. It looked to us like Mencken was yelling the same message in his magazine that we were trying to get across in our music: his words were practically lyrics to our hot jazz' (Mezzrow and Wolfe 1972, 94).[1]

F. Scott Fitzgerald's *Tales of the Jazz Age* appeared in 1922, when American literary magazines like *Soil* and *Broom* were promoting jazz as exemplary, and when a Serbian avant-garde journal took the title *Dada Jazz*. Jazz began to crop up as a reference in poetry. T. S. Eliot struggled unsuccessfully to write a jazz-inflected music-hall psychodrama called *Sweeney Agonistes*. In *Processional: A Jazz Symphony of American Life* (1925), John Howard

Lawson developed a theatrical method to reflect 'the wild disorder of contemporary life and the emotional exasperation which it produces' (Krutch
1939, 241). Meanwhile, popular writers in the 1920s availed themselves of
jazz to inject a period flavour into otherwise old-fashioned moralising tales.
In Germany, fiction writers such as Gerhard Schumann and Edwin Erich
Dwinger depicted the toxic allure of jazz for the Aryan spirit. In English,
jazz was sensationalist fodder in potboilers such as *The Great God Jazz* (n.d.)
by H. M. E. Clamp, *The Jazz Widow* (1930) by May Christie and *Jazz Mad*
(1928) by Svend Gade.

Literary uses of jazz were hardly restricted to motifs. The avant-garde
registered an affinity in numerous cases, as with Cocteau and Les Six in Paris.
Recognising in jazz 'the atavistic modernity they extolled', Berlin Dadaists
like Walter Mehring called for an 'international lingual work of art, the
language – ragtime' (Tower 1990, 89, 90). Dadaist sound poems do in fact
bear a striking resemblance to scat singing. Gertrude Stein's is the closest
literary equivalent to jazz improvisation, to which she pointedly refers in
Lectures in America: 'The jazz bands made of this thing, the thing that makes
you nervous at the theatre, they made of this thing an end in itself. They
made of this different tempo a something that was nothing but a difference in
tempo between anybody and everybody.' Stein's own compositional idiom is
not different in principle from that of jazz polyrhythms, or 'two times going
at once'. 'I kept wondering as I talked and listened all at once, I wondered is
there any way of making what I know come out as I know it, come out not as
remembering' (Stein 1935, 95, 180, 181). Is there a more concise definition
of improvisation? Stein, of course, has long been associated with cognitive
dissonance in literary circles, but jazz too was initially associated with noise
and discordant experiences. 'Of all the emphatic sounds of modernism,
noise is the most common and the most productively counterproductive'
(Kahn 1999, 20). Douglas Kahn's tantalising formulation applies to jazz as
well as to modernism, serving notice that while noise is the by-product of
any harmonious model of social or aesthetic relations, the affirmation of
noise imposes its own tacit field of relations.

A Chicago concert by James Reese Europe's band in 1919 concluded with
a sonic rendition of trench warfare called 'In No Man's Land', during which
the house lights were completely extinguished. This was precisely what the
Italian futurists had been doing in their public declamations; and Bell cited
Italian futurism as 'the nearest approach to a pictorial expression of the
Jazz spirit' (1928, 214). Had he known the latest developments, Bell might
have cited Dada instead of futurism. Certainly the insistent drumming that
accompanied recitations of sound poetry at Zurich's Cabaret Voltaire in 1916
served as prelude to the arrival of jazz. In Moscow, the state-sponsored jazz
ensemble led by Valentin Parnakh included not only music, but lectures,

demonstrations of dance steps and jazz poetry. A 1922 concert juxtaposed the band with N. N. Foregger's 'noise orchestra' (inspired by the Italian futurist art of noises). To Parnakh's distress, one critic detected no difference between the two groups. Even informed enthusiasts associated jazz with noise. André Coeuroy and André Schaeffner bluntly stated, in their 1926 book, *Le Jazz*, 'Jazz is not a matter of argument or doctrine. Jazz is rhythm and noise' (142).[2] Jean Cocteau pinpointed the challenge of jazz for vanguard artists: 'This noise drenches us, wakens us *to do something else*' (1970, 86).[3]

'The object of a jazz band, apparently, is to provide as much noise as possible', wrote a bewildered London critic in *The Times* in 1919 (Godbolt 1984, 3). Jazz was widely associated with noise, and drums were perceived as pre-eminent noisemakers. A jazz band, it was assumed, was an assortment of unfamiliar instruments meant to showcase a drum set. At that point, in Britain, drum kits were called 'jazz-sets'. The usage may have spread to Germany where, after the war, drums were called 'the jazz' (Kater 1992, 14). Even a *New York Times* article of 1921 asserted that 'the drum-and-trap accessories . . . constitute the jazz, the rest merely band' (Hershey in Walser 1999, 25). Michel Leiris recalled the first Parisian exposure to jazz in which 'each performance was dominated almost from beginning to end by the deafening drums' (1984, 108). The attraction proved infectious, as Cocteau, Picabia and Milhaud each made an attempt to learn jazz drumming. In 1927, Mendl looked back on the 'crude, weird sounds' of the previous decade: 'the jazz effects were produced by motor horns, rattles, squeaky whistles, tin cans, almost any means of making crude and raucous noises: usually these horrible embellishments were served up by the drummer, who was a veritable host in himself, or *homme-orchestre*' (1927, 48).

Noise was not an exclusive prerogative of drums. Ezra Pound predicted that 'The future of piano music lies in the Jazz'. In context this was a disparaging remark, for Pound viewed the 'pye-ano' as 'a sort of cheap substitute for an orchestra' (1977, 203, 205). In 1922 Wallace Stevens evoked the allure of the most durable jazz icon:

> our bawdiness
> . . . indulged at last . . .
> Squiggling like saxophones.
>   [1972, 77]

Two years later the *New York Times* cited 'that ghastly instrument, the saxophone' as an offence to musical taste (L. Levine 1993, 179); and an English dance hall in 1926 was able to renew its licence only on the condition that bands refrain from using saxophones. The exotic and risqué timbre of this novel reed instrument helped consolidate a musical soundscape, becoming in the process an internationally accessible cultural signifier, the logo for jazz. The saxophone might have given Rodchenko an indelible image for his photomontage but for the fact that saxophones were scarce in the Soviet Union. In fact, Rodchenko excludes musical instruments altogether, the space being filled instead with the floating signifiers of fashionable dance and nightclubs.

The serious study of jazz was initiated by discographers, leaving a permanent imprint on subsequent attempts to write its history. Martin Williams's influential *The Jazz Tradition* (1983), while exemplary in its attentiveness, is little more than a chronological examination of key recordings. Most symptomatic is that Williams never mentions any connection between jazz and dancing (an effacement perpetuated in his booklet for *The Smithsonian Collection of Classic Jazz*). But, until the rise of bebop, jazz was dance music. Its audience listened on its feet. The exceptions were in venues like the Cotton Club, where dance was displaced by floor shows of exotic spectacle catering to white clients. But the spectacle invariably involved dance; and Albert Murray reminds us that even in a concert setting jazz presents 'the dancing of attitudes' (1976, 189).[4]

In Europe, jazz arrived as a necessary accessory of the new dances – an extension, in effect, of the animation with which the musicians played. A Soviet enthusiast noted that, while the music was meant for dancing, the musicians' exertions constituted a dance of their own, making the jazz band a 'mimetic orchestra' (Starr 1983, 44). In both Europe and America, 'jazz' was often taken to refer to dancing rather than to a type of music: 'To Jazz or not to Jazz – that is the question', meaning, to dance or not to dance the latest dances, often bearing names like the Puppy Snuggle, the Terrapin Toddle and the Pollywog Wiggle. The American 'epidemic of mass social dancing' carried jazz with it around the world (Hobsbawm 1998, 268). The new dances did not go unprotested. The Vatican expressed official disapproval in 1914, and some municipalities arrested people for doing the foxtrot. A prominent American dance instructor charged that 'The music written for jazz is the very foundation and essence of salacious dancing' (Gelatt 1977, 213). In 1921 the *Ladies' Home Journal* condemned jazz as a subsidiary to lewd dances. The Salvation Army protested the 'implanting of jazz emotions' in babies at a maternity hospital proximate to a dance hall (Ogren 1989, 3). Indulging in the purple prose of the moral crusader, an American minister charged dance with every form of delinquency and social disgrace, but he never mentioned jazz or any other type of music, nor did he intimate any link between popular dances and African-American culture. For some, clearly, jazz was beneath notice, the mere sonic accompaniment to a menacing 'social pestilence' (Lamphear 1922, 38).

The dance audience was considerably larger than the listening audience, and even records were used mainly for dancing – a point made conspicuous on 78 rpm labels, in which most jazz releases bore a generic indicator: 'Fox trot'. Dance was recreational in America, but in Europe it took on other connotations in the post-war milieu. The hero of Hermann Hesse's *Steppenwolf* submits to a Nietzschean self-overcoming in order to learn the foxtrot. As for musical incitement, 'The Jazz Band is the orgiastic dance orchestra', wrote Paul Bernhard. 'It is the instrumental and rhythmic expression of primal instincts given naked and manifestly primitive agitation' (1927, 26). Primitivism in dance – and, by association, jazz – was Europe's way of purging itself of overcivilised neuroses and hypersophistication. (The irony, of course, is that cultivated primitivism merely added another layer of sophistication.) For many, Josephine Baker was the cure incarnate, 'a wand of golden flesh', 'neither infrahuman nor superhuman . . . equally nonprimitive and uncivilized', wrote e. e. cummings (1966, 162). Count Harry Kessler located Baker's dance 'somewhere between the jungle and the skyscraper. The same is true of her music, jazz, in its color and rhythm. It is ultraprimitive and ultramodern' (Gumbrecht 1997, 67). Parisian fashion capitulated to the Baker vogue: women could slick down their hair with Bakerfix and wear Baker perfumes.

Jazz was nothing if not fashionable. A poem by Juliette Roche captures the euphoria of the early Jazz Age:

> the woodwinds of the Jazz-Bands
> the ginfizzes
> the ragtimes
> the conversations
> contain every possibility.

A chorus of consenting Europeans agreed: 'In the period of great license that followed the hostilities, jazz was a sign of allegiance, an orgiastic tribute to the colors of the moment' (Leiris 1984, 109); 'It was the time of savage joys, crazy rascals, and wild pranks within the realm of propriety: in short, the whole program of the era was called "Jazz"' (Janowitz 1927, 10); 'jazz is just as precisely the outward expression of our time as the waltz was of the outgoing nineteenth century' (Weill in Kaes *et al.* 1994, 597). Ernst Křenek used jazz in his opera *Jonny spielt auf* to evoke 'the collective feeling of the age' (*ibid.*, 586). Dutch cabaret star Louis Davids caught the spirit of reckless abandon in his song 'Mother is Dancing':

> Crying for your mother, baby?
> Baby, give it up.
> Mother needs her daily whoopee . . .
> Mommy craves that mean ol' banjo
> And the saxophone.
>   [Senelick 1993, 220]

A character in J. Hartley Manners's 1922 play, *The National Anthem*, disparages its popularity: 'Why it's ridiculous. London is jigging to it . . . Paris is deafened by it. It has become the National Anthem of Civilization' (M. Moore 1985, 86). 'It is vulgar', a writer in *The Nation* conceded in 1922, 'but it is healthily frank – as frank as the conversation of a group of young people who cleanly and intelligently discuss birth control' (Schultz, 439).

Jazz was an ingredient of anything that people learned to call modern after World War I: 'in the jazz music what remains of the creative force of this sterile time unfolds: the genius of the eclectic, the cocktail mix of souls' (Gerstel in Kaes *et al.* 1994, 555). In Europe it was celebrated for its unpretentiousness, accepted with a sigh of relief as an alleviation from the burden of Art. Cocteau caught the precise nature of the appeal: 'The music-hall, the circus, and American Negro bands, all these things fertilize an artist just as life does. To turn to one's own account the emotions aroused by this sort of entertainment is not to derive art from art. These entertainments are not art. They stimulate in the same way as machinery, animals, natural scenery, or danger' (1926, 21). Commentators might offer different menus, but the ingredients always derived from a common stock of associations. In the USSR it became a useful suffix; people spoke of 'theatrical jazz', 'cinema-jazz', 'extra-jazz', 'joy-jazz', 'circus-jazz' and so forth (Starr 1983, 108). Jazz was one of a number of English loan words and phrases permeating European vocabulary, such as 'flirt', 'cocktail' and 'sex appeal'. Given such a panoply of associations, the music itself was subject to conceptual indeterminacy. Some took it to mean orchestrated ragtime; to others it meant hokum and novelty revues. Period references often include music patently unrelated to what we now call jazz. As the Jazz Age took off and recordings proliferated, we can ascertain with greater certainty what counted as jazz music, but the term itself continued to connote an intricate social panorama ranging from sports cars and safety razors to skyscrapers, comic strips, chewing gum, short hairstyles for women and the chorus line (or what the Germans called 'Girlkultur').[5] Oskar Schlemmer described a climate dedicated to 'the latest, the most modern, up-to-the-minute, Dadaism, circus, *variété*, jazz, hectic pace, movies, America, airplanes, the automobile. Those are the terms in which people here think' (Willett 1978, 119).

When André Breton said that beauty had to be convulsive in order to exist, he might as well have been speaking of jazz, which epitomised convulsiveness in social behaviour. Jazz incited a binge mentality. For a fashionable primitivism, the role of jazz was to 'apply the rouge on civilization', but, Ivan Goll lamented, 'these primeval people will be used up fast!' (Kaes *et al.* 1994, 560). That jazz itself might be a passing phase was registered by A. G. Bragaglia in 1929: 'The jazz-band already represents for us the physiognomy of nostalgia for our time' (1929, 9). As early as 1920 the French composer, Georges Auric, was writing its eulogy: 'Jazz woke us up', he conceded, but 'from now on let's stop our ears so as not to hear it' (Steegmuller 1970, 259); and his friend, Cocteau, wrote dismissively of 'a certain decor, a certain racket, a certain Jazz-bandism' as 'the froth of the modern movement' (Brown 1968, 200). Of course, the frenetic cycle of absorption and repudiation characterises not only the vanguard of the period, but also the routine turnover of fashion. Insofar as jazz was closely linked with fashionable activities, it was subject to commercial pressures to conform to fashion cycles, and was inevitably slated for obsolescence.

Much of the history has been written as if stylistic changes were strictly musical. But, in the larger cultural context, jazz was the servant of public fantasy, a condition to which musicians had to adapt. The reluctance of many black musicians to use the word 'jazz' is surely related to fashion. Why risk a promising career by being affiliated with a contested term? In its early years, jazz was conspicuously associated with hokum, 'spasm bands', and the 'nut jazz' of Ted Lewis and other novelty acts. Paul Whiteman's claim to have made a lady out of jazz was not altogether the infamous appropriation of black music it is often made out to be, but an attempt to keep it from sinking with its associations. By 1927, the editor of *Melody Maker* had alleged that 'it signifies everything that is old-fashioned' (Godbolt 1984, 35), and a few years later, before the swing phenomenon revitalised jazz and gave it a temporary name change, Constant Lambert observed that it had been reduced to 'a sort of aural tickling . . . a drug for the devitalised' in 'an age of tonal debauch' (1934, 228, 239).

Predictions of the demise of jazz proved irrelevant in the end, since the worldwide audience for Americanism meant that jazz would always benefit by the association. 'The rhythm of our time is jazz', said Kurt Weill, adding that it represented 'the Americanization of our whole external life' (in Kaes *et al.* 1994, 597). 'Jazz, filled with the youthful energy of America, is the pregnant outburst of a changed, untragic feel for life', another German affirmed (Warschauer in *ibid.*, 572). The Dean of the Yale Music School protested: 'America knows how to weep as well as how to laugh'[6] – a view epitomising genteel aspirations in America at a time when 'One could understand what Culture was by looking at the characteristics of jazz and reversing them' (L. Levine 1993, 174). During an American tour, Maurice Ravel reproached his hosts: 'you Americans take jazz too lightly' (Sullivan 1999, 199). Most of those who took it seriously did so because of the European attention it received. Lincoln Kirstein recalled that, for his set, 'Harlem was far more an *arrondissement* of Paris than a battleground of Greater New York' (1991, 34). Americans could use jazz to attain the sophistication of Europe, while Europeans sought in it the elixir of a primitive sagacity. In

Hesse's *Steppenwolf,* jazz awakens Harry Haller from his Old World lethargy. 'For me', he reflects, 'its raw and savage gaiety reached an underworld of instinct and breathed a simple honest sensuality . . . There was something of the Negro in it, and something of the American, who with all his strength seems so boyishly fresh and childlike to us Europeans' (1969, 43). For an American like Gilbert Seldes, jazz was an embryonic vernacular art, 'the normal development of our resources, the expected, the wonderful, arrival of America at a point of creative intensity' (1923, 151). Intensity, of course, need not mean sobriety or dignity. 'Jazz is just fun and foolishness', Frank Patterson wrote in 1922: '[It] expresses our American nature – and as long as our nature is expressed by anything so simple and straightforward we will have no cause to worry' (Collier 1993, 226) – to worry, that is, about degeneration or decadence.

The link with degeneracy was a persistent feature of the early jazz years. While its contribution to social effervescence was obvious, some composers heralded the potential of jazz for regeneration. In a 1924 *Vanity Fair* article, 'American Noises: How to Make Them, and Why', Seldes envisioned the tributary opening out on a global prospect: 'The discoveries which jazz has made, the freshness of tones – the American noises, in short – will be snapped up by composers in and out of the jazz movement. It is the musical world at large which will ultimately gain by the coming of jazz' (Kammen 1996, 118). The gains, in retrospect, were not restricted to signature jazz touches in a few bars of otherwise conventional art music. During the Jazz Age, however, imitation was the dominant form of appropriation, a circumstance Americans might view with anxiety. In its 'search for fresh booty', Matthew Josephson saw European colonialism in 1922 poised to devour jazz and its fashionable accessories 'on the hunch that the world is on its way to being Americanized in the next two decades' (1922, 347). Separating jazz from fashionable accessories has been the most consistent challenge for the music ever since, as the protagonists of high and low culture, seriousness and distraction, have laid equal claim to jazz, that durable Janus-faced icon of degeneration and regeneration.

The story of the jazz audience changes dramatically after the demise of the Jazz Age. By the time swing revitalised an industry hit hard by the depression, a new cadre of jazz enthusiasts had emerged. Early discographers played a notable role in winnowing out novelty items from the canon, heightening a sense of 'The Real Thing' to be excavated from distraction and pretence. However elusive this spectre continued to be, it enabled writers to impose highbrow criteria on the discussion of jazz, establishing the atmosphere to which Ellington was famously exposed on his first European tour in 1933, which emboldened him to pursue musical projects more ambitious than the 32-bar song. The impact of real innovation was slow to emerge, obscured by the miasma of swing. But, in any event, the monolithic aura of 'jazz'as a unitary musical and cultural event did not outlast the 1920s.

Why, then, has the term 'jazz' proven so durable, so insistent in its implication of continuity, despite contentious claims of rival factions for a pure lineage? Beginning in the 1930s, a jazz press developed in Europe and in North America, establishing criteria for the evaluation of jazz records and performances. Because these evaluations were musical, not cultural, what passed for jazz was increasingly subject to a logic of musical progress. The critics, predominately white, deployed a vocabulary of universalism, confining the African-American cultural background to a demographic footnote. In the hands of white critics – and discerning industry promoters such as John Hammond and Leonard Feather – jazz was endowed with a tacitly Hegelian destiny: the progressive self-realisation of musical potential in the stylistic achievement of innovators. This model, readily available in art criticism and in literary history, was easily adaptable to jazz.

The progressivist vision of jazz could also be inferred from the orientation of musicians, particularly after World War II. Popular music is restricted to basic and easily recognisable formats, and the musical ability of pop stars is often limited to their genre. Early jazz was so rudimentary in musical terms that educated musicians disdained it. But employment opportunities forced the issue, and legions of musicians found professional careers in a context in which their actual musical sophistication was underemployed. Many black musicians were looking for musical challenges to alleviate the routinisation of an increasingly homogenised swing idiom. The revolutionary impact of bebop – its eruption as revolt – marks a distinct moment in jazz history: the appearance of a counterforce contesting industry standards. Bebop has been mythologised as a blow struck for black freedom, a secession of the music from the burden of dance, an embrace of small-combo improvisation liberated from the prescriptive destiny of big-band charts; and, while such claims are not spurious, they overlook the most decisive role of bebop, which was the formation of a new audience.

Bebop impinged on the credentialling prerogative of white critics, with figures such as Charlie Parker, Dizzy Gillespie, Thelonious Monk and Bud Powell somersaulting beyond the going terms of musical approval with a flamboyance that could be construed as insolence. The piquant devil-may-care spirit attributed to jazz in the 1920s was remade by bebop into a posture of defiant musical fitness, and a definitive invitation to drop pretence. If jazz originally signified a fashionable hedonism, a requisite excess of gaiety following the Great War, bebop commemorated a new austerity passing oblique judgement on a world less easily assessed, a fitting counterpart to French existentialism. Insofar as bebop was initially a cult, its audience consisted of insiders, initiates and those in search of an initiation not necessarily musical. One might plausibly claim that the audience for jazz in the past fifty years has largely been oriented to bebop as benchmark – an ironic fate for a musical phenomenon that made the first serious claim for progressive jazz.

Despite its musical integrity, bebop re-established the association of jazz with fashion. As a conspicuously dissident and subterranean movement, bop was inseparable from a lifestyle mystique. Hipster subculture – which had incubated within the ranks of the big bands throughout the swing years – was extended to the culture at large through the notoriety of bop. Even as late as 1979, Gillespie felt obliged to devote large stretches of his autobiography to disentangling fact from innuendo. By that point, of course, bop had long been overtaken by rock as the exemplary purveyor of dissident posturing. As a lifestyle initiative, however, bebop was timely, playing a decisive role in the formation of white counterculture, most notably in the case of the Beats. Jack Kerouac in particular embodied a response to bop that was at once reverent and manic. His theory and practice of 'spontaneous prose' was explicitly modelled on jazz improvisation; and his free-associational essay, 'The Beginning of Bop' (1959), conveyed a white fan's virginal excitement with a shrewd understanding of the significance of the movement for black pride.

LeRoi Jones, who at the time was still associated with Beat poetry, made the telling observation that white musicians and fans were attracted to bop because of its nonconformity, while their black counterparts 'began to realize that merely by being a Negro in America, one was a nonconformist' (1968, 188). The mixed signals of nonconformity played a relentlessly intrusive role in the constellation of the jazz audience throughout the 1950s, as hot and cool, hard bop and third stream jostled for attention. The post-war years also imposed a new condition on jazz, which was the longevity of its earliest stars; so fans could also relish the continuing (and often inspiring) careers of figures like Benny Carter, Coleman Hawkins and Art Tatum. The spark of autonomy and independence ignited by bop remained a vital instigation to further transfigurations of the music. Much as the bop mystique degenerated into a conformism of nonconformity, it could also act as a standing challenge. Cecil Taylor and Ornette Coleman incarnated jazz as unrepeatable singularity; and Coleman's most famous album named not only a more open style of playing but served as an exhortation to his peers to 'free jazz' from prepossessing appreciations, dispossessions, appropriations and preconditions. It was a rare moment, when sheer unremitting intensity resurrected the oldest association of jazz with noise; a moment quickly kindling into the Black Power movement. Jones's *Blues People* marks the junction: it was the first history of jazz written by an African-American, but it was also the last book Jones published before he became Amiri Baraka. Novelist Ralph Ellison objected to the militant spirit of *Blues People*. Ellison had been one of the most insightful and devoted commentators on jazz since the publication of *Invisible Man* in 1952, but his review of Jones's book turned out to be a farewell gesture to the musical (and social) world of an older generation. The ensuing revolutionary turbulence of African-American politics elevated John Coltrane to the status of spiritual liberator, but his death in 1967 abruptly exposed the precarious footing of jazz in a musical marketplace dominated by *Sgt Pepper's Lonely Hearts Club Band*. As Miles Davis spliced jazz with rock in *Bitches Brew*, the liberatory demeanour of free jazz migrated to Europe with the Art Ensemble of Chicago, and exile has turned out to be a permanent state of affairs – figuratively if not always literally.[7]

The jazz audience, from the very beginning, has been global; and its American constituency has steadily declined since a brief zenith in the swing era. Professional jazz musicians now make their living largely abroad; and with the widespread establishment of jazz workshops and credentialling programmes, the American jazz audience may consist largely of aspiring musicians. If so, it follows a pattern of professionalisation symptomatic of American culture in general. Considering the historical impact of jazz, it is understandable that some might bemoan the shrinking audience, especially by comparison with film, television or pop-music audiences. But there is another order of available reference, ranging from the utterly non-commercial art of poetry to the esoteric glamour of opera. The jazz audience comprises a comparable constituency: increasingly knowledgeable, curious about the history of the music, disinclined to follow fashion, and often profoundly devoted to a form of cultural reckoning that shows no sign of depletion or attenuation for those ready for anything; and, for nearly a century, jazz has managed to find an audience ready for anything.

4 Jazz and dance

ROBERT P. CREASE

Jazz is often presented as a musical art form, which is fine for musical connoisseurship. But any serious inquiry into the nature, history, aesthetics and even future of jazz needs to examine the unique relation between music-making and dancing that existed at its origin and was mutually nourishing for decades. The severing of this relation brought about tremendous changes in both the music and the dance.

Popular dancing is an extremely important cultural activity, for bodily movement is a kind of repository for social and individual identity. The dancing body engages the cultural inscripting of self and the pursuit of pleasure, and dancing events are key sites in the working and reworking of racial, class and gender boundaries. For this reason Linda Tomko has argued that dancing is 'a social and cultural process operating in the midst, and not at the margins, of American life – indeed, as American life' (1999, xiii). Particularly significant are moments of transformation, when conventional forms of popular dancing are no longer sufficiently expressive, leading to experimentation with and development of new forms of bodily identity. New music emerges whose kinetic power reflects and reinforces the new bodily identity; the music and dance resonate with each other. These episodes of transformation inevitably generate alarm about the release of unbridled sexuality and trigger efforts to repress and supervise dancing and the places where it occurs.

Western dance historians have sometimes viewed dance forms as proceeding through cycles of innovation, consolidation, decline and then revitalisation through incorporating elements of the dances of peasants or foreigners (for example, see Sachs 1965, 350). In the revitalisation process that took place in the US during the Progressive Era (c. 1890–1920), Marshall and Jean Stearns note in their classic book, *Jazz Dance*, African-Americans played the parts both of the 'peasants' and the 'foreigners' (1968, 32), while also serving as innovators and revitalisers themselves.

Origins in the Progressive Era

The Progressive Era was a time of enormous social upheaval. The rapid expansion of mass-production technologies, new immigration patterns and the increasing number of people living in urban areas were having a deep impact on American economic and social life. The populist movement thrived, labour struggles intensified and suffrage became a popular movement. These and other developments brought challenges to existing patterns of power and privilege, a reconstitution of social identities and a restructuring of the patterns of leisure life, giving rise to collisions with existing forms of cultural expression.

One could hardly look for a more visible and dramatic manifestation of these changes than the transformations in popular dancing. Shortly after the turn of the century, American popular dance practices consisted of two currents. One included established ballroom dances mainly of European origin, such as the two-step, polka, tango (a special case) and waltz. While earlier in their histories these dances had been wilder and controversial themselves, in the transplanted American context of the day they had come to be characterised by a standardised formal and repetitive step pattern in which the couple moved in a circular path around the dance floor, the male leading, the female following. In upper social circles, such dancing was generally restricted to private ballrooms. The other current consisted of newer, cruder dances – often from lower-class African-American communities in the south or west of the US, which had long had their own distinctive dance styles – and included the grizzly bear, bunny hug, monkey glide, chicken reel, kangaroo dip, shimmy, Texas Tommy and turkey trot, in which the dancers imitated animals and their movements. These proto-jazz dances – called 'rag', 'tough' or 'animal' dances – were popularised and inspired by ragtime music, and tended to be found in the nightclubs, bar-rooms, cabarets, brothels and other places where such music was played.

The two types of dance were not incompatible – one might navigate the floor with the first, then stop and do the second – still, they contrasted. Rag dances involved greater use of the whole body, including many parts neglected by traditional ballroom dances: upper torso, waist, hips. Rag dances could be wild, earthy and erotically charged, had room for improvisation – what mattered were originality and style – and were generally done in place, with the creative agency vested in each individual. Rag dances, which would have been next to impossible to do in the corsets that until the recent past had been a regular feature of female clothing, opened up new possibilities of expression for the (white, middle-class) female body in particular. The often free sensuality of these dances helped trigger, in 1911, a vigorous campaign against them and the establishments in which they were performed. The campaign was waged far more against the dance than the music: the technology of the instrument mediates between the desire of the performer and the music performed, opening up a space that (supposedly) purifies the music of sexuality.

The two competing strands of social dancing – one relatively codified and repetitive, the other improvisational and sensual – always coexist in social dancing to some degree, but rarely as dramatically, or with as much interaction, as during the Progressive Era. Jazz dancing would develop, as it were, in the 'front' between them.

Meanwhile, in another development crucial to the development of jazz music and dance, a space was gradually opening up for the professional Negro performer. Towards the end of the nineteenth century, the decline of minstrelsy and the rise of travelling shows 'helped the Negro dancer establish himself as a small but necessary cog in the wheel of tent-show business', write Marshall and Jean Stearns, providing 'the seeds on a grass-roots level for the growth of a professional style of dancing' (1968, 63). By the 1880s, a few Broadway shows were including scenes with Negro dancers – though in the usual stereotypical roles – and by the 1890s, some Broadway shows had all Negro casts. In the late 1890s, the cakewalk, its parodic aspects partly a response to white popular dancing, was the focus of a dance craze which often centred around competitions. This 'furnished a springboard for the rash of dances to come, for during the competitions stress was placed upon individual invention', effectively allowing the cakewalk to serve as 'an incubator of talent, a framework for new steps, which helped to prepare the way for ballroom dances' (*ibid.*, 123–4). Because few white dancers were competitive, the cakewalk craze provided Negro dancers with additional visibility and status. The growing opportunities for Negro professional dancers, and the increasing number of venues where performers and audiences could be of different races, helped foster and spread particular dances and dance forms, including tap dancing.

By the beginning of the second decade of the century a dance 'craze' or 'revolution' was under way, helping to restructure American leisure life and the role of dancing in it. One contributing factor was technological – the spread of the phonograph – which not only popularised different kinds of dance music but allowed novice dancers to learn, with musical accompaniment, in private. Another factor was the growing commercialisation of American leisure life; the commercial promotion of the phonograph, for instance, did much to foster the acceptability of dancing in public. 'The ragtime dance craze', writes Susan Cook, 'could not have attained the unprecedented popularity and respectability it did without the new means of consumer access and artistic legitimization afforded by talking machines and the surrounding industry discourse of moral uplift' (Cook 2000).

Yet another important force was the popularity of exhibition dance teams such as Maurice Mouvet and Florence Walton, Vernon and Irene Castle, and others. These exhibition dancers helped blur the boundaries between formal and rag dances, and between informal dancing and professional theatre (see Malnig 1992). They borrowed from rag dances, and by eliminating the rough and erotic edges created exciting new forms of dancing which they made acceptable, even in high social circles. They also opened new possibilities for enjoying dancing as a form of expression – not for professionally trained and costumed bodies on stage doing formal routines, but for ordinary bodies improvising in ordinary clothes in ordinary spaces. 'Quotidian dancing', Tomko remarks, became 'an instance of performance, while performance came to be an activity available to any sociable body' (1999, 27). This was especially novel for the female body, which could now perform with a new vitality and originality rare in older social dances, but also without becoming a sexualised object as in theatre dancing. Dancing in socially mixed situations was less and less for professional performers only.

The dance craze sparked a vast increase in the number of places to dance. New ballrooms, cabarets and nightclubs opened, and many hotels and restaurants installed dance floors to cater to the dance-mad public. And, in a development of far-reaching significance to the history of jazz, the market for musicians soared – leading to a vast increase in the number and size of bands able to support themselves. This is one important subject for jazz dance studies: the dance was not spinning off the music; it was the other way around.

Most importantly, the dance craze made it fashionable for all classes to go out dancing. The result, in the words of F. Scott Fitzgerald, 'gave the modern dance a social position and brought the nice girl into the café, thus beginning a profound revolution in American life. The great rich empire was feeling its oats and was out for some not too plebeian, yet not too artistic fun.'[1] A new life force was beginning to announce itself, going under the name 'jazz'. The earliest known use of the term (1913), in a sports column, referred to the spirited motion that a certain pitcher put on the ball; but the term was soon widely applied to music and dancing, fiction, drama and the graphic arts. For this life force, fierce musical rhythms and sensuous bodily motions belonged naturally together:

And the rhythm whispered with the fierce unrest
Of a heart throbbing in a passionate breast

wrote Joseph March in his overwrought poem, 'Wild Party' (1928).

In 1917, an African-American pianist and songwriter named W. Benton Overstreet wrote a song called 'The Jazz Dance', the first known occurrence of the phrase in a song title. The lyrics name several dances of African-American origin, though the sheet music bills the song as a foxtrot (which was not an animal dance, and possibly named after a dancer called Fox). 'Jazz dance' was evidently broadly interpretable. It was not simply dancing to jazz music; other non-jazz dances could also serve. Nor was it dancing by African-Americans: though the distinctive rhythmic features of jazz music and dance are undeniably of African-American origin, African-Americans had other forms of dancing as well; references to a distinctive 'Negro dancing' date back at least to the beginning of the eighteenth century. And tap dancing – with its own multicultural provenance in the Irish jig and the English clog, thoroughly worked over by African-American vaudevilleans – could also be called jazz dance. 'Jazz dance', therefore, embraced those emerging new forms of social dancing that engaged the whole body, whose rhythms resonated with those of ragtime music and which united invention and execution through openness to improvisation. Jazz dancing, like jazz music, was a performer's art.

Dancing in the Jazz Age

In the 1920s, new forms of jazz dancing, including the Black Bottom and the Charleston, spread to a large audience; Roger Pryor Dodge ascribed the success of the Charleston to the fact that it was 'truly generic in character', able to be 'infinitely varied without losing any of the quality', but with an easily masterable basic step that was 'but one bar long' (1995, 282). Jazz dancing also moved on-stage in musical theatre and modern ballet. New forms of dancing are often spread and transformed in the interaction between vernacular and stage versions, but jazz was different. The interaction between jazz vernacular dances, versions of jazz vernacular dances as represented by musical theatre and modern ballet assimilations of jazz was complex, sometimes disturbing and often fraught with racial politics. In another key subject of jazz dance studies, deep and troubling questions arose about what jazz dancing was, who could perform it and what it meant in leisure and art.

Opportunities for African-American professional dancers expanded further with the success of African-American musicals. *Shuffle Along* (1921), the first to be performed in white theatres, was the breakthrough: 'Negro musicals were in demand thereafter, and dancing in musical comedy finally took wing' (Stearns 1968, 132). These always included at least one performance of a vernacular dance: *Shuffle Along* included a cakewalk, *Liza* (1922) and *Runnin' Wild* (1923) had Charleston numbers, and *Dinah* (1924) had a Black Bottom. These dances were inevitably altered in the process, and musicals thus began to play a crucial role of mediation and transformation as the dances were disseminated in new contexts in an unending cascade and recascade. The 'black musical served as a crucial stopover on the circuitous path of popular black dance forms', writes Anthea Kraut (1998, 27).

This process acquired a new dimension when, as Kraut notes, 'the same dance steps that appeared first in a black musical revue were imitated, re-worked, and re-staged in white productions' (*ibid.*). The Shimmy, for instance, was performed by Mae West in *Sometime* (1919) and Gilda Gray in *The Ziegfeld Follies* (1922) – both actresses claimed to have invented it – while Ann Pennington performed the Black Bottom in *Scandals of 1926*. Musical theatre, of course, was only doing what it does best: adopting something novel and exciting and reflecting it back to the audience. But the musical theatre was almost totally controlled by white producers, even when it featured a black cast. And certain Harlem Renaissance figures, concerned about the representation of African-Americans, noted the absence of the connection to African-American life in such reflections involving material of African-American derivation. 'I have never seen one yet entirely realistic', Zora Neale Hurston wrote. White performers think that 'the Negro is easily imitated, but nothing is further from the truth'. The white performers may 'have all the elements', but somehow always manage to accent 'the wrong element'. The result: 'Just about as Negro as caviar or Ann Pennington's athletic Black Bottom. When the Negroes who knew the Black Bottom in its cradle saw the Broadway version they asked each other, "Is you learnt dat *new* Black Bottom yet?" Proof that it was not *their* dance' (Hurston 1995, 844–5). Already at the very beginning of jazz dancing, therefore, different groups with different interests had come to have an investment in 'authentic' jazz dance. Ever since, jazz dance criticism (like jazz music criticism) has had its cartographers, critics who find it important to chart the boundaries of where dances came from, and who devote considerable energy to erecting or denouncing those boundaries, and praising or condemning those who transgress them.

Another process of mediation and transformation was involved in the work of modern dance choreographers who sought, not to represent vernacular jazz dances as such, but to use them as material or influence. These modern dancers were only doing what *they* do best: mixing an exciting, newly discovered form with their own traditions to produce something expressive, even liberating, and transforming their own traditions in the process. This provoked fewer immediate charges of cultural theft than musical theatre productions did – no group was seeming to supplant or speak for another, thus it seemed no more troubling than Picasso's use of African motifs – still, as Brenda Dixon Gottschild has observed in writing about white choreographers' appropriation of African-derived stylistic elements, 'It is too easy for the African American part of the equation to become invisible when jazz dance is described as an American folk dance' (1996, 49). For these early choreographers, usually European and much further from the milieu in which jazz was nurtured, 'jazz' might be virtually synonymous with 'American', almost as indistinguishable an influence as the music-hall motifs that appear, say, in *Parade*, the Cocteau–Picasso–Satie collaboration choreographed by Léonide Massine in 1917.

In 1922, for instance, Russian-born dancer-choreographer Adolph Bolm created the 'jazz-pantomime', *Krazy Kat*, but neither the movements nor the music (by American composer John Alden Carpenter) could be described as jazz or even jazz-inspired, and the term seems to be meant as a description of the eponymous comic-book protagonist's free-swinging impudence and flair.[2] At least Bolm was living in the US (where the work was premiered) and had some first-hand exposure to its popular culture. The same cannot be said for the dancers and choreographers of European 'jazz ballets' that were premiered in Paris before 1925, including the (Paris-based) Swedish Ballet's *Within the Quota* (1923; based on a Cole Porter score and panned when the company toured the US), Darius Milhaud's *La création du monde* (1923; inspired by African creation myths), Jean Wiener's ballet, *Arc en Ciel* (1925) and Nijinska's *Jazz* (1925; based on Stravinsky's *Ragtime*). It is true that Paris was an international cultural centre. Still, many of the artists involved had not been to the US and their exposure to jazz and US popular culture was modest, spotty, derivative and often confused; Nijinska included in her ballet hula-hoops, grass skirts and other Hawaiian touches. When the word 'jazz' is linked to these works it must be understood as an attempt to cast a contemporary 'American' edge on what were essentially European music-hall traditions. Things changed in 1925 with the arrival in Paris of Josephine Baker. Although Baker (who had first drawn attention in the US in *Shuffle Along*) was not the first African-American performer to appear in Paris, her show was a sensation and served to popularise some jazz dance elements. The term 'jazz dance' then came to name a movement style characterised by hip-centred motions, isolation, and sensual and quirky vitality.

Not all modern dancers thought jazz liberating. Isadora Duncan, who for her own reasons wanted to police a boundary she drew between high and low art, saw jazz as being on the wrong side. In 'I See America Dancing' (1927) she called it 'monstrous', denounced its 'tottering, ape-like convulsions', and rejected the 'sensual convulsion of the South African negro', who, according to her, had invented it. Jazz, with its 'rhythm from the waist down', was not fit music for dancing America, whose rhythm came from 'the solar plexus, the temporal home of the soul'.[3]

Yet another critical issue for jazz studies arises from the attempts by certain white performers, and especially white jazz critics, to 'elevate' or 'rescue' jazz from what they considered party-music status to that of a 'symphonic' art form that, they felt, properly belonged in concert halls. This was the explicit aim, for instance, of Paul Whiteman's 1924 Aeolian Hall concert – billed as 'The First American Jazz Concert' – which culminated in George Gershwin's *Rhapsody in Blue*, and the campaign continued for the next quarter-century. But for Hurston, Langston Hughes and others jazz was a music-dance phenomenon, an integral part of African-American life.[4] 'Music without motion was unnatural to Negroes', wrote Hurston (1995, 844–5), while in her plays the way her characters dance is an essential part of how they articulate themselves in the world, and structurally important to the plots. 'As a cultural form that requires interaction and thus forges social bonds', Kraut observes, 'vernacular dance has the potential to both assemble and disassemble the folk communities featured in Hurston's work' (1998, 35). At stake in these differing perspectives is nothing less than the nature of jazz itself: is it an art form, or a part of life? Whose life?

The Swing Era

By the end of the 1920s, the dance craze was well integrated into American leisure life. Dance spaces had proliferated. So had the bands needed to play in them, their local or national tours now handled by booking agencies such as Music Corporation of America (founded in 1924). Despite the fact that bands were generally characterised as 'sweet' or 'hot', the most popular bands generally had to be able to be both. And it was the 'hot' aspect of the music that was connected more to jazz development; a 'hot' dance band featured at least one jazz improviser, for what was sometimes called race dancing. Many future musicians of seminal importance in the history of jazz began their careers in high-school hot bands.

Early jazz composition and arrangement were heavily influenced by having to serve the dancers' need for respite, variety, partner changes and a fixed number of choruses for taxi dancing (where a dime would buy, say, two choruses' worth of partner). Linda Dahl writes, 'This was basic training for many bands, where the rudiments, primitive though they were, were established for arranging early jazz music: solo space was sparse, leading to a compact, compressed approach to playing' (1999, 65).

But by the end of the 1920s, a few black bands were exploring changes in the music. The still-popular ragtime, and the Charleston (see Spring), had a 2/4 rhythmic base, and the rhythm was grounded by the banjo and tuba, which played together on the downbeat. But the new tendency in certain bands was to play an even 4/4 rhythm instead of the Charleston's 2/4. The early jazz beat-carriers, banjo and tuba, were replaced by string bass and piano, and the off-beats were slightly anticipated. This generated a propulsive rhythm soon to be called 'swing'. Swing was less a conceptual feature of a musical structure than a kinetic bodily experience, something to be felt rather than explained; Benny Goodman compared the task of definition to trying to describe the colour red to a child who had never seen it. Jazz dancing could now be more precisely described as dancing animated by this kinetic force. One might compare, for instance, the simple *pas de bourrée*, a ballet step, and the 'fall off the log', a jazz step. Both have an essentially identical foot pattern – a three-step grapevine with a lift at the beginning – but in performance are very different. The ballet step is done with an erect posture, and is a formal element which is subordinated to a larger dance structure; the jazz step is done with much more vigorous upper-body movement, and shares with the others that precede and follow it principally a rhythmic pulse, together with a stylistic flair and originality.

Around 1927 a new dance, the Lindy Hop (named after the famous aviator Charles Lindbergh, whose solo flight across the Atlantic took place that year), began to emerge, characterised by an eight-count basic phrase. It was still more generic and open to improvisation than the Charleston, flexible enough to evolve with the developing swing style. In 1930, the Duke Ellington orchestra's recording of a song called 'That Lindy Hop'[5] illustrates the music in transition: Ellington plays an early 1920s stride piano, the horns play Charleston figures in late 1920s style emphasising the first and third beats, while the rhythm section, on the off-beat, is clearly headed towards swing. The lyrics capture the dance craze:

Come do that Lindy Hop
And you will never stop
I'm telling you, that's what the new rage is . . .
That dance will live on history's pages!

Song lyrics had hyped the latest dance crazes for almost two decades, but this one was on the money. While some regional dances clung to life – such as the Balboa at Balboa Beach, California – the Lindy effectively replaced all the others.

The Lindy developed mainly at the Savoy Ballroom in New York City, though it had numerous regional variants even in the boroughs of its home town. In the 1930s the Savoy was one of the most cosmopolitan places in the world, artistically speaking. It was not the only ballroom in Harlem, but it attracted the best bands and the best dancers. For about a quarter-century after its opening in 1926, the Savoy was a catalyst for innovation, where influences from all over the world were assimilated to pioneer new traditions in music and dance. Its principal feature was a 200 × 50 ft hardwood dance floor, with bandstands against the east wall. When Lindy Hoppers first appeared, the Savoy management deemed them too wild to mix with the other dancers and cordoned off a special area for them, but it soon became *the* dance at the Savoy. Most of the best dancers congregated to the north-eastern end of the ballroom in an area known as the 'Corner'.

Thanks mainly to the feverish activity at the Savoy, the Lindy was transformed during the 1930s. The dancers adopted a more relaxed pose by settling into their knees, giving their hips more swivel room and the dance a more horizontal look. Acrobatic 'air steps' developed in which one partner flipped another. Such changes made the dance suitable for the stage, and the Lindy appeared in movies and musicals of the era. In the Swing Era, the Lindy was the most popular jazz vernacular dance. It spread across the US and even the world, and came also to be called the 'jitterbug' and 'swing dancing'.

Meanwhile, modern dance choreographers continued to incorporate jazz, as in the 'Slaughter on Tenth Avenue' scene choreographed by George Balanchine for *On Your Toes* (1936). The assimilation of jazz vernacular dance into show dancing was the wave of the future. Writing in 1938, Lincoln Kirstein claimed that the future of American stage dancing lay, not in trying to imitate inimitable Russian dancers such as Pavlova and Nijinsky, but in drawing inspiration from America's vigorous and exciting amateur dancing; its national academies of the dance were the gymnasium on prom night, nightclubs and vaudeville stages. Three decades later, he would write that the 'strongest exterior influence on the development of the academic dance has derived (and still does, largely through Stravinsky) from jazz rhythm, beat, the shifting pulse and syncopation of styles and steps from ragtime to rock' (Copeland and Cohen 1983, 265). And in 1944, Katherine Dunham established the Dunham School of Dance, which paved the way for generations of African-American stage dancers who were strongly jazz-influenced, such as Talley Beatty, Geoffrey Holder, Eleo Pomare, Gus Solomons Jr and Alvin Ailey.

The big-band era ended soon after World War II, during another period of social transformation involving changed economics, entertainment patterns and musical tastes. The jazz alliance between music-making and dancing that had had a run of nearly four decades broke up – a development which is arguably the most significant single turning point in jazz history, and an important topic for jazz dance studies. For champions of jazz music as an art form, it was cause for celebration. At last, wrote André Hodeir on the first page of his book, *Jazz: Its Evolution and Essence*, Armstrong, Ellington, Bechet and Gillespie were appearing 'in the same concert halls as Gieseking and Menuhin', and it was no longer possible, as it had been shortly before, 'for an alert, reasonably well-informed person to confuse authentic jazz with cheap dance music' (Hodeir 1956, 7).

The music changed. True, the rhythm still swung, but the rhythm section began to function in new ways. Outside the dance-band context, drummers could play more lightly and emphasise different parts of the kit – cymbals and brushes, for instance – and serve the soloist more than before. The rhythmical demands of playing for dancers are so rigorous that the difference between a 'ghost' big band that has been performing the top 40s of the 1940s in concert halls and one that has worked a ballroom circuit is immediately recognisable. It is a different music.

The audience also changed: those who went to clubs tended to be wealthier and older than those who sought out dance events. For many youths restlessly seeking a new bodily identity in the new cultural context of the turbulent post-war years, the break-up of the jazz music–dance alliance meant that jazz was no longer a tool of self-discovery. This stunning cultural reversal is sent up in the movie, *Jailhouse Rock* (1957), in a scene in which Elvis Presley, a youth whose sensual new music makes his peers move their bodies, finds himself at a party where the adults are talking pretentiously about jazz. When asked his opinion, he explodes – 'I don't know what the hell you are talking about!' – and bolts from the cloying atmosphere.

But jazz had left a profound influence on popular dancing. The dancing of early rock-and-roll dancers was a modified jitterbug. And even after those dancers decoupled, different versions of swing dancing continued, performed to slowed-down music and in response to local conditions. These might be called 'allotropic' forms of swing, adapting the term for the different forms that hot metals can take when they cool and crystallise in different patterns. Allotropes of swing dance include the imperial style in St Louis, the shag in the Carolinas, the whip and push in Texas, and West Coast swing in California.[6] In the recent swing-dance revival, international swing-dance workshops and the video camera have intensified the spread and transformation of new styles. By the 1950s, too, jazz dancing – generally meaning a certain vocabulary of hip-centred steps, syncopated rhythms and isolated body motions – was thoroughly assimilated into show dancing, as can be seen in the works of Jerome Robbins and Bob Fosse.[7]

Alliances between jazz music and jazz dancing are now special events – temporary bridges between separate cultures. In 1960, John Lewis, a founder of the Modern Jazz Quartet, defended his composition of a piece for jazz ballet by saying that 'Jazz began as music that people danced to. We are not going out on a limb. We are just putting the music back where it belonged.'[8] But it didn't stay put. Jazz musicians may occasionally write for choreographers – Wynton Marsalis has been commissioned by companies as diverse as Garth Fagan and the New York City Ballet – but almost never for vernacular dancers. The contemporary jazz music scene is for listeners only; the 'jump' bands favoured by contemporary swing dancers work an entirely different scene.

For nearly half its history, dancers and musicians were co-creators of one cultural movement. To see the history of jazz as a series of musical performances and recordings – treating the dancers as simply those who paid the box office, or as people being entertained by the true artists who are up on the stage – amounts to a fundamental misunderstanding of jazz. Dance is an integral and indispensable part of jazz studies.

PART TWO

Jazz practices

5 Jazz as musical practice

TRAVIS A. JACKSON

Definitions of jazz as musical practice are contingent upon a host of factors, not least of which are the intellectual histories and life experiences that condition writers' approaches to definition. Some are likely to see as most distinctive jazz musicians' usage of rhythm, harmony, melody and/or timbre in jazz performance and composition, others the relative balance of oral/aural and textual materials, and still others the music's connections to African-American expressive culture. Early writers on jazz, for example, tended to have European concert music as their primary frame of reference. The 'work-' and 'score-centric' concepts and terminology of concert music almost dictated that these writers would focus on parameters of music-making amenable to staff notation and textual analysis – e.g., melody, harmony, form (and, to a lesser degree, rhythm) – and describe jazz chiefly through the ways in which it differed from concert music.[1] Whether or not one agrees with that approach, it is a manifestation of the desire to identify and describe jazz's distinctive character. In a world of diverse musical expressions displaced geographically and temporally, the practical necessity of making distinctions (Lakoff 1987, 5–6) has required those writing about jazz to find ways to distinguish it not only from concert music but also from Tin Pan Alley popular song, from other forms of African-American music and from other musics that prominently feature improvisation. This chapter will examine the ways in which other writers have defined jazz, taking account of the characteristics they have invoked and the usefulness of those items for definition.

Early jazz writers focused almost exclusively on what we might call the notatable characteristics of jazz *qua* music. One of the first to offer a sustained meditation on jazz's musical essence was Winthrop Sargeant in *Jazz: Hot and Hybrid* (1938).[2] A reading of his chapter headings indicates what elements he considered most important for defining jazz: 'elementary rhythmic formulas', 'hot rhythm', 'anatomy of jazz melody', 'scalar structures', 'derivation of the blues', 'harmony' and 'aesthetics and the musical form of jazz'. In each of those chapters, he describes the music's repertory and performance procedures for an audience presumably well-versed in concert music and not convinced of jazz's *musical* value. Thus, when writing on rhythm, he observes that to say that jazz is 'syncopated', although correct, overly simplifies a complex series of practices. Not only are there two kinds of syncopation, there are also rhythmic practices – e.g., multimetre and polyrhythm – that are often mistakenly classified as syncopation.[3] Understanding the distinctions between those different practices is essential if one is to grasp Sargeant's central point: that swinging rhythms, achieved by a variety of means, lie at the heart of jazz. He makes that position clear by considering rhythm prior to any other musical parameters and couching his discussions of melody, harmony, repertory and form in terms of rhythm. Improvisation is likewise presented as subsidiary to, and dependent upon, rhythmic practice. He mentions it primarily by placing jazz at the warmer end of a continuum ranging from 'sweet', largely pre-composed music to 'hot', largely improvised music (1938, 48–54).

Among those who followed Sargeant, two writers in particular were as concerned as he with musical practice. André Hodeir, in *Jazz: Its Evolution and Essence* (1956), reverses Sargeant's order – discussing improvisation before rhythm and swing – but otherwise shares with him the same focus. He uses them to explore an expansive range of materials, noting that effective improvisation emerges from the interplay of melody, harmony, articulation, timbre and blues feeling. In definitive jazz performances or recordings, those improvisatory inputs are made more compelling through swing, which he glosses as 'vital drive' (*ibid.*, 207–9). Furthermore, the perception of vital drive is dependent upon musicians' creative setting of tempo, use of accentuation and placement of sounds in the temporal flow of performance. Thus, for a given piece of music to be classified as jazz, it must effectively merge the different elements that define improvisation and do so through idiomatic use of rhythm. Writing from Europe and addressing himself, like Sargeant, to *aficionados* of classical music, Hodeir's analyses of performative conventions are illuminating, even if his disparaging assertions about jazz musicians' cognitive capacities betray his investment in notions of blacks as 'uncivilized'.[4]

The second writer to follow Sargeant, Gunther Schuller, has been praised for his meticulously notated analyses of the harmonic, rhythmic and orchestrational aspects of jazz performance. In *Early Jazz* (1968), he acknowledges a debt to both Sargeant and Hodeir and is, like them, concerned with explaining jazz to those from a concert-music background. His work differs from that of either of his predecessors in the emphasis he places on Africa as the ultimate source of jazz. He suggests that 'every musical element – rhythm, harmony, melody, timbre, and the basic forms of jazz – is essentially African in background and derivation' (*ibid.*, 62). While his insistence that jazz's origins and development are different from, rather than derivative of, concert music is laudable, his positioning of a singular African musical practice as the main source of that development – based on reading one book

(A. M. Jones's *Studies in African Music*, 1959) – devalues the *transformation* of African musical *practices* in the United States and leads him to extreme positions. In discussing the 'Africanness' of Charlie Parker's highly fluid rhythmic sense and use of quavers as primary rhythmic units, for example, he writes, 'Was [his playing] – like the emergence of some underground river – the musical reincarnation of impulses subconsciously remembered from generations earlier and producible only when the carrier of this memory had developed his instrumental technique sufficiently to cope with it?' (Schuller 1968, 25).

Despite the presence of romantic speculations like Schuller's, the value of his work and its two predecessors is a focus on what jazz musicians do – at least from the standpoint of observers better-versed in concert music. Each of those writers addresses the ways in which jazz musicians have approached rhythm, melody, harmony and form in performing. Their emphasis on the interlocking roles of many performative conventions notwithstanding, it is from work like theirs that the most simple and orthodox definitions of jazz emerge – those that locate its essence in the qualities glossed by swing and improvisation. The numerous pedagogical materials developed since the 1920s for novice jazz musicians are likewise complicit in that simplification process. Pedagogues have reinforced the status of swing as a *sine qua non* for jazz performance by counselling young musicians to play 'swing eighths', with an uneven 2:1 or 3:2 durational relationship between the first and second quavers in a single beat. By making that rhythmic approach normative, such pedagogy perhaps forecloses more creative and interactive ways of engaging with rhythm in performance, such as adjusting the degree of one's unevenness to create (or complicate) the perception of swing. Moreover, primers for novice jazz musicians tend to downplay timbre, blues feeling and articulation in favour of a focus on pitched elements: harmonies, harmonic substitutions and appropriate accompanying scales.[5] Similarly, jazz appreciation textbooks, while adding a historical and social dimension, also generally present swing and improvisation as the music's main attributes – if, for no other reason, because the pair functions as a convenient heuristic to apply across time, whatever distortions it might introduce into the historical narrative.[6]

Mark Gridley, Robert Maxham and Robert Hoff have outlined the problems with defining jazz based on only those two characteristics. A definition requiring both swing and improvisation, they observe, is useful for distinguishing jazz from musics that feature improvisation but don't swing, like Hindustani music, or those that arguably swing, but rely less on improvisation, like early rhythm-and-blues (1989, 517). Strict application of that definition, however, might force one to disqualify pieces usually described as jazz that neither swing nor prominently feature improvisation, such as

Duke Ellington's 'Single Petal of a Rose'.[7] Partly because of such difficult cases, those three authors reject the viability of defining jazz in strict terms (1989, 524). They propose instead two alternative strategies – a 'family resemblances' approach and a 'dimensional' approach – both of which leave room for pieces excluded by a strict definition. The first strategy, for example, draws from a larger inventory of characteristics that, like those visible characteristics that make family members resemble one another, help one to ascertain whether a given piece belongs to the jazz 'family'. One using that approach assumes that 'at least one [characteristic] must be present for any performance to be called jazz, but no one particular element must always be present; i.e., no single element is necessary and no single element is sufficient' (*ibid.*, 525). The second strategy slightly modifies the family resemblances approach, making jazz an 'open concept' whose definition can change over time. Whether or not a piece can be described as jazz 'hinges on the idea that, of those elements that have been previously associated with jazz, the more that are present and the more clearly they can be heard, the more a particular performance qualifies as jazz. In other words, jazz is not an all-or-none event, but is a continuum, a dimension: jazzness' (*ibid.*, 527).[8] When we confront a performance or recording that sounds like those things we already recognise as jazz, therefore, there is a greater probability that we can consider it to be covered by the term.

Using Gridley's, Maxham's and Hoff's ideas as a template, one might fruitfully return to the wider array of musical characteristics discussed by Sargeant, Hodeir and Schuller to determine the family resemblances or dimensionality of jazz recordings and performances. Because the early writers focused a great deal of attention on it, it might be wise to begin the expansion with jazz harmony. One of the most distinctive ways in which jazz musicians have approached harmony is that they have relied almost exclusively on harmonies with at least four distinct pitches – seventh chords, sixth chords and various extensions and alterations of them – rather than triads as primary building blocks. Such harmonies are connected to one another in composition and performance in quite specific ways, for example through series of ii–V chords (minor sevenths and dominant chords, e.g., Dmin7 and G7) that resolve to the next structurally important chord (e.g., a major seventh or major sixth chord – here Cmaj7 or C6: see Ex. 5.1). Moreover, since the 1930s, as jazz composers and improvisers have grown more adventurous in the manipulation of harmony, they have devised ever more ingenious and abstract ways of connecting chords – from tritone substitutions (Ex. 5.2) and common-tone diminished-seventh chords to more abstract quartal harmonies (Ex. 5.3) and tone clusters (Ex. 5.4) that defy functional classification.[9] Thus, while one can describe the development of jazz harmonic practice in terms of increasing complexity and ambiguity – particularly as evinced in the 'open' or 'extended' tonality of Wayne Shorter's 'E.S.P.'[10] – it is just as possible to present counter-examples that argue for greater harmonic simplicity, such as Miles Davis's 'So What' and Herbie Hancock's 'Maiden Voyage'.[11] The Shorter composition features a harmonic progression rich with major-seventh sharp-11 chords and possessing no clear key centre, while the Davis and Hancock compositions move in the opposite direction by minimising harmonic movement to two and four chords, respectively, that have the same basic quality (Dorian minor sevenths for Davis and dominant suspended-fourth chords for Hancock). Moreover, jazz harmonies are distinguished not only by the pitched resources they use, but by the way they are voiced, with closed, drop-two and drop-two-and-four voicings being among the most basic (Ex. 5.5).[12] The consideration of elements adapted from blues performance – particularly the alteration of thirds, fifths and sevenths that constitute 'blue tonality' – give jazz harmony an additional kind of uniqueness (see Tallmadge 1984). Such tonality is frequently, but incompletely, described as the usage of 'flattened' or neutral pitches, though in practice it is much more common to find musicians (including pianists) playing with the intonation of these and other pitches through whatever means their instruments afford. Use of such procedures makes possible the addition of other colours and extensions to the basic four-pitch building blocks of jazz harmony.

Ex. 5.1

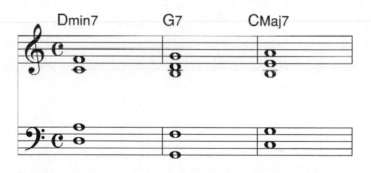

Ex. 5.2

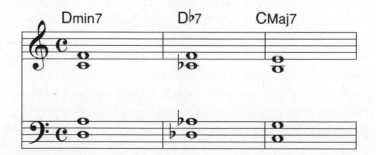

Ex. 5.3

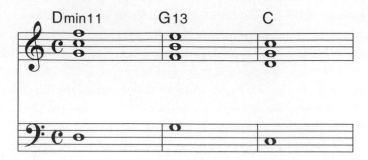

Ex. 5.4

Ex. 5.5

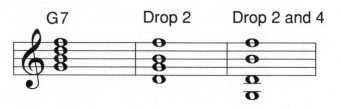

As with swing and improvisation, these aspects of harmonic usage provide a useful way to distinguish between pieces that employ those resources and those that do not, but harmony is not always a viable differentiator. In and of itself, harmony cannot mark jazz off from all other forms of music, particularly those that use the same kinds of harmonic resources, such as the Tin Pan Alley tunes that have become jazz standards or the rock music made by musicians familiar with jazz practice (e.g., Joni Mitchell, Steely Dan and Stevie Wonder). Again, therefore, the identity of a piece within the jazz family or jazz dimension is less a function of a specific characteristic than it is of that characteristic's deployment and articulation with respect to others.

The same might be said of instrumentation, timbre and texture. Small ensembles consisting of saxophone, trumpet, piano, acoustic bass and trap drum set, or big bands featuring choirs of trumpets, trombones and saxophones, are indelibly associated with jazz, even for those with little to no knowledge of the music. Instruments such as the electric piano, electric bass, French horn, cello, synthesizers, drum machines and even bagpipes, however, have also been used to great effect in 'jazz' performances and recordings. Whether or not an ensemble features conventional instrumentation, the parcelling of roles to different instruments seems a more definitive criterion for describing the sound of jazz. Instruments capable of producing multiple pitches simultaneously (pianos, keyboard and guitar) are grouped with basses and percussion instruments to form 'rhythm sections' that accompany 'single-line' instruments, such as saxophones and trumpets. In practice, though, even rhythm-section instruments can assume the foreground at the appropriate points in performance. The presence of rhythm-section/front-line organisation in pop and rock music, however, suggests that even instrumental roles are not always a reliable way of distinguishing jazz.

Discussion of instrumentation might be made more useful by examining how jazz musicians actually produce sound. Whatever the aggregation of instruments, jazz musicians and critics most highly praise those players with personally identifiable approaches to their instruments. Whether those approaches result from the technical details of fingering, blowing, tuning or striking an instrument; use of harmonic, melodic or rhythmic resources; or some combination of those, possession of a timbrally distinctive sound is perhaps more prized by the individual musician than anything else. Based on such sounds, well-informed listeners can upon hearing them identify the timbral signatures of musicians such as Miles Davis, Coleman Hawkins, Bill Evans, Thelonious Monk, Charles Mingus or Tony Williams. The sound of groups, then, becomes a function of the individual sounds of *musicians* rather than the sounds of *instruments*. While musicians of necessity adjust and adapt to one another's sounds to create 'group sound', the resultant textures are ideally heterogeneous mixtures. Olly Wilson describes this 'hetereogeneous sound ideal' in the following way: 'a kaleidoscopic range of dramatically contrasting qualities of sound (timbre) is sought after in both vocal and instrumental music. The desirable musical sound texture is one that contains a combination of diverse timbres' (Wilson 1992, in Wright and Floyd, 329). Thus, the kind of 'blend' that orchestra players seek is diametrically opposed to what jazz musicians seek. Wilson adds that, even in a solo performance, a musician seeks to differentiate even individual phrases from one another through varying attack, articulation, register and other performative nuances. As was the case with instrumental organisation, heterogeneity of this kind is not unique to jazz performance, especially given the adaptation of similar procedures in pop and rock music via amplification, stereo recording, multi-track recording technology and various electronic means of timbral manipulation.

Whether we describe jazz through swing, improvisation, harmony or timbre, or define it via family resemblances or dimensionality, however, the most fruitful understanding might result from shifting emphasis from static characteristics to a focus on the *processes* involved in jazz performance.[13] Those processes, to be sure, include ways of swinging (or not swinging) and ways of improvising, but they also reach more fundamentally into the realm of human action and decision-making. In other words, jazz might best be defined not on the basis of its characteristic forms, harmonies and rhythms, but based on what jazz musicians do with various performative elements.

Scholars interested in that kind of definition, among them Paul Berliner and Ingrid Monson, see jazz as a form of music-making that privileges the oral/aural over the literate, the processual and the performative over the executory and interpretive. In reducing oral or aural phenomena to notation and applying text-based analytical procedures, writers such as the three mentioned at the outset perhaps imply that their transcriptions have the same status as the sources used to generate them. Scores, lead sheets and transcriptions do make it possible for those who read music to *see* relationships they might not hear. But, at the same time, such texts encourage their readers to see them as 'objective' renderings of musical practice, when in fact they hide as much as they highlight (see M. Johnson and Lakoff 1980). Writing of whatever kind, Walter Ong observes, 'fosters abstractions that disengage knowledge from the arena where human beings struggle with one another. It separates the knower from the known. By keeping knowledge embedded in the human lifeworld, orality situates knowledge within a context of struggle' (1982, 43–4). By favouring oral/aural procedures, jazz musicians endeavour to keep their performing and recording vital and connected to the contexts in and out of which they make music rather than to those associated with textual analysis. Notated scores, sheet music and extant recordings of tunes are thus rarely, if ever, the final authority with regard to performance; instead they are starting points. A musician who wants to perform Bronislau Kaper's and Ned Washington's 'On Green Dolphin Street' might learn it from the sheet music published in 1947, from lead sheets published in various fake books or from recordings of the tune by musicians such as Miles Davis or Eric Dolphy.[14] From such sources, one learns that the tune is a thirty-two-bar, ABAC composition typically performed in E♭. Any performance or recording that faithfully replicated notated symbols or the sounds of those recordings would run counter to the general imperative that each performance is supposed to be different from all that precede it, that it should be as identifiable as the musicians who play it. Thus, while players are expected to be aware of, and conversant with, previous approaches to a tune, their versions ideally make more or less explicit reference to the tradition of performance on that tune while at the same time transforming it.[15] The rhythmic and improvisatory procedures discussed by Sargeant, Hodeir and Schuller are part of the act of transformation but so too are ways of approaching and altering form, melody, harmony, timbre, texture and intensity in performance (see Waters 1996). One might be able to sight-read well, but what matters more in the course of performance is being able to *hear* what other musicians are doing and to respond supportively.

Indeed, what is most important is inflecting those items and the moment-to-moment flow of performance with timbral shadings and interactive nuances that mark it as emanating from a particular group of performers at a specific location and point in time. Bill Evans's subdued introduction to the Davis recording of 'On Green Dolphin Street' seems more like the beginning of a solo piano piece than a group performance. His particular use of 'impressionist'-inspired harmonies identifies him as the pianist on the track as well as on Davis's 'So What' (*Kind of Blue*) in 1959. Likewise, once the solos are under way, the repeated two-bar cadential progression or 'tag' that marks their endings identifies the group as one of Davis's 1950s quintets and sextets, which often made such tags part of their performances on thirty-two bar tunes.[16] While Dolphy's recording more strictly maintains the thirty-two-bar form, one can recognise the distinctiveness of his version through other nuances: an evocative two-bar introduction featuring bass, bass clarinet, and drums and piano that continues through the first four bars of the tune; the timbral shadings of Dolphy's bass-clarinet playing and Freddie Hubbard's trumpet playing; and a more extensive exploration of dissonance in the solo and ensemble playing than is evident in the Davis recording.

Each recording is an intermusical exploration informed by the musicians' understanding of the tune, a particular arrangement of it, their experiences playing with one another and jazz performance practice more generally.[17] As each recording unfolds, the musicians make it *jazz* by virtue of the choices they make: syncopating and swinging, improvising, using harmonic substitutions, alternately raising and lowering the level of intensity, responding to and highlighting the work of other members of the group, stating or leaving implicit the metric framework, emphasising or obscuring the arrival of structural units (phrases, important cadences, four-, eight- or sixteen-bar sections, the ends and beginnings of choruses) among other things. The process is less aptly described by the literate metaphor of music-reading than it is by the oral/aural metaphor of conversation in the sense that these are 'musical personalities interacting, not merely instruments or pitches or rhythms . . . At any given moment . . . the improvising artist is always making musical choices in relationship to what everyone else is doing. These cooperative choices, moreover, have a great deal to do with achieving (or failing to achieve) a satisfying musical journey' (Monson 1996, 26–7).

The oral/aural emphasis in jazz performance is often described as emerging from African-American musical practices. Olly Wilson's previously cited comments on heterogeneity were applied to jazz when in fact he was describing practices common to musics in the 'black music cultural sphere' that includes west and central Africa, northern South America, the Caribbean and the United States. This sphere, more recently termed the 'black Atlantic' by Paul Gilroy (1993), is distinguished less by specific retentions of African rhythms or melodies than by a shared conceptual approach to music-making among African diasporic populations. Among the practices Wilson identifies as common in this sphere are the dominance of percussion and percussive playing, off-beat phrasing of melodic accents, polyrhythm and use of overlapping call and response (Wilson 1974, 6). To varying degrees, one can find examples of each of these practices in the work of jazz musicians and groups widely dispersed in time. What is crucial in Wilson's formulation is the notion that however the surface details of African-derived musics – including jazz – may change over time, a conceptual approach emphasising such elements is a primary animating force. His concern, therefore, is less the provenance of particular harmonic, rhythmic or timbral nuances than it is the way musical resources of whatever kind are realised in performance. One might see his position as an enlightened modification of Schuller's tracing of jazz's essential elements back to Africa. Rather than simply positing Africa as a source whose particulars have been transformed, he argues that processes of transformation are the real inheritance, and that their use in performance indicates the connection of African diasporic musics to one another in the present, not just in a mythical African past.[18]

Wilson's view of jazz's Africanness or African-Americanness is not uncontroversial. Since jazz emerged in the early twentieth century, commentators have debated its provenance and questioned whether it can indeed be called African-American music. Most recently such questions have been raised in the writings of James Lincoln Collier (1993), Gene Lees (1994), Terry Teachout (1995) and Richard Sudhalter (1999a). As evidence they cite the historical record – the absence of 'harmony' in the western sense in indigenous African musics, the early participation of whites in the making of jazz, the stellar achievements of white musicians such as Bix Beiderbecke, Benny Goodman and Bill Evans, and the dwindling African-American audience for the music – and a United States political climate that salves African-American feelings of inferiority by elevating their contributions to jazz's development while erasing the contributions of whites. For these writers, rather than being African-American, jazz is essentially American and intimately tied to democracy and racial integration. As they state their argument, the music may at one time have been African-American, but it is no longer exclusively so. Interestingly, their most frequent targets of criticism are LeRoi Jones (especially for his book *Blues People*, 1963), Albert Murray (*Stomping the Blues*, 1976), Stanley Crouch and Wynton Marsalis, but not European-American writers such as Schuller and the late Martin Williams, who have both described jazz not only as African-American but also as connected to notions of democracy and integration. By attributing the 'African-American version' of jazz history only to African-Americans, Collier and company are being as selective and loose with the facts of jazz history as those they criticise. Upon further examination, their revisionist position is based on a particular confusion: the mistaking of culture for race. The former refers to ways of acting and being in the world that one learns from observation, imitation and practical action over a long period of time. The latter, to the degree that one can say it exists at all, is a category that for many is based largely on visual perception.[19]

Some descriptions of jazz as African-American music have admittedly focused attention on the skin colour of the music's most influential performers but, if we return to Wilson's work, what seems paramount is how those performers have *approached* music-making and how their cultural backgrounds and knowledge have informed their work. While those musicians may have come from different socio-economic backgrounds and geographic regions, what they shared was a commitment to creating contexts for performance that were profoundly shaped by an African-derived understanding of performance. Those understandings, however, were not ones they were 'born with'; they are ones that each had learnt to come to from listening to recordings, interacting with other musicians and cultivating individual and collective sound. To say that jazz is an African-American music, therefore, is not the same as saying that it can be made only by African-Americans. Instead, such an assertion draws attention to the importance and greater relative influence of African-American musical practices in the music's development. Even when we consider the often-cited dyad of European harmony and African rhythm used to describe jazz's ancestry, we have to acknowledge that specific individuals mixed those elements in a way that had implications for the way that future musicians would perform.[20] The seemingly obligatory mentions of Jelly Roll Morton, Fletcher Henderson, Don Redman, Duke Ellington, Count Basie, Charlie Parker, Thelonious Monk, Charles Mingus, Miles Davis, John Coltrane and Ornette Coleman in jazz historical writing is not part of a conspiracy to denigrate the work of white musicians. It is instead a testament to the power and

persistence of ways of adapting and deploying musical resources in performance. Those practices, moreover, argue for more writing that connects
jazz not just to European music but also to African-derived and African-
American music contemporaneous with it.

Defining jazz as musical and cultural practice, then, seems more a matter
of defining an aesthetic, a set of normative and evaluative criteria utilised
by musicians in performing and judging performance. Through interviews
with a number of musicians in New York City in the mid-1990s I came to
understand that, specific musical parameters aside, working musicians –
African-American and otherwise – foregrounded the same group of concerns in discussing their work as well as the work of others: developing 'an
individual voice; developing the ability to balance and play with a number
of different musical parameters in performance; understanding the cultural
[and historical] foundations of the music; being able oneself to "bring something to the music"; creating music that is "open enough" to allow other
musicians to bring something despite or because of what has been provided
structurally or contextually; and being open for transcendence to "the next
level" of performance, the spiritual level' (Jackson 2000, 35). Using such
criteria as a guide, they could equally produce music identifiable as jazz
whether they were performing original compositions or adaptations of
jazz standards, rhythm-and-blues songs or pieces from the western concert repertory. Miles Davis and Eric Dolphy's realisations of 'On Green
Dolphin Street' are likewise excellent illustrations of that aesthetic at work.
As published or played by other musicians, the tune is a template which they
and their bandmates use to play with the history and conventions of jazz,
to present their distinctive approaches to performance, to interact with one
another, and to use the occasion to make a satisfying and engaging musical journey. As with the conceptual approach to music-making outlined by
Wilson (1992), they are concerned with making jazz anew each time they
perform, drawing upon and transforming it in real time.

Jazz as musical practice is thus more than the sum of its parts or any of
the ways in which we might configure them. While we can try to define it in
terms of swing, improvisation, harmony, instrumentation and timbre, those
characteristics are only a beginning. No single one nor any combination of
them is sufficient to capture the diversity of musical expressions gathered
under that rubric. At best, those different aspects are ingredients that have to
be combined by skilled cooks using the idiomatic and idiosyncratic knowledge they possess as well as whatever other tools they have at their disposal.
While musicians' ability to read a recipe (score or recording) or to abstract
it from someone else's realisation of it is surely important, in the end it
is what they do with the recipe that makes the difference. In decrying the
boundaries imposed by labels like 'jazz' in 1962, Duke Ellington asserted

that categories and characteristics, while useful at times, were potentially misleading. He explained to Stanley Dance that a satisfying dish was less a function of what went into it – whether one was having fish or fowl, served hot or cold – than of how it was prepared (Ellington 1962, 13–15). His seemingly offhand comment that 'the art is in the cooking' made clear that in the end it's not what goes into the music – the meat or how it is served – that makes the difference: it's what the musicians do with ingredients they have gathered.

6 Jazz as cultural practice

BRUCE JOHNSON

Since jazz emerged from its geographical origins it has travelled back and forth across the disputed terrain between high and low culture, variously located as folk, popular, art music and permutations. Its shifting position makes it a particularly instructive vehicle through which to study the matrix of cultural politics, the balances of power that determine which cultural forms carry authority. The migrations of jazz within musical politics and aesthetics depend upon negotiations between text (the particular jazz performance) and context (the physical and cultural space within which it is situated). The Eurocentric arbitration of musical value by the end of the nineteenth century was predicated on the stability of the musical text and of its relationship with context. Jazz appeared to demolish this model. As aurally based improvisation, in performance the 'text' evaded fixity, and the sites and conditions of performance blurred the distinction between art and social practice, music and noise. Even preserved on a sound recording, its formal components were scarcely intelligible in established musical terms such as background–foreground, melody–harmony and structural coherence. Jazz was a site of unruliness.

Jazz categorisations

The rapid international diaspora of jazz (see Chapter 2) meant that it could not be ignored; jazz was arguably the most pervasively influential development in twentieth-century music. Apart from the particular musical forms and practices in which it has been seminal, it was the most widespread musical vehicle of the progressive thrust into the experience of modernity in the early twentieth century, in such matters as gender, mass mediations and technological innovation. Jazz had to be spoken of. Yet there was no consensus as to how it should be categorised, or which of its formal and affective features should influence its categorisation. At one extreme it was deemed to possess no musical properties at all, being simply 'general noisy effects' (1922), a 'general din' (1918).[1] Society bandleader Vincent Lopez declared in 1924 that originally the word jazz meant 'contrary to music' (Walser 1999, 8). The acoustic disorder proclaimed itself in an apparent absence of melody; in timbral peculiarities arising from the unorthodox use of conventional instruments; the incorporation of 'noisemakers'; and most generally in rhythmic displacements.[2] The more disordered the sound, the more morally and aesthetically abominable. A definition of jazz in 1921 in the *Ladies' Home Journal*, as something in which 'the three simple elements of music – rhythm, melody and harmony – have been put out of tune with each other', was also framed by terms expressing the most extreme moral panic: 'evil influence', 'savage instincts', 'barbaric . . . brutality' (Walser 1999, 33, 34).

At the other extreme it was recognised that formal protocols were operating, particularly of course by its own pioneers. Jelly Roll Morton articulated the importance of melody, dynamics, structure, scored sections and European elements, all of which were elegantly embodied in his own work (*ibid.*, 19–21). Some attentive and well-informed European ears also recognised and respected a jazz aesthetic. Ernest Ansermet in a 1919 review paid the highest respect to the 'artists' of the Southern Syncopated Orchestra (which included Sidney Bechet); its 'astonishing perfection' and 'superb taste' were reflected in music which represented a 'veritable religious art' (R. Gottlieb 1996, 742–3).

Between these two extremes a spectrum of opinions refracted various aspects and permutations of jazz practices and its performance conditions. The African components paradoxically enabled the music to be declared barbarically primitive yet possessing the 'rhythmic aggressiveness' of 'the moderns' (Walser 1999, 6–7). Alternatively, these components marked jazz as a significant folk music through which African-American identity might be articulated with 'artistic finish' and having emancipative political potential (*ibid.*, 15, 55–7). For a writer in West Africa, however, the distinctive point about jazz was precisely its *non*-African elements (*ibid.*, 37–8). These categorisations of course were also determined by the particular performers and the performance sites and conditions associated with the label 'jazz'. Ansermet was writing of a concert format, while for the *Ladies' Home Journal* writer it was a dance music with disturbingly unruly affective manifestations. For others, as a cabaret music during prohibition, its links with bootleggers emphasised (glamorously or repellantly) the low-life licentiousness that already tainted its mythologised origins (Gabbard 1995a, 108).

Early responses to jazz thus ranged through bewilderment, outrage, fascination and respect, and depended on which version of the music was heard, in what conditions, and of course on the predispositions of the listener. These responses foreshadowed all the positions over subsequent decades, positions that both reflected and affected the range of jazz practices and venues. For its part, jazz obligingly provided exemplifications of whatever its partisans or opponents required of it, since its rapid diaspora was accompanied by a bewildering formal and functional pluralisation unique among musics.

Moral panic and aesthetic scorn have never entirely dissipated, partly because jazz has always lent its name to transgressive gestures of one kind or another. The anarchy and moral heedlessness of the 'Jazz Age' resurfaced in the extroverted ecstasies of the 'Swing Era' (Gendron 1995, 44–5). The drug-tainted *demi-monde* of bop and its argot strengthened an image that continued to pervade the jazz persona through subsequent developments such as psychedelic and later fusions. Such liaisons with dubious newcomers simply confirm its incorrigible nostalgia for the low-life.

By the mid-1930s, a growing body of articulate defenders of jazz were forced to agree that, in the theatrical excesses of swing, African-American music had surrendered to all that was crassly commercial in mass modernity. Rather than consign jazz in general to the artistic dustbin, however, they introduced a line of demarcation across the music itself. On one side it was an authentic folk art, and on the other its vulgarised commercial appropriations. In 1936, Alain Locke wrote: 'there is a vast difference between its first healthy and earthy expression in the original peasant paganism out of which it arose and its hectic, artificial and sometimes morally vicious counterpart which was the outcome of the vogue of artificial and commercialized jazz entertainment' (Walser 1999, 77–8).

This distinction would provide the most durable and versatile model for jazz discourse and the categorisation of jazz practices. It has been re-articulated in terms of race and colour, politics, musical form and gender. In the reaction against 'commercial' swing there emerged from the late 1930s a group that became known internationally as 'Mouldy Figs', invoking an authentic jazz which was a noble folk art in contradistinction to an early version of pop(ular) music which was a despised manifestation of mass culture (see Gendron).[3] The Figs' position frequently overlapped with the political left who found in pre-swing jazz an integrity that could be opposed to decadent bourgeois popular musics. The meretricious commercialism was held to be evident in a number of practices associated with swing, including ostentatious entertainment rhetoric and repertoire. The reductionist appeals to authenticity overlooked the fact that the idealised, rough-hewn, New Orleans folk musician eschewing commercial showmanship, and invariably black, was a denial of history and a form of 'postcardism' that ironically disempowered black musicians by discursive exclusion from the mainstream music industry.

At the same time, the debate created an aesthetic discourse for a music that in the 1920s had generally been dismissed as culturally negligible or reprehensible. In their condemnation of swing, the Figs echoed earlier attacks on contemporary African-American popular music, but in valorising a folk form, they were developing a version of the defence of jazz that some earlier avant-garde and art-music composers had foreshadowed: jazz as a

significant new art form. Australian composer and concert pianist Percy
Grainger had declared in 1932 that the 'three greatest composers who ever
lived are Bach, Delius and Duke Ellington' (J. Bird 1998, 239–40). Two years
later, Roger Pryor Dodge saw jazz musicians as heirs to a tradition of improvisation once practised by Frescobaldi, Handel, J. S. Bach, Haydn, Mozart
and Beethoven. Now moribund in art music, 'improvisation is absolutely
imperative to the development of an art form such as music or dancing'
(R. Gottlieb 1996, 749). The ambiguous layerings of discourse and practice
are evident even when the objective of securing art status for jazz was shared.
Paul Whiteman was a celebrated exponent of the durable belief that what
was required to lift jazz to an art form was increased symphonic discipline
and scoring (Walser 1999, 39–40).

A significant moment in the apparent resolution of the tensions
between African-American identity and high art was the bop revolution of
the mid-1940s, which provided new impetus in the transition of jazz from
entertainment to art (see Gendron 1995; and Elworth 1995). Regarded
largely as a black phenomenon, it also evinced a mystifying cerebral complexity, to the point of being apparently undanceable – a significant contrast with commercial swing. It defied the vulgar commercial imperative and
alienated itself from a bourgeois mainstream, boasting among its practitioners a number of spectacularly socially dysfunctional musicians available for
artistic romanticisation. It centralised the *agon* of the individual virtuoso and
was produced in the jazz equivalent of a Parisian garret. The relationship of
all this to the boppers' day-to-day lives was uneven and immaterial; there
was enough anecdotage available to patch together the identikit jazzman as a
driven outsider/genius, and the appropriate artistic discourse. Barry Ulanov
defined the position of the jazz musician in the late 1940s thus: 'behind him
is a history and a tradition. Before him is an art' (Elworth 1995, 67).

From the 1950s, particular kinds of jazz practice, particularly those associated with 'progressive' schools, became increasingly intellectualised (see
Chapter 10), especially through the music's association with undergraduate
audiences distancing themselves from emerging rock-and-roll. In doing so,
jazz found a place as an approved satellite of Eurocentric high culture and
increasingly situated itself in 'art' spaces. The Newport Jazz Festival was
established in 1954 to sponsor America's 'only original art form' (R. Gottlieb
1996, 686).

The simple fact of being so taxonomically evasive is sufficient to cause
nervousness among custodians of culture in a positivistic milieu. Additionally, however, several of the categories straddled by jazz exhibit characteristics that are at odds with the dominant discourses of aesthetic value in
the modern era. This aesthetic is layered. Its surface displays explicit criteria as to what kinds of music should be accorded greatest value. But these

are moulded over ideological templates with, at the deepest substrate, an Enlightenment episteme which is not hospitable to protocols historically associated with jazz. Our epoch privileges ways of knowing and experiencing that are not conformable with ways of knowing and experiencing manifested in jazz.

Epistemological frame

Because of its distinctive practices and taxonomic ambiguity, jazz (like other related musics) has not enjoyed artistic recognition commensurate with its character and influence. It must either eat in the scullery – 'down in the basement, a kind of servant's hall of rhythm', in the words of New Orleans's *The Times Picayune* on 20 June 1918 (Walser 1999, 8) – or gain admission to the dining room of funding, recognition and support only by donning a (sometimes implausible) disguise. The gatekeepers – traditional musicology, the forms and practices that it has canonised as the aesthetic and moral apogee of music, and the policies and attitudes arising from these – are in turn the musical agents of an Enlightenment epistemology. Although under increasing interrogation during the twentieth century, this epistemology remains dominant in the public discourse of western cultures and their satellites, the conditioned reflex that governs ways of thinking and practising culture. A defining contour is the connection between ocularcentrism and the intellect in maintaining a regime of knowledge-as-control, precipitating as, among many other things, a fixation on product rather than process. The more comfortably any cultural practice can be incorporated into such a model, the more privilege it will enjoy. It will be the argument of this chapter that in the general category of 'music,' jazz is less conformable than conventional art music to the dominant episteme, and that some practices associated with particular styles are even less so than others.

The episteme I am describing is particularly clear in the traditions of intellectual enquiry informed by the scientific revolution and the Enlightenment, in which virtue was eclipsed by power as the objective of knowledge. The desire to discover what is so has become instrumental to the desire to control what is so. The 'knower', the searcher for knowledge, is placed outside and above the field in which knowledge is to be found, manipulating and controlling through science's child, technology. It is a view of knowledge that seeks to open up the distance between Self and Other, empowering the former at the expense of the latter, 'that the mind may exercise over the nature of things the authority which properly belongs to it' (Bacon 1620, 7).

This is implicated also in the Cartesian mind–body dualism, with the mind as the central organising principle, exerting control over its objects, including the body – part of the mind's 'Other'. Clearly, however, in the materialist scientific regime the body must mediate the materiality from which knowledge is constructed. The classic experimental method, enunciated by Francis Bacon and later institutionalised in the Royal Society, harnesses the senses to reason. This hierarchy of mind over body in turn produced a hierarchy of the senses, in which the visual enjoys epistemological dominance:

> I . . . dwelling purely and constantly among the facts of nature, withdraw
> my intellect from them no further than may suffice to let the images and
> rays of natural objects meet in a point, as they do in the sense of vision.
>
> [*Ibid.*, 13–14]

Already, in this pioneering articulation of the project to link knowledge and power, Bacon instinctively enlisted its sensory trope. There is a range of reasons for this, and they bear on the arguments that follow. Different aspects of subjectivity are activated by each sense and, in some cases, the corporeal rather than the cerebral component of subjectivity is brought more powerfully into play. Smell, for example, 'is unique among the senses in not having connections through the thalamus to the . . . neocortex', while the visual system, however, directly accesses the cerebral cortex and has over 500 times the information-analysis capacity of the aural system (Gregory 1987, 720, 795). This facility makes vision highly appropriate to the dominant epistemology of the modern epoch. Vision is, more than any other sense, the faculty of distancing, control, intellectual analysis and analytical focus. Scopic cultural mapping and modelling distance us from the object in ways that other physical mediators do not. All the other senses are strengthened by physical proximity. The Self is vulnerably submerged in the wash of sound, intruded upon by touch, invaded by smell and taste. Sight is both the sense and the trope of objectivity and distance. As Foucault's work reminds us, as an instrument of knowledge devoted to control, vision is hegemonic in the modern epoch.[4]

That we are a scopocentric society has been the subject of note and critique. What is less often recognised is how deeply this traps us in a particular regime of knowledge itself. The visual is so deeply inscribed in cultural analysis, its 'perspectives', 'horizons', 'insights', that the language itself contests the exploration through alternative sensory fields, such as the acoustic.[5] In a paradigm that links knowledge with control, the enabling model is scopic. The post-Renaissance era organises knowledge through visual models: it is not merely a rhetorical ornament that the era is called the En*light*enment.

Aesthetic frame

Art music, its aesthetics, its most powerfully authorised production, performance and consumption protocols, and its public discourses are the musical realisation of these overlapping ideologies of the scopic, intellectual control and product fetishism. The privileged event of art music, the concert performance, is the social ritualisation of the convergence. To speak of a concert performance as 'spectacle' is clearly not to distinguish it from other forms of music performance. Stadium rock, for example, is one of the most visually theatricalised of all musical events. It is, however, a question of the relative emphases, of the balance with other criteria, and the content of the spectacle. Both the art music and the stadium rock concert are highly attentive to the appearance of the musical event, but they constitute a window on two very different kinds of visual statement. The rock concert relinquishes its purchase on the highest peaks of artistic seriousness by presenting a staged spectacle of unruliness and abandoned physicality, stylised anarchy that blurs the distinctions between performers and audiences (from aisle-jiving to mosh-pit). The rock spectacle is a ritualised refusal of other traditional components of the paradigm that defines 'serious' artistic achievement.

The traditional art-music concert is equally ritualised, but in celebration of a different ('higher') order of experience and value. The visual is equally respected in the art-music concert, but it is a spectacle of conformity to the other components of the aesthetic hegemony. It discloses regimentation, physical control in the interests of cerebral focus, the art work as a finished product, quarantined from social materiality in a bourgeois ritual of expiative transcendence, yet also imperialistically universalised, a 'celebration of the "sacred history" of the western middle classes' (Small 1987b, 19). The performance constructs an uncrossable divide between everyday world and artist, the masses and the genius, underlined by conventions of architecture, acoustics, lighting, dress, and temporal (order of appearance) and spatial hierarchies. The particular form of regimentation centralises the inviolable and completed score, the object of visual–mental focus for every musician either directly or as conducted from a central 'altar'. The programme centres on the 'opus': it is a spectacle of scopic hegemony, the eye engaging with a 'product'. All the musical skills on display are those of a body disciplined to a cognitive design inscribed in the score.

There is thus a template for high-status musical form and practice which celebrates the Enlightenment. Musics that evolved according to other templates must either endure trivialisation or disdain, or attempt to fit themselves into a Procrustean bed of values, which they can never occupy as convincingly as the music for which it was historically tailored.

Art-music discourses and jazz practices: performance

Jazz is an example of such other practices.[6] In whichever of the categories jazz has been situated, it has retained pre-eminently the practice of improvisation. Improvisation is so integral with jazz performance that jazz has in significant respects more in common with, and is therefore better understood in relation to, non-musical improvisational practices than with non-improvisational musical practices. Yet it is most frequently evaluated exclusively as a musical form. As such, in spite of its massive influence in the twentieth century, it has been accorded minor aesthetic significance in direct relation to the art-music tradition: an influence on it, but not an example of it (Johnson 2000, 47–52). We find the reasons for this in practices and competencies that distinguish jazz (and other similarly marginalised musics) from art music as it evolved throughout the nineteenth century. These practices are not inherently rebarbative, nor do they signal in any absolute sense a deficiency of creative imagination or a limit on performative competence. They are simply in tension with a dominant epistemology.

Central to the reasons for the trivialisation of jazz is that it is to a crucial extent an improvised music which comes into being in a moment of relatively unscripted performance and in response to social praxis. Paul Berliner's massive study documents the continuing centrality of improvisation as one of the distinctive elements of jazz in relation to western art music. This is not to posit an impermeable membrane between jazz and score-based music but, in practice and in print, jazz musicians almost universally hold improvisation to be a constitutive practice. This contends with the aesthetics and politics of a score-based tradition growing out of the episteme I have summarised above.

The marginalisation of improvisation is an outgrowth of the dialectics of modernism, reflecting the tensions between the elitist centralisation of cultural power and a form of mass enfranchisement achieved through the (re)production of music through aural and technological channels. This bypasses the (scopic) score-based aesthetics that serve 'First World' modernism. Key notions in the dominant cultural discourse have served to privilege particular artistic myths – the shaping genius (the composer) handing down the sacrosanct and autonomous work of art, a model of transcendence and permanence. One outcome of this ideology is the sacralisation of the scored composition – the Opus – as the centre of music production–consumption, against which all alternatives are to be seen as more or less imperfect deviations. Eminent Sorbonne musicologist André Pirro informed his pupil and successor Jacques Chailley: 'I never go to concerts any more. Why listen to music? To read it is enough' (quoted in Chailley 1964, 104).

Other interests converge with the aesthetic to favour musical practices that can be embodied as scored composition. One advantage of the 'Composition' is that its circulation can be controlled in a commodity economy, while the democratic enfranchising practices of improvisation are suspect because they represent a devolution of the control of cultural production. The moments and processes of production and consumption merge. There is relatively little intervening space for a mediating economic or critical network, as in a concert hall where interaction is controlled, or in a recording, which is only a static memory of the improvisational moment. A significant proportion of jazz performance is thus resistant to the usual dynamics of commodification. The organic process of interactive improvisation cannot be 'owned', but if that music can be frozen as a 'product' (a composition), it can be severed from the life that produced it, the conditions of production, and circulated as a commodity (see Johnson 1993). Jazz, of course, has its own commodified forms, and these are examined below.

A vernacular music like jazz has difficulty finding a place in this discourse. The aesthetics that frame the composer of 'serious' music, for example, are an inappropriate model for the relationship in jazz between composer, performer, audience, music-text and venue. When it seeks to situate itself within the domain of autonomous art, jazz finds it more difficult to mask its social specificity, especially those styles and performance practices in which the improvisational textures are most thickly entwined with the performance environment. The more overt the level of collective improvisation, and the more interactivity with audiences and supposedly extrinsic conditions, the less leverage jazz will have in a musicology that privileges the autonomous text.

The theoretical and instrumental competencies are very different for the jazz musician. Orchestral training does not normally develop the ability to improvise over sequences that change key, sometimes passing through different keys as often as every beat in a bar. Jazz instrumental skills also develop different dimensions of expressiveness, including spontaneously generated rhythmic and timbral ambiguities. That improvisation involves a differing repertoire of practices from those of score-based musics would not in itself disadvantage jazz were it not also the case that it is also a repertoire less oriented to the visual as a privileged channel and model of knowledge and experience.

Jazz is distinguished from art-music models in the priority of the ear in collective improvisational performance. Jazz is an earsite in an epistemology dominated by eyesight. It evades the authority of the score in both production and consumption. It is possible to become a successful jazz musician without ever having learned to read the conventional notation through which the art-music repertoire is definitively stored. It can thus be performed by musicians who have not subscribed to an approved symbolic order, access to which is restricted by class, race, economics and gender. Jazz performance also destabilised the rigid distinction between text and context by which musical experience was regulated in the prevailing aesthetic and political economy. The jazz ear constantly synthesises unexpected sounds into performance. Apart from the unpredictable contributions of other musicians in the band space, most jazz performances occur in the relatively unregulated soundscapes of pubs, dances, restaurants, malls, picnics or promotions, where they have to negotiate with audience interactivity, conversation and sounds such as dancers, dinnerware, glasses, poker machines and the intrusion of street noise.[7] Thus the myth of the artistic genius in full cognitive control of the act and conditions of creation has relatively little to do with improvisational performance, rooted not in a closed text, but in the unregimented acoustics of a vanishing moment.

Jazz musicians are working with contingencies over which they have little or no control, forming designs only to discover that they must be modified or abandoned, at one moment leading a line of development, at another, yielding to some other unexpected acoustic pattern. Unlike score-based art-music performances, jazz performance thus entails extraordinarily dense, unexpected and complex individual and collective decision-making processes in an acoustic field that is unscripted. Because the performance moment is everything, the soundscape is actually part of the 'text', part of the total sound being produced and consumed. Relative to art music, jazz is unprotected by the distinction between quotidian noise and music, a distinction preserved in the art-music score and central to the aesthetics of autonomy.

What these improvisational practices have in common, which sets them at odds with authorised musical aesthetics, is a tendency away from accepted forms of regulation, control and containment. To a greater extent than score-regimented art music, jazz is a music in which a degree of performance unruliness is a means to expressiveness. In terms of rhythm, pitch and timbre, jazz has broadly exhibited a resistance to the precise calibrations of western musicology and the score. Charles Keil's theory of participatory discrepancies is a recognition of the importance of this as a key to the expressive power of vernacular musics, including jazz.[8] This enabled its origins in 'primitive' (African) and contemporary mass (American) culture to be deployed as converging confirmations of its aesthetic deficiencies. Whatever apparent tensions might exist between the primitive and the modern, they were equally reprehensible in terms of Eurocentric Enlightenment criteria of civilised artistic practice. Thus, central to the expressive power of a jazz performance is a set of practices that are described by art-music discourse as musical incompetence or transgressiveness.

The centrality of performance rather than prior composition also destabilises the mind/body hierarchy that underpins high-art aesthetics. As performance music it is registered by and through the body in a way that is exuberant compared with 'classical' music. Jazz musicians and audiences are more physically animated, even in concert conditions, and this animation itself (as in shouted acclaim) in turn affects the character of performance. But the body is complicit, in a more profound and pervasive way, through the phenomenon of kinaesthetics (see, for example, Pressing 1987). The patterning motifs in a jazz musician's work represent a meshing of kinaesthetic and cognitive representation. Certain patterns are attributable not simply to cognitive design, but to the physical engagement with space, such as a habitual sequence of movements of the hand on the keyboard or fingers on keys and valves. The aesthetic implications are significant in violating formalist aesthetics based on the triumph of the heroic consciousness, the outcome of cognitive control. This means, for example, that among the determinants of 'artistic form' are physical contingencies associated with, for example, key signature. A musician's improvisational motifs will depend, among many other things, upon fingering sequences that have been habitualised in a particular key. On this basis, reed player Bob Wilber was able to restore the correct speed of an early Bechet recording (Kappler *et al.* 1980, 34). The relationship between cognitive and physical control in jazz performance is far too complex to be able to mythologise romantically the priority of the cognitive.

The internal politics of jazz reflect the same differentiated orientations to dominant discourses of value. In the attempt to increase its cultural capital, jazz is disadvantaged against art music; for the same reasons, certain jazz styles are disadvantaged against others, in particular to the detriment of sustained polyphony between three or four horns, supported by a rhythm section. This is virtually the distinguishing practice of all forms of so-called traditional jazz from New Orleans to Dixieland, re-emerging again in the 'free' jazz movement of the 1960s, with the difference (among others) that conventional concepts of tonality were now abandoned. Even so, its exponents frequently invoked the New Orleans tradition of collective improvisation as a model in terms of both form and social mission (see, for example, Wilmer 1977, 41).

Both traditional and free jazz are represented most sparsely in institutionalised support systems such as education, funding and media coverage. Continuous collective improvisation is both a formal musical skill involving the cultivation of a distinctive aural alertness, and a vehicle for a form of musical socialisation, that is peripheral to the tradition of the artist-as-individual, as 'soloist'. Collectivity does not construct the heroic individualism central to the aesthetics that equate artistic worth with formal virtuosity.

Improvisation, especially polyphonic, also destabilises a major structural principle by which romantic and modernist art works anchor themselves in, and confirm, their milieu: the figure–ground model. 'Where's the Melody?' asked the title of Martin Williams's introduction to jazz (1966), reflecting the nervous disorientation of many suspicious newcomers to the music. It is also singularly difficult to accommodate collective improvisation in a text-centred ethos, simply because it is so resistant to notation. As 'improvisation' (and this, of course, is as true of a bop solo as of traditionalist polyphony), it cannot be written down beforehand; but as 'collective' it is virtually impossible to transcribe later from a recording (see Munn 1960, 101). The intractability of collective improvisation to the form of a scored 'opus', as well as the effacement of individual virtuosic 'genius', the democratic dispersal of power in a collectivity, constitute radical disadvantages in any attempts it may make to secure legitimacy as high art.

Art-music discourse and jazz practices: dissemination

By the 1920s, jazz was linked with the sound recording so closely that an advertisement in the Australian journal, *Graphic*, on 20 January 1921 described the Melola record-player as being 'as effective as a full jazz band'. In this partnership, which represented the displacement of traditional musical practices by twentieth-century mass culture, jazz was already in tension with artistic values inherited from the nineteenth century. In many ways the sound recording became the jazz equivalent of art music's score. None the less, there are differences which also help to account for the lower status of jazz.

Of course, art music also enjoyed the benefits of the sound recording, but the recording determined the meaning of jazz to a far greater extent than it did in classical music, which had already situated itself aesthetically and politically through the more respectable authority of the score. For most of the world, however, jazz was first encountered and therefore inextricably linked with sound recording, and had no pre-existing purchase within the score-based nineteenth-century musical aesthetics that continue to dominate artistic standards. As in the case of live performance, the global generation of jazz was primarily by acoustic rather than visual means.

The fact that it was thus indiscriminately accessible on a global scale to the musically illiterate helped to lodge it in the category of 'mass culture'. This was seen by its opponents as evidence of its pernicious homogenising influence. The truth is by no means so simple. The art-music score, with its aura of sacral inviolability, constrains democratic interventions and reinterpretations. And the way in which the score is realised in the traditional concert setting reproduces that regimentation in social practice. Focused cognitive attentiveness is equally the approved protocol for domestic listening to classical recordings. All this is in the interests of a higher aesthetic (as well, however, as serving a political economy). By contrast, jazz is an example of musics that are performed and listened to (publicly and privately) in conditions that encourage interaction and reinterpretation. The recording also shifted attention away from composer and fixed or closed score, to performer and variable, open-ended performance. Mass mediations (historically the most symbiotic medium for jazz beyond earshot) place musical meanings up for grabs. The sound itself can be rearranged at the whim of the listener: by singing along, playing tracks in different orders, transferred, spliced, sampled. It can be listened to under a wide range of social conditions with personalised codings. The person sitting in a living room or car has greater freedom to mediate her/his individuality through a recording than the audience in a classical music concert. Indeed, it is precisely this – not homogenisation – that is antipathetic to the dominant aesthetic. While all musics, from 'art' to 'pop', are technologically accessible to such interventions, such unauthorised reconstructions of form and meaning are inherently offensive to an aesthetic tradition of privileged genius, transcendence and permanence.

The moral and aesthetic odium attached to mass culture, and to jazz by association, is less a manifestation of concern for 'the masses' becoming opiated or depraved, than a fear of the threat to centralised cultural control and its associated aesthetics. This control was once exercised by considerations such as class, race, gender and place. While these remain powerful instruments of inequity and exclusion, mass mediations such as the sound recording have not only given access to music without reference to score-reading skills or controlled-access concert settings, they have also made the (re)production of culture more democratic. This does not mean that unregulated cultural production must also be chaotic: spectators in a sports stadium are able spontaneously to sing together and in tune. Cultural democracy has proven no more likely to produce chaos and barbarity than any form of centralised control. The problem with cultural democracy is that representation and meaning can no longer be controlled by the established custodial classes. Thus, as a music stored for distribution in recording, jazz again cuts against the grain of the ideologies that determine artistic value.

The two generic categories, folk and mass culture, have most frequently hosted jazz. Jazz aspirants to a level of artistic respectability beyond the reach of such categories have therefore found it necessary to try to resituate the music as 'art'. Sometimes this is attempted by simply putting the music somewhere else. The effectiveness of this tactic is reflected in the increased respect and acclaim enjoyed by a jazz group when it performs in a concert hall exactly the same programme it presents in a pub. A more radical tactic is to try to develop a jazz form that attempts to conform to art-music criteria in terms of compositional practices, instrumentation and arrangement. In both cases this has amounted to resituating jazz into different performance and audience protocols, rhetoric, musical forms and taxonomies (from Paul Whiteman's 'symphonic jazz' to the increasingly ubiquitous 'Jazz Suite'). While this is no more or less 'valid' than any other of the numerous re-inventions of the music, it has most often produced curiosities isolated from what at this time appears to be the mainstream.

Popular-music studies and jazz

Certainly it has produced a hybrid, decentred discourse. While representatives of jazz were seeking a position within the art-music firmament, that aesthetic itself was under increasing critique with the emergence of popular-music studies. The latter specifically provided a counter-discourse to traditional musicology, drawing upon such fields as cultural studies and ethnomusicology. It might be expected that jazz would inevitably find a significant place in such scholarship and the public discourses it has helped to authorise, yet this has scarcely been the case. Simon Frith's incomparably well-informed perspective on the British scene is representative of a general pattern: 'In Britain the world of jazz scholarship remains far apart from the world of popular music studies. I can't recall a single article on British jazz being submitted to *Popular Music*' (Johnson 2000, vi).

Given jazz's history of general marginalisation and condemnation by the art-music establishment, this begs the question: why not? To some extent answers have already been provided. While cultural and popular-music studies have certainly evolved to a large extent as a reaction against established arts scholarship, they are nonetheless institutionalised in the same framework of Enlightenment intellectual traditions modelled on the knowledge/power/ocularcentrism axes. Although critiques of such traditions, they predominantly remain prisoners of its mental tropes of 'perspectives', 'horizons', 'viewpoints' and 'envisionings'. The resilience of the 'power' agenda in scholarly discourse will also impose the same limits on radicalism, producing the same blindspots as are found in its contestants.

Apart from such fundamental patterns, there are more particular reasons for the relative silence of jazz in popular-music scholarship. The tension between the two converges on the word 'popular' in a particular historical moment. The meaning of 'popular' in relation to culture in general and music in particular has itself been a major debate in the literature. There seems to be no satisfactory way of defining the term that corresponds to the powerful but inchoate understanding that drives its study; clearly there *is* such an understanding, or its various definitions would not be so vigorously debated. 'Popular' as 'liked by many' does not work. It is equally clear that it cannot be identified simply in the formal properties of a product. It possesses the characteristics of a process, of signifying practices, of negotiating spaces, of means of dissemination and consumption (see Storey 1993, Strinati 1995, and Middleton 1990). The point here is that by any definition, and by the logic of popular-music theory, the history and practices of jazz are substantially (if not wholly) case-studies in 'popular music'.

In practice, however, the territory thus designated has been colonised almost entirely by rock, post-rock and its derivatives. This is analogous to traditional musicology's tacit assumption that 'music' equals 'art music'. Tacitly, 'popular music' has coalesced with 'pop music'. The reasons are to some extent based in jazz practices, which manifested a level of improvisation that, its supporters in particular insisted, distinguished it significantly from rock. It became more difficult to sustain this distinction in relation to later developments in pop, however, particularly when jazz musicians themselves entered into crossover projects. Such developments unmasked the political and historical factors that opened the gap between jazz and post-rock. First, they disclosed the fact that the gap was more between the discourses than the practices. In practice, there has been a dynamic interaction between jazz, rock and pop, including sharing of blues forms by jazz and proto-rock styles such as jump, jive, rockabilly and rhythm-and-blues. Jazz musicians have always been found on what are regarded as rock sessions as well as later more self-conscious exercises in fusion.[9] Many bands and musicians securely located in the pop canon, such as Frank Zappa and Jack Bruce, have enjoyed the highest respect among jazz musicians, and pop figures such as Lou Reed have had a strong attachment to jazz.

The silence of jazz in popular-music studies thus reflects a great deal more about musical discourse than musical practices, though of course some of that discourse itself has been conducted by musicians. New Orleans revivalists in the late 1950s, for example, were determined to distance themselves from rock, while John Lennon helped kill the 'trad' boom when he reportedly declared a loathing for traditional jazz. Indeed, these two cases draw our attention to the historical moment at which the space between jazz and popular-music discourse began to open up. Anglophone cultural studies emerged largely as an interrogation of existing cultural hierarchies and assumptions, with Richard Hoggart's *The Uses of Literacy* (1957) paving the way for the seminal work of Raymond Williams, as in *The Long Revolution* (1961). While Hoggart dismissed 'juke box' culture, the redirecting of attention to popular culture under the sponsorship of a radical critique of value set the scene for the emergence of a serious and sympathetic popular-music discourse (Hoggart 1957, 247–8). This was largely initiated by a generation whose enthusiasms were shaped by the popular music of the late 1950s and 1960s. That is, the development of popular-music studies broadly coincided with the development of pop music itself: both new, both presenting themselves as oppositional.

At the apex of the high–low model under critique was art music ('Roll Over Beethoven') and its central legitimating discourse, musicology. However, other forms of arguably popular music were already positioned in the field that, in general, popular-music scholarship was writing against. Although the position of jazz within that field was subordinate, its own proponents, insofar as they participated at all in the high–low debate, were scrambling for the high ground. Whatever else might have divided the often fractious community of jazz writers, they largely closed ranks in scornful opposition to rock and its immediate successors. From the late 1950s a large section of the jazz community formed a united front with other cultural practices that were seeking or endowed with artistic *gravitas*. Alliances with the folk–gospel movement, with the university-campus population and the coffee-lounge set, with the Beats, through poetry and jazz ventures and collaborations with bohemian painters – all helped to stabilise jazz in an orbit, if at some distance, of 'art'. In earlier decades many would have agreed with American composer John Alden Carpenter, who insisted in 1924 that jazz was 'our contemporary popular music' (Walser 1999, 43). As rock invaded that category, jazz fled it, intensifying its efforts to gain admission to the sanctuary of art-music discourse, claiming allegiance to its ideologics, its conceptual models, and often its Schenkerian modes of 'textual' analysis (see DeVeaux 1991 and Gabbard 1995b). The apotheosis of this strategy was reached in the 1960s in the writing of what Elworth suggests were the Leavisites of jazz, Gunther Schuller and Martin Williams (1995, 71).

Rock–pop and its discourses were happy to live with the divide, to distance themselves from a music that, in a new culture of youth, carried the odour of the past, and that was publicly disdainful. While jazz was attempting to consolidate its position as art music (albeit incorrigibly second class), cultural and popular-music studies were seeking to articulate aesthetics appropriate to popular music (see, for example, Chester 1970). In the process they were privileging and glamorising contemporary subcultural sites that were deemed to be emancipatively and democratically oppositional. The immense range of cultural and specifically musical practices which appeared to be too prosaic, conservative or simply unfashionable were largely overlooked no matter how quantitatively popular, from philately to Julie Andrews, and included jazz. While it may seem to musicology that jazz is too demotically unruly to take equal place with high-art music, it is widely regarded as too elitist to warrant the attentions of popular-music scholars.

The coalface experience of David Horn, Director of Liverpool University's Institute for Popular Music, prompted him to comment that students at the Institute continue to feel that jazz improvisation 'seems to them to have its own brand of elitism'.[10]

Of course, this is all a matter of relativities, and relativities that are shifting. Gabbard's 1995 collections of essays represent themselves as an attempt to draw jazz into the new critical discourses.[11] Apart from registering a shift, their own bibliographies help to identify its prefigurations. The hitherto uncoordinated character of 'cultural studies' approaches to jazz, however, has thrown them into the shadow of the much larger body of literature in the tradition of high-art musicology which has most decisively framed the music. Jazz has left it very late to attempt to find a place in the discourses of popular culture. Trailing deferentially in the wake of traditional musicology and the Romantic and modernist ideologies that underpin it, jazz criticism has tethered itself to one of the most conservative of all critical discourses, gradually internalising and adopting its models even as they were being profoundly problematised.[12] It is strange that, for most of the century or so of its existence, a music that has been so pervasively influential, and that is such a potentially incandescent case study in modernity and cultural theory, has been treated so derivatively and unimaginatively by its major scholars, and almost completely overlooked by recent discourses that seem tailored to its history and practices. The resolute silence of jazz in those discourses has retrospectively occluded its historical status as the first music of urban modernity, to the extent that the pre-rock era is frequently regarded as being entirely bereft of oppositional youth music (Johnson 2000, 153). At the same time, with its fixation on formal high-art modernism, musicology has demonstrated the same insensitivity to the importance of jazz as the music of modernity (*ibid.*, 45–52).

Jazz aspirants to aesthetic legitimacy and its benefits are able to draw upon a critical commentary based on art music as well as bring into being projects that reconstruct jazz in ways that might allow it access to the category of 'art'. The attempt to accord jazz practices the status of art music can achieve important tactical gains, giving weight, for example, to arguments for its consideration in educational and funding policies. In broader strategic terms, however, the attempt will always bring jazz into unequal competition with the art music itself for which the 'rules' and criteria were created. As Walser comments, 'Virtually the whole tradition of musicological analysis of jazz . . . has been caught between the admission that jazz is different from classical music (and probably inferior), and the desire to legitimate jazz according to the criteria commonly used to analyze classical music' (Walser 1993, 171). At the same time, jazz distanced itself all the more from other musics that have enjoyed the attentions of popular-music scholarship and the policy recognition that has emerged in conjunction with the rise of cultural studies. Jazz has thus fallen between the two stools of traditional musicology and popular-music studies. The dialectical relationship between the music and its discourses, between the text and its contexts, is infinitely complex. The broad-ranging and durable debates it has generated are far more than just squabbles about naming and categorising. They reflect profoundly on how jazz has registered the distinctive twentieth-century convergence of musical practices, discourses and technologies.

7 Jazz improvisation

INGRID MONSON

The goal of this chapter is to provide an overview of the principal musical resources used in jazz improvisation as well as an approach to listening to jazz from the 'bottom up' – a way of hearing that will stress the interactive interplay between the soloist and the accompaniment. The melodic vocabulary of the improvising jazz soloist, which is what generally first catches the new listener's attention, must always be seen as emerging in a complex dialogue between the soloist and the rhythm section, and between the pre-existing musical knowledge of the band members and what they collectively discover in the process of improvisation.

Among the many musical characteristics associated with jazz are improvisation, syncopation, swing, blues feeling, call-and-response organisation and harmonic complexity. Improvisation and swing are often considered to be the most important elements of jazz, although defining them has proved elusive. Improvisation has been described as the spontaneous creation of music in performance,[1] but the sense of improvisation as elaborating upon something previously known is sometimes lost in this definition. Swing has generally been defined as forward propulsion through time resulting from the interplay between a fixed underlying pulse and the unevenly articulated subdivisions of that pulse which must ultimately be shaped into convincing phrases.[2] The improviser does this in call-and-response with a rhythm section (generally piano or guitar, bass and drums) – an ensemble within an ensemble whose function is both to keep time and interact with the soloist.

Rhythm sections define time feels or grooves of various types – two-beat, swing, Latin, ballad, jazz waltz – through a combination of distinctive bass lines, drum patterns and 'comping' (i.e., accompanying) styles. The musical resources just mentioned (from improvisation to swing to call-and-response) are deployed over a wide variety of time feels, some of which serve to distinguish the various historical styles of jazz improvisation such as New Orleans, swing, bebop, cool, hard bop, mainstream, free jazz and neo-classical. Recognising the various rhythmic feels in jazz as well as the typical melodic and harmonic gestures made by the improvising soloist is an important part of finding one's way around this remarkable music.

We will begin with some examples from early jazz and work our way through several others drawn from the rich variety of jazz styles in the twentieth century. The reader is encouraged to listen to the recordings cited (all of which are commercially available), locating the particular passages discussed by the timings indicated. I have tried to meet the needs of many types of listener by including some musical notation for the musically experienced, as well as general listening guidelines that require no technical expertise. Later we will consider how the basic elements of jazz improvisation have been used to articulate a variety of musical aesthetics – the value of which continues to be hotly debated among musicians and jazz *aficionados* today.

Swinging melody

Early jazz musicians learned repertory primarily by ear, internalising both the melody and its phrasing and articulation in one process. New Orleans brass bands and string bands embellished familiar tunes by paraphrasing and syncopating the melodies. New Orleans ensembles passed the melody from instrument to instrument, creating continuous textures of collective improvisation. By the early 1920s, the cornet had become the preferred melody instrument, while the clarinet improvised countermelodies, and the trombone and rhythm section (guitar, bass and drums, or banjo, tuba and drums) provided the rhythmic foundation against which the melodies were phrased. At first, solo improvisation took place during 'breaks' – two-bar units in which the rhythm section temporarily dropped out. Later, as the improvisational tradition expanded, gifted soloists – most notably Louis Armstrong – provided the model for lengthier and more varied improvisation that went beyond ornamenting and paraphrasing a known melody by relying increasingly on the underlying harmony as the basis of improvisation. The distinctive off-beat phrasing of a swung melody, which derives its push-and-pull effect from a weaving in and out of the underlying pulse of the rhythm section, had by this time become a distinctive element of the jazz sound.

A phrase from Armstrong's solo on 'Big Butter and Egg Man' illustrates this melodic style. The first staff of Ex. 7.1 provides a transcription of Armstrong's solo phrase in a style of notation from which a jazz instrumentalist might perform. The second staff provides a more literal rendition of the actual phrasing and articulation, illustrating several important features of melodic style. First, Armstrong subdivides the crotchet pulse into something closer to three units than two. Second, he often provides an accent on the final quaver of the beat, which propels the phrase forwards (bar 1, 2:14).

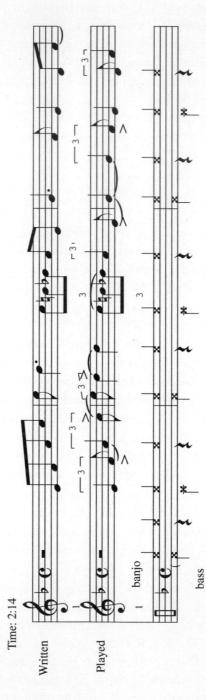

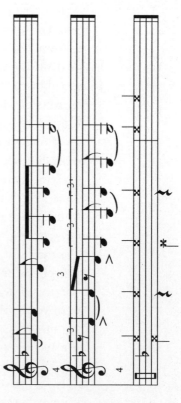

Ex. 7.1 Louis Armstrong, 'Big Butter and Egg Man', *Hot Fives & Sevens*, Chicago: 16 November 1926 (Columbia CK 44253). Staff 1: Gunther Schuller, *Early Jazz: Its Roots and Musical Development* (New York: Oxford University Press, 1968), 104, reproduced by permission of the publisher. Staff 2 and 3: edited by Ingrid Monson

Time: 2:14

Third, the accent is reinforced by Armstrong's articulation: slurring from the accented final triplet to the first note of the following beat. These elements are all aspects of the so-called 'swung' quaver. Fourth, Armstrong's phrasing pulls against the regular pulse of the banjo by accenting in between the four-square pattern. Although there is no bass line at this point in the recording (recordings of his Hot Five ensemble did not include a bass instrument), a two-beat feel is implied – and is actually played on trombone at the opening of the piece. The hallmark of the two-beat feel is a bass line on beats one and three of 4/4 metre.

Breaks and stop-time

Melodic improvisation, characterised by the swung quaver, typically takes place in dialogue with a more regularly repeating background played by the rhythm section. Jelly Roll Morton's 'Black Bottom Stomp' provides a classic illustration of the devices used by early jazz rhythm sections to provide contrast and excitement. Key to the excitement in the rhythm section is a two-bar break pattern that Morton uses to lead from one solo to the next (first heard at 1:32). This pattern is based on the Charleston rhythm, which is itself related to the Spanish *cinquillo* rhythm and the Cuban *son clave* (also known as the *tresillo*): see Ex. 7.2. As Christopher Washburne has noted, the 'Latin tinge' that Morton mentioned in his recollections of music in New Orleans at the turn of the twentieth century runs deeper than is generally acknowledged in the jazz literature. In 'Black Bottom Stomp', the break pattern (later called a 'riff') is used as a stop-time accompaniment to

Ex. 7.2 Jelly Roll Morton, 'Black Bottom Stomp', Chicago, 15 September 1926

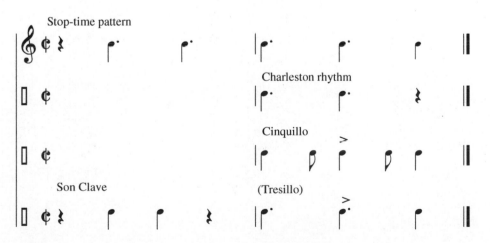

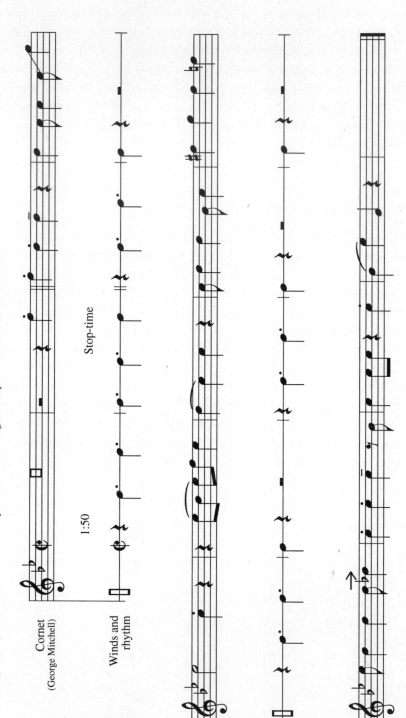

Ex. 7.3 Jelly Roll Morton, 'Black Bottom Stomp', *The Pearls*, Chicago, 15 September 1926: RCA 6588-2-RB

George Mitchell's cornet solo: see Ex. 7.3 (1:50–2:09). In stop-time, the rhythm section temporarily abandons continuous time-keeping, leaving open space for the soloist. The band punctuates the texture with either regular accents (a crotchet every two bars, for example) or a rhythmic figure as is the case here. In 'Black Bottom Stomp' the band returns to continuous time-keeping after Mitchell's solo. Bassist John Lindsay shifts temporarily from a two-beat to a four-beat bass line (double-time), intensifying the level of excitement even further (2:12–2:28). Early jazz ensembles made effective use of all these musical resources – breaks, stop-time and two-beat feels occasionally double-timed – to provide the foundation over which soloists such as Armstrong developed their distinctive melodic styles.

While Armstrong and other early jazz soloists developed an impressive melodic language, other musicians began learning favourite passages from phonograph recordings. In 1927, Melrose published in New York a book of transcribed Armstrong breaks (*125 Jazz Breaks for Hot Trumpet*) which was perhaps the first jazz publication with a pedagogical intent. Since they are presented without a rhythmic or harmonic context, they leave out much that is important, yet illustrate the constant interplay in jazz between aural and literate approaches to music. Ideas improvised in performance are learned by ear from recordings by other musicians and sometimes written down. Composers and arrangers may use some of these ideas as a basis for written arrangements that then serve as frameworks for other solos. Improvisers often take these fragments of melodies, practise them in several keys and use them as resources in the development of their own improvisational language.

The eternal cycle

These activities are all part of what Paul Berliner has called the 'eternal cycle' between newly created ideas and pre-composition in improvisation.[3] As Berliner's *Thinking in Jazz* (1994) has emphasised, it is best to think of jazz improvisation as a gradually acquired skill that consists of many different phases of learning. The first thing that an improviser must learn is a repertory of tunes that will serve as vehicles for improvisation. Next the student must learn to embellish melodies convincingly and master the melodic and harmonic language of jazz improvisation. Finally the improviser must learn to improvise in an ensemble setting and develop the ability to respond appropriately to the musical flow within the band. These different aspects of improvisational learning are ongoing aspects of the improviser's relationship to the music.

'Take the "A" Train', Billy Strayhorn
Recommended listening: *Duke Ellington: The Blanton-Webster Band*. RCA
5659-2-RB. r 15 February 1941

	1	2	3	4	5	6	7	8
A	C6	C6	D7b5	D7b5	Dm7	G7	C6	Dm7-G7
A	C6	C6	D7b5	D7b5	Dm7	G7	C6	Dm7-G7
B	Fmaj7	Fmaj7	Fmaj7	Fmaj7	D7	D7	Dm7	G7
A	C6	C6	D7b5	D7b5	Dm7	G7	C6	(Dm7-G7)

Fig. 7.1

Forms and feels

The repertory of early jazz included ragtime pieces, hymns, blues, marches, waltzes and other popular genres. In later styles, Tin Pan Alley tunes (most commonly in AABA song form) and the 12-bar blues become the most typical forms over which improvisation took place. Although there are styles of jazz improvisation that abandon these forms of fixed length, a budding jazz musician generally starts by learning a repertory of tunes and their chord progressions (Berliner 1994, 63–94). The tune or song defines the length of the improvisational cycle and the basic chord progression ('changes') that organise the improvising.

Figs 7.1 and 7.2 provide diagrams of two of the most common forms used in jazz. Thirty-two-bar song form (AABA) comprises four 8-bar phrases, and the 12-bar blues three 4-bar phrases. To help you hear the AABA form, try singing along with the melody on Duke Ellington's 1941 recording of 'Take the "A" Train'. When the saxophones repeat their opening melody, they have reached the 'second A' of the 32-bar form (0:17). The B section or 'bridge' is marked by the beginning of a new melodic phrase (0:28). When the opening melody returns, the band has reached the 'third A' of the AABA form (0:39). If you were to count in four (1-2-3-4, 2-2-3-4, 3-2-3-4, and so on) from the beginning of the melody, taking the bass line as your pulse, you would notice that each section of the form is eight bars in length. Once through the 32-bar form is called a 'chorus' and this is the unit used to describe the length of a solo. Here Ray Nance takes a one-chorus solo (0:51–1:35), that is, he plays once through the AABA form. Musicians learn to recognise the chord progression and phrase structure underlying the particular song they are playing, and hence learn to hear where they are in the form without having to count each bar individually.

The bass line heard on 'Take the "A" Train' is a 'walking bass', easily identifiable by the fact that a bass note is played on every beat of the 4/4 metre. The bassist shapes these notes into ascending and descending lines that

'McSplivens', Dexter Gordon
Recommended listening: Dexter Gordon, *A Swinging' Affair*, Blue Note CDP
7 84133 2, r 29 August 1962.

1	2	3	4	5	6	7	8	9	10	11	12
Bb7	Eb7	Bb7	Bb7	**Eb7**	Eb7	Bb7	Bb7	**F7**	Eb7	Bb7	F7
						alternate:	dm7 G7	**cm7**	F7	dm7 G7	cm7 F7

Fig. 7.2

move smoothly from chord to chord. The bass line plus the rhythmic figure
played by the drummer on the closed hi-hat cymbal (♪♫♪♫, with the quavers
swung) serve to define the basic 'time feel' or 'groove' of the piece, which in
this case is swing.

Dexter Gordon's 'McSplivens' illustrates the 12-bar blues form. Fig. 7.2
provides a diagram of the chord progression of 'McSplivens', which is a
typical blues progression found in hundreds of jazz compositions. Unlike
32-bar song form, the blues is associated with a specific chord progression
crucial to its identity. Although musicians frequently embellish this progression with a wide variety of alternative chords (one example is included in
Fig. 7.2), the three 4-bar phrases of the form almost always move from tonic
(in bar 1) to subdominant (in bar 5) and dominant or alternative (in bar 9).
Both 'Take the "A" Train' and 'McSplivens' make use of swing time – note
the walking bass line and the rhythmic pattern on the ride cymbal (♪♫♪♫).
This is the so-called 'ride-cymbal rhythm' that is characteristic of a swing
feel. Other commonly used feels in jazz include shuffle, 'in 2', jazz waltz, 6/8,
12/8, samba and various 'straight quaver' feels including Latin, rock and
funk.[4]

Melodic styles and harmony

The concept of the blues in jazz has several dimensions, including form,
chord progression, melodic style and emotional feeling. Indeed, the melodic
style of the blues is perhaps its most immediately recognisable characteristic.
Gordon's 'McSplivens' provides an excellent example of blues melody. The
entire 'head' (i.e. the melody of the composition) and many of Gordon's
solo passages are drawn from the blues scale (Ex. 7.4), which is an expressive resource that all musicians must master. Notice Gordon's great timbral
expressiveness as he bends, shapes and phrases the pitches of the blues
scale into meaningful music. Use of the blues scale is not restricted to
the blues form; indeed, melodies derived from the blues scale are often

Ex. 7.4

Blues Scale

heard at particularly expressive moments in a wide variety of jazz compositions.

Since the 1960s, jazz pedagogy has been dominated by the chord–scale approach to jazz harmony. Improvisers learn to associate scales with particular chords, which then guide their note choices while improvising. George Russell, whose *Lydian Chromatic Concept of Tonal Organization* (1959) generated much discussion among musicians of the 1950s and early 1960s (see Chapter 10), pioneered the concept of associating scales of various degrees of consonance and dissonance with particular chords. He based his musical philosophy and harmonic practice on the idea that the Lydian mode best expresses the harmony of the major triad. Since then, a chord–scale approach that takes the major mode as the best expression of the harmony of a major triad has been popularised by several instruction books including those by John Mehegan, David Baker and Mark Levine. Musicians now typically learn up to 21 scales and their associations with particular chords in the jazz harmonic vocabulary. In the 1940s, however, musicians focused on arpeggiating chords and playing the major, minor, Mixolydian and blues scales (see, for example, Eldridge 1946). Bebop added the diminished and whole-tone scales, both symmetrical in structure, to the commonly used tonal resources of jazz. Throughout the history of the music there has been a constant interplay between the disciplined study of music theory and the process of improvisation itself as a way of discovering new harmonic approaches.

Licks, sequences and interaction

Although scales and arpeggios are the building blocks of jazz's improvisational language, it is ultimately the melodic ideas invented by individual artists that make the music memorable. From a pragmatic point of view, the improviser is continually called upon to make musical decisions as he or she negotiates complicated harmonic progressions, often with dizzying speed and virtuosity. The melodic and harmonic solutions invented by the towering figures in jazz history – such as Louis Armstrong, Charlie Parker, Miles Davis and John Coltrane – have often been parsed into 'licks' that have been widely practised by subsequent jazz musicians. Since chord progressions often proceed with some regular structure (for example descending by step or ascending by perfect fourth) it is not surprising that melodic sequences moving in similar patterns have been a prominent feature of jazz melodic practice. Such licks are a crucial musical resource from which musicians build convincing solos and thematic continuity.

Ex. 7.5

Sequence
Chorus 1, B section 0:50–0:54

Parker's famous solo on 'Ko Ko' makes use of a distinctive sequence at the beginning of the first bridge (Ex. 7.5). The ascending arpeggio followed by a chromatic descent, beginning first on the pitch E and four bars later on D, is used to negotiate the tricky stepwise key changes in the bridge. Parker's idea expresses the so-called 'ii–V–I' progression, which is ubiquitous in jazz improvisation. There are countless ways to 'make the changes' with sequences, scales and thematic ideas that fit the harmonic context, but it would be a mistake to think of jazz improvisation as simply a matter of assembling short melodic licks into longer lines. Great improvisers such as Parker or Coltrane combine a facility with short melodic sequences and a keen ear for the tonal possibilities of larger stretches of music.

Another way to think of this is to envision an ascending or descending stepwise line of relatively long durations (crotchets or quavers) that the player keeps in mind while negotiating a long sequence of chord changes. The improviser may hear such underlying voice-leading as a scaffold on which many different kinds of patterns, scalar passages and phrases might be used. The swing of the rhythm section and the voice-leading of the bass and chordal instrument may play crucial roles in helping the improviser find harmonically and rhythmically satisfying ways to meet the demands of a particular tune. The improviser is constantly making choices about how to proceed, monitoring the dictates of the inner ear as well as the musical direction of the accompaniment. The improviser's choices may include making a musical quotation or allusion to a well-known tune or solo, which listeners familiar with the tradition may recognise with a smile. Ultimately it is the musicality of longer sections of music and the performer's ability to interact effectively with a band that distinguish the most admired improvisers.[5]

Aesthetics

The practice of jazz improvisation is indelibly shaped by the history of African-American musical aesthetics. The basic rhythm section/soloist configuration of the jazz ensemble, the call-and-response principles of musical phrasing and collective process, as well as the timbral variety expected of the jazz soloist, were all pioneered in African-American genres such as the ring shout, blues, congregational singing, gospel music, ragtime and jazz. Olly Wilson calls this basic approach to musical organisation the 'heterogeneous sound ideal', adding that African-American and many other African diasporic musics have a marked preference for timbral contrast, dense overlapping textures, the use of fixed and variable rhythmic groupings and a vocal communicative ideal (see Wilson 1992 in Wright and Floyd). 'Riffing' (i.e., repetition of short melodic or rhythmic figures) has been a particularly important resource in the expression of this aesthetic ideal.

Most cultural commentators have generally emphasised the secular heritage of jazz aesthetics with special emphasis on the blues as a musical process and cultural attitude. LeRoi Jones's *Blues People* and Albert Murray's *Stomping the Blues* both acknowledge the constant interplay between the secular and sacred in African-American music, but view the secular as the most liberating. More recently the sacred heritage of African-American musics has been stressed, as in Samuel Floyd's use of the ring shout as the interpretive lens through which to view the heritage of African-American musical genres (see Jones [Baraka] 1963, Murray, and Floyd 1995).

Whether sacred or secular, African-American musics in the twentieth century developed in constant counterpoint with a modernist aesthetic. Indeed the most widely acknowledged heroes of jazz – Armstrong, Ellington, Parker, Monk, Davis and Coltrane – were all pioneers in synthesising that blend of African-American heritage and modernism that is fundamental to jazz aesthetics and key to its appeal beyond the confines of any ethnic boundary. From very early in the history of the music, jazz was a musical form that mediated across the racial divide in a segregated United States, attracting generations of non-African-American youth to the freedom of improvisation and cultural sensibility whose emotional depth and intelligence it was difficult to deny. The mainstreaming of many aspects of the 'heterogeneous sound ideal' was a central component of twentieth-century American popular music.

The intersection of modernist aesthetic values (including virtuosity, abstraction, originality and the concept of the genius) with the African-American heterogeneous sound ideal has given rise to many different stylistic varieties in jazz. The musical elements we have already covered are widely accepted as components of most approaches to jazz, but it is important to understand that there have been sharp aesthetic divisions and debates that have taken place throughout the history of the music. Among the musical dimensions over which critics divide are the issues of virtuosity, repetition, harmony, rhythmic feel, form and timbre. A positive evaluation of virtuosity and harmonic complexity has made virtuosic musicians such as Parker, Coltrane and Lennie Tristano favourites of musical modernists from both jazz and classical-music backgrounds. Many *aficionado*s of classical music have had more difficulty accepting the riff-based approach of musicians such as Basie and Monk, whose artistic practice has seemed to argue that 'less is more'.

Riffing

Basie's 'Sent for You Yesterday' and Monk's 'Bag's Groove' provide two illustrations of the musical variety that can be achieved through means of the riff. There are four main ways in which riffs have been used in jazz improvisation: as melodies, in call-and-response, as continuous ostinato figures, and in layers. Eddie Durham's arrangement of 'Sent for You Yesterday' (a blues form) makes use of them all.[6] Fig. 7.3 illustrates the various uses of riffs in the arrangement. During the first chorus the melody is a riff played by the ensemble in call-and-response, with improvised fills from Earle Warren on alto saxophone. The second chorus reverses the order, with the improvised calls emanating from Basie's piano and the brass section answering with a riff. The third chorus features a solo by Herschel Evans on tenor saxophone, accompanied by a continuous riff figure (no space for an answer between repetitions) that adds an extra ostinato layer to the accompaniment. The final shout choruses of the arrangement illustrate the way in which different uses of the riff can be combined in layers. Chorus seven features the brass and reed sections trading riffs in call-and-response. The saxophone riff becomes a continuous ostinato layer in chorus eight, as the brass continues its riff in call-and-response with Jo Jones's solo drum fills.[7]

It is important to realise that riffs, unlike licks or patterns, serve to emphasise pitches shared between chords. Riffs generally serve to bridge across two or more harmonic changes rather than to emphasise the differences between them. As George Russell might put it, riffing takes a horizontal approach to harmony, as opposed to a vertical emphasis on expressing each

Intro.	Chorus 1 (0:11)	Chorus 2 (0:28)	Chorus 3 (0:43)
8 bars	12 bars	12 bars	12 bars
	Call and Response x 3	Call and Response x 3	Tenor sax solo
	Ensemble riff melody/Alto sax answer improvised	Piano call improvised / brass riff response	Continuous brass riff

Chorus 7 (2:04)	Chorus 8 (2:23)
12 bars	12 bars
Shout chorus, Call and Response x 3	Shout chorus, Call and Response x 3
Brass riff call/ Reed riff answer	Brass riff call/ drum solo answer
	Reed riff becomes continous riff layer

Fig. 7.3

Ex. 7.6

Led into by two bars of
triplets/semiquavers

Transcribed by I. Monson

individual chord change.[8] As such, riffs often serve both to sustain a tonal
area shared by more than one chord change and bring the rhythmic and
interactive dimensions of a phrase to the foreground.

Monk's solo on 'Bag's Groove' illustrates the importance of the riff as
a developmental resource in jazz melody.[9] In virtually every chorus Monk
begins with a riff that serves as a basis for variation throughout the remainder
of the chorus (Ex. 7.6). The first three choruses begin with riff figures that
emphasise progressively smaller note values: crotchets and quavers in chorus
two, triplet quavers in chorus two, and semiquavers in chorus three (6:47–
7:42).[10] The fourth chorus presents a riff in block voicings, while the fifth
and sixth choruses thematically develop a single riff. Monk's solo leaves a
great deal of space in the musical texture, illustrating that it is possible to
say a great deal with very few notes.

Stylistic diversity

In the late 1950s and early 1960s jazz musicians expanded the boundaries of the music in many ways: borrowing rhythmic feels from African-Caribbean and African music, exploring modal approaches to improvisation, experimenting with open-ended improvisational forms (moving away from chorus structures), developing harmonic voicings capable of expressing more than one chord, using non-duple metres, introducing non-western instruments and timbres into the music and exploring avant-garde means of expression. Charles Mingus's 'Pithecanthropus Erectus' (1956) provides an early example of an open-ended form which accommodated solos of variable length. A two-bar 'vamp' (an ostinato alternating between two chords) repeats for the duration of the solo, which is at the player's discretion. In this piece Mingus moves freely from 4/4 to 6/4 metre and back, and encourages the band to interject collective cries and shrieks at climactic points of the solo.

Bill Evans and McCoy Tyner developed piano voicings that have become essential knowledge for the modern jazz pianist. Evans developed the now ubiquitous rootless left-hand voicings, and Tyner demonstrated the tonal possibilities of voicings built on the interval of the fourth.[11] Tyner often used these voicings to construct the hypnotic vamps so central to his work with Coltrane. Open-ended improvisational structures and the simpler harmonic progressions of modal tunes (which often preserved chorus structures) tended to free the rhythm section to interact more intensely with the soloist. The recordings of the John Coltrane quartet and the Miles Davis quintet of the early to mid-1960s provide the best examples of this emerging aesthetic.[12]

Free jazz

A major aesthetic controversy erupted in the jazz world in early 1960 when alto saxophonist Ornette Coleman emerged on the New York scene. Coleman's dissonant harmonic style and abandonment of chorus structures and fixed harmonic changes as means of organising improvisational flow was claimed by some as *The Shape of Jazz to Come* (the title of Coleman's first album after his arrival in New York, recorded in 1959), by others as the destruction of jazz, and by some championed as a music of social critique. Over the next seven years an aesthetic community of jazz musicians, committed to what was variously termed 'free jazz', the 'New Thing' or 'avant-garde' jazz, emerged in New York. Among them were Coleman, Cecil Taylor, Albert

Ayler, Archie Shepp, Sun Ra and Coltrane. Coltrane's turn towards free jazz gave considerable prestige to the burgeoning free-jazz movement. The new approach also fostered the creation of collective musical organisations such as Chicago's Association for the Advancement of Creative Musicians (1965) and later St Louis's Black Artists Group (1968).

Among the greatest champions of free jazz as a political music was playwright, poet and critic LeRoi Jones (Amiri Baraka) whose *Blues People* (1963) viewed free jazz as the logical outcome of the black musician's centuries of struggle with racism in America. For many free-jazz artists, however, the political dimension of free-jazz expression was a by-product of its spiritual implications. For Ayler, Coltrane and Sun Ra, spiritual communion through avant-garde expression was a primary motivation for their expressive choices. Ayler's work drew heavily upon the African-American gospel and folk traditions, turning familiar hymn melodies into abstract wails and pleas of deep emotional intensity. Both Coltrane and Sun Ra were drawn to non-western modes of spirituality. Both men were widely read in spiritual traditions from locations as far-ranging as Africa, India, China and the Middle East. Sun Ra's aesthetic appealed to both ancient Egypt and outer space as metaphors for liberation and spiritual depth. Critics of free jazz failed to see 'progress' in the atonality and indefinite time feels of the music. They viewed the avant-garde as a decline, brought on by young musicians who 'didn't do their homework' or pay their dues in the tradition.

Fusion

Miles Davis's *Bitches Brew* (1969) augured a new direction for jazz in the 1970s, one that embraced rather than rejected popular musical styles. Widely heralded for its creative synthesis of jazz improvisation and rhythm-and-blues, *Bitches Brew* embraced electrified rock time feels, as well as many of the post-production techniques of popular music, including overdubbing and looping. Davis was particularly inspired by guitarist Jimi Hendrix, who was able to reach a broad audience with his creative guitar pyrotechnics. Later, Davis's fusion interests turned towards soul and funk in an effort to reach a younger African-American audience. His albums, *A Tribute to Jack Johnson* (1970) and *On the Corner* (1972), illustrate this trend. Several other bands, offering various mixes of jazz, rock, soul, rhythm-and-blues and non-western musics, emerged in the 1970s – including most prominently Weather Report, John McLaughlin's Mahavishnu Orchestra, Herbie Hancock's Headhunters and Chick Corea's Return to Forever.

Lincoln Center

By the early 1980s, many young jazz musicians found greater inspiration in the 'golden' age of modern jazz (*c*. 1945–65) than in much of the contemporary offerings of fusion and avant-garde. Trumpeter Wynton Marsalis made no secret of his disappointment in jazz of the early 1980s, passionately advocating a return to basic jazz values (e.g., making the changes and swinging) through studying the classic recordings of such masters as Art Blakey, Davis, Coltrane, Monk and Ellington. Marsalis's outspoken criticism of the jazz avant-garde and Davis's most recent fusion efforts polarised older jazz listeners who cast Marsalis as an aesthetic conservative and latter-day 'Mouldy Fig'. Marsalis nevertheless inspired and nurtured a group of young musicians who later became known as the Young Lions, among them trumpeters Roy Hargrove and Terence Blanchard, drummer Jeff 'Tain' Watts, bassist Christian McBride, and pianists Marcus Roberts and Cyrus Chestnut. Marsalis's prominent success in both jazz and classical music made him the ideal figure to actualise a longstanding dream: that some day jazz be treated as equal in stature to classical music, and accorded an institutional home. In 1988 the Jazz at Lincoln Center programme, dedicated to advancing jazz through performance, education and preservation, was launched with Marsalis as its artistic director. Marsalis organised the Lincoln Center Jazz Orchestra, and in the 1990s Lincoln Center offered a highly acclaimed series of jazz concerts and educational events, often devoted to the repertory of particular jazz figures such as Ellington.

Critics of the Lincoln Center have often decried the narrowness of Marsalis's programming decisions, objecting to his neglect of the avant-garde in jazz, his failure to commission more adventurous jazz compositions and his tendency to feature his own works over those of others. This 'left-wing' of critical opinion, which aims to retain the tradition of social criticism and musical experimentation in jazz, has found a leader in clarinettist Don Byron. Byron's more eclectic jazz series at the Brooklyn Academy of Music has been viewed as an alternative to the Lincoln Center.

As always the key elements of improvisation, syncopation, swing, blues feeling, call-and-response organisation and harmonic complexity are invoked to justify and defend one aesthetic perspective over another. Two of the key musical issues serving to divide different aesthetic constituencies are the rhythmic feel (groove) and the use of electronic instruments. To many critics of Davis's post-fusion music, his use of rock and funk grooves, synthesisers and electric guitars are sins that cannot be forgiven. These feels and instruments, for many jazz *aficionado*s, mark the music as more commercial than either the avant-garde or Lincoln Center. Musicians in the early years of the twenty-first century are now debating the admissibility of hip-hop feels into the family of acceptable grooves over which jazz improvisation can take place. Musicians as diverse as Steve Coleman, Kenny Garret, Cassandra Wilson and Don Byron have been exploring the boundary between jazz and hip-hop with interesting results. Despite the differences in aesthetic emphasis in various styles of jazz, the dialogue between the heterogeneous sound ideal and (post)modernism promises to continue unabated into the future.

8 Spontaneity and organisation

PETER J. MARTIN

'Improvisation', wrote Gunther Schuller in his groundbreaking study, *Early Jazz*, 'is the heart and soul of jazz' (1968, 58). Yet, as Bruce Johnson points out elsewhere (see Chapter 6), improvisation is only one of the distinctive elements of the music, and indeed Schuller immediately qualifies his assertion by pointing out that improvisation is also an essential ingredient of other folk and popular musical traditions. Even more to the point, improvisation is not a major ingredient in many celebrated jazz recordings. Louis Armstrong's classic 'Cornet Chop Suey' of 1926 was copyrighted almost as recorded (and in the trumpeter's own hand) more than two years earlier (Gushee in Nettl and Russell 1998, 298–9). Duke Ellington's 'Concerto for Cootie' of 1940 was described as a 'masterpiece' by another pioneering analyst, André Hodeir, yet one of the characteristics of the piece is 'the elimination of improvisation' (Hodeir 1956, 77). As the recorded evidence shows, other renowned soloists can be heard to repeat familiar solos in all essential respects, and over considerable periods of time (Berliner 1994, 240). As Armstrong himself put it: 'always, once you get a certain solo that fit in the tune, and that's it, you keep it. Only vary it two or three notes every time you play it' (quoted by Gushee in Nettl and Russell 1998, 313). Across the stylistic spectrum, too, performances have been praised mainly because they achieve the elusive quality of 'swing' (see Keil 1995), or when melodies are simply embellished but where the player's instrumental tone – as on *Clifford Brown with Strings* (1955) – is judged to be particularly expressive. Only the pedantic, however, would disqualify these and many other pieces from acceptance as jazz on the grounds that they lack a substantially improvised component.

The presence or absence of such a component, then, will not do as a distinctive criterion in determining what is, or is not, jazz. On the other hand, as Schuller suggests, neither will it do to minimise the importance of improvisation: the iconic figures of the music, from Armstrong and Bechet to Parker, Coleman and Coltrane, have been recognised above all for their abilities as improvisers, and even Ellington, whose reputation rests largely on his composing and arranging, was a distinctive piano soloist (who had a direct influence on Thelonious Monk, among others). Moreover, whatever the particular mixture of musical elements in a jazz performance, it is in the *practice* of improvisation – not rhythm, nor melody, nor harmony – that jazz differs most clearly from established procedures in the tradition of western art music. Indeed, some of the most interesting aspects of jazz as a music, as well as some of the most intractable difficulties affecting its reception, are highlighted in drawing this contrast, since we are inevitably led to consider not only the music in its technical aspects, but the distinctive character of what Becker (1982) terms the 'art world' in which its players and their performances are embedded.

In the present chapter, the concept of the art world will be used as a basic approach to understanding jazz improvisation as an organised, collaborative social practice occurring in the context of a specific artistic community. In approaching the subject in this way, it is possible to move beyond the remarkably tenacious, yet quite erroneous, view of the improviser as an inspired individual guided only by intuition and, in addition, to supplement psychological studies of improvisation by recontextualising the musicians and their performances. Moreover, even a cursory examination of the specific culture of the art worlds in which jazz players operate shows the fundamental importance of performance practice in the aesthetics of these groups, in marked contrast, for example, to the central position occupied by the composition of works in the European art-music tradition. With this in mind, it may be argued that, while jazz musicians have made contributions to music in a wide variety of ways, their greatest achievements have been the restoration of improvisation to the mainstream of western musical culture (see Peretti 1992, 112–13), and the creation of an art world in which the practice of improvisation is the musicians' fundamental commitment.

Irrespective of styles, unplanned self-expression is not, typically, what happens in jazz performances. As Albert Murray put it:

> no matter how deeply moved a musician may be, whether by personal, social or even aesthetic circumstances, he must always play notes that fulfill the requirements of the context, a feat that presupposes far more skill and taste than raw emotion ... Indeed on close inspection what was assumed to have been unpremeditated art is likely to have been a matter of conditioned reflex, which is nothing other than the end product of discipline, or in a word training.   [1976, 98]

Years earlier, Ralph Ellison had identified the essential paradox in speaking of 'true jazz' as 'an act of individual assertion within and against the group ... because jazz finds its very life in improvisation upon traditional materials, the jazz man must lose his identity even as he finds it' (1964, 234). Or in the words of Wynton Marsalis: 'It's a very structured thing that comes down from a tradition and requires a lot of thought and study' (quoted in Berliner 1994, 63). In the present context, it is the appearance of terms such as 'context', 'training', 'group' and 'tradition' that is of particular significance, suggesting the possibility of a sociological, as opposed to a purely psychological, approach to the understanding of improvisational practices.

Jazz as an 'art world'

In developing the concept of the art world, the sociologist Howard Becker is concerned to illuminate the cultural practices and institutional constraints that become established in any field of creative activity (see Becker 1974 and 1982, and Gilmore 1990). But Becker's purpose is not simply to reveal the features of the 'social context' of any process of artistic production (though these may be important); rather, the point is to demonstrate the ways in which such patterns of social organisation must be recognised as themselves having an effect on what gets created – what gets made, written, painted or played, and the ways in which it is done. As in other areas of social life, people engaged in artistic activities are seen as orienting themselves to recognised 'conventions' concerning what it is proper and appropriate for them to do – without this, no effective collective action would be possible (see Peter J. Martin 1995, 172ff.). As often as not, the conventions that are established in a particular art world are simply taken for granted as 'the way things are' by the participants, and consequently regarded as trivial or the common sense that 'everyone knows'. Yet, in bringing them to light, funda-mental features of the art world are revealed, since it is the orientations of individuals to such socially accepted conventions that constitute the links between them and the wider artistic community. This may be illustrated by considering the concept of performance 'style' in jazz (or any other music). From an art-world perspective, musical styles are to be understood as the inevitable configurations of conventions that guide performance practice; different styles of jazz – such as New Orleans, Dixieland, big band, bebop, fusion – are distinguished by particular conventions concerning instrumen-tation, repertoire, ensemble playing, the role of the soloist, rhythm and so on, right down to the fine details of performance practice. Within such styles, moreover, there may be different 'schools' of playing, as, for example, when musicians display their affinity to influential mentors. Once made, the point seems obvious, even trivial – yet in the present context it is quite fundamental, since it suggests some of the ways in which jazz musicians, op-erating within an art world that values musical creativity and self-expression above all else, are nevertheless guided and constrained in what they do by the normative conventions of the musical community to which they belong. We are dealing, in short, with the relationship between individual inspiration and the expectations of the collectivity in which it must be expressed.

As is well known, people involved in particular art worlds often form a deep attachment to specific ways of doing things, and a highly developed aesthetic sense which is related to them: the conventions of a particular musical style, for example, as well as habitual ways of playing in it, and a highly developed sense of musical rightness or wrongness, can become unconscious, embodied aspects of a player's taken-for-granted reality. In fact, as is also well known, many supremely capable musicians become relatively inarticulate when it comes to explaining why they do what they do – making remarks about how 'it felt right' or 'it just didn't work' and so on. For Becker, much of the explanation lies in the fact that 'editorial' decisions about what to do during the creative process have become 'acts rather than choices', as conventionally sanctioned ways of doing things are internalised: 'in those moments of simultaneous feeling and thinking what is being thought consists of a continual dialogue with the world relevant to the choices being made. The editorial and creative moment fuse in a dialogue with an art world' (Becker 1982, 204).

An important implication is that in order to become recognised as a capable performer, the aspiring jazz player will find it necessary not only to acquire the necessary high level of technical skills, but also to become immersed in the culture of this particular art world. And as Paul Berliner brilliantly shows in *Thinking in Jazz* (1994), this is just how things work in the jazz community. This authoritative study will be considered further below, but at this point it is worth simply noting some of the ways in which its results are consistent with Becker's art-world perspective: Berliner places particular emphasis on the ways in which jazz musicians acquire the culture of, and operate within, specific artistic communities with their own aesthetics and patterns of organisation, and the ways in which such communities may exert an influence on individuals' musical performances, their sense of self and their lifestyles in general. In contrast to many purely musicological analyses, Berliner is concerned to relate the details of performances to the social context in which they occur, and to emphasise the interactional, collaborative nature of jazz playing. By replacing performers in their social milieu, Berliner also goes beyond those studies which have approached improvisation from the perspective of cognitive psychology (e.g., Pressing in Sloboda 1988). Such investigations may ultimately reveal much about *how* music is played, but it may be suggested that studies such as Berliner's, and an art-world perspective more generally, may be more revealing about *what* gets played.

It is immediately apparent that the art worlds within which jazz musicians develop and practise their craft contrast in significant ways with those of classical (or rock) players. Whereas, for example, classical trumpet players are trained to produce a 'pure' tone (which would be very similar to others in an orchestral setting), jazz players will be encouraged to develop a recognisably individual sound, which, if achieved, may be regarded as evidence of originality and emotional depth. Further, while the classical player will tend to be rewarded for performances that act mainly as a medium for the realisation of a composer's putative 'intentions', jazz musicians (although nowadays expected to possess excellent reading and ensemble skills) strive above all to achieve an individual 'voice', and it is this attainment of a distinct, recognisable musical identity that is most highly valued in the jazz community. The process of acquiring the necessary skills, too, has been very different in the two musical worlds. While almost all classical players are trained from an early age in colleges and universities, with highly formalised programmes of instruction and examination, at least until the 1970s, most jazz musicians acquired their skills informally, through professional experience 'on the job', through studying privately with established performers, through immersion in a strong oral tradition in which knowledge of the music is passed on, and in collaboration with other aspiring musicians. (Since then, however, formal jazz courses have become an increasingly important aspect of music education in the USA, with implications which will be considered further below.[1])

Despite its informal pattern of organisation, the jazz world is highly centralised: since the 1940s, New York City – 'the world's largest jazz community' (Berliner 1994, 5) – has been recognised as the 'scene' where players must establish themselves if they are to be acknowledged as top performers. Whereas in the classical music world, performance standards are maintained through formal training and examination, the development of jazz musicians – though no less rigorous – is subject to the scrutiny of established elders in the jazz community and final recognition is only granted once a player has convinced these master performers of his or her capabilities. Here again it should be emphasised that the central figure in the jazz art world is not the composer of 'works' but the improvising soloist. This is a point that, although often not fully grasped by those who are schooled in the ways of other performance traditions, is of quite fundamental importance for an understanding of jazz as an art world, with far-reaching implications for its organisation, its aesthetic priorities and the activities of its members. To repeat, the primary aim of jazz musicians is not the production of 'works', but the creation of performances.

An understanding of the undoubted creativity and spontaneity of jazz playing thus requires that any particular instance is set in the context of the expectations of what Stanley Fish terms a particular 'interpretive community', whose conventions serve to guide the improviser's artistic decisions. Yet to avoid one possible source of misunderstanding, it should be emphasised that the art-world perspective does not entail an undue emphasis on conformity at the expense of innovation. Indeed, as Becker puts it: 'Every art work creates a world in some respects unique, a combination of vast amounts of conventional materials with some that are innovative. Without the first, it becomes unintelligible; without the second, it becomes boring and featureless' (Becker 1982, 63).

However, as Lester Young, Charlie Parker, John Coltrane and Ornette Coleman (among others) discovered, there may be a high price to pay in the pursuit of innovations that are perceived to threaten established conventions. Radical innovators, however talented, are likely at first to be marginalised or condemned as incompetent, and almost inevitably attract the hostility of those whose sense of security – musical, psychological or economic – is derived from their acceptance of the aesthetic status quo. Though it would be unwise to push the parallel too far, the succession of improvisatory styles in jazz thus displays some of the characteristics of the development of scientific thought as presented by Thomas Kuhn (1970; see also DeVeaux 1997, 42ff.). In both science and jazz, a high value is attached to creative thinking and the production of new ideas. Yet, Kuhn argues, most scientists, for most of the time, work quite productively and creatively within the constraints of a particular 'paradigm' – a general framework of assumptions and beliefs which holds the scientific community together. Revolutionary transformations in thinking – 'paradigm shifts' – take place relatively rarely and are experienced as periods of conflict and disruption, with a small number of individuals becoming identified as inspiring large-scale movements of thought. Just as Kuhn spoke of 'normal science' as characterising what most scientists do most of the time, so it seems appropriate in the present context to speak of 'normal' improvisatory practices, in the sense that most players, most of the time, while motivated by the goals of self-expression and finding their own 'voice', nevertheless operate within an accepted framework of stylistic conventions that both influences their artistic choices and provides a foundation for what they do.

The concept of improvisation

Improvisation now plays little or no part in the dominant art-music tradition of western societies, although this has only been the case in relatively recent times (see Chapter 9). A full discussion of the demise of the improviser is beyond the scope of this chapter; for present purposes, the essential point is that since the mid-nineteenth century the art world of 'serious' music has been organised around the composition of 'works' and their performance in formal concert settings, and the identification of a 'canon' of 'masterworks' produced by the great composers (see W. Weber 1992). One of the effects of these processes has been the consequent devaluation and marginalisation of improvisation in much of the discourse of 'classical' music: it has generally been regarded as a 'somewhat mystical art' (Tirro 1974, 285), but not one which could or should be incorporated into established performance conventions or aesthetic theories. Indeed, Derek Bailey suggests that the term 'improvisation' has acquired largely negative connotations among orthodox musicians as 'something without preparation and without consideration, a completely *ad hoc* activity, frivolous and inconsequential, lacking in design and method' (1980, 5). Since these words were written, there have been clear signs of reappraisal and a reawakening of interest in improvisation among music scholars, doubtless encouraged by their increasing interest in jazz more generally; yet, in introducing a recent collection of essays on the topic, Nettl still found it necessary to observe that 'within the realm of art music, improvisation is on a low rung, just as musics outside the realm of art music are often associated with the inferior practice of improvisation' (Nettl and Russell 1998, 9).

Where the practice of improvisation has been discussed, and often in consideration of the great jazz players of the twentieth century, it has tended to be seen as a gift bestowed on a few exceptional individuals. It has certainly not been regarded as part of the normal skill-set of 'trained' musicians, whereas reading (or better still, sight-reading) from notated music is a *sine qua non* of competence. Once again, it might appear as though this is simply a statement of the obvious: this is what is taken for granted in the world of 'serious' music. Yet one of the most interesting aspects of this situation is how unusual it is, when seen from the perspective of music cultures more generally. Indeed, for Max Weber, the degree to which western music had become 'rationalised' rendered it unique (1930, 15). Improvisation is an important aspect of the musical cultures of many societies (see Nettl and Russell 1998), and, of particular importance in the present context, improvised elements occur in all the styles of African-American music that have been increasingly influential in the western world during the second half of the twentieth century. From a cross-cultural perspective, then, the ability to improvise is not usually regarded as the special gift of a particularly talented individual; on the contrary, it is this belief itself that is exceptional.

In one sense, of course, there is an improvised element to all musical performance. Even the rank-and-file orchestral player confronted by a score must 'play', in the sense of making the sounds happen, and even the most detailed score allows some scope for 'interpretation'. (Indeed, all social interactions, such as conversations, are improvised in the sense that we do not – other than on ritual occasions – speak from scripts. The routine encounters that constitute social life must be *enacted*.) So what is at stake, then, is not the principle of improvisation, but the extent to which individuals have autonomy within the context of particular performance traditions (and, as we shall see, the conditions affecting such autonomy). The specific skills required for musical improvisation may be regarded, not as exceptional, but as normal and achievable in appropriate cultural contexts. This does not imply that in such settings everyone will become a skilled improviser, any more than that, in western societies, all children will become capable composers. The important point is that *in principle* a practical capacity for improvisation may be achieved, just as people of varying initial abilities usually manage, with practice, to ride bicycles and drive cars. What is crucial here is the extent to which individuals' expectations and aspirations are shaped by their cultural environment. As Berliner has put it: 'children who grow up around improvisers regard improvisation as a skill within the realm of their own possible development. In the absence of this experience, many view improvisation as beyond their ability' (1994, 31). Thus children in black American communities, however disadvantaged in other respects, have often been immersed in a cultural milieu that values both linguistic and musical improvisation, and affords prolonged exposure to the 'complex rhythmic juxtapositions, cadences, timbres, body movements and so on' that are characteristic of African-American music. It is this cultural factor, argues Kofsky, and not any alleged 'racial memory' or innate qualities, that can explain the pre-eminence of black musicians as jazz innovators (1998, 137).

I have suggested that the widely held view of improvisational ability as a gift possessed by a few exceptional individuals is a myth, the prevalence of which is related to the marginalisation of improvisation in the western art-music tradition. Indeed the fallacy of the basic premise is demonstrated by the number and variety of musical cultures in which improvisation is a normal element. At this point, however, it remains to dispose of another, related, myth. Kernfeld has put the matter succinctly: 'Somehow the casual and romantic notion that jazz is generated in an entirely spontaneous manner has become deeply rooted in our society' (1995, 99). Indeed, insofar as they have considered it at all, music scholars have often assumed that improvisation involved what Nettl called 'unpremeditated, spur-of-the-moment decisions' made in the 'suddenness of the creative impulse' (1974, 3). Nettl goes on to argue, however, that this view is misconceived – that the conventional distinction between composition and improvisation is not sustainable, and that improvisers in all musical cultures are oriented in their performances by a learned 'model' which serves as a guide to practical action. For Small, such a model is indispensable, since the spontaneity and creativity which are, rightly, taken to be characteristic of the accomplished improviser must nevertheless be set within the context of a musical culture with its own conventions and constraints. As he puts it: 'both improvised speaking and improvised musicking take place within a framework of rules. Neither is uncontrolled invention – indeed it is doubtful if the human mind is capable of such a thing – and both feed off a great deal of pre-existing material . . . musical responses will always be governed to a greater or lesser extent by the demands of the idiom' (Small 1984, 3, 4). In the present context, what is significant about the remarks of both Nettl and Small is not so much their dismissal of the idea of improvisation as unpremeditated (a notion that even a moment's serious reflection would show to be absurd), but – once again – their use of terms such as 'model', 'culture', 'framework of rules' and 'idiom'. For it is in the use of such terms that the practice of improvisation is revealed as collaborative and collectively organised, a social matter as much as a psychological one, in which the impulses and aspirations of individuals must somehow be reconciled with the configuration of normative conventions that confronts them. With this in mind, we may return to the art world of the jazz musician, and specifically to studies that have illuminated the model of performance practice to which the improvising player must attend.

Thinking in Jazz

Although the literature on jazz and its players has grown enormously in recent years, relatively little of it is concerned with actual musical practices, so the appearance of Paul Berliner's *Thinking in Jazz: The Infinite Art of Improvisation* in 1994 was something of a landmark. In this book Berliner reports the results of his meticulous ethnomusicological investigation of the jazz community in New York City. The account is structured so as to reflect the lengthy and rigorous process that players must go through if they are to acquire the necessary skills to perform at the highest level, and – of equal importance – if they are to achieve recognition from established performers. In contrast to the art world of the classical musician, most apprenticeships are organised through informal networks of players, as is the process through which bands and groups are formed and musicians recruited to them. In the present context, Berliner's title is particularly significant, as he demonstrates the ways in which the 'thinking' of improvising jazz musicians is shaped and influenced by the ethos of the jazz community in general and the particular networks of players in which individuals are involved. Just as socio-linguistic studies have shown how the function and meaning of language are dependent on the activities – and normative authority – of 'speech communities', so Berliner demonstrates how jazz players are socialised into accepting the values and performance practices of the wider community of players. Creativity and self-expression are central values in this community, but – and this is the point that must be emphasised – in order for players' efforts to be considered as aesthetically valid, or even competent, they must orient their practices to a specific set of musical conventions that represents, and constitutes, the performance tradition. This does not mean simply accepting such conventions; what is involved is a process of engagement with them. As Berliner puts it: 'from the outset an artist's ongoing personal performance history entwines with jazz's artistic tradition, allowing for a mutual absorption and exchange of ideas' (1994, 59).

It is this set of conventions, or what Berliner terms 'the formal structures of jazz', that constitutes the model, in Nettl's sense, with which improvisers work. In very general terms, an improvised 'solo' must conform in acceptable ways to the harmonic progression and formal structure of the piece (indicated by using the widely accepted system of chord symbols), which must normally retain a constant rhythmic pulse. There is, moreover, a standard repertoire of pieces in each jazz style that competent performers are expected to 'know' (in the sense of memorising both melody and harmonic changes), and a number of pieces generally recognised as suitable tests of a player's capabilities (such as the standards 'Body and Soul' and 'Cherokee', or John Coltrane's 'Giant Steps'). Though the principles of the model are simply enough explained, the acquisition of jazz performance skills is both musically and intellectually demanding, and Berliner documents the many ways in which aspiring players study, practise (alone and with others) and more generally immerse themselves in the ways of the jazz community. Typically, Berliner suggests, musicians will only achieve recognition as capable performers after 'seven to ten years of attention to the stringent routines . . . required for basic competency in jazz improvisation' (*ibid.*, 494).

Far from representing the free play of individual creativity, then, the jazz player's musical statements are tightly constrained by the demands of the model. In fact, from the perspective of the elders of the community, the extent to which a player can develop an aesthetically satisfactory synthesis of established conventions and personal expression is itself the supreme measure of aesthetic merit. Iconic figures are those such as Armstrong, Parker and Coltrane, whose musical imagination has been sufficiently powerful to transform the tradition from within; Berliner refers to 'the dynamic interplay between tradition and innovation within the jazz community as improvisers transform its musical conventions and imbue them with deep personal meaning' (92). Armstrong, Parker and Coltrane each inspired a host of followers, even imitators, as succeeding players sought to express themselves through the musical languages pioneered by these towering influences. Indeed, as in every other musical field, the great majority of players are not great innovators, seeking mostly to develop their own distinctive approach while accepting the constraints of the underlying musical model. Initially, this very often involves efforts to emulate a chosen mentor (see also Bailey 1980, 69).

It should also be emphasised that achieving an acceptable standard of performance is not simply a matter of obeying the rules in a technical sense, as the following account, taken from Berliner, illustrates. The pianist, Barry Harris, was conducting one of his widely renowned workshops for learners:

> At a fifth student's performance . . . he shook his head and remarked, 'No, you wouldn't do that in this music.' Stung by the rebuke, the student defended himself: 'But you said to follow the rule you gave us, and this phrase follows the rule.' 'Yes,' Harris admitted, 'but you still wouldn't play a phrase like that.' 'But give me one good reason why you wouldn't,' the student protested. 'The only reason I can give you,' Harris replied, 'is that I have been listening to this music for over forty years now, and my ears tell me that that phrase would be wrong to play. You just wouldn't do it in this tradition. Art is not science, my son.' The student left the workshop early that evening, not to return for months. [1994, 249]

The episode nicely captures some of the points that are relevant here. First, there is the evident authority of Harris, the acknowledged master performer and the student's mentor. Second, it is apparent that this authority is brought to bear on the finest nuances of the student's playing and, third, that it is concerned not only with matters of technical correctness but with questions of stylistic appropriateness that can only be decided on the basis of prolonged experience of the musical community and its expectations. It is clear that what is being communicated to these neophyte improvisers are ways of shaping performance practices – even in their most detailed aspects – that are dictated neither by musical requirements, nor by individuals' creative energies, but by the norms and values of an established 'interpretive community'. As with language more generally, and indeed all social interactions, the interests and idiosyncrasies of individuals must somehow be reconciled with an existing 'form of life' (Wittgenstein 1953, 11).

Ingrid Monson has drawn out some of the implications of the recognition that jazz improvisation must be understood as embedded in the culture of a 'community of interpreters' (1994, 305), emphasising that, as in other African-American cultural traditions, performances are shaped through an interaction between musicians and audiences who share an aesthetic frame of reference that allows them to make sense, and take a critical view, of what is being played. Monson also emphasises that the actual contents of performances are the outcome of ongoing interaction among the musicians; that is, they are fundamentally collaborative in a way in which (pre)composed western 'classical' music is not (1996, 74). As a consequence of these conventions, it may often be quite inappropriate to isolate the contribution of one individual for the purposes of analysis, or to treat the outcome as a 'text' similar to a composed score (*ibid.*, 80). Indeed, an important implication of Monson's examination of the interactive nature of jazz performances is the conclusion that analyses that restrict themselves to the notated 'text' can only yield a partial view of any music: 'the formal features of musical texts are just one aspect – a subset, so to speak – of a broader sense of the musical, which also includes the contextual and the cultural'; a deeper understanding of music, Monson suggests, will require the development of an 'interactive, relational theory of music and meaning' that will transcend the arbitrary distinction between musical structures and cultural contexts (*ibid.*, 186, 190). This theme cannot be pursued here, but its importance is evident in any attempt to examine the performance style of jazz players in the context of the art worlds in which they were situated. For present purposes, the career of Charlie Parker may serve as one brief illustration.

Charlie Parker

The alto saxophonist Charlie Parker was recognised as an outstanding musician by his contemporaries and associates, and by countless more who have only heard his playing on recordings. His work inspired a whole school of followers amongst saxophonists, and he was a major influence on players of all instruments. Indeed, Gary Giddins has argued that he was 'the only jazzman since Louis Armstrong whose innovations demanded a comprehensive reassessment of all the elements of jazz' (in Woideck 1998, 5). Yet it is clear from what is known of his musical development that he did not emerge as a fully fledged virtuoso. On the contrary, as a teenager he was regarded as the 'saddest' member of one of the first bands he was in (*ibid.*, 136), and is known to have experienced public humiliation on at least two occasions following his efforts to perform with established players. On one of these, probably in 1936, Count Basie's drummer, Jo Jones, threw a cymbal across the floor in protest at Parker's efforts (R. Russell 1973, 83–5). Such episodes are the stuff of legend, yet in the present context they may serve to illustrate two points. First, the laughter and contempt that the young Parker endured give some indication of the informal, yet highly effective, ways in which the community of established players sought to uphold accepted technical and aesthetic standards. Second, by his own account Parker's inadequacies had much to do with his lack of the conventional knowledge that was taken for granted within such communities, from the etiquette surrounding when and with whom to 'sit in', to the fundamental musical knowledge of appropriate repertoire, keys, harmonic progressions and so on (see, for example, Woideck 1998, 93).

In other words, for all his immense talent, Parker – like any other aspiring jazz player – had to work extremely hard to achieve mastery of both his instrument and the musical model on which conventional improvisation was based. In 1937 he accepted a summer job with George E. Lee's band up in the Ozark mountains primarily because it afforded the chance to practise and study: he learned to play several of Lester Young's recorded solos note-for-note, and studied harmonic progressions with the guitarist, Efferge Ware. When he returned to Kansas City, said the bassist, Gene Ramey, 'the difference was unbelievable' (*ibid.*, 136; R. Russell 1973, 93). It seems that Parker subsequently modelled himself on Buster Smith, then a leading local saxophonist, and was soon accomplished enough to impress bandleader Jay McShann, who recalls Parker as practising exercises constantly at this time (Woideck 1998, 147, 140).

The details of Parker's meteoric musical career (and personal disintegration) will not be rehearsed here.[2] What I wish to emphasise are some of the ways in which Parker's difficult apprenticeship and later acceptance demonstrate the effectiveness of the jazz community, as an established art world, in shaping the expression of his undoubted, but unschooled, talent. In all fundamental respects, this process seems to have operated in Kansas City during the 1930s in much the same ways that Berliner documented in New York fifty years later. I have already noted the ways in which established musicians indicated their dismissal of the young Parker's perceived incompetence, his determination to overcome this and the intense, even obsessive efforts that he made to this end (Woideck 1998, 151). Moreover, it seems that he quite consciously sought to emulate the playing of Lester Young, which he learned from records, and Buster Smith, with whom he worked in 1937–8. Mentors such as these feature prominently in the biographies of virtually all jazz musicians. It should also be apparent that the apprenticeship process is not simply one of acquiring musical skills in a technical sense. Parker learned to improvise on the foundations of the musical material in common use in Kansas City in the mid-1930s – the 12-bar blues (in a quite restricted number of keys) and a selection of standards (such as 'I Got Rhythm', 'Honeysuckle Rose' and 'Cherokee') – and used this material as the basis of his repertoire for the remainder of his life (Owens 1995, 37–8). In all these ways, then, the young Parker was inculcated by his elders into the aesthetic values and musical conventions of an established, and rich, musical tradition, a tradition that – despite the radical consequences of his own work – he never challenged.

Of course, by the early 1940s, when his personal style was approaching maturity, Parker's playing was recognised by his peers, and several of the elders, as innovative and exceptional. There was an undeniable freshness about the unprecedented combination of his melodic inventiveness, harmonic sophistication, rhythmic poise, instrumental virtuosity and the clear sense of structure that is evident in his solos. At the same time, it is apparent that Parker's work, far from constituting a challenge to the jazz tradition as it was evolving, was in fact a fundamental contribution to its development. As Martin Williams has suggested, Parker's work represented 'a truly organic growth for jazz', rather than the 'spurious impositions of a self-consciously "progressive" jazzman', and his conclusion was that 'What Parker and bebop provided was a renewed musical language (or at least a renewed dialect) with which the old practices could be replenished and continued' (Woideck 1998, 13). In this, then, Parker reached the aesthetic summit of the jazz community – the reconciliation of tradition and innovation in a personal style, the seamless integration of conventional and individual elements.

So Parker's achievements, far from representing a challenge to the conventions of the jazz musicians' art world, were based on his supreme mastery of them. A similar point could be made about Parker's collaborator, the trumpeter, Dizzy Gillespie – not initially a brilliant player, he became an instrumental virtuoso, a diligent student of harmony, and a master improviser (see Shipton 1999). Partly for this reason, of course, and partly because of his own remarkable inventiveness, Parker was perceived as 'something else' by contemporaries. As one of the great creative minds of jazz, Parker sounded distinct and original from his very earliest recordings. Thus, as Scott DeVeaux has argued, the 'gradual and altogether unexceptionable progression of musical style' was soon *perceived* as revolutionary, largely because the 'pace of evolutionary growth demanded of jazz at this juncture proved too brisk for the average listener to understand' (1997, 7). As the outcome of his explorations with Gillespie and others in their circle began to coalesce into the distinct bebop style (with Gillespie, as ever, aware of the benefits of suitably tantalising publicity), opposition – and a measure of conflict – began to emerge. All this is consistent with Becker's account of the likely effects of innovation on established artistic communities (1982, 306ff). For some listeners, the emergence of bebop simply emphasised the extent to which jazz had departed from the stylistic conventions associated with its origins, giving rise to the dispute between traditionalists and modernists, and adding impetus to the revival of the earlier New Orleans style. For many established musicians, the innovations and virtuosity of the bebop players were experienced as a real threat to their professional standing, both financially and aesthetically, so that 'older players of all colors reacted fiercely against the young innovators' (Peretti 1992, 200). In time, of course, the new musical language of bop became widely accepted as the basis for modern jazz in general and indeed in later decades was itself referred to as 'mainstream', often to differentiate it from jazz-rock and other forms of fusion (Owens 1995, 4; DeVeaux 1997, 2; Gioia 1997, 216).

It has been argued that Parker's improvisations cannot be understood as the unmediated expression of intuitive genius (indeed his initial efforts were perceived as simply incompetent), that the form of expression that he did develop was channelled and constrained by the conventions accepted by jazz players in 1930s Kansas City and that his ultimate pre-eminence as an innovator derived not from his rejection of these but his capacity to master and transcend them. It remains, briefly, to consider his distinctiveness as an improviser, in part because this serves to illuminate the process of improvisation more generally, and in part because it helps to dispel the notion that by focusing on conventions and constraints the art-worlds perspective somehow effaces the character of individual artists. In fact it is precisely because of their outstanding creativity that Parker and Armstrong have consistently been identified as the two supreme innovators whose influence was sufficient to transform the musical language of their day – and consequently the conventions of the jazz community – and whose work thus sets them apart from the vast majority of players. (In the more than half a century since Parker was in his prime, perhaps only Coltrane has approached his influence as an improvising soloist.)

Although recent authors, with the benefit of hindsight, have rightly emphasised the extent to which Parker's work had deep roots in the jazz tradition, there is no doubt that his playing seemed to many contemporaries to be radical and disturbing. Ellison, who heard Parker and the other bop pioneers at the legendary jam sessions at Minton's during the early 1940s, recalled their new music as

> a texture of fragments, repetitive, nervous, not fully formed; its melodic lines underground, secret and taunting; its riffs jeering – 'Salt Peanuts! Salt Peanuts!' – its timbres flat or shrill, with a minimum of thrilling vibrato, its rhythms were out of stride and seemingly arbitrary, its drummers frozen-faced introverts dedicated to chaos.   [1964, 203]

Moreover, this was intellectually demanding music, not the familiar, comfortable sounds that, as Ellison put it, 'give resonance to memory'. Indeed, as Thomas Owens has suggested, Parker's solos – despite their often breathtaking speed of execution – achieved a degree of 'internal logic and consistency' (1995, 35), a structural coherence, that only the greatest of players had previously attained. For Owens, this purposeful integration of elements was largely the result of Parker's habitual use of lengthy 'scalar descents', which underlie his fluctuating phrases and impart a sense of movement towards a definite goal: 'this scalar organisation is a device that he brought into jazz, for his predecessors' music does not contain it'. It was this 'system of improvisation' that allowed Parker to create great solos so consistently, and that was absorbed, consciously or otherwise, by his many followers (*ibid.*, 36).

Through his exhaustive analyses of Parker's work, Owens has done much to explicate the essential features of his style:

> Parker, like all important improvisers, developed a personal repertory of melodic formulas that he used in the course of improvising . . .
>   . . . he favored a certain repertory of formulas for the blues in B♭, a slightly different repertory for the blues in F, a much different one for *A Night in Tunisia* in D minor, and so on. Some phrases in his vocabulary came from swing, either unchanged or modified; others he created. But whether using borrowed or original melodic formulas, his way of combining and organising them was his own.   [*Ibid.*, 30]

Owens has identified sixteen such figures that form the basis of Parker's approach, with the most common short phrases each occurring, on average, 'once every eight or nine measures' in his improvisations (*ibid.*, 31). These are, so to speak, the conjunctions and prepositions of Parker's improvisational language, linking his more extended figures. One of the latter which Owens identifies is of particular interest, in that through it we can glimpse something of the way in which Parker transformed the tradition from within. In bars 55–7 of his famous solo on 'Shoe Shine Boy' (recorded on 9 November 1936), Lester Young played a phrase which reappears as the opening two bars of Parker's solo on Jay McShann's 'The Jumpin' Blues', recorded on 2 July 1942 (Buchmann-Møller 1990b, 4). The same phrase was then used by trumpeter Benny Harris as the opening of his theme 'Ornithology' (itself a contrafact on the chord changes of the standard 'How High the Moon'), which was recorded by Parker on 28 March 1946. In the early career of this little phrase, then, we can observe both Parker's creative appropriation of the work of one of his own mentors, and the way in which Parker's own figures and formulas were rapidly taken up by the 'modern' players of the day, contributing immensely to the codification of bebop as a musical language.

One further aspect of Parker's work, which Owens identifies, is of particular relevance to the present discussion. As the recordings of his live performances demonstrate, he was particularly fond of introducing quotations from the melodies of other pieces, so that to Ellison his solos 'added up to a dazzling display of wit, satire, burlesque, and pathos' (1964 [1967], 223). All this is testament – if it were needed – to Parker's dazzling imagination and matchless instrumental skills. Yet besides the introduction of humour, or a sudden change of mood, into a performance, some of Parker's quotations provide incontrovertible evidence of his profound immersion in the jazz tradition. In the fifth chorus of 'Cheryl' (a 12-bar blues in C), recorded at Carnegie Hall on Christmas Eve 1949, Parker produces an extraordinarily skilful paraphrase of Armstrong's celebrated introduction to 'West End Blues', recorded 21 years earlier. Exactly eight weeks later, during a performance taped at the St Nicholas Ballroom in New York on 18 February, Parker played another of his blues lines, 'Visa' (also in C). Once again, the 'West End Blues' introduction is paraphrased, only this time Parker plays the first part of Armstrong's line to complete his fourth chorus and uses most of the rest from the beginning of his fifth. Again, too, it is a brilliant and astonishing transposition, but beyond that it is also the clearest possible demonstration of the way in which Parker – widely perceived at the time as the arch-modernist – drew on the resources of the jazz tradition. For this is not simply a short quotation from some appropriate (or deliberately incongruous) pop song, but a quite complicated fragment which Parker – in the era before the availability of tape recorders – must have worked hard to master. It is tempting, but probably futile, to speculate on Parker's reasons for introducing this extract at a time when there was considerable animosity between certain traditional and modern elements in the jazz audience. What it does confirm is his deep roots in the tradition.

One further aspect of the 'West End Blues' quotation deserves comment. In the third and fourth choruses of his solo on 'Cheryl', prior to the quotation, Parker plays a series of figures which end on the off-beat prior to the third beat of every second bar. The drummer, Roy Haynes, soon picks up the pattern and plays the appropriate accents with Parker. Interestingly, a very similar pattern emerges on the 'Visa' performance, also prior to the quotation from Armstrong, only this time Haynes accents the first beat of every second bar, as well as the appropriate off-beat (as in a conga rhythm). This sort of evidence from tapes of Parker's live perfomances once again affords a fascinating glimpse of his improvisational method in mid-flight, so to speak. In both solos the conga-type rhythmic figures precede the Armstrong quotation, as if something in the former suggested the latter to him. Moreover, both are clearly routines, drawn from his repertoire of such devices, which his fellow musicians (on both occasions Haynes, pianist Al Haig, bassist Tommy Potter and trumpeter Red Rodney) recognise and respond to as part of the collaborative process of creating the performances. Indeed, such considerations may act as a reminder of the analytical limitations inherent in examining an improvisation independently of the context in which it was produced, and so neglecting the fact that, as Monson has put it, it must be understood as part of an 'interactive musical conversation in real-time performance' (1996, 185). Parker's brilliance may have ensured that his was the dominating voice in almost every group in which he played as an adult, yet his work was made possible only by that of others, and by the wider network of the jazz art world, with all its opportunities, challenges and constraints.

Even a very brief consideration of some aspects of Charlie Parker's career suggests the relevance of Becker's art-worlds perspective on cultural production: the ways in which Parker was informally but forcefully disciplined by the community of musicians, his intense motivation and dedicated practice, his learning from mentors, his acceptance of established perfomance conventions, his integration of innovations into the tradition, the opposition to his work by conservative elements, the formation of a self-conscious school of innovators, the codification of their style and its gradual acceptance into the mainstream, and so on. Above all, it should be apparent that this perspective is not concerned simply to document the cultural and institutional circumstances within which Parker performed – thus perpetuating the distinction between the 'art work' and its 'social context' – but to demonstrate the ways in which the former is shaped and constrained by the latter (and the arbitrary nature of the distinction itself).

It seems, too, that the art-worlds perspective may prove a fruitful basis for the investigation of further ways in which the 'editorial moments' (Becker 1982, 198ff.) when performers shape their solos are influenced by the context of their production. There is evidence, for example, that recordings made in a studio are likely to exhibit less risk-taking, and more signs of pre-planning, than those made by the same players in live performance, where the consequences of errors or accidents may be much less serious. Alternatively, soloists may work out ways of ensuring that the relatively brief time they have available to them on a recording still allows them to shine: even Parker's 'famous alto break' on 'A Night in Tunisia' (recorded at Radio Recorders Studios in Hollywood on 28 March 1946) appears to have been 'a precomposed, memorised phrase' since different takes of the piece reveal that Parker's break was 'virtually identical' on each (Owens 1995, 43). Conversely, many live recordings (including Parker's) often display a degree of exuberance, spontaneity and risk-taking that studio settings may inhibit. Indeed, it could be argued that not the least of the ways in which the conventions of the jazz world were changed by the modernism of Parker and his cohorts was to move players away from a conception of solos as more-or-less planned contributions intended to fit into a larger piece, and towards the idea of the solo as an extended personal statement. Of course, this process had been under way for some time, and – as DeVeaux has shown – many factors were involved, notably the institutionalisation of 'jam session' procedures, and the rise of small-group jazz. What is clear is that, after bebop, improvising soloists were firmly established at the centre of the jazz 'art world', and that Armstrong's advice to stick with 'a certain

solo that fit in the tune' was less and less heeded by the rising generation of
players.

Despite this increased emphasis on spontaneity and personal expression,
it has been the argument of this chapter that the art of the improviser is mis-
construed if it is still regarded as idiosyncratic, unpredictable or dependent
on flashes of inspiration. On the contrary, the art-worlds approach is particularly well equipped to investigate the way in which performers' decisions –
even down to the finest details – are shaped by their assessments of situa-
tional constraints, and the process through which they take into account the
expectations of others (P. J. Martin 1995, 192ff.). While the jazz solo is often
described as an act of self-expression, and while such a view may be used
to give aesthetic legitimation to jazz as a musical practice, it is none the less
the case that a variety of identifiable influences may bear upon the soloist in
the heat of the creative process. Deciding who the 'audience' is, for example,
is not a simple matter for either player or researcher. Is it the more-or-less
anonymous crowd on the other side of the stage lights, who may be roused
to appreciation with a few well-worn routines? Is it the other musicians in
the group, who may think little of this but will appreciate what they hear as
more genuinely creative work? Is it the bandleader, or the promoter, whose
musical opinions may be questionable, but whose approval is necessary for
future employment? Or is it some 'significant other' (a respected mentor,
or a lover perhaps) who is on hand at the time, or alternatively some other
'reference group' (Shibutani 1962) – perhaps of players who are not present,
but whose aesthetic ideals are respected? The point is that the player may
(or may not) take account of any of these in formulating a course of action
in performance, so that such influences are all possible contributors to the
shaping of the music that emerges.

As with all jazz players, then, the apparently uninhibited spontaneity of
Parker's solos was expressed through the organised conventions and situa-
tional constraints of the art world in which he found himself. Many conventions he accepted, others he transformed as a result of his own virtuosity and
remarkable creativity. But there was no sudden, unpremeditated flash of inspiration: rather, an intense and lengthy process of 'working on' the musical
materials available to him, from his teenage years well into his twenties. The
celebrated version of 'Ko Ko' (recorded on 26 September 1945), which
sounds as stunning now as ever, was the outcome of Parker's six-year exploration of its chord sequence – 'Cherokee' – and particularly its difficult
16-bar bridge section, so that over this period of time he had 'developed some
comfortable ways of moving through these chords' (Owens 1995, 39–40).
None of this should in any way be taken to diminish Parker's achievement –
even today the piece presents formidable problems for aspiring players – but
it is an indication of the way in which all capable players have over time

built up what Berliner (1994) calls a 'storehouse' of devices on which they can draw when constructing improvised solos. Similarly, Tirro (1974) has demonstrated the way in which players devise 'constructive elements', for example specific ways of negotiating unfamiliar harmonic progressions, which they employ in subsequent performances, and which may impart a distinctive, personal character to their work. As Berliner has observed, a jazz performance of a particular piece is very often just the latest realisation of work that has been in progress for a considerable time. Through the perpetual process of 'working on' material, players aim to ensure that their improvisations are well organised in a specifically musical sense; and, in making use of the conventions of a particular art world, they affirm their commitment to a pattern of social organisation that both facilitates and channels their self-expression.

There are striking similarities, then, between the jazz world of 1930s Kansas City, in which the young Parker struggled to find his voice, and that of New York in the 1980s, which Berliner explored in such fascinating detail. Increasingly since the 1970s, however, there have been profound changes in the jazz art world, as the informal apprenticeships of old have increasingly given way to formalised courses of study in colleges and universities (see Chapter 13). Already there have been dire warnings that the price of academic respectability – with its catalogue of canonic figures, standardised teaching methods and approved repertoire – may be the death of jazz as an individualistic, creative and spontaneous music (see, for example, A. Marquis 1998 and Tomlinson 1991). Such perils are real indeed. But before rushing to blame the educators for snuffing out the golden age of individualism, we should reflect that the social institutions that made such an age possible – the dance halls, nightclubs, theatres, bars and cafés and their jam sessions, radio shows, touring circuits and so on, where most of the music was actually played – have also disappeared. Moreover, even if there is no Armstrong, Parker or Coltrane among us, there is no shortage of fine musicians with fresh ideas, and there can be no doubt that through their collective efforts, jazz musicians have revitalised the art of improvisation in western music.

In this discussion, emphasis has been placed on the orderly and organised aspects of jazz improvisation, largely in an effort to dispel the persistent notion that the practice is intuitive or unpremeditated. This should not, finally, be taken as in any way an attempt to diminish the creative accomplishments of its players. As Berliner has put it, 'a soloist's most salient experiences in the heat of performance involve poetic leaps of the imagination to phrases that are unrelated, or only minimally related, to the storehouse' (1994, 216–17). It is precisely in reconciling the tension between innovation and tradition, spontaneity and organisation, that players seek to achieve that integration of the individual and the collective which is at the heart of the jazz aesthetic.

9 Jazz among the classics, and the case of Duke Ellington

MERVYN COOKE

There is [in 1957] an increasing interrelationship between the adherents to art forms in various fields. Contemporary jazz, for instance, has many enthusiastic listeners in its audience who are classical musicians of heroic stature. Indeed, some classical musicians in recent years have involved themselves with jazz as composers, soloists, or both. I am not pointing this out in any attempt to plead for tolerance, for jazz is not in need of tolerance, but of understanding and intelligent appreciation. Moreover, it is becoming increasingly difficult to decide where jazz starts or where it stops, where Tin Pan Alley begins and jazz ends, or even where the borderline lies between classical music and jazz. I feel there is no boundary line, and I see no place for one if my own feelings tell me a performance is good. [ELLINGTON 1973, 193]

Currently one of the least fashionable ways of looking at jazz is from the perspective of 'classical' music – a label still used in record shops, and still understood instinctively by almost everybody, in spite of its avoidance by commentators who have yet to find an acceptable substitute. (Of the alternative terms, 'art music' is just as politically incorrect as 'classical', while 'concert music' can be applied to almost everything; in America, classical music is deemed to be 'European' in a simplistic antithesis to African-American traditions.) The once common notion that jazz might be thought of as 'America's classical music' has long been discredited. Yet no amount of quibbling about labels will make the parallels between the classical and jazz worlds go away; and those who insist on the uniqueness of jazz and its incompatability with essential characteristics of classical music cut themselves off from the richness of allusion and crossover at the heart of all the best western music of the twentieth century. It was perhaps because of this limited outlook that Duke Ellington, on his own admission, stopped using the word 'jazz' in 1943 (*ibid.*, 452). In imposing on jazz musicians the necessity for artistic independence from allegedly inappropriate aesthetic and technical considerations, commentators often neglect to take the musicians' own views into account: for some jazz performers and composers, certain tenets of the classical world have been (however uncomfortably to modern sensibilities) something to aspire to rather than shun. As long as jazz is deemed to possess intellectual and emotional content worthy of respect and serious study, and as long as it is performed in public and recorded for posterity, the parallels with classical music – and the artistic tensions inherent in them – demand exploration.

A clear-cut distinction between jazz as improvised music and classical as pre-composed has been invalid since the very beginnings of jazz. In an attempt to soften the distinction, pianist Bill Evans coined the terms 'contemplative' (predominantly pre-composed) and 'spontaneous' (predominantly improvised) and stressed their common ground:

> you can't find in jazz the perfection of craft that is possible in contemplative music. Yet, oddly enough, this very lack of perfection can result in good jazz. For example, in classical music, a mistake is a mistake. But in jazz, a mistake can be – in fact, must be – justified by what follows it. If you were improvising a speech and started a sentence in a way you hadn't intended, you would have to carry it out so that it would make sense. It is the same in spontaneous music.
>
> In good contemplative composition, the creator tries to *recapture* those qualities – the trouble is that there are a lot of so-called composers who compose primarily by putting together tones in a logical structure they have set up. But spontaneous material can be worked over and developed, according to the limits of the person's craft. And the result will in some way be in touch with the universal language of understanding in music.
>
> [R. Gottlieb 1996, 426]

When jazz is pre-composed the results need not sound unspontaneous: the big bands of the swing era and since have been characterised by complex textures designed to sound like massed improvisations, with head arrangements often transmitted and refined by experimentation and oral communication rather than by written charts. A big-band number sounds spontaneous just as a late romantic symphony (which may have taken years to compose) should come across as a spontaneous outpouring of feeling in any good performance. In either case, whether the music was pre-planned or spur-of-the-moment becomes an irrelevance. This paradox is especially encountered in contemporary classical music, where detailed predetermination and aleatoric techniques can sometimes produce surprisingly similar results. Indeed, classical music since the 1950s has aspired to the condition of (sometimes random) spontaneity, an aspiration that clearly parallels the work of certain free-jazz artists of the 1960s. In some free jazz, only the presence of bass and drums lends a 'jazz' feel to the music, the 'gravitational pull' of such a rhythm section suggesting that recognition of characteristic sonorities and textures is a vital part of the jazz experience (see Schuller 1996, 72).

Ellington's scepticism on the validity of improvisation is well known, though he criticised the label more than the concept. When asked 'How important is improvisation in jazz?', he replied:

> The word 'improvisation' has great limitations, because when musicians are given solo responsibility they already have a suggestion of a melody

written for them, and before they begin they already know more or less
what they are going to play. Anyone who plays anything worth hearing
knows what he's going to play, no matter whether he prepares a day ahead
or a beat ahead. It has to be with intent.   [Ellington 1973, 465]

He offered more along the same lines in a programme note written for
his tour of the UK in 1958: 'Improvisation really consists of picking out
a device here, and connecting it with a device there; changing the rhythm
here, and pausing there; there has to be some thought preceding each phrase,
otherwise it is meaningless' (quoted in Rattenbury 1990, 14). That this
view appears to subscribe to the classical composer's traditional desire for
rational 'control' of material is symptomatic of Ellington's attitude to the
art in general.

It is easy to forget that classical music has enjoyed its own substantial
doses of spontaneity and widespread popular appeal over the centuries, and
it was largely the rise of modernism in the twentieth century that diverted
attention towards more esoteric considerations. Historical awareness of musical trends before the late nineteenth century is a useful factor in reassessing
attempts to segregate jazz and the classics on aesthetic grounds. Baroque
music, even in church, was heavily indebted to catchy dance rhythms, and
as a result undoubtedly sounded far more accessible to contemporaneous audiences than to the historically remote audience of today (though
the authentic-performance movement in the 1970s did much to restore a
buoyancy in Baroque performance lacking in the romantic approach of the
previous generation). Roger Pryor Dodge pointed out as early as 1934 that
reportage concerning spontaneous music-making in Rome in 1639 holds
as true for jazz as for early Baroque music, and went on to cite classical
parallels in an analysis of Ellington's *Black and Tan Fantasy* (see R. Gottlieb
1996, 748). Performers in the seventeenth and eighteenth centuries improvised elaborate melodic decorations and occasionally entire movements
from scratch (e.g., the slow movement of Bach's Brandenburg Concerto
No. 3, which survives only as a harmonic skeleton of two chords), even including complex fugal counterpoint, while the basso continuo was in effect
a prototypical rhythm section. The techniques of keyboard improvisation
have remained a vital component of the church organist's art to the present
day, and for those classical musicians who have not trained themselves in
this practice (which was much more widespread when Dodge made his
remarks on Baroque music in the 1930s, and is now a rapidly dying art),
the skills can seem just as remote and mysterious as jazz improvisation
(see Chapter 8).

Classical performers no longer improvise cadenzas when playing concertos from the eighteenth century, although they were expected to do so up

to at least the time of Beethoven. For those of today's jazz musicians trained in both classical and jazz styles, however, the situation is different. One rare modern exponent of the improvised cadenza is Chick Corea, whose jazz-inflected cadenzas for Mozart's piano concertos have shown him to be very much aware of this vital historical link between jazz and the classics. Corea's Mozart enterprise was turned to commercial advantage by Sony in the medium of televised concert in the 1990s: the broadcast depended for its success on the assumption that it would appeal simultaneously to two still reasonably distinct types of audience (to three, in fact, since the participants included bluegrass/new acoustic violinist Mark O'Connor). Wynton Marsalis's jazz ballets are now marketed on the Sony Classical label, while Django Bates's orchestral jazz is listed under the heading 'jazz/contemporary classical' by Decca.[1] This trend reinforces the comment made by George Avakian that the third stream – originally a provocative blend of jazz and classical techniques promoted in the late 1950s – has now simply become mainstream.[2]

Some jazz musicians, including Bates, nevertheless remain distinctly self-conscious in the classical arena. Skilled in both composition and improvisation, Bates remarked of his orchestral work, *Tentle Morments* (1989), that it had been conceived

> with the misguided intention of proving to the classical music world that I could write in various classical styles and must therefore be acceptable. I managed to rescue myself five-eighths into the piece, shaking some sense into me through the use of several badly executed Mozart trills which by their very ridiculousness reminded me how ridiculous I was being.[3]

Bates's disingenuous commentary on this witty and accomplished work misses a vital irony: the sudden intrusion of the Mozart keyboard cliché, far from saying 'look at me trying to be classical', reinforces the parallels between jazz and the classics because the formulaic trills are precisely those that invariably brought *improvised* cadenzas to an end in the eighteenth century. As a result, the Mozartean allusions can to some ears sound more spontaneous than the (pre-composed) jazzier sections surrounding them. The age-old tension between the 'clever' and the 'instinctive' refuses to go away.

Not all early jazz critics shared Dodge's wholesome attitude towards the problem in the 1930s. Winthrop Sargeant, versed in both classical and jazz styles, wrote scathingly in 1946 on both the then growing notion that jazz might be acceptable in the concert hall, and the attempts of various composers to bridge the stylistic gap between the two allegedly incompatible worlds:

Jazz concerts in Carnegie Hall and the Metropolitan Opera House have been hailed as cultural milestones when, in fact, they only proved that jazz can be played in uncongenial surroundings . . . Ever since the pundit Hugues Panassié discovered *le jazz hot* in a French chateau full of phonograph records, the world of intellectual jazz addicts has been calling a spade a *cuiller à caviar*. The ebullient, hit-and-miss ensemble of a New Orleans stomp is reverently described as 'counterpoint'; the jazz trumpeter's exuberant and raucous lapses from true pitch are mysteriously referred to as 'quarter tones' or 'atonality'. Jazz, as an art with a capital A, has become something to be listened to with a rapt air that would shame the audiences of the Budapest Quartet. To dance to it (which is just what its primitive Negro originators would do) becomes a profanation.

[R. Gottlieb 1996, 766]

Jazz, according to Sargeant, can only be described in enthusiastically emotive terms ('ebullient', 'exuberant', 'raucous') and not subjected to technical analysis. His conviction that jazz is a folk music, and that 'the distinction between folk music and art music is profound and nearly absolute', leads him inevitably to the conclusion that it 'has not proved itself an art of sufficient poetic or intellectual scope to take the place in civilized society occupied by the great art of concert and operatic music' (*ibid.*, 772). Even its emotional impact, he implies, has been enhanced more by comparison with the aridity of modern classical composers than by any inherent artistic merit, and it will appeal more strongly to a popular rather than highbrow audience. This view is, of course, severely dated, and entirely ignores the fact that arid technical analysis is equally capable of trivialising the emotional strengths of classical music. Why not describe the finale of Mozart's G major String Quartet (K387), for example, as 'ebullient' and 'exuberant' and forget about all the self-conscious – and undoubtedly tongue-in-cheek – counterpoint it contains? Mozart wrote plenty of entertainment music for social functions, too, though those who place him squarely in the pantheon of great composers may find this fact uncomfortable, as is the realisation that not all of his music can claim to be profound.

Attempts to reserve technical competence and intellectual complexity as the exclusive province of classical music became steadily less prominent in the 1950s, though not all commentators avoided confusion and inconsistency in their fluctuating attitudes. A good example is the case of bop, once lauded as the ultimate in spontaneity and then taken to task for its 'fetishizing technique' and the fact that it was 'too mesmerized by the devices and concepts of European music' (Gendron 1995, 49). By the 1960s, some jazz had grown so esoteric and complex in its technical procedures that it had become just as elitist as the classics; and the reaction against the commercial motivation behind jazz-rock fusion in the 1970s was, as Gary

Tomlinson has put it, 'a snobbish distortion of history by jazz purists attempting to insulate their cherished classics from the messy marketplace in which culture has always been negotiated' (in Bergeron and Bohlman 1992 82). Tomlinson's identification of 'the coercive power of the institutionalized jazz canon' suggests that some jazz has indeed attained the elitist status formerly the exclusive property of the classics. The nature of jazz's canonisation has been investigated by Krin Gabbard, who agrees with Scott DeVeaux that the concept of a jazz canon is as paradoxical as the jazz concert, and has drawn attention to those critics who – in his opinion – aim to 'theorize themselves and the music into positions of importance' and 'fetishize' the work of certain prominent musicians (Gabbard 1995b, 7).

Form and forming

Much analysis of jazz has taken as its starting point the old-fashioned classical notion that, in order for a work to be successful, it must display some kind of organic coherence – preferably goal-directed and founded on clear thematic developments. As Gabbard and others have pointed out, this approach can be inappropriate; Gabbard cites in particular the playing of Charlie Parker (often singled out as an exponent of so-called 'formulaic improvisation': see p. 148) and comments that 'Parker's work might just as easily be discussed in terms of how he *destroys* the illusion of organic unity in his solos by inserting easily recognizable fragments from other musical traditions' (Gabbard 1995b, 13). Gunther Schuller was in the 1950s one of the first commentators to realise that a basic misconception had blighted analysis of jazz:

> It has become increasingly clear [in 1956] that 'form' need not be a
> confining mold into which the tonal materials are poured, but rather that
> the forming process can be *directly* related to the musical material
> employed in a specific instance. In other words, *form* evolves out of the
> material itself and is not imposed upon it. We must learn to think of form
> as a verb rather than a noun.   [1996, 19]

In Schuller's view, the greatest exponents of this process of forming in jazz were Ellington and Charles Mingus. If the drawbacks of narrow-sighted analysis of classical music (chiefly when dealing with historically revered tonal structures) have to some extent been carried over directly into the analysis of jazz, it is important to note that certain classical theorists have lamented this trend even in their own field.

Charles Rosen remarks of the classical style that the 'relation of the individual detail to the large form even in apparently improvisational works, and the way the form is shaped freely in response to the smallest parts, give us the first style in music history where the organization is completely audible and where the form is never externally imposed' (Rosen 1976, 93). More provocatively, Rosen continues: 'The structure of a classical composition is related to the way its themes *sound*, not to what might be done with them' (*ibid.*, 94).[4] Both comments may be applied to the work of Ellington with singular appropriateness. Rosen's and Schuller's view that musical structures ideally evolve from the specific musical raw materials of a piece, and that form is not something to be imposed from without, compares directly with Bill Evans's criticism of 'a lot of so-called composers who compose primarily by putting together tones in a logical structure they have set up'. The more satisfying alternative is summarised in Rosen's memorable image of a piece taking shape as if 'literally impelled from within', which Joseph Kerman categorised as entelechy (Rosen 1976, 120, quoted in Kerman 1985, 151–2). In jazz, where sonority is paramount, such entelechy is even further removed from traditional classical notions of thematic development.

Sonority as structure

The concept of sonority as structure has become an increasingly valid way of approaching jazz, whether investigating the largely predetermined balancing of tonal contrasts in Jelly Roll Morton's music of the 1920s or comparable achievements by Ellington, swing bands, Claude Thornhill, Gil Evans or the Miles Davis nonet. The adaptation of idiosyncratic instrumental timbres to expressive ends has always been a characterising feature of the finest jazz improvisations, and a defining characteristic of Ellington's soloists from the late 1920s onwards. Schuller argues that the 'individual *personal* sonoric conception' of players and the music's 'timbral articulations' remain the true identifying features of jazz (1996, 29). This attitude allows him to assert, controversially but refreshingly, that the sound of Paul Whiteman's dance band is 'as original and as beautiful' as Ellington's – a comparison of which Ellington might well have approved, since he himself described the much-maligned bandleader in glowing terms, and wrote a piece specially for Whiteman's 1938 'Experiment in Modern Music' concert (*ibid.*, 45).[5] Ellington stated: 'To me, a musical instrument is in a sense a color instrument, and orchestral music should be scored to give full value to every possible shading and blending' (Tucker 1993, 247). Other writers, such as Sidney Finkelstein and Dan Morgenstern, have perceptively pointed out that Ellington's harmonies are inextricably linked with his timbres (*ibid.*, 353). Which listener, for example, can disassociate the evocative chords at the start of Ellington's famous 1930 recording of *Mood Indigo* from their extraordinary instrumental timbres? In Ellington's work, structure is thus articulated as much by what Schuller terms 'timbral articulations' (in other words, Rosen's 'the way themes sound') as by reliance on pre-existing formal frameworks or conventional techniques of development. The vividness of Ellington's orchestral palette and its indissoluble links with his equally distinctive harmonic language combine to make his style instantly recognisable, allowing for successive moments in a piece to be savoured as spontaneous and characteristic sonorous gestures; at the same time, these gestures are organised into highly sophisticated and often unpredictable patterns that repay detailed analysis.

Part of the inappropriateness of applying a classical analytical approach to jazz arises from the fact that romanticised notions of musical structure are unhelpful when considering much twentieth-century music (in any idiom). There is no point in relating Ellington's work to nineteenth-century ideas of thematic unity, when he owed a much more significant debt to twentieth-century composers whose work was mostly rooted in entirely different organisational principles: one example is Delius, whose music Ellington studied intensely in 1933 with the help of 'a whole bundle of scores', an influence noted by Ellington's son, Mercer (Nicholson 1999, 148). Jazz musicians have been quick to admit to such modern influences: Parker was outspoken about his admiration for Hindemith, Bartók and Stravinsky ('I dig all the moderns', he told *Down Beat* on 28 January 1953); Miles Davis commented that his modal techniques were inspired by listening to Ravel and Khatchaturian (Davis and Troupe 1989, 220); and the debt shown by Cecil Taylor to Webern and late Stravinsky is self-evident.

Stravinsky's compositional techniques highlight some revealing common ground between jazz and modern classical music. Not surprisingly, his penchant for metrical displacements, relentless ostinato patterns and added-note harmony drew him towards jazz, from which he liberally borrowed ideas both in the ragtime and swing eras; he was no stranger to the music of Ellington, and occasionally attended the band's later Cotton Club performances (Nicholson 1999, 124). In his *Ragtime for Eleven Instruments* and *Piano-Rag-Music* (both composed in 1918), and much later *Ebony Concerto* (written for Woody Herman in 1945), the parallels between jazz elements and rhythmical and textural devices already inherent in Stravinsky's music are strong, and these exerted considerable influence on younger musicians of both classical and jazz persuasions – and on 'in-between' exponents of the third stream such as Leonard Bernstein. The influence persisted into the fusion boom of the early 1970s: the electric-bass ostinati and syncopated octatonic pulsations of Jerry Goldsmith's main-title music to the movie, *Escape from the Planet of the Apes* (1971), for example, comprise a deft blend of elements reminiscent of both Stravinsky's *The Rite of Spring* and jazz-rock.

Stravinsky's characteristic structures, based on ostinato patterns and the interaction or juxtaposition of blocks of sound contrasted by sonority, were alien to traditional concepts of organic musical form, and it was not until Edward T. Cone wrote his pioneering article, 'Stravinsky: The Progress of a Method', in 1962 that analysts began to evolve a more appropriate way of approaching his music. Cone's suggestions provide a helpful starting point in reconsidering Ellington's work since both composers have at times been criticised for what Cone terms 'textural discontinuities', which have always been the life-blood of big-band jazz. In his celebrated analysis of Stravinsky's *Symphonies of Wind Instruments* (1920), Cone proposed concepts of 'stratification', 'interlock' and 'synthesis' through which blocks of discrete musical material are 'separated, interlocked, and eventually unified' (Cone 1962, 21). The musical ideas are essentially fragmentary, and therefore appear incomplete in conventional terms.

An understanding of the relationship between these concepts and the antiphony and riff patterns of jazz is essential to an adequate appreciation of how musical texture functions in much twentieth-century music. As a predominant feature of the swing style, the riff was bitterly resented by revivalists in the 1940s, who failed to see the creative potential such a fragmentary, gestural musical language – at once predictable and unpredictable – might have to offer. As Bernard Gendron has explained:

> On the one hand, the riff, perhaps more than any other musical device, revealed swing to be a simplistic, standardized, consumer package... On the other hand, the swing arranger would sometimes use a wide variety of different riffs in one piece to create a complex musical montage, generating an experimental, avant-garde sound, which glaringly excluded such pop requisites as a recurrent and easily recognizable melody. [1995, 44]

The tension between cliché and complexity was fully explored by Bernstein (under strong Stravinskyan influence) in his *Prelude, Fugue and Riffs*, written for Herman in 1949 but premiered by Benny Goodman six years later.

Precisely the same tension was a defining feature of some jazz many years before, and was brilliantly exploited in one of Ellington's most daring works of the swing years: the extraordinary original version of *Diminuendo and Crescendo in Blue*, recorded on 20 September 1937. One of Ellington's early experiments in extended jazz form that earned him a bad press at the time, its radical unpredictability ensured that it was not a popular success, and it was only when reinterpreted at the 1956 Newport Festival (in a much diluted version featuring a celebrated extended solo by tenor saxophonist Paul Gonsalves) that it came to wider public attention.[6] The original recording had been singled out for praise in 1938 by Aaron Copland, who (somewhat condescendingly) said of its composer that he 'comes nearer to knowing how to make a piece hang together' than other jazz musicians (Tucker 1993, 130). Significantly, Copland's own music at times drew rather heavily from Stravinsky's idiom.

In the 1937 version of *Diminuendo and Crescendo in Blue*, Ellington's novel structure is an exhilarating demonstration of Rosen's insight that 'the two principal sources of musical energy are dissonance and sequence – the first because it demands resolution, the second because it implies continuation' (1976, 120). By a cunning distortion of jazz clichés, Ellington applies dissonance and sequence in a resourceful scheme of interlocking and unpredictable antiphonal patterns, and creates harmonic instability by founding this highly fragmentary material on the roving changes of a 14-bar blues progression that is transposed several times. Only in the second half of the piece do the metrical and harmonic elements begin to stabilise into more familiar schemes and coalesce into a more conventional climax, and this shift from textural discontinuity to comforting coherence is managed with consummate compositional control.

Max Harrison commented that 'the continuing drive of *Diminuendo and Crescendo in Blue* arises from the productive tension between its simple basic materials and their complex treatment' (a comment equally applicable to Stravinsky), and added that 'one almost despairs at its further scope never having been extended on the scale it deserved and with the freedom which composers in the European tradition and its equivalents in America and elsewhere take for granted' (Tucker 1993, 390–91).[7] Harrison is, however, harsher on similar experiments by Ellington in other extended pieces, commenting that the first version of *Creole Rhapsody* (1931) 'consists of essentially a number of fragments . . . which, instead of being related organically, are merely strung together'; the second version is marred by there being 'too many disparate types of gesture in a small space of time' (*ibid.*, 388). Assessing precisely where incoherent rambling stops and masterly unpredictability begins is a challenge still confronting the analyst of twentieth-century music.

Jazzing up the classics, and classicising jazz

The tensions, parallels, contradictions and syntheses between various aspects of jazz and classical music are perhaps most clearly illustrated in numerous attempts to 'jazz up' classical scores, a practice which remains controversial even though it is as old as jazz itself. In the immediate prehistory of jazz, ragtime had been essentially a jazzed-up classical genre: widespread syncopation and (rarely) blue notes enlivened rigid harmonic structures borrowed from the most popular light classical forms of the 1890s (chiefly marches and duple-time dances) and the somewhat earlier salon music of composers such as Louis Moreau Gottschalk. When James Reese Europe appeared at Carnegie Hall in 1914, he played classical music alongside ragtime, apparently without incongruity (Schuller 1996, 123). In spite of Scott Joplin's attempt to establish ragtime as a new 'classic' genre in its own right, the extemporised embellishments habitually added to it by the first generation of stride pianists resulted in such reactionary titles as *Don't Jazz Me Rag – I'm Music*, published by James Scott in 1922 just as ragtime was pushed terminally out of fashion by the jazz craze. The early jazz pianists who built on the ragtime idiom were generally well versed in classical repertory and frequently applied their keyboard style to specimens drawn from it. The clear influence of Grieg is to be heard in the work of stride pianist Willie 'The Lion' Smith – Ellington's early mentor – and of Debussy in Bix Beiderbecke's piano piece *In a Mist* (1927), while harmonic devices paralleling those of French impressionism steadily crept into the music of dance bands in the later 1920s and remained a potent influence as late as the innovative style of pianist Bill Evans in the 1950s and 1960s.

In New Orleans, the famous Funeral March from Chopin's B♭ minor Piano Sonata was a staple for elaboration in funeral processions – a tradition alluded to when Ellington later quoted from it at the conclusion of *Black and Tan Fantasy*, recorded in 1927. Jelly Roll Morton was well known for his ragtime versions of popular arias from Verdi's operas, and cited an example from *Il Trovatore* in his memoirs (Lomax 1950, 278–9). In Baltimore and New York, flamboyant stride pianists took pride in their knowledge of the classics: Eubie Blake jazzed up the overture to Wagner's *Tannhäuser* and Chopin's Funeral March, and James P. Johnson gave a similar treatment to Grieg's *Peer Gynt*, Rossini's *William Tell* Overture, Rachmaninov's C♯ minor Piano Prelude (which became *Russian Rag*) and Liszt's version of Verdi's *Rigoletto* – the last therefore paraphrasing a paraphrase (Gioia 1997, 97). Whiteman built quotations from famous classical scores into his band arrangements, such as the allusions to Rachmaninov's C♯ minor Prelude in 'Hot Lips' (1922) and to Grieg's 'In the Hall of the Mountain-King' (from *Peer Gynt*) in his 1926 recording of 'St Louis Blues'. Ellington reworked Liszt's *Hungarian Rhapsody No. 2* in 1934, and Larry Clinton gave a jazz treatment to excerpts from Tchaikovsky's *The Nutcracker* in 1940 (Hajdu 1996, 204).

Many of these classical allusions were humorous in intent and, while they too showed the bandleader's knowledge of 'legitimate' music (as Ellington sometimes called it), were by no means out of place in the growing tradition of thematic allusion in other jazz styles. Even in the highly innovative soundworld of Mingus's *The Black Saint and the Sinner Lady* (1963), we encounter a quotation from *Peer Gynt*. Interestingly, accusations of pretentiousness have been far more promptly levelled at those jazz musicians who quote from the classics than at those who build into their improvisations equally prominent and sometimes contrived allusions to popular songs and jazz standards: the abrupt quotation from 'Country Gardens' at the end of Charlie Parker's 8 August 1951 recording of 'Lover Man', for example, is just as designedly silly as Whiteman's chirpy quotation from Grieg. (For further comment on Parker's quotations, see pp. 148–50.) Eric Lott has gone so far as to compare Parker's habitual quoting of 'Woody Woodpecker' with the surreal references to popular music in Mahler's style (1995, 249).

Significantly, those classical scores to have been given a wholesale jazz treatment have tended to be those already popular in their own right, and no longer considered to be elitist in appeal. The circumspect choice of classic 'hits', from Bach to Rodrigo, has increased the commercial value of recordings of these interpretations, while at the same time lessening the likelihood of severe attacks from purist critics from both jazz and classical camps; the humorous stance of many interpretations (e.g., Bob James's hillbilly version of Pachelbel's *Canon* from his 1974 fusion album *One*) disarms heavy criticism. If Bill Evans's choice of music by the Spanish composer Granados as raw material for jazzing-up in 1965 seems more esoteric, this is merely a reflection of changing tastes: Granados's *Goyescas* were a highly popular concert item in the 1960s.[8] Popular classics are often those with straightforward melodic appeal, strongly directional harmonies and uncluttered formal structures, and these features proved readily transferable to many different jazz styles.

Duke Ellington's Scandinavian scandal

Between 28 and 30 June 1960, Ellington and his orchestra recorded in Hollywood their interpretations of movements from Edvard Grieg's incidental music to Ibsen's play *Peer Gynt* (dating from 1874–6), which were released in the UK on a Philips LP (BBL 7470) jocularly subtitled 'Swinging Suites by Edward E. & Edward G'. The Grieg release was a follow-up to Ellington's reworking of material from Tchaikovsky's *Nutcracker Suite*, which had been recorded at the same sessions (BBL 7418). The sleeve notes for the Grieg project informed the listener: 'Duke has deep respect for all things of worth, and as a composer he has suffered a thousand times over the things that have been done to his own music through the years. His approach to the music of other composers is the approach he hopes he will receive from interpreters of his own music – a mixture of respect and innovation.' Ellington later recalled: 'We liked what we did, and we had fun doing it, but we did not try to do better than the symphony people. There was a certain amount of humor in it, and unfortunately the Grieg Society in Norway barred it. I don't think Grieg would have barred it' (1973, 466). In 1969, following a concert in Bergen at the conclusion of a world tour, Ellington told a Norwegian newspaper reporter: 'We shall never play it again. Billy Strayhorn made it with so much love that there is no fun in playing it now that it has been vetoed. Can you think of any bigger fools than us – to put in so much work only to have it refused? I believe that Grieg would not have been offended by our arrangement; he would certainly have taken it cheerfully.'[9] On the last point, Ellington was probably right: Grieg's own view of his *Peer Gynt* music was somewhat ambivalent, and he once reportedly dismissed 'In the Hall of the Mountain-King' for 'reeking of Norwegian cow pats'; its rustic quirkiness had been aped by Whiteman in his quotation from it in 'St Louis Blues'.

The Grieg Foundation in Bergen had prohibited performances in Norway of Ellington's *Peer Gynt* suite on the grounds that it constituted a violation of the original work (still in copyright in Norway in the 1960s but not elsewhere since 1957, the fiftieth anniversary of Grieg's death).[10] Under Norwegian copyright law, a fine could be levied in cases where a work was 'copied in a manner which damages the author's reputation',[11] and the Ellington incident occurred at a time when a strong faction was campaigning for these draconian restrictions to be extended permanently. The extraordinary tension surrounding the Ellington scandal resulted in a nationally televised debate on the subject, broadcast in a prime-time evening slot on Saturday 21 May 1966. The programme was led by Haagen Ringnes and entitled 'Has He Trampled on the Piano?'; it included extracts from the banned *Peer Gynt* music (for the broadcast of which special permission had to be obtained from the Grieg Foundation), which were played alongside the Grieg originals. The programme also featured Ellington's own view, as given in an interview for Swedish television, and a discussion between four Scandinavian composers: Egil Monn-Iversen and Karl-Birger Blomdahl defended Ellington, while Klaus Egge and Harald Sæverud attacked him on behalf of the Grieg Foundation. Blomdahl was Head of Music at Swedish Radio, and had already caused a considerable stir by allowing the broadcast of the complete Ellington *Peer Gynt* suite across the border. He dared to assert that Ellington's version was in some respects superior to Grieg's, and pointed out that banning it was an entirely futile exercise: if it is good it should be heard, while if it is bad it will fall by the wayside anyway, he argued.[12] He also pointedly demonstrated that Grieg had himself plundered material from Mozart and recomposed it in arrangements for two pianos, an observation swiftly echoed by Ellington himself when interviewed by a Norwegian newspaper some months later.[13] On the opposing side, Egge and Sæverud by all accounts acquitted themselves poorly: 'They may both be great composers', wrote one journalist afterwards, 'but as debaters they wouldn't be able to keep order in a musical nursery school. Sæverud was the worst: he had almost no argument to offer, his arguments consisting for the most part of persistent headshaking.'[14] The inference that the Grieg Foundation's spokesmen considered jazz to be inferior to classical music, hence the allegation of violating the *droit moral* of Grieg's music, was inevitable.

The heated debate (in which Ringnes had, on more than one occasion, to raise his voice in order to make himself heard from the chair) was repeated on Norwegian radio on 9 June, one newspaper on that date carrying a cartoon depicting a couple of young trolls dancing to the sounds of the Ellington orchestra – much to the disgust of a senior troll (see Plate 9.1).[15] Four days after the radio broadcast, Johann Gulbranson wrote in the *Oslo Dagbladet*: 'had the Beatles made a pop version of "The Hall of the Mountain King", it would certainly have avoided censure. If this problem is to be discussed, both parties must absolutely understand Ellington's and Grieg's music.' While memories of the debate remained vivid, Norwegian radio broadcast Ellington's *Nutcracker Suite* on 27 June 1966, lamenting that the *Peer Gynt* suite had only been heard in its entirety on Swedish radio so that no one in Norway could arrive at an informed opinion of its merits.[16] Tetchy correspondence on the matter was published in various newspapers, a supporter of the Grieg Foundation's position alleging that Ellington was guilty of 'artistic vandalism'.[17] One correspondent plaintively asked, 'When shall we Norwegians learn to end this painful national pride? Folk abroad laugh at us.'[18]

Plate 9.1 Erik Strøyer, cartoon inspired by Duke Ellington's *Peer Gynt* suite (*Arbeiderbladet*, Oslo, 9 June 1966)

In 1967, the copyright restrictions on Grieg's music in Norway finally lapsed, and Ellington's *Peer Gynt* suite was subsequently imported legally on the Columbia Jazz Odyssey label (32160252). Looking back at this incident, it is difficult to see what all the fuss was about. In jazz, the Norwegian 'national pride' has since found a commercially successful outlet in the shape of native saxophonist Jan Garbarek, the bestselling artist on the ECM label: 'the yearning cry of his sax', according to *Down Beat* reviewer Jon Andrews, is 'readily associated with fog-shrouded fjords and Nordic gloom'.[19] Garbarek's engagement with his Scandinavian heritage has involved not only the appropriation of Norwegian folk music, but also the music of Grieg: on *Twelve Moons* (1993), ECM's 500th release (519500-2), he included a plangent interpretation of the 'Arietta' from Grieg's *Lyric Pieces*. The critical acclaim accorded this album suggests that such appropriations are now viewed as entirely acceptable, especially in cases where the performer hails from the same cultural heritage as the music being appropriated and serves as an international ambassador for it. Garbarek's phenomenally successful *Officium* (1993) took medieval vocal music as its starting point, and it too managed to avoid offending listeners' historically conditioned sensibilities.

Discussing the newly imported recording of Ellington's *Peer Gynt* in the *Arbeiderbladet* on 31 May 1969, one reviewer perceptively pointed out that, while Grieg's famous 'Morning Mood' had a special resonance for Norwegian listeners, they tended to overlook the fact that it was inspired by an African wasteland in the original context of Ibsen's play (for which setting it is not, perhaps, especially appropriate); he went on to declare, 'why shouldn't Ellington's musicians think themselves in morning mood after a long night's work?' The review concluded: 'Duke Ellington and his musicians . . . have shaped a whole new tonal world out of Grieg's raw materials.' Since Ellington's 'tonal world' has traditionally been regarded as one of the strongest and most enduring idioms in jazz, it is instructive to examine precisely how Ellington and Strayhorn adapted their Nordic raw material to their own ends.[20]

The choice of Grieg as raw material was canny, not only for the obvious reason that the Grieg was already sufficiently popular a classic as to guarantee widespread interest in the venture, but more subtly because Grieg's compositional style is generally straightforward and free from complex structures and intellectual posturing (hence its popularity, one might argue). These observations apply equally to Tchaikovsky's *Nutcracker Suite*, the source for Ellington's previous classical project. Both Grieg and Tchaikovsky are celebrated melodists, and both have been criticised at times for their lack of structural sophistication. Because of this, it is much harder to take Ellington to task for destroying or distorting the original musical structures than it might have been had he chosen to rework the music of a more esoteric composer. The lack of organic 'development' (and reliance on simple sequential patterns) sometimes singled out for comment in Grieg and Tchaikovsky, which we have already shown to have been a misapplied preoccupation in the case of criticisms of jazz styles, was a positive advantage for Ellington's purposes. In Grieg's *Peer Gynt*, structures based on simple repetition include 'Morning Mood', 'Åse's Death', 'In the Hall of the Mountain-King' and 'Solveig's Song'. Both Grieg and Tchaikovsky savour local harmonic colouring (both are fond of augmented triads, for example, as was Ellington: see 'Morning Mood'), and the French augmented-sixth chords in 'Åse's Death' (e.g., bar 5) and the chromatic elaboration of 'Solveig's Song' (e.g., bars 18–24) would have appealed to Ellington, and are indeed lingered over in his versions of the Grieg originals.

Ellington's suite is organised schematically, alternating movements in slow tempo and lively swing style. 'Morning Mood' (No. 1) is, apart from a brief chordal introduction to establish the atmosphere, a bar-by-bar reworking of Grieg's original. The slow tempo and lack of swing are compensated for by Ellington's trademark richness in the bottom stratum of the texture (low saxophones and bowed double bass) and ominously pulsating cross-rhythms on tom-toms that are immediately suggestive of the Duke's famed 'jungle' style – a dash of exoticism that hints at the African setting of the relevant Ibsen context more than Grieg's original. Above this sensuous foundation, Grieg's melody is played without alteration by Paul Gonsalves (tenor saxophone), Jimmy Hamilton (clarinet) and finally Harry Carney (baritone saxophone). Improvised decoration (on clarinet) is reserved for the climactic moment at which Grieg's harmony is at its most static. The return of the main theme is subjected to an ingenious and lush chromatic reharmonisation; modernistic distortion reminiscent of Stravinsky is reserved for the eccentric trombone reworking of Grieg's evocative horn calls towards the conclusion. 'Åse's Death' (No. 4) reinstates the 'jungle' percussion from No. 1 and takes the same strictly bar-by-bar approach: it is little more than a reorchestration of the original material, albeit distinguished by the same characteristically Ellingtonian attention to rich sonorities sited low in the texture.

'In the Hall of the Mountain-King' (No. 2) is given a more liberal interpretation, replete with rich saxophone homophony and metrically disruptive unison riffs entirely typical of big-band swing. Grieg's melody is repeated over and over again in the original, so a jazz structure varying a set of repeating chord changes is a logical initiative. The bass line deftly changes function throughout (switching from main melody to walking bass to pedal notes and back), while the upper strata of the texture become increasingly complex in their antiphonal trading of abstract riff patterns based directly on the theme, recalling the heady textural discontinuity of *Diminuendo and Crescendo in Blue*. Ellington's analytical approach to his raw material is seen in the increasing abstraction of the interval of a rising semitone (the inversion of the falling chromatic patterns characterising Grieg's melody), isolated in the brief and stark coda for piano solo.

After an introduction virtually identical to Grieg's, the main theme of 'Solveig's Song' (No. 3) is transposed to sit comfortably as a high trombone solo in the 'ya-ya' vocalising style pioneered in Ellington's band by Joe 'Tricky Sam' Nanton decades before (and here imitated by Booty Woods). Straightforward arrangements of this melancholic theme, with some striking double-time chromatic reharmonisation, alternate with major sections in which Jimmy Hamilton's 'very "legitimate" clarinet'[21] supplies a decorated version of Grieg's subsidiary theme (its triple metre converted into a faster quadruple swing pattern); the trombone riffs directly recall the brass interjections in Ellington's *It Don't Mean a Thing (If it Ain't Got That Swing)* of 1932. As with No. 1, Grieg's straightforward original structure (here a simple ABA'B' form) is fully respected.

The final movement, 'Anitra's Dance' (No. 5), strikes an optimal balance between respect for the original structure and subtle reorganisation, and is arguably the most interesting experiment in the suite. Grieg's highly conventional rounded binary form (two halves, each repeated, with the second incorporating a modified recapitulation of the first) provides the foundation for Ellington's version. The A section is repeated in full, as in the Grieg, but with additional embellishment from a solo saxophone; but the B section is shortened so that it is repeated *before* the recapitulation of the main theme occurs, and the phrase lengths are subtly manipulated to make the harmonic sequences seem less predictable and four-square than in the original version; the dominant preparation for the recapitulation is also lengthened by Ellington for additional emphasis. In Ellington's version, the recapitulation is as a result heard only once instead of twice, and carries a correspondingly greater impact, leading directly into the catchy coda. The latter is based on the introduction, and the ease with which Ellington transforms a fragment of Grieg's melody into a catchy riff pattern shows how naturally the process of adaptation came to him; the simple ingenuity with which the metrical dislocation inherent in this transformation creates a modernistic feeling without unduly compromising the character of the original is impressive.

Ellington's and Strayhorn's reworking of Tchaikovsky's *Nutcracker Suite* is more radical in technique and satisfying in content than *Peer Gynt*, yet Ellington noted that it had not been met by a single critical objection at the time of its release.[22] This was in spite of the ostensibly (but misleadingly) flippant attitude towards the source material suggested by the heavy puns in certain of Ellington's titles, as shown in the following table (which also gives the location of Tchaikovsky's dance movements in the published suite):

Ellington (1960)	Tchaikovsky, Op. 71a (1892)
1. Overture	Ouverture miniature (No. I)
2. Toot toot tootie toot	Danse des Mirlitons (No. IIf)
3. Peanut Brittle Brigade	Marche (No. IIa)
4. Sugar Rum Cherry	Danse de la Fée-Dragée (No. IIb)
	[Dance of the Sugar-Plum Fairy]
5. Entr'acte	–
6. The Volga Vouty	Danse Russe Trepak (No. IIc)
7. Chinoiserie	Danse Chinoise (No. IIe)
8. Dance of the Floreadores	Valse des Fleurs (No. III)
9. Arabesque Cookie	Danse Arabe (No. IId)

This is a much more substantial venture than *Peer Gynt*. Ellington not only includes all the movements from Tchaikovsky's suite – adding, as the fifth movement, a recapitulation of the first not to be found in the original – but also re-orders the movements (as he had in the Grieg suite) with careful attention to balance and contrast, and with a clear desire to end enigmatically rather than in the grand flourishes of the 'Waltz of the Flowers' that closes the original Tchaikovsky sequence. As with the Grieg suite, Ellington juxtaposes movements in swing style with more relaxed and reflective pieces. The up-tempo swing movements are nos. 1, 3, 5, 6 and 8; perhaps predictably, these contain more jazz clichés than the slower movements, and the rambling riff patterns of 'Peanut Brittle Brigade' and 'Dance of the Floreadores', and the uninspired trumpet and clarinet solos in the former, are the low points of the work. The 'Overture', however, makes a greater impact as its deployment of big-band clichés is such a stark contrast to the gossamer lightness of the unorthodox scoring in Tchaikovsky's 'Ouverture miniature' (which lacks lower strings throughout), and Ellington makes a few deft alterations to the original structure. As in the Grieg suite, brief improvised solos are generally reserved for moments when the music is otherwise static or for the second statement of a theme that is immediately repeated; the most impressive solos are to be found in the recapitulation of the overture ('Entr'acte'), where they are accompanied by just bass and drums in a small-group texture that provides a welcome contrast at the centre-point of the suite.

Elsewhere, the recomposition is brilliantly inventive and unpredictable. As in the overture, much depends for its effect on the fact that the original scoring of certain of the dances is so well known. Thus the delicately fluttering flute trio of Tchaikovsky's 'Danse des Mirlitons' is transformed by Ellington into a squealing horn ascent with acerbic wrong-note harmony, with a strikingly modernistic introduction again recalling Stravinsky. Similarly, the tip-toeing celeste of the 'Dance of the Sugar-Plum Fairy' wittily metamorphoses into a ponderous and drunkenly lurching idea for low saxophones with support from trademark 'jungle' drumming. This movement, too, ends in fragmentation, suggesting that Ellington (no doubt subconsciously) approached his material with a clear distinction between swing-band stereotype in the fast movements and modernistic compositional techniques in the slow movements. Fragmentation also closes 'Chinoiserie', another of the more radical movements with its dislocated clarinet/saxophone heterophony (inspired by the original and paralleling the Mirliton reworking), dissonant bass interjections and quartal piano chords. The decision to locate Tchaikovsky's 'Arab Dance' at the end of the suite allows Ellington to close the work with a strikingly understated ending, in which the texture is gradually dismantled to leave just bass and tambourine in isolation.

Critics have either ignored Ellington's 'classical' suites, or roundly panned them. In a savage example of the latter extreme, Harrison declared:

> Altogether more desperate [than Ellington's other 1960s suites] as attempts at maintaining stylistic consistency over several movements were Ellington's grotesque assaults on major and minor European masters. The complaint is not about 'jazzing the classics', for the originals survive intact for those who want them. Rather is the complaint that he could, in these cases, find nothing better to do with his unique powers. It is a very long way down from great adventures like *Reminiscing in Tempo* [1935] to the contemptible Tchaikovsky and Grieg manipulations of 1960.
>
> [Tucker 1993, 393]

Harrison does not support his dismissal of these 'contemptible' and 'grotesque' ventures with specific musical evidence or rational argument and, given his positive insights into Ellington's earlier style, it seems likely that (*pace* his careful assertion to the contrary) the complaint really *is* about his 'jazzing the classics' by daring to 'assault' the sacred bastions of the classical canon.

Although one's opinion on the viability of such ventures is likely (for the foreseeable future, at any rate) to be so deeply rooted in matters of personal taste and canonical issues that objective assessment is virtually impossible, commentators might nevertheless do well to avoid the pitfall of allowing their extramusical preoccupations to colour their critical judgement. When Stravinsky transformed and distorted Pergolesi's Baroque melodies in his influential neo-classical ballet, *Pulcinella* (1919), we are told that the work's commissioner, the impresario Diaghilev, initially took offence and 'went about for a long time with a look that suggested "The Offended Eighteenth Century"'.[23] Today Stravinsky's score seems an unpretentious, freshly modern and certainly inoffensive reinterpretation of Baroque stylistic conventions, through which the force of Stravinsky's characteristic rhythmic and harmonic techniques always shines. In the case of Ellington's *Peer Gynt*, and even more so in the *Nutcracker Suite*, precisely the same situation obtains: the strength of Ellington's musical personality is imprinted on all his borrowed material and lends the reinterpretations a coherent character that entirely obviates the slightest criticism of his having violated the specious 'integrity' of the music on which the projects were based.

The same holds true for Miles Davis's and Gil Evans's interpretation of 'Gone' on their Gershwin-inspired album *Porgy and Bess* (1958), for example, which is a far more radical reworking of the original material than either of Ellington's suites, yet has never received the same barrage of criticism – undoubtedly because Gershwin's spirit is deemed to be closer to that of jazz than either Grieg's or Tchaikovsky's. This assumption may readily be dispelled by any intelligent examination of Gershwin's technical and aesthetic preoccupations, which were far more closely aligned to those of the classical composer he self-confessedly aspired to be. Our view of Ellington's general aspirations and achievements should be conditioned by the same awareness, and a refusal to give in to the still-prevalent myth of the incompatibility of jazz and the classics, whether in terms of musical technique, aesthetic outlook, or racial and sociological factors. A glance through Ellington's autobiography reveals that he was preoccupied throughout his career with musical issues that centred on craftsmanship, education, intellectualism, taste, and on a type of jazz that 'has grown up and become quite scholastic' (1973, 47) and which, in the hands of Strayhorn, shall survive as a legacy that 'will never be less than the ultimate on the highest plateau of culture' (*ibid.*, 161). Ellington's manager, Irving Mills, used this stance as a marketing tool as early as 1934 when he advised his clients to 'Sell Ellington as a great artist, a musical genius whose unique style and individual theories of harmony have created a new music. Sell his orchestra as a class attraction' (Nicholson, 1999, 153).

In his well-known analysis of Sonny Rollins's *Blue 7* in 1958, Schuller fired a broadside at those jazz purists who seemed to resent the then increasingly intellectual nature of modern jazz: he defined jazz intellectualism as 'the power of reason and comprehension as distinguished from *purely* intuitive emotional outpouring', and saw nothing wrong with those of its listeners (and exponents) who approached jazz with 'a roughly five-hundred-year-old musical idea, the notion of thematic and structural unity' (1996, 94). There can be no doubt that Ellington's views were broadly similar, though one may regret that the stunning originality of structural control in his early work later became replaced by the self-conscious and sometimes crude 'thematic unity' of diffusely extended works such as the *First Sacred Concert* (1965). It is difficult to believe that he would have agreed with Jed Rasula's assertion that the attempt to canonise jazz as part of Eurocentric culture is 'the *dominating fantasy* (and let me emphasize the domination) of the *predominantly* white world of jazz criticism and history' (1995, 153), for the simple reason that Ellington – and many other black jazz composers, for that matter – saw nothing wrong with inclusion in the classical canon, and indeed sometimes actively sought it. For Ellington, critical acclaim at Carnegie Hall was not something of which to be ashamed: 'our series there had helped establish a music that was new in both its extended forms and its social significance' (1973, 190).

Few jazz musicians have been subjected to (sometimes far-fetched) parallels with classical composers as was Ellington, who has variously been compared with Bach, Delius, Haydn, Mozart, Palestrina, Ravel, Rimsky-Korsakov, Schoenberg, Schubert and Strauss. Although he dismissed some of these comparisons as existing 'only in the minds of self-important, over-sophisticated musicologists', he nevertheless added that 'Brahms, Beethoven, Debussy and others of their calibre . . . have furnished us with wholesome musical patterns in our minds and have given us a definite basis upon which to judge all music, regardless of its origin' (Tucker 1993, 247). As Bill Evans put it, this compatibility ensures that jazz is 'in touch with the universal language of understanding in music'. One of the most memorable thumbnail descriptions of jazz is Lorenzo Thomas's assertion that the music is 'an extraordinary edifice of intellectualism balanced on the working-class eloquence of the blues' (258), and it is the tension of that balancing act that has always made the best jazz such a vital and all-embracing aesthetic experience.

PART THREE

Jazz changes

10 1959: the beginning of beyond

DARIUS BRUBECK

The idea for this chapter came from Mervyn Cooke's suggestion that we jointly organise a seminar – on jazz in 1959 – at the University of Nottingham. As soon as I began I found the choice of year felicitous both as a decisive cultural moment in establishing an autonomous art-form and as a year for musical landmarks recorded in every style of jazz (from main-stream to avant-garde). Nineteen fifty-nine was the year when jazz, as it is now, began.[1] Jazz before this time is now largely regarded as historic, as music usually identified by regional (e.g., Harlem school, Chicago style) and temporal (early jazz, Swing Era) associations. From 1959 onwards, it more strongly resembles universal current practice, indicating – and without con-descension to pre-1959 jazz – that this is the beginning of contemporary jazz. This is easily demonstrated by the still pervasive familiarity of certain of the recordings made in that year. *Kind of Blue* (Miles Davis), *Time Out* (Dave Brubeck), *Giant Steps* (John Coltrane) and Ornette Coleman's *The Shape of Jazz to Come* are albums that can scarcely be unknown or un-owned by jazz *aficionados* – and the 1960s had not even officially begun. Perhaps they began when John F. Kennedy was elected to the US Presidency and Robert Frost read his poetry at the Inauguration ceremony. In his speech, the young president raised the image of a relay in which 'the torch has been passed to a new generation of Americans'. This was turnover time in American culture and politics, as it was in jazz.

All reliable histories recount and analyse the musical achievements at and around this time and the broader discussion of American culture hinted at above is beyond the scope of this chapter. What is offered here is an interpretation of how and why so much happened when it did and the impact of this history on present-day jazz reality. The jazz life is as different from what it was 40 years ago as every other kind of life, but there has been surprisingly little discontinuity in the music. This is remarkable, given the breadth of outside influences and, of course, the many major artists who have flourished in the intervening years.

While the aforementioned album titles themselves proclaim new direc-tions and the artists involved were simultaneously pushing the boundaries of jazz outwards,[2] jazz in general was 'groovin' high' and definitely in forward gear that year. Wes Montgomery signed with Riverside, Thelonious Monk recorded his famous Town Hall Concert and two of Miles Davis's sidemen on *Kind of Blue*, John Coltrane and Bill Evans, were recording as leaders while Miles himself was working on *Sketches of Spain* with Gil Evans. Further, John Lewis and Duke Ellington composed feature-film scores, *Odds Against Tomorrow* and *Anatomy of a Murder* respectively. Nineteen fifty-nine also saw the term 'bossa nova' used for the first time (in connection with 'Desafinado' by Antonio Carlos Jobim) and the publication of the second edition of George Russell's almost mystical treatise on music theory, *The Lydian Chromatic Concept of Tonal Organisation for Improvisation*. It was the year Eric Dolphy moved to New York, of Johnny Dankworth's success and also of the infamous riot at Newport (the first regular US jazz festival, founded by George Wein in 1954), and much else. Studious fans could prolong this scene-setting recitative of 1959 to chapter length. The music that was recorded in that year is enough to flag it as one of unusual creativity in jazz even in the context of the extraordinary period from the mid-1950s through to the mid-1960s when American artists and intellectuals in every discipline were successfully modernising the cultural landscape. Indeed, it was a 'golden era' in terms of the high quality of art, music, dance, film, literature, drama and even television, one which was embraced by audiences large enough to confer full celebrity status on a few jazz musicians and many other artists in every field.

Historical records

The year 1959/60 is a sort of axis of symmetry between the first jazz recordings (1917) and the end of the twentieth century. It is often stated that jazz is the first music almost fully documented by sound recording. The annotated boxed set of records *From Spirituals to Swing*, made from Carnegie Hall concerts starring Benny Goodman in 1938 and 1939, only reached the market in 1959 and has remained the foundation of many enthusiasts' collections ever since. Prominently featuring Count Basie with members of his and Goodman's bands, with gospel, blues and boogie-woogie musicians representing African-American tributaries to the then modern music, the Carnegie Hall concerts were the first public presentation of jazz as a historical music, but it was really the 1959 release – which sold over a million copies – that popularised this idea. It is interesting to reflect that a sort of manufactured historical document in 1939 was, by 1959, really historical.

In the late 1950s, as compilations of archival jazz and folk recordings became available,[3] the relatively new medium of long-playing records made it possible to hear jazz history without being an expert collector. Anthologies compiled from early commercial releases of jazz, blues and 'field recordings' of African-American music in the Deep South posited and fixed (in time) musical traditions that became canonised as the roots of jazz. What had been mostly accessible to researchers as 'oral history' was becoming accessible to everybody as 'aural history', but always, of course, in the shape of a packaged product, which we now might see as somewhat suspect – not in terms of the authenticity or simple worthiness of the music presented, but for the criterion for selection. I have yet to be convinced that it is fundamentally wrong or misleading to teach a 'canon' in jazz studies,[4] but for better or worse this is how it started. Through the compilation of historical tracks, be they rescued from deepest archival obscurity or re-packaged hits, the musical past is constructed as leading up to something – in this case, modern jazz. This in turn encouraged people to believe, correctly, that modern jazz and jazz LPs could have long-term artistic and commercial value and would also be worth collecting; or, from the record companies' point of view, re-packaging.[5]

Even though members of the first generation of jazz musicians such as Louis Armstrong had some good years left, Sidney Bechet's death in 1959 foreshadowed the inevitable passing of the New Orleans/Chicago era. Billie Holiday and Lester Young, who directly influenced modern jazz, particularly the cool style of the 1950s, also died in 1959. The 1950s generation of musicians that grew up listening to them, to Fats Waller, Duke Ellington, Goodman and Basie, and later to Charlie Parker and Dizzy Gillespie, had all but taken over from those with local and historical connections with early jazz. Born in the 1920s and later, they were entering their prime in the 1960s as mature talents, hitting the scene just behind the watershed of bebop. They pursued careers with a full awareness that jazz is both a changing modern music and one with its own history and traditions. They were, on the whole, musically educated, experienced and inclined to experiment. This was not avant-gardism for its own sake. Making a living in jazz was going to depend on the appeal of the music *per se* rather than the previous built-in marketability of social dancing and jazz versions of popular songs. A 'personal voice', always prized and admired in jazz circles, was now also a personal 'approach' (in the jargon of the time) to music itself, more than just a 'sound' and some signature 'licks'. Many musicians felt that putting theory to work in practical and individual terms was going to be important to their survival, so it was important to 'study'.[6] Interest in music theory and theories about music was not 'academic' in the narrow sense, but part of finding an approach.

A critical debate at the end of the 1950s

The relationship between theory and practice, the pros and cons of jazz changing into a formalised discipline and getting closer to classical music and further from 'pop', are the background dynamics for ongoing musical and critical developments in jazz. Much of the jazz from around this time entered the canon and so did the issues debated. The arguments in favour of 'intellectualism' in jazz take on new, unanticipated meanings in the present era of academic Jazz Studies, but anti-intellectual attitudes have remained the same. I believe opposing sides of the intellectualism issue as understood around 1959 are well represented by two articles summarised below. Much of the jazz criticism written in the 1950s revolves around ideas about music, which criteria should apply, what jazz is and is not, the search for 'direction' and the catch-phrase 'where jazz is going'. Readers and writers, musicians and critics, often identified themselves with opposing, prescriptive concepts of 'jazz' in the abstract, and must have wanted very much to influence others. Participation in an ongoing debate about jazz was apparently part of the joy of being a jazz fan.

Down Beat: Special Silver Anniversary Edition (20 August 1959) features an article entitled 'The Case for Swinging' by John Mehegan, which sums up the history of jazz as 'evolutionary', but argues against further evolution.[7] It also contains André Hodeir's 'Perspective of Modern Jazz: Popularity or Recognition' (translated by Eugene Lees), a prescient rumination on the nature of jazz-as-art.

Mehegan was a working jazz pianist and academic, and an influential pioneer in jazz pedagogy – perhaps the first to believe jazz was teachable in a systematic way.[8] Given this background, it is surprising that he espouses a vehement, anti-intellectual line, although it was common in those days to do so. Let me assure the reader that I am not unfairly quoting Mehegan (with whom I studied briefly) in order to make fun of him or his ideas but, rather, because he is the best-informed and most coherent representative of this persuasion. He was not, though it is hard to tell from this article, against modern jazz, but indeed an admirer of Lennie Tristano and Bill Evans and a modern-jazz player himself. Because of his technical knowledge, arguments he used count as an insider's informed opinion and bear consideration if only to arrive at a better understanding of the underlying issues. In other words, they are not the vapourings of a disaffected journalist who 'couldn't swing a rope'. However, in print he adopts a crusty, hostile tone. Near the end of the article he writes:

> If we continue to smother [jazz] with a superstructure of complexity and
> intellectuality it cannot possibly support, we will eventually destroy it.
> This applies specifically to the cabalists, the metaphysicians, the formalists,
> the pretenders, the beatniks, the Zen Buddhists and the been-zootists.
>
> [Mehegan 1959b]

Given the date of publication, exactly at the time of the Lenox School of Jazz (see below), I believe that his real targets are Gunther Schuller,

George Russell and John Lewis, although his shotgun blast takes in the whole avant-garde. Collectively these three were promoting the principles of third-stream music, a meeting of jazz and classical music on an equal basis which contrasts with the random couplings of the distant past. Russell, as we shall see, might indeed qualify as a 'cabalist' and 'metaphysician', and Schuller and Lewis were uninhibited advocates of intellectualism.

One of Mehegan's pet hates is formalism, which 'has not been generally successful musically speaking for the reason that jazz is basically a folk music employing visceral or non-intellectual materials and, like all folk art, is pre-ponderantly *content* with a minimum of *form*'. This attitude should prepare us for the mindset of an academic but anti-intellectual conservative, with certain implicit beliefs about the world. Taking it 'from the top', Mehegan's article (drastically edited) reads:

> Did Charlie Parker leave a rich nourishing heritage for future jazz men – or did he finish off the art form? . . . The time composite of jazz has undergone extensive changes since 1920 . . . these changes, coupled with expanding instrumental and writing techniques, express in capsule the morphological history of the art form . . .
>
> Although the jazzman has displayed great ingenuity in the areas of time and horizontal extension, he has been singularly uninventive in dealing with the problems of vertical sound (harmony).

This is an odd opinion coming from a jazz pianist, but he does not stop to give reasons for it:

> Jazz is and always has been a tonal music employing the diatonic scale as its frame of reference.
>
> Parker himself never questioned the diatonic system in jazz harmony and never made any attempt to destroy it. In fact, as is well known, Parker returned to the most primitive harmonic materials, the blues, in order to deal freely with the horizontal line.

If the opposite of tonality is atonality, then few would fundamentally dis-agree, however much we might wince at the term 'primitive'.

With authoritarian bravura (and spectacular unintended irony), Mehegan concludes with a list of 'essentials' musicians in 1959 would question – or, using his words, 'attack' or 'destroy' – in order to arrive at a fresher conception of jazz:

> suppose we accept the circumscribed limits of a diatonic harmonic system, 4/4 time, eighth-note, quarter-note, half-note time composite, eight bar sections and the various attendant qualities we have been accustomed to. The point is that if we learned anything in the past 20 years, we have learned that to abandon or seriously alter any of these basic essentials of a jazz performance results in what can no longer be called jazz.

The four albums mentioned at the beginning of this chapter are remembered best for doing everything that 'results in what can no longer be called jazz'. Thus, in a strange way, one agrees with Mehegan. What was called jazz before 1959 is different from what is called jazz now, supporting the dichotomy between the historical and contemporary mentioned at the beginning of this chapter.

But we are not quite through with Mehegan's case. If we accept the circumscribed limits of jazz he proposes (and his is not a bad description of what – in a statistical sense – jazz is), then his later statement that 'all, it would seem [is] in a state of exhaustion' logically follows. For Mehegan writing in 1959, 'the evolution of jazz' is at an end.

Hodeir's article is not 'the case against swinging' but it is in all other respects an opposing and, indeed, formalist view. In contrast to Mehegan, he is not worried about the 'exhaustion' of jazz as creative music, but rather the time it takes for an increasingly specialised form of creativity to make it into the mainstream. Hodeir demands an active role in the service of creativity from an elite audience.[9] He plunges the readers (of *Down Beat*!) into the historical and aesthetic problems of modernism, high culture and popular art:

> Carried along by the prodigious cadence of constant renewal, jazz dies almost as quickly as it is created . . . But it happens that the public . . . does not keep correct time with the rhythm of change . . . This phenomenon has been observed in European art [when] Cézanne and Debussy unveiled the beginnings of a 'modern art' that is in no way of popular origin.
>
> [Hodeir 1959]

The new problem for modern jazz, according to Hodeir, is that recognition (for an artist or work of art) comes before and perhaps without popularity. For example, Monk was recognised as historically important (in 1959) without having experienced popular acclaim. Like Mehegan, Hodeir constructs the narrative of jazz history around the theme of 'evolution', but they really mean different things by it. Hodeir's evolution is punctuated by outstanding masterworks which 'show enough strength and strictness of conception' to transcend the norm. Mehegan wants to set out rules that define jazz in technical terms that are normative for the genre. (These rules and a concept of 'jazz' itself, rather than any particular manifestation in the form of jazz masterworks, are what evolved out of chaos.) Hodeir does not define jazz at all. Like Ellington and most musicians, he believes that an artist must be free to create without reference to pre-determined categories and that there must be valid 'universal' criteria of musical value not limited by genre (see heading quotation on page 153).

For Mehegan, generic boundaries are all-important because he is trying to rule out 'what can no longer be called jazz', so 'popular music' and jazz, while undeniably similar, are really antagonistic terms. The worst outcome of Mehegan's kind of evolutionary theory is that jazz musicians (he does not name any) looking for a way out of the 'cul de sac' of formalism (provided they have admitted they no longer live in the realm of 'folk-music') might opt for

> The final solution [which] is the oldest one in the world . . . Give the people what they want . . . So at last jazz has joined the other entertaining crafts that form the basis of what we call show business . . . The real difference between an art form and an entertaining craft is that an art form has a continuity which demands some contribution from each artist in order to insure its own succession; an entertaining craft makes no demand except that of popularity.   [Mehegan 1959b]

Hodeir spends rather more time considering the meanings of the term 'popular'. Although frankly elitist in outlook, he never equates popular with vulgar. He also does not slip into the present-day assumption that popular equals commercial:

> A musical work can be popular in two very different ways: by its origin and by its audience. They do not always coincide.
>   . . . the art of Ellington, and still more that of Armstrong, remained rather close to the popular origins [note the strict sense of 'popular' here] wherefrom jazz was little by little emancipated. Both won popularity before the cultural interest in jazz was fully realised. And it is only fair to add that they contributed powerfully to the recognition of jazz as an art. Better yet, jazz recognition was identified with their recognition.
>   With the advent of modern jazz, however, the problem of achieving popularity truly began to pose itself . . . For having wished to invent a complex language, suitable to convey a certain number of new truths, jazz became an art of specialists; in cutting itself free of its popular sources, it voluntarily limited itself to an audience of connoisseurs. Then it became risky to seek popularity if, deep down, one did not wish to give up what had been gained in modern jazz.
>   True popularity for a 'difficult work' is recognition by a reasonably large elite. The most celebrated masterpieces have taken this cultural route to success; it is a route that is necessarily long. A work, an artist, is recognised only thanks to the diffusing influence of a few clairvoyant souls . . .
>   And on a cultural level, the demand that this work show enough strength and strictness of conception to reach those whose sensibilities were nourished and developed by the greatest artists remains the least deceptive criterion of recognition.
>   Aside from those happy few who today appreciate it, the most advanced jazz has already launched invisible missiles toward the public of tomorrow.
>   [Hodeir 1959]

Conceptualising jazz

The familiar fault-lines in the generally accepted version of jazz history have always appeared immediately after an influential individual or group was in a position to articulate a conception of jazz. By this I mean defining what jazz was in their time, not a manifesto of which 'direction jazz should go in'. It is as if certain musicians in each generation, after a number of years of playing gigs and 'paying dues', gradually or suddenly find the hitherto hidden 'deep structure' of everything they have done or will ever do. These revelations, I believe, preceded and sometimes precipitated the new movements in jazz. Of course 'movements' or sub-genres do not have to happen consecutively and there is no reason that every new direction is inevitably 'forwards'.

Musicians have always been more concerned with ways of playing music than talking about it. Nevertheless thinking about the potential of what they do is as traditional as blue notes. In his chapter on Jelly Roll Morton in *Early Jazz*, Schuller uses Morton's own words (transcribed from the Library of Congress recordings made by Alan Lomax) and his own exhaustive case-study of Morton's work to show that what Morton called the 'invention' of jazz was the first conceptualisation of jazz:

> To Morton the composer, ragtime and blues were not just musical styles, but specific musical forms . . . These were as well defined as the sonata form was to a 'classical' composer, and Morton accepted them as active continuing traditions. At this point Morton's claim to be the 'originator of jazz' begins to take on a degree of plausibility. In his mind and perhaps in actual fact Morton had isolated as 'jazz' an area not covered by the blues or ragtime. Since he applied a smoother more swinging syncopation and a greater degree of improvisational license to a variety of materials, such as ragtime, opera and French and Spanish popular songs and dances, Morton's claim to have invented jazz no longer seems so rash.　[1968, 139–41]

Morton's statement that 'jazz is a style that can be applied to any type of tune' and his use of 'jazz' as a verb, as in 'jazzing' the 'Miserere' from *Il Trovatore* (see page 163), make it clear that the essence of jazz (noun and verb) is process and perhaps manner, but not content. It must be remembered that the American popular song was early, but not original, material for jazzing.

A final comment from Schuller's chapter on Morton lends some strong historical backing to the 'formalism' that was decried as infiltrating and diluting modern jazz: 'Morton's vision of jazz entailed contrast and variety – instrumental, timbral, textural; in short, structural.' This aspect of Morton's vision was de-emphasised by bebop with its formulaic head–solos–head approach to performance. (The 'structure' talked about when musicological terminology is used to explain why an improvised bebop solo is 'great' is not what Morton had in mind.)

Valid conceptualisations are holistic by implication but in practice it often seems that a disproportionate amount of attention is focused on one parameter at a time. In Morton's music, jazz was structurally complex but also harmonically primitive and improvisationally constrained compared to later styles. For soloists to soar it was found that one needed cyclical rather than additive forms and simpler arrangements. The professionally composed 'popular song' replaced traditional sources like hymns, marches and other borrowings referred to by Morton and his contemporaries and the great challenge ahead was the 'jazzing-up' of complex harmony.

Jazz changes and 'invisible missiles'

Bebop drew on various and new sources, including modern European composers, but by far the greatest influence was the immediate past and present of jazz itself. The conventions of jazz playing had attained stability in the Swing Era, and Art Tatum and other piano virtuosi, professional arrangers working for Benny Goodman, Woody Herman, Stan Kenton, the Ellington–Strayhorn team and composers working in Hollywood were constantly pushing harmony towards greater complexity. Harmony in the 1940s was dense, functional yet richly chromatic and highly mobile. Jazz musicians, though popularly celebrated as 'rhythm cats' in the commercial media, had become chord-meisters. Just being able to play 'the changes', let alone improvise a coherent chorus on songs like 'Have You Met Miss Jones', 'Invitation' or 'Stella By Starlight', is still an indication of sophistication.

Playing 'standards' means creating culturally and musically transformed versions of recognised Broadway or Hollywood songs. Eventually this became the art of playing an alternative version to prior jazz versions while the non-jazz original faded from memory, leaving only the tune and chord progression. In this way, a 'standard' is infinitely re-adaptable. For jazz musicians, hearing 'the changes' is so ingrained and natural that they barely notice that it is probably only jazz musicians who automatically relate to music as being essentially 'the changes'. Most can name a tune they know well within a few seconds of hearing it, even if the excerpt starts in the middle of a solo and is played with a different feel or tempo, using different instruments from those in any previous version. In other words they have developed a way of conceptualising music that has little to do with how it sounds in an ordinary sense of audition.

Jazz musicians adapted and improved a notational system of alphabetical chord symbols, originally used as early as the 1910s for labelling ukelele or guitar tablature in sheet-copy versions of popular songs. For example, the first two measures of 'I Got Rhythm' would have four box diagrams showing frets, strings and finger position labelled thus: C6, Amin., Dmin., G7 (not indicating chord function, as in the analytical notation I, VI, II, V). Published 'stock arrangements' for dance bands included piano parts consisting of chords in staff notation, but besides being literally harder to see, staff notation seemed to require restating identical chord voicings chorus after chorus and, worse, articulating them in the same rhythm. It is difficult to think of one recording where such a part was actually played. Similarly, bass parts were notated bass parts, but players who understood how to construct bass lines by connecting chord tones usually ignored them and wrote in the chord progression according to the alphabetical system, referring to staff notation only where a specific bass line was required. Guitar parts were always in chord symbols and therefore became the *lingua franca* of rhythm-section players even as the traditional role of 'rhythm guitar' was becoming obsolete in the 1940s. In small combos where every player (not only the soloist of the moment) is improvising most of the time, the normal and easiest way to co-ordinate performance by visual means is to give every player the same information. All musicians (including poor readers and regardless of instrument) know how to work from a lead-sheet consisting of the melody in treble clef with chord symbols above the line and sometimes the lyrics.

Chord symbols consist of the letter name of the root, a symbol such as a '-' for minor plus numbers if needed. F-7 therefore means F minor seventh. If F-7 occurs at the beginning of a measure of 4/4 time, it means the harmony starts on the downbeat (not that the pianist must play the chord on 'one') and if it comes near the middle of the bar, F-7 is the chord 'change' on beat three. The merit of this system is that it leaves so much up to the musician. Chord symbols do not specify register, inversion, top note, doublings or density. They do show the harmonic rhythm, in other words, the sequence and distribution of 'the changes'. You can write 'the changes' for a tune on any scrap of paper that comes to hand – menus and napkins become bass parts between sets – or, if there isn't even a pen available, the pianist or bass player can just call them out. (Not exactly professional behaviour, but who hasn't done this once or twice?)

There was no authoritative source for chord symbols so there were inconsistencies and disagreements, especially regarding notating extensions beyond the seventh. Does F-7 +9 mean add the ninth (G) or add and raise the ninth (G♯)? Of course musicians could decide for themselves which sounded best and which seemed logical. (G♯ is A♭ enharmonically, which adds nothing to an F minor chord, so G is the right answer.) Certainly by the 1950s, jazz musicians had to know some 'theory' whether or not they thought of it as that. Composers such as Milhaud, Stravinsky, Bartók and even Schoenberg were icons of highbrow modernism to jazz musicians, but not ones to emulate on the gig.[10] Playing changes was, at first anyway, an exploration and re-codification of the inherited tonal system before there could be an 'attack' on it. Rhythm-and-blues and urban blues used improvisation, a heavy beat and much else in common with 1940s jazz, but revealing the harmonic subtlety of the popular song was the defining, exclusive characteristic of jazz.[11]

'The way the music had to go'

'Whatever we were using had been around since Bach's time, or maybe Brahms's. Parker had the *style*', Dizzy Gillespie told me in an unpublished interview in 1987. In context it was clear that Gillespie was talking about harmony, possibly the seamless modulating sequences in Bach and Brahms's reassertion of functional harmonic relationships (analogous to Parker's use of ii–V?). He was not more specific. From a present-day perspective, harmony is the least difficult aspect of bebop. (Correctly reproducing the rhythms and phrasing of a Bud Powell or Charlie Parker solo in transcription takes considerable practice at a high technical level, but any jazz pianist can play the left-hand chords by ear.) I think the point about harmony that older musicians keep coming back to is simply that jazz harmony seemed to be the one aspect of music that was systematic and learnable. I suspect that the mystique of harmony has to do with not having an overview of tonality as a coherent, closed structural system. When I asked Gillespie if his colleagues in the 1940s saw themselves as part of a movement, he said he didn't think so. Were they consciously developing a new style? No, 'it was just the way the music *had to* go', insisting on inevitability almost as if 'music' were determined to 'go' somewhere of itself. But not quite, because, without 'the style' of Parker, without his specific and essential integration of all elements, it would not have been bebop. Along with the individual beauty and brilliance of Parker's music, a virtuosic and studied approach to playing 'the changes' was in tune with post-war modernism.

This is perhaps a good moment to reflect a little further on the question of the 'evolution' of jazz. This was not a problem in the 1950s because it was true for everyone coming into their own at the time. They had experienced a modern movement that demanded (but also began providing) ever greater knowledge and skill on the part of musicians and repaid their efforts with ever greater creative freedom and sometimes even a good living doing interesting, experimental music. In the 1960s it became difficult to see where 'the music' was trying to go, but 'evolution' was still tenable because developments that were taking place side-by-side claimed a shared past. The confusion and disunity of the 1960s was not the result of running into blind alleys and losing audiences to rock so much as an inconvenient profusion of overlapping epiphanies. There was no single way in which the 'music had to go' or just one 'genius' that had the 'style'.

The Lenox School and jazz education

The Lenox School of Jazz lasted only four summers (1957–60) but it had a great influence on the immediate and long-term future of jazz. Organised by John Lewis and Gunther Schuller, it was surely one of the main launch-sites of Hodeir's 'invisible missiles'. Simply intoning some other names of teachers and students who were there (Bill Evans, George Russell, Bill Russo, Kenny Dorham, Jim Hall and Jimmy Giuffre among the former, and Ornette Coleman, Don Cherry, Freddie Hubbard, Chuck Israels, Don Ellis and Steve Kuhn among the latter) risks making this School sound even more momentous than it was. Realistically, three weeks a year of intense study and interaction with great musicians is probably not enough to change the everyday world of jazz completely, unless that world is taking off in new directions anyway. But, strangely, the opposite of exaggeration has occurred and relatively few people know about Lenox. Even though literature about jazz is a high proportion of what I read, the only reason I know about this amazing School is because I was there as a 12-year-old in 1959, the year my father Dave was 'in residence', accompanied by his family.[12]

Situated at The Music Inn, a summer resort in the Berkshires and within walking distance of Tanglewood (the famous summer home of the Boston Symphony Orchestra), the School had, in effect, its own country hotel, concert tent, two bars and other venues for making music 'inside' and/or 'outside' – in every sense that those terms came to imply. When I recently interviewed Schuller about 'Lenox' (as it is referred to), he modestly played down the unique role of the School, because 'it was everywhere at that time'. Common sense nevertheless suggests that, as a result of the concentration of professionally active, highly skilled, creative and analytical musicians at a specific time and place, new 'discoveries' in jazz were mutually recognised and at least made known within the nuclear community. This in turn would inevitably accelerate the diffusion and acceptance of new ways of playing and thinking about music. How long would it have taken for Ornette Coleman to be recognised (and even popular in Hodeir's sense) had he not been there? And, in the theoretical realm, who would have spontaneously gone out and bought a book by a little-known composer named George Russell, especially one called *The Lydian Chromatic Concept of Tonal Organisation for Improvisation*? News gets out when musicians are gathered.

Furthermore, the formal practical study of jazz was, to a great extent, later developed by two Lenox students, David Baker and Jamey Aebersold.

They were recruited, along with Freddie Hubbard and bassist, Larry Ridley, by Schuller from Indiana, and it was here that they were all first exposed to jazz as a formal academic discipline. After Lenox, Aebersold created and published practical methods for learning jazz, eventually building his publishing and training courses into a multi-million-dollar international business. Baker is the long-serving Distinguished Professor and Head of Jazz Studies at the Conservatory at Indiana University and author of numerous analytical and pedagogical works years ahead of the wave of jazz studies now cresting in American universities.

The Lenox School of Jazz prospectus offered 'a conception of the history of jazz, the development of its styles and idioms, and its relationship to music as a whole . . . a point of view toward jazz as a significant and vital art form of our time'. Schuller told me that Coleman was extremely moved by hearing Jelly Roll Morton's music for the first time. The largest impact from an education 'missile' was, however, both directly and indirectly, the kind of music theory being taught at Lenox. It remains a major influence on what jazz students learn today.

Theories of music

The ability of African performance arts to transform the European tradition of composition while assimilating some of its elements is perhaps the most striking and powerful evolutionary force in the history of modern music. [G I O I A 1 9 9 7, 8]

The historical transformation of jazz from an entertainment music to an art music, initiated by the bebop revolution in the mid-1940s, represents arguably one of the most significant cultural shifts of the century . . . no form of mass culture seems to have crossed the boundary between 'entertainment' and 'art' as decisively or irreversibly as jazz. [G E N D R O N 1 9 9 5, 3 1]

A perennial difficulty with teaching music theory is forcing minds and ears more attuned to the jazz tradition to accept as provisionally true fairly essential 'facts' of the European harmonic tradition. To jazz ears, the final tonic major chord of a piece or section could easily have a flat seventh. A dominant seventh chord a tritone away from another chord is its freely interchangeable 'substitute'. Parallel octaves strengthen a line (but are seldom noticed given the common octave doubling of trumpet and tenor saxophone). In general, controlled 'dissonance' is more desirable than 'consonance', chord voicings without roots are 'hip' and simple triads with voices doubled are only used to convey an atmosphere of funky reverence.

What was still lacking in the 1950s was a self-contained, systematic theory of tonality and harmony that took for granted jazz chords and other devices that musicians actually had developed and put into practice over time. Such a theory was needed for 'irreversible development' as the 1950s drew to a close.

A body of information (generalities about music) and drill (exercises to demonstrate their application) is what academic music curricula refer to as 'theory'. Corresponding information came into jazz usage through invention, discovery and piecemeal appropriation by individual artists like John Coltrane, who was 'looking for something to play' (Porter 1998, 88) and for practical solutions to specific musical problems:

> A new influence [on Coltrane in *c.*1951–2] was the legendary pianist Hasaan Ibn Ali. Born in Philadelphia in 1931, Hasaan, as he was called . . . became known as an original composer and theorist. He was interested in the properties of fourths, in chord progressions that moved by thirds or seconds instead of fifths, in playing a variety of scales and arpeggios against each chord – all of which figured prominently in Coltrane's music later on.   [*Ibid.*]

Hasaan is reported to have used the chord-voicing of flat seventh, major third and thirteenth (without sounding the root) before it became common in the 1960s. This isolated piece of information (coupled with the fact that not many people today know about Hasaan) reads like erudite trivia, but actually provides a typical example of jazz musicians as 'a learning community' (see Berliner 1994, 36–62). Even better, this precise piece of 'trivia', the chord made up of an augmented fourth and a perfect fourth, is a distinctive feature of jazz harmony. It also represents the overvalued, fragmentary bits of information jazz musicians invented or collected to fill the vast space between 'legit' theory and jazz practice.

The Lydian Chromatic Concept

The first text written specifically as jazz theory was *The Lydian Chromatic Concept of Tonal Organisation* by George Russell, first published in 1953 and issued in a revised edition in 1959. Russell is a composer, teacher and some-time bandleader who had a great influence on the rising third-stream intelligentsia of the 1950s and early 1960s. He studied composition with Stephen Wolpe and also wrote scores for Gillespie. He taught at Lenox in 1958 and 1959, which gave his ideas the most important exposure imaginable at the time. (He later taught at New England Conservatory from the late 1960s.) As an academically trained composer he added unusual technical skill at manipulating structure, harmony and balance, affecting the usual concerns of jazz composition, which are the interplay of improvised solos and arranged ensemble passages. He was a daring and rigorous experimentalist as a composer (see, for example, 'All About Rosie' and 'Living Time'). Perhaps because he did not project himself enough as a performer (on piano) his music is little known to the public but it remains controversial, influential and respected within professional circles. Whatever the ultimate verdict on *The Lydian Chromatic Concept*, there is no doubt he was an inspirational teacher. 'All About Rosie' (re-issued on Schuller, *The Birth of the Third Stream*) is a singular accomplishment: it is mainly the exciting piano solo by Bill Evans that gives it an aura of historic specificity, but in style and conception it sounds as if it could have been written much more recently.

Unlike its respected author, *The Lydian Chromatic Concept of Tonal Organisation for Improvisation* (to use its full title) has a mixed reputation, probably because, according to Russell, 'The Lydian Chromatic Concept is as large as all of the music that has been written or that could be written in the equal tempered tuning system' ('Technical Appendix B'). Unfortunately, his attempt to present and prove such an audaciously comprehensive theory sometimes resulted in unreadably turgid discourse burdened with jargon, yet the work's influence has spread far beyond those who have actually read it:

> Russell codified the modal approach to harmony (using scales instead of chords) in a theoretical treatise that he says was inspired by a casual remark the eighteen-year-old Miles Davis made to him in 1944: Miles said he wanted to learn all the changes and I reasoned that he might try to find the closest scale for every chord . . . Davis popularised those liberating ideas in recordings like *Kind of Blue*, undermining the entire harmonic foundation of bop that had inspired him and Russell in the first place.
> [Giddins 1998, 6][13]

Davis, who according to this story was indirectly responsible for the Lydian Chromatic Concept, is reported to have given it its most succinct formulation, something like 'F should be where middle C is on the piano.' What this means is that instead of basing pitch relations on the major scale from C to C, our basic scale should be the Lydian mode, the white notes from F to F. The reasons given in Russell are acoustic (overtone series), historical (the major/minor scale system was a compromise which allowed for cadential harmony using the subdominant) and musical (the dissonant sound of fourth against major third making the fourth an 'avoid note' in major harmony). The series, moving up the cycle of fifths seven times starting from F, is as follows: F–C–G–D–A–E–B (–F). The augmented fourth (in either direction) is the last interval in this series, taking it back to F. Rearrange these notes in stepwise order and the result is the Lydian scale. To get to an enharmonic version of the 'perfect fourth' of the major scale (A♯) would require going right to the end of the series of fifths. (Continuing one more fifth would land on E♯ which is F, the starting note.) A♯, that is, B♭, is therefore the remotest possible note from the Lydian tonic. 'Enharmonic' distinctions are inaudible and therefore meaningless to Russell who takes equal temperament for granted. Why do we have a major scale with a perfect fourth rather than a Lydian scale and its derivatives?

> The major scale probably emerged as the predominating scale of Western music, because within its seven tones lies the most fundamental harmonic progression of the classical era . . . the tonic major chord on C . . . the sub-dominant major chord on F . . . the dominant seventh chord on G – thus, the major scale *resolves* to its tonic major chord. The Lydian scale *is* the sound of its tonic major chord.   [Russell 1959, iii, iv]

This is original, brilliant, even self-evident, but no one had quite said it before. The practical implications are indeed far-reaching and amount to a theory that works both for playing and teaching jazz. It follows then that Davis's original aim can be fulfilled by studying what are now called chord–scale relationships; this is, in fact, what jazz students are taught and there is of course much material (published by Aebersold) that supports teaching in this way. Davis's *Kind of Blue* is often used to illustrate what chord-scale relationships mean in practice and a pedagogy based on an ahistoric but serviceable system of modes (of major and melodic minor plus synthetic scales, etc.) is how improvisation is formally taught. For example, one of the first pieces I teach beginners is 'So What', which gives a convincing demonstration that the Dorian mode and the minor-seventh chord (with all extensions) are co-extensive; somewhat like describing light in physics as either a wave or a particle depending on what you need the description for.

Russell himself, perhaps thinking more as a composer and theorist than as a musician in search of an 'approach', took things in a somewhat more obscure direction, inventing special terminology (e.g., 'vertical polymodal-ity' and 'auxiliary diminished scale'). The details of this aspect of the Lydian Chromatic Concept seem so far not to have infiltrated practice today but the basic principle of chord–scale is now pervasive, even clichéd.

Russell was not merely tinkering with abstract relationships for the sake of it. His vision also had an observational and predictive dimension that was proven correct by the end of the 1960s:

> Since the bop period, a war on the chord has been going on I think . . . [Parker] probably represented the last full blossoming of a jazz music that was based on chords . . . Even the need to do extended form pieces, whether successful or not, is a desire to get away from a set of chord changes.   [Russell 1959, xx]

Ian Carr (1999) believes that Davis's mature career can be plotted as a gradual reduction of harmonic activity. The decade that started with *Kind of Blue* and *Sketches of Spain* ended with *In a Silent Way* and *Bitches Brew.*

The justifications, precedents and far-reaching claims Russell crowds into his oddly organised treatise tend to complicate rather than clarify, but the Lydian Chromatic Concept meant liberation from the obsolete concerns and dictates of 'legit' academic theory which is based on a different tradition of tonal organisation.

Even back in 1959, the 'war on the chord' escalated to thermonuclear proportions with the advent of free jazz and Coleman's harmolodic theory, which he has not systematically defined. His music generally seems to include reference to a tonal centre but no key or tonal hierarchy, accidental harmonies generated by moving parts (considerable parallelism) but no set sequences of chords, and communicative and often beautiful or humorous melodies.

In recent correspondence on these jazz theories, Barry Kernfeld wrote to me:

> the theoretical underpinnings of harmolodic theory are extremely suspect, even more so than those of George Russell's Lydian Chromatic Concept, but there is no question that these sorts of casual, home-made approaches to jazz theory have been of great value to performers and educators, helping them to capture, or to communicate, through inferential or emotive means, some of the processes involved in jazz improvisation.

To which I replied:

> I think the word 'theory' in Coleman's case has to be taken in a less technical – as in music theory – sense and recast as something like 'critical theory', 'reception theory'; even a musical version of relativity theory. It is an outlook or idea rather than a process of analysis or a set of instructions. My workaday answer to 'what does harmolodic mean?' is 'the theory that melody, harmony and rhythm should not be considered separately, especially in improvisation, because they all generate each other'.[14]

My workaday answer is an example of both the strength and weakness of formalism. It isolates a principle which Coleman has made the centre of his musical universe just as Russell has made the Lydian scale – 'the sound of its tonic major chord' – the centre of his. On the other hand, my quasi-definition cannot explain any particular musical result or why there was a need for harmolodic theory. Coleman must have had an intuitive cultural motive for dreaming up a word like 'harmolodic' and making it stick by playing out its implications throughout a career spanning decades. Coleman came from obscurity and gutbucket rhythm-and-blues gigs to the foremost intellectual forum of jazz in Lenox, encoding as 'theory' the emotional, primal and sacral substratum of a music now on the threshold of entering its academic phase. He renders unto academe a substantial and varied body of work and a word for it, a technical-sounding neologism of dual 'signifyin'[15] and formalist connotations. Now it is up to us, not him, to do the explaining. I think Kernfeld is right about the pedagogic importance of leaving a path open to continue communication 'through inferential or emotive means, some of the processes involved in jazz improvisation'. I would add, in the creation of music generally.

The third stream

'Third stream' ideology offered the potential of the two great mainstreams of western music, jazz and classical, blending into a third style. For those who have not yet heard *The Birth of the Third Stream*,[16] 'blending jazz and classical' could have kitsch connotations ranging from Paul Whiteman's orchestral jazz in the late 1920s to modern popularisations such as the often disparaged *Bird with Strings*, Jacques Loussier playing Bach accompanied by brushes on the snare drum, and orchestral 'pops' arrangements of Gershwin tunes sung by an opera star or even with a lonely jazz soloist in front. That third stream was entirely something else will become clear to any jazz fan looking at the list of composers on *The Birth of the Third Stream*: Jimmy Giuffre, J. J. Johnson, John Lewis, Charles Mingus, Gunther Schuller and George Russell. The majority of the players are jazz musicians (for example, Bill Evans, Bernie Glow, Miles Davis, Urbie Green and the composers) and, other than the basses and Barry Galbraith on guitar, there are no strings attached.

Despite well-made manifesto albums[17] on major labels in the 1950s and a prolific and respected advocate in Schuller, third-stream music seems at first to have been only a movement of its time. Did any 'invisible missiles' arrive in the future? Record producer George Avakian writes in the liner notes to *The Birth of the Third Stream*: 'With the passing years, it's been said that one doesn't hear much about third stream any more. There is a good reason for this; it has been absorbed into the mainstream.' Some of Schuller's new liner notes for this re-release contain the same message:

> Looking back to those heady, exciting days of 40 years ago, it is also fascinating to observe how the technical and stylistic horizons of musicians have broadened and deepened in the intervening years . . . it is commonplace today to find many performers who will readily deal with any kind of music: improvised or written . . . Varèse and Stravinsky . . . Mingus and Coleman . . . The world of music in the 1950s was still for the most part divided among sharply defined lines of musicians who, on the jazz side, could not (or preferred not to) read music . . . while on the 'classical side' musicians could not improvise, could not swing, could barely capture the unique rhythmic inflections and expanded sonorities of jazz.

This is a triumphal update of Schuller's original notes for *Modern Jazz Concert*. He wrote that this concert would have been impossible ten years before, and the existence of a number of musicians who can perform difficult written music and play jazz in 1957 is proof of the advantageous intermingling of jazz and non-jazz influences.

The main period of production under the third-stream banner was more like a series of premieres than the 'birth' of a new style that would (as real and metaphorical offspring do) take on its own life away from its original creators as bebop did. Or, if *really* a new kind of music, then *as jazz did*! So far it is not 'the way the music had to go', but it did foretell the 'birth' of a new kind of musician. The birth metaphor fits well with the advent of total instrumentalists like Keith Jarrett and Wynton Marsalis (their public mutual animosity notwithstanding) and so many young, relatively unknown musicians who make up the professional scene today. Third-stream composers had musicians such as these in mind.

The 1959 recordings

Since 1959, unresolved questions surround the alternative approaches to harmonic activity as the primary controlling factor in jazz performance and composition. If playing 'the changes' can be questioned, so can every other 'given'. The almost simultaneous popularisation of devices that were undoubtedly known but barely used in jazz is no accident. I will now turn to the four recordings I listed at the start of this chapter, without meaning to imply that four very different musicians were knowingly working in tandem or constituted a self-conscious 'movement'. Along the way I pointed out contemporaneous critical and technical concepts and now we can examine what these records 'mean' in jazz history and why these 40-year-old recordings remain both contemporary and historical. All recorded in 1959, they confirm that jazz was not just on yet another new course but was rapidly expanding like a galaxy. To risk stating the obvious, the collection of music represented here does not add up to a new style; on the contrary, it signals the break-up of a broad consensus (already charged with centrifugal forces) and perhaps, with hindsight, the last chapter of the collectivist and evolutionary narrative. Each record included in this set showcases an idea that contributes to the overall stockpile of jazz resources, and the net result was to remove from jazz Mehegan's 'circumscribed limits of a diatonic harmonic system, 4/4 time, eighth-note, quarter-note, half-note time composite, eight bar sections and the various attendant qualities we have been accustomed to' (see above, p. 181). Taken together, these landmarks of modern jazz at the end of the 1950s anticipate the 1960s as the epoch of stretching the form. And, by the way, they did call it 'jazz'.

Of all of the 'experimental' albums ever made, only *Kind of Blue* seems perfect and still able to please everybody. *Time Out* by Dave Brubeck was attacked as too 'commercial' while anything by Coleman is still too 'far out', just too different, for mainstream cultural assimilation. Leaving aside anything we know about the subsequent careers of the musicians involved, these three albums are high-quality realisations of their creators' artistic goals at the time; in every sense of the word, good records. In spite of its historic importance as a 'great' album, *Giant Steps* (with all due respect to Coltrane) sounds thrown together. Canonic status is accorded on other grounds: it represents a crucial stage in a celebrated artist's growth, premieres of compositions that will be performed for the rest of time, a strong declaration of stylistic stance.

An appreciation of jazz differs from the way one appreciates classical music. The 'rough edges', sloppy execution and inconsistency within some jazz performances are not there by design, but that they remain there at all in a medium that allows for re-takes, editing or rejecting a track that is unacceptable, points to other priorities. Jazz recordings that are considered good (and of course there is debate about which these are) have a long shelf-life and usually contain some brilliant unrepeatable moments framed within identifiable musical contexts that are interesting in themselves and capable of replication elsewhere. The context – composition, the ensemble, the style and maybe certain 'licks' in the solos – is all that alternate takes should have in common, so from the standpoint of a musician making a recording, the unrepeatable is most important. Next priority is the realisation of the composition, or concept, to the extent that there is one. Sometimes the first priority is to get down on record a prototype that can be improved on. But choosing between takes that equally get the idea across the brilliant improvised passage reverts to priority number one. Jazz musicians often hear or play 'what a piece is about' and are satisfied if the idea – in musical terms – is made sufficiently clear. Ideally, everyone plays the right notes, in time, in tune and with the right feeling and the instruments in perfect balance and sounding better under studio conditions with controlled reverberation than they would 'live'. Musicians accept that this cannot be always the case and listeners have learned too that high-quality jazz moments and imaginative ideas are worth more than flawless execution devoid of risk and freedom. That said, polished recordings such as those made by the Modern Jazz Quartet, the Miles Davis Sextet and the Dave Brubeck Quartet are not to be written off jazz-wise as less spontaneous, but rather the result of the same musicians working together long enough to develop a collective consistency of execution. (*The Shape of Jazz to Come* is spectacularly 'tight' in a less obvious way.) *Giant Steps* did not document the collective effort of a working band but the leader's material and musical ideas.

Miles Davis was first identified with the bebop movement of the 1940s and, from then on, seemed to lead the way in every new movement in modern jazz. *Kind of Blue* was not so much a revolution as a realisation, a supreme realisation of achieved simplicity. This is music that is expressive and cool, modern and simple, intellectually conceived – it is explicitly based on a theoretical idea – yet spontaneous in execution. Declaring 'war on the chord' meant no longer having to race around a slalom course of harmonic 'changes'. For example, the opening track, 'So What', uses just two chords in 32 bars. In the album notes, Bill Evans refers to Davis's compositions not as 'tunes' but as 'frameworks': 'As the painter needs his framework of parchment, the improvising musical group needs its framework in time. Miles Davis presents here frameworks which are exquisite in their simplicity and yet contain all that is necessary to stimulate performance with a sure reference to the primary conception.'

Kind of Blue has been extensively written about and has by now, in a Milesian, low-key way, worked its way into mass culture (see, for example, Khan 2000). I have already discussed some of the background to modal jazz. *Kind of Blue* is not the first jazz record to 'use modes' consciously and of course it is not just one technical factor but a fully integrated aesthetic achievement, including the performances of all members of the sextet, that make it the modal 'classic'.[18]

In the same year that he recorded *Kind of Blue* as a member of the Miles Davis Sextet, Coltrane pushed working with chord changes to the nth degree on his own *Giant Steps*. Poet and sociologist LeRoi Jones, writing in 1963, was also aware of the war on the chord:

> If Coleman's music can be called nonchordal, John Coltrane's music is fanatically chordal. In his solos, Coltrane seems almost to want to separate each note of the chord (and its overtones) into separate entities and suck out even the most minute musical potential. With each instance, Coltrane redefines his accompanying chords as kinetic splinters of melody, rather than using the generalised block sound of the chord as the final determinant of the music's direction and shape.   [228]

Certainly after *Giant Steps* Coltrane had nothing to prove as a virtuoso. Tunes using 'Coltrane changes' (progressions in thirds, semitones and fourths, perhaps inspired by Hasaan), along with transcriptions of his solos, are still the advanced literature of the tenor saxophone and indeed for chordal jazz in a modal era. If most musicians learned 'So What' because it was so simple, everyone had to learn 'Giant Steps' because it was so hard. Coltrane's short career at the top began with posing and solving technical problems (but with passionate commitment), and ended with smashing his way through layers of complexity to pure expression. Perhaps he was looking for the answer to the rhetorical question, 'So what?' The year 1959 finds him still near the beginning of this self-described spiritual journey and at this stage his music is intellectual; he is preoccupied with its technical elements rather than the esoteric musician as conduit for divine energy he later became.

For Ornette Coleman, playing on chord changes would have been just 'playing the background', the equivalent of not really improvising at all. Naming an album that demonstrated his harmolodic alternative, *The Shape of Jazz to Come* was an affront or at best a puzzle to many musicians. Coleman's approach seemed a crude abandonment of hard-earned skills and the collective wisdom of two or three generations. 'Free jazz' was a rejection of deeply felt criteria of 'validity' so painstakingly learned and observed by jazz musicians. By 1959, most took for granted that their work happened within a tradition that they had inherited and that would outlive them. Coleman's re-shaping of jazz 'to come' was uncomfortable in this context. Most disquietingly of all, his music could be quite beautiful. It was correctly predicted by the nay-sayers that whatever merit there might be in Coleman's own music, the influence of free jazz as a movement would have the effect of driving people away. It did, and this had real-world consequences. The resolute traditionalism of our present age is perhaps meant to protect the jazz scene against a similar economic catastrophe in the future. In the 1960s, free jazz won adherents even among established players like Coltrane. To the average listener, the problem with much of free jazz had less to do with not being 'based on the chord' than with the strident and deliberately 'un-musical' sounds often associated with it. Nevertheless, in the long run, the mainstream benefited from avant-garde explorations of an enlarged jazz sound-world, e.g., how instruments are played, which sounds are musical and how sound is organised. The avant-garde of the 1960s and 1970s gener-ously opened up a non-imitative space for improvisers, especially European musicians, for whom the disciplines and re-worked 'standards' (tunes) of bebop were of marginal relevance to their artistic goals and culture.

After the intellectual intensity surrounding the three above-mentioned albums, to include a popular hit like *Time Out* may seem like dragging *Star Wars* into a discussion of avant-garde cinema, but it really did open up a 'final frontier' of jazz. Like *Kind of Blue*, it was an album entirely dedicated to working out a particular musical idea. Steve Race's sleeve notes begin:

> Should some cool-minded Martian come to earth to check on the state of our music, he might play through 10,000 jazz records before he found one that wasn't in common 4/4 time . . . Dave Brubeck . . . is really the first to explore the uncharted seas . . . The outcome of his experiments is this album.

Experimenting was much closer to Brubeck's outlook than hit-making. In fact, the production of *Time Out* was undertaken somewhat in a spirit of artistic rebellion under a cloud of corporate disapproval. Columbia Records did not like the idea of an album of 'originals', the odd time-signatures concept or even the cover art he wanted. Because Brubeck (like Davis) was one of the top-selling jazz artists on the label, Columbia agreed to release *Time Out*, but only on condition that he also record an album of standards (*Gone with the Wind*).[19]

In spite of 'war' rhetoric, chords are not really destroyed by modes and/or free playing any more than 4/4 is rendered obsolete by 5/4. Soon after *Kind of Blue*, the chord-density Davis cleared out of his kind of jazz came back as second growth in the shape of 'modal' changes, compound harmonies, chord shapes and clusters over pedal points, primarily through the influence of McCoy Tyner, Coltrane's pianist during his 'classic' Quartet years. The chord, though weakened, has not yet surrendered completely and unconditionally, and jazz musicians still play and compose 'tunes' based on 'changes'.

The freedom to import or invent musical resources fundamentally changed the role of the composer-performer in jazz. Like Jelly Roll Morton, one could go on inventing jazz or take it as a given. The jazz composer-performer can choose to be a creator within a form and/or creator of forms. The difference, as of 1959, is that jazz was at last strong enough to venture beyond established conventions without losing its identity.

In the twenty first century the idealistic notion of an 'autonomous art form', especially one like jazz with popular roots, requires some qualification. What I have been writing about relates mostly to the internal methodologies of jazz because, as we have seen, this is what certain leading musicians and intellectuals were engaged with in 1959. Of course this engagement did not happen in a historical or cultural vacuum. Contributing factors ranged from the industry-wide changeover to the stereo $33\frac{1}{3}$ LP record around 1957 to broad social trends such as the surge in higher education affecting musicians and audiences in post-war America, economic growth and nationalism (the decline of regionalism) in culture, electronic media and commerce, the appearance of sub-cultures identified with alternative expressions in the arts and the vexed, pervasive, dynamics of race. Zen and Existentialism proclaimed the reality of the here and now and the modernist spirit encouraged experimentalism for its own sake. In the otherwise ambiguous jazz world, a new phase was clearly ushered in by 'music about music', as demonstrated in the four albums briefly discussed in this chapter. I therefore considered the background of intellectualism, technical means and critical expectation in order to understand the amazingly rapid success and recognition by an elite and canonisation of what was, of course, radical innovation. Mehegan's blustering in *Down Beat* would not seem ridiculous to us now if *Kind of Blue*, *Giant Steps*, *The Shape of Jazz to Come* and *Time Out* had not been by and large accepted first of all by the dynamic artistic community in which they arose.

There is a relatively simple answer to the question asked earlier about the similarity between jazz now and 40 years ago, but it does require a cultural perspective on 'internalist' matters. Jazz musicians and their advocates were entering a further stage of the long struggle for legitimacy. Of course, the greater part of this struggle had (and has) to do with minimising the practical consequences of longstanding elitist and racial prejudices. For cultural legitimacy to be a prize worth having, jazz musicians also had to succeed in their internal struggle to invent or discover appropriate values. Articulate critics, academics and musicians were inevitably drawn to formalist terminology and experimentation, and were challenged to create as well as replicate. Criteria in the classical world, though not usually useful in valorising performances in terms that jazz musicians themselves thought relevant, were much closer to the level of practical criticism that was needed.[20] There were many earlier victories on the socio-cultural level, for example, the 1938 and 1939 Carnegie Hall concerts, but the collective breakthrough in 1959 was the decisive emancipation of jazz from its popular past; a break not only from being seen as popular entertainment and dance music, but from being defined by the very (musical) characteristics that lasted even through the so-called bebop revolution. Modern jazz was not a rejection of tradition but, like modern 'classical' music, was built on re-conceptualising what was already possible. Present-day jazz pedagogy and theory within the jazz tradition is a lasting and powerful link with this period.

The pre-1959 historical canon was already in place; the best of Morton, Armstrong, Ellington, Basie, Goodman, Parker (and of course many names that fit alongside or in between) and the present-day canon – Miles, Coltrane and all the rest – was simply added to it and is now taught around the world. The evolutionary hypothesis (in its technical aspects) works deceptively well up to this point, but for the longer future and beyond, the organic analogy with its corollary of artistic progress breaks down. It would be unfair to write off all the music of the 1970s and 1980s, but this was not a period of comparable importance for the art-form as a whole. The recent re-emergence of acoustic post-bop based on the 1960s and the unassailability of the modernist canon would seem to mark, if not 1959 exactly, then not very long after as the beginning of the present era. The reason there has been relatively little change over such a period is that a secure sense of cultural legitimacy, musical values and intellectual purpose was achieved with reference to music that was produced at the end of the 1950s. Significantly, not by fixing limits but by destabilising them, jazz remains an open, experimental field grounded in now universally accepted traditions.

DISCOGRAPHY

The following albums referred to in the text are available as CD reissues at the time of writing:

Brubeck, Dave, *Time Out*, CK 65122
Coleman, Ornette, *The Shape of Jazz to Come*, Atlantic 7567-81339-2
Coltrane, John, *Giant Steps*, Atlantic 8122-75203-2, Rhino R275203
Davis, Miles, *Kind of Blue*, CK 64935
Goodman, Benny and various, *From Spirituals to Swing*, Vanguard VCD2-47/48
Mingus, Charles, *Mingus Ah Um*, CK 65512
Schuller, Gunther, *The Birth of the Third Stream*, CK 64929, 1996

[CK = Columbia Legacy]

11 Free Jazz and the avant-garde

JEFF PRESSING

'Free Jazz' refers to a historical movement that, despite earlier precedents, first significantly flowered in the late 1950s in the US. Its central focus was a liberation from musical conventions – but from a jazz player's perspective, since no liberation is ever complete. Initially known simply as the New Thing, it became Free Jazz after borrowing the title of a seminal 1960 album by saxophonist/composer Ornette Coleman. It subsequently has had international repercussions that seem set to continue well into the twenty-first century.

Its impact and relations to other developments remain controversial, and a variety of accounts of it are possible: as a culmination of the drive for individual creativity, a radicalisation of the scope of musical materials of jazz, a collection of statements by salient individuals and groups, or as a movement shaped by extramusical forces of political, cultural, racial and spiritual liberation – to mention only the most obvious. Here these are all taken as valid viewpoints, in need of reconciliation.

The seminal role of creative improvisation

The nucleus of all jazz is creative improvisational expression (Louis Armstrong's 'the sound of surprise'), a process that brings into the music the joy of discovery, the magic of communication, and the uniqueness of both the moment and the individual. Yet it also introduces several profound tensions which early on planted the seeds for the ultimate blossoming of free jazz.

First, in all but solo improvisation there is a tension between the freedom of expression of the individual and the need to form coherent relations with other performers in the group. The most traditional handling of this tension in jazz is via role-playing. Each instrument takes its nominal part in the play: the bass provides chord foundations and time, the comping instrument feeds chordal colorations, drums set up the rhythmic matrix and drive, and the soloist plays a main melody. Other instruments, as far as they are used, have well-defined roles of rhythmic or motivic support, as in call-and-response designs or early jazz polyphony. In this way there is both a functional framework promoting coherence and latitude for creativity.

Another tension is between freedom of expression and the song form. The recurring song cycle (most commonly the 12-bar blues or the 32-bar AABA form) provides harmonic propulsion and a time frame for phrasing; yet it can also act as a straitjacket, with too slavish a following of it yielding a vapid and predictable outcome. Experienced jazz performers and listeners handle this tension by using or recognising characteristic form-marking gestures (which may vary with instrument and performer), providing an extra level of surety for the imaginative introduction of form-threatening motivic processes, rhythmic overlays and accents.

A third tension is between freedom of expression and the conventional musical materials of African-American traditions, including styles and 'rules of the game' (see Jost 1974). These materials include technical resources such as scales, blues riffs, vamps, etc., and also aesthetic building blocks, such as swing, sound and feel. Such familiar materials and processes act psychologically, forming and invoking cultural and personal references that can bring forth powerful emotional associations in listeners. The common handling of this tension is to balance traditional materials with innovation, building a personal language that extends traditions but keeps the connection to them apparent.

Finally, there can be a profound tension between the creative urge and commercial viability, strongly affecting the jazz player's life conditions and view of self (see Rubington and Weinberg 1999). Jazz's origins are commercial, and it has built acceptance for its novelties by basing performances on the popular songs and styles of its own or earlier eras. When its expressions become too novel, its social functions are subverted: the music loses viability as a club music and has to move into the concert hall, alternative multi-stylistic venues or obscurity.

In mainstream song-form jazz, the containment of these tensions serves both improviser and listener, for constraints can spur both creation and intelligibility; the performer can react subliminally to the musical elements around him or her, saving precious cognitive facility for fluency and immediacy. Listeners can track the events in terms of the song. In short, listeners and performers have some sort of cognitive and emotional contract to experience and experiment with, and the ground rules ensure that everybody can have a good time.

But if one, or especially several or all, of these tensions are left unresolved, there are revolutionary consequences for perception, attitude and employability. And of course this is what free jazz set in motion. While jazz revolutions had been heralded before, notably with bebop, continuities with older traditions had soon become apparent and the fate of previous radicalism was rapid incorporation into an expanded view of the tradition. Not so here: many of the radicalisations of free jazz struck hammer blows at all these simmering tensions, blows with effects that were to force a reconsideration of the very nature of jazz.

The radicalisation process

Free jazz was a radical approach to music. Except for the choice of instruments, it ultimately radicalised every aspect of jazz: form, style, materials, context, relationships, sound, process – but not equally, nor at the same time. The changes to form were simple: the blues and 32-bar song forms might be abandoned, and new formats used, or form might emerge from process and interplay. Likewise, style was now a variable that players could adopt, extend, overlay and conceive anew, drawing on any source for materials, sometimes hearkening back to older roots like blues and the field holler for historical empowering.

With respect to context and relationship, there gradually came a realisation that nearly anything could be made to work in any context if the conceptual framework of expression were suitably broadened. Atonal clusters or discordant multiphonics (chords played on a reed instrument by cross-fingerings and overblowing) could sit in a complex polyphonic context, heard as avant-garde outpourings, or they could be a plaintive emotive cry within a traditional groove. Polyphony or heterophony could be replaced by an energetic collision of parts, by pantonal call-and-response, by conversational counterpoint or language-based gestures that might hearken back to early musical sources such as chant.

The radicalisation of sound was a deep and far-ranging process of individual exploration. The process was most powerful in instruments that provided continuous sustaining control of sound production, notably breath- and bow-based instruments. The scope of control intimacy was particularly acute with reed instruments, notably the saxophone (that most prototypical of modern jazz instruments), where the reed, mouthpiece, diaphragm, teeth, tongue, lips, cheeks and voice box provided an incredibly rich control apparatus. The cries of animals, the screechings of machines, the susurrations of the natural elements, the conversational twitterings of evoked harmonics and the gorgeous jazz ballad tone were now all equally possible. Novel fingerings were able to evoke luxuriant and unanticipated harmonic structures in a single note. What need for a melodic line when the single note was really a chord with internal movement, as could be heard in the centred urgency of tenor saxophonist Pharoah Sanders and later in the harmonic cascades of Evan Parker? But, was it still jazz?

The particular advantage that jazz brought to this putatively avant-garde language arose from its foundation as an aural tradition, since many of these saxophone sounds were unnotatable (this was also true of some other instruments, notably the winds and double bass). The results differed from instrument to instrument, and from embouchure to embouchure, requiring the construction of a personal language for each performer based on aural tradition and experimental self-evaluation. This was irreconcilable with mainstream traditions of notation, except under a stance of virtually or literally unplayable hyperprecise notation (e.g., the works of Brian Ferneyhough, which have little to do with jazz), but it fits well with the jazz idea of the soloist's personal voice.

A similar story applies to the brass traditions, although the scope of timbral resources proves to be more restricted, particularly on trumpet. Trumpeter Don Cherry, a vital partner for Ornette Coleman, was an early brass explorer; later, trombonist Albert Mangelsdorf and others showed the connection between free jazz and the sound world of extended brass techniques via chords, glissandi and vocalisings into the instrument.

The piano became radicalised in several ways: first, the vocabulary of chords grew without limit – every chord did not have to be either lush or funky. Second, the insides of the piano could be used, and its timbre possibly 'prepared' (under the inspiration of John Cage) by the addition of materials to the strings (e.g., bolts, paper, wood). Third, new percussive techniques of performance, for example, clusters and hand-alternation techniques, notably pioneered by Cecil Taylor, changed the palette of gesture and articulation. Finally, the piano became electric, and the keyboard (followed by the guitar) became the dominant interface for the synthesiser, which meant that any sound, digitally sampled or constructed, could be tailored to polyphonic presentation.

In practice, these keyboard innovations exhibited limitations. The emotive power of many complex chords and their sequences proved limited, and the piano's fixed tempered tuning clashed with the microtonal potentials of all other jazz instruments (hence it was an early casualty from Ornette Coleman's line-up). The prepared piano is not practicable in most club gigs, and it occupies a rather specific timbral world. The new percussive piano techniques often came at the expense of a lyrical touch. Lastly, the keyboard was not only a liberation for synthesised sound, it was also a prison. Keyboard players were not expert in pitch bending and real-time modulation actions, and most never mastered them to full fluency. Without this, many synthesised and sampled sounds lack the note-to-note variability that underlies expression; the exact repeatability of sounds tends to clash (though not ineluctably) with the idea of the essential uniqueness of the moment that forms part of the jazz attitude.

The bass kept its groove and melodic functions, but expanded into a world of explosive bow-guided timbres. It was some time, though, before the lessons of extended bass technique (as shown, for example, by Bert Turetzky) were fully incorporated into the playing of specific jazz bassists. Seminal in this transition were Dave Holland and Barry Guy.

The jazz drum kit evolved for jazz time; in early free jazz, it was the time which disintegrated first, replaced by clouds of activity that either played with or implied a pulse, via asymmetrical overlays, or soon abandoned pulse altogether. Drummers such as Rashied Ali and Sonny Murray saw to this. Major changes to the sound came later. The idea of percussion as a collection of timbral colorations of registral melody, with sounds drawn from found objects and many cultures, evolved more slowly. German percussionist Paul Lovens was among those who dramatically expanded the world of percussive sound. The free improvisation group, Kiva, with percussionist Jean-Charles François, was another.

The voice – the ultimate jazz source – was slower to find its freedom in a jazz context than it was in the hands of European composers such as Luciano Berio. Scat emphasises phonetics without semantic shackles, but the radicalisation of melody remained the province of only a few, such as the yodelling and falsetto techniques of Leon Thomas in the early free-jazz period. In the later 1990s, Kurt Elling emerged as a stunningly hip singer-commentator, showing a wealth of powers spanning impromptu sound poetry, transcendent rap and phonemic deconstruction.

Some historical threads

In this short chapter it is impossible to give a comprehensive or even fully balanced history of free jazz. Rather, I will recount some precedents and its period of origin, and then examine the consequences of these developments by focusing on a few selected individuals as exemplars.

Precedents

Free playing in jazz is not without historical precedent in other types of music. Although in the mainstream folk or traditional musics of the world, free self-expression reliably gives way to social function, something at least approaching free improvisation can emerge in some situations of religious ecstasy, trance or transcendence of the self – notably in traditional shamanism, and traditions of the Arabic world, India and many parts of Africa (though such situations often feature fixed music, too). In the West, such ecstatic musical behaviour was largely limited to certain melismatic church traditions (as in northern Scotland, or the spirituals of the American South), since the larger religious institutions attempted with considerable success to suppress them systematically.

Yet freedom came not only by ecstatic self-abandonment. Another path was driven by a frustration borne of the exhaustion of traditional materials. This can be documented in the West by written improvisational textbooks, which date back many centuries; while most such texts taught embellishment techniques, freer sources can also be found. For example, Carl Czerny, best known in today's educational traditions as a deviser of exercises, also wrote a book on free improvisation (*Systematic Introduction to Fantasy Playing on the Piano*, 1826),[1] emphasising the role of spontaneous intuition. This heightened emphasis on intuition was an inevitable outcome of the broader historical emphasis on the powers of the individual relative to received authority, seen in the Renaissance, the advent of empirical science, the Reformation, the Industrial and Information Revolutions.

Yet it unquestionably fell to the twentieth century to receive the ultimate consequences of these two approaches. Their timing was only roughly synchronous in composition and improvisation. In art-music composition, the exhaustively notated path to expressive freedom is traceable through diatonic extensions (Debussy, Ravel, Skryabin, Stravinsky), dodecaphony (Schoenberg, Webern, Berg), multi-serialism (Boulez, Babbitt) and hypercomplexity (Ferneyhough). This acted, of course, in tandem with its opposite: deliberate simplicity or primitivism (Satie, Reich, Glass, Pärt).

The more intuitionist path of abandon, focusing on the performance act via notation of deprecated specificity, is traceable through the works of Dada, the futurists, John Cage, Earle Brown, Cornelius Cardew, Pauline Oliveros, the Fluxus movement and many others. These two paths were roughly contemporaneous, supporting the idea that they were different responses to a widely felt underlying social condition, expressed in literature as alienation or existentialism.

In jazz these divisions were also apparent, as we will see below. The systematic extension of materials and their real-time performance potentials continues side by side with pure intuitionist stances.[2] The impact of electronics and computers via synthesis, loudspeaker culture and digital recording has also changed the concept of musical presentation drastically. Improvisations can be frozen and preserved, edited and reconstituted, fundamentally changing the face of the improvisation–composition continuum.

Early free jazz
The first unmistakably relevant evidence of free musical improvisation appears to be the home recordings made in the early 1940s in New York by jazz violinist Stuff Smith and concert pianist Robert Crum. Later, in 1949, pianist Lennie Tristano's jazz group recorded the first spontaneous studio tracks 'Intuition' and 'Digression'. These recordings were not a spur-of-the-moment idea, but documentation of a long-running practice by Tristano's

group. A measure of their shock value can be found in the facts that the engineer intentionally erased two other free tracks recorded in the same session and the recording company refused for years to release either 'Intuition' or 'Digression', or to pay royalties for them.

Tristano's path was incremental, in that his group interleaved stances of intuition (free playing) and rigour (public performances of tightly rehearsed complex jazz works and the *Inventions* of J. S. Bach). This led to a freedom which threw out formal design but maintained the inherited sound elements and phrasing of jazz, and the values of polyphony and the lyrical line.

There was then a gap of nearly ten years before significant others appeared. Important innovations occurred in this period that helped set the stage for free jazz, notably the interactive group processes developed by Charles Mingus and the modal approach to playing pioneered by Miles Davis and John Coltrane, but otherwise the jazz world was preoccupied with the dichotomy between hard bop and cool.

Then, in 1957–60, two artistic figures emerged of an individuality and influence sufficient to call all this into question, and a free-jazz movement was identified by jazz writers. Pianist Cecil Taylor and saxophonist Ornette Coleman were separately the architects of this movement, and their innovations were loudly decried as charlatanism and anti-jazz, even as they began to become widely influential.

Cecil Taylor

Taylor brought uncommon intellectual drive to his African-American heritage, as his literary writings reveal (e.g., album notes for *Unit Structures*, 1966). Drawing on variegated musical influences, such as impressionism, atonality, the dense voicings of pianist Dave Brubeck and the free linear approach of Tristano, he early on abandoned the lyrical touch and conventional jazz chords, and organised his compositional work as motifs for performer communication, with form emerging from the process of group interaction. Yet his most upsetting stance to jazz purists was the complete abandonment of swing. If the words to Duke Ellington's famous 'It Don't Mean a Thing . . .' were right, either Taylor's music was inconsequential or it was not jazz, and perhaps both. There was no question that this music occupied a different kinetic and emotional space from jazz that had gone before.

In a perceptive analysis of Taylor's early work, Jost notes how Taylor's extended free pieces, such as *Unit Structures*, had in practice a clear structural foundation, and that Taylor showed that 'the freedom of free jazz does not mean the complete abstention from every kind of musical organization. Freedom lies, first and foremost, in the opportunity to make a conscious choice from boundless material' (Jost 1974, 83).

Taylor's originality and iconoclasm left little scope for commercial success for many years. But by the time he gave a solo performance for Jimmy Carter at the White House in 1979, times had changed and the idiosyncratic virtuosity of Taylor's expression (likened by some to a pianistic field holler) was not only finely honed, but its expressive depth was evident even to the unconverted. His influence has become wide-ranging within and without jazz, even as it remains separate from the jazz mainstream, especially in the US.

Ornette Coleman

Alto saxophonist Coleman's early statement, 'Let's play the music and not the background' (cited in Jost 1974, 17), proposed an escape from the recurring chordal prison of the song form. His novel approach rapidly attracted attention through an extended seminal residency at New York's prestigious Five Spot in 1959.

Although clearly an original, he seemed to many to lack sufficient technical proficiency to justify his high public profile – and, in truth, he did not at this time approach the fluidity or clarity of line of the best bop and post-bop horn players. Also disconcerting was the conflict between his maintenance of a tonal framework and traditional song forms in his compositions (which were and continue to be widely admired), and the improvisations on them, which though bop-like in style often gave faint reference to the chordal progressions, acting instead more linearly via chains of association (see Jost 1974). Controversy flared again in 1965 when, after a two-year hiatus, he reappeared in public performance, now also playing violin and trumpet with unconventional and (to most ears) rather limited technique.

The spirit of free thinking in his early work gave rise to the historically important album *Free Jazz*, appearing in 1960, an unbroken single piece featuring a double jazz quartet including both those associated with free jazz, such as Don Cherry (trumpet) and Eric Dolphy (bass clarinet), and those from the mainstream, such as Scott LaFaro (bass) and Freddie Hubbard (trumpet). The result was complex and unlike anything heard before; with hindsight it appears both seminal and emotionally static. It was a direction Coleman did not pursue.

In the longer time frame, the characteristic piano-less sound of Coleman's group and his integrated 'harmolodic' tonal approach (see page 193) – a vaguely specified philosophy also underlying his subsequent ventures into fully notated string quartets, symphonies and ballets – were to be more influential. In more recent work, his rhythm-and-blues roots re-emerged, producing 'free funk', a free improvisation above a funk foundation. His original compositions remain widely influential with both mainstream and free-jazz musicians.

Taylor's and Coleman's groups also served as training grounds for others who subsequently became leaders in their own right, such as saxophonists Archie Shepp and Albert Ayler, and trumpeter Cherry. But other independent voices also soon arose.

Other early voices

Sun Ra, a keyboardist who played with Fletcher Henderson, took a developmental road to freedom in jazz, which involved the use of eccentric 'intergalactic' awareness (he claimed to have been born on the planet Saturn), a novel big-band instrumentation (including such unusual jazz instruments as timpani and bass marimba) and a pioneering use of electronics. Sun Ra's 'Arkestra' grew to encompass elaborate dance, theatrical and magic presentations which put him in the vanguard of performance art and at the same time hearkened to folk rituals of an earlier era.

Chicago not only gave us the Arkestra, but also the Association for the Advancement of Creative Musicians, which sought to heighten the creative potentials of jazz and also provide links to community that went beyond concertising to education and mentoring. Richard Abrams (piano) more than anyone else began the process, which led to the Art Ensemble of Chicago, which included Roscoe Mitchell (woodwinds), Lester Bowie (trumpet), Anthony Braxton (saxophones) and others, whose influence continues. Braxton has remained highly prolific to the present day, his output varying across standards, intimate small groups, and compositions for large ensembles incorporating both simple folk traditions (e.g., parade music) and developments in European contemporary music.

John Coltrane was not an early part of a free-jazz movement, but his personal path came to intersect with it, notably in the last two years of his life, when in the view of many he became its leading exponent. His path was one of intense exploration of materials, giving in the view of many his intuitive free-jazz developments a tremendous power and spirituality. His great 'free' epic is the single-track album *Ascension*, its title referring not only to the scaling of artistic heights but also the ascension of Christ. This work has a level of intensity uncommon in music of any style, and brought together a seminal big band of two trumpets, two altos and three tenors, with Coltrane's quartet of McCoy Tyner (piano), Jimmy Garrison and Art Davis (basses), and Elvin Jones (drums). The piece is a series of alternating solo and tutti sections, based on a simple diatonic motif, and presents a wide gamut of approaches to expression, from the iconoclastic sound sculpting of saxophonists Sanders and Shepp (smeared tones, animal cries, kinetic outpourings) to the motivic manipulations of trumpeter Hubbard, and Coltrane himself. A certain structural rigour informs Coltrane's work, even when it is at its most radical and confrontational, as here. In this same period,

Coltrane developed the free-jazz ballad within the traditions of the jazz small group, which juxtaposed lyrical directness with eruptions of broken quasi-atonality (e.g., 'Offering' and 'Ogunde' on *Expression*). The spiritual side of Coltrane's music was continued by his wife Alice (piano, organ, harp), as for example in *Journey in Satchidananda*.

Trumpeter Miles Davis also had a liberating influence on jazz language. The seminal role of modal playing in the late 1950s has already been mentioned. (For further on modal jazz at this time, see Chapter 10.) Although he himself did not play free solos, and spoke scathingly of free jazz, he later led moves to freer contexts by progressive small-group liberalisations of form and harmony with saxophonist Wayne Shorter and, most directly, by his electric free funk fusions, as heard on *Bitches Brew* (1969) or *Live at the Fillmore East* (1970), which brought together seminal musicians like Dave Holland (bass), Jack DeJohnette (drums), Chick Corea and Keith Jarrett (keyboards) in free-form gestures within a jazz-rock rhythmical matrix.

Beginning in the early 1970s, Jarrett has intermittently performed free solo-piano concerts, resulting in some stunning examples of the improviser's art, such as *The Köln Concert* and the *Solo Concerts*. This music connected not only with jazz but with the great nineteenth-century piano traditions, and while it often was based on traditional tonal materials, its high level of refinement and sheer beauty were incontestable.

In summary, this foundation period provided a real sense of a revolutionary movement and exhibited great diversity. Since it was founded predominantly by African-Americans, a natural interpretation of this period is as an expression of black liberation and cultural empowerment.

Later developments

Free jazz as a movement or foundation point may remain marginalised, diffuse and a thing apart, yet its influence – as a source of possibilities in jazz, contemporary concert music and even non-corporate rock music – runs deep. The variety of persons operating in the less traditional forms of jazz and improvised music is so great that it exceeds any ready classification scheme. In this short chapter it is impossible to do full justice to more recent developments, which are extensive and international.

Broadly, avant-garde jazz does not often appear at clubs, as it remains commercially suspect. It has a better chance at festivals, and is better-established in Europe than in the US, probably as a result of its cross-fertilisation with the European avant-garde traditions. The line between jazz and non-jazz is often blurred, with some mainstream jazz writers adopting an exclusive position based on use of jazz phrasing and forms, but with others taking inclusive positions based on the spirit of freedom of approach. At the close of the twentieth century, free-improvisation traditions emerging from jazz but with their own traditions of development of nearly 40 years were now well-established in many countries. At the same time, a common view (expressed, for example, by pianists Anthony Davis and Chick Corea) is that free improvisation is a useful process subserving the greater goal of richer musical expression, but that aiming towards freedom alone often leads to sterile or clichéd territory.

Strong traditions exist in Europe, notably in the UK (e.g., AMM, guitarist Derek Bailey, bassist Barry Guy, saxophonist Evan Parker), Holland (e.g., pianist Misha Mengelberg, drummer Han Bennink and saxophonist Willem Breuker) and Germany (e.g., the Globe Unity Orchestra, trombonist Albert Mangelsdorf). In the US, the dominant *Zeitgeist* at the end of the millennium remained retrograde, as in the case of 'rebop'. Many freer players there strove to keep some explicit links with the traditional elements of jazz, reflecting the greater American stake in the origins of black music. Nevertheless, a number of players are active in presenting extensions of the improvisational languages of the early free-jazz period, and others in setting out in fresh directions that either extend, or go well beyond, the frontiers of jazz. The diverse directions include the work of pianists Anthony Davis and Marilyn Crispell, electric guitarist James Blood Ulmer, the Rova saxophone quartet, influential composer Carla Bley, the Jazz Composer's Orchestra, electronic music systems designer and trombonist George Lewis, meditative musician Pauline Oliveros and eclectic composer-saxophonist John Zorn, to mention only a few.

Given the impossibility of adequate coverage, and the regrettable neglect here of significant performers in Japan, Australia, Eastern Europe, Russia, Scandinavia, South America, Canada and other locales, I have selected three players to serve as case-studies of the directions in which free-improvisation trends went in the last quarter of the twentieth century. These are the Australian violinist Jon Rose, the British saxophonist Evan Parker, and the US saxophonist and composer John Zorn. This choice may be controversial, in that all three of these performers perform in a much wider context than that of jazz. However, my view is that free jazz and the improvisational freedom it presupposes have had a critical influence on their development.

Jon Rose

An Australian who was born in England in 1951, Rose has since 1986 been based in Europe and has toured widely. He is dedicated to the development of improvisational languages on the violin (e.g., *Violin Music for Restaurants*) and on a myriad of other eccentric or extended string instruments of his own construction (e.g., *Fringe Benefits*). He has also used interactive digital electronics and interfaces extensively in recent work (e.g., *The Hyperstring Project*).

Trained early in classical music, he later (aged 15) abandoned formal music study to evolve a personal language, which had input from a great variety of musical genres, including jazz, soul, art-music composition, Italian club bands, Indian ragas and sound installations. He became a central figure in the development of free improvisation in Australia, both by prolific solo concert-giving and by a series of musical conversations with other significant players (e.g., drummer Louis Burdett), a project labelled *The Relative Band.*

With time, his focus came to include a project towards bowed string instrument extension of unparalleled invention and transmogrification, called *The Relative Violin.* This has embraced extra strings, multiple necks, multiple bows, attached metal resonators, gigantic scale-ups in size, and such imaginative creations as the half-size megaphone violin, nine-string elbow violin, automatic violin quartet, violin vivisection, violino del jesu, double-piston triple-neck wheeling violin, amplified windmill violin, triple humming bow and MIDI bow.

The textures of Rose's music are busy and extroverted, often distinctly nonlyrical, and give a central role to explorational improvisation and physicality of performance. His music is also highly contrapuntal, and he sees this latter attribute as the unique contribution of western music to world culture. For him, the new technologies are not only of value for their expansion of the world of sound, but for their expansion of the potentials of computer-interactive counterpoint for the solo improviser.

In technical terms, Rose is an impressive virtuoso and has a developed ear for all manner of tonal relations. His bowing is not only a means of controlling sound production, but an enactment of psychodrama. His work is in parts intense, in parts whimsical, in parts satirical (e.g., *The Fence*) and exhibits rapid changes of texture. He also combines high and low tech, incorporating junk, kitsch and trash in his constructions. They not only contribute light relief, but aid his central aims of unpredictability of interaction and comprehensive exploration of timbre.

For example, he has created a mythical musical protagonist, Johannes Rosenberg, and provided a detailed identity for him. His *Violin Music in the Age of Shopping* is a wry modernist projection which has been incarnated as a book and a CD, as well as numerous concerts. Another recent work, *Perks*, features a deconstruction of snippets of music by Australian composer Percy Grainger using a MIDI-controlled piano triggered by two badminton players, with video and text presentation, an improvised violin obbligato acting as commentary. The badminton strokes (as with the MIDI violin bow) are monitored by pressure sensors and accelerometers, which can call up different electronic sounds and video material, which can then be modified and manipulated in real time.

Evan Parker

Nowhere is the difference between the free-jazz paths of Europe and North America clearer than in the instance of Evan Shaw Parker, born in Bristol in 1944. Virtually unknown in the US, he is regarded in Europe as a uniquely powerful innovator who continues to disclose hitherto unknown potentials of the tenor and soprano saxophones. He has worked in a variety of formats, including small groups and duets, particularly with pianist Aleksander Schlippenbach, guitarist Derek Bailey, bassist Barry Guy and drummers Paul Lytton, Paul Lovens and John Stevens. He has taken part in all the major European large free-jazz ensembles (including the Globe Unity Orchestra, the London Jazz Composer's Orchestra and the Berlin Jazz Composer's Orchestra), and has been involved in electronic projects, notably with Lawrence Casserley in real-time digital signal processing using the IRCAM workstation.

The originality of his contribution is most clearly seen in his solo saxophone work. Particularly on the soprano saxophone, his repertoire of extended sounds is astonishingly diverse and well-controlled, establishing a sense to many of a principled extension of the sound-world explorations begun long ago by Coltrane, Ayler, Shepp and Sanders. His foundation technique includes a thorough mastery of circular breathing, effortless leaps between registers, and an uncommon tonguing approach (up/down motion of the tongue rather than the tu-ku stop of the tongue on the hard palette) that in his view allows more rapid sequences of very short notes, better articulated over a greater dynamic range, than would otherwise be possible. In his own words, 'the saxophone has been for me a rather specialised bio-feedback instrument for studying and expanding my control over my hearing and the motor mechanics of parts of my skeleto-muscular system'.[3]

Parker typically favours the use of additive and mutational procedures for developing the potentials of prefigured material, generating complexity from simple cells. He can achieve pauseless delivery of long solos (up to 30 minutes or more) via circular breathing, which veer from overtone cascades to motivic manipulations across several distinct registers, the latter a form of polyphonic melody that he likens to the simultaneous parallel actions of circus performers. A conventional sense of tempo is absent from his playing, replaced by a manipulation of the density of events in time. He is prolific, having recorded over 150 albums.

John Zorn

Zorn, born in 1953, is a saxophonist and prolific composer who draws on roots from many traditions. Whether he is really a free-jazz exponent (a typically European view), or an avant-gardist/postmodernist (a more American position), Zorn qualifies as one of the most eclectic musicians of any age. His eclecticism encompasses both high and low art, ranging from the most intricate of atonal structures to conceptual art, jazz tunes, whimsy, country music, reggae, klezmer and raging punk rock, not only in the same set, but often in 30-second blocks within the same song. Early examples of this mosaic style include the group Naked City, featuring Zorn on sax, Bill Frisell (guitar), Wayne Horvitz (keyboards), Fred Frith (bass), Joey Baron (drums) and Yamatsuka Eye (vocals).

Zorn's subsequent album *Spy vs. Spy* is a bent tribute to the tunes of Ornette Coleman. Zorn aimed to make the versions as iconoclastic as Coleman's early free jazz was, and so recast all the pieces in a confrontational hardcore punk style, using two drummers – a musical link not appreciated by everyone. In 1986, Zorn collaborated with Frisell and George Lewis (trombone) on *News for Lulu*, a tribute to four Blue Note hard-bop players of the 1950s and 1960s: Kenny Dorham, Hank Mobley, Sonny Clark and Freddie Redd. He has written many film scores.

Zorn also composes chamber music showing similar postmodern inclinations. For example, in his *Cat O'Nine Tails* (subtitled 'Tex Avery Meets the Marquis de Sade') for string quartet (1998), which is neither jazz nor improvised, we hear whimsically abrupt transitions between jazz standards, comical portamento whines, braying donkeys, polyphonic atonal textures, Jewish tangos and grinding solo cadenzas – a compressed version of the musical life of Manhattan.

Another tradition in Zorn's work is that of the game piece (e.g., *Cobra*), the use of sets of interactive instructions to determine the tactics and priorities of groups of improvising performers. Hand signals and cue cards are used to effect communication, making this a spectator sport as well as a sonic event. Such procedures have many precedents, such as the 1950s and 1960s explorations of the ensemble led by composer Lukas Foss (in a non-jazz style), and the graphic scores of composers such as Earle Brown (String Quartet, 1965) and John Cage (*Piano Concert*). Traditions of graphic composition for improvisers, though less fashionable than in the 1960s and 1970s, are still in active use, especially those involving mosaic techniques.[4]

The foundation of free jazz as a movement was a reflection of the richness and depth of the African-American musical culture. Its rise was associated with the cultural liberations of the 1960s, notably black power, and this early connection appears to have been essential in establishing vital directions. Subsequent developments have confirmed that this outpouring of freedom was the culmination of an individuation process in relation to received western culture of many centuries' duration, so that this freedom also very soon appeared strongly in European jazz and showed parallel development in contemporary art-music traditions, often yielding blurred stylistic boundaries. The potentials of free improvisation have been altered dramatically by international media developments, computers, mass education and ethnic interactions. While free jazz and the related improvisational avant-garde remain confined to specialist audiences and certain types of film score, their spirit of exploration continues to feed into more mainstream musical forms, buttressed by the increasing incidence of stylistic crossover in the late twentieth and early twenty-first centuries.

SELECT DISCOGRAPHY

AMM, *Generative Themes*, Matchless MR6, 1982

Braxton, Anthony, *Creative Orchestra Music 1976*, RCA ND86579, 1976

Coleman, Ornette, *The Shape of Jazz to Come*, Atlantic 7567-81339-2, 1959; *Free Jazz*, Atlantic 1364, 1960; *An Evening with Ornette Coleman*, Polydor 623246/7, 1965

Coltrane, Alice, *Journey in Satchidananda*, Impulse IMPD-228, 1970

Coltrane, John, *Ascension*, Impulse AS-95, 1965; *Expression*, Impulse AS-9120, 1967; *Sun Ship*, Impulse IMPD-167, 1965; *A Love Supreme*, Impulse A-77, 1964

Davis, Miles, *Bitches Brew*, Columbia G2K40577, 1969; *Live at the Fillmore East*, 1970

Jarrett, Keith, *The Köln Concert*, ECM 1064, 1975; *Solo Concerts Bremen/Lausanne*, ECM 1035–2, 1973

Parker, Evan, *The Topography of the Lungs*, Incus 1, 1970; *Six of One*, Incus 39, 1980; *Conic Sections*, AhUm 015, 1993; *Drawn Inward*, ECM 1693, 1998 (The Evan Parker Electro-Acoustic Ensemble)

Rose, Jon, *Violin Music for Restaurants*, ReR BJRCD1, 1990; *Perks*, ReRJR3, 1996; *Fringe Benefits*, Entropy 006, 1999; *The Hyperstring Project*, ReRJR6, 2000

Sun Ra, *The Heliocentric Worlds of Sun Ra*, 2 vols., ESP 1014 and 1017, 1965

Taylor, Cecil, *Unit Structures*, Blue Note CD 84237, 1966; *Silent Tongues*, Arista Freedom AL-1005, 1975; *Garden*, Hat Art 1993/94, 1981

Tristano, Lennie, *Sextet: Crosscurrents*, Capitol EASP 1–491, 1949

Zorn, John, *News for Lulu*, Hat Art CD 6005, 1986; *Spy vs. Spy*, Wea/Elektra Entertainment ASIN: B000002H6W, 1989; *Naked City*, Elektra/Nonesuch 9 79238–2, 1990; *Cobra*, Hat Art CD 2-6040, 1994

WEBSITES

Websites change with time, and so few URLs are given here. However, in the area of jazz research, websites have become an indispensable companion. They provide extensive discographies for all the artists mentioned in this chapter and can be readily accessed via keyword search for their names using any standard search engine. An excellent set of resources of major players on the European free-jazz scene is at the time of writing available at http://www.shef.ac.uk/misc/rec/ps/efi/. Availability of audio discs can also be ascertained by access to broad commercial retailers in music, such as www.amazon.com

12 Fusions and crossovers

STUART NICHOLSON

While it remains a fascination that one of the first recordings of African-American music was made in Sweden in 1899 – 'Cake Walk' (a version of 'At A Georgia Camp Meeting' by Kerry Mills), by the Kronoberg Society Regimental Band conducted by Erik Högberg – the first jazz recording is usually cited as 'Darktown Strutters Ball' by the Original Dixieland Jazz Band from January 1917. Prior to that we can only guess what the music might have sounded like as a deliquescent folk music in the rural southern states of America. But we do know that early jazz drew together several strands of vernacular music, including Negro spirituals, work and folk songs, ragtime, minstrel music, brass-band music and blues, that were freely mixed with elements from hymns, popular songs and popular classics of the day.

From the start, jazz was a pluralistic music. One of its great early practitioners, Jelly Roll Morton, argued that the music should always include a 'Spanish tinge' while the unambiguous *habañera* section in *St Louis Blues*, published by W. C. Handy in 1914, is revealing of jazz's practice of appropriation; an important, if often neglected, feature of a music that already comprised a diversity of elements drawn from a variety of sources both from within and without the African-American diaspora.

Appropriation is a recurring theme in the subsequent evolution of the music and reveals a continuing dialogue, not only with popular culture but other musical forms, in order to broaden the scope of jazz expressionism. After all, mass culture and modernist high culture had been in dialogue since the mid-nineteenth century, modernism appropriating whatever elements it needed for experimentation and articulation. Jazz, an exemplary expression of the modernist impulse in American culture, continued this practice, culminating in perhaps the most controversial moment in contemporary jazz history, the appropriation of rock.

This collision of genres was initially called 'jazz-rock' and subsequently 'jazz-rock fusion' or simply 'fusion'; there is no agreed meaning for these terms, despite their widespread use. The present account proposes exploring a distinction between 'jazz-rock', as originally applied to the first wave of experimenters in the late 1960s and early 1970s, and the term 'fusion' that crept into the lexicon around 1973–4. The term 'fusion' was first used in jazz in 1963 by record producer Orrin Keepnews as the title of an album by guitarist Wes Montgomery, who in mixing light, accessible improvisation with strings created an easy-listening album with an appeal extending beyond jazz audiences to 'crossover' into the popular market. 'Some of the words the dictionary uses to define *fusion* are "blending," "melting together," "coalition"', said Keepnews in his liner notes. Subsequently, the term would reappear in jazz in the mid-1970s and become associated with electric pop-jazz intended to 'crossover' into the youth market. In the 1990s and beyond, 'electric' jazz musicians would be at pains to distance themselves from this term, something this account will also seek to explore.

A socio-musical crisis: jazz and the emergence of rock music in the 1960s

When John Coltrane's restless experimentalism was silenced by his death in July 1967, a stillness overtook jazz that was perhaps more profound than when Charlie Parker died in 1955. It coincided with the sudden and unexpected rise of rock music that robbed jazz of the collegiate audience it had enjoyed throughout the 1950s. Charles Mingus and Ornette Coleman had temporarily withdrawn from the scene and, while Miles Davis had one of the finest small groups in jazz, it was popular with everyone except the general public. The free-jazz abstraction of the 'New Thing' was alienating potential young white fans who had hitherto formed a significant audience base for jazz, while older musicians were doing what they had always done, playing standards and the blues. 'The world's jazz output seems to fall into one of two categories', observed *Melody Maker* at the time, 'I've-heard-it-all-before or I-never-want-to-hear-it-again' (liner notes to Lloyd, *Forest Flower*).

While rock did not completely relegate jazz to exterior darkness, it did at least consign it to the commercial twilight. 'During the heavy rock years', wrote the popular culture critic Albert Goldman, it was 'an embarrassing scene. Jazz had lost its audience and was talking to itself' (1993, 236). With jazz clubs closing and reopening as discotheques, many leading American musicians moved to Europe in search of work, including Stan Getz, Phil Woods, Benny Bailey, Art Farmer and Johnny Griffin. Others took part-time jobs to supplement their wages, such as McCoy Tyner and Pete LaRocca (who drove taxicabs). Others went into non-jazz work, Lou Levy backing singers such as Peggy Lee and Steve Kuhn playing society music, while others found work in Broadway pit bands. It was a time when many commentators began to advance the prognosis that the end of jazz was in sight: 'Jazz As We

Know It Is Dead', pronounced *Down Beat* on its front cover on 5 October 1967, while *Melody Maker* contained a 'Requiem for a jazz we loved and knew so well' (2 September 1967).

As the end of the 1960s approached, it was gradually becoming clear that rock was not about to burn itself out like the Twist or the Loco-motion, and many musicians began making an accommodation with it. Pillars of jazz society such as Duke Ellington and Count Basie recorded versions of Beatles hits, the Modern Jazz Quartet signed with the Beatles production company Apple, while Ella Fitzgerald, an interpreter of the American popular song *par excellence*, began giving prominence in her repertoire to numbers such as the Carpenters' 'Close to You' and the Beatles' 'Something'. Both the Woody Herman and Buddy Rich big bands made in-creasing use of rock and pop material, while performances by Don Ellis's new band assumed the trappings of rock concerts with psychedelic light-ing, electrified saxophones and rock-style amplification. 'New Thing' saxo-phonist Albert Ayler made use of rock rhythmic patterns and 'soul singers' on his album *New Grass*, while Gerry Mulligan summed up this rush to be 'in tune with the times' by recording *If You Can't Beat Them, Join Them*. The latter included a liner photo that showed Mulligan shrugging his shoulders, as if to indicate a mood of futility and abandonment of principles.

Initially, jazz musicians sought to control rock music, attempting to make it conform to their notion of primitivism. But control is incompatible with rock's energy and to avoid its primitivism was to fail to acknowledge the source of its popularity. They found the concept of rock's volume, courtesy of Jim Marshall's monster 100-watt stacks, a denial of subtlety, failing to appreciate how volume contributed to rock's authenticity. Jazz musicians at first treated rock songs as they had the bossa nova, by adapting to the new rhythmic patterns. But the jazz rhythm section of acoustic piano, acoustic bass and drums missed the point by a mile. While albums such as Bud Shank's *Michelle* or Dizzy Gillespie's *My Way* showed that jazz musicians were quite prepared to take songs from popular culture, as they had in the past with Broadway show tunes, they also showed how they failed to realise their instrumental versions obscured those dimensions of the original hits that had made them compelling and subversive in the first place. Bud Shank covering 'Sounds of Silence' on flute sounds inauthentic because it is impossible to disentangle the memory of Simon and Garfunkel's original hit from the actual song itself. Singers and song had become bonded in a performance that exhausted the song's meaning because in pop and rock it is the recorded performance of the song that assumes an autonomous character, not the song in itself.

A resolution of opposites: jazz and the appropriation of rock

Clearly, any *rapprochement* with rock posed problems of authenticity in balancing the sounds associated with rock and jazz improvisation. Yet a working model of what a jazz-rock 'fusion' might sound like was revealed by the English band, Cream, formed in July 1966. Combining former jazz musicians Jack Bruce on bass and Ginger Baker on drums with blues purist Eric Clapton on guitar, they broke open the temporal limits of blues and popular songs with long, extended improvisations over rock rhythms. When the band toured the USA in 1967, *Rolling Stone* magazine pointed out that Cream 'had been called a jazz group'.[1] Indeed, during their tour many critics credited Cream with combining jazz and rock: 'The healthiest development in popular music these days is the extraordinary convergence of jazz and rock', said *Life* magazine in January 1968.

On the album *Wheels of Fire* is a performance of 'Spoonful' which provides a context for *Life* magazine's observation. Here the chord sequence is quickly abandoned in favour of a long Clapton solo in which Bruce's ostinato bass takes a prominent role in accompaniment, to the extent that it expands to provide contrapuntal lines more in the manner of a duet. Meanwhile the drums, after initially adopting a repeated rhythmic figure, gradually expand and develop this motif, colouring and commenting on the guitar and bass dialogue. As Clapton would later observe, 'I always felt . . . I [had] to fit into whatever concept [Baker] wanted to lay down . . . because he's much more of a jazz based musician; the Cream was really a jazz group, a jazz-rock group.'[2]

At this point it is important to note that jazz history has traditionally relied on canon formation and a chronological method of reconstructing jazz history based predominantly on 'masterpieces'. This exclusionary reading exalts favoured artists while bypassing others. Cream, a group which has generally been overlooked, had a considerable impact on the American scene; not only were rock bands forced to consider extended improvisation in their approach but many forward-looking young jazz musicians recognised that Cream's extensive use of improvisation over rock rhythms suggested a real possibility of a union between jazz and rock. For example, the youthful Chick Corea, while a member of Miles Davis's band in 1969, is on record as expressing admiration for Cream's synthesis of improvisation and rock.[3]

For young musicians coming of age in the 1960s, the social revolution was happening all around them. Tripping on acid had made the unthinkable commonplace and popular culture was swept with unusual connections and new ideas. In such a climate, integrating jazz and rock seemed not only natural but logical. 'Let's do something different!' said guitarist Larry Coryell, who in 1965 was 22 years old: 'We were saying, we love Wes [Montgomery], but we also love Bob Dylan. We love Coltrane but we also love the Beatles. We love Miles but we also love the Rolling Stones. We wanted people to know we were very much part of the contemporary scene, but at the same time we had worked our butts off to learn this other music [jazz]. It was a very sincere thing.'[4]

Musicians such as Coryell did not regard the prospect of combining jazz and rock as a commercial proposition, but as a way of moving the music in a new direction, as bebop and free jazz had done in the past. Coryell arrived in New York in 1965 and quickly made a reputation for himself, appearing in 1966 on the Chico Hamilton album, *The Dealer*, which flirted with combining jazz improvisation and rock rhythms. Given an opportunity to record under his own name, Coryell turned to his rehearsal group that included drummer Bobby Moses and saxophonist Jim Pepper. Calling themselves the Free Spirits, they cut their eponymous debut album, also in 1966. A somewhat self-conscious mixture of jazz improvisation with rock rhythms, these two albums were among the first in the USA to suggest the potential union of jazz and rock.

After Free Spirits broke up, Coryell joined vibraphonist Gary Burton to form a working quartet in January 1967. Their first album, *Duster*, from later in the year includes original compositions by Carla Bley and Mike Gibbs. Throughout the album Coryell used an acid tone customarily employed by rock guitarists, and on 'General Mojo's Well Laid Plan' unmistakable rock rhythms were employed; clearly Burton was working towards a synthesis of jazz and rock of his own. When the group appeared at the Berlin Jazz Days festival that year, they stunned German musicians who were unaware that a fusion of jazz and rock was being contemplated in the United States, the German writer, Alexander Schmitz, pointing out that they turned the German jazz scene around 'more or less overnight' (liner notes to Pike, *Masterpieces*). One of the first bands to reflect Burton's influence was the Dave Pike Set, whose inclusive vision of jazz extended into World Music and was years ahead of its time.

Experimentation was in the air; flautist Jeremy Steig, who had toured with Paul Winter and whose first album was produced by John Hammond, immediately became a Beatles fan when the group arrived in America. He formed a group in 1967 that included vibraphonist Mike Mainieri, pianist Warren Bernhardt, guitarist Adrian Guillery and bassist Eddie Gomez. Not only did they incorporate influences from rock, but each band member made a tape loop of sounds of their own choice and would play it at random on stage. However, their debut album, *Jeremy and the Satyrs* (1968), refrains from such abandon but nevertheless reveals a modestly successful combination of jazz and rock.

Burton's quartet continued to produce a series of well-conceived jazz-rock miniatures into the 1970s, and in 1968 he produced an album by a band that included tenor saxophonist Steve Marcus and pianist Mike Nock, both former fellow students from Berklee College of Music. Together with Coryell on guitar, the group called themselves Count's Rock Band and made their debut with *Tomorrow Never Knows*, including a version of the Byrds' 'Eight Miles High' where Marcus, the notional leader, plays in a middle-to-late Coltrane style over a powerful rock groove: so effective is Marcus's playing and so thoroughly had he absorbed the lessons of Coltrane that it is impossible not to speculate on what Coltrane's response to jazz-rock might have been had he lived another three years. Count's Rock Band worked infrequently, but before breaking up made a further two albums.

Coryell's subsequent career failed to capitalise either on his musical prowess or the fact that he was one of the first people to experiment with combining jazz and rock. Any potential his subsequent association with Marcus might have yielded was frustrated by personal problems, so it was with a sense of wiping the slate clean that he formed Eleventh House in 1973 with trumpeter Randy Brecker, Mike Mandel on keyboards, Danny Trifan on bass and Alphonse Mouzon on drums. Their debut *Introducing the Eleventh House* was recorded in September that year and might have had more impact had such an album been recorded earlier in the jazz-rock period. Events, however, had moved on and, as in much of Coryell's career, he gave the impression of following rather than leading.

After his period with Count's Rock Band, Mike Nock moved to the West Coast to join John Handy's quintet; Handy was flirting with rock grooves during his frequent appearances at Fillmore, where he appeared on the bill with popular rock acts of the day. The Fillmore was rock music's main emporium, masterminded by Bill Graham, who had helped launch the career of the Charles Lloyd Quartet – a group that included Keith Jarrett on piano, Ron McLure on bass and Jack DeJohnette on drums. Nimbly managed, the group had become the most popular in jazz with a fresh approach that moved in and out of rock rhythms with albums such as *Forest Flower* and *Dream Weaver*, the bestselling jazz albums of 1967.

'Lloyd's quick rise to international recognition provides an antidote to the disparaging commentary floating about the current state of jazz', observed *Down Beat*.[5] Adopting the colourful clothing of the prevailing Californian flower-power generation, instead of the lounge suits and ties typically associated with jazz musicians, and playing long, ecstatic versions of tunes with hip titles like 'Love Ship', Lloyd clicked with rock crowds. 'It was a time of idealism', said Lloyd: 'There were not these lines of demarcation in music.

Kids were listening to all kinds of music. So when we played the Fillmore we were very lovingly and warmly received and it opened a door because things were kind of depressed in the jazz scene. Jazz clubs were struggling for their existence.'[6] Such success in the then depressed market for jazz was sufficient to attract a feature in *Harper's* magazine, in which the group were hailed as the 'First psychedelic jazz group'. More than any other group of the time, Lloyd suggested that it was possible that rock could provide jazz with a source of energy and inspiration; and, more significantly, he demonstrated that there was a large, young audience receptive to new ideas. His success started the jazz world talking, increasing speculation that a fusion between jazz and rock could not be far off.

In fact, such a move had been widely predicted in the press; as early as August 1967, in a feature entitled 'A Way Out Of The Muddle', *Time* magazine expressed the hope that a marriage between jazz and rock might happen. And in 1968, *Down Beat* editor Dan Morgenstern wrote: 'A particularist, exclusive and non-proselytizing attitude ill behooves jazz in its present predicament, which briefly stated is the crying need of a bigger audience. If rock offers a bridge, jazz would be foolish not to cross it.'[7] More particularly, with a trade story in *Billboard* announcing that jazz would hit rock bottom in 1969,[8] rock music was now widely perceived as the catalyst that might well revitalise an ailing jazz.

Meanwhile, before Handy's group broke up in 1968 they had recorded *Projections*, which moved towards a synthesis of jazz and rock. Subsequently, Nock and Handy's violinist Michael White formed the group Fourth Way with bassist Ron McLure and drummer Eddie Gladden. Under Nock's leadership, the group convincingly stated a case for combining jazz improvisation and rock rhythms. Nock used one of the first electric keyboard set-ups in jazz, a stunning array of early synthesisers, ring modulators, flanges, a Fender Rhodes electric piano and wah-wah pedals, and he utilised their full potential from far reaches of white noise to guitar-like sounds. Combined with White's electric violin, his work seemed poised to usher in a new era of jazz. 'When the history of electronic music is written', said *Rolling Stone* magazine, 'the pioneering work of Fourth Way should neatly eclipse the influence of many other more highly publicized groups.'[9]

It was not to be. After three albums the band broke up in April 1970, its existence spent almost entirely on the West Coast, the wrong side of the continent to get the attention of the influential East-Coast critics who were effectively the opinion formers in jazz. The sense that a new page was being turned when jazz entered the age of rock-influenced music would be enacted out entirely on the East Coast under the eyes of a music press which had widely predicted such a move and were looking for a player around whom history could be constructed.

From the margins to the mainstream: the dialectics of jazz-rock

During the previous twenty years, Miles Davis had proved, not once but several times, that where he led others followed. With Lloyd's group the most successful in jazz in 1968 through their inclusive approach to popular culture, musicians and critics were waiting to see what Davis's response would be, and, with the break-up of his groundbreaking quintet that year, Davis began to reposition his music to reflect the changing times. After a series of inconclusive recording sessions, he went into the studios in February 1969 to record *In a Silent Way*. Reaching 134 on the *Billboard* chart, it demonstrated the aesthetic feasibility, if not the commercial viability, of jazz-rock.

Davis's ensemble – with an enlarged three-keyboard set-up, John McLaughlin's guitar, Wayne Shorter on soprano saxophone and cautiously stated rock rhythms from Dave Holland on bass and Tony Williams on drums – consciously distanced itself from the sound of Davis's earlier quintets. Another striking deviation was a concerted application of postproduction techniques by producer Teo Macero. In popular music, the notion that a recording should sound like a 'captured' live performance had given way to elaborate production techniques in the studio. In contrast, jazz had learnt hardly anything from this.[10]

In the eyes of many, Davis sanctioned a move into rock-influenced music. Because of his reputation as a musical pathfinder, the portents seemed clear: jazz-rock represented the way ahead because Miles Davis said so, and subsequently it has not been unusual for jazz histories to credit him with creating jazz-rock. In fact, Davis and his record company Columbia were keen to register the kind of success two popular groups on the label were already enjoying by combining jazz and rock. Blood Sweat & Tears and Chicago grafted a horn section on to a rock rhythm section and mixed jazz-influenced solos and ensemble passages with vocals, and were enjoying unprecedented pop sales. These groups were commercially produced and their recordings intended for a mass market, and their music was shaped accordingly. Actively promoted by Columbia, they reflected the music industry's constant drive to expand their market share by the mainstreaming and marketing of 'new' products from the margins, in this case creating a commercial jazz-rock hybrid.

The success of Blood Sweat & Tears' eponymously titled second album and the marketing push given it through corporate advertisements and radio play contributed to a climate where a financially beleaguered jazz world sat up and took notice of jazz-rock. It also suggested to the record industry a way of turning round their unprofitable jazz sales by giving the music a contemporary spin. 'Clive Davis was the President of Columbia Records and he signed Blood, Sweat & Tears in 1968 and Chicago in 1969', said Miles Davis. 'He started to talk to me about trying to reach this younger market and about changing' (Davis and Troupe 1989, 287–8).

If *In a Silent Way* represented a tentative move towards a jazz-rock synthesis, then *Bitches Brew*, recorded in August 1969, saw Davis embrace the concept wholeheartedly. By then Davis had come under the spell of rock guitarist Jimi Hendrix, who had a profound effect on his music. Davis's long-time friend and collaborator Gil Evans shared Davis's enthusiasm for Hendrix's music, and during a 1980 interview demonstrated how he and Davis incorporated the chords of Hendrix's 'The Wind Cries Mary' into the title track of Davis's 1969 album, *Filles de Kilimanjaro* (Enstice and Rubin 1992, 145). Indeed, there can be no mistaking how the deeply mysterious groove of Hendrix's 'Voodoo Chile' from his third, and final, Experience album, *Electric Ladyland* (released in September 1968), was echoed in 'Miles Runs the Voodoo Down' from *Bitches Brew*, recorded eleven months later. Here Davis avoids popular music's smooth contours with a grittiness and awkwardness that flies in the face of commercialism, using dissonant chords and angular open-ended improvisation. With Columbia aggressively marketing *Bitches Brew*, and in so doing assisting the passage of the jazz-rock 'concept' into the jazz mainstream, the album sold 400,000 units in its first year and won the 1970 Grammy for 'Best Jazz Record'.

The sound of *Bitches Brew* was in sharp contrast to Davis's music in live performance, which had taken on the proportions of free-form electronic abstraction. When Shorter left the group in December 1969, his replacement was a 19-year-old from Brooklyn, Steve Grossman. Saxophone solos were no longer as important a feature of Davis's music as they had been in the days of his acoustic quintet. Gone were the narrative certainties of Davis's own playing, which veered sharply in favour of fragmentation and coloration, often electrified and distorted through a wah-wah attachment. Columbia, in contrast to what Davis notes in his autobiography, did record the band and we do have bootleg recordings which document this radical shift in his music.[11] These changes, however, were not reflected on *A Tribute to Jack Johnson* (1970), where it was his stated intention to confront the music of Hendrix head-on.[12] The Davis/McLaughlin jam during the first half of 'Right Off' sees Davis's trumpet framed by the raw electronic energy inspired by Hendrix. He showed he had by no means abandoned the lyricism of his acoustic period, with a solo of such poise and structure that compares favourably with any from his earlier period.

Three days after *Jack Johnson*, Davis finally documented the electronic experimentation in which he was engaged in live performance on *Black Beauty: Miles Davis at Fillmore West* and, two months later, *Miles Davis at Fillmore*. Subsequently, Davis's output was uneven, although *Get Up With It*

(1974) contained a heartfelt tribute to Duke Ellington, who had died at the time of the recording sessions. In 1975, Davis embarked on a tour of Japan, although his health had been a cause for concern for some three years prior to this. The resulting albums, *Agharta* and *Panagaea*, provided the clearest indication of the impact of Hendrix on Davis's musical odyssey, this rather austere music belying any claim that Davis had sold out to the sirens of commerce (see, for example, Crouch 1996).

When *Rolling Stone* reviewed Davis's *In a Silent Way*, it was followed on the same page by a review of *Emergency!* by the Tony Williams Lifetime, so closely together were the two records released.[13] If Davis's album was characterised by an absence of significant musical events, favouring pastel tone colours and delicate shading, then Lifetime gave apodictic testimony that they had discovered a new way of reconciling jazz expressionism empowered by rock. Manic and desperate, for a moment at least, it seemed as if it were to Williams and not to Davis that destiny was beckoning. Lifetime comprised Williams (who had left Davis's employ in early 1969) on drums, McLaughlin on guitar and Larry Young on organ.

McLaughlin had moved from England to join Williams's band after playing in a variety of jazz ensembles in Britain and Europe and having worked as a session musician.[14] Prior to leaving he had recorded an album called *Extrapolation* with a group that included saxophonist John Surman. Rhythmically and harmonically fluid, it made use of both modal harmonies and the 'time, no changes' principle of improvising, in which the composition provides tempo, key and mood but leaves the chord changes to the spontaneous interaction of improviser and accompanists. It was these principles that McLaughlin brought to Lifetime. Davis was so impressed with McLaughlin's playing that, even before *Emergency!* had been recorded, he had invited the guitarist to join his own group. McLaughlin declined, but became a fixture on Davis's albums for the next two years.[15]

While early experiments such as those by Coryell, Burton, Steig, Lloyd and, just a few weeks earlier, Davis had incorporated rock's rhythms and tone colours, none had used the dynamics of electricity to such coruscating effect as Lifetime. Prior to the *Emergency!* session all the band members had jammed with Hendrix, and it is impossible not to think of this music as being touched by his terrifying electronics: 'I was heavily influenced by Jimi Hendrix', confirmed Williams.[16] After recording two albums, the band broke up in April 1971, but on subsequent albums without McLaughlin, Williams struggled to position his music in jazz.

Encouraged by Davis, McLaughlin decided to form his own ensemble after Lifetime disbanded. The Mahavishnu Orchestra, when it opened at Greenwich Village's Gaslight Café in July 1971, so mesmerised audiences it was immediately held over. McLaughlin, dressed in white, was a striking figure using a double-necked guitar (one neck of six strings, the other of twelve). With Jerry Goodman on electric violin, Jan Hammer on keyboards, Rick Laird on bass and Billy Cobham on drums, critics immediately expressed admiration for the band, which exhibited a high degree of ensemble cohesion at demandingly fast tempos, and revelled in unusual time signatures and abrupt changes of metre.

While performing at the Gaslight, the group recorded *The Inner Mounting Flame*, featuring compositions of McLaughlin's which were often as complex as any bebop lines and also reflected the influence of eastern cultures. The album was more influential in its time than even *Bitches Brew* which, for all its innovative importance, had often been turgid and congested with discursive melodies and soloing. *The Inner Mounting Flame* was more focused in structure and rhythm, collective ensemble interplay was reinforced with an intensity that belied its spontaneity and, with the bass often participating in the complex ensemble passages, the role of Cobham on drums was elevated to that of an equal voice within the ensemble.

Nothing like the sound of 'Meetings of the Spirit' or 'The Noonward Race' had ever been heard in jazz or rock. The newness was in the virtuosity itself; the group's 'coherence and control comes like a shaft of light in the muddied and confused', said *Melody Maker*, predicting that "The effects of this album will be far reaching."[17] Even today the album conveys a feeling of the new. It was followed by *Birds of Fire* (1973), which reinforced the startling first impression of their recording debut. The title track, in 18/8, opens with an ominous crashing gong that presages McLaughlin's thematic statement, with his overdriven guitar over a bass and violin ostinato that leads into passages of free-flowing improvisation over virtuosic drum accompaniment. It was not until autumn 1999 that *The Lost Trident Sessions* was released by Columbia/Legacy, the results of a recording session at London's Trident studios from 25 June 1973 intended to be their third album. Subsequently there were reports[18] suggesting artistic differences during recording, but in an interview McLaughlin gave in January 1974 he expressed optimism that the album would soon be released, saying, 'It's a terrific sound and some people have told me they think it's dynamite.'[19] Here was an empathy and cohesion that only a stable working band could achieve, and a degree of energy and animation that reached a level of emotional and creative intensity which, with hindsight, would appear almost impossible to sustain. Indeed, after just one more album, the live *Between Nothingness and Eternity*, the band was unexpectedly wound up on 29 December 1973.

With Mahavishnu's success, McLaughlin was quickly recognised as the most influential guitarist since Wes Montgomery, an inspiration to both jazz and rock guitarists, even helping to contribute to a rise in instrumental proficiency in rock (in London he had given lessons to Jimmy Page, for example). However, the Mahavishnu Orchestra set in train a host of imitators who copied the superficial aspects of their style, making virtuosity an end in itself at the expense of content – a trend which would arguably become the undoing of jazz-rock.

Art into artifact: the commodification of jazz-rock

Pianist Chick Corea was one musician who was sufficiently impressed by the Mahavishnu Orchestra to change musical direction. After leaving Davis in September 1970, Corea's first inclination was to explore the areas of abstraction pursued by Davis's group with an acoustic trio called Circle. A change of musical direction prompted the formation of Return to Forever, with Corea on electric piano plus multi-reed player Joe Farrell, bassist Stanley Clarke, drummer Airto Moreira and vocalist Flora Purim. An aesthetically pleasing fusion of jazz with Brazilian and Latin rhythms, their first album, *Return to Forever* (1972), contained Corea's widely admired composition 'La Fiesta'.[20] To keep the band together at a time when there was a lack of work under Corea's own name, the rhythm section played with Stan Getz, recording on *Captain Marvel* in March 1972 all but one of Corea's compositions for Return to Forever that would appear on the subsequent *Light as a Feather* (October 1972). In spring 1973 Farrell left, prompting another change of musical direction. 'I feel the formation of the Mahavishnu Orchestra was equally important [as Miles Davis's bands]. What John McLaughlin did with the electric guitar set the world on its ear', explained Corea. 'No-one ever heard an electric guitar played like that before and it certainly inspired me. I wanted to express that emotion. John's band, more than my experience with Miles, made me want to turn up the volume and write music that was more dramatic and made your hair move.'[21]

Corea took McLaughlin's virtuosity as a licence to demonstrate his own keyboard facility, combining somewhat grandiose orchestral effects with stunningly fast passages of meticulous precision for guitar, keyboards, bass and drums. Initially with Bill Connors on guitar for *Hymn of the Seventh Galaxy* (1973), he was replaced by Al DiMeola on *Where Have I Known You Before* (1974) and *No Mystery* (1975). It was perhaps inevitable that the band's virtuosity would take it over the top, as indeed DiMeola has acknowledged (liner notes to Corea, *Music Forever*). *No Mystery* has strong echoes of 'progressive' (or 'pomp') rock of bands such as Yes, and Emerson, Lake & Palmer, which becomes more apparent when considering Corea's *Romantic Warrior* from 1976 in the context of Rick Wakeman's *Myths and Legends of King Arthur and the Knights of the Round Table*. Opening with 'Medieval Overture', Corea performs four programmatically styled pieces before climaxing with 'Duel of the Jester and the Tyrant'. Clearly, this music was expected to sell into the jazz market, but it also had the potential of 'crossing over' into the 'pomp' rock market. It made Corea one of the most popular crossover artists of his day, albeit combining the worst of two worlds: a fusion of jazz's populist urges and rock's elitist ambitions, a theme that underwrites subsequent 'fusion' albums recorded by Clarke and DiMeola in their own right.

Like Corea's, the career of Herbie Hancock moved towards an accommodation with commercialism. Fired by Davis for returning late from his honeymoon in South America in September 1968, he formed a sextet that recorded five albums[22] and met with modest success on the touring circuits. However, when work dropped to just two bookings a month he was forced to concede that his excursions of free-form 'spacey' improvisation and occasional recondite interaction was not what the public wanted. A self-confessed Sly Stone fan, in 1973 he decided to form a jazz-funk band. 'Instead of getting jazz cats who could play funk, I got funk cats who could play jazz', he explained (Coryell and Friedman 1978, 162). The resultant album, *Head Hunters*, rocketed to 13 on the *Billboard* pop chart, and within a year had sold 750,000 units. The die was cast; with a pop hit under his belt, subsequent albums set about distancing his work from jazz. Hancock was annoyed at critics who continued to associate him with jazz, which he and his management considered an impediment to pop sales, citing his as a specific artistic choice to 'crossover' from jazz into pop. When his album *Future Shock* produced the single 'Rockit', one of the biggest instrumental dance hits of the 1980s, he said: 'I've been trying to take the pop stuff more into the pop area and leave out the jazz. I think I've pretty much succeeded at that because the last few records I don't consider jazz at all. "Rockit" has nothing to do with jazz.'[23]

Exploring the potential: Weather Report

Weather Report was formed in 1971, a musical partnership between Cannonball Adderley's former pianist Joe Zawinul and saxophonist Wayne Shorter, who had distinguished himself in the ensembles of Art Blakey and Davis. Their debut album, *Weather Report*, with an acoustic group of saxophone, piano, bass, drums and percussion, utilised this conventional line-up in highly unconventional ways. A point of departure was signalled in 'Eurydice', a piece free from metric and harmonic structure, while 'Milky Way' used the resonance of the acoustic piano to create an arresting tone poem. Their second album, *I Sing the Body Electric*, saw Zawinul adopting electric tone colours, using a Fender Rhodes piano on one side of the album to explore collective improvisation, while the other side included the ambitious impressionistic 'Unknown Soldier'. Their next album, *Sweet-nighter*, owed something to the complex rhythmic layering of post-'Cold Sweat' James Brown on numbers such as '125th Street Congress' and 'Boogie Woogie Waltz'. It was also the first album on which Zawinul used a synthe-siser, which pointed the way to the more orchestral approach of *Mysterious Traveller* that followed. Utilising the potential of the recording studio to a greater extent than on their previous albums, 'Nubian Sundance' featured complex layers of rhythmic patterns from two drummers, with motifs and orchestral effects overdubbed to present a constantly changing canvas of sounds. *Black Market*, from 1976, introduced the electric-bass player Jaco Pastorius, a virtuoso performer who galvanised the band. The title track, a programmatic piece that refines some of the ideas introduced in 'Nubian Sundance', announced a period of heightened creativity that saw the band become the top attraction in jazz.

In 1977 came *Heavy Weather*, with the structurally sophisticated track 'Birdland' receiving a Grammy nomination for 'Best Instrumental Compo-sition'.[24] Weather Report had now travelled some distance from the free-form collective improvisations on *I Sing the Body Electric*, taking in a wide variety of approaches to broaden the expressivity of the jazz combo. One important ingredient in the album's success (it reached 30 on the *Billboard* chart) was Pastorius's playing, opening up a new world for the electric bass just as Jimmy Blanton had with the acoustic bass 37 years earlier.[25] Although Weather Report went on to make 15 albums in all, with the ex-ception of *8.30* (1979), their finest work was now behind them. Their range extended from classical influences, most notably the French impression-ists, to World Music and bebop, big-band music and chamber music. They went from open-form collective improvisation to elaborately conceived forms, from structures with no apparent metre to straight-ahead swing. They achieved a successful integration of improvised lines and pre-written parts and adapted the new electronic technology to create a fresh and vital context for their playing. Alongside Duke Ellington, Weather Report cre-ated a body of work that numbers among the most diverse and imaginative in jazz.

From jazz-rock to fusion

In 1973, Columbia increased the advances against future sales to its top artists while at the same time increasing the amount spent on promoting them in order to put pressure on its competitors. By 1974, all guarantees to artists had skyrocketed against a background where recording costs had increased by 200 per cent, exacerbated by the energy crisis and a shortage of vinyl (i.e., polyvinyl chloride, a petroleum derivative). These factors combined to place unprecedented pressure on artists to attain sales targets or be dropped from the labels to which they were signed. In such a climate many jazz musicians were forced to reassess their artistic direction along the lines of socio-economic reality. Jazz artists were encouraged to record albums with – to use the new buzzword – 'crossover' appeal, music that has the potential to cross from one established market into another; for example, from jazz into pop, a market that offered the greatest potential for sales. Many musicians who had no affinity with trends in popular culture felt pressurised to respond accordingly – Barney Kessel recorded *Hair is Beautiful,* Paul Desmond recorded *Bridge Over Troubled Water* and Benny Golson went disco with the album *I'm Always Dancin' To the Music.*

When Hancock's *Head Hunters* went gold, Columbia immediately sought to establish itself as the major force in jazz-rock fusion, closely followed by Atlantic. Artists who ultimately failed to make the mark on the ledger in any significant way, such as Dexter Wansel, Rodney Frankin, John Blair, Walt Bolden and Jaroslav, began to crowd the major-label rosters. By now the promise of the early jazz-rock experimentation had given way to a more commercial music that was being called fusion, a key distinction between it and jazz-rock being that the dominant non-jazz elements of the jazz-rock equation no longer came from the creative side of rock but from pop with simple hooks and currently fashionable dance beats. Fusion completed the music marketing cycle continually enacted by record companies in popular music, taking a music from the margins (jazz-rock) and mainstreaming it for mass consumption (fusion). This process was summed up by Columbia's advertising of the period, which announced: 'Jazz has taken a long-overdue upbeat swing lately: the esoteric music of a relatively select few has become the music for just about everybody.'[26]

The jazz-rock continuum

When jazz-rock emerged at the end of the 1960s, it set a new agenda for change and continued to evolve in a way that many other areas of jazz would not. From the beginning, jazz-rock was never a static genre with clearly defined boundaries but a music in constant flux. As we have seen, one direction saw the colonisation of jazz-rock by record companies resulting in fusion, which with further commercial refinement during the 1980s and 1990s produced so-called 'smooth jazz'. A contemporary update (in terms of dance beats, melodic hooks and electronic technology) of 1970s fusion, smooth jazz was specifically designed for FM airplay, with musicians writing tunes and devising solos specifically to satisfy the rigid musical formatting requirements of FM radio stations. As one New York FM station manager put it, 'Primarily we are looking for bright tempos and melodies that are recognisable ... We want melodic strength that the casual listener or non-*aficionado* can pick up on.'[27]

In 1987, Radio KTWV in Los Angeles came up with an all-fusion rotation policy and quickly became the city's most popular radio station. Its 'smooth jazz' became the fastest-growing radio format of the 1990s, with revenue growth rising to a phenomenal 77.7 per cent, far outstripping 54.2 per cent for alternative music, 37.1 per cent for adult contemporary, 20.4 per cent for country and only 15.2 per cent for rock.[28] Fusion happened to click with the right money demographic, the 25- to 52-year-olds, and by the end of the 1990s there were over 200 radio stations across America that specialised in formatting fusion, with high rotation playlists often put together by market-research firms specialising in 'audience testing' to ensure recordings were selected on 'the basis of the broadest possible appeal' (or, to put it another way, the lowest common denominator).

Today, the spectre of fusion has grown so large it fills the viewfinder, to the extent it has been fashionable to ignore the distinction between it and jazz-rock, lumping them together and writing the whole lot off as having turned art into artifact – a classic case of throwing the baby out with the bathwater. No one would consider evaluating the swing era (which raises many issues similar to those posed by jazz-rock) in terms of Guy Lombardo, Jan Garber, Art Kassel, Tommy Tucker, Kay Kyser, Gus Arnheim, Abe Lyman, Fred Waring or Anson Weeks. Yet this is precisely what has happened with the perception of jazz-rock; it has become perceived in terms of fusion artists such as Kenny G, The Yellow Jackets, The Rippingtons, Kirk Whalum, Spyro Gyra, Grover Washington and Dave Sanborn.

Nevertheless, the eclecticism inherent in the original late-1960s premise of jazz-rock has continued to offer a set of possibilities warranting serious exploration. It has meant that for many musicians in contemporary times, a distinction between jazz-rock and fusion has become crucial when seeking to situate their music within the overall context of jazz. They distance their work from 'fusion' because of the pejorative connotations of a term that now implies a frankly commercial music, with more in common with pop than jazz. Pat Metheny has referred to fusion as 'The "F" word', asserting his work was inspired by 'the early jazz-rock experiments of the late sixties and early seventies'.[29] John Scofield has sought to make a similar distinction: 'The jazz-rock thing, the best of it, bands such as Weather Report, Miles, Mahavishnu, they all had their own style and their own way of doing things and I think they were really important. I guess I would like to be considered in that category somewhere, but putting the pieces together from my viewpoint.'[30]

For these musicians, jazz-rock and fusion are not one and the same thing; for them perhaps the most significant aspect of the jazz-rock of the late 1960s and early 1970s was the aesthetic potential suggested by key recordings that implied a whole range of new musical possibilities. Electronic tone colours suggested great scope for broadening the expressive range of jazz, while the big beat of 'rock' *per se* was never a characteristic of the music, at least not in the terms Grateful Dead or Led Zeppelin fans would recognise it; rather, a hunt for ever more sophisticated rhythms to invigorate compositional forms was set in motion. By the early 1970s the music of James Brown – 'Every man is a drum'[31] – inspired a new rhythmic complexity that did not come exclusively from the rhythm instruments. As Brown's influence along with World Music elements crept into the work of Davis and Weather Report, it was clear that jazz-rock had begun to transform the familiar tone colours and rhythms of jazz.

By the end of the 1970s, fusion seemed to have run its course and events elsewhere in jazz suggested a realignment of the avant-garde with the jazz mainstream (reflected in the work of musicians such as David Murray, Chico Freeman, Anthony Davis, Arthur Blythe and others) that presaged a return to a tradition-based synthesis of earlier styles that would dominate jazz for the next two decades. However, Miles Davis's return to the concert platform in 1981 after a furlough of some five years became the most publicised event in jazz history, with virtually every newspaper in the world carrying some reference to the event. Within a year he was commanding just under a million dollars for an eight-concert tour in Japan. His music, a well-calibrated mix of funk rhythms, electric tone colours and jazz improvisation, reignited interest in the possibilities of jazz-rock.

While Davis's albums over the next ten years lacked the ambition of his earlier work, somehow it did not seem to matter. He became a fixture on the international touring circuits and the biggest draw in jazz. The reason was simple: audiences wanted to consume the aura and physical presence of one of the great and enduring legends of jazz before it was too late. In many ways his music, paradoxically, was less important than the event. Of the albums he recorded during this period, the most dramatic was *Tutu*, which carried an arresting Irving Penn photograph on its cover that seemed to indicate a new beginning. Made for Warner Brothers in 1986 (and produced by Marcus Miller) after 31 years with Columbia, without his regular touring group, it featured synthesised orchestral effects made possible by the programming of Jason Miles that simultaneously evoked Gil Evans but suggested the mystery of things unforeseen. Davis's final three albums for Columbia, *Star People* (1982), *Decoy* (1984) and *You're Under Arrest* (1985), were recorded when guitarist John Scofield was a member of the band, his twisted blues lines inspiring Davis to extend himself beyond the rather modest aspirations of his improvisations on earlier, post-comeback recordings.

Scofield – a former Berklee College of Music graduate who, in addition to his work with Davis, had performed and recorded with Jay McShann, Lee Konitz, Gerry Mulligan, Chet Baker, Billy Cobham, Gary Burton, Charles Mingus and David Liebman – formed his own band in 1986. With Marc Cohen on keyboards, Garry Grainger on bass and Dennis Chambers on drums, the group's cohesion was much admired by musicians at the time, and Scofield's guitar had now matured into a readily identifiable style with his use of unusual intervals and rhythmic sequences and fluid, often polytonal harmonies. With this new group, Scofield succeeded in reawakening the potential inherent in the eclecticism of a jazz-rock union to a greater extent than perhaps the return of Davis had done. *Blue Matter* (1987) is one of the key albums of the 1980s, reminding a rather self-righteous acoustic mainstream that great jazz could still emanate from jazz-rock and suggesting the idiom was far from exhausted.

The Blue Matter group was disbanded after almost three years of constant touring. Scofield then formed a group with Joe Lovano on tenor, Anthony Cox on bass and up-and-coming drum star Bill Stewart in 1989. The group remained together until 1993, producing a run of critically acclaimed albums, most notably *Meant to Be* (1991) and *What We Do* (1993). Less equivocal than his previous group, this ensemble mixed elements of the jazz-rock equation with acoustic jazz, a powerful duality that pointed strongly to the continuing influence of jazz-rock. Scofield continued to produce albums reflecting this ethos into the new millennium, including *A Go Go* (1998), with the organ trio Medeski, Martin & Wood, and *Bump* (2000).

Scofield's predecessor in the Davis band was guitarist Mike Stern, who had not been displayed to best advantage by the trumpeter, who wanted his young charge to play like Hendrix. Strongly influenced by Wes Montgomery and Jim Hall, Stern's more considered side can be heard on bassist Harvie Swartz's *Urban Earth* and *Smart Moves* (1986), his own *In a Different Light* (1990) and *Give and Take* (1997). He made several albums with saxophonist Bob Berg, both under his own name and Berg's, where the emphasis was on wide-eyed soloing over an unsubtle backbeat, but the commercial stance of the music could not entirely conceal an original voice. When Stern left Davis, it was to join a band co-led by Pastorius. During his tenure with Weather Report, Pastorius (who had evolved a virtuoso technique on Fender and fretless basses) suggested he might exert a defining role in the music. It was not to be: just like one of jazz's earlier, tragically doomed young heroes, Pastorius was to die at the age of 35, his end hastened by drugs, alcohol and fast living. In his wake he left several albums which attested to his virtuosity but, for one so gifted, rather curiously lacked depth or substance. Yet on his debut album, *Jaco Pastorius* in 1975, he had taken the jazz world by surprise with just four choruses of Charlie Parker's 'Donna Lee'.

Pastorius had been a key element in a trio led by guitarist Pat Metheny for his recording debut as a leader, *Bright Size Life* (1976). Metheny had been a child prodigy, teaching guitar at the University of Miami at 17 and joining the faculty of Berklee College of Music in Boston at 19. Metheny left Berklee in 1976 to form the Pat Metheny Group with Lyle Mays on keyboards, Mark Egan on bass and Danny Gottlieb on drums. Through tireless low-budget barnstorming, piling into a cramped van and travelling hundreds of miles between gigs, he had built his band into an international attraction by the end of the 1980s. The success of their 1978 album, *Pat Metheny Group*, the Grammy-winning *Offramp* (1981) and *First Circle* (1984) was the key to the group's growing popularity. Alongside his endeavours with his touring group, Metheny continued with his trio in a more equivocal jazz climate, while *80/81* (with tenor saxophonists Mike Brecker and Dewey Redman) revealed a wide-ranging vision of jazz.

As the popularity of the Pat Metheny Group grew, so did Metheny's ambitions for it. *Still Life Talking* (1987) and *Letter From Home* (1989) saw both Mays and Metheny creating suave yet accessible musical soundscapes using extended forms, so that with the release of *Imaginary Day* (1997) he was able to say, 'We have been spending the last ten years getting deeper and deeper into extended compositions and it's been a fascinating challenge. I'm not talking about just a one shot thing with a bunch of solos. I really do feel that in writing for the group it's like writing for a large ensemble because of what electronic instruments can do. No one else is seriously dealing with the potential of what electric instruments are capable of doing at this point in the jazz world, to me it's such a rich territory.'[32] A good example of Metheny's ambitious structures and 'orchestral' writing for electronic instrumentation is 'The Roots of Coincidence', at one point juxtaposing thrash, dance rhythms and even a passage that evokes French impressionism in a deftly handled collage (none of which is sampled, incidentally), contrasted by an expansive developmental section that takes a germ of an idea and spreads it over a broad canvas.

Like the Pat Metheny Group, the group Steps drew inspiration from the early jazz-rock experiments, this time with musicians who had been around at its inception. Vibraphonist Mike Mainieri had been a member of Jeremy and the Satyrs while tenor saxophonist Mike Brecker and keyboard player Don Grolnick had been members of the early jazz-rock group Dreams, which in live performance in 1969 had impressed Miles Davis, who frequently attended their New York concerts. Drummer Steve Gadd had played with a group called Stuff, and with Chick Corea and

Chuck Mangione, while bassist Eddie Gomez was known through his work with the Bill Evans Trio. Steps attracted considerable underground interest through their performances at Seventh Avenue South, the New York jazz club owned by Brecker and his brother Randy. They were invited to Japan to play and record, and *Step by Step* and *Smokin' in the Pit* from December 1980 served notice that they had the potential to become a force in 1980s jazz. At the time, Mainieri called Steps a 'contemporary bebop band' and, indeed, many numbers they played were straight ahead and honoured the head-solos-head convention of bop, but often juxtaposed with square rhythmic patterns that suggested rock.

Paradox, recorded in 1981, revealed a more scrupulous attention to ensemble dynamics and articulation. In 1982 the band changed their name to Steps Ahead and their eponymous album was quickly dubbed 'the new acoustic fusion'. Largely misunderstood by critics at the time, the band's diligent application of sophisticated forms with a musical intent mediated by consistency of approach offered something fresh in the early 1980s. A unique, one-of-a-kind ensemble whose individual members succeeded in realising their collective potential, their frequent use of contemporary rhythms avoided the prevailing straight-ahead swing of the hard-bop renascence but meant they were frequently placed on the bill with electric jazz groups. To be heard, the band went electric themselves, sacrificing their astute acoustic poise, although *Modern Times* (1984) and *Magnetic* (1986) suggested they might take up the pathfinding role of electronic respectability vacated by the wind-up of Weather Report. But by 1987 the band had gone their separate ways. Brecker's own recording debut as a leader a year later, *Michael Brecker* (with Pat Metheny, Kenny Kirkland, Charlie Haden and Jack DeJohnette), remains a definitive statement in drawing together elements of post-bop, *ad hoc* song forms and shifting rhythmic densities that encapsulate not only the legacy of jazz-rock, but also the drawing together – fusing if you will – of many stylistic elements to create something new and fresh.

Appropriations and postmodernism: a contemporary dialectic

In the climate of renascence in the 1980s and 1990s, American impatience and intolerance with the contemporary, even to the point of displaying a refusal to acknowledge its place in the narrative of jazz history, had the effect of discrediting experimentation. Even so, it continued to flourish at the music's margins. In the 1980s, alto saxophonist Steve Coleman called his James Brown-inspired music M-Base, using funk rhythms as a basis for improvisation that by 1988 became the jazz critics' flavour of the

month – for months. Coleman's group Five Elements made their recording
debut with *Motherland Pulse*, which was followed by several albums on the
JMT label before they were signed by record giant RCA Victor, by which
time a certain monotony of tone and predictability had crept into their
music. With, at various times, like-minded musicians such as alto saxophonist Greg Osby, Graham Haynes on trumpet, Geri Allen on keyboards,
Marvin 'Smitty' Smith on drums and Cassandra Wilson on vocals, their
music was almost in determined opposition, perhaps even protest, to the
neo-classical movement. Osby, for example, called it 'a period of stagna-
tion', adding, 'If you wore a suit and are between 18 and 22 and played
like somebody on a Fifties Blue Note album, you got a record deal. That
can't be good for the future of jazz. Unless someone expresses themselves
with something they thought of, they conceived and brought to fruition,
you don't have complete artists.'[33] In the mid-1990s, Coleman moved away
from the chattering guitars and funk, and his experimental ensembles, The
Metrics and The Mystic Rhythm Society, explored ethnic rhythms, a study
that took him to Africa and Cuba in his search for authenticity.

M-Base was the first of several buzzwords that entered jazz at this time;
acid jazz, coined by British DJ Gilles Peterson to describe his musical mix for
dancefloor fans that included 1980s soul jazz, 1970s soul classics, jazz-funk,
1970s disco and 1960s classics from the Blue Note catalogue, reached New
York in 1990. It took hold at the Giant Step, a club in the basement of the
Metropolis Café in Union Square run by Jonathan Rudnick and Maurice
Bernstein. Digable Planets launched their hit 'ReBirth of the Slick' at their
club, home of the resident group Groove Collective, which combined bebop solos with a disco beat. However, much that passed for acid jazz was
no more than pop music, such as The Brand New Heavies' 'Dream on
Dreamer' or Jamiroquai's 'Blow Your Mind'. British guitarist Ronnie Jordan
was more convincing: his 'new-jazz-swing' album, *The Antidote* (1992), sped
up *Billboard*'s chart and numbered among the top five listings, selling over
200,000 copies on the strength of a funky version of Davis's 'So What'.

In its quest for novelty at the expense of substance, acid jazz soon had
turntable scratches and rappers added to the mix. The London group, US3,
with rappers Shabaam Sahdeeq and KCB, plus keyboardist Tim Vine and
producer Geoff Wilkinson, made their name by sampling Blue Note funk-
jazz hits with a heavy synthesised drum accompaniment. The success of
Hand on the Torch produced the hit single 'Cantaloop Island (Flip Fantasia)',
a heavily sampled version of Hancock's original from the album, *Empyrean
Isles* (1964), which had an inventive solo by British trumpet player Gerard
Prescencer added, thrusting hip-hop jazz into mainstream consciousness.
The group's popularity prompted a re-release programme by Blue Note
called the 'Rare Groove Series' dedicated to heroes of 1950s and 1960s soul

jazz such as Donald Byrd, Grant Green, Gene Harris, Ronnie Laws, Horace Silver and Lonnie Smith. By the mid-1990s acid jazz had spread to most US cities, its popularity giving impetus to the careers of several young musicians playing in a non-acoustic context, such as Medeski, Martin & Wood, and guitarist Charlie Hunter.

From the mid-1980s, New York's 'Downtown' scene became the centre of American experimental jazz, a broad spectrum of music that went from the free bop of alto saxophonist Tim Berne to the Jewish Alternative Movement. Echoing developments in European jazz by broadening jazz expressionism through the addition of indigenous cultural elements, the Jewish Alternative Movement used Jewish folk tunes and religious songs, or themes inspired by them, as a basis for jazz improvisation. Groups such as the Hasidic New Wave, led by Frank London on trumpet and Greg Wall on saxophones with David Fiuczynski on guitar, the Paradox Trio led by Matt Darriau (actually a quartet), David Krakauer's Klezmer Madness, The Klezmatics and Gary Lucas's Gods and Monsters were among many that brought tone colours into jazz that had not been heard since the (albeit legitimised) clarinet introduction to Gershwin's *Rhapsody in Blue* or Ziggy Elman's solos with the Benny Goodman Orchestra on 'Bei mir bist du schön' (1937) or on 'And The Angels Sing' (1939).

The doyen of the Downtown scene was alto saxophonist John Zorn, whose group Masada, formed in 1993, was named after the fortress in Israel where besieged Jews chose suicide rather than surrender to Titus's legions in the first century AD. Comprising Zorn plus trumpeter Dave Douglas, bassist Greg Cohen and drummer Joey Baron, they combined Hebraic folk music with the tradition of the Ornette Coleman Quartet of the late 1950s and early 1960s. With his stark and arresting solos, Zorn was revealed as a composer and conceptualist of great originality. Masada recorded prolifically, their repertoire eventually extending to some 600 compositions. Beginning with *Masada One* and progressing into double figures, their albums remained consistent in their artistic delivery, with *Masada Live in Jerusalem* (1994) a particularly vivid representation of the group.

Zorn's music, a substantial body of work, often makes widespread use of collage, a technique inspired by the modernists, but which postmodernism has made its own: a juxtaposition of seemingly incongruous elements where there is never one fixed configuration. Zorn has come to represent the postmodern impulse in jazz by his expropriation and transformation of practices, fragments and signifiers of sometimes different, sometimes alien musics and cultures to relocate them within his own expressionism. With *The Big Gundown* (1986) featuring boldly reworked movie themes by spaghetti-Western composer Ennio Morricone and *Spillane* (1987), a homage to B-movie private detectives in general and the Mike Hammer character in particular, Zorn not only garnered a kind of respectability for the Downtown scene but on 'Two Lane Highway' (from *Spillane*) broke the composition up with some 60 abrupt segues into contrasting moods.

Zorn called these segues 'jump cuts', which he likened to modern youth's compressed attention span that results in channel hopping on television. Here was postmodernism, streams of vivid fleeting images that destroyed the traditional organic unity of art, a matrix of internal relationships that appeared as a collage of musical events, one following closely on the heels of another. With the formation of Naked City in 1989, their eponymously titled album saw Zorn bring tight focus to the elements he had explored on *The Big Gundown* (movie themes) and *Spillane* (jump cuts) with elements reminiscent of the New Thing soundmakers of the 1960s with nine musical fragments (between 8 and 43 seconds in length) dotted throughout the album, refusing to yield to conventional meaning and thus experienced as a shock by the listener.

On 'Latin Quarter', Zorn uses jump cuts to programmatic effect, while 'Lonely Woman' (an Ornette Coleman composition) engages directly with postmodernism with its inclusion of the bass line from Henry Mancini's television theme, 'Peter Gunn'. The group, comprising Zorn on alto saxophone, Wayne Horvitz on keyboards, Bill Frisell on guitar, Fred Frith bass and Joey Baron on drums, made several further albums which add little to the group's startling debut. Perhaps with groups such as Naked City, with their unequivocal use of electric instruments and rock rhythms, we can trace the heritage of the original jazz-rock experimenters, pushing at the boundaries of jazz to find new horizons. Certainly this was true of several Downtowners. Horvitz with his own group produced two classic Downtown albums, *The New Generation* and *Bring Yr Camera*, while Frisell became celebrated as one of the most original guitarists of his generation, his own albums – some produced and directed by Zorn – drawing on elements of Americana including country and western and American folk tunes. The drummer Bobby Previte, who appeared on many Zorn recordings, equally established himself as a composer and conceptualist, introducing World Music elements and rock on albums such as *Claude's Late Morning* and *Empty Suits*. 'Now that adherence to a museum curator's idea of authenticity has become the rallying cry, Previte's music argues for divergence and freedom to ransack the tradition', observed *Down Beat* magazine in 1991.[34]

Postmodernism, reflected in the diversity of the Downtown scene, produced a myriad of highly personal styles and innovations that did not accede to commodification in the way previous styles of jazz had done. Marketing strategies as much as canon formation gather around unified concepts such as 'New Orleans', 'Chicago', 'swing', 'bop', 'hard bop', 'cool', 'West Coast', 'free', 'jazz-rock' and so on. The sheer stylistic diversity of postmodernism meant that it resisted convenient categorisation, so its impact was restricted to the recognition an individual player might achieve rather than the force generated by a community of similarly orientated and competing artists. Perhaps most importantly, postmodernism showed how the essentially teleological model of coherent evolution had now passed to individual contributors who refused to congregate around the security of established canons, but instead conceived and performed their own individual interpretations of jazz, drawing on a variety of sources, many beyond jazz. It was this juxtaposition of references, information-age sound bites decontexualised by juxtaposition, that created the 'new', and it was perhaps here that the future of jazz lay. Looking beyond established convention, these musicians sought to create something new and vital, a jazz reflecting their own time rather than that of previous generations, no matter how appealing it might have been to bask in the reflected glory of jazz's posthumous heroes.

Global fusions and the question of 'authenticity'

In the 1930s, Django Reinhardt showed just how close the camp-fire extemporisations of a Manouche gypsy guitarist were to jazz improvisation within the context of the Quintette du Hot Club de France. The group stood out because their jazz was so quintessentially European at a time when everyone else's was so quintessentially American. With violinist Stephane Grappelli playing ying to Reinhardt's yang, their boulevardier brio convincingly suggested that jazz could have a strong European component without sacrificing the elements that made African-American jazz compelling and subversive. It was a significant moment, revealing that jazz was not an exclusively American preserve – Reinhardt could count Duke Ellington, Benny Carter, Coleman Hawkins and Eddie South among his admirers.

Reinhardt was the first major European musician to propose an alternative to the dominant American style of jazz expressionism. Hitherto, and subsequently, it was the great American innovators who set the standards by which everyone was judged. Musicians such as Charlie Parker, Dizzy Gillespie, Bud Powell, Clifford Brown, Sonny Rollins, John Coltrane, Bill Evans, Ornette Coleman and Miles Davis emerged in such quick succession that the world was left gasping as it tried to keep pace with these pioneers. On the face of it, jazz appeared to be an American music with an international following, but in Scandinavia, musicians who had absorbed bebop at Parker's feet when he toured Sweden in 1950 began integrating elements of their own culture into the dominant American style of jazz expressionism. The evolution of what became known, in Scandinavia at least, as 'the Nordic tone' in jazz was the first major global 'fusion' of jazz and World Music beyond the shores of the USA.

Lars Gullin's childhood and teenage years were spent on the island of Gotland in the Baltic Sea where he developed a first-hand knowledge of rural and urban Swedish music traditions, providing the inspiration for a tonal vocabulary that evoked the Swedish folk tradition he applied within the context of bebop. One of the most accomplished baritone saxophonists in jazz, in 1952 he recorded a version of 'Sov du lilla vida ung' (Sleep, little pussy-willow), but his own compositions such as 'First Walk', 'Merlin', 'Danny's Dream', 'Ma', 'Fedja', 'Fine Together', 'It's True', 'Like Grass', 'Castle Waltz' and many others were imbued with a pensive melancholy characteristic of his Swedish folk heritage and of Swedish composers such as Wilhelm Peterson-Berger and Hugo Alfvén. In the 1960s, the development of a 'Nordic tone' was taken a stage further by Jan Johansson who, rather than seeking inspiration from Swedish folk music as Gullin had done, went straight to the source and interpreted indigenous folk melodies as a basis for jazz improvisation.

An accomplished pianist, Johansson had toured and recorded as a member of Stan Getz's quartet in 1960. In February 1961 Johansson recorded an album under his own name, *8 Bitar Johansson*, originally issued in Sweden. It was later released in America on the Dot label as *Sweden Non-Stop*, where it was awarded four-and-a-half stars by *Down Beat*. The record was a mix of Johansson's own compositions and jazz standards, but it also included an unconventional addition to a jazz record of the time: a Swedish folk melody called 'De salde sina hemman'. It garnered a favourable critical response, particularly in Scandinavia, something that encouraged him to record more Swedish folk songs during the course of 1962–3 with bassist Georg Riedel on three Swedish extended-play discs. These songs were taken from an anthology of some 8,000 indigenous melodies and folk songs published as *Svenska Latar* in 24 volumes. In 1964 the EPs were collected on the LP, *Jazz pa Svenska*.

The carefully nuanced sound of Johansson's piano, as revealed by the meticulous recording quality on *Jazz pa Svenska*, captured a new sound in jazz. 'Nordic tonality is in fact a sort of blues, Nordic blues, Scandinavian blues if you will', explained drummer Egil Johansen. 'For us jazz musicians it's but a short leap to experience that melancholy as a companion to joy' (Kjellberg 1998, 115). Two songs from this bestselling album, 'Visa fran Utanmyra' and 'Emigrantvisa', became widely played on Scandinavian radio, especially in Sweden, and were adopted as a symbol of Nordic tradition in the midst of an increasingly pluralistic culture. During the post-war years Scandinavia had readily accepted innovations from the US, from consumer products to social attitudes absorbed through film, theatre and literature.

But by the time of Johansson's premature death in 1968, the Vietnam War was causing a crisis of conscience, prompting a lively debate around nationalism and what constituted the national soul. Johansson's music fitted perfectly into a Scandinavian culture that had become intent on reclaiming its Nordic sensibility, and music from *Jazz pa Svenska* was in perfect synchronicity with the times, assuming the trappings of a 'visionary statement'. Odd Sneegen (of Svensk Musik) claimed it was 'a rural symbol of security in a [Scandinavia] marching towards anonymous big city wildernesses'.

While Johansson was not alone in attempting to find a Nordic voice within jazz – trumpeter Bengt-Arne Wallin's *Old Folklore in Swedish Modern* (1962) was also moving along similar lines – it was Johansson's work that was the most popular and influenced younger generations of Scandinavian pianists, including Bobo Stenson and Esbjörn Svensson. Yet in seeking to express a cultural identity quite removed from the essentially African-American characteristics of jazz, it raises the question of 'authenticity'. Does an indigenous American music shaped by the African–American experience become less meaningful when played by non-Americans, and specifically, non-Americans who seek to import elements of their own culture into the music?

Such questions have a striking resonance with the reaction to Charles Ives's Second Symphony, which he completed in 1901 or 1902 when the dominant culture in America was predominantly derived from Europe. Then critics resisted the introduction of Stephen Foster and 'American' themes suggesting gospel music into the 'European' symphonic tradition. The issue we are concerned with in jazz is, of course, precisely the reverse of this: that of elements suggesting European cultures and folk traditions introduced into a music with a strong 'African-American' tradition. In both instances, resistance to established convention is framed in terms of an idealised past violated by the crass and insensitive pluralism of the present. Yet progress is impossible without change – indeed, the essence of jazz has been realised in the process of change itself. Today, we regard the arguments voiced against Ives's symphony as quaint when seen in the context of composers such as Aaron Copland, Samuel Barber, William Grant Still and Elliott Carter, who consciously evoke elements of Americana in their writing. Jazz, which has continually been reinvigorated by the process of appropriation, has shown that in absorbing elements of quite different cultures it has successfully broadened the basis of jazz expressionism, as it had, for example, in the 1940s when Dizzy Gillespie introduced Cuban rhythms into bebop. 'You can apply any personal input coming from whatever part of the world and it's possible to find a way that will work in the jazz idiom', observed Norwegian saxophonist Jan Garbarek. 'We have players from any part of the world now doing their own, shall we say native version. They find their own direction, influenced by their culture, but still using the very strong basic elements of jazz' (Nicholson 1995, 325–6).

Garbarek evolved his approach against a background of Nordic cultural revival. Self-taught from the age of 14, he was invited to record with George Russell in Stockholm as a 17-year-old. In 1968 he became a 'saxophone sensation' when he backed singer Karin Krog at the Montreux Jazz Festival and shortly afterwards formed his own group with guitarist Terje Rypdal, bassist Arild Andersen and drummer Jon Christensen. In 1969 he formed an association with producer Manfred Eicher, then about to set up his own record company, Edition of Contemporary Music (ECM). Garbarek's first record, *Afric Pepperbird*, was among the very first albums released by the new label. From the outset, ECM professed a subtle 'aesthetic of atmospheres' that proposed a 'sound scenario of nature and history' (*ECM: Sleeves of Desire* 1996, 14). Despite the presence of several American musicians on his label (the first ECM album was by Mal Waldron and in the 1970s ECM produced a bestselling album by Keith Jarrett), Eicher consciously sought out European musicians who projected a specific European identity in their playing. In Garbarek he found a musician who at the very beginning of his playing career had won an amateur music contest playing his own original music after just two years' playing experience, and who had no desire to play compositions associated with the standard jazz repertoire. 'It's not really my tradition', asserted Garbarek. 'The so-called "standards" are not *my* standards. I don't feel a close attachment to that music, music that's made for Broadway shows. They're great compositions, but I've never had an urge to use that music as the basis of my playing.'[35]

Garbarek's music represented an ordered calm in the often frantic world of jazz, projecting the stark imagery of nature near the Northern Lights: 'I can't say what extent growing up in Norway would influence you, but I imagine deep down it must have some influence. There are very dramatic changes of the seasons and the landscape is also dramatic.'[36] Rigorous and highly disciplined, he created an evocative tranquillity strongly rooted in Nordic folk-forms that gave prominence to his saxophone tone as the main expressive force. Creating a context in which his haunting saxophone appeared to commune with nature, an effect heightened by his use of a wind harp on the album *Dis*, his working groups in the early 1980s included Bill Frisell on guitar, Eberhard Weber on bass and Michael Pasqua on drums, and a quartet with Keith Jarrett. Later work included a group with pianist Rainer Brüninghaus, solo recordings against electronic backdrops and a collaboration with the Hilliard Ensemble that produced *Officium* (which had passed one million sales by 2002). Garbarek's approach to saxophone improvisation was widely influential, British saxophonists Tommy Smith and Andy Sheppard being among many who adopted a less excitable approach to improvisation, giving prominence to the saxophone tone as the main expressive force in their playing.

The 'Nordic tone' can also be traced in the work of Rypdal and pianist Bobo Stenson, who co-led the Rena Rama group in the early 1970s with bassist Palle Danielsson. Both Danielsson and Stenson cite the music of Borje Fredriksson as an influence on their 'Nordic' outlook to jazz. Among some of the remarkably talented younger Swedish musicians are pianist Anders Widmark, trombonist Nils Landgren, drummer Per Lindvall, vocalist Jeanette Lindström and pianist Esbjörn Svensson, whose albums *Winter and Venice* and *From Gagarin's Point of View* both won Swedish Grammy awards. Full of complex motifs and thoughtful stylistic allusions, Svensson's trio was one of the most original of Sweden's crop of young jazz musicians. Svensson also collaborated with Nils Landgren in his funk unit and on *Swedish Folk Modern*, reflecting the continuing use of folk themes within Nordic jazz. Keyboard player Bugge Wesseltoft, who appeared on Garbarek's albums (including *Rites* from 1998), took the moody electronic soundscapes that evoked the Nordic climate and mixed them with rhythms from contemporary dance culture. *Sharing* (1998) included turntable scratches and dancebeats but was imbued with distinctly European hues. Conceptually, it sounded far in advance of American fusion of the period. 'In Norway, once you reach a certain point you are encouraged to find your own voice', said Wesseltoft: 'I was taught it's no good copying McCoy Tyner or Bill Evans or whoever. There are already hundreds of musicians in America who do that.'[37]

In 1973, the group Garbarek co-led with Stenson recorded *Witchi-Tai-To* with Palle Danielsson on bass and Jon Christensen on drums, and included a 20-minute version of trumpeter Don Cherry's *Desireless*. Cherry, who established his reputation in Ornette Coleman's quartet in the late 1950s, recorded under his own name for the Blue Note label before embarking on a peripatetic existence that brought him in touch with a variety of cultures from Africa, the near East and the Far East. *The Sonet Recordings* from 1969, for example, were made in the US Embassy in Ankara, Turkey, and include improvisations using a wide variety of ethnic instruments. Resident for a long while in Sweden from 1970, Cherry's role in the development of improvised music in Europe in general, and Scandinavia in particular, is a subject not adequately addressed by jazz history. It was Cherry, for example, who suggested to Garbarek that he investigate Norwegian traditional music.

In later years, Cherry's collaboration with Collin Walcott on sitar and percussionist Nana Vasconcelos produced *Codona, Codona 2* and *Codona 3*. His last superior recording before his death in 1995 was *Multikulti*, primarily a collaboration with tenor saxophonist, pianist and percussionist Peter

Apfelbaum in 1989–90, made after touring with Apfelbaum's Hieroglyphics Ensemble. Born and raised on the West Coast of America, Apfelbaum was a musical prodigy and by the time he was 16 was already working on concepts that united a wide variety of World Music elements with jazz. His debut album from 1990, *Signs of Life*, drew on elements of Yoruba praise singing, scales found in the Gnawa music of Morocco and Bambara music of Mali, the Rhumba Obatala of Afro-Cuban origin, reggae, African rhythms and free jazz as well as incorporating his own method of writing for a large ensemble that he calls 'rhythm block'. The integration of these elements into a cohesive whole, the sure handling of simple forms, detailed part writing, use of tension and release, and integration of the improviser into the rhythmic complexity of the compositions made this one of the finest albums in jazz during the 1980s and 1990s.

Apfelbaum's ensemble included several musicians who went on to record in their own right, including Josh Jones, Will Bernard and Jai Uttal who brought a distinct Indian flavour to the band. Uttal led his own Pagan Love Orchestra, swept with sounds of Indian culture, the sitar, dotor, kartals, dubdubbi and raga-like sequences set against contemporary rhythms. But Indian music was hardly a novelty in jazz: Coltrane had applied some of its precepts to his music and the Joe Harriott/John Mayer Double Quintet successfully adopted Indian ragas (scale-like patterns of selected notes from which melodic material is derived) for jazz improvisation in London in 1967 and 1968. *Indo-Jazz Fusions* and *Indo-Jazz Fusions II* seemed to point jazz in a new direction in the late 1960s, although the potential was not fully realised until the formation of McLaughlin's Shakti in 1974. The latter's eponymously titled first album, recorded in 1975, revealed the guitar virtuoso's playing *en règle* with the conventions of Indian music. The band recorded three albums during their three-year existence, but left the question of achieving a larger synthesis between World Music and jazz moot. When the band was reformed in the 1990s, McLaughlin allowed allusions to western harmonies to illuminate his improvisations, bringing that larger synthesis closer to realisation: see *Remember Shakti* (1997).

Less subtle than Shakti, Trilock Gurtu aimed for a more forthright fusion of Indian, World Music and jazz. His albums on the German CMP label included guests Cherry, L. Shakar (formerly of Shakti), Ralph Towner, Garbarek and (on *Crazy Saints* from 1993) Metheny and Zawinul. Yet despite the romance and deferred promise of the 'east-meets-west' fusions, it was primarily European musicians who seemed to be extending the boundaries of jazz in new and interesting ways. Edward Vesala was one of the key musicians in the burgeoning Finnish free-jazz scene of the late 1960s and early 1970s with the likes of Juhani Aaltonen, Eero Koivistoinen and Pekka Sarmanto, and came to international attention in 1973 as a member of

Garbarek's trio on *Triptykon*, which stands as the saxophonist's most abstract recorded statement. Subsequently, Vesala toured extensively as a co-leader of the Tomasz Stanko–Edward Vesala Quartet which was wound up in 1978 after recording five albums.

Stanko, a highly original Polish trumpeter was, with Zbigniew Namyslowski and Krzysztof Komeda, one of the three most significant influences on Polish jazz. Komeda, a self-taught pianist and composer, became a legend and cult hero after his early death in 1969. Komeda provided the music for more than forty films, including classics of the Polish cinema by Roman Polanski and Andrzej Wajda. While improvisation was central to his film music, he regarded the latter as a separate activity from his career in jazz. His 1965 album, *Astigmatic*, with Namyslowski and Stanko, was one of the most important contributions to the shaping of a European aesthetic in jazz composition. Stanko continued to have a distinguished career on recordings after Komeda's death and in the 1990s recorded for ECM, including *Litania: Music of Krzysztof Komeda* (1997), widely acclaimed on release, and *Leosia*, *Matka Joanna* and *Balladyna*.

Vesala, as well as his involvement in free jazz, also played blues, rock tango, classical and film music. He began his career with two years of study at the Sibelius Academy, concentrating on music theory and orchestral percussion that helped establish him as a drummer while developing a parallel reputation as a composer in a variety of multi-media projects. His music for theatre included settings of the Finnish national epic *Kalevala*, which drew on very old folk ballads, and his experiences growing up in the remote forests of eastern Finland, where he became conscious of Finnish folk music's magical/religious function and the role music and myth played in the lives of the rural community. In 1974 he recorded *Nan Madol*, a mixture of brooding Scandinavian melancholia, freely improvised episodes and sinister folk-dance imagery that established him as one of a handful of European jazz composers to make sense of his cultural heritage alongside the dominant African-American ideology of jazz expressionism.

Satu (1977) continued Vesala's restless experimentation with a larger ensemble, this time built around the Vesala–Stanko Quartet with some impassioned playing from Rypdal. Vesala entered the 1980s heading his Sound & Fury music workshops, part percussion clinics and part music school, from which emerged his experimental ensemble Sound & Fury: see *Lumi* (1986). As Vesala observed the American jazz renaissance during the 1980s he became disturbed at what he saw as glib revivalism with its surface slickness, he believed, masking the music's loss of faith. His opposition to this perceived emotional sterility was voiced most forthrightly on his next album, *Ode to the Death of Jazz* (1989), a denunciation of the status quo that he felt had come to prevail in jazz. In the liner notes he wrote: 'This music is first of all about feeling and the transmission of *feeling*. This empty echoing of old styles – I think it's tragic. If that is what the jazz tradition has become then what about the tradition of creativity, innovation, individuality and personality?'

The Netherlands has a long tradition of adapting the impulse of the jazz improviser within new and challenging musical environments, and although *Machine Gun* (1968) by Peter Brötzman may not have been the first album by European 'free' improvisers to move away from the American model of jazz and attempt to establish their own specific identity, it remains the most famous and most memorable: a landmark album that has come to represent a seismic shift in the thinking of the European free movement. But while England, Germany, Denmark, Norway and Sweden all produced important free-jazz musicians, it was the Dutch jazz scene that came to epitomise the diverse ways in which 'freedom' could be managed. Gaining momentum in the late 1960s, the Dutch musicians embraced political issues, blurred the boundary between theatre and music, replaced the seriousness of the American avant-garde with humour and parody, embraced classical influences such as Terry Riley and Charles Ives, and drew on a variety of cultural influences including elements that reached back into Dutch colonial history. The separateness of the Dutch jazz scene is illuminated by the resolute individuality of players like Willem Breuker, Han Bennink and Maarten Altena, who in 1978 had proclaimed his independence from American jazz, and Peter Kowald, who called his music 'Kaputt-play', the main objective of which was 'to do without the musical influence of most Americans'.[38]

Drummer Han Bennik emerged as one of the most important figures on the Dutch jazz scene. His first recording was with Eric Dolphy and in the 1960s he was the first-choice drummer for many touring American musicians, including Sonny Rollins, Dexter Gordon and Hank Mobley. At the same time he was immersing himself in the European improvised-music scene and was quickly recognised as one of its most original exponents. One of the first drummers to assemble a drum kit from all manner of 'found' percussion (i.e., almost anything from hub-caps to kitchen pans that could be banged, shaken or rattled), his recordings include work with Cecil Taylor, Derek Bailey, Peter Brötzman and during the 1990s the Clusone Trio (sometimes Clusone 3) which revealed a perfect context for his talents, not least in providing a forum that gave vent to his reputation as a 'performance' artist.

The Clusone Trio brought together cellist Ernst Reijseger and American saxophonist/clarinettist Michael Moore. A graduate of the New England Conservatory, Moore moved to Holland permanently in 1982, observing, 'In America there's more pressure to be conformist and players who were once pioneers of new music can work a lot more if they play tunes in a traditional way. In Europe there's a larger audience that grew up listening to guys like Han over a 25 year period, and they appreciate not hearing the same thing every time.'[39] A fluid mixture of pre-arranged forms and free expression, the Clusone Trio broadened the emotional range of jazz through humour, parody and visual theatre, elements conspicuously avoided in the American model. Such elements were not displayed so conspicuously in the work of tenor saxophonist Yuri Honing, one of the most influential of the young players in Holland. Artfully deconstructing songs associated with popular culture from the likes of Sting, Abba, Prince, Blondie and Björk, he succeeded in disentangling each tune from the memory of the original hit to create something new and subversive beyond the pop artifact: see *Star Tracks* (1996) and *Sequel* (1999).

That the national sensibilities of European jazz musicians could broaden the emotional range of jazz improvisation in new and fresh ways was increasingly felt in jazz after the 1970s. The success of ECM in building a catalogue of some of Europe's finest jazz musicians who brought elements of their own culture played a significant role in broadening the expressive range of jazz at a time when the American model had become increasingly inward-looking. The British saxophonist, John Surman, evoked English atmospheres on albums such as *The Biography of the Rev. Absalom Dawe*, *Road to St Ives* and *Proverbs and Songs*. Indeed, ECM's success helped shift the centre of jazz innovation ever closer to Europe. The low-key ardour of precisely articulated, rigorous yet emotionally intense improvisation was in contrast to the prevailing American approach which favoured a technical display increasingly seen, in Europe at least, as excessive.

Elsewhere on the Continent, Austrian Max Nagl combined the sensibilities of jazz and chamber music with the Viennese tradition of folk and café music on *Café Electric* (2000). The Vienna Art Orchestra under the direction of Mathias Rüegg has, since its formation in 1977, revelled in affectionately disrespectful adaptations of American jazz and has long taken pride in its particular European stance. Rüegg's compositions are often missions into uncharted territory for jazz improvisation, with beguiling titles like 'Nightride of the Lonely Saxophone Player', 'The Innocence of Clichés', 'Freak Aesthetics', 'Concerto for Voice and Silence' and 'Blues for Brahms'. There is an openness in which Rüegg embraces other musical forms, from classical to folk, Ellington to Erik Satie, that makes American jazz of the 1980s and 1990s seemed narrow and blinkered.

As Reinhardt revealed, lusty camp-fire rhythms and gypsy extemporisation are but a small step from jazz. In contemporary times, the work of violin virtuoso Roby Laktos and his ensemble moves convincingly between the two idioms without incongruity; the virtuostic Laktos inhabited the twilight zone between European folk music, classical music and jazz, and succeeds in showing the close interrelationship between all three, suggesting a continuation of the gypsy tradition that looked back to both Reinhardt and the gypsy flavours that once coloured the music of Haydn, Liszt and Ravel. The Dresch Quartet from Hungary represent a small touch on the tiller to bring these elements more directly into the forum of jazz. Led by Dudás Mihály Dresch on saxophones, with Ferenc Kovács on violin, Mátyás Szandai on bass and Jstvan Balo on drums, the quartet successfully invokes Coltrane's intensity and spirituality in themes inspired by Hungarian/gypsy folk songs. The step from Laktos to the Dresch Quartet may be small but, as *Riding the Wind* (2000) illustrates, it enriches jazz with exciting tone colours, rhythms and folk forms as the basis of improvisation.

Similar principles are used by Yugoslavian pianist (now resident in Paris) Bojan Zulfikarpasic, who combined a wide range of contemporary jazz idioms with ethnic Bosnian and Serbian folk melodies. On *Bojan Z Quartet* (1994) the fusion of these idioms suggested potential rather than a complete realisation, but with *Yopla!* (1995) Zulfikarpasic's well-rounded contemporary piano technique and conceptualisation produced moments of genuine musical excitement that on *Koreni* (1998) included 'La Petite Gitane', moving from free jazz to Balkan rhythms to straight-ahead jazz and the sound of an overdriven electric guitar. Native French musicians such as Louis Sclavis, Michel Portal, Aldo Romano and Henri Texier all imported quintessentially French elements into their music. At a time when the Lincoln Center Jazz Band and the Carnegie Hall Jazz Band were turning to the jazz repertory with re-creations of the likes of Ellington, Sy Oliver and Benny Carter, the Cartatini Ensemble's masterful deconstruction of Louis Armstrong offered something that was new and fresh in a way that the American note-for-note reconstructions did not: see *Darling Nellie Gray* (2000).

Today, without the dominant figures who have providentially appeared in the past to provide the catalyst for change, American jazz has increasingly turned in on itself. As Scott DeVeaux has pointed out, there is 'a revolution under way in jazz that lies not in an internal crisis of style, but the debate over the looming new orthodoxy: jazz as "American classical music"' (in O'Meally 1998, 505). The terms in which jazz was being appropriated to form part of the nation's cultural heritage suggested that the role of many American jazz musicians was increasingly becoming that of custodians of a music with clearly proscribed parameters.

As colleges and universities produced more and more students conscious of a limit to their art, usually terminating in the hard-bop era of the late 1950s and early 1960s, musicians appeared less eager to participate in staking out new ground. As American jazz paused in the 1980s and 1990s to move towards 'an alternative conservatory style for the training of young musicians' and 'an artistic heritage to be held up as an exemplar of American or African-American culture' (*ibid.*), it seemed apparent that academicism was breeding revivalism. With the 1990s and early-millennium New York scene given over in the main to neo-conservatism, and major recording companies fulfilling their commitment to jazz via young neo-conservative jazz musicians, a belief was being widely expressed among European jazz musicians[40] that the evolutionary zeal that had carried American jazz forward for almost a century had now burnt itself out; the task of carrying the music forward had crossed the Atlantic to Europe – Holland, Germany, Scandinavia, Italy, Spain, France and Britain – and eyes turned elsewhere in search of the evolutionary continuum. Held in check for almost two decades, the momentum for innovation, the *sine qua non* of modernism, had become irresistible – not least as evidence that the music was continuing to evolve as an art form.

With American jazz's preoccupation with its past came a failure to acknowledge that the music had become so big it had finally outgrown its country of birth, and that its stewardship was no longer an exclusively American preserve. The centre of jazz had failed to hold and had shifted. As critic Kevin Whitehead has pointed out, in America there was 'a touching naivete about the impact the music was making around the world' (vi) and an apparent unawareness that, in relinquishing its pathfinder role, others would jump into the void. It raised the hitherto unimagined possibility of the vanguard of jazz, its cutting edge, no longer resting in its country of origin but in Europe.

SELECT DISCOGRAPHY

Apfelbaum, Peter, *Signs of Life* Antilles 422 848 634-2

Blood Sweat & Tears, *The Best of Blood Sweat & Tears: What Goes Up!* Columbia/Legacy 481019-2

Brecker, Mike, *Mike Brecker* Impulse MCAD 5980

Burton, Gary, *Duster* RCA Victor 74321 25730-2

Cartarini Ensemble, *Darling Nellie Gray* Label Bleu 6625 HM 83

Chicago, *Chicago Transit Authority* Columbia GP8

Clusone Trio, *Love Henry* Gramavision DCD 79517

Coltrane, John, *Impressions* Impulse! AS42; *Olé* Atlantic AT 1373

Corea, Chick, *Chick Corea: Music Forever and Beyond* GRP GRD–5–9819

Coryell, Larry, *Introducing the Eleventh House* Vanguard VMD 79342

Cream, *Wheels of Fire* Polydor 827578-2

Davis, Miles, *Miles Davis and Gil Evans: The Complete Columbia Studio Recordings* Columbia/Legacy C4K 67397; *Filles de Kilimanjaro* Columbia/Legacy 467088-2; *In a Silent Way* Columbia/Legacy 450982-2; *The Complete Bitches Brew Sessions* Columbia/Legacy C4K 65570; *Live at the Fillmore (March 7, 1970)* Columbia/Legacy C2K 85191; *A Tribute to Jack Johnson* Columbia/Legacy 471003-2; *Black Beauty: Miles Davis at Fillmore West* Columbia/Legacy C2K

65138; *Miles Davis at Fillmore East* Columbia/Legacy C2K 65139; *Agharta* Columbia/Legacy 467897-2; *Panagaea* Columbia/Legacy 467087-2

Dresch, Dudás Mihály, *Riding the Wind* November NVR 20003-2

Fourth Way, *The Fourth Way* Capitol ST-317; *The Sun and Moon Have Come Together* Harvest SKAO-423; *Werewolf* Harvest ST 666

Free Spirits, *Free Spirits* ABC Records ABC-10872

Garbarek, Jan, *Afric Pepperbird* ECM [G] 1007; *Dis* ECM [G] 1093

Getz, Stan, *Captain Marvel* Columbia COL 468412-2; *The Girl from Ipanema: The Bossa Nova Years* Verve 823611-2

Gillespie, Dizzy, *The Complete RCA Victor Recordings* RCA Bluebird 07863 66528-2; *My Way* Solid State SS 18054

Gullin, Lars, *Vol. 4 Stockholm Street* Dragon DRCD 264

Hancock, Herbie, *Head Hunters* Columbia/Legacy CK 64983; *Future Shock* Columbia/Legacy 471237-2

Handy, John, *The Second John Handy Album* CBS BPG 62881

Hawkins, Coleman, *Body and Soul* RCA Bluebird ND85717

Hendrix, Jimi, *Electric Ladyland* Polydor 847 233-2

Herman, Woody, *Giant Steps* Fantasy F9432

Johansson, Jan, *8 Bitar Johansson* +Heptagon [Sd] HECD 005; *Jazz pa Svenska* +Heptagon [Sd] HECD 000; *Folkvisor* Heptagon HECD-000

Komeda, Krzysztof, *Astigmatic* Power Bros. 00125

Laktos, Roby, *Live From Budapest* Deutche Grammophon 45964-2

Lifetime (Tony Williams), *Emergency!* Verve 539117-2; *Turn It Over* Verve 539118-2

Lloyd, Charles, *Forest Flower: Charles Lloyd at Monterey* Rhino Atlantic 8122 71746-2; *Dream Weaver* Atlantic P-4539A (Japan)

Mahavishnu Orchestra, *The Inner Mounting Flame* Columbia/Legacy CK 65523; *Birds of Fire* Columbia/Legacy 468224-2; *Between Nothingness and Eternity: Live* Columbia CDCBS 32114; *The Lost Trident Sessions* Columbia/Legacy CK 65959

Marcus, Steve (Count's Rock Band), *Tomorrow Never Knows* Vortex 2001

Metheny, Pat, *Imaginary Day* Warner Bros. 9362 46791-2

Montgomery, Wes, *Fusion! Wes Montgomery with Strings* (OJCCD 368-2)

Mulligan, Gerry, *If You Can't Beat Them, Join Them* Limelight 82021

Pastorius, Jaco, *Jaco Pastorius* Epic/Legacy EK 64977

Pike, Dave, *Dave Pike Set: Masterpieces* MPS 531 848-2

Previte, Bobby, *Empty Suits* Gramavision GV 79447-2

Return to Forever (Chick Corea), *Return to Forever* ECM 811978-2; *Light as a Feather* Verve 557 115-2; *The Anthology: Return to the Seventh Galaxy* Verve 533 108-2; *Romantic Warrior* Columbia 468205-2

Scofield, John, *Blue Matter* Sonet/Gramavision SNT 965

Schuller, Gunther, *The Birth of the Third Stream* Columbia/Legacy 485103-2

Shank, Bud, *Michelle* World Pacific 21840

Steig, Jeremy, *Jeremy and the Satyrs* Reprise RS 6282

Steps Ahead, *Steps Ahead* Elecktra Musician 96 0168-1

Stern, Mike, *In a Different Light* Blue Moon R2 79153

Svensk Jazz Historia Vol. 1 (1899–1930) Caprice 22037

Svensson, Esbjorn, *From Gargarin's Point of View* Act 9005-2

Us3, *Hand on the Torch* Blue Note 829585-2

Vesala, Edward, *Ode to the Death of Jazz* ECM [G] 1413

Weather Report, *Weather Report* Columbia/Legacy 468212-2; *I Sing the Body Electric* Columbia/Legacy 468207-2; *Sweetnighter* Columbia/Legacy 485102-2; *Mysterious Traveller* Columbia/Legacy 471860-2; *Black Market* Columbia/Legacy 468210-2; *Heavy Weather* Columbia/Legacy CK 65108; *8:30* Columbia CD884455

Weseltoft, Bugge, *Sharing* Jazzland 538278-2

Zorn, John, *Naked City* Elecktra Nonesuch 979238-2

Zulfikarpasic, Bojan, *Koreni* Label Bleu LBLC 6614 HM 83

PART FOUR

Jazz soundings

13 Learning jazz, teaching jazz

DAVID AKE

Not everyone has subscribed to the idea that all people can learn to play jazz. Since the time of the earliest accounts of the music, many writers and audiences have perceived jazz as a 'natural expression' of the performers rather than as a learned and practised behaviour. This perception has taken two predominant modes: that the ability to play jazz passes mysteriously from some invisible source through select 'great' individuals (i.e., geniuses), or that jazz springs forth from a subconscious and unmediated 'voice of the people', more specifically, an apparently unified African-American population. Prevalent as these notions have been, however, neither of them explains certain fundamental aspects of musical performance, and this chapter will focus on some of the ways in which jazz musicians have acquired and handed down to others the practical knowledge of their craft. It will investigate both the informal venues in which individuals learn how to play jazz and, in somewhat greater depth, some of the methods, values and influences of the relatively recent institutionalisation of jazz pedagogy, commonly referred to now as 'jazz education'. But before turning to these issues, it may be helpful to review briefly the attitudes and beliefs behind the aforementioned 'natural expression' perceptions.

'Some folks got it and some folks ain't'

Public notions of jazz as the product of either biology or genius are rooted in a number of historical and cultural domains. First, white audiences and critics around the turn of the twentieth century had come to understand music largely as a notated phenomenon, the craft of improvisation in European-based styles having gradually died out over the course of the previous decades. Consequently, these listeners marvelled at the ability of jazz musicians to vary, embellish and invent melodic lines, seemingly effortlessly and 'out of thin air' (see, for example, Ansermet 1919). Those same milieus had also come to view select painters, poets, writers, and especially musicians, as Artists, separate from and seemingly 'above' the rest of humanity. The public venerated classical virtuosi and composers; in the eyes of many, these musicians replaced the clergy as those most closely attuned to spiritual insights beyond the ken of ordinary men and women (see Horowitz 1998, and L. Levine 1988). In time, this reverence for classical Artists extended to jazz musicians as well.

Second, although a virulent and violent racism still gripped much of white America at this time, a frequently misinformed fascination with things African and African-American pervaded the country. It is no small fact to bear in mind that, during the nineteenth century, blackfaced minstrelsy – wherein white and, after the Civil War, even African-American entertainers darkened their faces and presented sometimes cruel, sometimes sympathetic, but generally simplistic visions of southern black life – stood as the most popular form of entertainment. And though the minstrel show's popularity had waned by the turn of the twentieth century, one need only recall Al Jolson's blackface scenes in and as *The Jazz Singer* (1927) to see that many of the images and understandings associated with that institution persisted (see Lott 1993, Cockrell 1997 and Mahar 1999).[1] In Europe, meanwhile, the primitivist bent among painters such as Paul Gauguin and, later, Pablo Picasso also reflected and fuelled the public interest in cultural exotica, including Africana (see Lemke 1998). In all such situations, white Americans and Europeans viewed the 'darker' populations as exceedingly virile and 'instinctive', less guided by intellect or social mores. These understandings certainly contributed to the initial success of such performers as Josephine Baker and Sidney Bechet in Paris, and Duke Ellington at the Cotton Club in Harlem, though only those performers' prodigious abilities can account for their phenomenally long and productive careers.

The two 'natural expression' perceptions described above continue to some degree to this day, and both warrant further investigation. To be sure, Afro-diasporic individuals *have* contributed most of the significant innovations in and influential models for jazz, and that music remains a central component of many African-American communities. However, not all musicians from these communities have played or even cared about jazz; indeed, many black civic and musical leaders, particularly during the first three decades of the twentieth century, distanced themselves from blues and jazz in favour of the perceived 'civilised' and 'sophisticated' music of Europe.[2] On the popular-music side, rhythm-and-blues, soul, funk and rap have held a decidedly broader black listening population in recent decades than has jazz. Still more crippling to the explanation of jazz as innate to all of African-blood lineage is the fact that only a small percentage of those who do play that music attain the level of competence necessary to earn the respect of audiences and fellow players. That is to say, if all African-Americans automatically created music on the level of a Louis Armstrong or Lester Young, black cultures would not celebrate those and other players as outstanding models.[3] Clearly, though jazz continues its strong connections with black America, it reflects no more an intrinsic or exclusive expression of Afro-diasporic peoples than country and western music does for southern whites, or symphonies do for the Viennese. Musical style remains a cultural expression, not a biological one.

Though such bio-musical perceptions appear less frequently now than in the music's earliest decades (at least in the press), the first mode of natural expression outlined above – that jazz passes from The Great Beyond through select musicians – endures in many circles. For instance, the solemn, ritual-like aura that surrounds Keith Jarrett's solo-piano concerts stems in large measure from audience understandings that Jarrett uniquely connects to a type of universal/musical consciousness. Similarly, the existence of San Francisco's St John's African Orthodox Church, where parishioners revere the late saxophonist John Coltrane as 'the divine sound Baptist', reveals the degree to which many listeners (and not just church members) view that musician as one deeply and singularly attuned to a 'higher power'.[4] We can even see that the oft-bandied dictum about jazz to the effect that 'if you have to ask what it is, you'll never know' also supports understandings of the music as somehow outside the realm of general and rational understanding.

I do not wish to suggest that jazz cannot lead, or has not led, to profoundly moving experiences for its adherents, or that it means the same thing to all cultural communities. But we should keep in mind that jazz, as with any cultural product, involves the manipulation of certain materials and the enactment of certain behaviours. And like painters, or writers, or weavers, jazz musicians can learn, indeed must learn the skills necessary to work effectively with those materials and to affect those behaviours. For even in order that audiences may hear and see a particular musician's work as 'jazz', that musician must have already grown familiar with a wide variety of tunes, timbres, rhythmic feels and demeanours specific to jazz communities. Individuals are not 'born to play jazz'; they play the music because they have heard it somewhere and, for a number of reasons, feel themselves intrigued enough to want to learn how to create it.

Of course, not all individuals possess equal aptitudes for all activities: 'talent' does affect the rate at which, and the degree to which, individual players develop their skills. But talent always implies ability within a particular field, and even the most precocious prodigies must internalise the rules, styles and norms of their discipline, if only to reject some of them later. With that in mind, we can now turn to the ways in which musicians teach and learn the various rules, styles and norms of jazz.

Learning jazz

The community

For the first decades of the twentieth century, jazz remained predominantly an urban genre, with players and listeners living and working in close proximity to each other. Such an environment facilitated a phenomenon in which older or more established musicians from local neighbourhoods acted as models for succeeding generations, enacting a 'passing down' that continues in many cities today. Most obviously, mature musicians serve as teachers in the traditional sense: guiding beginners through the earliest stages of musicianship, including selecting an instrument, learning fingerings and embouchures, note reading, technical exercises, as well as the idiomatic songs, sounds, licks and other fundamentals of jazz. Such teachers normally, but not always, receive some sort of remuneration for their services, usually in the form of money, although food, drink and other commodities have substituted for cash.

But local jazz learning also occurs outside formal student–teacher relationships. Hearing a parent, sibling, friend or neighbour during a performance or practice session may motivate a child to pick up an instrument and to follow that older player into music. For instance, Coleman Hawkins stood as a neighbourhood hero to Harlem youths in the 1930s and 1940s, his exceptional musical ability and professional success inspiring a number of local children, including Sonny Rollins, to learn to play.[5] Similarly, authors Lewis Porter and Gene Lees have both written extensively on the Philadelphia neighbourhood in which John Coltrane, Benny Golson, Jimmy Heath and others honed their skills and, in turn, became the models for younger players, among them Coltrane's future pianist, McCoy Tyner (Porter 1998, chapters 2–6; Lees 1994, 123–42). Such neighbourhood musicians do more than encourage youngsters to play instruments. As role models, their approach to jazz helps to determine local aesthetics regarding all parameters of the music, and accounts in large measure for recognisable regional styles such as the penchant for marching-band figures from New Orleans drummers, or the 'big sound' blues approaches associated with Texas-raised saxophonists. At the same time, local leaders also shape jazz in less directly musical ways, setting norms for such aspects as jargon, codes of dress and public behaviour, and attitudes towards other musics and peoples.

Jam sessions play a central role in configuring and perpetuating this local-education process. Sessions establish and maintain the core jazz repertoire as well as the performance and behavioural guidelines just outlined. In short, the jam session audibly and visibly presents for beginning players what their particular jazz community expects of them, some or all of which might transfer to jazz scenes elsewhere. (We should note in passing that any city might serve as home to multiple jazz communities, each carrying its own ideals and practices. For instance, the musicians who congregate around New York's Knitting Factory nightclub learn and maintain very different models of jazz performance, dress and demeanour from those who play in the Lincoln Center Jazz Orchestra, or from the 'Dixieland' musicians who perform at Michael's Pub and other such locales. Musicians may participate in more than one scene, though they will generally adjust their playing and behaviour in accordance with the accepted norms of each. Similarly, we should bear in mind that while any or all of these musical and extra-musical parameters may be passed down locally, the meanings and attitudes surrounding them seldom remain constant as they move from generation to generation. Changing historical realities may change attitudes toward established social institutions or cultural practices.)

One of the most important educational services jam sessions provide is the opportunity for beginning and intermediate musicians to play, or 'sit in', with their more established colleagues. Sitting in allows the beginner to experience 'under fire' subtle yet crucial aspects such as the feeling of an effective swing groove or the ways of group interaction on a bandstand. Sessions also serve as meeting points where players often make their first professional contacts. One outstanding performance at a session can lead to a string of gigs which, in turn, leads to broader playing experience and hopefully a more mature style, as well as an expanding circle of musicians and patrons as a source of future professional engagements.

Finally, the competitive 'cutting contest' mentality frequently underlying this setting also exposes each player's ability in relation to his or her peers, while the almost inevitable 'train wrecks' that occur in a musician's first attempts should suggest areas requiring improvement. For example, a famous story circulates of a Kansas City jam session in *c.* 1936 during which drummer Jo Jones apparently threw his cymbal in disgust at the young and struggling Charlie Parker (see page 144). This episode supposedly spurred the humiliated saxophonist into a period of intense secluded practising, or 'woodshedding', from which he emerged a giant of the instrument. Though the tale may be apocryphal, it clearly shows the importance of jam sessions as both a training ground and as a stage for demonstrating one's ability, and leads us to perhaps the most significant realm of jazz skill development: practising (R. Russell 1973, 83–5).

'Shedding'

We have seen that 'talent' always refers to ability within a specific field, and that not all musicians possess equal aptitude in assimilating new ideas. This phenomenon has led many non-playing listeners automatically to equate playing skills with innate ability, again implying that all performers simply 'have it'. Such a perception overlooks the fact that, at least at some point, every successful musician has spent long hours in solitary practice sessions.

While each player develops a practice routine according to the specific requirements of the instrument concerned, current strengths and weaknesses, and the aesthetics handed down within the chosen jazz community or school, some aspects seem to remain particularly common among jazz musicians. For instance, most work diligently on tone production, referred to by many simply as their 'sound'. Horn players especially may spend hours playing 'long tones' as they check the consistency of their air stream and pitch, as well as the timbre itself. Rhythm-section players also work on sound: drummers experiment with different tunings, cymbals and stick sizes; pianists vary their 'touch'; and bassists strive toward consistent intonation. Since the advent of amplification in jazz, electric bassists, guitarists and keyboardists have searched for synthesizer, amplifier and effects-processor settings that offer the richest and most expressive tone. As shown below, the rise of jazz programmes in schools has affected how these players conceive of and work on their sound.

Another common area of practising entails developing dexterity on the instrument. Scales, arpeggios and other exercises, either self-designed or culled from instruction manuals, provide a framework for musicians wishing to attain a degree of virtuosity that many feel is required since the innovations of Art Tatum, Charlie Parker, Clifford Brown and others. Players possessing outstanding technical ability, or 'chops', often fare well at jam sessions where tempos may tend toward the fast side. A formidable technique can mean the difference between earning a gig or being passed over, especially in bop-oriented communities. For that reason, players may spend the vast majority of their practice time working towards virtuosity.

Finally, jazz musicians practise melodic patterns and tunes specific to their community. This may involve memorisation and repetition of frequently played material (i.e., 'standards'), common phrases or 'original' compositions in preparation for an upcoming gig. If a particular song is based on a harmonic structure, players may devote their time to finding creative yet idiomatic ways of negotiating the chord changes. Contradictory as it may sound, even free-jazz players work on such aspects, as they explore different possibilities for expressive nuance within various improvisational frameworks. Ultimately, musicians practise those areas of performance that will help them sound creative and meaningful within a particular jazz community. We should note at this point that such communities are not always bounded by local geographical area or by a shared time period. The proliferation of recording technology in the twentieth century has profoundly affected the ways in which communities function, leading us to our next topic of discussion.

Listen and learn

No pedagogical tool has left as widespread or as long-lasting an impact on jazz skill acquisition as have the various media of sound recording.

Records, tapes and CDs not only act as the physical 'texts' of jazz, they also serve as the pre-eminent 'textbooks' of the music, providing study materials for virtually all players. Recordings facilitate learning in at least two ways.

First, the repeatability of recordings enables musicians to familiarise themselves thoroughly with the general sound of the music, as well as the specific nuances of select practitioners. After repeated listenings, many internalise jazz subtleties by singing or playing along with a record, mimicking the melodic lines, dynamic shifts, timbral gestures and rhythmic feels of each recorded player. In addition, repeatability also facilitates transcription, wherein an individual writes down as closely as possible the notes (if not the timbres) of a performance, creating a visual representation of the music to which the student may refer for further study. During the 1970s, music publishers began marketing such transcriptions as pedagogical tools in their own right, reflecting the emphasis on 'note choice' in most jazz-education programmes, a subject to which we will return below.

Second, the combined replicability and portability of recordings facilitates a situation in which musicians who grow up outside the predominant jazz eras and neighbourhoods can still learn the sounds and tunes used by players within those scenes. More than just documents of performances, records create a shared, enduring and mobile body of compositions, melodic fragments, timbres and rhythmic feels. Moreover, experience has shown that records (and also radio broadcasts) can cross racial, national and other boundaries in a way that people often cannot (or will not). That is, individuals who would otherwise have no access to cultures different from their own can experience alternative possibilities of music-making. And while jazz innovations have tended to move from African-American communities to others, the well-documented influence of Frankie Trumbauer's recordings on Lester Young is only one example showing that streams of influence flow in more than one direction. That is not to say that the meanings associated with the music necessarily travel with records. The short-lived furore surrounding Ornette Coleman's music in the late 1950s tells us that Coleman sounded very different to the New York musicians of that time from the way he sounded to, say, guitarist Pat Metheny who was listening in a small Missouri town in the early 1970s. Still, Coleman's recordings remain available, and each subsequent player may adopt and adapt one or more aspect of that saxophonist's approach to jazz.

In formal teaching situations, too, records become a kind of 'shorthand', a form of non-verbal communication, as a teacher or mentor 'prescribes' a certain recording for a student to listen to rather than attempting to notate or verbalise the musical conception. Musicians even use records as a teaching aid amongst themselves when preparing unfamiliar material.

For instance, a bandleader desiring a particular approach or effect from a group might refer to a famous recorded performance that draws on a similar style.[6]

Teaching jazz

Jazz goes to college

Since 1968, the International Association of Jazz Educators (IAJE) has served as the leading organisation for school-based jazz pedagogy. Each year, the group sponsors and coordinates hundreds of workshops, programmes and conferences devoted to teaching jazz, and functions as an unofficial clearinghouse for instructors and their materials. Though based in the small midwestern town of Manhattan, Kansas, the association reaches around the globe, even extending to Colombia, Russia, South Africa, Kazakhstan and Turkey – areas not generally regarded as jazz centres. And though the following discussion focuses specifically on jazz education in North America, the influence of the IAJE and its membership has been such that the methods and aesthetics discussed below reflect those of teachers, programmes and schools everywhere.

Select college courses in jazz had surfaced long before the emergence of the IAJE and contemporary jazz education. For instance, author Marshall Stearns taught a jazz-history class at New York University in 1950 (his impressive list of guest lecturers and performers included Louis Armstrong, Duke Ellington, Benny Goodman, Count Basie, Dizzy Gillespie and author Ralph Ellison).[7] Even earlier, Len Bowden began a long and productive career as a jazz educator in 1919 when, as a student-teacher, he led a band at the Tuskegee Institute. Bowden later taught at Georgia State College (now Savannah State College) and Alabama State Normal College, and held a respected position as director of the African-American musicians at Great Lakes Naval Air Station outside Chicago during World War II (see Murphy 1994, and McDaniel 1993).

These individuals aside, one could argue that jazz education, as we understand it today – institutionalised training in jazz performance – emerged in the 1940s. Nineteen forty-five saw the opening of Boston's Berklee School of Music (now the Berklee College of Music) and the Westlake College of Music in Los Angeles (no longer in operation), both of which offered instruction in jazz. Two years later, North Texas State Teachers College (later North Texas State University, and now the University of North Texas) founded a degree major in Dance Band, which focused on big-band performance. All of these programmes turned out excellent performers; Berklee and North Texas continue to do so.

Yet even these examples stood as exceptions, not as the rule in American colleges, universities and conservatories, the vast majority of which remained staunchly dedicated to providing instruction in the western classical tradition. For, despite the success of the music programmes just mentioned, few offered students jazz in any form during the 1940s, 1950s and 1960s. Some of the more prestigious conservatories not only omitted the genre, but also actually forbade the playing of jazz on school property, with transgressions possibly leading in extreme cases to students' expulsion from the institution.[8]

Even in less prim surroundings, school big bands (sometimes called 'lab' or 'stage' bands) frequently defined the sole jazz outlet, and these were usually offered only as extracurricular activities with few students earning college credit for their participation. Conservatory-trained directors led most institutional big bands of this period: their main responsibilities typically included the concert or marching band (but not the more prestigious symphony orchestra). Not surprisingly, these jazz-band directors generally stressed the same musical ideals that were valued in the other ensembles: centred and stable intonation, correct note reading, section balance and the like, while improvisation often went overlooked.

As demonstrated by recent articles in the IAJE's *Jazz Educators Journal* entitled 'The Improvised Jazz Solo: An Endangered Species' (Jarvis 1990) and 'Don't Neglect Improvisation' (Reeves 1991), discussions of improvisational concepts in big-band rehearsals remain minimal in many schools even now. Exceptions aside, band directors possess little insight into improvisational skills, an absence reflecting their training in European-rooted practices. Meanwhile, to satisfy the demand for amateur jazz-band material, a growing cottage industry of school-oriented big-band composers and arrangers has emerged. These writers, mindful that most ensemble directors still view improvisation as a somewhat mysterious phenomenon (recall the first 'natural expression' mode above), write performers' solos into their charts. Directors often encourage players to rely on these notated passages rather than to improvise, avoiding precarious moments in school concerts or in the annual competitions and festivals held in many countries.

Answering calls for a more 'relevant' and diverse cultural landscape within the academy, jazz-studies programmes have appeared with increasing frequency since the 1970s. In 1972, only fifteen American colleges or universities offered degrees in jazz studies (Murphy 1994, 34). By September 1998, the Music Educators National Conference counted 67 undergraduate and 30 graduate programmes specifically devoted to jazz. In addition, dozens of other schools now offer a 'jazz emphasis' or 'jazz track' under the umbrella of their music performance, composition or education degrees. In all, almost 2,000 music staff in North American colleges teach jazz improvisation or jazz lessons of some kind, while over 1,500 direct jazz ensembles.[9] At the same time, jazz-history classes now constitute some of the largest enrolments among the 'general education' courses offered by music or fine-arts departments.

In order to justify their existence, fledgling jazz programmes need to entice new students. An early solution to this problem sought to foster a reputation through local highschool recruiting or band appearances at festivals. Eventually, the schools hoped, one of their 'products' would find commercial or critical success, engendering word-of-mouth distinction for the institution. A more recent trend involves the hiring of 'name' teachers who hold impressive credentials as professional performers and recording artists. In the US, Charlie Haden at the California Institute of the Arts, Kenny Burrell at UCLA, Max Roach at the University of Massachusetts and Anthony Braxton at Wesleyan University exemplify a few of the well-known jazz musicians who have found that academia can provide a pleasant, creative and stable adjunct to performing. Such academic positions appear particularly attractive to musicians in the light of the medical and retirement benefits available through school employment, especially given the uncertain future that hung over so many jazz performance venues and record labels at the turn of the twenty-first century. This new generation of musician/teachers belies the adage that 'those who can, do; others teach', as jazz musicians – young and old – increasingly consider the college classroom, rather than neighbourhood sessions, to be the prime training ground for beginners.

One significant consequence of the increase in jazz programmes has been the emergence of smaller ensembles (from three to eight players) coexisting alongside the ubiquitous big bands. In turn, the greater soloing responsibilities inherent in the small-group format have necessitated the creation of classes devoted to improving students' improvisational skills. For reasons both practical and accreditational, clear-cut methods and standards of teaching and adjudicating these skills require development: and instructors, administrators and textbook authors have set about devising guidelines. Their concerns have spawned a number of questions. What does an aspiring jazz player need to know in order to be considered a 'good musician'? How does a teacher best go about conveying that information, and how does one test a student's knowledge and understanding of these principles? Should every jazz student be required to study 'classical' music? What is the optimal and practical balance between private lessons, ensembles and classroom instruction (both musical and general)?[10]

The responses of jazz programmes to these questions have varied according to each music department's size, financial resources and, just as important, the values and concerns of its faculty members. But even with the hiring of experienced performers and a new small-group emphasis, jazz programmes and published educational materials have tended to valorise the same musical parameters and skills as those stressed earlier by the band directors – that is to say, jazz-pedagogy aesthetics remain decidedly European-based.

Along with the traditional conservatory backgrounds of so many college-level instructors, a significant factor in this musical Eurocentricity involves genre prestige. In order that jazz receives the institutional respect and financial support that its adherents covet, many teachers and authors have resorted to a 'jazz has all of the things that classical music has' approach. For instance, many early academic studies of jazz stem from nineteenth-century European aesthetics that valued 'organic unity', 'motivic development' and harmonic complexity (see Chapter 9, and Walser 1997). By demonstrating that certain jazz solos or compositions worked 'just like the classics', music departments could rest assured that they were still teaching their students 'serious' music. To be sure, such efforts have served to elevate the status of jazz. But as we will see, these ideals also brush aside or ignore much outstanding jazz that counters conservatory-based measures of excellence.

Harmony and the jazz programme's *Gradus ad Parnassum*
One musical area rarely considered in jazz pedagogy includes the sonority-based aspects of timbre and intonation. Music teachers or ensemble directors may raise these issues as they relate to creating a 'good sound', usually thought of as a stable ideal. But discussion of timbral manipulation – employing a variety of tone colours within a musical performance or, for that matter, on one note – seldom arises. The classical orientation of most instructors returns here, for traditional conservatory training provides students with the tools necessary to work within a large-ensemble setting (soloist prodigies excepted). Players win and keep orchestral jobs by realising as cleanly and consistently as possible the notes set down on the printed page in a manner dictated by the conductor. As many very fine musicians have discovered, it can lead to disastrous results, musically and professionally, for players in an orchestral setting to alter their sound radically during a performance (see Vigeland 1991).

Jazz education programmes reinforce these same ideals, setting norms for tone, vibrato and pitch. This pedagogical approach appears somewhat understandable where the big band is concerned, with that larger ensemble's increased possibility for sounding chaotic. Yet it makes less sense in small-group settings where so many important jazz musicians – Lester Bowie, Dewey Redman, Sidney Bechet, Ornette Coleman, Cootie Williams, Miles Davis, Evan Parker and Bill Frisell, to name only a few – earned their reputations through unique manipulations of timbre.

A concept such as timbral manipulation is most effectively explored in one-on-one lessons. Yet though most music departments provide these for their students, they remain the least cost-effective means of education for colleges and many schools simply cannot afford to provide a teacher on every instrument. Where private instructors are used, departmental hiring policies still favour 'legit' (classically oriented) instructors over jazz-based teachers by a wide margin. For example, in 1997 the College Music Society listed approximately 2,100 oboe and bassoon teachers in US and Canadian colleges and conservatories – more than their entire listing for jazz instructors. In fact, the Society does not provide sub-categories such as 'jazz piano' or 'jazz saxophone', though they do have categories for harpsichord, recorder and even timpani.[11] It goes almost without saying that those instructors schooled in the European traditions will encourage – if not require – their students to adopt the same ideals of sound and technique in which they were themselves trained.

Given that the written score has long stood as the document with which conservatory-trained music teachers and departmental administrators are most familiar, it seemed almost inevitable that the focal points of 'note choice' and harmony would carry over into jazz education. Notation- and harmony-based improvisational theory suits classroom use: notes, chords and harmonic progressions translate easily to paper, blackboard and text-books. Meanwhile, teachers can 'objectively' measure the students' grasp of the materials through written exams. All of which has unquestionably guided the direction of jazz education.

Getting the notes right: the chord-scale system
Since the 1970s, the 'chord-scale system' has stood as the most widely used method for teaching jazz improvisation in college. This approach enables students to identify quickly a scale or mode that will offer the fewest 'wrong notes' against a given harmonic structure. While most college jazz pro-grammes advocate some form of this system, saxophonist, publisher and jazz educator Jamey Aebersold reigns as its most widely influential propo-nent, as well as its chief codifier. His enormously popular summer camps, and even more popular mail-order books and recordings of the 'music-minus-one' type, have served as the foundation for two generations of be-ginning improvisers and as the primary texts for many college improvisation classes.

Aebersold's ever-expanding 'Play-A-Long' books and recordings feature standards, typical jazz chord progressions and canonic jazz compositions. The cornerstone of the system is the 'Scale Syllabus' printed on the back cover of each volume. Here Aebersold provides a list of chords commonly found in jazz 'fake-books' along with a series of scale possibilities for each chord. His chart illustrates quite clearly that this improvisational approach encourages a concept of note choice: the student sees a chord and plays a corresponding series of pitches.

Teachers advocating this method encourage their students to recognise chord-scale relationships through all keys and may test them on their ability to memorise them. Beyond familiarity with the typical chord progressions and their concomitant note-choice possibilities, persistent practising of this system also builds technical facility, the ability to 'run' scales and arpeggios in all ranges of the instrument. Yet while this pedagogical approach does succeed for the most part in reducing 'clams' (notes heard as mistakes) and building 'chops' (virtuosity), it ignores important conceptions concerning timbre, rhythm and musical interplay among players.

Even within the advantages that the chord-scale method purports to offer, a number of issues arise. For one, by dividing the twelve possible pitches of the western scale into a binary series of 'right notes' and 'wrong notes', this system precludes the non-scale tones that characterise so much bop and 'free' playing, as well as the 'in between' sounds characteristic of the blues. Such a categorisation also ignores the fact that, even within the list of acceptable pitches, each note always achieves a different effect: playing the flattened seventh degree on a dominant chord does not function in the same way as playing the root of that chord. In other words, players trained in the chord-scale method learn to play on individual chords, and so gain little insight into generating musical direction within a harmonic sequence. The disadvantages of this system may become clear when students begin to question why their own playing does not sound like such outstanding linear-oriented players as Charlie Parker, Sonny Stitt or Johnny Griffin (or, for that matter, the freer jazz stylists). However, this method does present fewer problems over chord-based but harmonically non-functional forms, which helps to account for the popularity among college level players of less 'teleological' tunes such as John Coltrane's 'Giant Steps' and 'Countdown'.

Free jazz and the classroom
As suggested above, another realm of jazz performance overlooked by the chord-scale method involves the various 'extended techniques' associated with the freer jazz that emerged during the 1960s (see Chapter 11). While many musicians and audiences of that period came to associate unconventional sounds with mystical or transcendental states, the techniques involved in producing those sounds remain teachable and learnable.[12] Yet in order for a teacher and student to begin the process of exploring such devices, both must recognise them as useful, that is to say, 'musical', skills to develop. And to instructors who prize a clear, clean, stable tone, the seemingly

otherworldly shrieks, screams, honks, clucks and clicks produced by many avant-garde musicians can sound like sheer incompetent caterwauling.

Even beyond the music, other issues come into play when we discuss the marginalisation of free jazz in the academy. For one, though the quest for the Infinite was not uncommon in the heady days of the mid-1960s, these sorts of goals have proven less acceptable in the very rational world of the university (and they are certainly difficult to grade). More to the point, encouraging students to play 'like that' might to the denizens of music institutions undermine the authority of – even the necessity of – instrumental teachers. Schools run on the tacit understanding that their instructors possess specialised knowledge that they can pass on to their pupils. Instances such as the time when Ornette Coleman recorded *The Empty Foxhole* with his 10-year-old son Denardo on drums (who, though refreshingly devoid of clichés, was not a child prodigy) throw into question the conservatory's *raison d'être*: that individuals require extensive training to earn the title of 'musician'. Meanwhile, parents footing the bill for this sometimes very expensive training might wonder just what sort of school it is that would encourage that type of 'noise', and if their son or daughter might not receive a better education elsewhere.

In addition to these aspects, the increasing collectivity of some freer jazz raises problems for a jazz-conservatory system that, somewhat paradoxically, pushes for standardised performance norms at the same time that it extols individual improvisers. Jazz educators – whether through workbooks, private lessons or in-class improvisation courses – orient their students to esteem the soloist. Consequently, beginners learn to hear recordings of early New Orleans-style bands as quaint reminders of what jazz sounded like in its 'primitive' stages, and to view more recent collective performances as a type of musical deception, cloaking the players' soloing inadequacies. As schools have a mandate to turn out competent, professional musicians, structuring individual displays of versatility and virtuosity offers one way for jazz programmes to ensure that they are producing employable musicians capable of 'making it' in the outside world. At the same time, avoiding freer styles of playing decreases the possibility that a student may be 'faking it', and makes the grading process much more 'objective'. Even for a young player inclined towards collective playing, it is virtually impossible to practise group improvisation alone. With lessons, assignments and practice spaces geared towards the development of individual skills, little if any time or space remains for the development of the very different musical tools necessary to improvise successful collective jazz.

To be sure, much can be gained by fostering professional individual skills in jazz students as they prepare for life as working musicians. Yet by ignoring the musics of the avant-gardists and the early New Orleans players, jazz pedagogy marginalises other skills and traditions that have circulated in various guises since the genre's earliest days, resulting in a skewed view of jazz history, practices and ideals.

Ultimately, the issue boils down to knowledge: what sorts of knowledge will be esteemed in a given setting? How will that knowledge be transmitted, by whom, and to whom? In many instances, tests and grades measure only a student's ability to reproduce, rather than to apply, a given knowledge system. All of which points out the difference between the playing of jazz, which involves a type of practical knowledge, and the academic theorising about jazz. These knowledges – musical practice and its codifications – do not always overlap completely.

In closing, we should note that the insistence of jazz education to remain based on note-choices might be coming into question among some programmes. For instance, during the Banff Summer Jazz Workshops of the 1980s, saxophonist Steve Coleman taught students his oftentimes extremely intricate compositions by ear. Likewise, the Vail Jazz Foundation workshops for promising highschool players rely solely on aural skills. Most encouragingly, the Music Educators National Conference published *Teaching Jazz: A Course for Study* in 1996. Their four-page section on 'Skills and Concepts' (26–9) recommends that teachers develop students' rhythmic and aural skills as well as their knowledge of scales and harmony. All of which may signal a return of sorts, recalling the early local-community learning process where sound and gesture, and not just notes, formed the core of each jazz musician's schooling.

DISCOGRAPHY

Coleman, Ornette, *The Empty Foxhole*, Blue Note BN 4246/BST 84246, 1966; reissued as CDP 7243 8 28982 2 1, 1994

FILMOGRAPHY

Bach, Jean (producer), *A Great Day in Harlem: A Historic Gathering of Jazz Greats*, ABC Video, 41110, 1995

Jeff Swimmer, Jeff and Gayle Gilman (producers), *The Church of Saint Coltrane*, Tango Films, 1996

14 History, myth and legend: the problem of early jazz

DAVID SAGER

There are many tantalising tales of early jazz and its origins that conjure up both romantic and tragic images of an evolving musical tradition. These tales become a bit hazy as they are passed down, and the truth often obscured. Because jazz has frequently been accorded great reverence by its loyal fans, the tales of its heroes and their exploits have grown in great proportion, often leading to misunderstandings. It is only recently through accurate and patient research that we have come to some less colourful but more informative conclusions about the origins of this music. Likewise, viewing a faded old photograph may cause us to wax nostalgic about the persons staring at us across a century or more. If we could find a pristine negative of the photo and could make a new print of it, we would have a truer representation of that moment in time. There would be greater detail and clarity. However, with the sharper, truer image, we would miss some of that faded quality from which mystique and legend emerge.

One of the great legends of the pre-history of jazz was an African-American cornettist from New Orleans named Buddy Bolden (1877–1931). To many he is considered to be the first of all jazz musicians. Stories of his powerful cornet are among the earliest and most prominent in jazz. Legend tells us that Bolden played loud and low down, drank heavily, ran with fast women. His music was exciting and intoxicating. No recordings exist of Bolden (despite the persistent rumours of an Edison cylinder having been made) and what little we know about his playing style comes from the comments of a few old-time musicians, his contemporaries, who were interviewed. For many years the only known hard evidence of him having existed at all was an eerie, faded photograph showing Bolden and the men of his band. The Bolden group stare toward the camera, their eyes barely discernible due to the faded quality of the photograph (see Plates 14.1 and 14.2, and pages 275–7 below).

The Bolden photo stands out as a unique and priceless document of the earliest days of jazz, taken over a decade before the term came into common use. However, if we could filter out the scratches and faded quality and restore some crispness, the picture would speak more as a truthful hint at the past than as a departure point for myth and legend. So it is with discipline and restraint that we look to Buddy Bolden to raise and hopefully help to answer some nagging questions.

While maintaining its significance as a jazz artifact, the Bolden photo is not in itself unusual, and we cannot assume that such a photo could have been taken only in New Orleans or even in Louisiana. Looking at it as part of the American picture album of 1900, we are reminded that this photograph could have been taken anywhere in the US during the early 1900s. Further-more, a scene depicting a black rural string ensemble would not be surprising. During the early nineteenth century, professional black musicians such as Francis Johnson and Peter Guss could be found leading successful brass bands in northern cities (Philadelphia and Boston respectively). Free blacks in the north were likely to mix their instilled musical culture with that of their surroundings. The same is true in more rural locations in the south, particularly after the Civil War. In the early 1900s, the brass band was still holding its own as the most pervasive form of entertainment in the US, as it had been since the 1860s. Early twentieth-century photographs of professional and amateur bands from all parts of the United States are rather commonplace, and although not as common as white organisations, there were many black bands and orchestras of which photographs survive.

One question which the photograph inevitably raises is whether jazz was born solely in New Orleans or whether, as Robert Hickok suggests, 'jazz began to emerge wherever African and European music came into contact – which is to say, wherever black and white Americans came into contact' (1979, 422). Discussions of early jazz frequently pivot around a notion that all components of the music are considered organic and exclusive to New Orleans. But the fact remains that brass-band and dance-orchestra music was popular throughout America at the time and thousands of antique photographs exist to prove it.

Hickok refers to the distinction of the 'birthplace of jazz' that has been granted to 'the great cosmopolitan city of New Orleans' as 'honorary', imply-ing that he doubts its accuracy. Others have held less equivocal views, some for quite specific reasons. Thomas Fiehrer, for example, accuses Hickok of 'missing the catalytic variable – Creole civilisation' (1991, 36). Fiehrer's ar-gument is that the Creole ingredient was not only the catalyst that bridged African-American and European styles to create jazz, but was also responsi-ble for New Orleans having been *the* birthplace. He states unambiguously:

> Early jazz was the product of a thoroughly suppressed civilisation – namely
> Louisiana's variant of the French colonial or Creole universe – which came
> via geopolitical happenstance under the aegis of the United States in the
> early decades of the past [i.e., nineteenth] century.   [21]

By 'Creole universe', or, as he later calls it, 'Creole sensibility', Fiehrer means the combined culture of both the descendants of the 'native' white *ancienne population* and the coloured Creoles, whose lineage was a mixture of African, Caribbean and European. 'Creole sensibility' for Fiehrer is a product of European, African and Caribbean factors, the first major encounter having taken place in the Caribbean. The influx of St Domingan and Haitian refugees – whites, blacks and coloureds – who came to the city in droves during the winter of 1809–10 was especially significant as it provided a catalyst which energised the Creole population as a whole, eventually creating an environment that allowed jazz to flourish.

Fiehrer has a particular problem with those who propose a 'melting pot' theory for New Orleans. For him the ingredients of jazz did not converge on to the Crescent City, but exploded from it. He sees New Orleans as a place where diverse cultures coexisted with and without incident and produced memorable music. Fiehrer's opposition to the 'melting pot' theory is strong and his explanation complex. Citing the example of ragtime, he is unimpressed by those who argue that ragtime's independent existence from jazz, but close connections to it, are evidence against the uniqueness of New Orleans as the source of jazz. 'On the contrary', he declares, 'so potent was the Creole creative impulse . . . between 1840 and 1865, that its products permeated as far as the West Indies, Europe and even the interior of farm-town America.' Bearing in mind, as Fiehrer reminds us, that 'ragtime Missouri' and St Louis were once part of upper Louisiana, one can argue for 'the role of Creoles in the trajectory of ragtime as well as jazz' (1991, 26). Also, legendary ragtime composer Louis Chauvin shared his surname with one of Louisiana's premier early families. In short, 'the same "foreign" influences that generated early jazz were contemporaneous with ragtime and represent not a break, but a topographical as well as aesthetic continuum' (*ibid.*, 27).

Fiehrer's closing paragraph offers a succinct summation of his argument that tells us that jazz could have emerged only in the colonial subtropics. This is due not only to the Euro-African synthesis, but also to the igniting factor of an emergent Creole culture. If that 'catalytic variable' had not been present, jazz could not have occurred:

> Like its Cuban cousin charanga, jazz could have only issued from a unique Euro-Afro synthesis . . . and could have only made its appearance where it did . . . Otherwise jazz would have appeared in South Carolina, Mississippi, Jamaica or even Angola, but it didn't.   [36]

In *Jazz: A History*, Frank Tirro attempts to show the happenings that led to the emergence of jazz by examining different geographic locales in the United States. He seems to be in agreement with Hickok with this uncontroversial statement:

> it is clear that the story of jazz begins neither with the origin of the word
> nor with the magic of a single creative genius in a specific isolated
> locale ... Jazz developed in America during the last decades of the
> nineteenth century with a kind of spontaneous combustion that singed
> both coasts.   [1977, 53]

Tirro is of the 'melting pot' school refuted by Fiehrer. He also has a stab at the relationship between jazz, ragtime and blues, and briefly lumps them together as one genre. While discussing the first published blues and rags, Tirro boldly – and, one might suspect, with alarming unconcern – states: 'If we count ragtime as jazz, and there seems to be no stylistic reason for not doing so, then we can find an even older publishing history' (*ibid.*, 52).

Between these more extreme positions, Lewis Porter offers a middle way. He points out there is much evidence that jazz was a product of New Orleans. Among such evidence are the facts that pioneers of the music such as Jelly Roll Morton, King Oliver, Louis Armstrong and Sidney Bechet had an amazing impact on the music scene in Chicago during the late 1910s and early 1920s. These men were all products of New Orleans and each added a distinctive, unique ingredient to popular dance music in the Windy City. Early sound recordings tell us that these styles were absent prior to the arrival of these musicians. Between the extremes of Fiehrer's Creole argument and the 'spontaneous combustion' notions of Tirro and Hickok, Porter offers a sober middle ground:

> It is undeniable that ragtime was being played and partially improvised
> elsewhere, and the blues was gradually spreading out of the South, and as a
> result something like jazz probably developed in other cities. Yet it seems
> equally undeniable that the music we think of today as jazz was initially a
> product of New Orleans and its environs.   [Porter *et al.* 1993, 19–20]

The ethnicity of jazz

The question 'is jazz black music?' has been answered in as many different ways as there are genres of jazz. Jazz was first created by black musicians and therefore is a type of black music. However, white musicians were involved very early on and in significant ways. Porter states, 'jazz is black music – not that whites were not involved with its creation, but it did originate in the black neighborhoods of New Orleans ... Sure it was a mixture from different cultures, but it was the black musicians who did the mixing.'[1]

Fiehrer calls jazz a 'Latin-American type of music' and says that terms such as 'African-American' or 'black' are simply vague adjectives when describing the music. Going back to the 'melting pot' briefly, we should remember the disparate cultures in and around New Orleans – many cultures, many skin colours. Hickok's view is that jazz was created every time Negro and White music met in rural America. Tirro's contribution ('no specific locale') echoes this theme. But was the music created in rural America something that pointed towards jazz?

Gunther Schuller's pioneering work, *Early Jazz*, emphasises the importance of rhythm and inflection in jazz. Schuller explains that the basic elements of jazz rhythm 'derive exclusively from African musical antecedents' (1968, 6). Unfortunately, through complex example and illustration Schuller eventually undermines his own theory. He cites A. M. Jones's pioneering work, *Studies in African Music*, as a breakthrough to understanding African music on its own turf as an alternative to the perspective of European classical theory. Porter points out that Jones's work was in fact rather Eurocentric. Jones conducted his research in British-occupied lands only, thus missing many traditions of African music, for example, those that emphasise strings and not drums. He also notated African music in polymetres, with different metres for each part. More recent published research by David Locke has shown that Africans hear all the parts in a common metre (either duple or triple, depending on the piece in question), and hear all the seemingly conflicting rhythms as cross-rhythms rather than as different metres. Porter adds that polymetre is a device that exists only on paper and not in any aural culture.[2]

Thornton Hagert's excellent and unfortunately unpublished work 'Before Jazz'[3] focuses on traits in various types of music, black and white, formal and informal. Hagert carefully explains two disparate musical traditions of nineteenth-century America and how one of them leads us in a direction towards understanding the ethnicity of jazz. This tradition is described as 'the everyday music making of ordinary people'. This would include congregational singing and music which would accompany dancing 'of a sort now called "square dancing"', he adds. It was simple uncomplicated music, the type which was easily learned by ear and 'changed at a relatively slow rate'. The newer type to which Hagert refers was a style of composed music mostly imported from Europe. It usually was labelled as 'high art' or 'up-to-date',

> and it included elaborate pieces for the newly-improved pianoforte, songs
> from opera and the theater, hymns 'approved' by a committee of
> hymn-writers, and the new couples-dances such as the waltz, galop and
> schottische. Some of it was hard to learn by ear and required trained
> musicians to perform.   [2]

As this newer style began to take hold in the cities, the older style was found to survive mostly in northern backwater regions and rural areas of the South. As enslaved blacks were sold off and dispersed through the newer territories, the older style of music found new life. 'By 1860', Hagert writes, 'the majority of Blacks in the United States were heavily concentrated in rural areas of the South and near West.' In these regions blacks, retaining whatever they could of their cultural traditions from Africa and the Caribbean, mixed with whites who had retained the older style of music-making, although some significant mixing also took place nearly sixty years earlier. There were whites and blacks living in eastern cities who had never heard this older style.

Hagert also offers comments on black hymn-singing styles in the nineteenth century. Whereas white congregational singing frequently used a five-note scale that avoided use of the fourth and seventh degrees, black styles of the 1820s included repeated use of the flattened seventh, a slower pace and elaborately subdivided rhythms. Since written evidence is all we have to go on, the subject of mid-nineteenth-century singing styles is rather speculative. However, a song collector of the 1860s reports that: '[the Freedmen] strike sounds which cannot be precisely represented by the gamut [i.e., scale] and abound in slides from one tone to another' (Hagert, 16).

The image of jazz

So far the Bolden image has raised questions which it cannot answer alone, however much it may make answers desirable. But what of the specifics of the image itself? It famously contains a particular conundrum. The musicians are posed in a manner that opposes the orthodox playing postures of the various instruments. Donald Marquis, in his outstanding biography of Bolden, errs when he states, 'As originally printed in *Jazzmen* the fingering position of the clarinetists indicate that the picture may have been printed backward' (1978, 79). However, the photo, as it was originally published in *Jazzmen*, shows both guitarist Brock Mumford and bassist Jimmy Johnson addressing their instruments left-handed and clarinettists William Warner and Frank Lewis holding their instruments correctly. Also Bolden is holding his cornet in his flat palmed right hand – usually a cornettist would pose using the left hand to hold the instrument and the right to work the valves.

The Bolden photograph is sometimes printed with the orientation reversed (see Plates 14.1 and 14.2). Marquis diplomatically had it shown both ways in his Bolden biography. But in the flipped image, clarinettists Warner and Lewis are holding their instruments backwards and valve-trombonist Willie Cornish is using his left hand to work the valves of his instrument. Bolden, while assuming a more common cornet-holding posture, has another problem. Upon close examination his cornet is seen to have its leadpipe to the left of the shepherd's crook (if he were to have it up to his mouth). Also, Cornish's valve-trombone has been assembled backwards. One could easily achieve a backwards trombone since the bell and slide (or in this case, valve) sections come apart for storage, but the cornet would have to be

Plate 14.1 Buddy Bolden and his New Orleans band

Plate 14.2 Buddy Bolden and his New Orleans band (orientation flipped)

un-soldered to achieve such a configuration. My opinion is that the photo-graph as originally printed in *Jazzmen* is correct. Perhaps the photographer had the guitarist and bassist pose backwards, or perhaps Mumford and Johnson were engaging in some hijinks as musicians are frequently wont to do! Bolden was most likely holding his cornet right-handed as if he were go-ing to play with the right hand both supporting the cornet as well as fingering the valves, a commonly seen practice amongst cornettists and trumpeters.

The sound

The greatest question posed by the faded Bolden photograph is 'what did the players sound like?' Like their counterparts in northern cities – Boston for example – these men, both professional and amateur, attempted to make music to the best of their abilities and stick closely to generally accepted no-tions of musicality. However, contemplating the cloudy images of Bolden's musicians seems to bring out a romance and mystery which to this day still characterises the city of New Orleans. It is a place where musical sounds can seem to come from anywhere, magical and exciting sounds that bounce about easily in the humid atmosphere. Having lived for some time myself in the Crescent City, I can attest to the acoustic properties of the French Quarter, with its narrow building-lined streets acting like a series of sound chambers; hearing a band off in the distance and walking in that direc-tion only to find that the sound is now behind me . . . and the sound of the calliope coming from the Natchez Steamboat some eight blocks away.

As New Orleans guitarist and banjoist Danny Barker (1909–94) recalled, these magical sounds were especially enticing to children:

> One of my pleasantest memories as a kid growing up in New Orleans was
> how a bunch of us kids, playing, would suddenly hear sounds. It was like a
> phenomenon, like the Aurora Borealis – maybe. The sounds of men
> playing would be so clear, but we wouldn't be sure where they were coming
> from. So we'd start trotting, start running – 'It's this way!' 'It's that way' –
> And, sometimes, after running for a while, you'd find that you'd be
> nowhere near that music. But that music could come on you any time like
> that. The city was full of the sounds of music.   [Shapiro and Hentoff 1955, 3]

Barker's comments are similar to many of the stories of early jazz, which promoted the romance and mystique of New Orleans and gave rise to many of the myths and legends of early jazz. Many who remembered Bolden said his horn could be heard 'for miles' from where he was playing. In one instance, Jelly Roll Morton claimed it was 'ten or twelve miles'. It is commonly believed that Bolden blew loudly – but loudly enough to project for several miles? Music teacher Manuel Manetta recalled being able to hear Bolden's horn coming from Globe Hall (just west of the French Quarter) all the way in Algiers, Louisiana (east of the French Quarter and across the Mississippi). Although both claims sound like tall tales, Manetta pointed out in a 1957 interview that it was a relatively short distance (about nine small city blocks plus the narrow width of the river) from Algiers to Globe Hall. Without the noise from traffic it was much quieter in those days and it is well known that sound does carry across water. It is not too difficult to imagine how such stories grew into legend. The legend of Buddy Bolden blowing his horn so loudly that it could be heard for miles is quite clearly an exaggeration, but it does inform us that Bolden was a loud player. In this regard, the legend is invaluable (D. Marquis 1978, 102–3).

But we continue to speculate. What complicates our speculation is that such a question presupposes that the Bolden band and bands like it played something that sounded like early jazz as we know it. The thirst for aural evidence is not easily quenched – there is little recorded evidence prior to 1917 to suggest the sound of bands in 1900 New Orleans. In addition, for years a rumour of a cylinder recording made by Bolden's band has persisted. If such a recording were to be discovered, we would probably be somewhat disappointed. For while Bolden and his New Orleans contemporaries may have been influenced by the vast musical and cultural diversity of their city, their music was still part of a national trend in band music. These New Orleans musicians were not setting out to make jazz happen, they simply were playing music for dancing and parading just as bands were doing in, for example, Allentown, Pennsylvania. What caused jazz was not their musical integrity but an unconsciousness regarding their skill as musicians. They played 'hot' and improvised not out of intention but out of necessity.

Improvisation

Probably the most frequently discussed component in jazz is improvisation. Over the years this has become the rule for understanding and misunderstanding not only how jazz is played, but also how it came to be. The basic theme is simple, the setting feverish and romantic: itinerant New Orleans musicians 'jam' feverishly into the night and come up with 'a new kind of rhythm', and new works of music which would pass into the canon of early jazz – a spontaneously improvised music, one that is created in the head and heart. Musicians would gather and magically create wondrous new melodies and then spin endless variations on them. This type of thinking has done wonders for the mystique of the jazz musician, regardless of the style performed. It has ignited similar thoughts by writers such as Rudi Blesh, who described a 'beater . . . hunched over the battered upright piano . . . a lonely figure, tapping his foot, humming in a rough voice the bare and melancholy phrases' (Oliver 1991, 13).

We can turn to the pioneering work *Jazzmen* for more excitement and mystery. We learn that the authors of this popular work referred to the early jazz musicians as 'fake' players – i.e., musicians who could not read music, and had to rely on their seemingly natural ability to *hear* the music. The authors romanticise notions of natural ability: 'Although naturally influenced by the music of their former masters, the Negroes retained much of the African material in their playing . . . characteristic New Orleans polyphony . . . became a dissonant counterpoint that antedated Schoenberg' (Ramsey and Smith 1939, 9–10).[4] The same paragraph in *Jazzmen* tells us that young aspiring Negro musicians, who could not afford music lessons, went beyond the technical limitations of their instruments since there was no teacher to show them these limitations: 'In classical music the wind instruments had always lagged behind in their development. Especially the brasses were subordinated to the strings.' Obviously consideration was not given to the myriad of brass soloists who were truly the pop stars of the late nineteenth century. Players like Jules Levy (cornet) and Arthur Pryor (trombone) were just two of the many brass virtuosos who could play with a speed and accuracy approaching that of a fine violinist. On the other hand, the point is made that, with the lack of a traditional education, the young jazz pioneer was free from the restraints that might inhibit the creation of a unique jazz style.

As far as music education is concerned, we must remember that New Orleans was a major centre for classical music and opera. Young children learning a musical instrument generally took lessons with an experienced player/teacher and read from any number of standard 'note spellers' (i.e., method books). There was a fierce sense of pride in learning music. Hopefully one day the fruits of practice would pay off and a student would be allowed to join a marching band or an orchestra. This was the case not only in the more privileged Creole families residing downtown but also in the black African-American families in the more dingy uptown area. White families lived scattered all over the city, sometimes sharing the street with black families uptown. For example, white clarinet-playing brothers Harry and Larry Shields were next-door neighbours to Buddy Bolden, and Larry went on to become a member of the Original Dixieland Jazz Band, the first group to record jazz. Musicians in New Orleans at the turn of the twentieth century possessed a wide variety of musical skills. To put it simply: some were adept at reading music and had a somewhat 'classical' training; others were not and did not. The music publishing business at the time was booming. Werlein's Music Store on Canal Street sold not only music sheets for voice and piano, but also dance orchestrations and band arrangements. Many of the early black music groups in New Orleans used these published arrangements which could be purchased almost anywhere in the country. Those who were better music readers coached the others in learning their parts. The semi- or non-reading participants could play a semblance of the written part and more than likely improvise a part that was even better.

It may well have been this kind of 'by the seat of the pants' approach that gave legendary cornettist Freddie Keppard his unique style. Keppard, basically a non-reader, was one of the many cornet 'Kings' of New Orleans. The stories of his powerful and imaginative playing abound. He recorded relatively late in life after some physical decline, but there is enough left to give a glimpse into his musical persona. Being a non-reader did not prevent Keppard from working with high-class reading dance and show orchestras like that of Charles 'Doc' Cook, whose orchestra was in residence during the mid-1920s at Chicago's Dreamland Ballroom. On his recordings with Cook, Keppard plays fiercely with a wild vibrato, playing a second cornet part too loud to balance with first cornettist Elwood Graham's lead. It is possible to surmise that during his tenure as a New Orleans brass-band musician, Keppard grew accustomed to being given the easier second cornet parts and proceeded to learn them, after a fashion. What his reading lacked, his ear and ego more than made up for and the second duly became the lead.

There is another route we must take in order to 'fill out' our discussion of the development of improvisational playing during the late nineteenth and early twentieth centuries. The orchestrations designed for both theatre- and dance-orchestra pit often had a written out obbligato part to be played by the first violinist, who invariably was the orchestra's leader. Hagert's unpublished essay, 'Before Jazz', notes how,

> In European Art music, the term *obbligato* usually indicated an elaborate counterpart to a melody written for an especially skilled performer. The part was necessary for the piece, and was therefore, 'obligatory'. . . In dance orchestras of the early 1900s, this term obbligato took on a new meaning, nearly the reverse of 'obligatory'. The obbligato, usually written out for the leader-violinist, was intended to be played *only if* there were not enough instruments in the group to play all the normal parts.   [25]

Hagert points out that, eventually, even when there was a full complement of instruments on hand, the leader could signal certain players to drop out of the ensemble while he would play an obbligato. The obbligato became more and more a solo part, and was often played even with the main melody absent. Eventually it became common for players to embellish on written obbligatos or make up their own, as had already been done in baroque and classical music (but of course in very different styles).

Repertoire

Published band and orchestral arrangements were the foundation of what was to become the jazz repertoire. The chief forms of musical entertainment largely included both the (military) band and the (salon) dance orchestra. Many selections offered were popular tunes of the day such as 'O Didn't He Ramble', 'High Society', 'Panama', 'Maple Leaf Rag' and others. These tunes have become part of historic jazz lore and by the late 1930s the new breed of jazz scholars were regarding these as folk melodies, which sprang up from a fountainhead of African-American inspiration. These selections were composed by tunesmiths based in New York, and recorded frequently by the city's bands, orchestras and vocalists. Today, these numbers are often thought of as 'traditional' and have become the staple of repertoires of old-time jazz bands.

Some of the classic recordings of early jazz have also generated a mystique around the musicians involved. An example of this is the Jelly Roll Morton recording of 'Steamboat Stomp'. Certainly Kid Ory's simple and memorable solo has been regarded as a true moment of pure improvisation. By looking at the Melrose stock arrangement, however, we see that Ory was trying to capture the line originally intended to be played by the trombone and saxophone section. A similar incident involves another Jelly Roll Morton recording, his 1924 accompaniment to Joe Oliver's rendering of Morton's 'King Porter Stomp'. This is a record that has long been prized by collectors for its rarity more than for its value as a dynamic musical experience. I have often heard collectors wonder why Oliver played so conservatively and 'unhot' on this recording. Indeed, Oliver is not playing here with the bluesy abandon for which he is usually noted. Instead it is a straight, rather workmanlike rendering of Morton's melody. A look at the Melrose stock orchestration explains the reason: Oliver plays the first cornet part notatim, and he reads it directly from the sheet music. This realisation may well dash some of our fantasies about the creativity of our jazz heroes, but it also excuses Oliver for not being the legend we had imagined him to be. In fact, it tells us that he must have been a rather good reader of musical notation.

The dance at Place Congo

The Bolden photograph has no direct connection with a site in New Orleans that has taken on almost mythical significance, but the emergence of bands such as his by the end of the nineteenth century is sometimes linked to the availability and popularity of this space as a site where the music came together. The space in question was known as Congo Square. This open place at the back of the town, adjacent to the turning basin of the canal, was known in the eighteenth century as 'Place des Nègres', then as 'Place Publique'. By the late 1810s it was called 'Circus Square', after the Congo Circus that performed there, and later as simply 'Congo Square'. In 1817 a law was passed restricting slaves from dancing and playing music in public, with one exception. These activities could take place on Sundays at Congo Square before sundown. Here, the enslaved blacks were allowed to dance and make music freely in their native manner. The standard jazz histories seem to be based on various New Orleans tourist guidebooks going back to the 1840s. Many accounts tell of Negroes dressed in elaborate costumes, men wearing jangling anklets, and performing traditional African dances such as the *Calinda* and the *Bamboula*. They would shout '*Dansez bamboula, dansez calinda – badoum, badoum!*' Actually these dances were African-Caribbean and had apparently spread to other cultures before they reached the shores of Louisiana; for example, a citing exists of nuns dancing the *Calinda* in seventeenth-century Martinique (Fiehrer 1991, 24).

Many accounts of the 'Dance at Place Congo' have been written, representing differing views. Tirro points out that drumming by slaves was often outlawed, particularly in the South. Hand-clapping and foot-stomping were soon substituted so that typical African rhythms could be 'practised and perpetuated without offending the white master'. Tirro then briefly cites Place Congo as the important exception to the drumming problem: here slaves could gather on Sundays to 'dance, sing and play percussion instruments' (Tirro 1977, 47).

The estimable book, *Music in New Orleans*, by Henry Kmen devotes a chapter to 'Negro Music' and goes into some detail regarding Negro dances at Congo Square and at other places before the 1817 law came into effect. According to Kmen's research, a tourist reported in 1799 that 'vast numbers of negro slaves, men, women and children, assembled together on the levee . . . dancing in large rings' (1966, 227). Similar reports emerge from 1804 and 1819. The 1804 report obliquely makes the ritual sound quite exciting with great masses of Negroes making themselves 'glad with song and dance'. The report goes on to describe the costumes of the principal dancers as 'wild and savage . . . ornamented with a number of tails of the smaller wild beasts'. Kmen also cites a contrasting view made by architect Henry Latrobe. Latrobe described two women who 'set to each other in a miserably dull & slow figure, hardly moving their feet or bodies' (*ibid.*, 226–7). The Sunday dances began to meet with some objections by the early 1820s and were shortly thereafter forbidden. Kmen tells us that the privilege was restored in 1845, possibly because of the popularity of the dances with tourists.

A vehement discussion of the Congo Square dances appears in *New Orleans Jazz: A Revised History* by R. [Ralph] Collins, who dismisses the free dances at Congo Square as an absolute myth. Where Kmen cites references from 1799 and 1804, Collins reaches no further back than 1845. Collins quotes from Norman's *New Orleans and Environs*. The quotation refers to 'olden times' when 'thoughtless' Negroes whiled away their cares dancing to tunes such as 'Old Virginia Never Tire', performing 'the unsophisticated break-down double-shuffle'. Collins refers to this passage as 'the most authentic description of the slave dancing in Congo Square that we are likely to encounter' (1996, 17). (Since Mr Norman mentions the 'Old Virginia' tune, Collins insists that this is proof that slaves were not dancing the *Calinda* or *Bamboula*, 'whatever they may be' (he adds). Collins asserts that they were dancing to the same popular tunes as white people.)

Collins seems to miss the point entirely by ignoring the many references made to the dancing prior to 1845. When he does cite a more reliable work, such as Kmen's, he does so disparagingly. Collins insists that the 'myth' of Congo Square was invented to motivate tourism. His further explanation tells us that it was in 1845 that the city council passed an ordinance permitting the public dances. Prior to this 'slaves were prohibited from such time wasting activities'. The ordinance was to show the abolitionists that the slaves were truly happy. Unfortunately, no slaves appeared at the Square and the *Daily Picayune* fictionalised the whole thing! (*ibid.*, 18). In Collins's summary of Congo Square he finally admits that some unpaid 'servant-slaves' occasionally held neighbourhood dances on the local village green. The only point upon which Collins and Kmen agree is in acknowledging that the restoration of the 1845 dancing privilege was probably a ploy to promote tourism.

Perhaps the most balanced recent account is that of Jerah Johnson (1991). Johnson draws a picture of the role of the square over a hundred or so years, from the 1750s to the 1850s, as a marketplace where slaves (many of whom were carrying on trading practices they had followed in Africa) gathered on their free days to trade the goods they were permitted to grow and make for themselves. Music and dance were important elements, to mark out ownership of the space and to while away the time between trades. Dance styles would have been markedly African in nature for many years, as the peak period for importation of slaves into Louisiana occurred around the 1760s. Gradually, dancing became more cosmopolitan, while remaining deeply influenced by its African roots.

So, were the Sunday dances wild, joyous, uninhibited affairs, or were they solemn and staid? Perhaps a clue lies in a report from a missionary named Timothy Flint, who visited the Crescent City in 1823. Flint describes joyous, boisterous gatherings, but suggests that the joy and boisterousness did not occur every Sunday:

> Every year the Negroes have two or three holidays, which in New Orleans and the vicinity are like the 'saturnalia' of the slaves in ancient Rome. The great Congo-dance is performed. Everything is license and revelry. Some hundreds of Negroes, male and female, follow the king of the wake . . . For a crown he has a series of oblong, gilt-paper boxes on his head, tapering upwards, like a pyramid . . . They dance and their streamers fly, and the bells they have hung about them tinkle.   [Kmen 1966, 227]

But how long did the Sunday dances continue? Kmen does not address this, probably because his work does not cover history beyond the year 1841. In Johnson's view, the Americanisation of New Orleans, following the Louisiana Purchase of 1803, gradually led to greater civic control of activities, until by the end of the 1850s dancing on Congo Square had effectively ceased.

The question has caused many debates amongst jazz historians because of the possibility of actual contact that some of the first-generation jazz musicians had with the dancing and African traditions. The venerable and myth-laden *Jazzmen* claims that Buddy Bolden was already a teenager before the free dances were discontinued. If this is true, then Bolden's 1877 birthdate would put the existence of the dances in the 1890s (Ramsey and Smith 1939, 9). However, most jazz histories give Bolden a much earlier birthdate, usually *c.* 1868, which would likewise place his encounter with the dancers a decade earlier. In a similar vein, soprano saxophonist and clarinettist Sidney Bechet (born in 1897) tells a long and colourful tale about his enslaved grandfather Omar's drumming in Congo Square. Bechet's tale takes place in 1855, which is plausible according to Kmen. Thanks to jazz historian John Chilton, however, we know that Bechet's story is pure fiction. In his biography of Bechet (1987), Chilton details the family lineage and we learn that Omar was actually Bechet's father and the paternal line can be traced back to Illinois. Johnson prefers to see Bechet's story as a metaphor, his way of saying that jazz was a part of the New Orleans experience.

While the accounts of various aspects in jazz history may be quite different and even at odds, we must not forget to regard each as part of an intricate puzzle. When we attempt to assemble the pieces we see many layers of fact and fiction, scholarly revelations and popular myths. It is that attempt at completion that allows us to see a broad picture with one scene disqualifying or perhaps validating another. Collins's extreme scepticism cannot be fully appreciated without the balance of Kmen's more sober and conservative efforts. Similarly, Tirro's scattered observations on the diversity of music in America is made much clearer when juxtaposed with more carefully explained works such as Hagert's or Fiehrer's.

Scores of scholars are today chronicling all genres of jazz. Those who document jazz since the advent of bebop have the advantage of accessibility, either to musicians still living or to the documented interviews they left behind. We hope that today's careful chronicling and accessibility to reliable information will ensure greater historical accuracy. This will save a great deal of time and effort in untangling myths and sorting legend from lies and myths. Or will it? The 'pre-preservation' of jazz lore will not destroy the music's mystique, nor will it preclude the evolving of legends and perhaps some myths. No amount of careful record-keeping will diminish the spark of a jazz performance, nor will such meticulous attention to detail suppress the storytelling of a jazz musician. May the legends live, but let us also keep sacred thorough research and accurate reportage.

15 Analysing jazz

THOMAS OWENS

In reply to the . . . question, 'What is jazz, Mr Waller?' the late and great Fats is supposed to have sighed: 'Madam, if you don't know by now, DON'T MESS WITH IT!' [STEARNS 1956, 11]

Though Waller (if he actually made that remark) was speaking to a neophyte jazz fan, had he lived to see scholars 'messing' with jazz he probably would have disapproved of that activity as well. They spend lengthy amounts of time listening to it, reading and thinking about it, for they find the music fascinating, irresistible and sometimes mysterious. Ever curious, they examine it, using a variety of skills and approaches. Then they write about it in their spare time (no one makes a living analysing music), hoping to reach an interested audience with their insights into the music. Readership and book sales are minuscule by popular-press standards. But if the readership is small, jazz analysts still may take pride in providing informed alternatives to the pseudo-intellectual verbiage and scrambled terminology that sometimes characterises jazz writing for the general reader.[1]

Music analysts strive to describe or explain musical phenomena with some combination of words, musical notation and graphic representation. But while a jazz piece, like any other piece of music, may be a fixed object – an audio recording or written score – analyses may be dramatically different, as John Brownell has pointed out (1994, 23), depending upon what each analyst listens for and finds in a piece.

For example, in the 1920s the educators who published the first jazz teaching materials often illustrated their ideas with generic musical examples rather than with transcriptions of specific recordings. Though not usually regarded as analysts, they clearly had analysed the aspects of jazz that interested them in order to compose their examples. Glen Waterman, perhaps the first jazz educator to use triplet quavers in notating jazz rhythms, composed some idiomatic examples and made some cogent observations about improvising in his *Piano Jazz* of 1924; the following year Art Shefte added many more examples in a series of instruction books (1925).[2]

In general, the first jazz analysts were dabblers whose primary interests lay elsewhere. Roger Pryor Dodge, for example, was a dancer, choreographer and performing-arts critic who began writing occasional articles about jazz in the 1920s. In 1934, one such article included transcriptions and a discussion of solos from four Ellington recordings of *Black and Tan Fantasy*.[3] In so doing, according to Wolfram Knauer (1999, 31), he became the first jazz analyst. Four years later, Winthrop Sargeant entered the field with his well-known book, *Jazz: Hot and Hybrid* (1938). Sargeant had been an orchestral violinist in major symphony orchestras in San Francisco and New York during the 1920s, and in 1934 began a long career as a classical music critic. In his book of 1938, he discussed jazz syncopation (it is mostly 'anticipative', not 'retardative', resulting from arriving early rather than late on a note that would otherwise be on a beat), a blues scale (the major scale plus the blue third and blue seventh), some aspects of jazz harmony and a few other topics. Though clearly enthusiastic about jazz, he apparently found no pieces worthy of extended discussion among the few jazz recordings he cited. His book is a general survey of the music, written for readers who, like himself, were interested primarily in the classical tradition of European concert music. To Sargeant, jazz was a foreign country that he visited occasionally; his book is a souvenir album containing his textual and musical 'snapshots'.

André Hodeir was more than a casual visitor to jazz when he wrote his *Hommes et problèmes du jazz* in 1954; he was a jazz violinist, jazz critic, editor of the journal, *Jazz Hot*, and a jazz-influenced composer. His daily involvement with the music gave him a far broader perspective than Dodge and Sargeant had; he knew, for example, the multiple takes of Charlie Parker's Dial recordings, which had only recently become available. This involvement led him to posit some terms that many analysts continue to find useful: 'theme phrase', 'variation phrase', 'paraphrase' and 'chorus phrase'. It also equipped him to make some pithy observations about eight of Armstrong's Hot Five recordings, and to write his centrepiece chapter on Duke Ellington's *Concerto for Cootie* (reprinted in Walser 1999, 199–212).

Among the musical analyses that strive to reveal the beauties within fine jazz recordings, Hodeir's chapter on Ellington's *Concerto* is surely one of the first great landmarks; no one before Hodeir had devoted 21 pages to a single three-minute jazz work. He enlivens his detailed description of the music with a contagious enthusiasm for both Ellington's composition and trumpeter Cootie Williams's performance; after reading the chapter it is hard to resist rushing to the recording that inspired remarks such as these (taken from the English-language version):

> Few records do more than the CONCERTO to make possible an
> appreciation of how great a role sonority can play in the creation of jazz.
> The trumpet part is a true bouquet of sonorities. The phrases given to it by
> Ellington, which have a melodic beauty of their own that should not be
> overlooked, are completely taken over by Cootie. He makes them shine

forth in dazzling colors, then plunges them in the shade, plays around with
them, makes them glitter or delicately tones them down; and each time
what he shows us is something new.   [Hodeir 1956, 93]

The one frustrating segment of the chapter concerns the modulation (from
F to Db) leading into the middle (C) section for open trumpet. Hodeir tells
us the passage is extraordinary but does not illustrate it or describe it in
any detail (*ibid.*, 84–5). Still, overall, the chapter holds up well; it is a classic
analysis of a classic piece.

During the 1930s, 1940s and 1950s a scattering of analytical articles appeared, most often in jazz periodicals. In the 1930s, for example, *Down Beat*
magazine began publishing musical transcriptions with accompanying descriptions. Though brief, these descriptions called the reader's attention to
a few points of interest in the transcriptions. Leonard Feather, one of the
magazine's writers at one time, followed the same tradition in the chapter entitled 'The Anatomy of Improvisation' in *The Book of Jazz* (1957). His transcription and discussion of Armstrong's 'Muggles' is particularly engaging
and illuminating (*ibid.*, 216–19). Feather was capable of more writing of
this kind, for he was an amateur pianist and had composed some jazz tunes.
But he was primarily a jazz journalist, and evidently preferred to leave the
analytical writing to others.

In 1958, four years after Hodeir's book first appeared, Gunther Schuller
wrote perhaps the most famous jazz analysis of all: his article on Sonny
Rollins's *Blue 7*. Schuller, a professional French-horn player, composer, conductor and educator, had recorded with Miles Davis and Gigi Gryce and
had conducted a recording jazz ensemble by 1958. He shared with Hodeir a
thorough and intense background in twentieth-century music, and a similar
analytical perspective on jazz.

Early in the article Schuller states some of his criteria for judging a solo's
worth:

to a very great extent, improvised solos . . . have suffered from a general
lack of over-all cohesiveness and direction – the lack of a unifying
force . . . [They] have been the victims of one or perhaps all of the
following symptoms: (1) The average improvisation is mostly a stringing
together of unrelated ideas; (2) Because of the *independently* spontaneous
character of most improvisation, a series of solos by different players
within a single piece have very little chance of bearing any relationship to
each other . . . (3) In those cases where composing (or arranging) is
involved, the body of interspersed solos generally has no relation to these
nonimprovised sections; (4) Otherwise interesting solos are often marred
by a sudden quotation from some completely irrelevant material.
                                                        [M. Williams 1962, 240–41]

While acknowledging that some improvisations may succeed solely because they are 'meaningful realizations of a well-sustained over-all feeling', Schuller clearly prefers something more. He is pleased to find that

> there is now a tendency among a number of jazz musicians to bring thematic (or motivic) and structural unity into improvisation. Some do this by combining composition and improvisation, for instance the Modern Jazz Quartet and the Giuffre Three; others, like Sonny Rollins, prefer to work solely by means of extemporization. Several of the latter's recordings offer remarkable instances of this approach. The most important . . . of these is his *Blue 7* (Prestige LP 7079). It is at the same time a striking example of how *two* great soloists (Sonny and Max Roach) can integrate their improvisations into a unified entity. [*Ibid.*, 241]

The core of the article is Schuller's illuminating explanation of how both Rollins and Roach ingeniously based their 17 improvised blues choruses on two motives each, a fact that Rollins was unaware of until he read Schuller's analysis (Blancq 1977, 102). Though Schuller does not mention pianist Tommy Flanagan's two solos and downplays the role of bassist Doug Watkins, we must be grateful that he led us to this 11-minute musical treasure.

A decade later, Schuller's book on 1920s jazz appeared (Schuller 1968), eclipsing all previous efforts at jazz analysis – including his own. Unlike earlier writers, Schuller listened to every available jazz recording made between 1917 and the early 1930s. One wonders how he found the time to hear all those recordings, much less write the book; during the 1960s he also composed a ballet, an opera, three sets of songs, five film and television scores and about three dozen other instrumental works (including two concertos and a symphony); he conducted frequently, at Carnegie Hall and elsewhere; he taught composition at Manhattan School of Music and Yale School of Music; and he began serving as president of the New England Conservatory of Music.[4] In the light of these numerous other obligations his fine book on jazz is indeed a remarkable achievement.

As with Hodeir, Schuller brings to his writing a contagious passion for the recordings he likes. But unlike Hodeir, who clearly preferred later styles of jazz, Schuller finds much to admire in earlier jazz, and with his numerous expert transcriptions and his keen perceptions, he delves deeply into his subject. It is hard to imagine anyone exploring the music of King Oliver, Louis Armstrong, Jelly Roll Morton, Bix Beiderbecke, Sidney Bechet, Johnny Dodds, Jimmy Noone, Jabbo Smith, Fletcher Henderson, Duke Ellington and others without first reading what Schuller had to say. There are many inspiring pages in this book; among the best are those devoted to Armstrong's 'West End Blues' (1928), Morton's 'Black Bottom Stomp' (1926) and the chapter on Ellington (1968, 115–19, 155–61 and 318–57 respectively). In its sequel, *The Swing Era* (1989), Schuller brought his encyclopaedic approach to a much larger body of recorded music, and created another indispensable work.

Enter the musicologists

In the last decades of the twentieth century, musicologists specialising in jazz research dominated the field of jazz analysis. At first there were only a few graduate studies on jazz; I know of three in the 1940s, two in the 1950s and four in the 1960s (including the first PhD dissertation devoted to jazz analysis, Pyke's study of early jazz recordings [1962]). By the 1970s, the trickle of academic works began to grow. Encouraged by earlier efforts, aided by valuable discographical tools and inspired by an increased awareness of African-American contributions to American culture, scholars delved into a variety of topics. During that decade there were at least eight master's theses and twenty-seven doctoral dissertations. Five of these writers saw their work, or revisions thereof, published: Milton Stewart (1975, on Clifford Brown), Franz Kerschbaumer (1978, on Miles Davis), Dietrich Noll (1977, on free jazz), Lewis Porter (1985, on Lester Young) and Billy Taylor (1975, on the jazz piano tradition; internationally known pianist Taylor was, of course, not the typical jazz scholar of the 1970s). In the 1980s, at least 64 theses and dissertations appeared; seven were published. In the 1990s, the number far exceeded 100. In addition, during these decades numerous articles and several books appeared that were not linked to graduate studies.

As might be expected, these authors, trained to research and analyse a topic exhaustively, approach their subjects in ways that differ markedly from those of Hodeir and Schuller. Many reject the colourful descriptive style of Hodeir's essay on *Concerto for Cootie*, opting for a more impersonal dissection of the music according to one criterion or another. Many also reject the value judgement that guided Schuller to *Blue 7*, contending that he was too biased towards 'classical' musical criteria and ignored the true intentions of the jazz idiom. About half of them focus on over 60 individual musicians or ensembles,[5] and within these single-subject studies is a corresponding greater focus on detail. Stewart scrutinises the structure and performance refinements of a single recording by Clifford Brown; I look with much less individual scrutiny at about 250 solos by Charlie Parker (1974a); others use a sampling that falls somewhere between these numerical extremes.

Several studies – including Stewart, Owens, Simon (1978), J. Williams (1982), Elliott (1987), Larson (1987), G. Davis (1990) and H. Martin (1996) – draw upon reductive analysis to show underlying structural logic in themes and/or improvisations. This analytical approach, developed by Heinrich Schenker (1933), Felix Salzer (1952) and others, looks beneath the surface features of melodic ornamentation and harmonic embellishment to show the structural melodic tones and chords that support entire pieces. Though used primarily to study European concert music of the eighteenth and nineteenth centuries, this method can also be helpful in understanding jazz solos (see Exx. 15.3 and 15.4 below). Some studies – including Owens, Howard (1978), Kernfeld (1981), Davison (1987) and H. Martin – de-emphasise the beauties of specific pieces and emphasise features common to many related improvisations (such as solos on the 'I Got Rhythm' chord structure in Bb). One such feature of Parker's solos that I studied intently was his vocabulary of favourite phrases and patterns ('licks'). I realised that, as an experienced jazz musician, Parker had developed a repertory of musical figures which he used while improvising. Thus, he actually pre-composed his solos to some extent. To my knowledge, however, he never repeated a solo notatim; instead he continually found new ways to reshape, combine and phrase his well-practised melodic patterns. An awareness of these patterns allowed me to listen with an increased insight into his improvising habits (Owens 1974a, vol. 1, 167–75). Henry Martin studied many of the same solos and found that those patterns often had subtle connections with the themes that preceded the solos. He found that 'Parker would often absorb the *underlying* foreground motives and voice-leading structures of the themes, then fashion his solos in light of that larger-scale thematic material. That is, Parker connects to the source material through middleground voice leading, and by abstracting, internalizing, then projecting essential, if sometimes less evident, qualities of the head [i.e., theme]' (1996, 3).

At least one analyst – Pressing (1982) – has applied set theory to jazz. In contrast, several writers – including Kernfeld (1981), Perlman and Greenblatt (1981), Smith (1983), Strout (1986), Floyd (1995) and Walser (1993) – have found useful the writings of scholars working primarily outside music, such as Parry and Lord in epic poetry, Chomsky in linguistics and Gates in African-American literary criticism. Noting analogies between spoken languages and musical languages, these writers have developed fresh concepts to illuminate jazz.

R. Bird (1976), Gushee (1981), Potter (1990) and Brownell (1994) have written thoughtful discussions of various approaches to jazz analysis. Brownell argues that analysts tend to view jazz improvisation either as product or process. In the former group are Hodeir, Schuller, Stewart and others, who look for notable recordings to single out and discuss at length. These superior performances, the writers find, contain features common to great works in the European concert-music tradition, such as melodic coherence gained through motivic development and/or discoverable underlying structure. Those who view jazz as process, including Owens and Smith, downplay the importance of individual performances and look for the general patterns a player used in putting together solo after solo. Gushee, in his excellent study of Lester Young's various 'Shoe Shine Boy' solos, postulates four approaches: the 'motivic' (Brownell's 'product'), the 'formulaic' (Brownell's 'process'), the 'schematic' (also part of Brownell's 'product') and the 'semiotic' (Floyd, Walser, and others; a group, absent from Brownell's categories, that finds extramusical significance in musical gestures).[6]

Nearly every analytical writer, from Sargeant on, shares one common trait: they are jazz scholars first, players second. Though they may play jazz professionally or semi-professionally, few have spent years developing distinctive playing styles and earning a living as a player. Thus, when they listen, evaluate and analyse this music, they are outsiders to some degree. But the players they admire and study are (or were) jazz analysts, too, pondering and perfecting every nuance of their personal jazz language. Some concentrated largely on one particular role model; thus, alto saxophonist Sonny Stitt created an aural dissertation on Parker every night he performed. Others, such as John Coltrane, blended musical ingredients gleaned from several masters with their own ideas in the creation of unique *magna opera*. The difference, of course, is that they rarely wrote about what they did. (David Liebman's *Lookout Farm* (1978) and Todd Coolman's dissertation (1997) are exceptions.) Sometimes they did not even talk much to one another about their music. For example, Coltrane's sidemen report that there was scant verbal communication about musical matters, but, of course, the most intense and eloquent musical communication. When the players did talk to reporters or researchers, they often made only general remarks, using terms different from the technical language of analysis. Thus, there is a gap between players and scholars.

One scholar, Paul Berliner, has gone to monumental lengths to close that gap. His *Thinking in Jazz* (1994) delves deeply into the nature of improvisation as viewed by over 50 improvisers, whom he interviewed at length. By interweaving numerous musical examples with information provided by his informants, he has written vivid and perceptive descriptions of the processes these players followed to develop their musical vocabularies, construct solos and interact with one another. The 150 pages of transcription and description he devotes to rhythm-section players constitute the most extensive discussion in print of the harmonic, melodic and rhythmic procedures that are at the heart of the jazz process. Almost 900 pages long and filled with important information, Berliner's book is presently the Mount Everest of jazz ethnomusicology and analysis (see Peter J. Martin's comments on pages 141–3).

Transcription

Though the interviews and commentary are vitally important in Berliner's book, so are his excellent transcriptions. Indeed, almost any musical analysis is notation-dependent; and, since jazz is largely improvised, jazz analysts usually are also jazz transcribers. As such, they must grapple with sometimes formidable aural challenges, especially if the music is complex or the acoustical quality of the recordings is poor. The level of detail that they strive for in transcription depends upon what they want to examine in the music. Typically they have centred on melodic issues, especially those having to do with chorus phrases, where there is little or no connection with the original theme. In such cases, pitch shapes and patterns are the primary focus, so an uncluttered notation should be perfectly adequate, especially for a moderately fast solo passage (see Ex. 15.1). If, on the other hand, the analysis embraces small details of rhythm (such as swing quavers versus simple quavers), phrasing (often weak-to-strong) and articulation (often a mix of on-beat and off-beat accents), or dynamics and vibrato are germane, more refined transcriptions are necessary (see Ex. 15.2). To reach this level of detail, analysts may use tape recorders and slow the music to half, quarter, or even eighth speed; newer devices, such as the Digital Music Study Recorder, can reduce the speed without lowering the pitch.

Master musicians in any tradition play in exceedingly subtle and complex ways, and the transcriber wishing to convey that complexity but still keep the transcriptions comprehensible faces difficult issues. Schuller bracketed two successive measures from Armstrong's recording of 'Weather Bird' with the ratios $5^1/_2$:4 and 5:4, subsuming a half-measure triplet within the second ratio (1968, 125). Though few readers may be able to ideate this phrase, the notation serves at least two important purposes: it suggests Armstrong's rhythmic subtlety, and it encourages readers to listen to the recording for themselves.

As Frank Tirro (1974) and other analysts have pointed out, our notational system often fails us when we wish to represent pitches and rhythms accurately. Years ago I spent many hours trying to make a detailed and accurate transcription of the first complete take of 'Parker's Mood'. Then the sound technician in the UCLA ethnomusicology programme produced a frequency and amplitude graph of the piece with the now-defunct Seeger Melograph Model C, and I spent many more hours examining the graph, using a ruler and calculator. It was a humbling experience to learn how crude my aural transcription actually was. Parker's wonderfully expressive solo contained not only quavers, semiquavers, demisemiquavers, triplets and so on, but also fifteenth notes, nineteenth notes, twenty-first notes and other

Ex. 15.1

Ex. 15.2

lengths for which we have no precise symbols. Additionally, he employed a variable range of frequencies for many of the notes; he used, for example, a 'family of Fs' above and below the F on the piano (Owens 1974b). How can we show these things notationally?

If traditional notation is inadequate, perhaps a different approach is in order. Craig Woodson used a proportional notation for his transcriptions of Tony Williams's drum solos: a graduated series of dots (with diameters ranging from 0.055 inch to 0.125 inch) to represent loudness, with these dots placed proportionally along the staff to represent durations. It is an intriguing solution, but feasible only because he had graphs of the music available for study (from the Melograph again). Perhaps the solution is a linking of graphs and modified musical notation, though the large size of graphs makes long examples impractical.[7]

Other problems arise when the analytical focus is on group interaction rather than individual solo lines. Full-score transcriptions are often filled with educated guesses: was that note on the string bass or the bass drum? How many notes are in that pianist's soft, quick chord? Is that G in the piano part or in the guitar part? Is the drummer actually using the high-hat under those all-enveloping ride-cymbal sounds? Older recordings are particularly difficult; Launcelot Pyke decided to transcribe only wind parts plus chord symbols in his study of 1920s ensembles, partly because much of the rhythm-section playing is an indecipherable acoustic mush in recordings made before the introduction of the electrical process in 1925.

No matter how simple or complex the transcriptions, however, analysts must provide readers with legible transcriptions. Publishers no longer wish to absorb the costs of transferring hand-written examples into camera-ready copy. Further, reproductions of handwritten music should no longer be acceptable, even for theses and dissertations, for with the versatile music-writing programs now available we can generate professional-looking examples on personal computers. Though some of these programmes are complex to learn and tedious to use, the end results can be impressive. Berliner's excellent, reader-friendly examples (1994, 513–757), and Franz Krieger's example-rich study of solo piano performances of 'Body and Soul' (1995), are models for all analysts to emulate. Both writers say much of importance in their texts, but the elegant notation of their fine transcriptions also speaks volumes.

Sometimes analysts avoid the use of transcriptions, perhaps for fear of discouraging the general reader, and sometimes, unfortunately, to avoid unpleasant copyright issues. Copyright laws say nothing about written transcriptions of recorded improvisations, but some attorneys and publishers feel that the rights of composers extend even to athematic improvisations on the harmonies of their compositions. A writer who has had to track down the current copyright owners of themes and then to negotiate permission fees may well reflect upon this strange exercise (what happened to the rights of the *improviser*?) and say 'never again' to the use of transcriptions.

The 'right' approach?

With so much analytical material currently available, the reader may find several different analyses of the same recorded performance. Ekkehard Jost (1999) has stated correctly that there is no single reliable method for analysing jazz. His observations on jazz analysis form the opening article in an array of papers on the subject, and the varied nature of these papers proves his point. A particular phrase might represent signifyin(g) or signifyin' to Floyd or Walser, an astonishing musical gesture to Hodeir or Schuller, a rapid scalar run in C minor that ends on the diminished fifth of chord ii to Owens, or a descending, direct, homogeneous, passing pattern elided with an ascending, direct, homogeneous passing pattern to Smith. Some writers argue forcefully that his/her approach is the most informed way in which to listen to the music, and argue just as forcefully that earlier analysts espoused erroneous, misleading or ambiguous theories. How does a reader decide which is the 'right' approach? In many cases there are no real conflicts among the various analyses; rather, different approaches often afford the reader complementary views of the same music.

Consider, for example, Armstrong's famous recording of 'West End Blues' (28 June 1928, Okeh 8597). Schuller, in discussing the final chorus, called it 'the perfect climax, structurally and emotionally', and used such adjectives as 'ecstatic', 'extraordinary' and 'astonishing' (1968, 118–19). The features that stimulated his enthusiasm are the long initial high Bb (concert pitch) and the ensuing rush of notes, all of which add up to an 'impassioned finale'. His well-crafted transcription provides the reader with an excellent visualisation of these features. H. David Caffey, in an essay on Armstrong's style, includes his own transcription and discussion of the solo. He points out, among other features, that the four-note figure of bars 5–6 appears in Armstrong's unaccompanied introduction (1975, 90).

There are other noteworthy aspects of this solo chorus. For one, Armstrong's improvised melody maintains clear connections with the initial 'West End Blues' theme recorded by Oliver earlier that month (11 June 1928, Vocalion 1189); his initial motive, F♯–G–Bb, occurs in bar 2 of Oliver's theme, and that repeated four-note figure in Armstrong's bars 5–6 derives from bar 5 of the theme. Further, Armstrong's dramatically extended high Bb is the ultimate summary of Oliver's first phrase, which is framed by two Bbs an octave apart.

The structures of Oliver's and Armstrong's melodies, though not easily heard at first, are similar as well. Both choruses begin by prolonging Bb, step 5 of the Eb scale. Oliver maintains that structural pitch by emphasising it at the beginning of each four-bar section (bars 1, 5 and 9 of Ex. 15.3); then in bar 10 he descends chromatically, ending on Eb when the tonic chord arrives in bar 11. Armstrong's diatonic descent from Bb to Eb (Ex. 15.4) is

Ex. 15.3

Ex. 15.4

more gradual, for he embeds the structural tones A♭–G (steps 4–3) in the ornate phrase after the long B♭, and presents the final F–E♭ descent only after a brief interpolation by pianist Earl Hines.

Of course, we do not treasure Armstrong's recorded performance because it adheres to a logical melodic structure (one, incidentally, which figures prominently in the European concert tradition), but because of its melodic and rhythmic details, many of which Schuller and Caffey discuss. None the less, just as a brilliantly crafted sentence has a structure dictated by the syntax of its language, and just as a beautiful building must have a solid foundation and superstructure, so we might expect a fine musical statement to have a structural underpinning. And if we listen for it as the music unfolds, we may well hear the music in a new way, enhancing our enjoyment and appreciation.

Is there any conflict between Schuller, Caffey and Owens? I think not. Are there things of importance to say about Armstrong's chorus that we have omitted? Probably so. Indeed, perhaps each analyst who continues to 'mess' with jazz, in defiance of Fats Waller's admonition, has a truth to reveal about the music. Each is, after all, saying the same thing: this music has value; let me show you why.

PART FIVE

Jazz takes

16 Valuing jazz

ROBERT WALSER

When the United States Congress declared that jazz deserved to be 'preserved, understood, and promulgated', 1987 became a watershed year in the history of valuing jazz: a music that had first entered the written historical record as 'discordant jass' now possessed the status of 'a rare and valuable national American treasure'.[1] Yet it could be said that such a statement attempts to erase the history that made it necessary. Even the Congressional discussion that preceded the resolution shows that the conflicted history of jazz is not so easily swept away.

Although John Conyers, the resolution's chief sponsor, at one point mentioned the 'Afro-American roots' of jazz, he, like the other speakers, emphasised the music's global success. He spoke of having encountered jazz in Japan, Moscow, Africa and the Caribbean, and he hailed the spread of jazz, along with its generative force to produce musical fusions, as bases for international respect and understanding. However, he raised important issues of ownership and identity when he commented: 'I have been in countries throughout Europe in which many people thought that the art form [jazz] was their art form.'

Constance Morella underscored the idea that the global success of jazz is a sign that it has transcended its origins when she remarked that 'jazz is no respecter of political philosophies, and in fact jazz belongs to the world'. However, when Mervyn Dymally praised the rise of first-rate Japanese jazz composers and musicians as a sign of the music's importance, Conyers steered this line of thought to the success that American jazz musicians have found in Japan. He praised Japanese people not as participants in jazz, but because 'in Japan our jazz artists have been afforded great honor and recognition, as well as remuneration . . .'; in Japan, jazz 'is studied with great care'.

Texas representative Henry Gonzalez touched on the origins of 'the Afro-American rhythm, which we now call jazz', but spoke more admiringly of the 'truly 100 percent American contribution to bringing it out of the purely Afro-American center', citing for the record three Texans – one black, one Mexican-American and one white – who contributed much to its history. Lindy Boggs of New Orleans and Ike Skelton from Kansas City spoke for the record about the special contributions of their home cities to the development of jazz but, like the other speakers, they made no reference to the historical factors that explain why the recognition they were seeking had been so long coming; it appears to have been simply an oversight.

The tensions and elisions of this debate left their mark on the language of the resolution itself: 'Whereas, jazz has achieved preeminence throughout the world as an indigenous American music and art form, bringing to this country and the world a uniquely American musical synthesis and culture through the African-American experience . . . ' Jazz is thus at once African-American in its origins and universal in its achievements but, most of all, it is somehow uniquely American in its essence. The resolution promotes a particular vision of Americanness in an international context, one that strikingly erases the history of American racism and thus evades the question of why this resolution was sought – primarily by members of the Congressional Black Caucus. Jazz is reified, treated as a thing, a product, a collective achievement rather than as a variety of ways of music-making in which particular people have engaged in particular historical circumstances. History is not welcome here because truth is divisive; one imagines that only by inviting all of their colleagues to share in the credit for jazz could the resolution's sponsors have hoped to get it passed.

All of the participants in this debate agreed implicitly that there *is* one thing called jazz that has a continuous history of artistry and a coherent generic identity – a tacit stipulation that effaces the long history of contestation that has accompanied the music (see DeVeaux 1991). Jazz is compared to classical music once during the discussion, but no one compared jazz to other forms of music so as to explain why it should be elevated above them, beyond making generally admiring references to the artistry and popularity of jazz. And ultimately, the resolution is purely symbolic: it urges recognition, understanding, documentation, archival support, preservation, celebration and promulgation, but it proposes no actual plans to accomplish any of this. That Congress has seen fit to recognise the artistry of jazz is an important fact to which others might later appeal, and from which they may draw support, but the resolution itself allocates no funds to anyone.

This Congressional colloquy throws into relief a number of enduring tensions among the ways in which jazz can be valued, and has been valued over the century of its existence. Considered as part of the long history of criticising jazz and arguing about its merits, the scope of the debate is limited; absent, for example, are the sorts of overtly racist denunciations of the music that would have been part of the record had such a resolution somehow been introduced in an earlier decade. Still, this part of the day's proceedings ended with a final sign of anonymous dissension: 'A motion to reconsider was laid on the table.' Even in 1987, the artistic stature of jazz could simply be gainsaid by those who preferred not to dispute the issue openly.

To proclaim that jazz *is* something – whether African-American, American, universal, or somehow all of these things at once – is to assert that a set of historically contingent cultural practices has a fixed, universal *essence*. It is an attempt to ground value outside one's own experience, however much it is motivated by one's own experience of value. It could thus be called a religious impulse and, as such, its conclusions may be respected but not proven. To value something is to make a kind of use of it. Proclamations of value are always interested, partial and polemical, all the more so when they deploy the rhetoric of universality, which is a claim to special privilege; were it not, it would not need to be made.

Much writing about jazz resists such thinking. Mark Gridley, the author of the most widely used jazz textbook, forthrightly urges enjoyment of jazz rather than understanding of its history: 'teaching "jazz HISTORY" for the sake of history might prevent teaching the essential listening skills that truly develop APPRECIATION for jazz' (Gridley 1984, 2). But what has enabled such pleasures, and what are their consequences? Exactly this attitude was criticised by LeRoi Jones in 1963:

> Usually the critic's commitment was first to his *appreciation* of the music, rather than to his understanding of the attitude which produced it. This difference meant that the potential critic of jazz had only to appreciate the music, or what he thought was the music, and that he did not need to understand or even be concerned with the attitudes which produced it, except perhaps as a purely sociological phenomenon ... The major flaw in this approach to Negro music is that it strips the music too ingenuously of its social and cultural intent. It seeks to define jazz as an art (or a folk art) that has come out of no intelligent body of socio-cultural philosophy.
> ['Jazz and the White Critic': quoted in Walser 1999, 257]

Such an approach, Jones might say, is ultimately narcissistic: Gridley is promoting consumption of the music, and to do this he aims to increase the pleasure that listeners experience from jazz, and insists that too much historical knowledge can subvert this primary goal. He thus attempts to increase one aspect of the value of jazz – the pleasure it can give certain contemporary audiences – at the expense of all others. Jones mounts the counter-argument that jazz history must aspire to be as complex as the history of jazz has been. And that history, I would add, is a history of multiple pleasures, interpretations, arguments and uses – a thorny, sometimes unpleasurable history of how jazz has been valued.

Thus this chapter broaches an aspect of jazz history with which scholars seldom engage directly, by sketching and comparing a sampling of the ways in which jazz has been valued. If I will mostly neglect what many people would consider one of the most common aspects of value – money – it is because I maintain that all financial transactions involving jazz are secondary to the fact of its being valued for other reasons. However much financial transactions shape the social worlds of jazz by affecting the lives of musicians, fans, critics, club owners, concert promoters, record company owners and employees, money is never exchanged for jazz unless something else of value is believed to be provided in return, and it is those other things that will be my concern here. A history of jazz styles is a history of sensibilities, values and ways of valuing.

Arguing about values

Consider the index of a published collection of readings in jazz history, comprising nearly a hundred years of critical, personal and analytical commentary (Walser 1999). One list of references steers the reader to various understandings of the nature, character or purpose of jazz:

as African-American music
as American music
as ceremony or ritual
as classical music
as entertainment
as experimental music
as folk music
as instinctive music
as intellectual music
as play
as primitive music
as symptom of modernity
as universal music
as youth music

These are contradictory assessments of the essence of jazz and, as such, they are ways of valuing it, of defining its significance, of simultaneously using and exalting it. The historian's task, I would argue, is not to sift through the evidence and issue a ruling that declares only one of these valuings to be true, but rather to embrace them all in order to apprehend the music's full cultural significance.

A little further down the same index we find the category of 'jazz, effects of, beneficial':

awakens interest in music
cathartic release
communication
creation of community

emotional escape and rejuvenation
enriches understanding of classical music
expresses attitudes about the world
expresses a variety of emotions
expresses freedom
expresses identities
expresses individuality
fun
gratifies sexual impulses
'healthy paganism'
heroic action
'musical socialism'
orgasm
overcomes racism
protests injustice
promotes wind instruments
provides examples of African-American achievements
reconciles individuality and group identity
records the spirit of its times
source of pride and self-knowledge
spiritual experience
unifying force
used to explore and affirm identities and relationships

And there is also a list of 'jazz, effects of, harmful':

atrophy of the brain
corrupts youth
defiles musical culture
degenerating effect on popular songs
demoralizing effect on workers
expresses negative emotions
intoxicating effect
mental, physical, and moral damage
'morbid eroticism'
orgasm
promotes sloppy technique among music students
'triumph of sensuality'
violates natural law

This last list is useful because a historian cannot really account for the appeal of a mass-mediated cultural phenomenon for some people without thinking about how it also produces dislike or indifference in others. (That 'orgasm' appears in both lists is a tribute to the cultural complexity of sexual pleasure.)

As sounds, images and people move around the planet, they find themselves in new contexts within which their significance and worth is assessed. Because jazz coalesced during the age of mass-mediated culture, its scope has been global for nearly all of its history. Constant recontextualisation produced a host of contradictory arguments, speculations and declarations of its meanings in various times and places, all of which are now a dauntingly complex but precious part of its legacy. As early as 1922, a journalist for the *New York Times Magazine* traced the global diffusion of jazz (although most of what went by that name we might now categorise as Tin Pan Alley song with ragtime inflections) through the media of recordings, sheet music and peripatetic musicians, marvelling at the music's ability to win converts in many cultures and to stimulate cross-cultural fusions. Lands the west had thought exotic now thrilled to the exotic sounds of the west's most popular music.

When *The Appeal of Jazz*, the first British book on the topic, was published in 1927, its author, R. W. S. Mendl, wrestled with the problem of how to account for jazz's attractiveness for many different audiences: 'That a form of music which originated among black people should have developed into . . . the most widely popular form of music in the world's history is a phenomenon sufficiently remarkable to lead us to probe it still further.' On the one hand, he suggested that syncopation offered many people an 'instinctive delight in emphasizing with your feet a beat which was not stressed by the players', the pleasure of breaking with convention. On the other hand, he related the popularity of jazz to the upheavals of modernity, including the World War and new forms of speedy transportation, implying that jazz expressed, fitted and made sense of these restless times. Not everyone experienced these historical changes similarly, though, and Mendl even points to how the British reception of jazz necessarily differed from the American, most importantly because the absence of African-Americans in one context and their fraught presence in the other affects the music's significance, but also because he and others associated the speed and dynamism of modernity most strongly with the United States.

The perception that jazz was a means of breaking with convention, of resisting regimentation, has sometimes acquired a dimension that is overtly political. Novelist Josef Škvorecký has recounted the Nazi restrictions on jazz in occupied Czechoslovakia, attributing to the music an *élan vital* that evades, for as long as it sounds, totalitarian control. Ben Sidran explains the political value of jazz as the result of its preservation of the sensibilities and priorities of oral culture: 'Black music was in itself revolutionary, if only because it maintained a non-Western orientation in the realms of perception and communication . . . This strength has been shared by all Americans, black or white, who at any point took exception to the underlying assumptions of mainstream society and has been available simply through the experience of black music' (quoted in Walser 1999, 301). Jazz critic Charles Delaunay hailed jazz as civilisation's lifeline to France during the dark days of World War II. For him, jazz was not black music and 'much more than American music': it was 'the first universal music', New Orleans's blend of the 'artistic sensibility and wit' of Franco-Spanish culture, the 'methodical precision and coolness' of Anglo-Saxon culture, and the 'epic temperament' and vigour of Africa (Walser 1999, 131). For both Škvorecký and Delaunay, the power of jazz to furnish hope and strength in the face of barbarity proved that wherever it came from, it could speak emotionally to anyone and it belonged to the world. Although certainly not everyone has valued the music in this way, Škvorecký and Delaunay spoke for many when they praised jazz for its positive capacity to create shared human bonds and life-affirming experiences. Both furnished examples of how jazz could, through mass mediation, come to be vitally important in contexts that were far removed from the music's origins.

The rhetoric of universalism, however, can also be used to celebrate the particular. When Billy Taylor and other African-American musicians call jazz 'America's classical music', they are appealing for the same transcendent status that German music has enjoyed: 'Americans of African descent, in producing music which expressed themselves, not only developed a new musical vocabulary, they created a *classical* music – an authentic *American* music which articulated uniquely American feelings and thoughts, which eventually came to transcend ethnic boundaries' (*ibid.*, 328). Without disguising the music's origins, Taylor elides its meanings so that a small, marginalised group of musicians could become spokespersons for a kind of unified American essence, which despite this specificity had universal appeal. As with the classical canon that served as the model for this representation of jazz, many styles, uses and meanings must be blurred together. Taylor sought respect for the black originators of jazz and pointed to the widespread appeal of their music as evidence that they had created real art, which for him was art that had transcended the conditions of its origin. His argument implies nothing less than the claim that jazz musicians triumphed over the inequities and brutalities that limited their lives to produce something better – something that, if not exactly reflective of American realities, represented, we might say, what America ought to be, presented a vision that others also recognised as an ideal worthy of celebration. This is a powerful rhetorical move that is grounded in important truths.

Still, this influential formulation papers over fundamental contradictions. As Everett Taylor Atkins remarks in his study of jazz in Japan, 'few cultures are as concerned with "authenticity" as jazz is. It is an obsession that potentially undermines the rhetoric of jazz as a "universal language", for "authenticity" implies particularism, not universalism' (1997, 11). Atkins analyses a long history of Japanese participation in jazz that has been marked by anxieties about authenticity – the nagging feeling that no matter how much Japanese audiences were moved by this music, no matter how well Japanese musicians learned to play it, it was not really theirs. Moreover, he points out that 'Jazz's "universal" pretensions are subverted not only by its fetish for "authenticity", but also by its close association with American military might and cultural arrogance, particularly in the Cold War era' (*ibid.*, 8). In such a context, the value of jazz could not be considered apart from larger issues of cultural identity, modernisation and American hegemony. Indeed, when it was promoted by the government and the mainstream media during the Cold War, jazz became celebrated for exemplifying the value of individuality, in ways that effaced, for political purposes, the cooperative and collective aspects of jazz.[2]

For Atkins, the concept of authenticity is divisive and unfair: 'one historical crime – robbing black artists of their rightful profits and credit for creating this music – does not justify another – denying the significance of non-black artists in shaping jazz' (41). Thus does the very idea of what constitutes African-American culture become a matter of debate. For example, Jelly Roll Morton absorbed ragtime, blues, hymns, minstrel songs, French and Italian opera, Tin Pan Alley songs and the 'Spanish tinge' of Caribbean music on his way to becoming one of the most influential of jazz musicians. Morton himself celebrated the richly multicultural environment within which jazz developed: 'we had so many different styles that whenever you came to New Orleans, it wouldn't make any difference that you just came from Paris or any part of England, Europe, or any place – whatever your tunes were over there, we played them in New Orleans' (Walser 1999, 17).

Indeed, the role jazz has played in breaking down social barriers is another reason it has been valued. As early as 1919, the *Chicago Defender*, one of the country's pre-eminent black newspapers, pointed with pride to the accomplishments of black jazz musicians whose excellence had attracted white audiences: 'It is a well-known fact that the white people view us largely from the standpoint of the cook, porter, and waiter, and his limited opportunities are responsible for much of the distorted opinion held concerning us.' Through their demonstrations of musical excellence, black musicians were 'jazzing away the barriers of prejudice' (Walser 1999, 15–16). Leonard Feather, John Hammond and other critics have made strong claims in this regard, but perhaps no one has put it as elegantly as Joseph Bechet (Sidney's brother): 'this jazz music helps to get this misunderstanding between the races straightened out. You creep in close to hear the music and, automatically, you creep close to the other people' (Lomax 1950, 121).

Sometimes, however, the value of the music is that it marks difference, as when participation distinguishes 'hip' from 'square', or musicians from others. Howard Becker characterised jazz in the late 1940s as a 'service occupation', in which professional musicians hired to play dances had to accommodate their employers' choices of repertoire, style and tempo, and made up for their lack of artistic control by isolating themselves socially (Walser 1999, 179–91). Insider status also means different things as the music's cultural location changes: in the late 1930s to be knowledgeable about jazz was to participate in a broadly shared public culture, but in the 1960s there were many possible subcultural affiliations that involved jazz. Like any other cultural activity, jazz can be 'articulated' (as Stuart Hall puts it) to particular ideologies; the meanings of jazz changed somewhat when *Playboy* presented it among the trappings of a swinging bachelor's luxury life, distancing it from earlier associations with social dance, exotic spectacles or black artistry (Walser 1999, 261–2).

Such articulations are complex cases within the general set of reception issues, one of the most enduring of which is the possibility that what white people heard might be different from what black musicians thought they were playing. One of the earliest published discussions of jazz, a 1917 article in the *New York Sun,* shows how enthusiasm about jazz could easily be based in the same fantasies that supported blackface minstrelsy. On the one hand, its author praises jazz musicians' musical skills and links their innovations to modern life and art. On the other hand, he imagines that jazz puts him in touch with the exotic spectacles of the African jungle, quoting a musicologist to make this point: 'The music of contemporary savages taunts us with a lost art of rhythm. Modern sophistication has inhibited many native instincts, and the mere fact that our conventional dignity usually forbids us to sway our bodies or to tap our feet when we hear effective music has deprived us of unsuspected pleasures' (Walser 1999, 6). With one hand, such explanations criticise white society for having repressed too much that is valuable and thank black musicians for giving it back; with the other hand, those same musicians are labelled 'savages' for having successfully done so. This is the same mechanism that Nathan Irvin Huggins identified at the heart of the minstrel show: white performers in blackface could indulge in every vice that they had forsworn in everyday life, and at the same time pin the guilt for such indulgence on black people as they imagined them.[3]

The same tensions are at work in one of the most often-cited documents of jazz history, Ernest Ansermet's 1919 review of Will Marion Cook's Southern Syncopated Orchestra, which included at the time a young clarinettist named Sidney Bechet (reprinted in Walser 1999, 9–11). Jazz critics and historians value Ansermet's enthusiastic comments because he was a respected orchestral conductor, one of the very first classical musicians to go on record with favourable evaluations of jazz. Even as he marvelled at their complex timbres, their rhythmic innovations, their ability to play without written music and Bechet's virtuosity as a soloist, however, he was troubled by his inability to understand why Cook's musicians were doing the things they were doing: 'I couldn't tell whether these artists feel it is their duty to be sincere.' He sees that their improvisatory freedom is not absolute: 'they can let themselves go, in a certain direction and within certain limits, as their hearts desire'. But when he struggles to describe the effects of their music, he spills out similes that seem very distant from the disciplined efforts of professional musicians: 'it seems as if a great wind is passing over a forest or as if a door is suddenly opened on a wild orgy'. He also imagined that the relative lack of harmonic innovation he heard in Cook's music was a sign that Negro musicians had not yet ascended high enough 'in the scheme of musical evolution'. Still, Ansermet was excited by these musicians' own pleasure in playing, by the way they exulted in their creativity and mastery.

Thus those who would universalise jazz are responding to a long history of denigrating jazz and its makers. The city of New Orleans today glories in (and markets) its reputation as the birthplace of jazz, but in 1918 the editors of the New Orleans *Times-Picayune* emphatically denied that jazz had been born in their city, or declared at least that they could take no pride in such an origin (Walser 1999, 7–8). They created a striking image of cultural and racial hierarchy, a house containing a 'great assembly hall of melody', where many are welcomed to music, and an 'inner court of harmony', to which fewer pass on to enjoy 'truly great music'. In the basement is the 'servants' hall of rhythm', where one can hear 'the hum of the Indian dance, the throb of the Oriental tambourines and kettledrums, the clatter of clogs, the click of Slavic heels, the thumpty-tumpty of the negro banjo'. The tapping foot appears again as a locus of taste and social order; the *Sun* had endorsed it but the *Times-Picayune* sternly denounced such vulgarity. The very fact that jazz engaged and energised the body proved to many its essential meretriciousness.

Black bandleader and writer Dave Peyton was similarly concerned about the rough timbres and techniques, with the added anxiety that 'mushy, discordant jazz' would hold back racial progress: 'We listen to many of the famous white orchestras with their smoothness of playing, their unique attacks, their novelty arrangement of the score and other things that go to make for fine music, and we wonder why most of our own orchestras will fail to deliver music as the Nordic brothers do' (Walser 1999, 59). Like the editors of the *Times-Picayune*, Peyton assumed that there was but a single scale of musical value, and he worried that black musicians had some catching up to do. In contrast, Langston Hughes, writing at the same moment, cared more about celebrating difference than proving equality according to white standards: 'Let the blare of Negro jazz bands and the bellowing voice of Bessie Smith singing Blues penetrate the closed ears of the colored near-intellectuals until they listen and perhaps understand' (*ibid.*, 57). Ways of valuing jazz do not simply split along the fault-line of race; it is crucial to realise that arguments about the value of jazz proceeded within communities as well as among them.[4]

Tom Turino has analysed a fascinating transformation of musical values among Peruvian musicians in his book, *Moving Away from Silence* (1993). Traditionally, music of the Andean highlands is composed collectively: musicians sit together improvising until one of them hits upon a musical idea that some of the others like, whereupon they may imitate and confirm it or suggest alternatives. Once it gains enough support, a melody becomes part of the new composition, and this non-verbal process of joint composition continues until the new work is complete. When highland people emigrated from the Andes to metropolitan Lima, the music of their origin became a crucial symbol and enactment of their newly fragile and marginalised cultural identity. In order to preserve this symbolic power, urban musicians found themselves travelling back to the mountains to learn the latest songs, which they would memorise and reproduce back in the city. But by faithfully copying the sounds of their homeland colleagues, they necessarily abandoned the process of collectively improvised composition that had always been used to produce those sounds. The urban musicians replicated their rural counterparts' songs, but their values had radically changed: achieving certain sounds became more important than following certain practices; copying replaced composing; music acquired a single, authoritative point of origin instead of arising from spontaneous collaboration and interaction; product succeeded process; authenticity triumphed over creativity.

It is easy enough to see such musicians as Wynton Marsalis, the jazz repertory ensembles and virtually the whole of jazz education as having managed a similar shift of values (see David Ake's comments in Chapter 13[5]). When jazz enters the institutional context of the academy, it must contend not only with the classical measuring stick, but also the tendency to teach whatever can be easily or efficiently taught and measured, which may have little to do with how jazz is valued in other contexts. And whatever the worth of live recreations of music of the past – and it is considerable – the old sounds can no longer express or engage the same values. Musical innovations become frozen in repetition, the cutting edge becomes a classic model, experiments become lessons. Miles Davis complained that jazz had become stagnant in the 1980s: 'I didn't even go to listen to most jazz groups anymore, because they were only playing the same musical licks that we played way back with Bird, over and over again' (Walser 1999, 374). Davis blamed jazz critics for rejecting expressive innovations – at the end of his life, he was championing Prince as the musician he admired most: 'For me, he can be the new Duke Ellington of our time if he just keeps at it' (*ibid.*, 376) – and he was always sensitive to shifts in values and the opportunities they present, as when he wrote around 1968: 'We were playing a searching kind of music, but the times had changed. Everybody was dancing' (*ibid.*, 369).

One of the most heated controversies in jazz history was sparked by the appearance of free jazz. Its supporters heard it as the next step in the evolution of jazz, one that mirrored classical music in its harmonic development but also restored the early jazz tradition of collective improvisation. Some went even further: 'It's a vision that considers self-expression synonymous with social responsibility, and individuality synonymous with spirituality ... In discussing his harmolodics music system, where every player is free to take the lead at any time, Ornette [Coleman] poses it not just as a liberating paradigm for jazz performers, but for everybody' (Tate 1992, 117). The other side regarded free jazz as the barbarous noise of 'nihilists' trying to 'destroy the music that gave them birth'.[6] Critics and musicians alike divided according to a set of binary oppositions that ascribed values to the new music:

progressive	retrogressive
creative	destructive
explorative	self-indulgent
democratic	nihilist
restoring tradition	repudiating tradition
saying something new	abandoning coherent statement

Because the critical commentary on free jazz bristled with such terms of value, it is an excellent example for the argument that musical evaluations are underpinned by moral and ethical commitments.[7] All judgements of value are specific to the judge's goals and needs, and limited by that person's perspective and attitudes about what is good: play, order, rebellion, transcendence, esteem for originality versus the respect due to past models that establish the boundaries within which excellence must be sought.

Scott DeVeaux (1991), building on the historiographical work of Hayden White, identifies two modes of emplotment that have shaped a great deal of jazz history: the Romance, the triumph of musicians and their music against indifference and racism to become a central part of twentieth-century culture; and the Tragedy, the moving tale of musicians whose genius could not save them from self-destruction. DeVeaux also discusses two other concerns that have shaped jazz narratives: racial authenticity and agoraphobia, or fear of the marketplace. We might add to this list adherence to innovative musical technologies of the nineteenth century (piano, saxophone, valve trumpet – arguably jazz's most important instruments – and, around the turn of the twentieth century, the drum set) rather than the innovative musical technologies of the twentieth century (synthesiser, multi-track recording, effects, electric bass, sequencing, turntables, sampling, pedal steel guitar). The main exceptions to this division are the electric guitar (and, to a lesser extent, the vibraphone and the Hammond B3 organ), which in jazz utilises only the most basic amplification and tone modification, and the microphone, which is skilfully used to capture a wide range of timbres that would be inaudible without it. Even so, to both of these means of performance has been attached a certain amount of suspicion – unlike the amplified acoustic bass, piano or other instruments, where technology is perceived as transparent and unproblematic. These larger narratives about jazz have affected not only historiography but also our perceptions of the music itself. We enjoy jazz in part because we enjoy the stories it seems to tell us about triumph and tragedy, identity, commerce and technology. And we also enjoy it because of the stories it enables us to tell about the world.

Performing values

To this point, I have developed my discussion of valuing jazz through examples of verbal discourse. But musical discourse can also be a source of historical information and, despite the fact that the preceding survey of ways in which people have valued jazz could continue indefinitely, I will turn now to the question of how values are performed. It has often been said that the best jazz solos are not simply virtuosic displays; a good solo must tell a story, it must say something. But what are jazz musicians saying? This is a question that is as difficult as it is fundamental; few writers have raised it and even fewer have persuasively answered it. Ingrid Monson takes the trope of 'saying something' as the title of her important book (1996) yet, beyond noting that quotation and allusion are meaningful practices within jazz improvisation, Monson has relatively little to say about what jazz musicians are saying when they perform. In that book at least, Monson chooses to remain true to a fieldwork paradigm that requires discussions of value to be tightly grounded by what informants tell the ethnographer. This is a method that is of limited value to jazz history, then, because it is so attached to present contact, verbal articulation and the insider's perspective. It is not at all easy to correlate the pleasures that musicians experience with what they say about music, since their thinking and speaking about music takes place within complex discourses that both enable and limit various kinds of conception and expression. As Michael Denning puts it, 'a culture's own understanding of its genres is an important part of its rhetoric and must be attended to', but 'To be content with the terms the culture used, with the culture's self-understanding, is to abdicate the historian's task, which is to understand the way a culture's social and political unconscious overdetermines its self-consciousness' (1987, 77). Analysing music, which requires attention to non-verbal discourse and multiple perspectives, can thus be an important means of fulfilling the historian's task.

This is tricky business, of course; a host of formalist analyses of jazz have revealed less about their objects of study than about the power of entrenched analytical methods to set the terms of legitimation and other kinds of valuing. But these difficulties should not discourage us from trying to create a more substantial hermeneutic tradition for jazz studies. As LeRoi Jones put it, 'Failure to understand, for instance, that Paul Desmond and John Coltrane represent not only two very different ways of thinking about music, but more importantly two very different ways of viewing the world, is at the seat of most of the established misconceptions that are daily palmed off as intelligent commentary on jazz or jazz criticism' (Walser 1999, 260–61). If this is true, we should be able to hear these differences and to analyse them.

I want to contribute to the project of developing the hermeneutics of jazz by discussing a warhorse of the repertoire, Louis Armstrong's 1928 recording of 'West End Blues'. The opening cadenza of this performance is perhaps the most praised solo in all jazz, yet there has been little contextual analysis of its power and meanings. From Hugues Panassié and Robert Goffin to Martin Williams and Gunther Schuller, we run the gamut of marvelling at Armstrong's exuberant escape from convention to celebrating his logical constructions and technical advancements. What is largely missing is analysis of Armstrong's performances in terms of their rhetorical force, and interpretation of the significance of such performances within the contexts that shaped their production and reception.

In formal terms, Armstrong's cadenza is easily enough described. It consists of two contrasting phrases, the first starting high but dropping quickly before climbing to a sustained note at the top of the trumpet's range, and the second picking up from there and then swinging down two octaves to pause on a low note, before the rest of the players enter and the song's verse commences. Harmonically, the cadenza begins by articulating what will turn out to be the song's relative-minor key area, with the second phrase moving through some bluesy licks and proto-bebop angular circumlocutions to arrive on the seventh of the dominant chord.

Armstrong develops a number of motivic notions during the cadenza: repeated whole-tone and minor-third descents, chromatic ascending triplets in the second phrase that are not unrelated to the ascending triplet arpeggios of the first. Though it is unmeasured, the cadenza is nevertheless swung, and each of its moments seems to develop or comment upon previous moments. It thus achieves – and this particularly pleased Schuller – organic unity.[8] But one does not need to share Schuller's formalist and Eurocentric agenda to perceive and be affected by such details, for this is just another way of describing Armstrong's engagement with powerful blues conventions of variation and response. Even when they do not use the same terms to describe their experiences, different audiences may well be excited about the same things.

I am going to begin with my own experience, too, because I think that the process of figuring out how to perform a reasonable facsimile of Armstrong's cadenza has taught me a few things. This is an approach that my colleague Elisabeth Le Guin, in her forthcoming book on Boccherini, has dubbed 'carnal musicology', the premise of which is that attention to the physicality of performance – how various parts of the body must bend and tighten and vibrate and stretch – can perhaps be as valuable as any other means with which we try to recover and understand musical meanings.[9] Armstrong's is a virtuoso performance, one that extended both the higher and the lower limits of what was considered the trumpet's usable range. Having benefited from Armstrong's model and the achievements of other players he influenced, as well as from other traditions of trumpet virtuosity and pedagogy, I am, at my best, able to play it. But few if any of Armstrong's contemporaries could have nailed it night after night as he did, let alone composed it in the first place. Working on this cadenza and other Armstrong solos reminds me that he redefined the instrument: after a hiatus of more than one hundred years, the extreme range, power, precision and improvisatory skills of the eighteenth-century *clarino* trumpeters were reborn with him.[10] That it is difficult for many people, even trumpet players, to recognise Armstrong's virtuosity now is simply due to his success: no player who came after him was untouched by his influence, and so the breathtaking creativity and prowess that impressed Armstrong's contemporaries can pass unnoticed by many people today.

The 'West End Blues' cadenza inscribes a number of historical developments and aspects of its context. Armstrong had switched from cornet to trumpet around 1926 and the OKeh record label had changed over to the electrical recording process in 1927; both of these factors helped make this recording sound newly crisp, real and powerful. The strength of Armstrong's playing recalls the pre-amplification days during which he developed his style so as to include the commercially advantageous attribute of volume. And the very idea of a fanfare, which this cadenza clearly evokes, comes most immediately from the deployment of such in theatre and cabaret bands (in which Armstrong often played) to announce new events and to quieten audiences.

The first note of the cadenza is very risky: as one goes higher on a brass instrument, the notes of the overtone series get closer together, and since this particular note (a concert G, or an A as it is played on the B♭ trumpet) requires a fingering that adds a significant amount of tubing to the instrument's length, it turns out that one could just as easily hit the note a whole step above or the one below as the right one. I found that hitting this note consistently depended entirely on approaching it with total concentration and the right attitude and posture. As I got better at imitating Armstrong's sound, my physical stance came to resemble his: body erect and balanced with weight slightly forward, a feeling of power focused throughout the chest and arms as they encompass the trumpet, in a manner that is wholly unlike the sensations I experience when playing in the styles of, for example, Miles Davis or Clifford Brown. That feeling of power is essential if a solo this difficult is to be played persuasively and without missing or cracking any notes; it is in fact virtually impossible to play this cadenza softly.

It could easily be objected that my identification with Armstrong is wholly imaginary, that there are perhaps many possible ways of playing such a solo without purporting to stand as he stood and feel what he felt. Certainly, many aspects of Armstrong's identity and experience are distant from my own: he was Southern, black, born in New Orleans near the turn of the century, and so on. But we both have played the trumpet at a high level of skill, and that is not an irrelevant connection. In fact, there are not infinite means of producing the same sounds on any instrument, and my identification is grounded in a keen sense of the limits of the human body for manipulating an airstream in collaboration with a piece of brass tubing. Once, as I was about to undergo some dental work, I confided to a friend my worries: one miscalculation, and I will have lost an octave of my range. He cheerfully suggested that I could just as well look forward to a slip that gave me an extra octave, but it doesn't work that way. Trumpet players evolve their technique for greatest efficacy with certain configurations of bone, muscle and air column. I approach Armstrong's music much as he did as a simple matter of efficiency – and efficiency is paramount when working near the limits of what the body can do. Approaching those limits, one is warned by pain, and sometimes I have had to do what Armstrong did innumerable times: put the pain aside, and not let it affect the concentration, the focus, the occupation of a physical stance of power and confidence that this cadenza both requires and articulates.

For what Martin Williams has described as Armstrong's 'power, sureness, firmness, authority, such commanding presence' (1983, 59) is surely evident throughout 'West End Blues'. The strength and accuracy, the unfaltering rhythmic complexity and swing, the long spun-out phrases that play against the periodic tendencies of the tune – the latter two in particular more than foreshadow what would be taken to be core innovations of bebop. Yet a paramount influence is the blues, a complex mixture of oral and written traditions, of rural and urban entertainment. We hear this in Armstrong's phrasing, his pitch choices and alterations, in his vocal call-and-response with clarinettist Jimmy Strong – although Armstrong's 'commanding presence' turns this into call-and-RESPONSE.

Armstrong's vocals are often compared to his trumpet style, and in phrasing and pitch choice this is apt enough. But the daring leaps, wide tessitura and clear, brilliant timbre that are so characteristic of Armstrong the instrumentalist contrast sharply with the gentle, albeit sometimes raspy, probing of a few notes that often marks Armstrong's vocal recompositions of melodies. Unlike his trumpet playing, his vocals reflect the influences of the popular crooners of the 1920s and of the microphone, the technological innovation that enabled this whole approach to singing. According to one source, Armstrong himself traced his practice of scat singing, unrestrained by fixed lyrics, to his experiences of Jewish *davening* (ritual praying and head-banging) when he worked and lived closely with the Karnofsky family as a boy in New Orleans (Bergreen 1997, 267).

Armstrong's trumpet playing, specifically the rhetorical style of his phrasing and vibrato, reflects the strong influence of the recordings of Caruso and other operatic singers, to whom he listened devotedly, often improvising along with the records, from the moment he first could afford a phonograph until the end of his life (Giddins 1988, 151).[11] Armstrong perfectly exemplifies what is true of jazz more generally: it not only instantiates the persistence of African retentions and what has been called the 'changing same' of African-American culture, it reminds us that African-American traditions do not simply articulate some essence of African-American character or practice but rather embody the agency and creativity of African-Americans as they engage with and adapt to a changing world by appropriating styles and mixing discourses. Armstrong's music (like all music, perhaps) is thoroughly multicultural. So is Earl Hines's piano solo, which combines swing, elegance and flourishes that betray the influence of Chopin and other European composers.

It is worth emphasising that all of these sounds come to us from a record – an object that was manufactured for sale. Armstrong was denounced throughout much of his career for being too 'commercial': such accusations were common in the 1940s, but Schuller dates Armstrong's fall from late 1928 (1968, 130), only months after he recorded 'West End Blues'! 'By January 1930', Schuller argues, 'the creepy tentacles of commercialism had begun to exert an alarming degree of stylistic constraint' (1989, 165). This charge simply would not have made any sense to Armstrong, whose career as a professional musician freed him from hauling coal and rags, and who saw nothing wrong with wanting to reach lots of people with his music. For his part, Armstrong complained about the beboppers with their 'weird chords' in 1948: 'These young cats now they want to make money first and the hell with the music . . . And look at them young cats too proud to play their horns if you don't pay them more than the old-timers' (Walser 1999, 153–4). That each side could blame the other's failings on the same cause is a reminder that the commercial context of popular music is not a symptom of that music's artistic failure; rather, how we understand that commercial context has much to do with how we value the music. When one writer cites *Kind of Blue* as the only jazz album to reach double-platinum sales status (Nisenson 2000, ix), he is certainly appealing to the album's commercial popularity as some sort of corroboration of its artistic worth, but he is just as surely thereby defining jazz such as to exclude Kenny G, a multi-platinum artist whose recordings can be found in the jazz section of any record store. Arguments over whether certain music is good jazz, or is jazz at all, depend less on simple facts of musical procedure or commercial context than on complicated investments in prestige, identification and values.

One of the main points of this chapter is the claim that self-awareness about our values is important, at least as much so for historians as for anyone else. This directly contradicts the approach of many eminent jazz critics and scholars, such as Schuller: 'In writing this book, my approach to the subject was essentially simple. I imagined myself coming to jazz without any prior knowledge or preconceptions and beginning, *tabula rasa*, to listen to the recordings – systematically and comprehensively' (1989, ix). Schuller thus attempts to forget that he has values, not to mention expertise. But there is no way he can escape either, and his insights spring from his allegiance to the values of modernism. How many jazz musicians would agree with his proclamation that 'the greatness of jazz lies in the fact that it never ceases to develop and change' (*ibid.*, 846)? Miles Davis might, but Louis Armstrong would not; Herbie Hancock perhaps, but not Wynton Marsalis. As Sidney Finkelstein argued in 1948, 'the entire fetish of originality, which causes the most creative musicians often to be called "unoriginal" and the greatest fakers to call themselves "original" composers, is a product of commercialism . . . With the rise of the market and the music industry, "originality" became a necessary part of a salable commodity' (Walser 1999, 137). Schuller's modernism is inseparable from the commercial contexts that enabled jazz to spread around the globe and enabled someone like Armstrong to climb to stardom. We have no way to think about jazz apart from the context within which it is being thought about, apart from the values that lead us to think about it in the first place. And the tactics we use to legitimate jazz produce their own investments and new pleasures. The meanings of jazz change even as we try to explain it or justify our pleasures, and ways of valuing have consequences that can be evaluated in terms of value.

'West End Blues' ends with the trumpet sustaining a high C (i.e., sounding B♭) for four bars – hanging on to that gloriously yearning fifth scale degree, which appears so often in J. S. Bach's trumpet parts because it is such an effective use of the instrument. Armstrong follows with urgent repetitions of a high, bluesy riff, played out of strict time in a rhapsodic burst, with a deft squeeze back up to the high C and an elegant wind-down. After an almost melancholic piano interlude, the band delivers its closing figure, with Armstrong landing in the middle register on the tonic, his warm, vibrant sound radiating assurance and fulfilment. For Armstrong's contemporaneous audience – many of them, like him, black migrants from the South to northern urban centres – this was the sound of success and achievement.[12] Other musical figurations of fulfilment have arisen, yet the powerful, inventive, confident persona Armstrong projected in his performances and recordings has continued to move and attract many people over the years.

Cootie Williams, a trumpeter for many years in Duke Ellington's band, was known for two distinct approaches to the instrument: high, clear, lead trumpet playing, and the growling, gutbucket sound that was an essential component of Ellington's 'jungle music'. Williams used to say of this contrasting pair of voices: 'Those were my two ways of being' (quoted in Dance 1970, 106). Similarly, Christopher Small's work has called our attention to the performative and relational aspects of what he accordingly calls 'musicking'. Small highlights the ways in which music serves as a means of trying on identities, living out ideals, articulating and performing relationships.[13] Sidney Bechet would have agreed: 'The man singing it, the man playing it, he makes a place. For as long as the song is being played, *that's* the place he's been looking for' (Walser 1999, 4). For Bechet, jazz is supremely valuable because it helps us understand the world, it tells us who we are and where we came from, it teaches us what to do, and, most of all, it lets us experience utopia.

One person's utopia, of course, is another's purgatory. We now take it so much for granted that jazz is a soloist's art that we can easily fail to notice how Armstrong at this moment was perhaps the strongest force in transforming jazz's primary orientation from collective improvisation to the dominance of soloists. This is a change in values. King Oliver's band, for example, offered an experience that combined individual freedom with social harmony as horn players interwove their lines with relative equality. With Armstrong, we celebrate the individual virtuoso, for whom other musicians provide an accompaniment, a framework or a stage.

While he was recording 'West End Blues', I doubt that Armstrong was thinking about relationships or identities, nor about revolutionising music, nor about the daily challenges and potential humiliations of being a black man in a racist society. But all of these aspects of his context contributed to making his artistry possible, meaningful and powerful. He was, at least in one sphere, supremely capable, and his heroic stature as a musician sustained and inspired him in his whole existence.[14] He lived this way of being for himself and for everyone who listened. Many of us can still recognise and respond to Armstrong's pride, extraordinary mastery, dignity and sureness. When we do, when we value his jazz, we are valuing a way of being that was more important to him and to many others than anything else, because in a perfect world, that's the way everyone would feel all of the time.

17 The jazz market

DAVE LAING

One of the most striking aspects of the writing on jazz is a reluctance to relate the history of the music to the messy and occasionally sordid economic circumstances of its production. [DEVEAUX 1997, 12]

The purpose of this chapter is to contribute towards a systematic study of those 'economic circumstances' by suggesting two frameworks within which jazz can be situated as part of the wider music business.

The three music markets

The first framework is a 'horizontal' dimension which allows jazz to be viewed in relation to the three general types of music market to be found in the twentieth century: those of traditional (or folk) music, of popular music and of art (or classical) music. At different times jazz has been part of each of these markets.

The principal characteristic of a traditional music market is the close relationship of music to social ritual: the main occasions for music are such events as weddings, funerals, carnivals and festivals. Early jazz activity in New Orleans – the parades, picnics and funerals – included elements of this music culture (see Buerkle and Barker 1973).

In societies subject to such processes as urbanisation and industrialisation, traditional music markets give way to the popular music market that supplies entertainment as a commodity to be consumed within leisure time (see Laing 1969). And from the beginning in New Orleans, the musical elements of a traditional culture were interwoven with the dance jobs, the mobile advertising jobs and other elements of a de-ritualised and commercialised leisure and entertainment economy. From this early period until the demise of the big bands in the mid-1940s, most jazz was performed and recorded according to the demands and protocols of the popular music business.

After big-band jazz had been supplanted by jump-jive (and later rhythm-and-blues and rock-and-roll) as the primary form of popular music for dancing, jazz made only intermittent appearances within the changing popular-music economy, either through its 'crossover' into the world of pop radio and mass record sales or through its 'fusion' with rhythm-and-blues, rock or soul music.

Simultaneously with the decline of the big bands, the bebop emphasis on jazz as music to be listened to, rather than as an accompaniment for dancing, gave credence to the idea that jazz deserved recognition as one of the arts, as a 'concert music, a form of art, not just music you hear in clubs or places where they serve whiskey' (Gillespie 1979, 448) and as 'America's classical music' (see Taylor 1986). As such, jazz would be entitled to share in the economic privileges of western art music, notably its access to subsidy and sponsorship. Apart from some isolated cases, however, jazz has been relatively unsuccessful in attracting institutional support as well as subsidy for individual tours or festivals.

The three sectors of the music business

Jazz occurs within the context of an international music industry, and the image we have of musicians is constructed through the activities of many types of agents: musicians, concert promoters, booking agents, record company executives, recording engineers, jazz club owners and employees, radio producers, critics, audience members and academics . . . any individual might simultaneously or consecutively occupy several positions within the larger jazz world.
[MONSON 1996, 14–15]

A second framework is a 'vertical' approach to the jazz business that considers jazz musicians' position within the three main sectors of the music business – performing, composing and recording.

This discussion must, however, be prefaced by the recognition that any cultural activity rooted in twentieth-century United States will inevitably be marked by the facts of racist exploitation. When writers such as Amiri Baraka (formerly LeRoi Jones) and Frank Kofsky emphatically denounced the omnipresence of racism in the American jazz business, they were often ignored or resented, but much direct testimony from musicians bears out the view that jazz has always had its own form of what today would be called 'institutionalised' racism.[1] This fact has even been recognised by such authors as Richard M. Sudhalter who prefaces his somewhat quixotic attempt to champion 'white jazz' with the admission that 'life for members of the Duke Ellington, Count Basie, Jimmy Lunceford, Cab Calloway and Chick Webb orchestras was neither as comfortable nor as well rewarded as it was for Benny Goodman, Artie Shaw or Dorsey Brothers sidemen' (1999, xi).

Michael Ullman puts the matter in a less emollient way when he writes that 'historically jazz as a commercial product has been manipulated and promoted largely by white businessmen, sometimes dedicated like John Hammond and George Wein, but often irresponsible and uncaring' (1980, 1). This comment also points up the crucial importance to the jazz business of the ensemble of activities practised by the posse of intermediaries or gatekeepers who connect (or stand between) the musician and his or her potential audience.[2] Jazz history provides numerous examples of such intermediaries playing a significant economic role in the careers of musicians.

Performing

Despite the enormous growth of the music recording industry in the latter half of the twentieth century, performing face-to-face to audiences in real time has always been the primary activity of jazz musicians and very few derive greater income from record or composer royalties than from gig fees. A recent survey of musicians in Britain found that, on average, jazz musicians derived 43 per cent of their earnings in 1998 from gigs, 15 per cent from teaching and 30 per cent from non-music sources. Recording, royalties and broadcasts represented only 12 per cent (York and Laing 2000, 11).

The range of performance venues and situations has been wide. From the mid-1920s to the mid-1940s jazz performance in the United States was dominated by the big bands and orchestras that toured constantly or, occasionally, had residencies at theatres, nightclubs or hotels in major cities. Even outside the major metropolises, in the cities of the southwest states there were 'ballrooms, hotels, night clubs, outdoor amusement parks and a Negro population large enough to keep one or more big bands and smaller combos working' (Driggs 1959, 193).

Bebop encouraged the emergence of smaller nightclubs specialising in jazz performance for seated listeners and jazz was promoted at larger concert halls through tours like Norman Granz's Jazz at the Philharmonic and at festivals such as George Wein's pioneering Newport Jazz Festival, launched in 1954. Europe alone now has 300 major jazz festivals including Montreux, North Sea and London. The headline artists of all but the smallest festivals tend to be American and popular US acts can now spend much of the summer in Europe, moving from festival to festival.

The key intermediaries in jazz performance have been booking agents, bandleaders and club-owners. Particularly in the years of Prohibition, jazz musicians' work in nightclubs brought them into contact with organised crime whose interests frequently included investment in entertainment venues (see Morris 1980 and, for a later era, Dannen 1990).

In the big-band era it was vital for bandleaders to gain the favour and support of booking agencies such as Julius Steyn's MCA (Music Corporation of America, known in the 1930s as The Octopus), William Morris and TOBA (the Theater Owners' Booking Agency, colloquially known as 'Tough on Black Asses'). Within the agencies, individual bookers became closely associated with specific bands and in some cases combined the role of booking agent with that of personal manager. This was the role played by Joe Glaser with Louis Armstrong (see Collier 1984) and Willard Alexander with Count Basie and Benny Goodman. Alexander has been described as 'the architect of the big band era' (see Levinson 1999).

While the direct involvement in jazz musicians' careers of agents and other intermediaries such as record companies, publishers and managers is clear, the role of the print and broadcast media in establishing musical reputations should not be ignored. Jazz magazines and jazz radio stations are both economic entities in their own right (providing employment and – sometimes – profits) but also an important influence on public taste. There is no space to discuss the media role further here, except to point to the key role of jazz disc jockeys in promoting new music and the significance of both record reviews and polls of critics and readers in jazz journals.

In the big-band era, bandleaders were sub-contractors, responsible for supplying the musical services guaranteed to venue owners by agents. The management style of many, if not most, leaders was decidedly authoritarian. Harry James's biographer quotes a typical James response to requests for higher wages from his sidemen: 'Anybody who doesn't like what he's getting – he can get lost' (Levinson 1999, 89).

Perhaps the best-documented business career of any bandleader is that of Duke Ellington. In his early years as leader of The Washingtonians (1923–4), each member received $30 a week. This was not a high wage but it was supplemented by tips from nightclub customers, sometimes amounting to $20 a week per musician (Collier 1987, 39). In the late 1930s and early 1940s the Ellington band commanded a fee for a single performance of between $1,250 and $2,000. Ellington paid each of his 16 musicians between $125 and $185 per week, a wage bill of about $2,500. In addition there were travel costs, payments to administrative staff and fees to agents and managers. The overall profit and loss depended directly on the quantity of work offered to the band and the level of fees paid by promoters. According to Richard O. Boyer, the Ellington band made a loss on touring of $1,500 in 1941 when its income was $135,000, but a profit of $4,000 in 1942 on the considerably higher income of $210,000 (Tucker 1993, 244–5).

The musicians in the Ellington band and other leading jazz orchestras were the elite players. At the Ritz Café in Oklahoma City in August 1939, Charlie Christian received $7.50 for three nights' work. A few days later, his weekly wage from Benny Goodman was $150, 'a jump of 2000 per cent!' as Rudi Blesh commented in *Combo USA* (1971).

As a labour-intensive activity, jazz performance is arguably subject to Baumol's Law. Applying economic principles to the performing arts, the American economist William J. Baumol argued that these industries (theatre, opera, classical music) could not benefit from the gains in productivity achieved by automation in conventional production industries and therefore had 'priced themselves out of the market', a situation only to be remedied through subsidy and sponsorship. This external funding (external in the sense that it comes from outside the market) fills the gap between what the consumer is willing to pay and the costs of mounting a performance (see Towse 1997).

The maximisation of audience numbers at festivals can be seen as one strategy to mitigate the effect of Baumol's Law, as can the jazz clubs' 'subsidy' for music from sales of liquor, the recycling of recording income by musicians' unions and the acceptance by musicians of paltry fees so that, in effect, jazz players are subsidising themselves! In the United States, a musician on a local jazz scene in the early 1990s would be paid anything from $25 to more than $100 per gig. Only a few of these, playing 100 or more gigs a year, earned more than $5,000 from jazz. Similarly, one British musician played 197 dates in 1991 and was paid a total of only $8,000 (*Review of Jazz in England* 1995, 9).

In the second half of the twentieth century, however, modern jazz musicians had some success in attracting conventional subsidy and sponsorship, sometimes by presenting jazz as a contemporary concert music worthy of parity of treatment with western classical genres. In the post-bebop era the Modern Jazz Quartet was invited to appear at state-subsidised contemporary music festivals in Europe in the late 1950s (Hentoff 1962, 147), while Keith Jarrett's fee for concert-hall solo appearances in the early 1980s was between $10,000 and $15,000; he also received subsidy through a Guggenheim Award (Carr 1991, 140, 62).

Bridging the gap between the world of commercial music business and the subsidised arts are jazz organisations, made up of musicians, fans or promoters (or a mixture of these). In a number of countries such non-profit bodies have acted as promoters, record labels, publicists, educationalists and pressure groups. Among these groups have been: the United Hot Clubs of America, the fan organisation that initiated the jazz record reissue business in the late 1930s; musicians' self-help bodies such as the Association for the Advancement of Creative Musicians and Jazz Composers Orchestra Association in the United States; and lobbying groups such as the Danish Jazz Association and, in Britain, Jazz Services.

Partly as a result of the work of these bodies, some musicians have been commissioned to write substantial works, tours have received financial support and occasionally CD production has been supported with small grants. The most advanced European country in this respect may be Denmark where in 1994 the Ministry of Culture paid tour support for 40 bands and helped to finance six CDs by local jazz musicians (see *Euro Jazz Book 1996/7*). In addition, many festivals now receive commercial sponsorship, albeit often from alcohol and tobacco companies that also support rock events rather than from the philanthropists and banks that sponsor classical music events.

With two outstanding exceptions, jazz has seldom been granted large-scale institutional funding that is commonplace for symphony orchestras, piano competitions and opera companies. Those exceptions are the Jazzpar Prize of about $35,000 given annually by a Danish jury to an outstanding international performer, and the controversial Jazz at Lincoln Center scheme in New York City whose purpose-built education, performance and broadcast facility will cost $115 million.

Composing

Globally, the business of music composition and publishing was worth over $6 billion annually in the 1990s.[3] This sector of the industry includes sales of printed music, royalties from recordings and performance royalties from broadcasting, concerts and other gigs, background-music companies, the juke-box business and elsewhere. These revenues are directly dependent on the legally established system of music copyright that grants to the author of a composition the right to be paid when that work is performed or reproduced.

That concept of the author was consonant with the nineteenth-century roles of classical music composer and Tin Pan Alley songwriter, each of whom had a clearly defined place in the division of labour within the music business as a whole. Many jazz musicians from Ellington to Marsalis also fit the authorial mould, but the importance to jazz of the skills of interpretation and improvisation on already composed works has placed many of its most inspired practitioners at an economic disadvantage. Equally, there is a history in jazz and other popular musics of the appropriation of the ownership of newly created compositions by individuals who played no part in their creation. The result was a 'confusion that existed, particularly in the minds of business people, concerning the overlapping roles of improvisation, composition and arrangement' (Feather 1986, 147).

Copyright law offers little assistance in resolving this confusion, except to state that copyright can only be granted to the realised form of an idea (in music, a score, a recording or even a performance) and not the idea itself. In legal and business practice the composer of a musical work is simply he or she whose name is attached to it through registration of a piece with a government agency or an author's collection society or simply through attribution when the piece is published as sheet music or is recorded.

Jazz history provides considerable evidence that the originator of a composition was often not credited as the author, or had to suffer a joint credit with someone who had taken no part in the creation of a piece. In the jazz world and the adjacent world of rhythm-and-blues it was commonplace for a publisher or even a bandleader to 'have exercised what might be called a sort of *droit de seigneur* so far as their sidemen's compositions were concerned, either taking over the rights completely or at least sharing them' (Carr 1982, 109).[4]

The economic importance of authorship increased significantly with the growing popularity of records and radio. National copyright laws stipulate that radio and television stations as well as other users of music, including concert halls, juke-box operators and retailers with background music, must pay royalties for music use. The mechanism for collecting such fees and distributing them to composers is the 'collection society' of which the American Society of Composers, Authors and Publishers (ASCAP) and Broadcast Music Inc. (BMI) in the US are among the best-known examples. These organisations are among the most powerful in the music business and have a complex history. BMI was formed in 1941 in part as a counterweight to ASCAP's prejudice against composers in idioms other than classical music and Tin Pan Alley pop (see Ryan 1985). Outside ASCAP, composers had no means by which to claim royalties and Jelly Roll Morton claimed that he had lost $75,000 because he had been refused membership of ASCAP in the 1930s (DeVeaux 1997, 311).

The financial rewards due to the composer or co-author of a recorded work could be considerable. Under national copyright law, the composer receives a proportion of the statutory 'mechanical' royalty (until the 1970s this was usually split 50/50 between the writers and the music publisher). If the music was also printed and sold by the publisher, the composer would be paid a proportion of the retail price of the sheet-music copy, typically 10 per cent. The potential importance of such income can be seen from the example of Duke Ellington: between 1924 and 1944 he was paid a total of $250,000 from these sources (Tucker 1993, 244).

Music publishing was itself a separate and potentially lucrative sector of the music business. Some early jazz composers, notably W. C. Handy and Clarence Williams, formed their own publishing companies with which other composers placed works. It was commonplace for pieces to be sold outright for cash to publishers but composers with market power could demand royalties (see Singer 1992). More recently, jazz composers have formed their own publishing companies and used larger firms for administration purposes only.

Composers of art music have always been dependent on patronage of one kind or another and jazz has received a small amount of such patronage. In 1957 Brandeis University commissioned jazz or 'jazz-oriented' works from six composers, three of whom were working jazz musicians – Jimmy Giuffre,

Charles Mingus and George Russell (Carr 1982, 109). Oscar Peterson's *Easter Suite* was commissioned by the British television company LWT in 1984 (Palmer 1984, 63), though it is difficult to imagine any such commission today.

Recording

The retail value of global sales of recorded music was $37 billion in 2000. The vast majority of this represented spending on popular music of all types. Classical music accounted for about 7 per cent and jazz for little more than 1 per cent.[5] Based on these estimates, the retail value of jazz recordings was between $400 million and $500 million and the number of jazz albums sold between 40 million and 50 million.

At a national level, in 1998 jazz represented 2 per cent of the recorded music market in the US, Russia and the Netherlands but only 1 per cent in Germany and the UK (IFPI 1999, 151). In 2000, jazz sales in the US received an unexpected boost from the publicity surrounding the television series, *Jazz*, produced by Ken Burns, although even then jazz sales remained lower than a decade earlier when jazz was reported to be 4 per cent of the US market.

In the mid-1950s most jazz albums sold fewer than 5,000 copies and the bestsellers between 30,000 and 50,000. Only Miles Davis, Dave Brubeck and a handful of others sold more than this. Fifty years on, the situation has, if anything, deteriorated. In 1996, *Billboard* reported that the latest Sonny Rollins album had sold only 9,000 copies in the US while typical sales for titles issued by Milan's Red Records were between 1,000 and 10,000 in 2000,[6] and 1,000 was the maximum figure for domestic sales of new Finnish jazz albums in the late 1980s (Konttinen 1989).

The recorded-music business has been dominated from its inception by a few vertically integrated record companies (generally known as 'the majors') that control the artist-and-repertoire function (choosing whom to record), manufacturing, marketing and distribution, and have an international network of branches.[7] Today, such companies are mostly divisions of even larger media or electronics corporations. The 'big five' of the present-day record business are BMG (owned by the German media group Bertelsmann), the British-based EMI, Sony of Japan, Universal Music Group (owned by the French firm Vivendi) and Warner Music Group (owned by the US media conglomerate AOL Time Warner).

In the pre-1945 period the majors' predecessors, such as Columbia (now Sony), RCA Victor (now owned by BMG) and Decca (now part of Universal), were significant jazz recording firms, issuing titles by small groups, blues singers and big bands like those of Ellington, Basie and Goodman. Goodman sold millions in the Swing Era, while in the 20-year period from 1924 to 1944, Ellington received $500,000 in record royalties from sales of 20 million discs, i.e., 2.5 cents per disc (Tucker 1993, 245).

The major labels became more fickle in their commitment to jazz as rhythm-and-blues and rock replaced it as a mainstream popular dance music. The former head of Columbia, Clive Davis, summed up their position when he wrote (apropos of Miles Davis's average album sales of 50,000 in the mid-1960s) that '50,000 barely takes you out of red ink' (Davis and Willwerth 1975, 151). Some intrepid producers such as Steve Backer nevertheless attempted to operate a jazz line for a major company, usually with negative results (Ullman 1980, 215–22).

While the majors have intermittently maintained a commitment to jazz, hundreds of smaller specialist 'independent' labels in North America, Europe, Japan and other parts of the world have made the vast majority of new recordings since 1950. The principals of these 'independent' labels have sometimes been owners of jazz record stores, such as Milt Gabler of Commodore in New York, Ross Russell of Dial in Los Angeles and Doug Dobell in London, promoters and club-owners such as Norman Granz (Verve) and Morris Levy (Roulette), managers such as Francis Dreyfus of the Paris-based Dreyfus, or musicians themselves: Charles Mingus's Debut in 1952, Betcar (owned by Betty Carter in the 1970s), the Jazz Composers Orchestra Association label in the 1960s and, in Britain, Carlo Krahmer's Esquire.

In contrast to the transparency of the exchange relation in performance, the economics of recording could be extremely opaque for the musician. While there were (and are) fixed session fees for attendance at the studio and many featured singers and leaders got only fees not royalties, any further payment was based on retail sales and on the record company's ability to account for those sales accurately and honestly. Even those musicians who appeared to have been treated 'fairly' were subject to onerous contractual terms. For example the singer Ruth Brown 'got about $69 for each tune she recorded, she recalls, against a promised royalty of 5 percent. But she actually received little in royalties, because costs of hiring musicians and arrangers, renting recording studios and so on were billed to her account, and – at least on paper – her records did not appear to be making much money for Atlantic' (Deffaa 1996, 38).

Some owners of the new 'independent' labels were unscrupulous and criminal in the way they withheld royalties or exploited the drug habits of musicians. Among the most notorious were such as Herman Lubinsky of Savoy (Deffaa 1996, 85–8) and Bob Weinstock of Prestige (Carr 1982, 79). Many independent label owners also insisted that jazz musicians placed their recorded compositions with the label's in-house publishing company thus ensuring they had a cut from the composer royalties that flowed from record sales.

The most recent phase in jazz recording has been the era of the compact disc, during which the major companies and others (such as Fantasy, owner of the Prestige catalogue) made exceptional profits from reissuing old recordings from their archives in digital form. In the process of concentration of ownership that characterised the record industry from the 1960s, the majors had acquired the catalogues of numerous small jazz labels. EMI/Capitol has Blue Note and Roulette; Universal has Verve, Chess, Impulse, ABC, etc.; and Time Warner has Atlantic. Reissues incur few origination costs and the record companies were initially able to charge high prices because of the novelty of the CD. Along with other forms of music, jazz was subjected to the reissue process, although the original musicians did not often share in the record industry's bonanza, either because the reissues were out of copyright (being older than 50 years) or because the labels claimed they had no contractual obligation to pay royalties on them.

While the Internet holds out the possibility of promoting jazz records to a global audience for a nominal price, the contemporary picture of jazz recording mirrors that of 40 years ago. The major companies have very few active jazz musicians signed to long-term contracts, and there is also a flourishing independent sector. It was reported in 2000 that 200 labels 'regularly release jazz or jazz-related albums in Europe'.[8] With the exception of a few relatively large firms such as ECM (whose *Köln Concert* by Keith Jarrett is one of the few jazz albums to have sold over one million), these were very small companies owned by enthusiasts for whom sales of 10,000 were exceptional. In France, a network of 15 labels had active catalogues totalling 600 titles by 300 artists with annual sales of 200,000 units and exports to 30 countries (see Queroy 1996).

This brief resumé of the jazz business highlights the fact that jazz continues to occupy an uneasy and precarious place within the music business as a whole. While there continue to be occasional 'crossover' successes as new forms of pop music 'discover' jazz and integrate elements into their sound, the unpredictability of an improvised genre does not fit with the mainstream pop-music business. On the other side, the strenuous attempts to brand jazz as 'art' have resulted in a few spectacular successes such as the Lincoln Center project, but more generally jazz's share of subsidy and sponsorship remains a fraction of that given to western classical music. An anonymous Belgian contributor to the 1996 edition of the *Euro Jazz Book* described the three types of explanation offered by different interest groups for the lack of state support for jazz as art. These were 'the elitist explanation ("the public at large will never understand jazz"), the paranoid explanation ("stuck between classical and popular music, jazz is the victim of a conspiracy") and the ideological explanation ("as it is the music of rebellion and organised anarchy, jazz cannot and must not expect more than a formal consideration on the part of the public authorities")' (1996, 16).

In business terms, then, jazz remains a music 'in between' the two economic models of market entertainment and subsidised art (see Haynes *et al.* 1982); or, to borrow DeVeaux's description of bebop, it 'occupies a precarious position on the outskirts of the business as an art-music without portfolio'.

18 Images of jazz

KRIN GABBARD

Although novelists, film-makers and photographers are likely to rely upon familiar myths when they create images of jazz, they can also bring new life to a music that can be opaque, even to the initiated. As David Yaffe has argued, a novelist such as Ralph Ellison can surpass both musicologists and critics when, for example, he links Louis Armstrong's music with his metaphor of invisibility: 'Sometimes you're ahead and sometimes behind. Instead of the swift and imperceptible flowing of time, you are aware of its nodes, those points where time stands still or from which it leaps ahead. And you slip into the breaks and look around' (Ellison 1952, 8). In Ellison's metaphors, Yaffe hears a definition of swing more convincing than one based on empirical data or formal analysis.[1] At their best, fiction, cinema and photography produce illuminating, often startling representations of jazz through different sets of metaphors appropriate to the history and aesthetics of each medium. In hopes of identifying these metaphors and how they function, I devote special attention to 'tutor texts' that facilitate a long view of jazz within specific art forms. Although these texts may not be the most canonical, they may be the most representative. I begin with a book that sums up how images of jazz were presented during the twentieth century.

Jazz in fiction

The eponymous hero of *The Bear Comes Home*, by Rafi Zabor (1997), is a Kodiak grizzly of smaller proportions than most.[2] (Grizzly bears generally achieve an adult weight of approximately 410 kilos but, perhaps so that Zabor's bear can pass for human in a bulky trenchcoat and a big hat, the author has given him only half that weight.) Otherwise, the Bear, as he is called throughout the novel, is indistinguishable from other members of his species. He also speaks perfect English and plays the alto saxophone in the tradition of Charlie Parker, Jackie McLean and Ornette Coleman. The *Encyclopaedia Britannica* describes grizzlies as 'unpredictable, often sullen and ill-tempered'. Accordingly, the Bear has difficulties with record producers, children and policemen; at one point he is literally hunted down by the police and confined in a cell. Nevertheless, the Bear is extremely learned, witty and emotionally capable, ultimately achieving a satisfying romantic relationship with a human female. The 'sullen and ill-tempered' aspects of his character are ultimately attributable to his artist's temperament and the usual exploitation of jazz artists and trained animals.

The Bear Comes Home is intended for an audience of intellectual jazz connoisseurs. Mozart, Stendhal and Kafka are cited almost as often as Parker, Charles Mingus and Thelonious Monk. The narrator regularly refers to jazz lore, casually mentioning Carla Bley's stint as a cigarette girl at Birdland, Mingus's increasing tendency to resemble his bass as he aged and the ironies in King Pleasure's lyrics to 'Parker's Mood'. The novel also abounds with playful references to bears in literature, including a climactic nod to Goldilocks as well as a direct quotation of Shakespeare's most famous stage direction, 'exit, pursued by a bear' (*The Winter's Tale*, Act III, scene 3). Zabor frequently ignores the line between fiction and documentary by enlivening his narrative with walk-ons from real-life artists such as Coleman, Lester Bowie, Arthur Blythe, Charlie Haden and Billy Hart. He also finds room for other figures well known to New York jazz *cognoscenti*, including the notoriously long-winded jazz disc jockey who discourses at length about what Monk and his sidemen had for lunch between takes of 'Bye-ya'. When the Bear first begins playing in public, he is denounced by Wynton Marsalis for presenting 'a degrading image of the jazz musician'.

The choice of a bear as protagonist is especially appropriate for this hulking, often overwritten novel. But as the hero of a jazz novel, a saxophone-playing bear wryly invites allegorical readings. On the one hand, there is virtually no discussion of race for much of the first half of *The Bear Comes Home*. The Bear could represent African-American men, whose complex inner lives have little in common with the menacing beasts for which they are regularly mistaken. On the other hand, any jazz musician – black or white – is a stranger in a strange land, inhabiting a subculture that seems completely bizarre to many but utterly natural to its denizens. And as Will Straw has observed in a discussion of writing about jazz and popular music (1997, 8), the figure of the 'brute' often appears among the masculine types favoured by followers of the music. Straw points out that 'pure and uncultivated instinctuality' can be an admired aspect of a musician's stance. There is also a certain brutish power even in the connoisseur's constructions of the jazz artist, especially when the artist is African-American. As we shall see, aspects of the black jazz artist as brute were still present as late as 1988 in *Bird*, Clint Eastwood's film about Parker. Indeed, the hypermasculine image of the black jazz artist is a regular element in what David Meltzer has called the 'permissible racism' of jazz *aficionados*, who celebrate the beauty and spontaneity of the music while also harbouring – at least in some cases – fantasies of idealised primitivism (Meltzer 1993, 4). Although

Zabor's Bear resembles many of the most admired jazz artists by possessing substantial knowledge of the jazz tradition and by deploying it regularly in his performances, he is also capable of distancing himself from that tradition and playing with spontaneity, strength and, in keeping with the metaphor, instinct. If, in fact, an allegorical reading is the best way to approach *The Bear Comes Home*, then a highly intellectual, musically inspired bear may be an ingenious way of representing the best jazz artists' careful acquisition of a revered tradition as well as the brute instinct necessary for remaking that tradition.

Stripped of its allegory, *The Bear Comes Home* may even provide a familiar characterisation of jazz artists and the jazz life. Sudhalter has insisted that the book 'easily transcends its genre' (1999b, 1), but the book treads several paths well known to readers of jazz fiction. In particular, *The Bear Comes Home* plays with two of the most important tropes in jazz fiction identified by Michael Titlestad (1999): the notion that the improvising jazz artist becomes inseparable from his (the protagonist is almost always male) instrument, and the idea that the improvising musician can achieve some kind of transcendence.

As Titlestad demonstrates, writers of jazz fiction frequently adopt the conceit of an artist's body fusing, sometimes mystically, with a musical instrument. An especially honoured text that exploits this convention is Michael Ondaatje's *Coming Through Slaughter* (1976), in which a fictionalised Buddy Bolden lives out many of the myths that make up his legend. Jelly Roll Morton, for example, said that Bolden 'went crazy because he really blew his brains out through the trumpet' (Lomax 1950, 60). In one of Bolden's internal monologues in Ondaatje's novel, the trumpeter combines sexual experience with musical performance, ultimately describing how his own blood 'comes up flooding past my heart in a mad parade, it is coming through my teeth, it is into the cornet' (*ibid.*, 131). Anchored in the body of the musician, the instrument that expresses so much sexuality becomes itself sexualised.

But even when sexuality is not explicitly evoked, the jazz artist in fiction often fuses with an instrument. In James Baldwin's 'Sonny's Blues', the narrator realises the sacrifices his jazz-pianist brother must make in attempting to make music out of 'the roar rising from the void'. Watching the face of his brother, the narrator understands 'how awful the relationship must be between the musician and his instrument. He has to fill it, this instrument, with the breath of life, his own. He has to make it do what he wants it to do' (Baldwin 1965, 127). We can find another type of yoking of musician to instrument in John Clellon Holmes's novel, *The Horn* (1958). The protagonist is a tenor saxophonist named Edgar Poole, based closely on Lester Young. Like Young, Poole holds his tenor away from his body and parallel to the floor, like 'some metallic albatross caught insecurely in his two hands, struggling to resume flight' (Holmes 1958, 8). As with so many images of jazz artists, this one suggests that musicians struggle with both their bodies and their instruments in order to create music.

Trapped in the body of an animal, Zabor's Bear plays the saxophone with that additional degree of bodiliness that allegedly separates the jazz artist from 'ordinary' musicians who merely use an instrument to read off music written by someone else. According to this myth, non-jazz musicians do not achieve that oneness that characterises jazz performance at its most inspired. As Titlestad argues, jazz writers have taken this myth into religious, even mystical territory. At a climactic gig at a Brooklyn club called 'The Bridge' (in honour of Sonny Rollins), the Bear takes a solo that allows him a rare moment of self-transcendence in which he is 'plucked out of existence like a cheap suit' (Zabor 1997, 454). A (typically) long passage describes the Bear's visions as he solos with an exhilaration previously unavailable to him. Here is an excerpt:

> He saw the treasured geometry of his lights and vitals, the wellscanned signature of his timeless self erased by waves of greater light, the vessel bursting, and as the Bear sped to the limits of his own transcendent outline, he could discern details – gardens, geometrics, geometric gardens, fine dust and starry singularities, all the declensions of Life into lives – rushing toward annihilation and embrace, their mayfly constructions swept away, since under these circumstances even metaphysical flesh was grass.   [453]

In the midst of this vision, the Bear even sees the face of Coltrane, the one figure in jazz history who has inspired an organised religious following. The Saint John Coltrane African Orthodox Church is in San Francisco and has figured prominently in at least one jazz novel, a mystery about a serial killer of successful 'jazz-lite' musicians.[3]

The quasi-religious moment of transcendence through jazz takes different forms in different narratives. In 'Sonny's Blues', the jazz artist behaves like a mystic, 'wrapped up in some cloud, some fire, some vision all his own' (Baldwin 1965, 114). Edgar Poole of *The Horn* makes dangerous pilgrimages into the unknown with his saxophone, identified as 'the holy vessel of American song' (Holmes 1958, 36). The spiritual dimensions of jazz seem especially important to African-American writers. Amiri Baraka hints at why this may be the case when he clarifies the cultural positions of two canonical trumpeters from the 1920s. Armstrong, according to Baraka, functioned as 'an honored priest of his culture', while Bix Beiderbecke, a member of the white bourgeoisie from Davenport, Iowa, was 'an instinctual intellectual' with an emotional life 'based on his conscious or unconscious disapproval of most of the sacraments of his culture' (L. Jones [Baraka] 1963, 154).

At the risk of essentialising jazz writers according to race, I would suggest that, on the one hand, African-American authors are more likely to characterise jazz musicians in Baraka's terms as priest-like. White writers, on the other hand, are more likely to celebrate the subversiveness of jazz artists as they refuse their culture's 'sacraments'. Especially in the 1950s, the Beats and other oppositional writers found great opportunity for rebellion in jazz. *The Sound* (1961), Ross Russell's *roman à clef* about Parker, has many of these elements, as do the novels of Jack Kerouac. Thomas Pynchon, who expressed sympathy with the Beats and their desire to *épater le bourgeois* (1984, 7), falls back on this tradition in a memorable scene in *Gravity's Rainbow* (1973). Parker's legendary discovery of bebop harmony while soloing on 'Cherokee' in 1939 becomes a kind of cinematic soundtrack for the hallucinatory moment when Pynchon's character Slothrop vomits up a hamburger, a Clark bar, a half-bottle of Moxie and 'the cherry from some Radcliffe girl's old-fashioned' (1973, 63). In other words, Parker subverts 'Cherokee', which Pynchon calls 'one more lie about white crimes' (*ibid.*), while the hero expels the familiar garbage of white American culture from his body. By contrast, James Baldwin's 'Sonny's Blues' often invokes religious imagery to describe Sonny's life in jazz. Think also of Ellison's Invisible Man, who finds Armstrong to be the perfect muse as he retreats into invisibility, presumably to create a novel that will tell the truth about Negroes in the United States. Even when jazz strikes a character in an African-American novel as shocking and vulgar, as seems to be the case for the young and innocent Sandy of Langston Hughes's *Not Without Laughter* (1969), the experience of watching musicians and dancers gracefully sway and gyrate together becomes a crucial moment in the child's maturation. Previously protected from jazz and the corresponding aspects of African-American culture by his puritanical aunt, Sandy suddenly senses the transformative, even redemptive power of jazz: 'Four homeless, plug-ugly niggers, that's all they were, playing mean old loveless blues in a hot, crowded little dance-hall in a Kansas town on Friday night. Playing the heart out of loneliness with a wide-mouthed leader, who sang everybody's troubles until they became his own' (Hughes 1969, 105).

In much of the jazz fiction written outside the United States, the potential of jazz to upset bourgeois decorum becomes a central motif. The novels and stories of Josef Škvorecký are probably the most celebrated examples of jazz as the Dionysian alternative to the repressions of a totalitarian regime. In stories such as 'The Bass Saxophone' and 'Red Music' and novels such as *The Cowards* and *The Swell Season*, Škvorecký repeatedly holds up jazz – even ragtag versions played by clowns and barely musical teenagers – as 'a sharp thorn in the side of the power-hungry men, from Hitler to Brezhnev, who successfully ruled in my native land' (1979, 26). Milan Kundera found a similar function for jazz in his novels, including *The Joke* (1992), in which the music takes on great political significance, representing everything that is free, vital and forbidden. According to Titlestad (1999, 45), a black South African poet named Kelwyn Sole even looked to the repression of jazz in Eastern Europe as a vehicle for critiquing his own country's policies during the height of the apartheid era.

Like many poets inspired by jazz, Sole uses the music as a paradigm for writing even more than as a subject for impressionistic description. As Michael Jarrett has brilliantly demonstrated (1999, 45–56), Ondaatje's *Coming Through Slaughter* may be the best example of a novel that looks to improvised jazz for its structure. Toni Morrison's *Jazz* (1993) and Xam Wilson Cartiér's *Be-Bop, Re-Bop* (1987) also attempt to appropriate the eccentricities of jazz harmony and rhythm into the texture of the novel. Leland Chambers has even argued (1995) that the several accounts of Gypsy's death in Eudora Welty's story 'Powerhouse' (in Breton 1991) can be read as parallels to the fourteen choruses that Powerhouse performs at the piano. But, however much we might admire these books, they take us away from the *images* of jazz that are the subject of this chapter. Much the same can be said for the jazz-inspired paintings of Jackson Pollock, Piet Mondrian and Stuart Davis, not to mention the paper cut-outs of circus figures that Henri Matisse called 'Jazz' (see Hadler 1983).

Jazz and photography

Certainly the best place to find compelling images of jazz is photography. William Claxton may have transformed the image of jazz musicians (and edged popular representations of masculinity closer to androgyny) when he extensively documented the youthful beauty of Chet Baker in the early 1950s. As Jarrett has pointed out (1995), Claxton was especially imaginative when he posed Rollins wearing a cowboy outfit in the Californian desert for the cover of the 1957 LP, *Way Out West*, thus comparing the saxophonist to a gunslinger and suggesting a connection between innovation in jazz and America's westward expansion.

The photos that Francis Wolff took for the celebrated Blue Note album covers of the 1950s and 1960s consistently portray black artists as good-natured, dignified and even a bit adventuresome (see Marsh *et al.* 1991). With their dark glasses, their cigarettes and their streamlined cars, they represent a standard of 'cool' to which subsequent generations still aspire. Rock-and-roller Joe Jackson actually posed for an album cover that unambiguously recalled the front of *Sonny Rollins, Vol. 2*, the tenor saxophonist's 1957 LP with J. J. Johnson, Horace Silver and Art Blakey. The

Blue Note album covers were of course designed to promote the recordings of the artists, and they are not unusual in idealising jazz musicians and their artistry. Even Lee Friedlander's stark photos of Coleman's 1960 quartet with Ed Blackwell, Don Cherry and Charlie Haden suggest purposefulness, strength and even a touch of the black nationalism that was then on the rise. (See, in particular, the cover of the Atlantic LP, *This Is Our Music.*)

The African-American photographer, Roy DeCarava, creates images of jazz that are seldom as idealised as those on Blue Note albums. Like Milt Hinton, the black bassist and photographer who worked regularly as a jazz artist from 1931 until the end of the century, DeCarava surely benefited from his ability to put black artists at ease. He often finds new ways of presenting important artists, including a playful Duke Ellington from 1967, a flirtatious Sarah Vaughan from 1956 and a quizzical Mary Lou Williams from 1952. But DeCarava also seems interested in rendering the transcendence that jazz writers have attempted to describe in prose. Often allowing his images to blur and even presenting them in semi-darkness, DeCarava depicts the labour of jazz that can lead the perspiring, grimacing musician to a level of consciousness that few have witnessed, let alone experienced. Many of DeCarava's photographs of Coltrane carry this valence, including the extraordinary photo of him in a tight embrace with Ben Webster in 1960 (Galassi 1996, 46). Webster, who is taller than the younger man, appears to be pulling Coltrane to his neck in a gesture that connotes a nurturing spirit as much as affection. Coltrane presses his face against Webster as if to absorb some of his revered and beloved predecessor's essence. Few photographers have presented so revealing an image of the relationship between two jazz musicians, an image that is even more remarkable for its absence of musical instruments.

The best-known photographs of William P. Gottlieb tend to be less intense than DeCarava's, at least in part because they come from *The Golden Age of Jazz* (1995), the title of Gottlieb's famous collection of images. Jazz became less golden when it lost its popularity in the 1950s and 1960s, perhaps because too many white Americans began associating the term with black artists such as Coltrane who appeared to be angry or simply inaccessible. Nevertheless, Gottlieb's work does more than simply promote the artists. His late-1940s photograph of a dignified Ella Fitzgerald in a white, feathery hat is typical (see Plate 18.1). The singer had dropped by a 52nd Street club to hear Dizzy Gillespie as well as his bassist, Ray Brown, whom she would later marry. While the singer closes her eyes and seems to lose herself in the lyric, Gillespie appears in the right margin smiling dreamily and perhaps flirtatiously at Fitzgerald. Ray Brown, at the other side of the photo, seems to be eyeing Gillespie with a trace of suspicion. In the bottom foreground of the picture is the balding head of the Danish jazz connoisseur

Plate 18.1 Ella Fitzgerald with Dizzy Gillespie and Ray Brown: photograph © William P. Gottlieb

and record producer, Timme Rosenkrantz. In his note to the photograph, Gottlieb points out that Rosenkrantz was a titled aristocrat. With this one image Gottlieb has played with the complex social (and sexual) milieu in which the music takes place, as well as the vastly diverse levels on which people can listen to it. In many of his photographs, Gottlieb tries hard to frame his artists with the spellbound faces of people watching and listening. Even when his subjects are alone, he frames them with mirrors in dressing rooms where the various accessories always tell us a great deal. In a well-known photograph from the 1940s, a smiling, dapper Duke Ellington poses in front of a piano. This is the same dressing room in which Gottlieb also photographed white bandleader Glen Gray with his golf clubs and a target pistol.

Jazz and cinema

In turning to cinematic images of jazz, I start with another representative text, but one that has little in common with either Zabor's *The Bear Comes Home* or the photographs of DeCarava. *The Benny Goodman Story*, directed in 1955 by Valentine Davies, may be the most typical of all American jazz films. As I have suggested elsewhere (1996, 54–8), *The Benny Goodman Story* resembles several other biographical films in recalling *The Jazz Singer* (1927), the breakthrough film that first presented large audiences with the image *and* the sound of a man singing. Like the blacked-up singer played by Al Jolson in the 1927 film, the protagonist of *The Benny Goodman Story* is a poor Jewish boy who overcomes his father's opposition to popular music and becomes extremely successful playing music associated with African-Americans. Along the way, the protagonists of both films acquire beautiful gentile women while maintaining the uncritical adulation of their mothers. Both artists also have the uncanny ability to maintain strong roots in their Jewish heritage even as they forge ahead with a music beloved by a large American audience. Just as Jolson can sing 'Kol Nidre' in the temple on the holiest day of the Jewish calendar and then perform 'Mammy' in blackface in the Wintergarden Theatre, so can Benny arrange for the pop tune 'And the Angels Sing', performed by the whiter-than-white Martha Tilton, to segue into a klezmer-inflected solo by Jewish trumpeter Ziggy Elman at the film's climactic concert at Carnegie Hall. Even though *The Jazz Singer* is presented as fiction and *The Benny Goodman Story* is presented as biography, an American narrative of ethnic assimilation through jazz has become the inevitable backbone of supposedly true stories. Even earlier, the story of bandleader Ted Lewis's ascent was given a *Jazz Singer* plot in *Is Everybody Happy?* (1943), as was – not surprisingly – Al Jolson's early history in *The Jolson Story* (1946). Both men overcome the obstacles of Jewish fathers opposed to secular music before they become stars, and both transform the supposedly primitive music of black Americans.

But whereas Al Jolson does not interact with African-Americans in the original *Jazz Singer*, the hero of *The Benny Goodman Story* has several encounters with 'authentic' jazz artists of colour. In fact, the Goodman film makes the African-American artists, Teddy Wilson and Lionel Hampton, significant presences throughout the narrative. The hero's first and most significant encounter with a black artist, however, takes place just after the teenaged Benny has been humiliated by a young woman who laughs at him for wearing short trousers. Moments after this sexualised degradation, Benny wanders into a ballroom to hear the music of a group of New Orleans musicians led by trombonist Kid Ory, appearing as himself in the film (as do, later on, Wilson and Hampton). Fascinated by the unfamiliar sounds, Benny asks Ory where the music comes from. In a speech that probably does not reflect Ory's own attitudes, the trombonist insists that the music is 'nothing special', that most of the musicians cannot read music, and that they just 'swing on out and play what they feel'. Benny asks if he can join in and immediately plays a convincing solo in New Orleans style (Goodman himself dubbed in the clarinet solos throughout the film). With only the vaguest familiarity with jazz, the young clarinettist has no difficulty keeping up with the New Orleans veterans. The film seems to suggest that Benny's romantic mishap has given him a new depth of feeling that finds expression through the medium of jazz, in which untutored artists simply play what they feel. As is frequently the case in American narratives, the untutored artists are people of colour.

Later in *The Benny Goodman Story* the mature Benny (played by Steve Allen) supposedly transforms the music of New Orleans by giving it a new sophistication. The film goes so far as to acknowledge the role that the black composer and orchestra-leader Fletcher Henderson played in the band's first successes with audiences. It was Henderson's arrangements, after all, that were crucial to Goodman's success with a large audience in 1935. In fact, Henderson (played by Sammy Davis, Sr) is nearby when Ory returns to tell Benny that he has 'the best band I ever heard anywhere'. Significantly, Ory reappears just as Benny has begun to fall in love with Alice Hammond (Donna Reed), the woman he eventually marries. Benny thanks Ory for the compliment, casually hands his clarinet to Henderson ('Fletch, could you hold this, please?'), and quickly moves to the side of Alice as she enters the room.

These are crucial moments in the familiar narrative of the white jazz artist: an older black artist acknowledges the superiority of the white artist at the same time as the sexual maturity of the white jazz hero is tied to his mastery of black music. The scene is staged so that Henderson is there to assist the hero in his romantic progress as much as to provide the arrangements that made Goodman a millionaire. Throughout the 1940s and 1950s, Hollywood repeatedly told the story of white jazz artists in which black musicians played these kinds of marginal but essential role. The music of the white hero is sanctified by a black musician in *Birth of the Blues* (1941), *Blues in the Night* (1941), *Carnegie Hall* (1947) and *Young Man with a Horn* (1950). And in both *The Glenn Miller Story* (1954) and *The Five Pennies* (the filmed biography of Red Nichols, released in 1959), a white brass-player performs with the real-life Armstrong in a Harlem nightclub just before he consummates a romantic relationship with a woman. By the implicit logic of the film, Armstrong authorises the musical *and* the sexual success of the white musicians.

Conventions drawn from *The Jazz Singer* as well as myths of white artists surpassing black veterans were so well established by 1959 that they were even recapitulated in *St Louis Blues*, the biography of the black composer W. C. Handy (played by Nat King Cole). Like Jolson, Goodman and many other white heroes, Handy learns from 'primitive' black musicians, overcomes the opposition of his clergyman father to popular music, indulges in a flirtation with the highly sexualised Gogo Germaine (Eartha Kitt, essentially standing in for the gentile goddess), and crosses over to mainstream success at the finale when he performs with a symphony orchestra made up entirely of white musicians. In large part because he was played by Cole, one of the few black artists to attract a substantial white following in the 1950s, Handy was effectively configured as a white hero.

By the time of *St Louis Blues*, however, jazz had ceased to be America's popular music, and the nostalgia for older jazz had run its course. There were no more biopics about white jazz musicians after 1959 (although films about Chet Baker, Stan Getz and Louis Prima are 'in development'). But as jazz became a music for the elite, it could easily be denounced as pretentious in a film such as *Jailhouse Rock* (1957), a vehicle for Elvis Presley (see page 79). In more ambitious films, the music could be associated with highly ethical artists like the characters played by Martin Milner in *The Sweet Smell of Success* (1957) and Gerry Mulligan in *The Subterraneans* (1960). Significantly, both of these glorified white musicians perform with black artists, who validate the white men's broadmindedness while subliminally shoring up their masculinity. The actual black artists in these films (Chico Hamilton in *The Sweet Smell of Success*, and Art Farmer and Dave Bailey in *The Subterraneans*) have little else to do except play the music.

This is not to say that black jazz artists were never allowed centre stage in the American cinema. Both Bessie Smith and Duke Ellington starred in short films directed by Dudley Murphy in 1929. Smith plays an abused, gin-swilling woman in *St Louis Blues* (not to be confused with the Handy film from 1959), and Ellington plays a stylishly dressed but principled composer/bandleader in *Black and Tan*. The degraded image of Smith and the idealised portrait of Ellington in two films from the same year by the same director surely reflect the personal charisma of Ellington as much as the racist stereotypes associated with dark-skinned women such as Smith. And, of course, black artists frequently starred in 'race films', made with all-black casts explicitly for African-American audiences. *Jivin' in Be-Bop* (1947) provided generous portions of Gillespie's big band, not to mention his witty repartee with a master of ceremonies. A much more ambitious film was *Broken Strings*, directed by Clarence Muse in 1940. In one sense another remake of *The Jazz Singer*, *Broken Strings* showed the healing effects of jazz on a classical violinist (played by Muse himself) who had forbidden his son to play popular music. After his hands have been paralysed in an accident, the violinist miraculously recovers and finds himself clapping in spite of himself when his son uses the occasion of a classical concert to break into a joyous jazz performance.

But these films were not typical of the dominant American film industry. In the 1930s and 1940s, black jazz artists often appeared in short scenes that could easily be removed for audiences unnerved by the sight of African-Americans. Even the most estimable artists were usually presented as grotesques. Think of Cab Calloway wildly waving his hair in *The Big Broadcast* (1932) or Fats Waller exercising his lips and eyebrows in *Stormy Weather* (1943), an image that surfaced even earlier when Eudora Welty created the macabre character 'Powerhouse' after she saw a performance by Waller in the 1930s (Breton 1991, 29–43). By the 1950s, black jazz musicians might appear as dignified if marginal attachments to the hero, as in *The Benny Goodman Story*, or as the providers of a romantic atmosphere, as when Benny Carter elegantly serenades Gregory Peck and Ava Gardner in *The Snows of Kilimanjaro* (1952).

In the 1960s and after, African-American jazz artists occasionally became the subjects of feature films, although the films were almost always low-budget and independently produced. In 1966, for example, two black-and-white films appeared that were loosely based on the lives of black jazz musicians. *Sweet Love Bitter* starred Dick Gregory as Richie 'Eagle' Stokes, based on Charlie Parker, and Sammy Davis, Jr played the eponymous hero loosely based on Miles Davis in *A Man Called Adam*. Both films went well beyond familiar Hollywood practice by representing the climate of hatred and neglect in which black artists have historically performed, but the two films also chose to frame the lives of the jazz musicians within the gaze of attractive white actors. In *Sweet Love Bitter*, the narrative begins and ends with the actions of Dave (Don Murray), a college teacher who befriends Richie and struggles to make sense of the saxophonist's self-destructive behaviour. Similarly, in *A Man Called Adam*, the young trumpeter Vincent (Frank Sinatra, Jr) endures abusive treatment from Adam but is there to mourn when the black hero dies, the victim of the even greater abuse that a black artist must suffer.

Little had changed by the 1980s with the appearance of *Round Midnight* (1986) and *Bird* (1988), both made on small budgets and mostly ignored by audiences. Like the black biopics of the 1960s, neither film sought to represent the kind of transcendence that occurs in jazz literature. *Round Midnight* starred Dexter Gordon as a figure based on both Bud Powell and Lester Young, while *Bird* starred Forest Whitaker as Charlie Parker. Significantly, both Gordon and Whitaker are large men, embodying that aspect of white mythology that sees black jazz artists as idealised brutes. Both musicians in the two films turn to drugs and alcohol in hopes of easing their sufferings in a world that cannot accommodate their bulkily talented souls. And, again, important white characters stand between the black musician and the audience to interpret the otherwise incomprehensible behaviour. In *Round Midnight*, the French commercial artist Francis (François Cluzet) is the one character who truly understands the music and the needs of Dale Turner (Dexter Gordon) and protects him from a large group of people, both black and white, who would take advantage of him. In *Bird*, Parker's common-law wife Chan (Diane Venora) and the trumpeter Red Rodney (Michael Zelniker) consistently look after the welfare of Parker and interpret his actions for the spectator. At one point in *Bird*, Chan explains that her saxophonist-husband's unprovoked attack upon a white inmate in an institution is the result of his need to feel *something*, even the pain that comes with a fight, after he has been deprived of drugs and alcohol. The film seldom gives Parker the opportunity to give his side of the story. Unlike Benny Goodman, Glenn Miller and the white hero of *The Jazz Singer*, the protagonists of the black biopics live on a downward trajectory in spite of their abilities as artists. Audiences for the black jazz biopics were invited to condemn America's neglect of great artists at the same time as white liberal spectators could identify with their surrogates in the films who understood the music, often better than the black artists themselves.

But there are also narratives of white jazz musicians laid low by substance abuse and the philistine attitudes of the public. Bix Beiderbecke, who drank himself to death at the age of 28, inspired what may have been the first jazz novel, Dorothy Baker's *Young Man with a Horn* (1938), as well as the 1950 film with the same title. For Vance Bourjaily, Baker's novel was the first version of 'The Story':

> The Story goes like this: a musician of genius, frustrated by the discrepancy between what he can achieve and the crummy life musicians lead (because of racial discrimination, or the demand that the music be made commercial, or because he has a potential he can't reach), goes mad, or destroys himself with alcohol and drugs. The Story might be a romance, but it is a valid one. [1987, 44]

Bruce Weber's documentary film on Chet Baker, *Let's Get Lost* (1988), certainly adopted this narrative, and the feature film of Baker's life, in which Leonardo DiCaprio is scheduled to star, will probably also be a desultory experience.

The view of jazz artists as self-destructive and intentionally marginal began to wane at the end of the twentieth century. Partially in response to the old clichés of 'The Story', and partially because jazz was gaining serious cultural capital, new forms of the jazz narrative were invented. I'm thinking in particular of the documentaries broadcast on American public television and the cable network Bravo as part of a series titled, appropriately, 'American Masters'. These programmes presented artists such as Ellington, Parker, Coltrane, Armstrong, Sarah Vaughan, Billie Holiday and Monk as significant figures whose lives are consistent with their achievements as artists. Kendrick Simmons and Gary Giddins say much at the outset by naming their 1987 documentary *Celebrating Bird: The Triumph of Charlie Parker*. The programmes soft-pedal the troubling incidents in the biographies of Monk, Parker and Holiday, often bordering on the kind of hagiography that until recently has only been afforded to canonical figures from classical music.

The best evidence that there is a viable middle path between 'The Story' and the saints' lives of the 'American Masters' series may be two films directed by Robert Altman in the 1990s. In *Short Cuts* (1993), based on the short fiction of Raymond Carver, the Jazz Singer Tess (Annie Ross) and her cellist daughter Zoe (Lori Singer) provide a key to understanding how the many narratives of the film might fit together. Tess and Zoe represent, respectively, characters who wear their emotions on their sleeves, and those who repress their feelings until they explode – or, like Zoe, commit suicide. In addition, some characters in *Short Cuts* are improvisers like Tess, while others seem to need scripts such as Zoe reads when she plays classical music on her cello. Altman's film is remarkable enough in showing Annie Ross/Tess singing in real time with her band; it is even more unusual in making her story central to all the narratives and in refusing either to pathologise or idealise her career as a jazz artist.

On one level Altman's *Kansas City* (1996) is about kidnapping and politics in the midwestern city, but the film is also about the jazz of 1934 with biographically accurate references to Parker, Count Basie and Bennie Moten. The highlight of the film is the musical competition between Lester Young (Joshua Redman) and Coleman Hawkins (Craig Handy). As Hawkins, Handy even pauses to remove his coat as in the perhaps mythological account of how the upstart Young overwhelmed the revered Hawkins when he passed through Kansas City with Henderson's orchestra in 1934. The cutting contest between musicians takes place at the same time as another 'cutting session' in which a group of African-American gangsters repeatedly stab a turncoat member of their group. When the saxophonists finally bring their contest to an end, they shake hands as a sign of mutual respect. The saxophone competition and the brutal stabbing of the gangster are cut together so that the black men in the alley are killing one of their own at the same time that the black musicians are engaging in the richest kind of co-operation. Like *The Bear Comes Home*, the film is an especially thoughtful appropriation of jazz after many years of images that used jazz to promote ideological and racial agenda rather than the music itself.[4]

Notes

The publisher has used its best endeavours to ensure that the URLs for external websites referred to in this book are correct and active at the time of going to press. However, the publisher has no responsibility for the websites and can make no guarantee that a site will remain live or that the content is or will remain appropriate.

1 The identity of jazz

1 *Livery Stable Blues*, Victor 18255, 1917; *Tiger Rag*, Victor 18472, 1918; and others. Goddard notes that, within a few weeks of the first of these releases, 'the market was flooded with dozens of imitations' (1979, 23).

2 Perhaps most notable of these were the recordings, beginning in 1902, of Italian tenor Enrico Caruso

3 The term was first used on advertising for OKeh records and became commonplace from 1923: see Dixon and Godrich 1970, 17.

4 For example, 1929 saw the emergence of the first modern entertainment corporation, Radio Corporation of America (RCA).

5 No entry for copyright or performing right appears in *The New Grove Dictionary of Jazz* (Kernfeld 1988).

6 For further discussion of improvisation, see the essays by Ingrid Monson and Peter J. Martin (Chapters 7 and 8).

7 Duke Ellington, *Carnegie Hall Concerts, January 1946* (Prestige P 24074, 1977).

8 See Gerard 1998, especially 35–6, for some examples of these paradoxes.

9 The Browne quotation was taken from recordings in the archive of Tulane University.

10 The exact contribution of harmony to the distinctiveness of jazz is difficult to assess. For many musicians, their use of harmony was a key factor in the badge of difference, but public recognition of jazz seems to have proceeded without much conscious awareness of harmony's role.

2 The jazz diaspora

In researching this article I received indispensable assistance from a number of sources. I would therefore like to acknowledge with the greatest appreciation the following: the Finnish Jazz and Pop Archives and the Finnish Music Information Centre, for making print and sound resources available; the Department of Cultural Research (Kulttuurintutkimus) at the University of Joensuu, Finland, which provided a research base in the form of a Visiting Fellowship in 1999; the Department's Administrator (Amanuenssi), Leena Waismaa, for her general assistance and in particular her patient and considered advice on translations from Finnish to English.

1 The date, however, is unlikely to be correct, as 'Yes Sir, That's my Baby' was not published until 1925.

2 Ballantine's 1991 article is virtually reprinted in Ballantine 1993, 1–38, but as this is out of print at the time of writing I refer to the *Popular Music* articles where they duplicate each other.

3 The emergence of the recording industry in Australia has been recently surveyed by Laird.

4 This is a well-documented phase; see, for example, Kernfeld 1988, I, 585.

5 See also Frank Whitford, *Bauhaus: The Face of the Twentieth Century*, video documentary (BBC/RM Arts, 1994).

6 Will Earhart, Director of Music, Pittsburgh Pa., writing in *The Etude* (1924); cited in Walser 1999, 49.

7 Anne Shaw Faulkner, writing in *The Ladies' Home Journal* (August 1921); cited in Walser 1999, 35–6.

8 This connection and its implications are documented and developed at length in Johnson 2000, 63–76.

9 [*Finnish Music Quarterly*] 1992, 2–23; Juha Niemi, 'The Finnish American Songs in the 1920's and 1930's' (unpublished paper, University of Turku, Finland), 137; and unpublished correspondence between Bruce Johnson and Juha Niemi.

10 Accounts of the impact of the *Andania* musicians include Haavisto 1996, 12–14; Konttinen 1987; and Jalkanen 1989, 393.

11 The Bell band's first international tour, and its impact, are chronicled and documented in detail in Johnson 2000, 147–63.

3 The jazz audience

1 Ironically, Mencken did not have reciprocal feelings about jazz, which he generally disparaged.

2 The citation is in fact a quotation from Leon Werth.

3 Cocteau's essay, 'Jazz-Band', dates from 1919.

4 Murray is troping on Kenneth Burke, who wrote that 'the symbolic act is the "dancing of an attitude"': see Burke's *The Philosophy of Literary Form* (New York: Vintage, 1957), 9. For further on jazz as dance, see Chapter 4 of the present volume.

5 See Giese, who writes that 'the Girl' was known in earlier incarnations like the 'Gibson Girl', whereas 'the Girls' as a plural phenomenon made their European appearance in 1923 (1925, 15). The best-known treatment of the phenomenon is by Siegfried Kracauer in 'The Mass Ornament' (1927).

6 In an unsigned article 'Putting Jazz in its Place', *Literary Digest* 82 (5 July 1924), 32.

7 See Chapters 11 and 12 of the present volume for further comment on the development of European free jazz and Davis's jazz-rock.

4 Jazz and dance

I am greatly indebted to Elizabeth Aldrich, Anthea Kraut, Danielle Robinson, Stephanie Stein Crease and Linda Tomko for help with this chapter.

1 F. Scott Fitzgerald, 'The Perfect Life', quoted in Erenberg 1981, 146.

2 On Bolm, see Carbonneau in Garafola and Baer 1999.

3 Duncan in Copeland and Cohen 1983, 265. On the background to Duncan's view of jazz, see Daly 1995, ch. 3.

4 The intimate role that contexts of music-making and dancing play in African-American life can also be seen in Hughes's first novel, *Not Without Laughter* (1930), and other writings of that era.

5 'That Lindy Hop', written by Andy Razaf and Eubie Blake for Duke Ellington and his Cotton Club Orchestra.

6 For more on these developments, and on the history of swing in general, see Crease 1986; Crease 1995; and Crease 2000.

7 For more on jazz and modern dance, see Daly 2000.

8 *Down Beat*, 7 July 1960.

5 Jazz as musical practice

1 For discussion of the weaknesses of these analytic paradigms, even for concert music, see Treitler 1989, 50–55. For a more expansive argument tracing the emergence and 'regulative function' of the concept of the musical work, see Goehr 1992.

2 While I am linking Sargeant's work to what seems today a very conservative paradigm of writing on music, it is important to point out that his work was also quite forward-looking in viewing jazz in diasporic terms (i.e., as connected to the musics of the Caribbean and Africa), in questioning the utility of musical notation for musical analysis, and in defining all music as 'social' and dependent upon human activity. These viewpoints have been more recently celebrated by Christopher Small (1998). One might cite the earlier work of Henry Osgood as an entry point into consideration of jazz, but his work has been much less influential than the work surveyed here.

3 Most properly, syncopation involves a displacement of rhythmic accents that does not contradict the prevailing metre of a passage. Polymetric or multimetric playing (e.g., $3 + 3 + 2$ groupings of quavers in 4/4 time) is often described as syncopation when in fact it involves a different procedure, one that challenges rather than confirms an existing pattern of metric accents: see Sargeant 1938, 57–63.

4 He writes, for example, that unlike composers jazz musicians do not meditate. They work instead through 'intuitive assimilation' (Hodeir 1938, 18).

5 See, for example, Jaffe 1983, Benward and Wildman 1984, and Reeves 1989. For a historical overview of jazz pedagogical materials and their impact on jazz education, see Witmer and Robbins 1988. One might argue that the emphasis placed on pitched materials makes it possible for writers to address young musicians regardless of the instruments they play.

6 Many of the most widely used textbooks on American university campuses reveal this emphasis to varying degrees: see, for example, Tirro 1977, Collier 1978, Porter *et al.* 1993 and Gridley 1997.

7 Duke Ellington, *The Ellington Suites*, Pablo 2310, 1976; reissue: Fantasy/Original Jazz Classics 446 (CD), 1990.

8 For a discussion of open concepts, see Goehr 1992, 93.

9 A tritone substitution involves the replacement of Dmin7 and G7 in the previous example with chords having the same quality but roots a tritone – i.e., three whole steps – away from D and G. Thus, the previous progression becomes A♭min7–D♭7–C. Extended use of the technique could result in progressions like A♭min7–G7–C or Dmin7–D♭7–G. Common-tone diminished-seventh chords generally

elaborate a preceding harmony with which they share certain pitches. An F♯ diminished seventh following an F7 shares with it three pitches: A, C and E♭. Quartal harmonies are those that use fourths, rather than thirds, as the building blocks for harmonies. In practice, their tonal implications are more ambiguous than triadic harmonies and give a soloist more freedom in the choice of pitches to use in improvisation.

10 Miles Davis, *E.S.P.*, Columbia CL 2350, 1965; reissue: Columbia/Legacy CK46863 (CD), 1991.

11 Miles Davis, *Kind of Blue*, Columbia CL1355, 1959; reissue: Sony Jazz CK 64935 (CD), 1997; Herbie Hancock, *Maiden Voyage*, Blue Note 84195, 1965; reissue: Blue Note 46339 (CD), 1986.

12 For more extensive discussion of jazz harmonic resources, see Steven Strunk, 'Harmony (I)', in Kernfeld 1988.

13 This kind of shift was first suggested by Charles Keil, who exhorted researchers to place less emphasis on the syntactical characteristics of jazz, i.e., those that are easily notated, and more on the processual and performative dimensions of jazz. A similar change of emphasis motivated composer Olly Wilson's call for those interested in defining African-American music to focus on the continuity of certain *ways* of using sonic material rather than search for retentions or literal correspondences between rhythms, pitches or forms. See Keil 1966, and Wilson 1974.

14 Miles Davis, *Jazz Track*, Columbia CL1268, 1958; reissue *'58 Sessions*, Columbia Legacy CK47835 (CD), 1991. Eric Dolphy, *Outward Bound*, New Jazz 8236, 1960; reissue: Original Jazz Classics 022, 1987. A fake-book version of the tune – whose harmony and form, but not its melody, conform to the Davis version – can be found in Sher 1995.

15 For a more considered, if somewhat overstated, discussion of how musicians re-create and transform compositions over time, see Bowen 1993.

16 Such tags were generally positioned in the bars preceding the final cadence on the tonic chord, e.g., in the two bars preceding the thirty-first bar. The eventual cadence on the tonic would likewise mark the beginning of a two-bar break leading back to the first bar of the form. One can hear the same procedure in the Davis quintet's recording of 'All of Me' on *Round About Midnight*, Columbia CL949, 1956; reissue: Columbia CK 40610, 1991.

17 And, one might add, the procedures involved in recording rather than performing for a live audience. Monson describes intermusicality in part as a historical awareness of jazz performance practice, the work of specific jazz performers, particular kinds of grooves and forms of interaction, as well as repertory (1996, ch. 4).

18 See also Mensah 1972, and E. Collins 1987.

19 See Omi and Winant 1994 for an excellent review of writings on race and the problems with them.

20 A recent work that repeats that dyad and reviews extant literature on the subject is Brothers 1994.

6 Jazz as cultural practice

1 See Gabbard 1995a, 107, and Johnson 1987, 4. As with other primary sources used in this chapter, the earliest published versions are often difficult to access. Where possible I have therefore used recent invaluable anthologies, most frequently R. Gottlieb 1996, and Walser 1999.

2 See for examples: Walser 1999, 6, and Gabbard 1995a, 109; Walser 1999, 13; Johnson 1987, 4; Walser 1999, 6–7, 8.

3 Much of the debate is reprinted in R. Gottlieb 1996, 722–38; for an Australian case study, see Johnson 1987, 34–7; Johnson 1998, 26–37.

4 The proposition is pervasive in Foucault's work: for a range of discussions, see Levin 1993.

5 Arguably, Foucault conducts his critique from within a scopic framework: see Flynn in Levin 1993, 273–86. Soundscape studies, largely pioneered by R. Murray Schafer, provide alternative models of acoustically based cultural analysis. For a collection of such studies with particular reference to music, see Järviluoma 1994.

6 Parts of the following section are adapted from Johnson 2000, 175–83.

7 A specific example of dense, improvised musical interactivity between jazz musicians, audience and street noise is analysed in Johnson 1996, 8.

8 Keil and Feld 1994, 96–108; Keil 1995, 1–19. The latter appears in an issue of *Ethnomusicology* largely devoted to debate on the theory.

9 See, for example, the *Roots of Rock 'n' Roll* series issued by Savoy Records in 1981; more recently, the work of such bands as Blood, Sweat & Tears; Chicago (Transit Authority); Chris Barber in England; and, of course, the influential later work of Miles Davis.

10 Email correspondence with the author, November 1999.

11 Gabbard, 1995a and Gabbard 1995c; see his comments in the 'Acknowledgements' section of *Jazz Among the Discourses*.

12 On the conservatism of musicology, see the introduction to Scher 1992, xiv. Other assertions to this effect are cited in Johnson 2000, 46 and endnotes.

7 Jazz improvisation

1 See Barry Kernfeld's article 'Improvisation' in Kernfeld 1988.

2 For various definitions of swing see Berliner 1994, 244–5; 'Swing' in Kernfeld 1988; and Schuller 1989, 224–5.

3 Berliner's comprehensive account of jazz improvisation is an excellent source for those readers who wish to delve more fully into the topics presented here.

4 Those interested in musical explanations of these feels can consult John Riley's text on bop drumming. Listening examples include: 1) Shuffle: Art Blakey, 'Moanin'', *Moanin'*, rec. 30 October 1958, Blue Note CDP 7 46516 2; 2) 'In 2': John Coltrane, 'Good Bait' (A sections), *Soultrane*, rec. 7 February 1958, Prestige OJCCD-021–2; 3) Jazz waltz: Bill Evans, 'Someday My Prince Will Come', *Portrait in Jazz*, rec. 28 December 1959, OJC (Riverside RLP-1162) OJCCD-088–2; 4) 6/8: Miles Davis, 'All Blues', *Kind of Blue*, rec. New York, 2 March and 22 April 1959, Columbia CK40579; 5) 12/8: Max Roach, 'Garvey's Ghost', *Percussion Bitter Sweet*, rec. New York, August 1961, Impulse GRD-122; 6) Samba: Airto Moreira, 'Samba de Flora', *Samba*, rec. Los Angeles, 1988, Montuno Records, MCD-528; 7) Latin: Art Blakey, 'Split Kick' (A sections of the head), *A Night At Birdland Vol. 1*, rec. New York, 21 February 1954, Blue Note CDP 7 46519 2.

5 For detailed comment on soloist–rhythm section interaction and musical quotation, see my *Saying Something: Jazz Improvisation and Interaction* (1996), and Berliner 1994, 348–446.

6 Count Basie (with Eddie Durham and Jimmy Rushing), 'Sent for You Yesterday', rec. New York, 16 February 1938, Smithsonian RD 030–2.

7 Transcriptions of these choruses can be found in my 'Riffs, Repetition, and Theories of Globalization' (1999).

8 Russell defines three possible ways that the improviser may relate to chord changes. The musician may 1) allow each chord as it passes to determine his or her choice of scales (Vertical Tonal Gravity); 2) impose a single scale on a sequence of chords that resolves to a tonic (Horizontal Tonal Gravity); or 3)

improvise his or her chromatic melody in relationship to the overall tonic of the entire piece (Supravertical Tonal Gravity).

9 Miles Davis, 'Bags Groove (take 1)', *Bags Groove*, rec. Hackensack, NJ, 24 December 1954, Prestige OJCCD-245–2 (P-7109).

10 Unlike all but the last chorus of the solo, the main figure in chorus two is not repeated at the same pitch level during the chorus. For this reason it is not, strictly speaking, a riff.

11 Bill Evans, *Portrait in Jazz*, rec. 28 December 1959, OJC (Riverside RLP-1162) OJCCD-088–2. McCoy Tyner can be heard on John Coltrane, *My Favorite Things*, rec. New York, 21, 24, 26 October 1960, Atlantic 1361–2.

12 Recommended listening: John Coltrane, *Africa/Brass Vol. 1&2*, rec. Englewood Cliffs, NJ, 23 May and 7 June 1961, Impulse! MCAD-42001; John Coltrane, *Crescent*, rec. Englewood Cliffs, NJ, 27 April and 1 June 1964, Impulse! IMPD-200; Miles Davis, *The Complete Concert 1964: My Funny Valentine + Four & More*, rec. 12 February 1964, Columbia CK 40609 (reissued material from LPs CL 1812 and CS 8612); Miles Davis, *Miles in Berlin*, rec. 25 September 1964, CBS/Sony CSCS 5147.

8 Spontaneity and organisation

1 See A. Marquis 1998; see also the present volume, Chapter 13.

2 See the accounts in Vail 1996, Woideck 1996, R. Russell 1973 and Reisner 1962.

9 Jazz among the classics, and the case of Duke Ellington

1 Wynton Marsalis, *Jump Start and Jazz* (Sony SK 62998, 1997); Django Bates, 'Good Evening . . . Here is the News' (Argo 452 099–2, 1996).

2 George Avakian, liner notes to *The Birth of the Third Stream* (Sony 01-485103–10, 1996), 18. For further on the third stream see Schuller 1996, 114–33.

3 Django Bates, liner notes to 'Good Evening . . . Here is the News', 6.

4 Elsewhere Rosen remarks (1976, 129): 'Any discussion of second themes, bridge passages, concluding themes, range of modulation, relations between themes – all this is empty if it does not refer back to the particular piece, *to its character, its typical sound*, its motifs' (my emphasis).

5 For Ellington's encomium on Whiteman, see Ellington 1973, 103; see also Nicholson 1999, 199–200.

6 For Gonsalves's ambivalent attitude towards this event ('It was a thing that just happened by chance. I never guessed it would get that

much attention'), see Nicholson 1999, 308–9.

7 For a detailed description of the structure of *Diminuendo and Crescendo in Blue*, see Schuller 1989, 90–92. Schuller does not find the piece entirely satisfying: 'the dichotomy between the innocuousness of the melodic-thematic material and the comparatively sophisticated and perhaps overly complex fragmentation of underlying component material constitutes a weakness of the work, although an interesting risk-taking one. The necessary equilibrium between horizontal (melodic) and vertical (harmonic) elements is not achieved' (92).

8 Bill Evans's 1965 recordings of 'Granados' and 'Pavane' (the latter a jazz interpretation of Fauré's haunting melody) are included on the compilation *Compact Jazz: Bill Evans* (Verve 831 366–2, 1987).

9 *Oslo Aftenposten*, 4 November 1969. The author is greatly indebted to Mrs Sheila Husson for her tireless assistance in tracking down (from the Norsk Jazzarchiv and Norske Argus) the press cuttings cited here, and for supplying English translations from the Norwegian texts.

10 *Oslo Dagbladet*, 21 May 1966. See also *Arbeiderbladet*, 21 May 1966, for clarification of the copyright details.

11 *Lofotposten*, 11 May 1966.

12 *Trondheim Adresseavis*, 23 July 1966.

13 *Oslo Aftenposten*, 23 January 1967.

14 *Oslo Dagbladet*, 23 May 1966.

15 *Arbeiderbladet*, 9 June 1966.

16 *Oslo Dagbladet*, 27 June 1966.

17 Letter from Håkon Hansen, *Arbeiderbladet*, 3 June 1966. On 9 June, the newspaper printed a robust response by Jens Halvorsen, who declared: 'If a tiny percentage of Norway's population absolutely cannot tolerate the appropriation of Grieg's works, they should lock themselves up with all Grieg's music on records.'

18 *Arbeiderbladet*, 9 June 1966.

19 Review of Garbarek's *Twelve Moons*, *Down Beat*, February 1994, 46. For further on Garbarek, see Stuart Nicholson's comments on pp. 242–4 of the present volume.

20 The exact extent of Strayhorn's involvement in the Grieg and Tchaikovsky projects is uncertain. Strayhorn was no stranger to the idiom of Grieg, having performed his Piano Concerto in A minor, Op. 16, with his school orchestra on 1 March 1934: see Hajdu 1996, 15. For Strayhorn's vital role in the Tchaikovsky adaptation, see Hajdu 1996, 203–6. According to bassist Aaron Bell, the recordings were made at 'a very loose session . . . It always seemed to

me that [Ellington and Strayhorn] weren't prepared': see Nicholson 1999, 323.

21 Irving Townsend, sleeve notes to Philips BBL 7470 (1961).

22 Interview for *Oslo Aftenposten*, 23 January 1967.

23 From Stravinsky's programme note to *Pulcinella*, reproduced in the booklet accompanying Sony SMK 46 293 (1991).

10 1959: the beginning of beyond

1 Dr David Baker, Distinguished Professor of Jazz Studies, Indiana University, concurs in his jazz history course outline, which includes 'The Breakthrough Year Into the Contemporary Period: 1959'. He showed me this after I interviewed him in connection with this chapter.

2 A recently circulated National Public Radio (USA) list of the '100 most important American musical works of the 20th century' admits 17 jazz works – perhaps 18, if you count Hoagy Carmichael singing 'Stardust' (1927). Of these, two from 1959 are 'Take Five' (from *Time Out*) and *Kind of Blue* in its entirety, and John Coltrane is on the list for *A Love Supreme* (1964). Ray Charles's 'What'd I Say' was also recorded in 1959. NPR's definition of 'most important' is as follows: 'By virtue of its achievement, beauty, or excellence, the work is an important milestone of American music in the 20th century. It significantly changed the musical landscape, opened new horizons, or in itself had a major effect on American culture and civilization.'

3 See, for example, Frederic Ramsey Jr's multi-volume series *Jazz* for Folkways Records, beginning with *The South* (FJ2801) in 1958, and George Avakian's four-volume *The Bessie Smith Story* for Columbia, launched with *Bessie Smith with Louis Armstrong* (CL855) in 1956.

4 For a full discussion of the canon issue, see Gabbard 1995b.

5 Al Bendick, president of Fantasy Records (which owns several other major jazz-specialist catalogues, e.g., Prestige) told me in 1992 that most of the company's income came from CD re-issues of LPs made in the 1950s and 1960s.

6 See Berliner 1994 for an in-depth study of 'study' within the jazz community. Students who went to the Lenox School of Jazz and John Coltrane as a learner will be mentioned later in this chapter. Also mentioned here are some of the relatively few jazz musicians at the time who studied music formally at postgraduate level, such as Dave Brubeck,

John Lewis, John Mehegan, Bill Evans, George Russell and David Baker.

7 According to the prevailing modernist view, jazz had evolved *from* African-American folk music, etc. The opposing view was that 'true jazz' *was* African-American folk music but long-since diluted and overwhelmed by 'Tin Pan Alley' cosmopolitanism. A current, widespread critical perspective is that 'evolution' requires a teleological view of history which, besides funnelling the whole musical past into whichever version of 'the story of jazz' one prefers, implies that 'jazz' is metaphorically an organism. The evolution of jazz is assumed to be analogous over a short time-scale with the history of European art music with its succession of periods. The movement from polyphony to homophony offers a striking parallel.

8 See Mehegan, *Jazz Improvisation* (1959a), the first in a series of four instructional volumes completed in 1965.

9 In Mehegan's article, 'the poor listener' (to modern jazz) is afflicted with 'an inferiority complex' and 'rampant ambivalence', and either 'leaves the scene in an unhealthy state' or 'remains to allow this total content to wash over him in a final Götterdämmerung of beatnik ecstasy'. Had this been written one or two years later he might have been attacking Brubeck's *Take Five* or Coltrane's *My Favorite Things*, in which rampantly unambivalent record-buyers did find 'beatnik ecstasy'. It is not clear to me how the names Mehegan mentioned (Sonny Rollins, Miles Davis, Thelonious Monk and Max Roach) relate to his point.

10 Parker often mentioned the above composers in interviews (see p. 160). Brubeck studied with Milhaud and often did incorporate polytonality and counterpoint into jazz performances, as did John Lewis. Nevertheless, whatever devices were used in arranged sections, the form and 'changes' of a tune were considered immutable during improvised solos.

11 To many competent but untrained working musicians, jazz means music with 'jazz chords'. I was once cautioned during a rehearsal with Don McLean (of 'American Pie' fame) not to put chords 'with numbers in them' behind his vocals and of course he was right in assuming my normal style would clash with his.

12 I wish to thank George Schuller, who is currently writing an article on Lenox, for sharing research material and also Michael Fitzgerald for maintaining a Lenox website on which is posted student and faculty lists, the original brochure, contemporaneous newspaper stories and the like.

13 George Russell's website gives the date of Davis's remark as 1945. Russell's version adds technical substance to 'fresh approach'. Russell, or his website ghost writer, explains: 'Knowing that Davis already knew how to arpeggiate each chord, Russell reasoned that he really meant he wanted to find a new and broader way to relate to chords' (http://www.georgerussell.com – 8/5/00).

14 This attempt to define harmolodic came after reading the following passage in Giddins: 'Coleman's music remains so singular that, forty years after his debut recordings, I still can't hear it without marvelling anew at how his privileged ear resisted all of the laws of harmony, melody, rhythm and pitch, all of which he ultimately revised in the abracadabra of harmolodic ... If you can resolve any note in any chord, why not do away with the chords and allow harmony to proceed serendipitously from the melody?' (1998, 468).

15 According to Robert Walser, 'Signifyin' ... works through reference, gesture, and dialogue to suggest multiple meanings through association' (1993, 168). Walser acknowledges borrowing this term from literary critic Louis Gates.

16 Columbia Legacy CK 64929, 1996 is a composite of *Music for Brass* CL941 (1956) and *Modern Jazz Concert*, WL127 (1957).

17 *Third Stream Music* by the Modern Jazz Quartet (1957, 1959–60; Atlantic 1345) being the third, followed by *The Modern Jazz Quartet and Orchestra* (1960; Atlantic 1359).

18 For a readable and accurate track-by-track technical description, see Gridley's 'Listening Guide for *Kind of Blue*'(1997), 217ff. As for mainstream culture, Clint Eastwood's character in the movie *In the Line of Fire* (1993) aims his lethal-looking remote control at his stereo and 'All Blues' starts.

19 Columbia CD 450984, recorded in April 1959.

20 'Although a jazz musicologist influenced by Hodeir may not overtly argue that Ellington is the equal of Brahms, his use of analytical methods designed for Brahms makes the argument all the same' (Gabbard 1995b, 15). Critical or interpretive difficulties related to jazz have not been fully worked out to this day, but awareness of them seems a good place to start.

11 Free jazz and the avant-garde

1 Carl Czerny, *Systematische Anleitung zum Fantasieren auf dem Pianoforte* (1826), trans.

Alice Mitchell, New York, Longman, 1983.

2 The extensions and potentials are described in detail by Dean 1992.

3 Evan Parker, programme notes for *Man and Machine* (Zaal deUnie, May 1992), 'De Motu' for Buschi Niebergall.

4 See, for example, Pressing 1994.

12 Fusions and crossovers

1 *Rolling Stone*, 11 May 1968, 14.

2 *Rolling Stone*, 15 October 1970, 22.

3 *Down Beat*, 3 April 1969, 22.

4 *Down Beat*, May 1984, 16.

5 *Down Beat*, 1 June 1967, 35.

6 Interview with Stuart Nicholson, 31 July 1997.

7 *Down Beat Yearbook 1968*, 13.

8 Quoted in *Down Beat*, 30 April 1970, 12.

9 *Rolling Stone*, 15 April 1971.

10 With the release in 1996 of *Miles Davis and Gil Evans: The Complete Columbia Studio Recordings*, however, it became clear how many final takes were spliced composites, sometimes with overdubs by Davis, on *Miles Ahead* (1957), *Porgy and Bess* (1958) and *Sketches of Spain* (1959).

11 In 2001 Columbia released *Live at the Fillmore: March 7, 1970*, which had languished in its vaults for thirty years, while the bootleg *Double Image* (Moon MLP 010/11) had come out in the mid-1980s.

12 *Rolling Stone*, 13 December 1969, 22–3.

13 *Ibid.*, 33.

14 His session work included albums by Tom Jones, Engelbert Humperdinck, Petula Clark, David Bowie and the Rolling Stones. 'This session thing was driving me completely crazy', he said later, 'I had to do it in order to survive, yet more things were happening musically that I wanted to do. Finally one day I woke up and I said I cannot do this anymore.' He promptly moved to Germany and immersed himself in free jazz with Gunter Hampel's group.

15 Including *In a Silent Way, Bitches Brew, Circle in the Round, Directions, Live-Evil, On the Corner* and *Get Up With It*.

16 *Down Beat*, 29 January 1976, 17.

17 *Melody Maker*, 1 April 1972, 28.

18 E.g., Rick Laird in *Rolling Stone*, 28 February 1974, 11.

19 *Melody Maker*, 2 February 1974, 15.

20 One notable version of the song was recorded by the Woody Herman band on the Grammy-winning album *Giant Steps*.

21 *Down Beat*, September 1988, 19.

22 *The Prisoner, Fat Albert Rotunda, Mwandishi, The Crossing* and *Sextant*.

23 *Down Beat*, July 1986, 17.

24 See Nicholson 1998, 176–7, for a detailed discussion of this piece.

25 It has taken some while for the jazz community to come to terms with Pastorius's importance, but a measure of his acceptance was signalled in 1998 with a four-part radio series devoted to his life on BBC Radio 3.

26 Columbia trade advertisement, autumn 1974.

27 *Down Beat*, 9 August 1979, 23.

28 Figures for the period January 1993 to December 1995, quoted in *Newsweek*, 20 May 1996.

29 Interview with Stuart Nicholson, 8 September 1987, for *The Observer*, although the quotation was not used in my subsequent article (28 September 1997).

30 *The Times*, 7 March 2000; interview with Stuart Nicholson. In interviews for both my book *Jazz-Rock: A History* and *The Observer* (1996–99), many musicians sought to make a distinction between 'jazz-rock' and 'fusion', so this account follows how the musicians themselves sought to situate their music, rather than imposing any arbitrary definitions.

31 This quotation from an unknown source is often used in discussion of Brown's music and refers to an African drum choir, where each instrument has an independent role yet the totality of them forms an overall rhythmic tapestry. Often many of Brown's instruments seem to have an independent rhythmic as well as rhythmic function that together form the James Brown sound.

32 Interview with Stuart Nicholson, 8 September 1997.

33 Interview with Stuart Nicholson, *The Observer*, 19 October 1997.

34 *Down Beat*, February 1991, 31.

35 *Down Beat*, July 1986, 27.

36 *Ibid.*, 26.

37 Interview with Stuart Nicholson, *The Independent*, 4 February 2000, 14.

38 *Jazz Podium*, December 1972, 22–5.

39 Record company press release to accompany the Clusone Trio's album, *I Am An Indian* (+Gramavision GCD 79505).

40 My own interviews for *The Observer* between 1996 and 1999 with John Surman, Bobo Stenson, Gary Crosby, Louis Sclavis, Mike Westbrook, Ian Carr, Gerard Presencer and Kenny Wheeler (among others) all suggest this belief is widely held among European musicians.

13 Learning jazz, teaching jazz

I would like to thank David Borgo, Larry Engstrom, Susan McClary, Robert Walser and the book's editors for their insightful comments on this chapter.

1 See also Daniel Goldmark, *Happy Harmonies: Music in Hollywood Animated Shorts, 1928–1960*, PhD dissertation, University of California, Los Angeles (forthcoming).

2 See Dave Peyton, 'The Musical Bunch', *Chicago Defender* (28 April, 10 March and 12 May 1928), reprinted in Walser 1999, 57–9; see also Floyd 1995, ch. 6.

3 This is one of the fundamental themes of Albert Murray's important *Stomping the Blues* (1976).

4 For more on the jazz musician as mystic, see the video documentary *The Church of Saint Coltrane* by Swimmer and Gilman; see also Ake 1999, and David Beer, 'The Coltrane Church,' *Image* (6 March 1988), 18, 20.

5 See Rollins's comments in Jean Bach's film, *A Great Day in Harlem.*

6 For a more in-depth phenomenology of jazz-skill acquisition, see Paul Berliner's monumental *Thinking in Jazz* (1994).

7 Stearns's course syllabus is reprinted in Walser 1999, 195–9.

8 A colleague informed me that, as recently as the early 1990s, she and her fellow clarinet majors at a leading midwestern university were forbidden to play jazz: classical instructors feared that such musicking would 'destroy' their embouchures. Ironically, this attitude persists at a school with a long-running jazz programme, which demonstrates that although jazz has established a foothold in the academy, a cultural hierarchy remains in place.

9 See *Music Data Summaries 1997–98*, Reston, Va., Higher Education Arts Data Services, 1998.

10 Some jazz educators raised these concerns as early as the 1960s: see Baker 1965.

11 *Directory of Music Faculties in Colleges and Universities*, 1997.

12 David Borgo, 'Music, Metaphor, and Mysticism: Avant-Garde Jazz Saxophone and the Ecstatic State', paper delivered at Society for Ethnomusicology Southern California Chapter Meeting, Northridge, California (February 1997).

14 History, myth and legend: the problem of early jazz

The author acknowledges the help of the following in preparing this chapter: Robert Bamberger, Dorothy Geller, Thornton Hagert, Henry Jova, Lewis Porter, Natalie Sager and Richard Spottswood.

1 Lewis Porter, lecture at Rutgers University's Institute of Jazz Studies, 1998.

2 Personal communication.

3 This was to be a chapter for a work to be published by the Smithsonian Institution but unfortunately the work was never published. The references for subsequent quotations in the text are to pages in the manuscript.

4 If it seems odd that the writers of *Jazzmen* should compare their beloved New Orleans jazz with the very different harmonic language of composer Arnold Schoenberg, we should remember that one of the authors who made this comparison was William Russell, himself a musically diverse composer. In addition to his love and involvement with early New Orleans jazz, Russell also composed atonal music, most notably for percussion ensemble.

15 Analysing jazz

1 For examples, see Stern 1999, and George Avakian's liner notes for Dave Brubeck Quartet, *Jazz Goes to College*, Columbia 566, 1954.

2 Excerpts from Waterman's publication are to be found in Porter 1997, 41–5.

3 Roger Pryor Dodge, 'Harpsichords and Jazz Trumpets', *Hound & Horn* (July–September 1934); reprinted in Toledano 1994, 13–31, and in Dodge 1995, 247–59.

4 Austin Clarkson, 'Schuller, Gunther (Alexander)', in Hitchcock and Sadie 1986, iv, 164–6.

5 The subjects of these studies, besides those mentioned earlier, include Louis Armstrong, Chet Baker, David Baker, Bix Beiderbecke, Jimmy Blanton, Anthony Braxton, Randy Brecker, Dave Brubeck, Betty Carter, Sid Catlett, Charlie Christian (three), Ornette Coleman, John Coltrane (seven), Chick Corea, Miles Davis (two others), Buddy DeFranco, Duke Ellington (four), pianist Bill Evans (four), Gil Evans (two), Clare Fischer, Ella Fitzgerald, John Graas, Robert Graettinger, Freddie Green, Urbie Green, Jimmy Heath, Fletcher Henderson, Earl Hines, Freddie Hubbard, Keith Jarrett (two), J. J. Johnson, Stan Kenton, Rahsaan Roland Kirk, Hubert Laws, Warne Marsh, Pat Metheny, Charles Mingus, the Modern Jazz Quartet (two), Thelonious Monk, Wes Montgomery (two), the Bennie Moten band, Jelly Roll Morton (three), King Oliver's Creole Jazz Band, Charlie Parker (eight), Oscar Peterson (two), Bud Powell, Sonny Rollins, George Russell, Gunther Schuller, Art Tatum (three), Cecil Taylor, Claude Thornhill, Lennie Tristano, Sarah Vaughan, Julius Watkins, Mary Lou Williams (three), Tony Williams and Lester Young (Porter 1979 and one other).

6 See R. Bird 1976, Gushee 1981 and Brownell, 9–29.

7 See Woodson 1973, vol. 1, 70; Owens 1974b, 171; Kerschbaumer 1978, 229–38; and Kiroff 1997.

16 Valuing jazz

1 *Congressional Record – House*, 23 September 1987, p. 7827. Actually, the printed record reads 'perserved'. The resolution itself is reprinted in Walser 1999, 332–3.

2 See, for example, the 1955 *New York Times* article, 'America's "Secret Sonic Weapon"', reprinted in Walser 1999, 240–41.

3 See Huggins 1971, especially Chapter Six, 'White/Black Faces – Black Masks'. There are now several fine studies of blackface minstrelsy but, to my knowledge, Huggins was the first to produce such an analysis.

4 Black bandleader James Reese Europe briefly broached this complicated issue when he commented in 1919: 'I have come back from France more firmly convinced than ever that negroes should write negro music. We have our own racial feeling and if we try to copy whites we will make bad copies . . . The music of our race springs from the soil, and this is true today of no other race, except possibly the Russians, and it is because of this that I and all my musicians have come to love Russian music. Indeed, as far as I am concerned, it is the only music I care for outside of negro' (Walser 1999, 14).

5 I also want to acknowledge the impact on my thinking of Ake's PhD dissertation, *Being Jazz: Issues and Identities*, UCLA, 1999, subsequently published as *Jazz Cultures* by the University of California Press in 2002.

6 John A. Tynan, quoted in Walser 1999, 255. See the debates from *Down Beat* reprinted in *ibid.*, 253–5 and 395–400.

7 This is the argument of Mitchell Morris's extraordinary but as yet unpublished paper, 'Musical Virtues'.

8 See the chapters on Armstrong in Schuller 1968 and 1989. For a critical discussion of such approaches to analysing jazz, see my article 'Deep Jazz' (1997).

9 See also Elisabeth Le Guin, '"Cello-and-Bow Thinking": Boccherini's Sonata in E-flat Major, "*fuori catalogo*"', in the online journal, *Echo* 1:1 (1999) http://www.humnet.ucla.edu/echo/. For an example of this sort of thinking applied to jazz, see my 'Out of Notes: Signification, Interpretation, and the Problem of Miles Davis' (1993).

10 Here I am speaking simply of the trumpet's own history, without meaning to imply anything about the relevance of these practices to Armstrong's musical development. See Edward Tarr, *The Trumpet* (Portland: Amadeus Press, 1988), and my 'Musical Imagery and Performance Practice in J. S. Bach's Arias with Trumpet', *International Trumpet Guild Journal* 13:1 (September 1988), 62–77.

11 See also Joshua Berrett, 'Louis Armstrong and Opera', *Musical Quarterly* 76:2 (summer 1992), 216–41.

12 Charles Garrett has written a fascinating, as yet unpublished, article that focuses on just this point.

13 See Christopher Small, *Music of the Common Tongue* (1987a), as well as his *Music-Society-Education* (1996 [1977]), and especially *Musicking: The Meanings of Performing and Listening* (1998).

14 The 'heroic action' of the jazz or blues musician is a value that Albert Murray has celebrated and analysed in much of his writing: see, for example, his *Stomping the Blues* (1976).

17 The jazz market

1 Among many examples, see Roach 1972, and Deffaa 1996.

2 On the concept of 'cultural intermediaries', see Bourdieu 1986; on 'gatekeepers', see Hirsch 1972.

3 See 'Value of music publishing rose 7% in 1998; performing right represented 44%', *Music & Copyright* 186 (19 July 2000), 12, 14.

4 From the 1920s on, Irving Mills had mastered this art of 'cutting in' on composer credits and on the subsequent royalties paid for pieces actually written by Duke Ellington and others (see Feather 1986, 168). Ellington himself claimed credit for works substantially created by Billy Strayhorn, although there the overlap between Strayhorn's roles as arranger and composer made the issues complex (see Hajdu 1996, 120–22).

5 'The dollar value of global soundcarrier sales fell 4.5% in 2000', *Music & Copyright* 204 (25 April 2000), 5–11.

6 Terry Berne, 'The State of Independents', *Music & Media* (23 September 2000), 10.

7 Horizontal integration has been defined by Keith Negus as 'a process whereby one company acquires and integrates into its operations numerous firms that are producing the same product'. Vertical integration, by contrast 'involves the consolidation of processes occurring at different levels of an industry . . . An example here would be the way that the Disney

Company owns film production studios, film distribution networks and cinemas along with video production companies, distribution outlets and television channels' (see Negus, 'The Production of Culture', in *Production of Culture/Cultures of Production*, ed. Paul Du Gay, Milton Keynes, Open University Press, 1997, 67–118; quotation from 86).
8 Terry Berne, 'Labels that Keep The Flame Alive', *Music & Media* (23 September 2000), 12–13.

18 Images of jazz
1 David Yaffe, 'Thriving on a Riff: Representing Jazz in American Literature', Ph.D dissertation, City University of New York Graduate Center (forthcoming).
2 Zabor's novel won the PEN/Faulkner Award for fiction in 1998, but was initially ignored by audiences. Thanks to an article by Richard M. Sudhalter ('Composing the Words That Might Capture Jazz', *New York Times*, 29 August 1999, 2:1) and solid but slow word-of-mouth, the book seems to have found its audience among jazz *aficionados*.
3 Bill Moody, *Bird Lives* (1999). Moody's other jazz mysteries include *Solo Hand*, *Death of a Tenor Man* and *Sound of the Trumpet*.
4 This chapter has only scratched the surface of a large body of fiction, film and photography. The author apologises for the many important texts and images that have been overlooked. Interested readers should consult Richard Albert's bibliography (1996) for a more complete inventory of jazz fiction. Ambitious critical studies of jazz in novels and stories are now the subject of dissertations and may soon become scholarly books, most notably the work of Titlestad and Yaffe. For film, see David Meeker's *Jazz in the Movies* (1981) and my own *Jammin' at the Margins* (1996). The essential essay on jazz in painting is Hadler's 'Jazz and the Visual Arts'. Although there are many attractive collections of jazz photography, I know of no extended treatment of the subject comparable to Hadler's essay.

Works cited

Adorno, Theodor W., 1991. 'On Popular Music', in Simon Frith and Andrew Goodwin (eds), *On Record: Rock, Pop and the Written Word*, London, Routledge, 301–14

Ake, David, 1999. *Being Jazz: Identities and Images*, PhD dissertation, University of California, Los Angeles

Albert, Richard N., 1996. *An Annotated Bibliography of Jazz Fiction and Jazz Fiction Criticism*, Westport, Conn., Greenwood Press

Ansermet, Ernest, 1919. 'Sur un Orchestre Nègre', *Revue Romande*, October 1919; repr., with trans. by Walter E. Schaap, in *Jazz Hot*, November–December 1938, 4–9; trans. reproduced in Walser 1999, 9–11, and Toledano 1994, 111–18

Atkins, Everett Taylor, 1997. 'This is Our Music: Authenticating Japanese Jazz, 1920–1980', PhD dissertation, University of Illinois at Urbana-Champaign

Bacon, Francis, 1620. *The New Organon*, version of 1620, ed. Fulton H. Anderson in *The New Organon and Related Writings*, Indianapolis, New York, Kansas City, Bobbs-Merrill, 1960

Bailey, Derek, 1980. *Improvisation: Its Nature and Practice in Music*, Ashbourne, Moorland Publishing

Baker, David, 1965. 'Jazz: The Academy's Neglected Stepchild', *Down Beat* 23/20 (23 September 1965), 29–32

———, 1969. *Jazz Improvisation*, Chicago, Maher

Baldwin, James, 1965. 'Sonny's Blues', in Breton 1991, 112–29

Ballantine, Christopher, 1989. 'A Brief History of South African Popular Music', *Popular Music* 8/3 (1989), 305–10

———, 1991. 'Concert and Dance: The Foundations of Black Jazz in South Africa Between the Twenties and the Early Forties', *Popular Music* 10/2 (1991), 121–45

———, 1993. *Marabi Nights: Early South African Jazz and Vaudeville*, Johannesburg, Ravan Press

Bechet, Sidney, 1978. *Treat It Gentle: An Autobiography*, New York, Da Capo Press

Becker, Howard S., 1974. 'Art As Collective Action', in *American Sociological Review* 39 (1974), 767–76

———, 1982. *Art Worlds*, Berkeley and Los Angeles, University of California Press

Bell, Clive, 1928. *Since Cézanne*, New York, Harcourt, Brace

Benward, Bruce and Joan Wildman, 1984. *Jazz Improvisation in Theory and Practice*, Dubuque, Iowa, William C. Brown Publishers

Bergeron, Katherine and Philip V. Bohlman (eds), 1992. *Disciplining Music*, Chicago, University of Chicago Press

Bergreen, Laurence, 1997. *Louis Armstrong: An Extravagant Life*, New York, Broadway Books

Berliner, Paul F., 1994. *Thinking in Jazz: The Infinite Art of Improvisation*, University of Chicago Press

Berne, Terry, 2000a. 'Labels that Keep the Flame Alive', *Music & Media* (23 September 2000), 12–13

———, 2000b. 'The State of Independents', *Music & Media* (23 September 2000), 10

Bernhard, Paul, 1927. *Jazz: Eine musikalische Zeitfrage*, Munich, Delphin

Berrett, Joshua, 1992. 'Louis Armstrong and Opera', *Musical Quarterly* 76/2 (Summer 1992), 216–41

Bird, John, 1998. *Percy Grainger*, Sydney, Currency Press

Bird, Robert Atkinson, 1976. 'Methods and Categories of Jazz Analysis: A Critical Review of Five Approaches to Jazz History and Musical Analysis', MA thesis, University of Wisconsin at Madison

Bisset, Andrew, 1987. *Black Roots White Flowers: A History of Jazz in Australia*, Sydney, ABC Enterprises, revised edn

Blancq, Charles Clement III, 1977. 'Melodic Improvisation in American Jazz: The Style of Theodore "Sonny" Rollins, 1951–1962', PhD dissertation, Tulane University

Blesh, Rudi, 1958. *Shining Trumpets: A History of Jazz* [1946], second edn, New York, repr. Da Capo Press, 1975

———, 1971. *Combo USA: Eight Lives in Jazz*, Philadelphia, Chilton,

Bourdieu, Pierre, 1986. *Distinction. A Social Critique of the Judgement of Taste*, London, Routledge

Bourjaily, Vance, 1987. 'In and Out of Storyville: Jazz Fiction', *New York Times Book Review* 13 (December 1987), 1, 44–5

Bowen, José A., 1993. 'The History of Remembered Innovation: Tradition and Its Role in the Relationship between Musical Works and Their Performances', *Journal of Musicology* 11/2 (1993), 139–73

Bradley, Dick, 1992. *Understanding Rock 'n' Roll: Popular Music in Britain 1955–1964*, Buckingham, Open University Press

Bragaglia, A. G., 1929. *Jazz Band*, Milan, Edizioni Corbaccio

Breton, Marcela (ed.), 1991. *Hot and Cool: Jazz Short Stories*, London, Bloomsbury

Brothers, Thomas, 1994. 'Solo and Cycle in African-American Jazz', *Musical Quarterly* 78 (1994), 479–509

Brown, Frederick, 1968. *An Impersonation of Angels: A Biography of Jean Cocteau*, New York, Viking

Brownell, John, 1994. 'Analytical Models of Jazz Improvisation', *Jazzforschung/Jazz Research* 26 (1994), 9–29

Buchmann-Møller, Frank, 1990a. *You Just Fight For Your Life: The Story of Lester Young*, New York, Praeger

———, 1990b. *You Got to Be Original, Man: The Music of Lester Young*, New York and Westport, Conn., Greenwood Press

Buerkle, Jack V. and Danny Barker, 1973. *Bourbon Street Black. The New Orleans Black Jazzman*, Oxford University Press

Burian, E. F., 1928. *Jazz*, Prague, Aventinum

Caffey, H. David, 1975. 'The Musical Style of Louis Armstrong, 1925–1929',
     Journal of Jazz Studies 3 (Fall 1975), 72–96
Carbonneau, Suzanne, 1999. 'Adolph Bolm in America', in Garafola and Baer
     1999, 219–44
Carr, Ian, 1982. *Miles Davis: A Critical Biography*, London, Quartet
     ———, 1991. *Keith Jarrett, The Man and his Music*, London, Grafton
     ———, 1999. *Miles Davis: The Definitive Biography*, London, Harper Collins
Cartiér, Xam Wilson, 1987. *Be-Bop, Re-Bop*, New York, Available
Cassidy, Donna M., 1997. *Painting the Musical City: Jazz and Cultural Identity in
     American Art, 1910–1940*, Washington, Smithsonian Institution Press
Chailley, Jacques, 1964. *40,000 Years of Music: Man in Search of Music*, trans. Rollo
     H. Myers, London, Macdonald
Chambers, Leland, 1995. 'Improvising and Mythmaking in Eudora Welty's
     "Powerhouse"', in Gabbard, *Representing Jazz*, 54–69
Chester, Andrew, 1970. 'Second Thoughts on a Rock Aesthetic: The Band', *New
     Left Review* 62 (1970), 73–82
Chevigny, Paul, 1991. *Gigs: Jazz and the Cabaret Laws in New York City*, New York,
     Routledge
Chilton, John, 1987. *Sidney Bechet: The Wizard of Jazz*, Basingstoke, Macmillan
Chomsky, Noam, 1957. *Syntactic Structures*, The Hague, Mouton
     ———, 1964. *Current Issues in Linguistic Theory*, The Hague, Mouton
Christie, May, 1930. *The Jazz Widow*, New York, Grosset & Dunlap
Clamp, H. M. E., n.d. *The Great God Jazz*, London, Hurst & Blackett
Cockrell, Dale, 1997. *Demons of Disorder: Early Blackface Minstrels and Their World*,
     Cambridge University Press
Cocteau, Jean, 1926. *A Call to Order*, trans. Rollo II. Myers, London, Faber &
     Gwyer
     ———, 1970. *Professional Secrets*, ed. Robert Phelps, trans. Richard Howard,
     New York, Farrar, Straus & Giroux
     ———, 1972. *Cocteau's World*, ed. Margaret Crosland, London, Peter Owen
Coeuroy, André, and André Schaeffner, 1926. *Le Jazz*, Paris, Claude Aveline
Collier, James Lincoln, 1978. *The Making of Jazz: A Comprehensive History*, Boston,
     Mass., Houghton Mifflin
     ———, 1984. *Louis Armstrong*, London, Michael Joseph
     ———, 1987. *Duke Ellington*, Oxford University Press
     ———, 1993. *Jazz, The American Theme Song*, Oxford University Press
Collins, Edmund John, 1987. 'Jazz Feedback to Africa', *American Music* 5 (1987),
     176–93
Collins, R. [Ralph], 1996. *New Orleans Jazz: A Revised History. The Development of
     American Music from the Origin to the Big Bands*, New York, Vantage Press
Cone, Edward T., 1962. 'Stravinsky: The Progress of a Method', *Perspectives of New
     Music* 1 (1962), 18–26; repr. in Benjamin Boretz and Cone (eds), *Perspectives
     on Schoenberg and Stravinsky*, Princeton, N.J., 1968, second edn 1972, 156ff
Cook, Susan C., 2000. 'Talking Machines and Moving Bodies: Marketing Dance
     Music before World War I', in Juliette Crone-Willis (ed.), *Dancing in the*

  Millennium: Conference Proceedings, July 19–23, 2000, Stoughton Wisc., The Printing House Inc., 75–8

Coolman, Todd F., 1997. 'The Miles Davis Quintet of the Mid-1960s: Synthesis of Improvisational and Compositional Elements', PhD dissertation, New York University

Copeland, Roger and Marshall Cohen (eds), 1983. *What is Dance?*, Oxford University Press

Coplan, David, 1985. *In Township Tonight: South Africa's Black City Music and Theatre*, Johannesburg, Ravan Press

Corbett, John, 1984. *Extended Play: Sounding Off from John Cage to Dr. Funkenstein*, Durham, N.C., Duke University Press

Coryell, Julie and Laura Friedman, 1978. *Jazz-Rock Fusion*, London, Marion Boyars

Crease, Robert P., 1986. 'Swing Story', *Atlantic* (February 1986), 77–82

———, 1995. 'Divine Frivolity: Hollywood Representations of the Lindy Hop, 1937–1942', in Gabbard, *Representing Jazz*, 207–28

———, 2000. 'Jazz and Dance', in Kirchner 2000, 696–705

Crouch, Stanley, 1996. 'On the Corner: The Sellout of Miles Davis', in R. Gottlieb 1996, 898–914

Crow, Bill, 1990. *Jazz Anecdotes*, Oxford University Press

cummings, e. e., 1966. *A Miscellany*, ed. George J. Firmage, London, Peter Owen

Dahl, Linda, 1999. *Morning Glory: A Biography of Mary Lou Williams*, New York, Pantheon

Dahlhaus, Carl, 1982. *Aesthetics of Music* [1967], Cambridge University Press

Daly, Ann, 1995. *Done into Dance: Isadora Duncan in America*, Bloomington, Indiana University Press

———, 2000. 'New World A-Comin': A Century of Jazz and Modern Dance', in Myers 2000, 31–9

Dance, Stanley, 1970. *The World of Duke Ellington*, New York, Charles Scribner

Dannen, Fredric, 1990. *Hit Men: Power Brokers and Fast Money Inside the Music Business*, New York, Times Books

Davis, Clive with James Willwerth, 1975. *Clive: Inside the Record Business*, New York, William Morrow & Company

Davis, Glen Roger, 1990. 'Levels Analysis of Jazz Tunes', DMA dissertation, Ohio State University

Davis, Miles, with Quincy Troupe, 1989. *Miles: The Autobiography*, New York, Simon and Schuster

Davis, Stuart, 1971. *Stuart Davis*, ed. Diane Kelder, New York, Praeger

Davison, Michael Allyn, 1987. 'A Motivic Study of Twenty Improvised Solos of Randy Brecker Between the Years of 1970–1980', DMA dissertation, University of Wisconsin

Dean, Roger T., 1992. *New Structures in Jazz and Improvised Music Since 1960*, Milton Keynes, Open University Press

Deffaa, Chip, 1996. *Blue Rhythms: Six Lives in Rhythm and Blues*, Urbana and Chicago, University of Illinois Press

Denning, Michael, 1987. *Mechanic Accents: Dime Novels and Working-Class Culture in America*, New York, Verso

DeVeaux, Scott, 1989. 'The Emergence of the Jazz Concert, 1935–1945', *American Music* 7 (1989), 6–29

———, 1991. 'Constructing the Jazz Tradition: Jazz Historiography', *Black American Literature Forum* 25/3 (1991), 525–60; repr. in O'Meally 1998, 483–512; abridged version in Walser 1999, 416–24

———, 1997. *The Birth of Bebop: A Social and Musical History*, Berkeley, University of California Press

Directory of Music Faculties in Colleges and Universities, U.S. and Canada, 1997. Missoula, College Music Society

Dixon, Robert M. W. and John Godrich, 1970. *Recording the Blues*, London, Studio Vista

Dodge, Roger Pryor, 1995. *Hot Jazz and Jazz Dance: Collected Writings, 1929–1964*, Oxford University Press

Driggs, Frank, 1959. 'Kansas City and the Southwest', in Hentoff and McCarthy 1977, 191–230

Drdla, Franz, 1999. 'The Jazz Problem', in Walser 1999, 44–5

Duncan, Isadora, 1983. 'I See America Dancing', in Copeland and Cohen 1983, 264–5

ECM: Sleeves of Desire, 1996. Switzerland, Lars Müller

Eldridge, Roy, 1946. *Shortcut to Good Ad-Libbing*, London, Little Jazz Music

Ellington, Duke, 1962. 'The Art Is in the Cooking', *Down Beat* (June 1962), 13–15

———, 1973. *Music Is My Mistress*, Garden City, N.Y., Doubleday, and London, W. H. Allen

Elliott, Scott Nelson, 1987. 'A Study of Tonal Coherence in Jazz Music as Derived from Linear Compositional Techniques of the Baroque Era', MM thesis, Duquesne University

Ellison, Ralph, 1952. *Invisible Man*, New York, Random, repr. 1972

———, 1964. *Shadow and Act*, New York, Random House; London, Secker & Warburg, 1967

———, 1970. 'What Would America Be Like Without Blacks?', *Time* (6 April 1970)

Elworth, Steven B., 1995. 'Jazz in Crisis, 1948–58: Ideology and Representation', in Gabbard, *Jazz Among the Discourses*, 57–75

Enstice, Wayne and Paul Rubin (eds), 1992. *Jazz Spoken Here*, Baton Rouge, Louisiana State University Press

Epstein, Dena J., 1977. *Sinful Tunes and Spirituals*, University of Illinois Press

Erenberg, Lewis A., 1981. *Steppin' Out: New York Nightlife and the Transformation of American Culture, 1890–1930*, University of Chicago Press

———, 1998. *Swingin' the Dream: Big Band Jazz and the Rebirth of American Culture*, University of Chicago Press

Euro Jazz Book 1996/7. International Jazz Directory, Paris, IRMA Publishing, 1996

Eyerman, Ron and Andrew Jamison, 1998. *Music and Social Movements: Mobilizing Traditions in the Twentieth Century*, Cambridge University Press

Faulkner, Anne Shaw, 1999. 'Does Jazz Put the Sin in Syncopation?', in Walser 1999, 32–5

Feather, Leonard, 1957. *The Book of Jazz*, New York, Horizon

———, 1986. *The Jazz Years. Earwitness to an Era*, London, Quartet

Fiehrer, Thomas, 1991. 'From Quadrille to Stomp: The Creole Origins of Jazz',
   Popular Music 10/1 (1991), 21–38

[*Finnish Music Quarterly*], 1992. 'A Musical History of Independent Finland',
   Finnish Music Quarterly 4/92 (1992), 2–23

Fish, Stanley, 1980. *Is There a Text in the Class? The Authority of Interpretive
   Communities*, Cambridge, Mass., Harvard University Press

Fitzgerald, F. Scott, 1956. *The Crack-Up*, ed. Edmund Wilson, New York, New
   Directions

Floyd, Samuel A., 1995. *The Power of Black Music: Interpreting Its History From
   Africa to the United States*, Oxford University Press

Flynn, Thomas R., 1993. 'Foucault and the Eclipse of Vision', in Levin 1993,
   273–86

Foucault, Michel, 1977. *Discipline and Punish: The Birth of the Prison*, trans. Alan
   Sheridan, New York, Pantheon

Gabbard, Krin (ed.), 1995a. *Jazz Among the Discourses*, Durham, N.C., and
   London, Duke University Press

———, 1995b. 'The Jazz Canon and Its Consequences', in *Jazz Among the
   Discourses*, 1–28

———, (ed.), 1995c. *Representing Jazz*, Durham, N.C., and London, Duke
   University Press

———, 1995d. 'Signifyin(g) the Phallus: *Mo' Better Blues* and Representations
   of the Jazz Trumpet', in *Representing Jazz*, 104–30

———, 1996. *Jammin' at the Margins: Jazz and the American Cinema*, University
   of Chicago Press

Gade, Svend, 1928. *Jazz Mad*, New York, Jacobsen-Hodskinson Corp.

Galassi, Peter, 1996. *Roy DeCarava: A Retrospective*, New York, Museum of Modern
   Art

Garafola, Lynn and Nancy Van Norman Baer (eds), 1999. *The Ballets Russes and Its
   World*, New Haven, Conn., Yale University Press

Gates, Henry Louis, Jr, 1988. *The Signifying Monkey: A Theory of African-American
   Literary Criticism*, New York, Oxford University Press

Gelatt, Roland, 1977. *The Fabulous Phonograph 1877–1977*, New York, Macmillan

Gendron, Bernard, 1995. 'Moldy Figs and Modernists: Jazz at War (1942–1946)',
   in Gabbard, *Jazz Among the Discourses*, 31–56

Gerard, Charley, 1998. *Jazz in Black and White: Race, Culture, and Identity in the
   Jazz Community*, Westport, Conn., Praeger

Gerstel, Alice, 1994. 'Jazz Band', in Kaes *et al.* 1994, 554–5

Giddins, Gary, 1987. 'Bird Lives!', in Woideck 1998, 3–9

———, 1988. *Satchmo*, New York, Doubleday

———, 1998. *Visions of Jazz: The First Century*, Oxford University Press

Giese, Fritz, 1925. *Girlkultur: Vergleiche zwischen Amerikanischem und europaischem
   Rhythmus und Lebensgefuhl*, Munich, Delphin

Gillespie, Dizzy, 1979. *To Be Or Not . . . To Bop: Memoirs.* New York, Doubleday

Gilmore, Samuel, 1990. 'Art Worlds: Developing the Interactionist Approach to
   Social Organisation', in Howard S. Becker and Michael M. McCall (eds),
   Symbolic Interaction and Cultural Studies, University of Chicago Press, 148–78

Gilroy, Paul, 1993. *The Black Atlantic: Modernity and Double Consciousness*, Cambridge Mass., Harvard University Press, and London, Verso

Gioia, Ted, 1997. *The History of Jazz*, Oxford University Press

Godbolt, Jim, 1984. *A History of Jazz in Britain 1919–50*, London, Quartet

Goddard, Chris, 1979. *Jazz Away From Home*, London, Paddington Press

Goehr, Lydia, 1992. *The Imaginary Museum of Musical Works: An Essay in the Philosophy of Music*, Oxford, Clarendon Press

Goffin, Robert, 1932. *Aux frontières du jazz*, Paris, Editions du Sagittaire
———, 1999. 'Defining "Hot Jazz"', in Walser 1999, 82–6

Goll, Ivan, 1994. 'The Negroes are Conquering Europe. The Negroes are Conquering Europe', in Kaes *et al.* 1994, 559–60

Goldman, Albert, 1993. *Sound Bites*, London, Abacus

Gottlieb, Robert (ed.), 1996. *Reading Jazz*, New York, Pantheon, and London, Bloomsbury, 1997

Gottlieb, William P., 1995. *The Golden Age of Jazz* [1979], San Francisco, Pomegranate Artbooks, expanded edn

Gottschild, Brenda Dixon, 1996. *Digging the Africanist Presence in American Performance*, Westport, Conn., Greenwood Press

Gray, Herman, 1988. *Producing Jazz: The Experience of an Independent Record Company*, Philadelphia, Temple University Press

Gregory, Richard L. (ed.), 1987. *The Oxford Companion to the Mind*, Oxford University Press

Gridley, Mark C., 1984. *How to Teach Jazz History: A Teaching Manual and Test Bank*, Manhattan, Kansas, International Association of Jazz Educators, second edn
———, 1997. *Jazz Styles: History and Analysis*, Englewood Cliffs, N.J., Prentice-Hall [1985]; sixth edn

Gridley, Mark, Robert Maxham, and Robert Hoff, 1989. 'Three Approaches to Defining Jazz', *Musical Quarterly* 73 (1989), 513–31

Gronow, Pekka, 1986. 'Things Happen That Way', *Finnish Music Quarterly* 3/86 (1986), 20–24
———, 1989. 'The Recording Industry in Finland', *Finnish Music Quarterly* 4/89 (1989), 3–8
———, 1992. 'Wartimes Sounds', *Finnish Music Quarterly* 3/92 (1992), 22–32
———, 1996. *The Recording Industry: An Ethnomusicological Approach*, Tampere, University of Tampere

Gumbrecht, Hans Ulrich, 1997. *In 1926: Living at the Edge of Time*. Cambridge, Mass., Harvard University Press

Gushee, Lawrence, 1981. 'Lester Young's "Shoe Shine Boy"', in Daniel Heartz and Bonnie Wade (eds), *International Musicological Society: Report of the Twelfth Congress, Berkeley, 1977*, Kassel, Bärenreiter, 1981, 151–69; repr. in Porter 1991, 224–54
———, 1998. 'The Improvisation of Louis Armstrong', in Nettl and Russell 1998, 291–334

Haavisto, Jukka, 1996. *Seven Decades of Finnish Jazz: Jazz in Finland 1919–1969*, trans. Roger Freundlich, Helsinki, Finnish Music Information

Hadler, Mona, 1983. 'Jazz and the Visual Arts', *Arts Magazine* (June 1983), 91–101

Hajdu, David, 1996. *Lush Life: A Biography of Billy Strayhorn*, New York, Farrar, Straus & Giroux

Haynes, Tony, Julie Eaglen and Dave Laing, 1982. *Music In-Between*, London, Gulbenkian Foundation

Helasvuo, Veikko, 1987. 'The 1920s: Fresh Breezes from Europe', trans. William Moore, *Finnish Music Quarterly* 3–4/87 (1987), 2–10

Hentoff, Nat, 1962. *The Jazz Life*, London, Peter Davies

Hentoff, Nat, and Albert McCarthy (eds), 1977. *Jazz*, London, Quartet

Hershey, Burnet, 1999. 'Jazz Latitude', in Walser 1999, 25–31

Hesse, Hermann, 1969. *Steppenwolf*, trans. Basil Creighton, New York, Bantam

Hickok, Robert, 1979. *Exploring Music*, Philippines, Addison-Wesley, second edn

Hinton, Milt and David G. Berger, 1988. *Bass Line: The Stories and Photographs of Milt Hinton*, Philadelphia, Temple University Press

Hirsch, Paul M., 1972. 'Processing Fads and Fashions: An Organization-set Analysis of Cultural Industry Systems', *American Journal of Sociology* 77 (1972), 639–59

Hitchcock, H. Wiley and Stanley Sadie (eds), 1986. *The New Grove Dictionary of American Music*, 4 vols., London, Macmillan

Hobsbawm, Eric, 1998. *Uncommon People: Resistance, Rebellion and Jazz*, London, Weidenfeld & Nicolson

Hodeir, André, 1956. *Jazz: Its Evolution and Essence*, trans. David Noakes, New York, Grove Press, and London, Secker & Warburg

———, 1959. 'Perspective of Modern Jazz: Popularity or Recognition', *Down Beat* 26/17 (20 August 1959)

Hoggart, Richard, 1957. *The Uses of Literacy*, Harmondsworth, Penguin, repr. 1965

Holbrook, Dick, 1974. 'Our Word JAZZ', *Storyville* (December 1973 – January 1974), 46–58

Holmes, John Clellon, 1958. *The Horn*, New York, Thunders Mouth, repr. 1988

Hopkins, Ernest J., 1913. 'In Praise of "Jazz"', *San Francisco Bulletin*, 5 April 1913

Horn, David, 2000. 'Some Thoughts on the Work in Popular Music', in Michael Talbot (ed.), *The Musical Work: Reality or Invention?*, Liverpool University Press, 2000, 14–34

Horowitz, Joseph, 1998. '"Sermons in Tones"': Sacralization as a Theme in American Classical Music', *American Music* 16/2 (Fall 1998), 311–40

Hosokawa, Shuhei *et al.* (eds), 1991. *A Guide to Popular Music in Japan*, Kanazawa, International Association for the Study of Popular Music – Japan

Howard, Joseph A., 1978. 'The Improvisational Techniques of Art Tatum', 3 vols., PhD dissertation, Case Western Reserve

Huggins, Nathan Irvin, 1971. *Harlem Renaissance*, Oxford University Press

Hughes, Langston, 1969. *Not Without Laughter*, New York, Simon and Schuster, repr. 1995

Hurston, Zora Neale, 1995. *Folklore, Memoirs, and Other Writings*, 'Library of America' series, Literary Classics of the United States, New York

IFPI [International Federation of the Phonographic Industry], 1999. *The Recording Industry In Numbers 1998*, London, IFPI

Jackson, Travis A., 2000. 'Jazz Performance as Ritual: The Blues Aesthetic and the African Diaspora', in Monson, *The African Diaspora*, 23–82

Jaffe, Andrew, 1983. *Jazz Theory*, Dubuque, Iowa, William C. Brown Company

Jalkanen, Pekka, 1989. *Alaska, Bombay Ja Billy Boy: Jazzkulttuurin murros Helsingissä 1920-luvulla*, Suomen etnomusikologisen seuran julkaisuja 2, Helsinki, University of Helsinki

———, 1993. *The Roots of Finnish Popular Music*, trans. Susan Sinisalo, [Helsinki], Finnish Music Information Centre

Janowitz, Hans, 1927. *Jazz*, Berlin, Verlag die Schmiede

Jarrett, Michael, 1995. 'The Tenor's Vehicle: Reading *Way Out West*', in Gabbard, *Representing Jazz*, 260–82

———, 1999. *Drifting on a Read: Jazz as a Model for Writing*, Albany, N.Y., State University of New York Press

Järviluoma, Helmi (ed.), 1994. *Soundscapes: Essays on Vroom and Moo*, Tampere, Department of Folk Tradition, University of Tampere

Jarvis, Jeff, 1990. 'The Improvised Jazz Solo: An Endangered Species', *Jazz Educators Journal* 22/4 (Spring 1990), 70–74

Johnson, Bruce, 1987. *The Oxford Companion to Australian Jazz*, Melbourne, Oxford University Press

———, 1993. 'Hear Me Talkin' To Ya: Problems of Jazz Discourse', *Popular Music* 12/1 (January 1993), 1–12

———, 1996. 'Resituating Improvisation', *Journal of Improvisational Practice* 2/1 (1996), 6–11

———, 1998. 'Doctored Jazz: Early Australian Jazz Journals', *Perfect Beat: The Pacific Journal of Research into Contemporary Music and Popular Culture* 3/4 (January 1998), 26–37

———, 2000. *The Inaudible Music: Jazz, Gender and Australian Modernity*, Sydney, Currency Press

Johnson, Jerah, 1991. 'New Orleans's Congo Square: An Urban Setting for Early Afro-American Culture Formation', *Louisiana History* (Spring 1991), 117–57

Johnson, Mark and George Lakoff, 1980. *Metaphors We Live By*, University of Chicago Press

Jones, A. M., 1959. *Studies in African Music*, Oxford University Press

Jones, LeRoi [Amiri Baraka], 1963. *Blues People: Negro Music in White America*, New York, William Morrow & Company

———, 1968. *Black Music*, New York, William Morrow & Company

Josephson, Matthew, 1922. 'After and Beyond Dada', *Broom* 2 (1922), 346–50

Jost, Ekkehard, 1974. *Free Jazz*, Graz, Universal

———, 1999. 'Über einige Probleme jazzmusikalischer Analyse', *Jazzforschung/Jazz Research* [*Jazz Analyze: Lectures of the 5th Jazz Musicological Congress*] 31 (1999), 11–18

Kaes, Anton, Martin Jay and Edward Dimendberg (eds), 1994. *The Weimar Republic Sourcebook*, Berkeley, University of California Press

Kahn, Douglas, 1999. *Noise, Water, Meat: A History of Sound in the Arts*, Cambridge, Mass., The MIT Press

Kammen, Michael, 1996. *The Lively Arts: Gilbert Seldes and the Transformation of Cultural Criticism in the United States*, Oxford University Press

Kappler, Frank K., Bob Wilber and Richard M. Sudhalter, 1980. *Sidney Bechet*, Chicago, Time-Life Books Inc.

Kater, Michael H., 1992. *Different Drummers: Jazz in the Culture of Nazi Germany*, Oxford University Press

Keil, Charles, 1966. 'Motion and Feeling Through Music', *Journal of Aesthetics and Art Criticism* 24 (1966), 337–49

———, 1995. 'The Theory of Participatory Discrepancies: A Progress Report', *Ethnomusicology: Journal of the Society for Ethnomusicology* 39/1 (Winter 1995), 1–19

Keil, Charles, and Steven Feld, 1994. *Music Grooves*, University of Chicago Press

Kennedy, Rick, 1994. *Jelly Roll, Bix and Hoagy: Gennett Studios and the Birth of Recorded Jazz*, Bloomington, Indiana University Press

Kenney, William, 1993. *Chicago Jazz: A Cultural History*, Oxford University Press

Kerman, Joseph, 1985. *Musicology*, London, Fontana

Kernfeld, Barry, 1981. 'Adderley, Coltrane, and Davis at the Twilight of Bebop: The Search for Melodic Coherence (1958–59)', PhD dissertation, Cornell University

——— (ed.), 1988. *The New Grove Dictionary of Jazz*, 2 vols., Macmillan, London; single-volume reprint, 1994

———, 1995. *What to Listen For in Jazz*, New Haven, Conn., and London, Yale University Press

Kerouac, Jack, 1959. 'The Beginning of Bop', in Ann Charters (ed.), *The Portable Jack Kerouac*, New York, Viking, 1995, 555–9

Kerschbaumer, Franz, 1978. 'Miles Davis: Stilkritische Untersuchungen zur musikalischen Entwicklung seines Personalstils', PhD dissertation, Universität Graz [1976]; revised edn in *Beiträge zur Jazzforschung* 5, Graz

Khan, Ashley, 2000. *Kind of Blue: The Making of a Masterpiece*, New York, Da Capo Press

Kingsley, Walter, 1999. 'Whence Comes Jass?', in Walser 1999, 5–7

Kirchner, Bill (ed.), 2000. *The Oxford Companion to Jazz*, Oxford University Press

Kiroff, Matthew John, 1997. '"Caseworks" As Performed by Cecil Taylor and the Art Ensemble of Chicago: A Musical Analysis and Sociopolitical History', DMA study, Cornell University

Kirstein, Lincoln, 1938. 'Popular Style in American Dancing', *The Nation* 146 (16 April 1938), 450–51

———, 1983. 'Classic Ballet: Aria of the Aerial', in Copeland and Cohen 1983, 264–5

———, 1991. *By With To & From: A Lincoln Kirstein Reader*, ed. Nicholas Jenkins, New York, Farrar, Straus & Giroux

Kjellberg, Erik, 1998. *Jan Johansson*, Stockholm, Svensk Music

Kmen, Henry A., 1966. *Music in New Orleans, The Formative Years, 1791–1841*, Baton Rouge, Louisiana State University Press

Knauer, Wolfram, 1999. 'Der Analytiker-Blues Anmerkungen zu Entwicklung und Dilemma der Jazzanalyse von den 30er Jahren bis heute', *Jazzforschung/Jazz Research* 31 (1999), 27–42

Kofsky, Frank, 1970. *Black Nationalism and the Revolution in Music*, New York, Pathfinder Press

———, 1998. *Black Music, White Business: Illuminating the History and Political Economy of Jazz*, New York, Pathfinder

Konttinen, Matti, 1987. 'The Jazz Invasion', trans. Susan Sinisalo, *Finnish Music Quarterly* 3–4/87 (1987), 20–25

———, 1989. 'Finnish Jazz Records', *Finnish Music Quarterly* 4 (1989), 33–9

Kracauer, Siegfried, 1927. 'The Mass Ornament', in *The Mass Ornament: Weimar Essays*, ed. and trans. Thomas Y. Levin, Cambridge, Mass., Harvard University Press, 1955

Kraut, Anthea, 1998. 'Reclaiming the Body: Representations of Black Dance in Three Plays by Zora Neale Hurston', *Theatre Studies* 43 (1998), 23–36

Krenek, Ernst, 1994. 'New Humanity and Old Objectivity', in Kaes *et al.* 1994, 586–8

Krieger, Franz, 1995. 'Untersuchungen zum Stilwandel im Jazz-Solopianospiel am Beispiel ausgewählter "Body and Soul"-Aufnahmen zwischen 1938 und 1992', PhD dissertation, University of Graz [1994]; published as 'Jazz-Solopiano: Zum Stilwandel am Beispiel ausgewählter "Body and Soul"-Aufnahmen von 1938–1992', *Jazzforschung/Jazz Research* 27 (1995)

Krutch, Joseph Wood, 1939. *The American Drama Since 1918*, New York, Random House

Kuhn, Thomas S., 1970. *The Structure of Scientific Revolutions*, University of Chicago Press, second edition

Kundera, Milan, 1992. *The Joke*, London, Faber & Faber

Laird, Ross, 1992. *Sound Beginnings: The Early Record Industry in Australia*, Sydney, Currency Press

Laing, Dave, 1969. *The Sound of Our Time*, London, Sheed & Ward

Lakoff, George, 1987. *Women, Fire, and Dangerous Things: What Categories Reveal About the Mind*, University of Chicago Press

Lambert, Constant, 1934. *Music Ho! A Study of Music in Decline*, London, Faber and Faber; New York, Scribner

Lamphear, Guy A., 1922. *The Modern Dance: A Fearless Discussion of a Social Menace*, Chicago, Glad Tidings Pub. Co.

Larkin, Philip, 1985. *All What Jazz: A Record Diary 1961–1971*, London, Faber and Faber, revised edn

Larson, Steven, 1987. 'Schenkerian Analysis of Modern Jazz', PhD dissertation, University of Michigan

Lawson, John Howard, 1925. *Processional: A Jazz Symphony of American Life in Four Acts*, New York, Seltzer

Lees, Gene, 1994. *Cats of Any Color: Jazz, Black and White*, Oxford University Press

Le Guin, Elisabeth 1999. '"Cello-and-Bow Thinking": Boccherini's Sonata in E-flat Major, "*fuori catalogo*"', *Echo* 1 (1999), 1

Leiris, Michel, 1984. *Manhood*, trans. Richard Howard, San Francisco, North Point

Lemke, Sieglinde, 1998. *Primitivist Modernism: Black Culture and the Origins of Transatlantic Modernism*, Oxford University Press

Leonard, Neil, 1962. *Jazz and the White Americans: The Acceptance of a New Art Form*, University of Chicago Press

Leonard, Susan, M., 1988. 'An Introduction to Black Participation in the Early Recording Era, 1890–1920', *Annual Review of Jazz Studies* 4 (1988), 31–44

Levin, David Michael (ed.), 1993. *Modernity and the Hegemony of Vision*, Berkeley, Los Angeles and London, University of California Press

Levine, Lawrence W., 1988. *Highbrow/Lowbrow: The Emergence of Cultural Hierarchy in America*, Cambridge, Mass., Harvard University Press
———, 1993. *The Unpredictable Past: Explorations in American Cultural History*, Oxford University Press

Levine, Mark, 1995. *The Jazz Theory Book*, Petaluma, Calif., Sher Music

Levinson, Peter J., 1999. *Trumpet Blues: The Life of Harry James*, Oxford University Press

Liebman, David, 1978. *Lookout Farm: A Case Study of Improvisation for Small Jazz Group*, Hollywood, Almo

Lipsitz, George, 1990. *Time Passages: Collective Memory and American Popular Culture*, Minneapolis, University of Minnesota Press

Lomax, Alan, 1950. *Mister Jelly Roll*, New York, Grosset and Dunlap; repr. Berkeley, University of California Press, 1973, London, Virgin, 1991, and New York, Pantheon, 1993

Lord, Albert B., 1960. *The Singer of Tales*, Harvard Studies in Comparative Literature, No. 24, Cambridge, Mass., Harvard University Press

Lott, Eric, 1993. *Love and Theft: Blackface Minstrelsy and the American Working Class*, Oxford University Press
———, 1995. 'Double V, Double-Time: Bebop's Politics of Style', in Gabbard, *Jazz Among the Discourses*, 243–55

Mahar, William J., 1999. *Behind the Burnt Cork Mask: Early Blackface Minstrelsy and Antebellum American Popular Culture*, Urbana and Chicago, University of Illinois Press

Major, Clarence, 1994. *Juba to Jive: A Dictionary of African-American Slang*, New York, Viking

Malnig, Julie, 1992. *Dancing Till Dawn: A Century of Exhibition Ballroom Dance*, New York University Press

Mandel, H., 1999. *Future Jazz*, Oxford University Press

Marquis, Alice Goldfarb, 1998. 'Jazz Goes to College: Has Academic Status Served the Art?', *Popular Music and Society* 22/2 (1998), 117–24

Marquis, Donald M., 1978. *In Search of Buddy Bolden, First Man of Jazz*, Louisiana State University Press

Marsh, Graham, Felix Cromey and Glyn Callingham (eds), 1991. *Blue Note: The Album Cover Art*, San Francisco, Chronicle Books

Martin, Henry, 1996. *Charlie Parker and Thematic Improvisation*, Lanham, MD, Scarecrow Press

Martin, Peter J., 1995. *Sounds and Society: Themes in the Sociology of Music*, Manchester University Press

McDaniel, William T., Jr, 1993. 'The Status of Jazz Education in the 1990s: A Historical Commentary', *International Jazz Archives Journal* 1/1 (1993), 114–39

Meeker, David, 1981. *Jazz in the Movies*, New York, Da Capo, enlarged edition

Mehegan, John F., 1959a. *Jazz Improvisation 1: Tonal and Rhythmic Principles*, New York, Watson-Guptil

———, 1959b. 'The Case for Swinging', *Down Beat* 26/17 (20 August 1959)

Meltzer, David (ed.), 1993. *Reading Jazz*, San Francisco, Mercury House

Mensah, Atta Annan, 1972. 'Jazz – The Round Trip', *Jazzforschung* 3–4 (1971–72), 124–37

Mendl, R. W. S., 1927. *The Appeal of Jazz*, London, Philip Allan

Mezzrow, Mezz and Bernard Wolfe, 1972. *Really the Blues*, New York, Anchor

Middleton, Richard, 1990. *Studying Popular Music*, Buckingham, Open University Press

Mitchell, Jack, 1988. *Australian Jazz on Record 1925–80*, Canberra, Australian Government Publishing Service

Monson, Ingrid, 1994. 'Doubleness and Jazz Improvisation: Irony, Parody, and Ethnomusicology', *Critical Inquiry* 20 (1994), 283–313

———, 1996. *Saying Something: Jazz Improvisation and Interaction*, University of Chicago Press

———, 1999. 'Riffs, Repetition, and Theories of Globalization', *Ethnomusicology* 43/1 (Winter 1999), 31–65

———, (ed.), 2000. *The African Diaspora: A Musical Perspective*, New York, Garland

Moody, Bill, 1999. *Bird Lives*, New York, Walker

Moore, Joe B., 1998. 'Studying Jazz in Postwar Japan: Where to Begin?', *Japanese Studies* 18/3 (1998), 265–80

Moore, Macdonald Smith, 1985. *Yankee Blues: Musical Culture and American Identity*, Bloomington, Indiana University Press

Morris, Ronald L., 1980. *Wait Until Dark: Jazz and the Underworld 1880–1940*, Bowling Green, Ohio, Bowling Green University Popular Press

Morrison, Toni, 1993. *Jazz*, New York, Knopf

Munn, H. O., 1960. *The Story of the Original Dixieland Jazz Band*, Baton Rouge, Louisiana State University Press

Murphy, Dan, 1994. 'Jazz Studies in American Schools and Colleges: A Brief History', *Jazz Educators Journal* 26/3 (March 1994) 34–8

Murray, Albert, 1976. *Stomping the Blues*, New York, McGraw-Hill; Vintage, 1982

Myers, Gerald E. (ed.), 2000. *Modern Dance, Jazz Music, and American Culture*, American Dance Festival and the John F. Kennedy Center for the Performing Arts

Negus, Keith, 1997a. *Popular Music in Theory: An Introduction*, Oxford, Polity Press

———, 1997b. 'The Production of Culture', in Paul Du Gay (ed.), *Production of Culture/Cultures of Production*, Milton Keynes, Open University Press, 67–118

Nettl, Bruno, 1974. 'Thoughts on Improvisation: A Comparative Approach', *Musical Quarterly* 60 (1974), 1–19

———, 1998. 'An Art Neglected in Scholarship', introduction to Nettl and Russell 1998, 1–23

Nettl, Bruno, and Melinda Russell (eds), 1998. *In the Course of Performance: Studies in the World of Musical Improvisation*, University of Chicago Press

Newton, Francis [Eric Hobsbawm], 1960. *The Jazz Scene*, Boston, Mass., Monthly Review Press

Nicolausson, Harry, 1983. *Swedish Jazz Discography*, Stockholm, Swedish Music Information Centre

Nicholson, Stuart, 1995. *Jazz: The 1980s Resurgence*, New York, Da Capo
———, 1998. *Jazz-Rock: A History*, New York, Schirmer Books; Edinburgh, Canongate
———, 1999. *A Portrait of Duke Ellington: Reminiscing in Tempo*, London, Sidgwick & Jackson; repr. London, Pan, 2000

Nisenson, Eric, 1997. *Blue: The Murder of Jazz*, New York, St Martin's Press
———, 2000. *The Making of* Kind of Blue: *Miles Davis and His Masterpiece*, New York, St Martin's Press

Noll, Dietrich J., 1977. 'Struktur Untersuchungen zum deutschen Free Jazz von 1964–1974', PhD dissertation, University of Marburg; published as *Zur Improvisation im deutschen Free Jazz: Unters. zur Ästhetik frei improvisierter Klangflächen*, Hamburg, Verlag der Musikalienhandlung Wagner

Ogren, Kathy, 1989. *The Jazz Revolution: Twenties America and the Meaning of Jazz*, Oxford University Press

Oliver, Paul, 1991. 'That Certain Feeling: Blues and Jazz . . . in 1890?', *Popular Music* 10/1 (1991), 11–19

O'Meally, Robert G., 1998. *The Jazz Cadence of American Culture*, New York, Columbia University Press

Omi, Michael and Howard Winant, 1994. *Racial Formation in the United States: From the 1960s to the 1990s*, London, Routledge, second edn

Ondaatje, Michael, 1976. *Coming Through Slaughter*, New York, Norton

Ong, Walter J., 1982. *Orality and Literacy: The Technologizing of the Word*, London, Routledge

Osgood, Henry O., 1926. *So This is Jazz*, Boston, Little, Brown

Ostendorf, Berndt, 1982. *Black Literature in White America*, Brighton, Harvester Press

Owens, Thomas, 1974a. 'Charlie Parker: Techniques of Improvisation', 2 vols., PhD dissertation, University of California at Los Angeles
———, 1974b. 'Applying the Melograph to "Parker's Mood"', *Selected Reports in Ethnomusicology* 2 (1974), 167–74
———, 1995. *Bebop: The Music and its Players*, New York, Oxford University Press

Palmer, Richard, 1984. *Oscar Peterson*, Tunbridge Wells, Spellmount

Parry, Milman, 1971. *The Making of Homeric Verse*, ed. Adam Parry, Oxford, Clarendon Press

Pattee, Fred Lewis, 1925. *Tradition and Jazz*, New York, The Century Co.

Peretti, Burton, 1992. *The Creation of Jazz: Music, Race, and Culture in Urban America*, Urbana, University of Illinois Press

Perlman, Alan M. and Daniel Greenblatt, 1981. 'Miles Davis Meets Noam Chomsky: Some Observations on Jazz Improvisation and Language Structure', in Steiner 1981, 169–83

Porter, Lewis, 1985. 'The Jazz Improvisations of Lester Young', MA thesis, Tufts University [1979]; revised as *Lester Young*, Boston, Twayne

――――, (ed.), 1991. *A Lester Young Reader*, Washington, DC, Smithsonian

――――, 1997. *Jazz: A Century of Change*, New York, Schirmer Books

――――, 1998. *John Coltrane: His Life and Music*, Ann Arbor, University of Michigan Press

Porter, Lewis, Michael Ullman and Ed Hazell, 1993. *Jazz: From Its Origins to the Present*, Englewood Cliffs, N.J., Prentice-Hall

Potter, Gary, 1990. 'Analyzing Improvised Jazz', *College Music Symposium* 30 (Spring 1990), 64–74

Pound, Ezra, 1977. *Ezra Pound and Music: The Complete Criticism*, ed. R. Murray Schafer, New York, New Directions

Pressing, Jeff, 1982. 'Pitch Class Set Structures in Contemporary Jazz', *Jazzforschung/Jazz Research* 14 (1982), 133–72

――――, 1987. 'The Micro- and Macrostructural Design of Improvised Music', *Music Perception* 5/2 (1987), 132–72

――――, 1988. 'Improvisation: Methods and Models', in Sloboda 1988, 129–78

――――, (ed.), 1994. *Compositions for Improvisers: An Australian Perspective*, Melbourne, La Trobe University Press

Pyke, Launcelot Allen II, 1962. 'Jazz, 1920 to 1927: An Analytical Study', 2 vols., PhD dissertation, State University of Iowa

Pynchon, Thomas, 1973. *Gravity's Rainbow*, New York, Viking

――――, 1984. 'Introduction', *Slow Learner: Early Stories*, Boston, Mass., Little Brown

Queroy, Jean-Claude, 1996. 'Labels indépendants et le jazz français contemporain', *Ecouter Voir* 54/55 (June/July 1996), 17–20

Ramsey Jr, Frederick and Charles Edward Smith (eds), 1939. *Jazzmen*, New York, Harcourt Brace

Rasula, Jed, 1995. 'The Media of Memory: The Seductive Menace of Records in Jazz History', in Gabbard, *Jazz Among the Discourses*, 134–62

Rattenbury, Ken, 1990. *Duke Ellington: Jazz Composer*, Westport, Conn., Yale University Press

Reisner, Robert, 1962. *Bird: The Legend of Charlie Parker*, London, Quartet

Reeves, Scott D., 1989. *Creative Jazz Improvisation*, Englewood Cliffs, N.J., Prentice-Hall

――――, 1991. 'Don't Neglect Improvisation', *Jazz Educators Journal* 23/3 (Winter 1991), 65–7

Review of Jazz in England, 1995. Consultative Green Paper, Arts Council of England, London

Riley, John, 1994. *The Art of Bop Drumming*, New York, Manhattan Music

Roach, Max, 1972. 'What Jazz Means To Me', *The Black Scholar* (Summer 1972), 3–6

Roche, Juliette, 1920. *Demi Cercle*, Paris, Editions d'Art 'La Cible'

Rogin, Michael, 1996. *Blackface, White Noise: Jewish Immigrants in the Hollywood Melting Pot*, Berkeley, University of California Press

Rose, Arnold M. (ed.), 1962. *Human Behaviour and Social Processes*, London, Routledge

Rose, Jon, 1994. *Violin Music in the Age of Shopping*, Melbourne, NMA [New Music Articles]

Rose, Jon, and Rainer Linz, 1992. *The Pink Violin*, Melbourne, NMA

Rosen, Charles, 1976. *The Classical Style*, London, Faber and Faber, revised edn

Rubington, Earl, and Martin Weinberg (eds), 1999. *Deviance: The Interactionist Perspective*, Boston, Mass., Allyn and Bacon

Russell, George A., 1959. *The Lydian Chromatic Concept of Tonal Organization for Improvisation*, New York, Concept Publishing, second edn

Russell, Ross, 1961. *The Sound*, New York, Dutton

———, 1973. *Bird Lives! The High Life and Hard Times of Charlie 'Yardbird' Parker*, London, Quartet

Ryan, John, 1985. *The Production of Culture in the Music Industry: The ASCAP-BMI Controversy*, Lanham, MD, University Press of America

Sachs, Curt, 1965. *World History of the Dance*, trans. Bessie Schönberg, New York, W. W. Norton

Salzer, Felix, 1952. *Structural Hearing*, New York, Boni; repr. New York, Dover, 1962

Sargeant, Winthrop, 1938. *Jazz: Hot and Hybrid*, New York, Arrow; new and enlarged edn, New York, E. P. Dutton, 1946; revised as *Jazz, a History*, New York, McGraw-Hill, 1964

Schafer, R. Murray, 1977. *The Tuning of the World*, Toronto, McLelland & Stewart

Schenker, Heinrich, 1933. *Fünf Urlinie-Tafeln*, New York, Mannes; repr. as *Five Graphic Music Analyses*, New York, Dover, 1969

Scher, Steven Paul (ed.), 1992. *Music and Text: Critical Enquiries*, Cambridge University Press

Schiff, David, 1997. *Gershwin: Rhapsody in Blue*, Cambridge University Press

Schuller, Gunther, 1958. 'Sonny Rollins and the Challenge of Thematic Improvising', *Jazz Review* 1/1 (1958), 6–11; repr. in M. Williams 1962, 239–52; Schuller 1996, 86–97, and Walser 1999, 212–22

———, 1968. *Early Jazz: Its Roots and Musical Development*, Oxford University Press

———, 1989. *The Swing Era: The Development of Jazz, 1930–1945*, Oxford University Press

———, 1996. *Musings: The Musical Worlds of Gunther Schuller*, Oxford University Press; repr. New York, Da Capo Press, 1999

Schultz, William J., 1922. 'Jazz', *The Nation* 115 (25 October 1922), 438–9

Seldes, Gilbert, 1923. 'Toujours Jazz', *The Dial* 75 (August 1923), 151–66

Senelick, Laurence (ed. and trans.), 1993. *Cabaret Performance, Volume II: Europe 1920–1940. Sketches, Songs, Monologues, Memoirs*, Baltimore, Md., Johns Hopkins University Press

Shapiro, Nat and Nat Hentoff (eds), 1955. *Hear Me Talkin' To Ya*, New York, Rinehart and Company, Inc.

Shefte, Art, 1925. *Jazz Breaks, Blue Breaks, Hot Breaks and Jazz Bass for Piano*, 4 vols., Chicago, Forster

Sher, Chuck (ed.), 1995. *The New Real Book, Volume 3*, Petaluma, Calif., Sher Music Co.

Shibutani, Tamotsu, 1962. 'Reference Groups and Social Control', in A. Rose 1962, 128–47

Shipton, Alyn, 1999. *Groovin' High: The Life of Dizzy Gillespie*, Oxford University Press

Simon, Tom, 1978. 'An Analytical Inquiry into Thelonious Monk's "Ruby, My Dear"', MA thesis, University of Michigan

Singer, Barry, 1992. *Black and Blue: The Life and Lyrics of Andy Razaf*, New York, Schirmer Books

Škvorecký, Josef, 1979. *The Bass Saxophone*, trans. Káca Poláclová-Henley, New York, Knopf

Sloboda, John A. (ed.), 1988. *Generative Processes in Music: The Psychology of Performance, Improvisation, and Composition*, Oxford, Clarendon Press

Small, Christopher, 1977. *Music-Society-Education*, Hanover, N.H., Wesleyan University Press, 1996
    ———, 1984. 'No Meanings Without Rules', in *Improvisation: History, Directions, Practice*, London, Association of Improvising Musicians, 1–5
    ———, 1987a. *Music of the Common Tongue: Survival and Celebration in Afro-American Music*, London, Calder
    ———, 1987b. 'Performance as Ritual: A Sketch for an Enquiry into the True Nature of a Symphony Concert', in White 1987, 6–32
    ———, 1998. *Musicking: The Meanings of Performing and Listening*, Hanover, N.H., Wesleyan University Press

Smith, Gregory Eugene, 1983. 'Homer, Gregory, and Bill Evans? The Theory of Formulaic Composition in the Context of Jazz Piano Improvisation', PhD dissertation, Harvard University

Spring, Howard, 1997. 'Swing and the Lindy Hop: Dance, Venue, Media, and Tradition', *American Music* 15 (Summer 1997), 183–207

Starr, S. Frederick, 1983. *Red and Hot: The Fate of Jazz in the Soviet Union 1917–1980*, Oxford University Press

Stearns, Marshall, 1956. *The Story of Jazz*, Oxford University Press

Stearns, Marshall, and Jean Stearns, 1968. *Jazz Dance: The Story of American Vernacular Dance*, New York, Macmillan; repr. Da Capo, 1994

Steegmuller, Francis, 1970. *Cocteau, A Biography*, Boston, Mass., Little, Brown

Stein, Gertrude, 1935. *Lectures in America*, New York, Random House

Steiner, Wendy (ed.), 1981. *The Sign in Music and Literature*, Austin, University of Texas

Stern, Chip, 1999. 'The Emperor of the Cool; Jim Hall', *Jazz Journal* 29 (August 1999), 32–41

Stevens, Wallace, 1972. *The Palm at the End of the Mind*, ed. Holly Stevens, New York, Knopf

Stewart, Milton Lee, 1975. 'Structural Development in the Jazz Improvisational Technique of Clifford Brown', PhD dissertation, University of Michigan [1973]; published in *Jazzforschung* 6/7 (1974–5), 141–273

Stites, Richard, 1992. *Russian Popular Culture: Entertainment and Society since 1900*, Cambridge University Press

Storey, John, 1993. *An Introductory Guide to Cultural Theory and Popular Culture*, Hertfordshire, Harvester Wheatsheaf

Straw, Will, 1997. 'Sizing Up Record Collections: Gender and Connoisseurship in Rock Music Culture', in Whiteley 1997, 3–16

Strinati, Dominic, 1995. *An Introduction to Theories of Popular Culture*, London and New York, Routledge

Strout, Nicholas, 1986. 'I've Heard That Song Before: Linguistic and Narrative Aspects of Melodic Quotation in Instrumental Jazz Improvisation', MA thesis, Indiana University

Such, David G., 1993. *Avant-Garde Jazz Musicians: Performing 'Out There'*, University of Iowa Press

Sudhalter, Richard M., 1999a. *Lost Chords: White Musicians and Their Contribution to Jazz 1915–1945*, Oxford University Press

———, 1999b. 'Composing the Words that Might Capture Jazz', *New York Times*, 2, 29 August 1999, 1

Sullivan, Jack, 1999. *New World Symphonies: How American Culture Changed European Music*, New Haven, Conn., Yale University Press

Szwed, John F., 2000. *Jazz 101: A Complete Guide to Learning and Loving Jazz*, New York, Hyperion

———, and J. Marti, 1997. *Space is the Place: The Life and Times of Sun Ra*, New York, Pantheon

Tallmadge, William, 1984. 'Blue Notes and Blue Tonality', *Black Perspective in Music* 12 (1984), 155–65

Tarr, Edward, 1988. *The Trumpet*, Portland, Amadeus Press

Tate, Greg, 1992. *Flyboy in the Buttermilk: Essays on Contemporary America*, New York, Simon & Schuster

Taylor, Arthur, 1983. *Notes and Tones: Musician-to-Musician Interviews*, London, Quartet

Taylor, William Edward [Billy], 1975. 'The History and Development of Jazz Piano: A New Perspective for Educators', EdD dissertation, University of Massachusetts; revised as *Jazz Piano, a Jazz History*, Dubuque, Iowa, William C. Brown, 1982

———, 1986. 'Jazz: America's Classical Music', *Black Perspective in Music* 14/1 (Winter 1986), 21–5

Teaching Jazz: A Course of Study, 1996. Reston, Va., Music Educators National Conference

Teachout, Terry, 1995. 'The Color of Jazz', *Commentary* (September 1995), 50–53

Thomas, Lorenzo, 1995. 'Ascension: Music and the Black Arts Movement', in Gabbard, *Jazz Among the Discourses*, 256–74

Tirro, Frank, 1974. 'Constructive Elements in Jazz Improvisation', *Journal of the American Musicological Society* 27 (1974), 285–305

———, 1977. *Jazz: A History*, New York, W. W. Norton

Titlestad, Michael Frank, 1999. *Representations of Jazz Music and Jazz Performance Occasions in Selected Jazz Literature*, MA thesis, University of South Africa

Toledano, Ralph de (ed.), 1994. *Frontiers of Jazz* [1947], Gretna, La., Pelican, third edn

Tomko, Linda, 1999. *Dancing Class: Gender, Ethnicity, and Social Divides in American Dance, 1890–1920*, Bloomington, Indiana University Press

Tomlinson, Gary, 1991. 'Cultural Dialogics and Jazz: A White Scholar Signifies', *Black Music Research Journal* 11/2 (1991), 229–64; shortened repr. in Bergeron and Bohlman 1992, 64–94

Tower, Beeke S., 1990. 'Jungle Music and Song of Machines: Jazz and American Dance in Weimar Culture', in *Envisioning America: Prints, Drawings, and Photographs by George Grosz and His Contemporaries, 1915–1933*, Cambridge, Mass., Busch-Reisinger Museum, 87–105

Towse, Ruth (ed.), 1997. *Baumol's Cost Disease. The Arts and other Victims*, Cheltenham and Northampton, Mass., Edward Elgar

Treitler, Leo, 1989. *Music and the Historical Imagination*, Boston, Mass., Harvard University Press

Tucker, Mark (ed.), 1993. *The Duke Ellington Reader*, Oxford University Press

Turino, Thomas, 1993. *Moving Away From Silence: Music of the Peruvian Altiplano and the Experience of Migration*, University of Chicago Press

Ullman, Michael, 1980. *Jazz Lives: Portraits in Words and Pictures*, New York, Perigee Books

Vail, Ken, 1996. *Bird's Diary: The Life of Charlie Parker 1945–1955*, Chessington, Castle Communications

Vigeland, Carl A., 1991. *In Concert: Onstage and Offstage with the Boston Symphony Orchestra*, Amherst, University of Massachusetts Press

Vincent, Ted, 1995. *Keep Cool: The Black Activists Who Built the Jazz Age*, London, Pluto Press

Walser, Robert, 1988. 'Musical Imagery and Performance Practice in J. S. Bach's Arias with Trumpet', *International Trumpet Guild Journal* 13/1 (September 1988), 62–77

———, 1993. 'Out of Notes: Signification, Interpretation, and the Problem of Miles Davis', *Musical Quarterly* 77/2 (summer 1993), 343–65; repr. in Gabbard, *Jazz Among the Discourses*, 165–88

———, 1997. 'Deep Jazz: Notes on Interiority, Race, and Criticism', in Joel Pfister and Nancy Schnog (eds), *Inventing the Psychological: Toward a Cultural History of Emotional Life in America*, Westport, Conn., Yale University Press, 271–96

———, (ed.), 1999. *Keeping Time: Readings in Jazz History*, Oxford University Press

Warschauer, Frank, 1994. 'Jazz: On Whiteman's Berlin Concerts', in Kaes *et al.* 1994, 571–2

Washburne, Christopher, 1997. 'The Clave of Jazz: A Caribbean Contribution to the Rhythmic Foundation of an African-American Music', *Black Music Research Journal* 17/1 (Spring 1997), 59–80

Waterman, Glen, 1924. *Piano Jazz*, Los Angeles, Waterman

Waters, Keith, 1996. 'Blurring the Barline: Metric Displacement in the Piano Solos of Herbie Hancock', *Annual Review of Jazz Studies* 6 (1996), 19–37

Weber, Max, 1930. *The Protestant Ethic and the Spirit of Capitalism* [1904–5], London, Allen and Unwin

Weber, William, 1992. *The Rise of Musical Classics in Eighteenth Century England: A Study in Ritual, Canon, and Ideology*, Oxford University Press

Weill, Kurt, 1994. 'Dance Music', in Kaes *et al.* 1994, 577

Welty, Eudora, 1991. 'Powerhouse', in Breton 1991, 29–43

White, Avron (ed.), 1987. *Host in Music: Culture, Style and the Musical Event*, London and New York, Routledge & Kegan Paul

Whitehead, Kevin, 1998. *The New Dutch Swing*, New York, Billboard Press

Whiteley, Sheila (ed.), 1997. *Sexing the Groove: Popular Music and Gender*, New York, Routledge

Whiteoak, John, 1999. *Playing Ad Lib: Improvisatory Music in Australia 1836–1970*, Sydney, Currency Press

Willett, John, 1978. *Art and Politics in the Weimar Period: The New Sobriety 1917–1933*, New York, Pantheon

Williams, James Kent, 1982. 'Themes Composed by Jazz Musicians of the Bebop Era: A Study of Harmony, Rhythm, and Melody', PhD dissertation, Indiana University

Williams, Martin (ed.), 1962. *Jazz Panorama: From the Pages of Jazz Review*, New York, Crowell-Collier Press

———, 1966. *Where's The Melody? A Listener's Introduction to Jazz*, New York, Pantheon

———, 1983. *The Jazz Tradition*, Oxford University Press, second edn

Williams, Raymond, 1961. *The Long Revolution*, Harmondsworth, Penguin

Wilmer, Valerie, 1977. *As Serious As Your Life: The Story of the New Jazz*, Melbourne, New York and London, Quartet

Wilson, Olly, 1974. 'The Significance of the Relationship between Afro-American Music and West African Music', *Black Perspective in Music* 2 (1974), 3–22

———, 1992. 'The Heterogeneous Sound Ideal in African-American Music', in Wright and Floyd 1992, 327–38

Witmer, Robert and James Robbins, 1988. 'A Historical and Critical Survey of Recent Pedagogical Materials for the Teaching and Learning of Jazz', *Bulletin of the Council for Research in Music Education* 96 (1988), 7–29

Wittgenstein, Ludwig, 1953. *Philosophical Investigations*, Oxford, Blackwell

Woideck, Carl, 1996. *Charlie Parker: His Music and Life*, Ann Arbor, University of Michigan Press

——— (ed.), 1998. *The Charlie Parker Companion: Six Decades of Commentary*, New York, Schirmer Books

Woll, Allen, 1989. *Black Musical Theatre: From Coontown to Dreamgirls*, Baton Rouge, Louisiana State University Press

Woodson, Craig DeVere, 1973. 'Solo Jazz Drumming: An Analytical Study of the Improvisation Techniques of Anthony Williams', MA thesis, 2 vols., University of California at Los Angeles

Wright, Josephine, and Samuel Floyd, Jr (eds), 1992. *New Perspectives on Music: Essays in Honor of Eileen Southern*, Warren, Mian, Harmonie Park Press

York, Norton and Dave Laing, 2000. *Nice Work – If You Can Get It! A Survey of Musicians' Employment 1978–98*, London, Musicians' Union

Zabor, Rafi, 1997. *The Bear Comes Home*, New York, Norton

Principal musicians cited

Armstrong, Louis; trumpet, vocal
b. New Orleans, 1901; d. Queens, New York, 1971
An outstanding pioneer in jazz and popular entertainment, Armstrong set new standards in instrumental style and technique and vocal style and played the single most important role in the emergence of the jazz soloist. From small groups in the 1920s in Chicago (most influential of which were the ones which made the Hot Five and Hot Seven records) he turned to fronting a swing band in the 1930s and early 1940s. In 1947 he returned to the small-group format with his All Stars, remaining with them for the rest of his life. Later years also saw the recording of several popular song hits, most notably 'Hello Dolly' and 'Wonderful World'.

Basie, Count (William Basie); piano, bandleader
b. Red Bank, New Jersey, 1904; d. Hollywood, 1984
Basie took over leadership of Bennie Moten's Kansas City-based orchestra in 1934 and, with the help of arrangers such as Eddie Durham, turned it into one of the leading bands of the swing era. His own piano style, spare and understated, was the basis of a simple, exciting, riff-based sound that also featured outstanding soloists such as Lester Young and Dickie Wells. Though adversely affected by the decline of big bands in the later 1940s he came back with a new band in the 1950s and continued to record and tour with it till his death.

Bechet, Sidney; clarinet, soprano saxophone
b. New Orleans, 1897; d. Paris, 1959
With Armstrong, Bechet played a major role in altering the nature of early jazz to provide a key role for the soloist. A more passionate player than Armstrong (with whom he performed only rarely), Bechet was also a more volatile individual and this, combined with lengthy spells in Europe (especially France, where he was idolised by fellow musicians), resulted in less recognition in the USA. He was the first jazz musician to master the soprano saxophone.

Beiderbecke, Bix; cornet, piano
b. Davenport, Iowa, 1903; d. New York, 1931
Influenced by Armstrong, Beiderbecke created his own distinctive style, with a clear, luminous tone and relaxed approach. He became known through his recordings with the Wolverines (Chicago 1924), later moving into bigger ensembles such as Paul Whiteman's orchestra. One of the few early white musicians for whom black musicians had a high regard, his health was undermined by alcoholism.

Bell, Graeme; piano, bandleader
b. Melbourne, Australia, 1914
A very influential figure in the popularisation of jazz in Australia, Bell was also central to the revival of traditional jazz in post-war Europe. In 1947–8 he and his band performed for four months in Czechoslovakia, inaugurating a jazz movement there, and for eight months in England, where their approach to jazz as a dance music contrasted sharply with the more intellectual attitude that had grown up in the jazz record clubs. Other international tours followed in later decades, during which Bell and his All-Star band were based in Sydney.

Blakey, Art; drums, bandleader
b. Pittsburgh, 1919, d. New York, 1990
The Jazz Messengers of 1947 was the first version of a group with which Blakey's name became inseparably linked. From the mid-1950s on, the Messengers played a fierce hard bop, driven along by Blakey's powerful drumming, with its innovative use of high-hat and snare. The Messengers also provided opportunities for a great many young musicians beginning their careers, from Keith Jarrett and Wayne Shorter to Wynton Marsalis and Terence Blanchard.

Bolden, Buddy; cornet
b. New Orleans, 1877; d. Jackson, Louisiana, 1931
The one inescapable figure from the period before jazz was recorded (though legend has it he made a cylinder recording), Bolden led a small band that performed in New Orleans, in dance halls and in the open air, from 1895 to 1907. His cornet playing was highly celebrated locally for its excitement and attack, and he gave prominence also to blues and 'slow drags'. He was committed to a mental institution in 1907.

Braxton, Anthony; alto saxophone, multi-instrumentalist, composer
b. Chicago, 1945
Braxton joined the black avant-garde cooperative organisation, the Association for the Advancement of Creative Musicians (AACM), in Chicago in 1966 and was influenced by experimentalism, multi-instrumentalism and the group's social ideals. Working in succeeding years in both Europe and the USA he developed a career as a composer alongside that of soloist and group leader. In all roles he was frequently considered highly controversial. In his compositions he developed an original form of diagrammatic notation, in order to express (among other things) his strong sense of synaesthesia.

Brubeck, Dave; piano
b. Concord, California, 1920
The classically trained Brubeck became a household name with his Quartet's recording of the 5/4 tune 'Take Five' in 1959. The melody was by the group's saxophonist, Paul Desmond, but, like Brubeck's own 'Blue Rondo à la Turk', it reflected Brubeck's interest in the challenges of unusual time signatures and metres, and his lifelong attraction to serious composition. The Brubeck Quartet of the 1950s and 1960s

avoided developments such as hard bop and free jazz and was especially popular with an audience on the North American college circuit and at festivals. As well as forming subsequent quartets, some with his sons, Brubeck produced numerous compositions from the 1970s on, including cantatas, oratorios and works for jazz ensembles.

Carter, Benny; alto saxophone, trumpet, arranger

b. New York, 1907

Carter became a noted arranger for Fletcher Henderson's orchestra in 1930 before forming his own orchestra in 1932. From 1935–8 he lived in London, where he wrote arrangements for the BBC Dance Orchestra and was influential in the development of jazz in Britain and Europe. In subsequent years he wrote and arranged music for several films and helped to open Hollywood up for black musicians. Noted for his versatility and for the elegance of his performing style, Carter's outstanding achievement was his part in the creation of the big-band sound.

Christian, Charlie; guitar

b. Texas, 1916; d. New York, 1942

A pioneer of the amplified guitar, Christian first performed on the instrument in Oklahoma in 1937. In 1939 he joined Benny Goodman in Los Angeles, before coming to New York in 1940. His recording of 'Solo Flight' with Goodman in 1941 was one of several marking the arrival of the guitar as a solo instrument. Christian's ability to create long improvised single-note lines for chorus after chorus was captured on a live recording of 'Swing to Bop' at Minton's Playhouse in Harlem. He died of tuberculosis.

Coleman, Ornette; saxophone

b. Fort Worth, Texas, 1930

From a background in rhythm-and-blues bands in the west and southwest of the USA, Coleman became one of the pioneers of free jazz, playing a major role in creating a form of the music that departed radically from conventional structures and harmonic changes. Especially influential were the albums, *The Shape of Jazz To Come* (1959) and *Free Jazz* (1960), involving a new approach to collective performance.

Coltrane, John; tenor and soprano saxophones

b. Hamlet, North Carolina, 1926; d. New York, 1967

Coltrane's early career in big bands and rhythm-and-blues groups did little to suggest the hugely influential musician he was to become. His first major exposure came in two spells with the Miles Davis band in 1955–7 and 1958–60. He formed his own group in 1960 (with, among others, McCoy Tyner and Elvin Jones) and in the period from then till his death it built an international reputation as a supremely innovative ensemble. Coltrane himself combined an unprecedented technical mastery and improvisatory imagination, often expressed in overwhelming performances, with a quiet spirituality. His playing moved from being dominated by complex harmonic changes through his famous 'sheets of sound' to a style based on motivic variation.

Corea, Chick; piano
b. Chelsea, Massachusetts, 1941
Following early involvement with Latin-style groups, Corea joined Miles Davis in 1968 at the beginning of the jazz-rock movement, leaving in 1970 to form the avant-garde group Circle with Dave Holland and Barry Altschul. His own interests lay in a more lyrical, Latin-influenced approach with a wider market, and in 1971 he formed the first of three Return to Forever groups (the third, which included a string ensemble, disbanded in 1980). In the later 1980s he formed his Akoustic and Elektric bands.

Davis, Miles; trumpet, bandleader
b. Alton, Illinois, 1926; d. Santa Monica, California, 1991
A dominant figure in jazz for over forty years, Davis was also remarkable for his persistent interest in radical stylistic change and experiment. Switching from the particular challenges of bop to a smoother, more sonorous approach (dubbed 'the cool') in the late 1940s, he went on in the mid-1950s to make a series of seminal recordings, with his own quintet and with the orchestra of Gil Evans, that are especially notable for his own intense but relaxed, spare but complex trumpet playing. In the late 1950s, especially on what became perhaps his best-known album, *Kind of Blue* (1959), he explored a modal approach. Following the rise of rock in the 1960s, Davis was at the forefront of jazz-rock experimentation, on albums such as *Bitches Brew* (1969). In later years he continued to explore new possibilities, while also revisiting earlier styles.

Ellington, Duke (Edward Kennedy Ellington); piano, bandleader, composer
b. Washington, DC, 1897; d. New York, 1974
In one of the most productive careers in jazz, Ellington led his celebrated orchestra for almost fifty years. His first major opportunity came in 1927–31, when his band was the resident ensemble at Harlem's Cotton Club, providing atmospheric cabaret and dance music for the white clientele. Experimenting with sonorities and structures alongside popular songs and big-band numbers, he found himself lauded in Europe as a composer in the early 1930s, and continued from then on to develop new conceptions of the jazz piece, especially through a long series of suites, from *Reminiscing in Tempo* (1935) and *Black Brown and Beige* (1943; subtitled 'a tone poem to the American Negro'), to the *New Orleans Suite* of 1971. In later life an underlying spirituality showed itself more openly in a series of 'sacred concerts'. Central to Ellington's approach to composition and arrangement was an awareness of the qualities and timbral character of each of his musicians, a large number of whom remained with him for many years.

Evans, Bill; piano
b. Plainfield, New Jersey, 1929; d. New York, 1980
Evans was a member of the Miles Davis group who recorded the landmark modal album, *Kind of Blue*, in 1959. For much of the rest of his career he recorded with his own trio, forming a particularly creative relationship with bassist Scott LaFaro. In this context Evans developed his highly influential style, introducing greater lyricism and reflectiveness alongside rhythmic intricacy and innovative voicings.

Evans, Gil; bandleader, arranger
b. Toronto, 1912; d. Cuernavaca, Mexico, 1988
Evans came to attention as arranger for Claude Thornhill in the 1940s. His interest in the subtle timbres of what became known as a 'cool' sound was a major contribution to Miles Davis's *Birth of the Cool* recordings of 1948–50. Evans teamed up with Davis again in the late 1950s to record a set of albums (including *Porgy and Bess*) in which his highly textured, chromatic orchestral sound perfectly sets off Davis's solo trumpet.

Fitzgerald, Ella; vocal
b. Newport News, Virginia, 1917; d. Beverly Hills, California, 1996
Considered by many to be the first female vocal equivalent of virtuoso instrumentalists, Fitzgerald established herself as a big-band singer in the 1930s, before going solo in 1942. Her performances at Jazz at the Philharmonic concerts, from 1946, were celebrated for her scat singing. Beginning in the 1950s a series of 'songbooks', featuring interpretations of songs by major songwriters performed in a style merging jazz and popular singing, brought her to a wider audience.

Garbarek, Jan; tenor saxophone
b. Mysen, Norway, 1947
In his recording career Garbarek has been particularly closely associated with the German-based label ECM and its owner Manfred Eicher, who shares a liking for a spacious concept of recording sound, influenced by the atmospherics of Scandinavia, and an interest in combining jazz, classical and ethnic music. Garbarek played with Keith Jarrett and worked also with Don Cherry, Chick Corea and George Russell among many others. By the late 1980s he was widely regarded as the leading tenor saxophonist in Europe.

Gillespie, Dizzy; trumpet, bandleader
b. Cheraw, South Carolina, 1917; d. Englewood, New Jersey, 1993
From an early career in big bands, including Cab Calloway's, Gillespie became one of the young generation experimenting, mainly in New York, with the new style (which Gillespie himself may have christened), bebop, or bop. Throughout his subsequent career he led both small groups and big bands, often mingling bop approaches with Afro-Cuban rhythms. His trademark image, in which he performs with puffed-out cheeks on a trumpet whose bell is raised at an angle of 45 degrees (the result of an accident to an instrument in 1953), became widely recognised around the world. His trumpet style was extrovert and dramatic, with a brilliant sound.

Goodman, Benny; clarinet, bandleader
b. Chicago, 1909; d. New York, 1986
Following an early career in California, Chicago and New York, Goodman formed his own band in 1934. The band became famous nationwide due to its radio broadcasts. Particularly popular with the young, it proved one of the most exciting bands of the swing era, earning Goodman himself the title 'King of Swing'. Noted for his discipline,

Goodman achieved a new level of recognition for jazz with a Carnegie Hall concert in 1938. A virtuoso instrumentalist, he was the first jazz musician to venture successfully into performing works from the classical repertory.

Hancock, Herbie; piano, composer
b. Chicago, 1940

A member of Miles Davis's quintet from 1963 to 1968, Hancock participated in Davis's move into jazz-rock and in the band he himself subsequently formed pursued the overall idea of fusion widely, making use of African and Indian elements alongside rock and jazz, and introducing electronic instruments. With the album *Head Hunters* (1973) he turned consciously to appeal to a wider, disco-orientated market and continued in this vein into the 1980s, returning to jazz with an award-winning score for the film *Round Midnight* in 1986.

Hawkins, Coleman; tenor saxophone
b. St Joseph, Missouri, 1904; d. New York, 1969

Hawkins played a major role in transforming the tenor saxophone from a component of the dance band into a premier jazz solo instrument. His long career began uncertainly, his first major opportunity coming when he joined Fletcher Henderson's band in 1924. Hawkins stayed with Henderson for ten years, during which time he developed the basis of a virtuoso technical style combined with a high level of emotional intensity. He spent the years from 1934 to 1939 in Europe, returning to make his seminal – and bestselling – recording of 'Body and Soul'. He toured extensively from the late 1940s on with his own and other groups and made many festival appearances.

Henderson, Fletcher; piano, bandleader, arranger
b. Cuthbert, Georgia, 1897; d. New York, 1952

A key figure in the development of the big-band style, Henderson came to New York in 1920 to seek employment as a chemist (he had a degree in chemistry) but drifted into music when work did not materialise. After accompanying various classic blues singers he formed his first band and obtained a residency at the Roseland in 1924, remaining there for ten years. Under various influences, including the brief presence of Louis Armstrong and the skills of arrangers Don Redman and Benny Carter, Henderson turned this orchestra from a dance band to one of the first jazz big bands. By the late 1920s he was writing his own arrangements, and after the demise of his own band, these charts were taken up by Benny Goodman at the start of the swing era. Lacking the leadership qualities of others, Henderson was unable to capitalise fully on the swing boom, but continued to contribute many arrangements.

Holiday, Billie (Eleanora Fagan); vocal
b. Baltimore, 1915; d. New York, 1959

Holiday's career as an internationally known vocalist began when she was spotted by entrepreneur John Hammond singing at a Harlem nightspot in 1933. Recordings and tours with various bands followed, including those of Benny Goodman, Teddy Wilson and Count Basie. With Artie Shaw's orchestra in 1938 she was one of the first black singers to front a white band. In 1939 she departed from her practice of interpreting popular songs to perform and record the anti-lynching song by Lewis Allen, 'Strange Fruit'. Voted top vocalist in the early 1940s her subsequent career was affected by drug and emotional problems, but these also invested many of her later performances – by which time her light voice had taken on a rough edge – with a deeply affecting voice of experience. Her approach to her material was based on a combination of subtle phrasing against the beat and stretching of the melody.

Jarrett, Keith; piano

b. Allentown, Pennsylvania, 1945

Jarrett's outstanding technique first attracted widespread attention as a member of Charles Lloyd's quartet in 1966–69. He moved on to join Miles Davis, playing organ and electric piano. On leaving Davis he returned to acoustic piano and in 1972 performed his first solo piano concert. With the support of the ECM label Jarrett not only revived solo piano playing, he developed it in unprecedented ways with extended improvisations that integrated many styles and could last more than thirty minutes. His best-known record, *The Köln Concert* (1975), was a remarkable example of his ability. It also demonstrated his appeal to a wider audience. He has continued to perform in small groups, with Jan Garbarek and others, and has performed numerous works from the classical repertoire.

Lewis, John; piano, composer

b. LaGrange, Illinois, 1920; d. New York, 2001

Formally trained in music and anthropology at the University of New Mexico, Lewis became interested in jazz during wartime military service, through contact with drummer Kenny Clarke, and joined Dizzy Gillespie's big band in 1946. In 1952 he joined Milt Jackson's Quartet, soon to be renamed the Modern Jazz Quartet (MJQ). The ensemble was to dominate his life (it disbanded in 1974, but reformed in the 1980s), but he also taught at the Lenox School of Jazz and at Harvard University and formed the cooperative big band, Orchestra USA. Lewis's style, and that of the MJQ, was based on a restrained version of bebop. He was known as a delicate but subtle improviser with a fondness for countermelodies when accompanying soloists. In his own compositions he integrated jazz with stylistic approaches from eighteenth-century European music.

Lewis, Ted; clarinet, bandleader

b. Circleville, Ohio, 1892; d. New York, 1971

An ex-vaudevillean performer, Lewis led a novelty band in the 1920s and 1930s that often included significant jazz musicians, such as Jimmy Dorsey and Benny Goodman.

McLaughlin, John; guitar

b. Yorkshire, England, 1942

McLaughlin's approach to jazz was strongly influenced by rock (he played with rock musicians including Eric Clapton in London, before emigrating to the USA in 1969) and Indian music. After collaborations with Tony Williams and Miles Davis in 1969–70 on pioneering jazz-rock albums, he founded his own Mahavishnu Orchestra (which he would later re-form twice) and the group Shakti. In addition to conventional electric and acoustic guitars, he played a specially designed double-necked electric instrument.

McShann, Jay; piano, bandleader
b. Muskogee, Oklahoma, 1916
As a young musician McShann absorbed the southwestern blues and boogie-woogie traditions. His subsequent big bands featured blues prominently, and his own piano style retained the strong flavour of boogie-woogie. His first, Kansas City-based big band provided an early professional opportunity for Charlie Parker. In the 1940s McShann led bands in New York and California, before returning to Kansas City.

Marsalis, Wynton; trumpet
b. New Orleans, 1961
Highly proficient in both jazz and classical music from a very early age, Marsalis joined Art Blakey's Jazz Messengers in 1980. While there he made his first album as a leader and attracted wide attention for the brilliance of his technique. In 1984 he received two Grammy awards, one for a jazz recording, the other for a recording of classical trumpet concertos. In 1987 he co-founded the Jazz at the Lincoln Center programme in New York, becoming its artistic director. From this position he has argued passionately for the greater recognition of jazz and has been involved in numerous educational and media initiatives. The 1990s saw several jazz-centred compositions, including the oratorio, *Blood on the Fields* (1994), and the growth of an interest in dance, expressed in works for Twyla Tharp and for the Alvin Ailey American Dance Theater.

Mezzrow, Milton 'Mezz'; clarinet
b. Chicago, 1899; d. Paris, 1972
Only an average performer, Mezzrow's main claim to fame lay in his autobiography, *Really the Blues* (1946), with its colourful, if self-centred, account of the jazz scene of the 1920s and 1930s, and of how he was deeply attracted to African-American culture. Mezzrow also organised a number of important recording sessions with musicians such as Sidney Bechet.

Miller, Glenn; trombone, bandleader
b. Clarinda, Iowa, 1904; d. in air crash over English Channel(?), 1944
The leader of one of the most popular bands of the Swing Era, Miller based his approach on precise arrangements that left little room for improvisation. Some of his best-known numbers ('Moonlight Serenade', 'In the Mood') became popular music hits. He died travelling to France to arrange for his British-based wartime band to play for the troops.

Mingus, Charles; double bass, bandleader
b. Nogales, Arizona, 1922; d. Cuernavaca, Mexico, 1979
As an instrumentalist Mingus transformed double-bass playing, raising the standard of performance to a virtuoso level to rival that of 'front-line' instruments. As band-leader and composer he merged techniques from different styles of jazz and black

music (including the blues and gospel music he had grown up with in Watts, Los Angeles) in often complex pieces, which nevertheless had a distinctively sonorous individual style, capable of a huge range of expression. In performance, Mingus's music blurred divisions between composition and improvisation.

Monk, Thelonious; piano
b. Rocky Mount, North Carolina, 1917; d. Weehawken, New Jersey, 1982
As pianist at Minton's Playhouse in Harlem in the early 1940s Monk was at the very heart of the nascent bebop movement. However, he did not record under his own name till 1947, and his career did not fully take off till the late 1950s. His idiosyncratic style, lacking the more obvious trappings of virtuosity, exposed him to charges of incompetence, but was actually a very demanding approach, full of displaced rhythms and harmonic surprises. As a composer (he is best known for 'Round Midnight'), he created many pieces that mixed the warmly melodic with the asymmetrical.

Montgomery, Wes; guitar
b. Indianapolis, 1923; d. Indianapolis, 1968
Montgomery's mid-1960s recordings fronting large ensembles, including string orchestras, brought him to a wide audience, but it is the trio recordings he made, beginning in 1959, that show him most clearly to have been a highly innovative jazz guitarist in the tradition of Charlie Christian. Combining Christian's development of long, finely phrased single note lines with chordal passages and octave playing, Montgomery created a subtle, influential style that was widely admired.

Morton, Jelly Roll (Ferdinand Lamothe); piano, bandleader
b. New Orleans, 1890; d. Los Angeles, 1941
One of the most colourful figures in early jazz, Morton reached the peak of his career as bandleader-composer with the recordings made with his Red Hot Peppers in 1926–28. Basing his music on his own multi-thematic piano pieces, he produced highly crafted arrangements incorporating the elements of New Orleans collective playing. In his Library of Congress interviews in 1938 he recalled his early life in New Orleans, its many musical idioms (including the Caribbean 'Spanish tinge'), and the role of the 'piano professors'.

Oliver, King (Joe Oliver); cornet, bandleader
b. New Orleans, 1885; d. Savannah, Georgia, 1938
From 1922 to 1927 Oliver led highly influential bands in Chicago. Drawing principally on New Orleans musicians, he famously provided the first major opportunity, in 1922, for Louis Armstrong. The recordings made by Oliver's Creole Jazz Band in 1923 made a powerful impact on fellow musicians. Oliver's own style – sometimes dubbed 'preaching trumpet' – was especially noted for its use of the mute.

Parker, Charlie; alto saxophone
b. Kansas City, 1920; d. New York, 1955
Parker grew up in the competitive atmosphere of Kansas City, where he absorbed the local swing idiom with its characteristically strong blues influence. Following a period

in Jay McShann's big band he moved to New York in the early 1940s, where he met and performed with other young musicians involved in what would become bebop. He led his own group for the first time in 1945, working in New York and California. He established a considerable reputation, but fell victim to a destructive lifestyle associated with drugs and alcohol. Generally regarded as one of the most innovative musicians in jazz, he raised improvisation to new levels. Within the convention-challenging context of bebop he introduced a concept that blended virtuosity with innovative approaches to melody, phrasing and rhythm.

Russell, George; composer, piano
b. Cincinnati, 1923

Russell developed his influential theory, the 'Lydian Chromatic Concept of Tonal Organization', in the late 1940s, publishing it in 1953. Compositions embodying his principles were performed by his own ensembles and by groups led among others by Dizzy Gillespie, Lee Konitz and Bill Evans. Russell was an influential teacher at the Lenox School of Jazz, the New England Conservatory and the University of Lund (Sweden).

Stanko, Tomasz; trumpet
b. Rzeszow, Poland, 1942

Stanko's 1962 group Jazz Darings was strongly influenced by American free jazz, especially that of Ornette Coleman. In 1974 he formed a quartet with Edward Vesala (drums; b. Mäntyharju, Finland, 1945). In the 1980s he played with many American free-jazz musicians, and formed his own group, Freelectronic.

Sun Ra (Herman Blount); keyboards, composer, arranger
b. Birmingham, Alabama, 1914; d. Birmingham, Alabama, 1993

Sun Ra formed his Solar Arkestra in Chicago in the 1950s, performing an influential precursor of free jazz. Keeping many musicians with him for many years, he moved to New York in the 1960s and Philadelphia in the 1970s, all the time using his complex ensemble-based music to explore different tonal and timbral combinations. His recordings, all made for his own label, were not widely known and he often had little work. An enduring interest in Egyptian culture (which he contrasted to Biblical culture) and in astronomy and cosmology earned him a reputation as an eccentric in some quarters, but his interests were part of deeply held beliefs and concerns about the future and the past, especially for black peoples.

Surman, John; baritone and soprano saxophones, composer
b. Tavistock, England, 1944

Surman first came to attention in workshops run in Plymouth, England by Mike Westbrook, later becoming a member of his orchestra in London. Here, and in the groups he formed himself from 1968, he demonstrated an outstanding technique on baritone saxophone, extending the possibilities of the instrument. In 1969 he made a jazz-rock recording with John McLaughlin. In the 1970s and 1980s he performed with many European musicians and formed a saxophone trio, SOS, with Mike Osborne and Alan Skidmore. He continued to play with big bands, including the British orchestra organised by Gil Evans.

Tatum, Art; piano
b. Toledo, Ohio, 1909; d. Los Angeles, 1956
Although from the time he first came to New York in 1932, as an accompanist for blues singer Adelaide Hall, to his death Tatum regularly played with small groups and made group recordings, it is as a solo pianist that he is best known. His first solo recordings, in 1933, were regarded with astonishment by fellow musicians, who marvelled at the fullness and accuracy of his technique, coupled with his sense of exploration and his interpretation of swing. Never part of the bebop movement in the 1940s, his career was revived by a series of solo and group recordings for producer Norman Granz in the 1950s. These show at its best Tatum's ability to retain the heart of an existing piece of music and yet transform it with a range of techniques.

Waller, Fats (Thomas Waller); piano, organ, composer
b. New York, 1904; d. Kansas City, 1943
Waller's main early influences were the stride piano playing of James P. Johnson, (whom he met in Harlem around 1920), the songwriting and performance style of black vaudeville, and the classical studies he also undertook. His reputation as a songwriter, an accompanist and a hugely entertaining performer (much in demand at after-hours parties) grew in the mid-1920s. His collaboration with lyricist Andy Razaf proved particularly fruitful, leading to the Broadway show, *Hot Chocolates*, in 1929, with its hit song, 'Ain't Misbehavin''. He made a number of solo recordings for the Victor label between 1929 and 1934 that demonstrate a fascination with harmonic alteration and rhythmic variety, within the context of a stride-based approach. He toured extensively in the USA and Europe in the late 1930s and 1940s, and appeared in several films, including *Stormy Weather* (1943).

Weather Report; jazz-rock group
Founded in 1969, its principal and most consistent members were Joe Zawinul (keyboards; b. Vienna, 1932) and Wayne Shorter (soprano and tenor saxophones; b. Newark, New Jersey, 1933). Among other musicians featured before the group was disbanded in 1986 were Airto Moreira (percussion; b. Itaiopolis, Brazil, 1941), Jaco Pastorius (electric bass; b. Norristown, Pennsylvania, 1951; d. Fort Lauderdale, Florida, 1987) and Peter Erskine (drums; b. Somers Point, New Jersey, 1954). Weather Report built a considerable following and moved more towards rock in the 1970s. Their playing continued to be characterised by a group approach which emphasised interaction and overall sound textures, and avoided foregrounding the soloist.

Whiteman, Paul; bandleader
b. Denver, 1890; d. Doylestown, Pennsylvania, 1967
Often derided in jazz circles because the music that earned him the title 'King of Jazz' in the 1920s was jazz-inflected dance music, not 'real jazz', Whiteman created an alternative to jazz that was acceptable to worried guardians of public morality. He also commissioned and featured compositions – most famously, George Gershwin's *Rhapsody in Blue* (1924) – that incorporated classical and jazz idioms (so-called 'symphonic jazz'), and gave employment opportunities to a number of white jazz musicians.

Williams, Tony; drums
b. Chicago, 1945; d. Daly City, 1997
One of the most highly regarded drummers of the last forty years, Williams joined
Miles Davis before he was 18, staying till 1969. He left Davis to form his own influential though short-lived fusion band, Lifeline, which also featured John McLaughlin.
He returned to jazz with the band V.S.O.P. in the late 1970s, joining forces with
Herbie Hancock and Wayne Shorter. His drumming style, more assertive than his
predecessors' without sacrificing clarity, was especially notable for his ability to anticipate – and therefore interact with – improvising soloists.

Young, Lester; tenor saxophone
b. Woodville, Mississippi, 1909; d. New York, 1959
A central member of the Count Basie Orchestra when it came from Kansas City to
New York in 1936, Young made his first recordings with a small group drawn from that
band. Musicians and listeners saw a striking contrast with another tenor saxophonist,
Coleman Hawkins, with Young offering a gentler, less intense elegiac approach, and a
partiality for long melodic lines. In recordings with Billie Holiday he showed himself
to be a superb accompanist. Highly regarded by the next generation of musicians, he
was a deeply sensitive, private man who led a nomadic existence and never occupied
a central position. His later playing often took on a deeper tone.

Index